Land Law

DIRECTIONS

5th E...

SAN...

SAR...

Birmingham · Bristol · Chester · Guildford · London · Manchester · York

OXFORD

UNIVERSITY PRE...

OXFORD
UNIVERSITY PRESS

Great Clarendon Street, Oxford, OX2 6DP,
United Kingdom

Oxford University Press is a department of the University of Oxford.
It furthers the University's objective of excellence in research, scholarship,
and education by publishing worldwide. Oxford is a registered trade mark of
Oxford University Press in the UK and in certain other countries

Second edition 2010
Third edition 2012
Fourth edition 2014

Impression: 1

Published in the United States of America by Oxford University Press
198 Madison Avenue, New York, NY 10016, United States of America

British Library Cataloguing in Publication Data
Data available

Library of Congress Control Number: 2015958812

ISBN 978–0–19–874845–8

Printed in Italy by
L.E.G.O. S.p.A.

For our law students, past, present, and future, at the University of Greenwich and the University of Worcester

Guide to using the book

The fifth edition of *Land Law Directions* is enriched with a range of features designed to help support and reinforce your learning. This guided tour shows you how to fully utilize your textbook and get the most out of your study.

Learning objectives

These serve as a helpful signpost to what you can expect to learn by reading the chapter.

LEARNING OBJECTIVES

By the end of this chapter, you will be able to:

- explain what is meant by 'adverse possession';
- understand the rationale for adverse possession;
- distinguish between the old law and the new law in this are

Examples

We encounter real examples of land law every day, whether we recognize them or not. In each chapter you will find everyday scenarios illustrating how land law applies to real life situations.

EXAMPLE

Matthew owns the freehold title to The Grange, a large Victorian prope tered land. He decides to divide it up into three flats, and grants two 120- and Will. He decides to keep one of the flats for himself and rents it out

How many separate titles would be registered at the Land Registry?

Diagrams and flowcharts

Numerous diagrams and flowcharts illustrate this book, providing a visual representation of concepts, processes, and cases. Use these in conjunction with the text to gain a clear understanding of even the most complex areas.

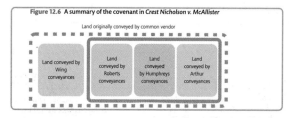

Figure 12.6 A summary of the covenant in *Crest Nicholson v. McAllister*

Photographs and sample documents

Photographs and sample legal documents demonstrate the role of land law in the real world, helping to clarify abstract ideas and develop skills to support your future career.

Photo 1.4 The Cutty Sark
© Sandra Clarke

Statute boxes

Land law is very much based on statute. Relevant provisions are set out and clearly explained in the text.

STATUTE

Infrastructure Act 2015 s.43 Petroleum and geothermal energy: deep-level land

(1) A person has the right to use deep-level land in any way for the pur petroleum or deep geothermal energy.

Case close-ups

Summaries of key cases are clearly highlighted for ease of reference and to develop your understanding.

CASE CLOSE-UP

Swift 1st Ltd. v. Chief Land Registrar [2015] EWCA Civ 330

Mrs R was the registered proprietor of a house which was her home at a 2006, someone took out a loan from Swift 1st Ltd, the appellants, and crea (mortgage) over Mrs R's house as security. The charge was registered on Mr When the loan was not paid back, the appellants sought to repossess M

Definition boxes

Key terms are highlighted and clearly explained when they first appear, helping you to quickly understand important terminology while reading. These terms are also collected in a glossary at the end of the book.

> **easement**
> a right enjoyed by the owner of land to a benefit from other land

ill see numerous
rs might well be
eded; there may

Thinking points

Why was a particular decision reached in a certain case? Is the law on this point rational and coherent? Is land law fit for its purpose? Thinking points within chapters draw out these issues and help you to reflect.

> **THINKING POINT**
>
> Think about the facts of *Pye v. Graham* under the new law. Would an application by the Grahams to be registered as proprietors?
>
> Pye Ltd would have objected. It still wanted the land and had not ab

Cross references

Clearly marked cross references ensure the book is easy to navigate, pin-pointing particular sections where related themes or cases are covered.

> **▶ CROSS REFERENCE**
>
> For more on mortgages and repossession, see Chapter 13.

n it, particularly
on what will be
possesses land
d in its security,

Chapter summaries

The central points and concepts covered in each chapter are condensed into useful summaries. These provide a mechanism for you to reinforce your understanding and can be a helpful revision tool.

> **Summary**
>
> 1. If the land register records a sole legal owner of property, the
> 2. The sole legal owner may also be the sole equitable owner, i land arises.
> 3. The sole legal owner may hold the land entirely on trust for so

End-of-chapter questions

Problem and essay questions at the end of each chapter help you to develop analysis, essay writing, and problem-solving skills, which are essential for successful study and in the workplace. The Online Resource Centre provides suggested approaches to answering these questions.

> **? Questions**
>
> **Self-test questions**
>
> 1. Jac, Steve, and Sam are all friends from university. They decide to buy a They have to decide whether they want to hold the land as joint tena common. Advise Jac, Steve, and Sam, giving your reasons.
> 2. They agree to be tenants in common. How would this be reflect

The bigger picture

Further advice, study suggestions, and additional cases are provided at the end of each chapter to help you build upon your knowledge of land law and prepare for assessments and examinations.

> **☐ The bigger picture**
>
> • If you want to know more about registers of title, look at Chapter possible exam questions on this area, see Chapter 15, 15.5. If yo information on the formation of a contract for the sale of land und please see the Online Resource Centre under 'Advanced topics', cl
> • More information on registration can be found in Chapters 2 and

Further reading

Selected further reading is included at the end of each chapter to provide a springboard for further study. These suggestions help you take your learning further and provide a guide to some of the key academic literature.

> **≡ Further reading**
>
> Dixon, M., 'Trusts of land, bankruptcy and human rights' [2005] This article discusses *Barca v. Mears* and the implications of the HRA 199
> Ferris, G. and Bramley, E., 'The construction of sub-section 6(5) of th Appointment of Trustees Act 1996: When is a "right" not a "right An interesting discussion of what TOLATA 1996, s. 6(5) might actually

Glossary

A useful one-stop reference point for clear definitions of all the keywords and terms used within the text.

> # Glossary
>
> **1925 property legislation** a series of Acts of Parliament that came into effect on 1 January 1926. These Acts consolidated earlier piecemeal changes in the law—particularly from 1922–24—and brought them all
>
> **assignor** the person assigning t lease (cf assignee)
>
> **bankruptcy** a state under whic been judged by a court to be involving the appointment of

Guide to the
Online Resource Centre

The Online Resource Centre that accompanies this book provides students with ready-to-use learning resources. The resources are intended to be used alongside the book and are designed to maximize the learning experience.

 www.oxfordtextbooks.co.uk/orc/clarke_directions5e/

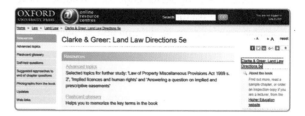

Regular updates

An indispensable resource that allows you to access recent changes and developments in the law that have occurred since publication of the book. These updates are accompanied by references to the textbook, so you can see how the new developments relate to the existing case law.

Chaudhary v Yavuz [2011] EWCA Civ 1314 - *update to 4.5.1.1*

The Court of Appeal has considered the effect of an unregistered equitable easement on a purchaser of the registered estate who was registered with absolute title.

The defendant had bought a property (no35) next door to a property owned by the claimant (no 37). The previous owner of no35 had allowed the claimant to use an exterior metal staircase which was part of no35 to access the first floor flat at no37. This created an equitable easement in the claimant's favour. However, that easement had not been registered by notice under LRA 2002 s.34.

Once he became owner, the defendant removed the part of the staircase and balcony giving

Advanced topics

Additional details on selected topics help to broaden and deepen your understanding of land law.

Mabo and others v. Queensland (No. 2) (1992) 175 CLR 1 F.C. 92/014

The case was brought by Eddie Mabo, a member of the Meriam islanders, who live on a group of islands off the north coast of Queensland. They had lived on those islands since before settlement of Australia by the British, and before the islands were annexed by the Queensland government in 1879. Eddie Mabo claimed that the property rights of the Meriam islanders survived the change in government, and that the doctrine of tenure did not mean that the Crown took a beneficial title to all the land in Australia, but only a radical title.

The case is most famous for overruling the doctrine of '*terra nullius*' – that is that Australia was 'empty territory', belonging to no-one at the time the British arrived. The question then

Self-test questions

Self-test questions for each chapter provide instant feedback to help you consolidate your knowledge of land law and prepare for assessments.

Instructions

Answer the following questions and then press 'Submit' to get your score.

Question 1

What is meant by the terms 'realty' or 'real property'?

- a) Freehold land
- b) Freehold and leasehold land
- c) All types of property
- d) Tangible property

Suggested approaches to end-of-chapter questions

Advice is given on answering the example problem and essay questions from the text to help you develop essential skills in analysing problems and constructing well-balanced arguments.

1. Daisy's neighbour has started to build an extension to his house. The extension adjoins Daisy's back garden. The foundations for the extension and the new drainage pipes run under Daisy's garden. Has Daisy any grounds for complaint?

    Answer: Daisy does have grounds for complaint. She is the owner of the land included in her garden, and that land includes not only the surface of the land, but also the subsoil and subterranean space. Authority for this can be found in LPA 1925 s. 205(1)(ix), which states that land includes mines and minerals, which are below the surface. Houses may have cellars, and these form part of the land. Also, in *Bocardo v Star Energy* [2010] UKSC 35, [2011] 1 AC 380, oil wells drilled far below the surface were held to trespass on the claimant's land. See 1.1.2.1.

Web links

Don't spend time using search engines. The authors have selected links to useful websites so you can go directly to reliable sources of online information, allowing you to work efficiently and effectively.

Chapter 3: Web links

On Crown Land

Law Commission/HM Land Registry (2001) *Land Registration for the Twenty-First Century: A Conveyancing Revolution* , Law Com No. 271, available online at http://www.justice.gov.uk/-lawcommission/publications/land-registration-for-the-21st-century-a-conveyancing-revolution.htm, paras 2.7, 11.5–11.19
This Law Commission/HM Land Registry report introduced the LRA 2002. You can see here details of provisions about Crown land.

Flashcard glossary

A series of interactive flashcards containing key terms and concepts allows you to test your understanding of land law terminology.

Clarke & Greer: Land Law Directions Flashcards

Instructions: Click on the card to flip it, use the navigational arrow buttons to view the previous/next cards, and the links below for additional functionality.

dominant tenement

Photographs

All photographs from the book can be viewed in more detail, and are available to download.

Photo 1.4 **The Cutty Sark**
© Sandra Clarke

New to this edition

The courts continue to be busy in the area of co-ownership of the family home. This edition considers the post-*Jones v. Kernott* [2011] UKSC 53 cases, including the Court of Appeal decision in *Capehorn v. Harris* [2015] EWCA Civ 955, which makes it clear that a two-step approach to ascertaining beneficial shares is still needed in sole legal owner cases. It also considers *Re North East Property Buyers, Scott v. Southern Pacific Mortgages Ltd* [2014] UKSC 52, and its implication for the timing of the acquisition of proprietary rights and the creation of overriding interests.

A topical area considered is the right to 'frack' under land without consent, following the passing of the Infrastructure Act 2015, s. 43, and its limiting effect on *Bocardo v. Star Energy* [2010] UKSC 35 where petroleum and natural gas are concerned.

The problem of forged dispositions of registered titles has been considered by the Court of Appeal in *Swift 1st Ltd. v. Chief Land Registrar* [2015] EWCA Civ 330, which held that earlier cases had been decided *per incuriam*, and that the innocent transferee under a forged transfer does have the protection of LRA 2002, s. 26. *Gold Harp Properties Ltd v. MacLeod* [2014] EWCA Civ 1084 (CA) has considered the effect of rectification of the register on priority of interests.

The interesting question of the effect of Legal Aid, Sentencing and Punishment of Offenders Act 2012, s. 144 on the adverse possession of residential buildings seems to have been resolved by *Best v. Chief Land Registrar* [2015] EWCA Civ 17, in which the Court of Appeal held that a squatter may still get title to residential premises despite the criminality of the act.

We have also considered the effects of *Coventry v. Lawrence* [2014] UKSC 13 on the *Shelfer* rules for granting damages instead of injunctions, something only touched on in the fourth edition, which went to press just as the decision was reported.

Preface

We wrote the first edition of this book almost a decade ago, and so much has happened in that time, both in land law and our lives. The law in this area continues to evolve and develop, bringing us new directions and challenges. We have tried, as always, to make the often very complicated principles of land law as clear and accessible as we possibly can—although the courts do not always make that an easy task. We have dedicated this edition to our students at our respective universities. We are grateful for their questions, suggestions, and surprising enthusiasm for land law.

Thank you to Felicity Boughton, our Oxford University Press editor, for her help and good humour in the process of writing this edition. Many thanks too to our colleague, Professor Mark Pawlowski, for his helpful comments on some of the chapters, and to Lynne Hanmore for her invaluable help in being willing to discuss *Coventry v. Lawrence* over lunch for days if necessary!

Finally, the biggest thank you, as always, must go to our families. Sarah would like to thank Steve and Hamish for their love, help, and patience. She promises that she will now resume dog-walking duties at the weekend. Sarah would also like to thank Di Fisher, for making sure that she actually had the time to manage to finish this book. Your kindness and support are very much appreciated, Di, as were the chocolate biscuits. Sandra would like to thank Pete for his willingness to brave the supermarket run whilst she finished her final edits, and for being the best husband in the world. She would also like to thank Andrew and Lolly and David and Becci for just being their lovely selves and such fun to be around.

Sandra Clarke and Sarah Greer

Publisher acknowledgements

Figure 3.1 is reproduced by kind permission of Mr and Mrs S. C. Williams.

Figure 3.2—Land Registry form TR1—is Crown copyright and is reproduced by kind permission of the Land Registry.

Figure 5.10—Tenancy agreement—is reproduced for educational purposes only by kind permission of Oyez Professional Services Limited.

Contents

PART 2   LEGAL ESTATES   67

Chapter 3   The freehold estate   69

Chapter 4   Registration of title   94

Table of cases

Bold page numbers indicate Case close-ups. Other references may occur on the same page.

Table of legislation

Bold page numbers indicate where text is reproduced in full. Other references may occur on the same page.

UK secondary legislation

European secondary legislation

International legislation

PART 1

INTRODUCTION

1   What is land?

☐ **LEARNING OBJECTIVES**

By the end of this chapter, you will be able to:

- recognize what is meant by 'land';
- understand the extent of land—in particular, how it exists in three dimensions;
- explain which objects form part of the land and which keep their separate character;
- understand what is meant by 'intangible rights' in land;
- discuss the ownership of objects found on, or within, the land, including the Crown's right to 'treasure'.

Introduction: how relevant is land law today?

Land law has always been important to people. From the beginning of civilization, people have needed to regulate land ownership and use. Although land law has its roots in ancient times, it is of vital and growing importance in today's world. Everyone, every day, comes into contact with rules relating to the ownership, occupation, and use of land. To begin with, everyone has to live somewhere. Some people live in a freehold property; others live in a leasehold home. Although most people have heard the terms 'freehold' and 'leasehold', they may not really understand what the words mean. Many people have a fairly hazy idea about their rights over their land, but it is an important topic. The owners of a freehold house need to know what they can and cannot do with their land. Owners of a leasehold property need to know how their rights differ from those of a freehold owner. People renting their homes from week to week, or month to month, also need to know what they can and cannot do in relation to the property in which they live. Even students living at home with parents, or people living in a property owned by a partner, need to know what rights, if any, they have in their homes. Land law is important—as important as the roof over your head.

Despite its very practical relevance, students sometimes say they find land law dull. Land law has a specialized vocabulary, with some words dating from medieval times, but that does not mean that it cannot be explained in modern English. Words such as 'covenant' and 'easement' have an old-fashioned sound, but they describe concepts that are as relevant today as they were when the words were first coined. Throughout this book, although we may use dusty old cases as authorities, we will also give modern examples and photographs of real pieces of land to illustrate and explain. Land law is a living, dynamic subject—and it is an increasingly relevant one in these days of housing shortages and increasing competition for land.

1.1 The definition of land

It is always helpful to begin by defining the subject matter being studied. Unfortunately for those who like simplicity, although there are many statutes that regulate land law, there is no single, authoritative, statutory definition of 'land'. There are a number of different definitions in various statutes—but they tend to repeat and expand upon one another in a less than helpful way.

As a starting point, however, we can look at the partial definition of land in the Law of Property Act 1925 (LPA 1925), s. 205(1)(ix). The LPA 1925 is one among the body of statutes that makes up the 1925 property legislation: an impressive attempt to rationalize and codify the law relating to land.

 STATUTE

Law of Property Act 1925, s. 205(1)(ix)

'Land' includes land of any tenure, and mines and minerals, whether or not held apart from the surface, buildings or parts of buildings (whether the division is horizontal, vertical or made in any other way) and other corporeal hereditaments; also a manor, advowson, and a rent and other incorporeal hereditaments, and an easement, right, privilege, or benefit in, over, or derived from land; … and 'mines and minerals' include any strata or seam of minerals or substances in or under any land, and powers of working and getting the same … ; and 'manor' includes a lordship, and reputed manor or lordship; and 'hereditament' means any real property which on an intestacy occurring before the commencement of this Act might have devolved upon an heir.

As a definition for a new student of land law, this leaves a lot to be desired. For a start, it is only a partial definition, because it begins '"Land" *includes*', and this means that land may also include things that are *not* mentioned in this definition. Further, it uses words and phrases that are not in common use today, so it can be difficult to grasp immediately what it means.

Despite these shortcomings, however, it is worth persevering with this definition, because it can teach us quite a lot about the basics of land law. It also introduces some of the vocabulary needed for further study, which will make it much easier for you to understand later chapters.

1.1.1 Land of any tenure

Firstly, the section states that land 'includes land of any tenure'. Broadly speaking, this means that both freehold and leasehold land count as land for land law purposes. The concepts of freehold and leasehold are dealt with in later chapters.

For now, it is sufficient to understand that freehold land is owned effectively 'forever', whereas leasehold land is owned by a tenant for a definite period, which may be short or long, but is not 'forever'. A leasehold is created out of a freehold.

It might seem obvious to you that both are 'land', but, for historical reasons, this was not always the case. Originally, the distinction was not made between 'land' and other types of property, but between **real property (**or **realty)** and **personal property (**or **personalty)**. Personal property can also be described as **chattels** —a word that is thought to be derived from cattle, which were a common type of personal property in early farming societies.

CROSS REFERENCE
For more on freehold land, see Chapter 3.

CROSS REFERENCE
For more on leasehold land, see Chapter 5.

> **real property, or realty** this term refers to freehold land
>
> **personal property, or personalty** all property that does not comprise freehold land
>
> **chattels** all property that is not real property, including leasehold land, and is also often used as the opposite to 'fixture'—see 1.1.3.1. Leasehold land came to have such importance, however, that it was called a 'chattel real', because it has many of the characteristics of real property.

Originally, all land was freehold, so real property meant freehold land. The word 'real' comes from the Latin *res*, which means 'the thing itself'. Real property could be protected in law by the real actions. This meant that a court action could be brought to restore the land itself to the true owner, rather than an award of money damages as compensation for its loss. It is still true today that courts will usually order specific performance of a contract to sell land. In other words, they will order the seller to transfer the land to the buyer rather than awarding damages.

By the time the idea of a lease developed, the definition of real property as freehold land was too fixed to be altered. Leasehold land was regarded as personal property, although it was clear that it was different from most types of personalty. The real actions were not available to leaseholders.

You will be relieved to hear that, because land now 'includes land of any tenure', leasehold land is now included squarely within the definition of land for all modern purposes.

CROSS REFERENCE
For more detail on 'tenure', see Chapter 2.

1.1.2 The extent of land

Turning back to LPA 1925, s. 205(1)(ix), you can see that land includes mines and minerals, whether they are owned by the owner of the surface of the land or owned separately from it. This illustrates a very important fact about land, which is that land is three-dimensional. There is the surface of the land, the ground beneath the surface, and the airspace above. Different people can own different strata (or levels) of land.

 EXAMPLE

Anna owns a house that is built on land above a coalfield. She owns the surface of the land (and the house built on it), but the land beneath the surface—that with the coal in it—may be owned by the British Mining Company.

This same principle can be seen at work in the next part of the definition—that land includes 'buildings or parts of buildings (whether the division is horizontal, vertical or made in any other way)'. Not surprisingly, buildings form part of the land, but interestingly, different people can own different parts of buildings and the building can be divided in any way (see Figure 1.1).

Figure 1.1 Ways in which a building can be divided

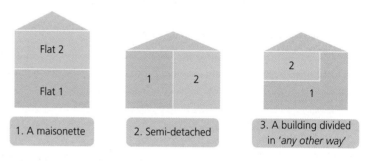

1. A maisonette   2. Semi-detached   3. A building divided in 'any other way'

> ### → EXAMPLE
>
> Maisonettes are buildings that are divided horizontally (1); semi-detached houses (2) are buildings that are divided vertically.
>
> There is, however, no reason why a building should not be divided unequally, so that one person owns all of the ground floor and part of the first floor, and the other person owns the rest of the first floor. This last example (3) is of a building divided in 'any other way'.

cuius est solum eius est usque ad coelum et ad inferos
'he who owns the land owns everything reaching up to the very heavens and down to the depths of the earth'

The extended definition of land is sometimes expressed in the maxim ***cuius est solum eius est usque ad coelum et ad inferos***, or 'he who owns the land owns everything reaching up to the very heavens and down to the depths of the earth'. This maxim, approved in *Bocardo v. Star Energy* (see 1.1.2.1), is useful in reminding us that land includes not only the surface, but also the air above and the space beneath the ground. However, whilst it is true that land includes airspace and subterranean space (the space beneath the ground), it is not true that the owner's rights are unlimited, particularly with regard to airspace.

1.1.2.1 Subterranean space

The landowner owns the subterranean space below the surface of his land. He can dig down into it to form a cellar or underground room.

As s. 205(1)(ix) states, mines and minerals form part of the land—but certain minerals do not belong to the landowner and belong instead to the state. Gold and silver belong to the Crown as of right—*Case of Mines* (1568) 1 Plowd 310. The Crown is also entitled to oil, petroleum, coal, and natural gas (including shale gas obtained by fracturing the land or 'fracking') by statutory right—see the Coal Industry Act 1994 and the Petroleum Act 1998. In addition, the Crown has the right to treasure found in the land (see 1.2.3).

CASE CLOSE-UP

Bocardo v. Star Energy [2010] UKSC 35, [2011] 1 AC 380

This case contains an interesting point about ownership of the land 'down to the depths of the earth'. The claimants were the owners of an estate in Surrey. The defendants were holders of a licence under the Petroleum Act 1934 to search and drill for and pump out petroleum products from an oilfield that extended partly under the claimants' land. The defendants carried out their drilling operations from land next to the claimant's estate but, unknown to the claimants, their oil wells extended under the claimants' land.

The claimants eventually found out about the oil wells and claimed damages for trespass to their land. The defendants argued that the oil wells were so deep underground (a minimum depth of 800 ft) that they did not affect the claimants' use of the land in any way; the claimants had been unaware of them for years and therefore they did not trespass on the claimants' land.

The Supreme Court held that the oil wells were a trespass. Although they were deep below the surface, the subsoil belongs to the owner of the surface unless it has been granted to someone else. The petroleum products belonged to the state by statute (Petroleum Act 1934), but not the subsoil. It was not a trespass to remove the petroleum, but it was a trespass to drill wells under the claimants' land without permission. The defendants were therefore ordered to pay compensation to the claimants.

Recently, landowners have sought to use this decision to prevent fracking under their land. However, the Infrastructure Act 2015 provides that:

 STATUTE

Infrastructure Act 2015 s.43 Petroleum and geothermal energy: right to use deep-level land

(1) A person has the right to use deep-level land in any way for the purposes of exploiting petroleum or deep geothermal energy.

…

(4) deep-level land is any land at a depth of at least 300 metres below surface level.

This right to use deep-level land expressly includes fracking under s. 44 of the Act. Provisions are made in later sections for notice and payments to landowners.

The land beneath the surface can be extended if land borders a roadway. There is a presumption that the landowner owns the subsoil of the roadway adjoining the land up to the middle of the roadway—***ad medium filum***, as the cases often say, meaning 'to the mid line'. Landowners can construct cellars that extend into this space below the ground.

> ***ad medium filum***
> 'to the mid line'

Should you happen to be visiting a pub, take a closer look: often trap doors enabling delivery of barrels to the beer cellars are set in the pavement outside the pub (see Photo 1.1).

Photo 1.1 Pub trapdoor
© Sandra Clarke

1.1.2.2 Airspace

The owner of land also owns the airspace above that land—but he or she does not own 'up to the very heavens', as the case of *Bernstein v. Skyviews* [1978] QB 479 shows.

Q CASE CLOSE-UP

Bernstein v. Skyviews [1978] QB 479

Lord Bernstein, the owner of a large country estate, brought an action in trespass against a company for flying over, and taking photographs of, his land. The case turned on whether the airspace formed part of the claimant's land.

Griffiths J held that the rights of the owner of land in the airspace above it extends 'to such height as is necessary for the ordinary use and enjoyment of his land and the structures upon it'. Above that height, the landowner has no more rights than the general public. Aircraft flying at a normal height do not trespass upon land, so Lord Bernstein lost the case.

It is clear, however, that lower regions of airspace do belong to the landowner. Cases have been brought in respect of overhanging signs, for example.

Q CASE CLOSE-UP

Kelsen v Imperial Tobacco Co [1957] 2 QB 334

The claimant leased a ground floor shop. The defendants had erected an advertising sign that projected into the airspace above his shop by about eight inches (30 cm). McNair J held that this was a trespass to the claimant's airspace, and granted him an injunction for the sign's removal.

Even if a neighbour has a real need to infringe on the landowner's airspace, this will not prevent an injunction being granted.

CASE CLOSE-UP

John Trenberth v. National Westminster Bank (1979) 39 P & CR 104

In this case, the defendant needed to repair his building, because it was unsafe. The claimant refused to allow scaffolding to be erected on his land, but the defendant proceeded anyway. The claimant was granted an injunction to prevent this. An earlier case, *Woolerton and Wilson Ltd v. Richard Costain Ltd* [1970] 1 WLR 411, in which an injunction had been delayed to allow time to complete the work, was not followed and the correctness of that decision was doubted.

It is also clear from more recent cases that the landowner does not have to prove that the trespassing object has affected his use of the land.

CASE CLOSE-UP

Laiquat v. Majid [2005] EWHC 1305 (QB)

In this fairly recent first-instance case, there was an extractor fan at about 4.5 m above ground level, which protruded 750 mm into the claimant's garden.

Silber J, relying on *Kelsen v. Imperial Tobacco Co. Ltd* [1957] 2 QB 334, held that it was a trespass into the claimant's airspace. It was well within the height which the older authorities considered to be trespass and it did not matter that the fan had not actually interfered with the claimant's normal use of his garden.

It is clear, then, that lower regions of airspace, to the height necessary for ordinary use of the land, form part of the land. Any objects intruding on that airspace from next door are a trespass and will entitle the landowner to either an injunction or damages, even if they do not, in fact, affect the ordinary use of the land.

It is interesting that the courts have held that there is a limit to the height above the land over which landowners have control, but apparently no limit to the depth over which they have control—see *Bocardo v. Star Energy* (see 1.1.2.1). In that case in the Court of Appeal Aikens LJ, at [2009] EWCA Civ 579 [61], said that it is not helpful to draw analogies between rights to airspace and rights to substrata, because there are many uses which can be made of airspace whilst the general public has no right to enter substrata, and because the use of airspace is regulated by statutes and regulations concerning aircraft. This view was endorsed by the Supreme Court, although as we have seen, Parliament has since intervened in respect of underground petroleum products and natural gas.

In the same way that cellars can extend under the surface, the owner of land next to a highway can build out over that highway above the height required for the passage of traffic.

Photos 1.2 and 1.3 show buildings that extend out over pavements and alleyways. Room is left for the passage of pedestrians underneath. It is quite possible for the part of the building over the alleyway in Photo 1.2 to be owned separately from other parts of the building. It may have no connection with the earth itself, but it is still 'land'. (Such pieces of land are sometimes called 'flying freeholds', although, for practical reasons that we shall see later on in the book, they are often leasehold rather than freehold.)

Photo 1.2   Building over alleyway
© Sandra Clarke

Photo 1.3   Balconies
© Terraxplorer

1.1.3 **Corporeal hereditaments**

It can be seen from the definition in LPA 1925, s. 205(1)(ix) that minerals and buildings are part of a wider category of **corporeal hereditaments**. This is a very old expression, but it is actually quite easy to understand. The word 'corporeal' means 'having a physical form', so it includes not only minerals and buildings, but also other physical things, such as plants, fences, etc.

The word 'hereditaments', meanwhile, is defined in the last sentence of LPA 1925, s. 205(1)(ix) as *'any real property which on an intestacy occurring before the commencement of this Act might have devolved upon an heir'*. Again, this is a definition that is less than helpful for the new student: it is referring back to concepts that have little place in modern land law. It was meant at the time to indicate that the old cases on real property were to remain good law.

In the past, cases were brought to establish the extent of real property for inheritance purposes. This was because the heir was entitled to all real property, but not to chattels. It was therefore important to know which items formed part of the land (real property) and which remained separate from it (chattels). Despite their age, these cases are still authority in a more modern context for establishing the extent of land.

> **corporeal hereditaments**
> any real property having a physical form

1.1.3.1 **Fixtures**

Many of the old cases that discussed real and personal property did so in the context of **fixtures**. The law on fixtures is important for reasons other than determining who should inherit property such as pictures fixed to the wall or statues standing in a garden.

> **fixture**
> an object that is attached to the land in such a way and for such a reason that it becomes part of the land

---

THINKING POINT

In today's world, when do you think it would be important to work out which objects form part of the land?

It is important when buying and selling land to know what is included within it, particularly when it is bought and sold at auction, as there is no further chance to bargain on what will be included in the sale. Also, if a mortgagee such as a bank or building society repossesses land where the borrower has defaulted on the loan, it needs to know what is included in its security, and what is not.

> **CROSS REFERENCE**
> For more on mortgages and repossession, see Chapter 13.

It can also be relevant for tax purposes to know whether an object forms part of the land.

Before land is sold, the freehold owner of the property may, of course, fix things to the property and remove them again at will (although different rules apply to tenants—see 'Tenant's fixtures'). It is only when land is to be sold, or when you need to know who owns an object for tax purposes, that the law on fixtures is relevant. When land is sold in the 'normal' way, by contract, the parties are free to come to an agreement about fixtures and fittings. They generally do this by filling in a list, supplied by their solicitors, in which they specify exactly what is included in the sale and what is excluded. It is only if this is not done that the general law on fixtures will be relevant.

EXAMPLE

Sandra bought a new house from Pete. Sandra and Pete specifically agreed that the carpets of the house were included in the sale, but that the curtains were excluded. It did not matter whether fitted carpets would form part of the land under the general law,

---

> because Sandra and Pete had already reached an agreement about them. If, when he was moving out, Pete had changed his mind and taken the carpets, he would have been in breach of contract.

quicquid plantatur solo, solo cedit

'whatever is fixed to the land becomes part of it'

Yet again, there is an old Latin maxim that sums up the law on fixtures: ***quicquid plantatur solo, solo cedit***, or 'whatever is fixed to the land becomes part of it'. However, you should approach the maxim with some caution: it is useful as a general guide, but it does not state the law with complete accuracy. You must look at the case law to understand which objects are likely to become part of the land and which will remain as chattels.

The best place to start is with the test in the leading case of *Holland v. Hodgson* (1872) LR 7 CP 328.

🔍 CASE CLOSE-UP

Holland v. Hodgson (1872) LR 7 CP 328

In this case, the question arose whether looms installed in a factory formed part of that factory—that is, were they part of the land?

Blackburn J said that whether an object is a fixture or a chattel depends on two tests:

1. the degree of annexation;
2. the purpose of the annexation.

In explaining the test, Blackburn J went on to say that articles that are attached to the land only by their weight are not usually considered to be part of the land, unless they were actually *intended* to form part of the land.

He gave the useful example of a dry-stone wall—the kind you often see when you are in the countryside. A pile of stones, randomly stacked in the middle of a field, would not be part of the land—but when they have been arranged, packed, and formed into a stone wall, then they clearly are intended to be part of the land. It is for the person claiming that such an object is part of the land to prove it.

On the other hand, an object fixed to the land—however lightly—is initially considered to be part of the land, unless circumstances indicate that it was always intended to remain a chattel. In this case, it is for the person claiming that the object is a chattel to prove it.

This case tells us to look first at whether the object is attached in any way to the land. If it is, then it is to be classified as a fixture unless there is good reason to classify it as remaining a chattel. If it is not attached, the presumption is reversed: it is to be classified as a chattel unless there is good reason to classify it as a fixture. These rules have been considered in a large number of cases, of which only a selection can be considered here.

🔍 CASE CLOSE-UP

Berkley v. Poulett (1976) 120 Sol Jnl 836

The Court of Appeal considered whether pictures fitted into panelling on a wall, a heavy marble statue resting on a plinth in the garden, and a sundial formed part of land being sold by auction. The test in *Holland v. Hodgson* was applied.

The Court concluded that the pictures, although attached to the walls, were not fixtures: they were put on the walls to be enjoyed as pictures, rather than with the intention of making them part of the land. The statue, also, was not attached to the land, but was placed on a plinth that was attached to the land. The Court of Appeal concluded that the plinth formed part of the land, but the statue did not, because there was no evidence that the statue was designed to go in just that spot in the garden as part of an 'architectural scheme'. The sundial was also held to be a chattel rather than a fixture, because it had been detached from its pedestal many years earlier.

Berkley v. Poulett shows that objects may remain chattels even though they are fixed to the building, as were the pictures in this case. Note the test proposed by this case: were the pictures brought onto the land to be enjoyed as pictures, or to enhance the land permanently? It can also be cited as authority that Blackburn J's 'purpose of annexation' test is regarded as more important than his 'degree of annexation' test in modern times.

It appears, however, from older cases, that statues—even if resting only by their own weight—can form part of the land in some cases, as can pictures.

 CASE CLOSE-UP

D'Eyncourt v. Gregory (1866) LR 3 Eq 382

The court held that articles, such as tapestry, pictures in panels, and frames filled with satin, which were attached to the walls, were fixtures and thus part of the land. In the garden, statues, figures, vases, and stone garden seats that were part of the architectural design of the grounds were fixtures, whether or not they were attached to the ground. Glasses and pictures not in panels, however, were not part of the building and so were chattels.

D'Eyncourt v. Gregory is one of these old cases about inheritance, but it is still useful in illustrating the rule that objects fixed as part of an 'architectural design' are more likely to be fixtures.

Not all cases on fixtures are as old as these: in 1997, the House of Lords had the opportunity to consider the rules expressed in *Holland v. Hodgson* in a modern context.

 CASE CLOSE-UP

Elitestone v. Morris [1997] 2 All ER 513

This case concerned a chalet or bungalow resting on concrete blocks on the ground, which had been brought onto the land many years before. It had been occupied by the defendants since 1971. The landowner and the occupiers seem to have proceeded on the assumption that the chalet belonged to the occupier and not the landowner, and rent was paid for the use of the land on which it stood.

When there was a change in landowner, the rent for allowing the chalet to remain on the ground was increased steeply and notice was served on the occupiers to remove the chalet.

As part of their legal fight to stay on the land, the occupiers needed to argue that the chalet formed part of the land. (This was so that they could claim that they were tenants protected by the Rent Acts—an argument that is not relevant to the point which we are looking at now.)

The Court of Appeal decided that the chalet did not form part of the land, because it merely rested on—but was not attached to—the concrete blocks that formed its foundations.

The House of Lords reversed the decision of the Court of Appeal. It found that the chalet was not designed to be removed from the land without being destroyed. It was not like a Portakabin, or a mobile home: it could not be taken down and erected elsewhere. Therefore, the House of Lords decided that, whatever the parties had originally assumed, the chalet had become part of the land.

Lord Lloyd of Berwick said that he thought the terms 'fixture' and 'chattel' were confusing ones in the context of a house or building. He preferred a different approach, using a threefold classification:

> An object which is brought onto land may be classified under one of three broad heads. It may be (a) a chattel; (b) a fixture; or (c) part and parcel of the land itself. Objects in categories (b) and (c) are treated as being part of the land.

The chalet fell into category (c)—part and parcel of the land itself—as do most buildings. It appears that, if an object cannot be removed from the land except by destruction, it has become part and parcel of the land.

Elitestone v. Morris seems to give more weight again to the 'degree of annexation' part of the test, because it is clear that, if objects are so much part of the land that they cannot be moved without destroying them, they will be classed as fixtures (or, to use Lord Lloyd's preferred terminology, '*part and parcel of the land*'). On the other hand, the purpose test was also used, because the chalet was brought onto the land with the intention that it was to stay there permanently.

This case was applied in *Mew v. Tristmire* [2011] EWCA Civ 912.

 CASE CLOSE-UP

Mew v. Tristmire [2011] EWCA Civ 912

The claimants lived in old houseboats on wooden platforms around a harbour. Just like Mrs Morris, they wanted to claim that the houseboats formed part of the land so that they could claim rights under the Rent Acts.

The Court of Appeal held that the houseboats were chattels. They had been brought to the harbour as moveable objects which could have been easily removed without being destroyed. They could not be considered as one object with the platforms onto which they had later been lifted. It did not matter that they were now very fragile and could not be moved without damage—it was the intention at the time they were brought to the land which was relevant.

THINKING POINT

Look at Photo 1.4 of the Cutty Sark, a tea clipper built in 1869. She has been in dry dock in Greenwich since 1954 and has recently been restored and refixed into a glass exhibition centre.

Do you think that the Cutty Sark is a chattel, a fixture, or part and parcel of the land? Why?

Photo 1.4 The Cutty Sark
© Sandra Clarke

 THINKING POINT

What about the vessel pictured in Photo 1.5, the Gipsy Moth IV, in which Sir Francis Chichester sailed around the world. She was on display in Greenwich, close to the Cutty Sark.

Is she a fixture, a chattel, or part and parcel of the land? Why?

Does your answer differ from that which you gave for the Cutty Sark? Why?

Photo 1.5 How the Gipsy Moth IV was fixed to the ground
© Scott Hortop

It is submitted that the Cutty Sark forms part and parcel of the land, based on the fact that she was brought onto the land with the intention that she stay there permanently as a visitor attraction and has been in dry dock ever since. Gipsy Moth IV, on the other hand, is a chattel. Although she was attached to the land, it was simple to detach her from her fixings and take her elsewhere. In fact, she has been away from Greenwich for some time now and has since sailed around the world again! She was fixed to the land to display her as a chattel, not with the intention of making her part of the land.

Photo 1.6 A narrowboat moored on a canal
© Chris Crafter

Finally, the houseboat in Photo 1.6 is definitely a chattel, because she can be untied and moved at any time. Relevant cases are *Chelsea Yacht and Boat Club v. Pope* [2001] 2 All ER 409, in which it was held that a houseboat always remains a chattel, and of course, *Mew v. Tristmire*.

Everyday items

 THINKING POINT

Have a look around at the room that you are in at the moment.

What do you think about the everyday items that you see?

What about carpets or curtains, or fitted kitchen units? Are they fixtures or chattels?

The best guidance on everyday items is the Court of Appeal decision in *Botham v. TSB plc* (1997) 73 P & CR D 1.

CROSS REFERENCE

See Chapter 13 for more on mortgages.

> ### 🔍 CASE CLOSE-UP
>
> **Botham v. TSB plc** (1997) 73 P & CR D 1
>
> The appellant was behind with his mortgage payments, so the respondent bank was entitled to possession of his flat. The appellant claimed that he had transferred the contents of the property to his parents. The court therefore had to decide which of the contents were fixtures, and so the property of the bank, and which were chattels, and so the property of the parents. The trial judge had divided the 109 items into nine categories and considered each of the categories. He found almost all of the items to be fixtures.
>
> The Court of Appeal differed, however, in its interpretation of the law. A summary of its decision can be seen in Table 1.1.
>
> It is important to note that all cases will depend upon their facts. If curtains or carpets were fixed in a different way, or were part of an 'architectural scheme', for example, the decision as to whether they are fixtures or chattels could vary. This case is, however, a very useful starting point in considering everyday items.

Table 1.1 Summary of the Court of Appeal's decision in *Botham v. TSB plc*

Item	Decision
Fitted carpets	Held by the Court of Appeal to be chattels, because they are easily removed
Lights fixed to walls or ceilings, some of which were in recesses in the ceilings and some of which were attached to the ceiling by tracks	Only those recessed into the ceiling were held to be fixtures; the others could be easily removed
Gas flame-effect fires	Held by the Court of Appeal to be chattels, because they could be easily disconnected and removed
Curtains and blinds, including a shower curtain	Held by the Court of Appeal to be chattels, because they are easily removed
Towel rails, soap dishes, and lavatory roll holders	Held by the Court of Appeal to be fixtures, because they constituted a permanent improvement to the land
Fittings on baths and basins, such as taps, plugs, and shower heads	Held by the Court of Appeal to be fixtures, because they constituted a permanent improvement to the land
Mirrors and marble panels on the walls in the fitted bathroom	Accepted by the defendants to be fixtures
Kitchen units and work surfaces, including a fitted sink	Held by the Court of Appeal to be fixtures, because they constituted a permanent improvement to the kitchen
White goods in the kitchen, such as fridge-freezers, washing machines, and dishwashers	Held by the Court of Appeal to be chattels, because they could be easily removed

Tenant's fixtures

The law on fixtures could act harshly in relation to tenants, because they occupy the land for a limited period only and have to return the land to their landlord at the end of the tenancy. If they have attached items to the land in such a way that the items have become fixtures, they become part of the land and belong to the landlord. In order to avoid such unfairness, a separate set of rules has been established concerning **tenant's fixtures**.

A tenant who attaches a tenant's fixture may remove it at any time during the tenancy or at the end of the lease, or even after the tenancy has ended, provided that he or she is still lawfully in possession. The tenant must make good any damage done in removing the fixture.

> **tenant's fixtures**
> fixtures attached to rented property by a tenant that the tenant is entitled to remove

 CASE CLOSE-UP

Mancetter Developments Ltd v. Garmanson Ltd [1986] QB 1212

The tenant had installed pipework and extractor fans in a factory. These were tenant's fixtures. When they were removed, large holes were left in the factory walls. The tenant was entitled to remove the fans and pipework, but was liable in damages for failing to make good the holes.

There are three categories of tenant's fixture: trade fixtures, ornamental fixtures, and agricultural fixtures.

* Trade fixtures

  These are objects used by the tenant in his or her trade. They have been held to include boilers, machinery, etc., and also the fittings of a public house. This is the category under discussion in *Mancetter Developments Ltd v. Garmanson Ltd.*

When looking at tenant's trade fixtures, it is important to consider the question in two steps:

1. Is it a fixture at all?

2. If it is a fixture, is it a trade fixture and therefore removable by the tenant? This may be decided by the wording of the lease: see *Peel Land and Property Ltd v. Sheerness Steel Ltd* [2014] EWCA Civ 100, in which the Court of Appeal held that the lease prevented the removal of any tenant's fixtures.

The reason for this two-step approach is that it is often necessary to decide whether an article is a fixture, even if it is a trade fixture that the tenant may ultimately have a right to remove. The ownership of the object may be important for tax or rent-review purposes during the tenancy. If it is a fixture, it belongs to the landlord until the tenant removes it under the tenant's fixture rules. If it is not a fixture, it is a chattel, which belongs to the tenant throughout.

* Ornamental fixtures
  Older cases—such as *Martin v. Roe* (1857) 7 E & B 237—recognized the tenant's right to remove articles attached to the land for ornamental purposes, which could be removed without damage to the land. It is arguable that, in the light of the 'purpose of annexation' test, these items would probably not be regarded as fixtures at all today and so would be removable by the tenant anyway.

* Agricultural fixtures
  Farm tenants are given statutory rights under Agricultural Tenancies Act 1995, s. 8 to remove any fixture they have affixed to the land. They must make good any damage caused by removal of their fixtures. Unlike trade fixtures, agricultural fixtures belong to the tenant at all times.

1.1.3.2 **Water**

LPA 1925, s. 205(1)(ix) does not mention water at all, but the Land Registration Act 2002 does.

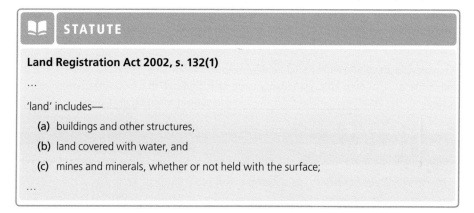

STATUTE

Land Registration Act 2002, s. 132(1)

…

'land' includes—

    (a) buildings and other structures,

    (b) land covered with water, and

    (c) mines and minerals, whether or not held with the surface;

…

Section 132(1) makes it clear that 'land covered with water' is still 'land' (and indeed, English law does not regard the water as being in separate ownership to the land it covers). Therefore, a lake or pond in the middle of your land is part of the land, and the bed of a river and the seabed also form part of the land.

So far, so good—but then it gets a little more complicated. Rights over the water itself depend on whether the water is still or flowing, and, if it is flowing, whether it is tidal or not. Still water, such as a pond or lake, is regarded as forming part of the land on which it rests and landowners can do as they like with it, subject to any statutory controls under the Water Resources Act 1991. Landowners have certain natural rights over rivers flowing through their land: they can fish in the river (unless that right has been granted to someone else) and they have the right to an undiminished flow of the water. They cannot, however, take water from the river to the detriment of landowners downstream and they are entitled to prevent owners upstream from abstracting (removing) water to a noticeable extent. In any case, abstraction is now regulated by statute.

In contrast, landowners have no natural right to water simply percolating through the land—that is, to water that is not in a defined stream, but is just ground water. Subject to statutory restrictions, other landowners can pump out naturally percolating water, or even increase the amount of naturally percolating water reaching lower land, as long as they are acting reasonably—see the discussion of the law in *Palmer v. Bowman* [2000] 1 WLR 842.

If the boundary of land is a non-tidal river, the landowners on each side of the river own the bed of the river up to the centre line—*ad medium filum*. They can fish as far across the river as they can cast their lines—possibly a good excuse for a longer fishing rod.

Tidal water is treated somewhat differently. For a start, there is a presumption that the Crown owns the **foreshore**, although the Crown may have granted it to another body (for example, a local authority).

foreshore

the land between the high-water mark and low-water mark

In addition, the public has rights of navigation and fishing over tidal waterways.

If the boundary of land is tidal water, the boundary may be fixed, or it may vary with the changing of the coastline over the years—see *Baxendale v. Instow Parish Council* [1982] Ch 14. Similarly, in the recent case of *Loose v. Lyn Shellfish Ltd* [2014] EWCA Civ 846, the extent of land over which a fishery (a right to harvest shellfish) could be exercised altered with the movement of the low water mark from time to time.

1.1.3.3 **Animals**

Wild animals and birds do not form part of the land while they are alive, and belong to landowners only when they are found dead on the land. Landowners, however, have the right to hunt them and thus bring them into possession by killing them.

1.1.3.4 **Plants**

Trees and other plants are attached to the land, and form part of it. It is possible to own the plants separately from the land—another example of land having different strata or levels.

 EXAMPLE

It is possible for Farmer Brown to own the land on which trees are planted, but for Forestry Ltd to own the trees.

1.1.4 **Incorporeal hereditaments**

Have another look at the definition in LPA 1925, s. 205(1)(ix).

 STATUTE

Law of Property Act 1925, s. 205(1)(ix)

'Land' includes land of any tenure, and mines and minerals, whether or not held apart from the surface, buildings or parts of buildings (whether the division is horizontal, vertical or made in any other way) and other corporeal hereditaments; also a manor, advowson, and a rent and other incorporeal hereditaments, and an easement, right, privilege, or benefit in, over, or derived from land; … and 'mines and minerals' include any strata or seam of minerals or substances in or under any land, and powers of working and getting the same … ; and 'manor' includes a lordship, and reputed manor or lordship; and 'hereditament' means any real property which on an intestacy occurring before the commencement of this Act might have devolved upon an heir.

You will have noticed that it also includes reference to **incorporeal hereditaments**.

'Incorporeal' means things without a physical form (intangible property), such as rights to receive rent from the land, rights of way, rights of light, and the two ancient rights mentioned in the definition in LPA 1925, s. 205(1)(ix)—an 'advowson' and a 'manor'. You need not worry about an advowson (the right to present a priest to a parish), because it is largely obsolete. Manorial rights, meanwhile, are mainly ceremonial nowadays—but there have been two modern cases showing that manorial rights are not quite dead and buried:

> **incorporeal hereditaments**
> intangible rights in land

⟩ CROSS REFERENCE

If you want to know more about this case, see Chapter 11.

 CASE CLOSE-UP

***Bakewell Management Ltd v. Roland Brandwood and Ors* [2004] UKHL 14**

A businessman who bought the lordship of a manor tried to charge large sums of money for granting rights of way over the common land of the manor to the residents who owned houses around the common. They had been driving over the common to reach their houses for years, but he claimed that they had no right to do so. He was eventually unsuccessful, but the residents had to appeal all the way to the House of Lords to stop him.

 CASE CLOSE-UP

Crown Estate Commissioners v. Roberts [2008] EWHC 1302 (Ch)

The defendant bought up a number of titles to ancient manors and tried initially to claim ownership of large areas of the foreshore of the Pembrokeshire coastline. This claim failed because of a decision in an earlier case (*Roberts v. Swangrove Estates* [2008] EWCA Civ 98), so Mr Roberts instead claimed a number of manorial rights, including wreck de mer, a several fishery, treasure trove, sporting rights, and estrays (these ancient terms are explained in a glossary in an appendix to the judgment). However, all he was able to prove title to was 'a moiety' (half) of a right to wreck.

Although both these cases led to very little in the final analysis, there was a good deal of expensive litigation and anxiety before the matters were settled. It might be better if such ancient rights were either abolished or their extent set out clearly by statute.

Incorporeal hereditaments form part of the land just as much as corporeal hereditaments. If you reflect for a moment, you will see why this is.

 EXAMPLE

Ali lives in a first-floor flat. The stairs and hallways belong to his landlord, Ben. If Ali is to use his flat, he must have a right of way over the stairs and hallways. This right of way needs to form part of land and needs to be transferred with the physical land each time it is transferred to a new owner, or the flat will be valueless.

It is therefore necessary, when looking at the extent of a piece of land, to consider the incorporeal hereditaments that may form part of it. These rights form an important part of the land.

The other side of the coin is that other people may have rights over your land. These may be incorporeal hereditaments, such as rights of way—Ben, in the example just given, has a right of way over his land that will bind any future owner of his land. Such rights are described as **proprietary rights**. They are not personal to the original parties, as are ordinary contractual rights, but are binding on future owners, who were not parties to the original contract.

proprietary rights
rights that are not personal to the original parties, but which are binding on future owners

Many of these proprietary rights will be studied in later chapters, but it is worth noting now that the courts have always sought to limit the number of proprietary rights, precisely because they have such far-reaching effects. In the leading House of Lords decision, *National Provincial Bank Ltd v. Ainsworth* [1965] AC 1175, Lord Wilberforce made the following statement:

CASE CLOSE-UP

National Provincial Bank Ltd v. Ainsworth [1965] AC 1175

Per Lord Wilberforce at 1247:

> Before a right or an interest can be admitted into the category of property, or of a right affecting property, it must be definable, identifiable by third parties, capable in its nature of assumption by third parties, and have some degree of permanence or stability.

This definition means that a proprietary right needs to have three qualities:

1. It must be definable—that is, it must be possible to say what the right is and what it is not.

2. It must be able to be transferred to a new owner—that is, it must not be personal to the person now claiming that right.

3. It must last a reasonable amount of time—that is, it must not be a very fleeting right, or one that changes frequently.

The definition is somewhat circular, in that the *consequence* of a right being proprietary is that it can be transferred to a new owner and the *definition* is that it is a right that can be transferred to a new owner. Also, the degree of stability of the right will depend in some measure on whether it is held to be proprietary. This definition however, does set out the most important features of proprietary rights and, in practice, the law is slow to add new rights to the category of proprietary rights, although this can still happen.

1.2 Objects lost and found in and on the land

Sometimes questions arise as to the rights of landowners to objects found lost or hidden on, or buried within, the land. The rules that apply differ depending on whether the object is found in (or attached to) the land or on the land. In both cases, however, these rules apply only if the true owner of the object (the person who lost or hid it, for example) cannot be found.

1.2.1 In the land

Objects found in, or attached to, the land belong to the occupier of the land.

CASE CLOSE-UP

AG of the Duchy of Lancaster v. Overton (Farms) Ltd [1981] Ch 333

In this case, the court had to decide whether coins were treasure trove (see 1.2.3) or not. It was accepted that if they were not they would belong to the owner of the soil in which they were found.

1.2.2 **On the land**

Objects found on the surface of the land may belong either to the finder or to the occupier of the land. The lost object can be claimed by the occupier only if a manifest intention to control the land can be shown.

CASE CLOSE-UP

Parker v. British Airways Board [1982] 1 All ER 834

A passenger found a gold bracelet on the floor of the executive lounge. He handed it to an employee of British Airways, with a request that it be returned to him if the true owner was not found. British Airways could not find the owner, so they sold the bracelet and kept the proceeds. The claimant sued for damages, on the basis that he had a better right to the bracelet than British Airways. The Court of Appeal held that the claimant did, indeed, have a better right to the bracelet.

The bracelet was not attached to the ground, so the occupier did not have automatic priority over the finder. The claimant was lawfully in the lounge and not a trespasser, and he did not have dishonest intentions. The test, therefore, was whether the defendants had shown 'a manifest intention to exercise control over the lounge and all things which might be in it'. They had not done so, because there was no evidence that they searched regularly, or at all, for lost articles.

It was accepted by the court in *Parker v. British Airways* that, in some circumstances, there was a clear 'manifest intention to exercise control' by the very nature of the premises. Donaldson LJ agreed that a bank vault would fall into such a category. At the other end of the spectrum, a public park clearly gives rise to no such implications. Most premises fall somewhere in between these two extremes.

CASE CLOSE-UP

Waverley Borough Council v. Fletcher [1995] 4 All ER 756

In this case, the defendant, who was using a metal detector in a park owned by the claimant council, found a brooch some 9 in below the surface of the land. He dug it up and reported his find to the Coroner, who determined that it was not treasure trove (see 1.2.3). The question arose as to who had the better right to the brooch: the finder or the landowners.

The Court of Appeal held that the claimant council had the better right to the brooch. It had been found within, or attached to, the land, rather than on the surface, so that it belonged to the owner of the soil in which it had been found. The defendant's claim that he was enjoying lawful recreation in the park was rejected, because metal detecting and digging for finds were not recreations of the sort permitted in local parks.

Both of these cases show the importance of the lawfulness of the finder's presence on the land. A trespassing finder will have no right to the found object. This may occur because the finder was not invited onto the land at all, or because the limits of the permission (known in land law as a licence) that was granted by the landowner have been exceeded. For example, in *Waverley*

Borough Council v. Fletcher the defendant had a licence to be in the park for recreation, but not to use a metal detector, nor to dig up the park.

1.2.3 Treasure

At common law, items of gold or silver found hidden in land belonged to the Crown.

In *AG of the Duchy of Lancaster v. Overton (Farms) Ltd*, it was held that coins had to contain a substantial quantity of gold or silver to be **treasure trove**. Finders of treasure trove were paid compensation.

The common law was defective however, in not protecting archaeological finds unless they were of gold or silver and so the Treasure Act 1996 was enacted with effect from 24 September 1997. This Act abolished treasure trove and made fresh provision in relation to treasure. It removed the requirement that the objects had to have been hidden in the land to be treasure, it defined the amount of precious metal that had to be present for a find to count as treasure, and it made provision for other items of archeological importance found with treasure to be included within the definition.

> **treasure trove**
> under common law before 1997, items of gold and silver found in a concealed place, having apparently been hidden by their owner and not reclaimed, to which the Crown had the right of possession, now replaced by the Treasure Act 1996

📖 STATUTE

Treasure Act 1996, s. 1 [Meaning of 'treasure']

Treasure is—

any object at least 300 years old when found which—

    (i) is not a coin but has metallic content of which at least 10 per cent by weight is precious metal;

    (ii) when found, is one of at least two coins in the same find which are at least 300 years old at that time and have that percentage of precious metal; or

    (iii) when found, is one of at least ten coins in the same find which are at least 300 years old at that time;

any object at least 200 years old when found which belongs to a class designated under section 2(1);

any object which would have been treasure trove if found before the commencement of section 4;

any object which, when found, is part of the same find as—

    (i) an object within paragraph (a), (b) or (c) found at the same time or earlier; or

    (ii) an object found earlier which would be within paragraph (a) or (b) if it had been found at the same time.

Treasure does not include objects which are—

unworked natural objects, or

minerals as extracted from a natural deposit,

or which belong to a class designated under section 2(2).

Under s. 2(1) of the Act, the Secretary of State was given power to designate further objects as treasure and, under the Treasure Designation Order 2002, SI 2002/2666, the following items were added to the definition of treasure.

> ### 📖 STATUTE
>
> **Treasure Designation Order 2002, art. 3 [Designation of classes of objects of outstanding historical, archeological or cultural importance]**
>
> 3. The following classes of objects are designated pursuant to section 2(1) of the Act.
>
>   (a) any object (other than a coin), any part of which is base metal, which, when found, is one of at least two base metal objects in the same find which are of prehistoric date;
>
>   (b) any object, other than a coin, which is of prehistoric date, and any part of which is gold or silver.

The Act and the Order apply to objects within these definitions that are found anywhere within England, Wales, and Northern Ireland, whether attached to or within land, or on the surface. In practice, most treasure is discovered during archaeological digs or by people using metal detectors. Very little treasure is likely to be found on the surface of land.

Finds of items that might be treasure have to be reported to the Coroner within 14 days and an inquest held to determine whether the find is treasure or not. It is a criminal offence not to report a find. A Code of Practice for offering finds to museums, and for rewarding finders and landowners has been drawn up—see the Treasure Act 1996 Code of Practice (second revision). This Code sets out the division of the reward between the finder and the landowner. It starts with the presumption that the reward is to be split 50/50, but an agreement between the finder and landowner as to the split may be observed. If the finder is a trespasser or has committed an offence related to finding, or dealing with, the treasure (such as not declaring it in a timely way to the Coroner), his or her reward may be reduced or refused altogether.

1.2.4 Summary

The law on objects lost and found in and on the land is summarized in Figure 1.2.

Figure 1.2 A summary of the law on objects lost and found in and on the land

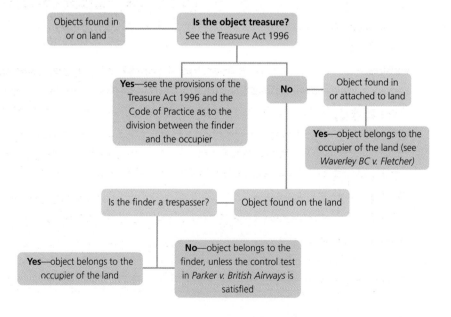

Summary

1. Land extends both below and above the ground.

2. Both corporeal and incorporeal hereditaments form part of the land.

3. The law distinguishes between fixtures and chattels, and the test used by the courts to identify them relates to the degree and purpose of annexation.

4. Items lost or hidden on land belong to their true owner if they can be found, or, if they cannot, to the occupier of the land within which the items are buried or to which they are attached.

5. If the item is merely on the surface of the land, however, the finder may well have better rights than the landowner, depending on the 'manifest intention to control' test. An exception to these rules is found within the law of treasure.

 The bigger picture

- If you want to see how this area of land law fits into the rest of your studies, you can look at Chapter 14, especially 14.2.1 and 14.2.2. Before you can answer any question on land law, you need to be able to identify the land!

- For some guidance on what sort of exam questions come up in this area, see Chapter 15, 15.3.

- If you need to find extra cases for research on coursework in this area, the following may be helpful.

Extent of land

Anchor Brewhouse Developments Ltd v. Berkley House (Docklands Developments) Ltd [1987] 2 EGLR 173

London & Manchester Assurance Co Ltd v. O & H Construction Ltd [1989] 2 EGLR 185

Mitchell v. Mosley [1914] 1 Ch 438 (this case was approved by the Supreme Court in *Bocardo v. Star Energy*)

Fixtures

Caddick v. Whitsand Bay Holiday Park Ltd [2015] UKUT 0063 (LC)

Hamp v Bygrave [1983] 1 ELGR 174

Melluish v. BMI (No. 3) Ltd [1996] AC 454

Smith v. City Petroleum Co Ltd [1940] 1 All ER 260

Stokes v. Costain Property Investments Ltd. [1984] 1 WLR 763

Young v. Dalgety plc [1987] 1 EGLR 116

Webb v. Frank Bevis Ltd [1940] 1 All ER 247

Objects found on or in land

Armory v. Delamirie (1722) 1 Stra 505, 93 ER 664

Bridges v. Hawksworth (1851) 15 Jur 1079

Elwes v. Brigg Gas Co (1886) 33 Ch D 562

Hannah v. Peel [1945] KB 509

? Questions

Self-test questions

1. Daisy's neighbour has started to build an extension to his house. The extension adjoins Daisy's back garden. The foundations for the extension and the new drainage pipes run under Daisy's garden. Has Daisy any grounds for complaint?

2. Mai Ling's neighbour has just installed a new boiler. The flue extends some 10 cm into Mai Ling's garden, at a height of about 4 m. Has Mai Ling any grounds for complaint?

3. Olu has just bought a house. When he saw the house before buying it, the garden contained a large shed and a number of beautiful plants. The shed and some of the plants were removed before he moved in. Does Olu have any grounds for complaint?

4. Haminder is walking across Farmer Jones' field when he sees a golden bracelet half-buried in the soil. He loosens it with his fingers and takes it home to clean it up. Haminder hands the bracelet to the police, but they have handed it back, saying that they cannot trace the owner. Can Haminder keep the bracelet?

Exam questions

1. Abdul owns a metal detector, which he enjoys using to find objects buried below the surface of land. Early in 2003, he went out with his metal detector onto Bill's farm. Bill was a tenant farmer, leasing his farm from Cuthbert.

   Abdul had seen Bill a few days earlier and asked if he could look for 'buried treasure' in Bill's fields. Bill had laughed and said: 'Okay, but I doubt you'll find anything there—I plough it up pretty regularly.'

   In fact, Abdul found a cache of metal objects, which turned out to be silver goblets and arm-rings, dating from Saxon times. They have been valued at £250,000. He also found a Rolex watch lying on the surface of the field. No one knows who lost or buried any of the items.

   Advise Abdul whether he can lawfully keep these items and, if not, to whom they belong.

2. 'As a matter of legal definition, "land" is both the physical asset and the rights which the owner or others may enjoy in or over it.' (M. Dixon, *Principles of Land Law*, 8th edn)

   Discuss.

   ⓐ For suggested approaches to answering these questions visit the Online Resource Centre.

Further reading

Caldwell, D., 'Don't get in a fix over fixtures' (2014) 164(7616) NLJ 15

This article examines the case of *Peel Land and Property Limited v. TS Sheerness Limited* [2014] EWCA Civ 100.

Conway, H., 'Case comment on *Elitestone v. Morris*' [1998] Conv 418

This case comment examines the leading case of *Elitestone v. Morris*.

Thompson, M. P., 'Must a house be land?' [2001] Conv 417

This article looks at the case of *Chelsea Yacht and Boat Club v. Pope*, and considers the nature of land and of dwelling houses.

 ## Online Resource Centre

www.oxfordtextbooks.co.uk/orc/clarke_directions5e

For more advice relating to this chapter, including self-test questions and an interactive glossary, visit the Online Resource Centre.

2 The structure of land law

 LEARNING OBJECTIVES

By the end of this chapter, you will be able to:

- understand the origins of the structure of modern land law;
- explain the doctrines of tenure and estates;
- identify the different roles of common law and equity in land law;
- explain the doctrine of notice and the modern equivalent—registration;
- identify the significance of the 1925 property legislation;
- discuss the two schemes of registration and their importance.

Introduction

Arguably, the single most important provision in land law is in the Law of Property Act 1925, s. 1.

STATUTE

Law of Property Act 1925, s. 1

(1) The only estates in land which are capable of subsisting or of being conveyed or created at law are—

    (a) An estate in fee simple absolute in possession;

    (b) A term of years absolute.

(2) The only interests or charges in or over land which are capable of subsisting or of being conveyed or created at law are—

    (a) An easement, right, or privilege in or over land for an interest equivalent to an estate in fee simple absolute in possession or a term of years absolute;

    (b) A rentcharge in possession issuing out of or charged on land being either perpetual or for a term of years absolute;

(c) A charge by way of legal mortgage;

(d) ... and any other similar charge on land which is not created by an instrument;

(e) Rights of entry exercisable over or in respect of a legal term of years absolute, or annexed, for any purpose, to a legal rentcharge.

(3) All other estates, interests, and charges in or over land take effect as equitable interests.

...

This section lies at the heart of modern land law, because it sets out the estates and interests in land that can be legal and then says that all other interests in land are equitable.

The section raises a huge number of questions for someone with no knowledge of land law:

- What is an estate?

- What does it mean to be 'conveyed at law'?

- What is the difference between an estate 'at law' and an 'equitable interest'?

- Why does it all matter?

The aim of this chapter is to explain what land lawyers mean by legal estates and equitable interests, and why it matters which you own.

2.1 The historical context

At first sight, the history of land law may seem completely irrelevant—after all, why does it matter what the law used to be? Surely what is important is the modern law, not what used to happen in the past?

Our experience, however, suggests that some explanation of the history of land law is vital to understanding the modern law. Many of the concepts and words that confuse students starting out in land law have ancient origins and, once these are explained, the structure of land law becomes clearer, and it is easier to understand how land law works today.

Table 2.1 sets out the main periods in the development of land law. This chapter does not cover any of these in depth, but uses them to explain the main concepts.

Table 2.1 A historical outline of land law

Period	Development
1066 (the Norman Conquest)–c. 1300	**Tenures and estates** Land law in England and Wales dates from 1066. During this early period, the doctrines of tenure and estates were established, as the common law courts worked out the fundamental principles of land law. At the end of this period, in 1290, the statute Quia Emptores was passed, which began to end the feudal system.

(Continued)

Table 2.1 Continued

Period	Development
1300–1535	**Common law and equity**
	The body of law known as equity grew and became established. Equitable estates and interests came to exist alongside common law estates and interests. One of the most important developments of equity was the 'use', which later developed into the trust.
1535–c. 1650	In 1535, the Statute of Uses was passed. This was intended to abolish 'uses'—the forerunners to trusts. In fact, lawyers found ways round the statute and a great deal of new law was created as a result.
c. 1650–c. 1800	In 1660, the Tenures Abolition Act was passed, which further reduced the effect of the feudal system of tenure. Trusts were developed further, the strict settlement was invented, and the modern form of mortgage was developed.
1800–1925	During this period, there was a series of statutory reforms of land law. These culminated in the 1925 property legislation—a series of Acts of Parliament that consolidated earlier changes in the law.
1926–	Since the 1925 property legislation, there have been further developments in equity, such as 'new model' constructive trusts and proprietary estoppel. In addition, there have been further statutory reforms, the most important of which have been the Trusts of Land and Appointment of Trustees Act 1996, and the Land Registration Act 2002.

CROSS REFERENCE

For more on modern trusts, see Chapters 8–10.

For more on mortgages, see Chapter 13.

CROSS REFERENCE

For more on proprietary estoppel, see Chapter 9.

For more on the Trusts of Land and Appointment of Trustees Act 1996, see Chapter 10.

For more on the Land Registration Act 2002, see Chapter 4.

2.2 The earliest developments: tenures and estates

The structure of land law traditionally dates from 1066: the date of the Norman Conquest. William, Duke of Normandy, invaded England and fought the Saxon King, Harold, at the Battle of Hastings. King Harold was killed and the victorious Duke became King William I, the first Norman King of England.

The significance of this event for English land law was that the Normans brought with them their own system of landholding, known as the **feudal system**. Under that system, only the King was able to own land outright. All others were granted land by the King, to hold from him for a certain period of time. This holding of land is known as **tenure** and the period of time for which it is held is known as an **estate**.

> **feudal system** a political, economic, and social system under which only the monarch was able to own land outright
>
> **tenure**
>
> 1. *freehold tenure*—in the feudal system, the grant of an estate in land by a lord to a tenant. The tenant 'holds the land of the lord' for the period defined by the estate.
> 2. *leasehold tenure*—the relationship between a landlord and a tenant in leasehold land

estate the length of time for which land has been granted to a tenant under the system of tenure. It means the duration of the grant. Note that this is a use of the word 'estate' that differs from the general use of the word; estate is used in this technical sense in land law.

2.2.1 Tenures

In this chapter, we will be looking at the first meaning of tenure—that is, freehold tenure.

When William I became King of England, he became the 'paramount lord' of all the land in England, which gave him the power to make grants of that land to anyone he wished. In practice, he no doubt left many of the Saxon noblemen in residence on their land and either granted estates in that land to them, or granted an estate in it to a Norman lord, who would, in turn, grant an estate in it to the Saxon already in residence. In return for the grant of the estate, the new tenant would be obliged to perform services for his new lord.

CROSS REFERENCE

For more on leasehold tenure, see Chapter 5.

 EXAMPLE

The King might grant the Duke of Borsetshire an estate in the whole of Borsetshire, in return for the provision of 100 fully equipped soldiers for 100 days each year. The Duke might provide these soldiers by making grants of parcels of his land to ten lesser noblemen, in return for ten soldiers each for 100 days a year. He might also make grants to farmers in return for quantities of food, etc.

Each of the tenants might, in their turn, make grants of part of their land in return for services.

Tenure also carried with it certain 'incidents', which meant payments to the lord or rights that the lord could exercise. For example, when an estate in land passed on the death of a tenant to his heir, a sum of money was usually payable to the lord. If a tenant died without leaving an heir, the estate would revert back or **escheat** to the lord.

escheat the right of the lord to the tenant's land if he were to die without leaving an heir. This survives into modern times as the right of the Crown to land left without an owner (bona vacantia), although it is now regulated by the Administration of Estates Act 1925. Common law escheat survives, under which land is disclaimed by a debtor on insolvency (bankruptcy).

The granting of estates in land in return for services and incidents led to the development of the feudal pyramid.

Figure 2.1 The feudal pyramid under William I

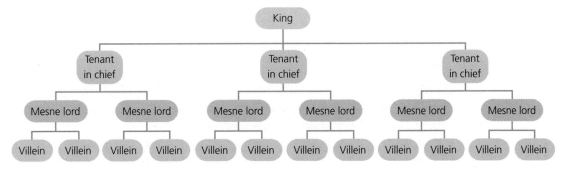

As you can see, the King is at the top of the pyramid as the owner, or more correctly, as 'paramount lord' of all land in the kingdom. The 'tenants in chief' held estates directly from him; the 'mesne' lords held from the tenants in chief, etc. At the very bottom are the 'villeins' or peasants, who held on the 'unfree tenures'. They would be granted strips of land in their lord's fields, to grow their own food, in return for working on the lord's land for part of the time. It is important to note that there could be many more levels in the feudal pyramid than are shown in Figure 2.1. New grants could be made at any time and the process of making such grants of land was called **subinfeudation**.

> **subinfeudation**
>
> the process of making new grants of land under the feudal system

The feudal system's use of the land as a means to obtain services did not last very long. Over time, many services were replaced by a payment of money instead. With inflation, those sums of money became less valuable.

In 1290, the statute Quia Emptores (which is still in force) began the dismantling of the feudal system, because it prohibited subinfeudation. From the passing of that statute to present times, estates in land can be transferred only by **substitution** —that is, one owner taking the place of another. No further levels could be added to the feudal pyramid and, over the course of time, the pyramid began to flatten.

> **substitution**
>
> the process of transferring estates in land under which one owner takes the place of another

This flattening process was accelerated by the Tenures Abolition Act 1660 and completed by the Law of Property Act 1925 (LPA 1925). Today, there is only one form of tenure left and only one lord. Everyone holds their land directly from the Crown on 'freehold tenure in socage', a tenure that has no services and only one relevant incident—escheat. So, the feudal pyramid has flattened completely, as shown in Figure 2.2.

Figure 2.2 The feudal pyramid today

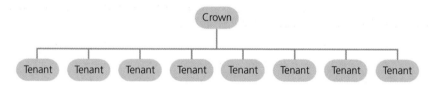

It is fair to say that the doctrine of tenure itself now has limited importance in everyday land law in England and Wales. But it 'is a doctrine which could not be overturned without fracturing the skeleton which gives our land law its shape and consistency', according to Brennan J of the High Court of Australia in the case of *Mabo v. Queensland (No. 2)* (1992) 175 CLR 1 FC 92/014.

See the Online Resource Centre for an excerpt from this case, with some questions.

🔍 **CASE CLOSE-UP**

Mabo v. Queensland (No. 2) (1992) 175 CLR 1 FC 92/014

In this case, the doctrine of tenure was minutely examined to establish whether, when the Crown acquired sovereignty over Australia, this destroyed all prior interests held by Aboriginal Australians. It was held that the Crown's 'radical title' as paramount lord did not destroy native title rights that had existed since before the Crown acquired sovereignty; it was only if the Crown had granted the land to settlers or used the land itself that native title had been destroyed.

The case contains a fascinating discussion of the details of the doctrine of tenure.

2.2.2 Estates

The doctrine of estates follows on directly from the doctrine of tenure and is a consequence of it. If land is to be 'held of' a lord, then the parties must specify the length of time for which it is to be held. It is this length of time that is the estate in land. In the very ancient *Walsingham's Case* (1573) 2 Plowd 547, it was said that: 'An estate in the land is a time in the land, or land for a time.'

Before 1925, there were three common freehold estates, as shown in Table 2.2.

Table 2.2 Types of common freehold estate pre-1925

Estate	Duration
Fee simple	For as long as there were heirs to inherit. The estate would not end unless all possible heirs (blood relations of the grantee or any of his heirs, etc.) were dead. The estate could therefore potentially last forever. It would come to an end only if the present tenant were to die without leaving an heir.
Fee tail	For as long as the grantee's lineal descendants (children, grandchildren, etc.) lasted. A variant of the fee tail was the fee tail male, under which only male lineal descendants could inherit. (Note that these estates could, in later times, be 'barred' to create a fee simple.)
Life estate	For as long as the life of the grantee or the life of a named person. Note that this is not a fee, because it is not inheritable.

The common feature of all the freehold estates is that they are of uncertain duration: no one can say with certainty when a person will die, or when all of his or her heirs will die. This is the hallmark of the freehold estates and distinguishes freehold from leasehold.

One question that might occur to you is how one is to know what sort of estate is under **conveyance** (being transferred): did the **conveyancer** intend to transfer the fee simple, the fee tail, or merely a life estate?

Historically, conveyancers have used 'words of limitation'—that is, a particular phrase that is known to have the correct legal effect—to mark out the limits of the estate they intended to transfer. In modern times, however, this is simplified by statute under LPA 1925, s. 60.

> **STATUTE**
>
> **Law of Property Act 1925, s. 60(1)**
>
> A conveyance of freehold land to any person without words of limitation, or any equivalent expression, shall pass to the grantee the fee simple or other the whole interest which the grantor had power to convey in such land, unless a contrary intention appears in the conveyance.

conveyance
the transfer of a legal estate in land from one person to another

conveyancer
a person who specializes in the transfer of estates in land—usually a solicitor or licensed conveyancer

Therefore, the grantor is assumed to have transferred the largest estate he or she held in the land, unless it is made clear in the transfer that a lesser interest was intended.

2.2.3 Crown land

The only land in England and Wales that is not held as an estate from the Crown is land that belongs to the Crown itself, including **demesne land**.

demesne land
'land belonging to [the monarch] in right of the Crown'

STATUTE

Land Registration Act 2002, s. 132

...

'demesne land' means land belonging to Her Majesty in right of the Crown which is not held for an estate in fee simple absolute in possession;

...

> **CROSS REFERENCE**
> For clarification of the meaning of 'foreshore', see Chapter 1.

Such land is also referred to as **allodial land**, which means land that is owned outright, rather than as an estate in land held of a lord. Examples of demesne land include the foreshore and land that has escheated to the Crown, as well as land that has belonged to the Crown since ancient times and in which an estate was never granted.

> **allodial land** land that is owned outright, rather than as an estate held of a lord

2.3 Common law and equity

> **common law**
> the law developed by the Royal Courts—that is, the law applicable to the whole country, not purely local law

Tenures and estates are creations of the **common law** and their development dominates most of the early history of English land law. At that time, however, the common law itself was developing, as law moved out of local courts and into the Royal Courts (the King's Bench, the Common Pleas, and the Exchequer). Actions in these courts were by 'writs', which were very prescriptive. Like many modern-day government forms, these writs were appropriate only for certain cases. Other cases simply could not be 'fitted into' any writ, so it was difficult to bring the case at all—particularly after the Statute of Westminster II 1285, which severely restricted the invention of new writs. This led to obvious injustice in a number of cases.

The remedy for such injustice was for the injured party to appeal directly to the King as the 'fountain of all justice'. The King's Council, including the King's most important minister, the Chancellor, heard these petitions and, gradually, the Chancellor rather than the King's Council came to be responsible for hearing such claims. In this way, the Court of Chancery developed.

> **equity**
> the law developed by the Lord Chancellor and the Court of Chancery to remedy defects in the common law

From the end of the seventeenth century until the Constitutional Reform Act 2005, only lawyers were appointed to the post of Lord Chancellor and each sat as a judge in the Court of Chancery. The system of justice called **equity** developed, from one-off decisions in the early stages, to become a body of law that was as settled as the common law. The principles of equity, however, were based on conscience, in contrast to the common law's emphasis on technicality.

> **CROSS REFERENCE**
> For an example of this rule in action, see *Walsh v. Lonsdale* in Chapter 5.

Because equity developed from the position of the King as fountain of all justice, in cases of conflict between the two systems, equity prevailed over the common law. This means that, if there are two possible answers to a legal problem—one given by the common law and one given by equity—the equitable answer takes priority.

Eventually, by the Judicature Acts 1873 and 1875, the two systems of law came to be administered by all courts, so that there were no longer courts of common law and courts of equity. The two systems of law still operate side by side, and, even today, it is possible to distinguish equitable rights and remedies from legal ones.

2.3.1 **The effect of equity on land law**

The easiest way to describe the effect of equity on land law is by giving examples of the types of interest rejected by the common law, but recognized by equity. One important example is the **trust**.

CROSS REFERENCE

For the use of trusts in modern land law, see Chapter 10.

> **trust** an arrangement by which someone (called a 'settlor') transfers property to others (called 'trustees') on terms that the trustees will hold that property for the benefit of certain persons (called the 'beneficiaries')

To understand how the trust developed, think about the following example.

 EXAMPLE

Sir Robin of Locksley was about to go off to war abroad. He wanted to ensure that his family was provided for while he was away. He therefore transferred his estate in Locksley Hall to his good friend, Sir Guy of Gisborne, trusting him to use the property for the benefit of Sir Robin's wife, Lady Marian, and children.

In this example, Sir Robin was the settlor, Sir Guy was the trustee, and Lady Marian and the children were the beneficiaries.

The common law courts, after a little hesitation, refused to recognize the rights of beneficiaries under trusts. The common law recognized only the trustee as having legal rights in the land, because he was the person with legal title to the land: it had been transferred to him. The courts of equity, meanwhile, recognized the rights of the beneficiaries.

 EXAMPLE

Suppose that after three years, Sir Guy of Gisborne were to have received news that Sir Robin was dead. He may have decided to keep Locksley Hall for himself and have therefore thrown Lady Marian and the children out into the streets.

If Lady Marian were to have brought an action in the common law courts for the return of the land, she would have been unsuccessful. The common law courts recognized only the legal title of the trustee.

If Lady Marian were to have gone to the Court of Chancery, however, she might have obtained a remedy. The Court recognized the equitable rights of the beneficiaries as the true or 'beneficial' owners of the estate. The Court would have issued an order to the trustee (Sir Guy) to carry out the terms of the trust, and Lady Marian and the children could have moved back in.

> *in rem*
> a right enforceable against everyone— that is, a right in the property itself

The order for the trustee to carry out the terms of the trust is an example of equity acting *in personam* —that is, 'on the person'. Because equity acts on the conscience of the individual, equitable rights are enforceable only against those 'whose conscience is affected by them'. This can be contrasted with the common law, under which legal rights can be enforced against anyone, no matter what the state of their conscience. Legal rights are said to be *in rem*—that is, in the property itself, rather than against a particular person.

> *in personam*
> a right enforceable against certain persons or classes of persons

The history of the development of the trust is a fascinating one, but its details are outside the scope of this book. It started as the 'use', developed in the fifteenth century. The use proved so effective as a means of avoidance of feudal dues (taxes) that it was prohibited by Parliament in the Statute of Uses 1535. Lawyers found ways around the statute, however, and the use returned as the trust. Trusts are still used for tax avoidance today, as well as for many other purposes in land law and other areas of law.

⟫ CROSS REFERENCE

For more on mortgages, see Chapter 13.

mortgage
a way of using land as security for a loan

equity of redemption
the rights of a mortgagor over the mortgaged property—particularly, the right to redeem the property

charge
a legal or equitable interest in land, securing the payment of money

Another example of the effect of equity on land law is the development of the **mortgage**.

The earliest type of modern mortgage dates from the seventeenth century. The borrower would convey (transfer) his estate in the land to the lender, in return for the loan. The lender would promise to reconvey (return) the land to the borrower on a date that was fixed for the repayment of the loan. The common law was inflexible about this date for repayment, even if the failure to pay was as the result of an accident or mistake. Equity began to intervene in these cases to extend the date for repayment; at first, where there were special circumstances, but eventually in all cases. Over time, the equitable right of the borrower (mortgagor) to redeem the land long after the agreed date had passed became a recognized right in the land called the **equity of redemption**. Although modern mortgages do not work by conveyance and reconveyance, but by way of a **charge**, the equity of redemption is still a valuable right.

Because the courts of equity regularly upheld both the interests of the beneficiaries under trusts and the equity of redemption held by the mortgagor, these rights came to be equitable estates and interests in land. Therefore, a beneficiary under a trust (such as Lady Marian in our examples) had an equitable estate in the land, whereas her trustee (Sir Guy) had a **legal estate** in the land. This is still true today, although the interests of beneficiaries are nowadays referred to as **equitable interests** rather than as estates, in line with the wording used in LPA 1925, s. 1(3).

> **legal estate** an estate in land that is recognized by the common law
>
> **equitable interest** an interest in land that is recognized by equity

2.4 Legal and equitable estates and interests

From section 2.3, you should have understood that two kinds of estates and interests developed in land law: those recognized by the common law (legal rights) and those recognized by equity (equitable rights).

If you take a minute to look back at the introduction to this chapter, you will see that this distinction is a fundamental one in the modern law and that LPA 1925, s. 1 lists those estates and interests in land that can be legal, and then says that all other rights in land can only be equitable. We have established so far what we mean by estates in land, and what we mean by legal and equitable rights—but that is only part of the story. We must now go on to examine the differences between these two different types of rights and explain why it matters whether a right in land is legal or equitable.

The main difference stems from the way in which common law and equity enforce rights. As we saw earlier, common law acts *in rem*, whereas equity acts *in personam*. You can understand the difference that this makes in practice by thinking about the following situation.

THINKING POINT

Consider again the trust in the examples above. Sir Guy of Gisborne is the legal owner of Locksley Hall, but Lady Marian and the children are the equitable owners of Locksley Hall. As we established earlier, the Court of Chancery would oblige Sir Guy to carry out the terms of the trust, as he had originally agreed to do.

Suppose that Sir Guy were to sell Locksley Hall to the Sheriff of Nottingham and keep the money for himself. The Sheriff would become the legal owner of Locksley Hall, because he has bought Sir Guy's legal estate in the land. The vital question, however, is whether he would have to hold it on trust for Lady Marian and the family—after all, he did not agree to be a trustee.

If Lady Marian's rights in Locksley Hall had been legal rights, they would have been enforceable against anyone, because they would be rights *in rem*. As equitable rights, however, they would be enforceable only *in personam*—against certain persons. Would the Sheriff of Nottingham be such a person?

The answer to this question can be found in the origins of equity as a doctrine of conscience. Equity would enforce the trust against anyone whose 'conscience was affected' by it. This would come down, ultimately, to whether that person had notice of (knew about) the equitable interest. Therefore, the answer to the question whether the Sheriff of Nottingham would be affected by Lady Marian's equitable interest under the trust would depend upon whether the Sheriff knew about it.

If the Sheriff bought the land knowing of Lady Marian's equitable interest, he would be ordered by the Court of Chancery to carry out the trust. If he knew nothing about the trust, the Court of Chancery would not require him to carry it out, so Lady Marian would have no remedy against him. Instead, she would have to bring an action against Sir Guy of Gisborne, against whom equity could act *in personam*. The problem with that solution, however, would be that Sir Guy no longer owned the land. Therefore, he could only be ordered to pay damages. If he had run away with the money and could not be found, Lady Marian would be left with no remedy at all.

This shows the disadvantage of equitable estates and interests over legal ones.

2.4.1 The doctrine of notice

Gradually, the rule developed that equitable interests could be enforced against anyone *except* those who bought a legal estate in the land and who had no notice of the equitable interest in it. There is a classic statement of this rule in the old case of *Pilcher v. Rawlins* (1872) LR 7 Ch App 259, which sets out the importance of someone now referred to as the **bona fide purchaser of the legal estate for value without notice**.

bona fide purchaser of the legal estate for value without notice broken down, this phrase refers to someone who has bought the legal estate in the land—the 'purchaser of the legal estate'—who has acted honestly in the purchase—that is, in good faith or 'bona fide'—and has bought the land without knowing about the equitable interest in the land—that is, 'without notice'

Such a person was held to have an 'absolute, unqualified, unanswerable defence' to any claim in equity. He could not be deprived of the full value of his legal estate by equity, but had to be allowed to 'depart in possession' of it.

The differences between legal and equitable interests might therefore be expressed as in Table 2.3.

Table 2.3 The differences between legal and equitable interests

Legal estates and interests	Enforceable against everyone—that is, 'good against the whole world' Common law acts *in rem*
Equitable estates and interests	Enforceable against everyone *except* the 'bona fide purchaser of the legal estate for value without notice' Equity acts *in personam*

Because equitable interests were not enforceable against the bona fide purchaser of the legal estate for value without notice—sometimes quaintly called 'equity's darling'—it is necessary to examine in more detail the definition of that person.

2.4.1.1 'Bona fide'–in good faith

bona fide

'in good faith'

It is clear from James LJ's statement of the law in *Pilcher v. Rawlins* that **bona fides** (good faith) is a separate requirement from that of notice and one that may be tested by the courts. In *Midland Bank v. Green* [1981] AC 513, Lord Wilberforce defined it as 'genuine and honest'. In practice, it is closely related to the lack of notice and particularly to the doctrine of constructive notice, which is considered later at 2.4.1.4.

2.4.1.2 'Purchaser of the legal estate'

CROSS REFERENCE

For more on the fee simple absolute in possession, see Chapter 3.

For more on the term of years absolute, see Chapter 5.

This means that the person must buy a legal estate in the land. In the past, this could have meant any freehold estate, or a legal lease. Since 1925, it means a fee simple absolute in possession, or a term of years absolute, which are the two remaining legal estates under LPA 1925, s. 1(1).

A purchaser is someone who gives value for the land—so someone who receives it as a gift, or as an inheritance, for example, would not qualify. The meaning of purchaser is extended to those who take 'a charge by way of legal mortgage' under LPA 1925, s. 87(1): that is, a person who lends money on the security of a mortgage over the estate.

Note that the definition is limited to those who purchase a legal estate in the land; it does not apply to someone who buys only an equitable interest. If an equitable interest is purchased, then the rule 'if equities are equal, the first in time prevails' applies, meaning that an earlier equitable interest will usually be enforceable against the purchaser of a later equitable interest.

2.4.1.3 'For value'

'Value' means consideration in money or money's worth. Historically, it also included marriage, which was viewed as consideration for a transfer of property. It does not mean that full value must have been paid for the land. For example, in *Midland Bank v. Green* [1981] AC 513, a payment of £500 for land worth £40,000 was held to be within the definition of 'a purchaser for money or money's worth'.

2.4.1.4 'Without notice'

The doctrine of notice lies at the heart of the definition of the person against whom equity would enforce interests. A bona fide purchaser for value of the legal estate who had no notice of the equitable interest would not be bound by it—but notice was not confined to matters of which the purchaser actually knew. It was extended to situations in which the purchaser should have known of the equitable interest.

There are three types of notice: actual notice, constructive notice, and imputed notice.

Actual notice

A purchaser had actual notice of any interests about which he actually knew, by whatever means. He need not, however, have attended to vague rumours—*Barnhart v. Greenshields* (1853) 9 Moo PCC 18.

Constructive notice

A purchaser had constructive notice of any interests about which he was deemed to know:

 CASE CLOSE-UP

Jones v. Smith (1841) 66 ER 943

In this case, Lord Wigram identified two categories of constructive notice:

1. cases in which the purchaser has knowledge of some defect or incumbrance in relation to the property, enquiry into which would reveal others, so is deemed to have notice of what those enquiries would have revealed;

2. cases in which the purchaser has deliberately abstained from enquiries to avoid having notice.

The first type of constructive notice means that, if a purchaser discovers a problem with, or equitable interest in, the estate being purchased, further enquiries must be made. The purchaser will be deemed to have notice of any interest that would have been discovered by further enquiries, whether or not they were actually made.

The second type of constructive notice means that a purchaser cannot decide to make no enquiries at all, in the hope that this will avoid being fixed with notice of any equitable interests. In this case, the purchaser will be treated as if he knew anything that proper enquiries would have revealed.

A third category of constructive notice is that the purchaser is also deemed to have notice of all those matters that a reasonable or prudent purchaser, acting with skilled legal advice, would have investigated—*West v. Reid* (1843) 2 Hare 249.

These rules are now summarized by statute, under LPA 1925, s. 199.

 STATUTE

Law of Property Act 1925, s. 199

1. A purchaser shall not be prejudicially affected by notice of—

   ...

   (ii) any other instrument or matter or any fact or thing unless—

   (a) it is within his own knowledge, or would have come to his knowledge if such inquiries and inspections had been made as ought reasonably to have been made by him;

   ...

The purchaser therefore needs to investigate the title to the estate to the same standard as a skilled lawyer. There is also a requirement to inspect the land and to make enquiries of the occupiers as to their rights. A purchaser who fails to do these things might be fixed with notice of matters which should have been discovered.

Imputed notice

This is notice imputed to the purchaser by virtue of actual or constructive knowledge possessed by the purchaser's agent.

STATUTE

Law of Property Act 1925, s. 199(1)(ii)(b)

(b) in the same transaction with respect to which a question of notice to the purchaser arises, it has come to the knowledge of his counsel, as such, or of his solicitor or other agent, as such, or would have come to the knowledge of his solicitor or other agent, as such, if such inquiries and inspections had been made as ought reasonably to have been made by the solicitor or other agent.

A purchaser is deemed to know what his or her solicitor (or other agent) knew and even what that solicitor would have known if the job had been done properly.

THINKING POINT

Do the doctrines of constructive notice and imputed notice make it easier or harder for someone to be a bona fide purchaser of the legal estate for value without notice?

These doctrines make it harder, because they expand the meaning of 'notice'. It includes not only what the purchaser actually knew, but also what they, or their solicitor, ought to have known if they had made proper enquiries. Therefore, equitable interests affect more purchasers than they otherwise would have done.

2.4.2 **Summary**

The situation before 1925, therefore, was that legal estates 'bound the whole world'—that is, that any person coming to own a legal estate in land would be bound to give effect to any existing legal interest in it.

EXAMPLE

Sir Guy of Gisborne granted a legal lease (tenancy) of one wing of Locksley Hall to John Little. When Sir Guy sold Locksley Hall to the Sheriff of Nottingham, there is no doubt that John Little's lease would have been binding on the Sheriff—that is, the Sheriff could not have thrown John Little off the land, but would have had to permit him to remain there for the term of his lease.

A person coming to own a legal estate in land would be bound by existing equitable interests in it only if he was *not* a bona fide purchaser of the legal estate without notice.

EXAMPLE

Consider again the position of Lady Marian after Locksley Hall had been sold to the Sheriff. She did not have a legal estate or interest in the land; she had only an equitable interest in it. Therefore, the Sheriff would have had to give effect to her interests only if he was not a bona fide purchaser of the legal estate for value without notice. This would have depended upon whether the Sheriff knew, or ought to have known, about the trust. If Lady Marian and the children were actually living in Locksley Hall, it is very likely that at the very least, the Sheriff would have had constructive notice of their interests and would thus have been bound by them. This would have meant that Lady Marian and the children would have been able to continue living in the hall.

2.5 The 1925 property legislation

The **1925 property legislation** marks a watershed in the history of land law. Although based on older concepts and previous reforms, the effect of this body of legislation cannot be overstated. In many ways, modern land law can be dated from this legislation.

By the nineteenth century, land law in England and Wales had become hopelessly complex. Attempts at reform were made throughout the nineteenth century, but most of them were concerned with the process of conveyancing (transferring land), rather than with the substantive law. It was not until after World War I that professional legal opinion finally accepted the need for real reform of land law. It was this acceptance that led to the 1925 property legislation.

> **1925 property legislation** a series of Acts of Parliament that came into effect on 1 January 1926. These Acts consolidated earlier piecemeal changes in the law—particularly from 1922–24—and brought them all together as a body of law, which made substantial changes to the common law of property.

The Acts that are bundled together under this heading are (in alphabetical order):

- Administration of Estates Act 1925;
- Land Charges Act 1925;
- Land Registration Act 1925;
- Law of Property Act 1925;
- Settled Land Act 1925;
- Trustee Act 1925.

As you might expect after more than ninety years, all of these Acts have been amended, and some of them have been repealed and replaced by later legislation. Nonetheless, the 1925 property legislation remains a fundamental landmark in the development of modern land law and the basic scheme that it introduced continues.

It is, of course, very difficult to sum up the policy of so many Acts of Parliament in a few words, but some underlying themes can be seen running through the legislation.

Put simply, the legislation tried to achieve two main objectives:

1. Land must be freely alienable—that is, it must be possible to transfer it (and interests in it) to others.

2. Land must be capable of fragmentation of ownership, for both family reasons and commercial reasons—that is, it must be possible to create numerous different interests in land in favour of others.

These two objectives are in tension with each other: if land is to be easy to transfer, the fewer interests that exist in it, the better. A purchaser is less likely to buy land if he or she cannot buy the estate free of **prior adverse interests**.

---

prior adverse interests

interests that come before an estate in time and that are not for the present landowner's benefit

---

 EXAMPLE

It is 1800. Locksley Hall, and its surrounding outbuildings and land, are now owned by the Earl of Huntingdon. He, however, has only a life estate in the Hall, after which it is to go to his eldest son, Lord Locksley for life, then to his eldest son in fee tail. The Earl of Huntingdon's mother, Lady Huntingdon, has a life interest in one of the houses in the grounds, as well as an annuity (annual payment of income) secured on the estate. Under the terms of the settlement (trust) that governs the Hall, various other beneficiaries—such as the Earl's sisters—have rights in parts of the property. There are several mortgages on the Hall—some legal and some equitable—and some of the land has been leased to the Huntingdon Mining Corporation.

It is clear that this kind of complexity will make it very difficult to sell Locksley Hall. No one has the right to sell an unencumbered freehold in the Hall: the Earl has only a life estate and so does his eldest son. The land is encumbered (burdened) with many different interests, some of which are legal and some equitable. A purchaser would have to work very hard to pay all of these off and to be sure that every interest had been discovered.

This example shows that land is capable of fragmentation of benefit—many different people have rights in it, and the land is being used to support a whole family and some commercial purposes. But it lacks alienability—it is much harder to transfer.

If land is to be more freely alienable, then the number of interests allowed to exist in it must be limited in some way and/or those interests must not be binding on a purchaser. This, however, would decrease the availability of fragmentation of benefit, which could be a disadvantage in utilizing the land fully. In other words, it would make it easier to sell the land, but it would make it harder for lots of people to share in it.

Although landowners before 1926 could easily share the land (fragment the benefit), the differences between legal and equitable rights could leave some beneficiaries vulnerable. Those with equitable interests had a share in the land, but they might lose it to a purchaser.

 EXAMPLE

Under the settlement, Jane Goodwill, the Earl's cousin, has been granted a right to live in one of the cottages on the estate. While she is away on holiday, the Earl grants a legal lease of the cottage for ten years to Peter Farmer.

Because Peter Farmer has purchased a legal estate in the land (a lease) and Jane's rights are equitable, Jane will be unable to enforce her rights against Peter unless he has had notice of them. If he is held to have had neither actual nor constructive notice, she may lose her home for the next ten years.

On the other hand, if Peter Farmer had no actual notice of Jane's rights when he took the lease, but is deemed to have had constructive notice, then he will be bound to give effect to her interests. This could be very unfair to Peter, who planned to live in the cottage.

In both cases, there would be a remedy against the Earl, but that would lie in damages only and would depend on him having enough money to pay damages. It would also not result in the injured party keeping the land—a remedy that he or she would probably prefer.

So, if we consider the position before 1925, some problems become clear. A purchaser of a legal estate in land might have had to deal with a number of interests already existing in the land: some of them legal and some of them equitable.

As we have seen, a purchaser who had no notice of an adverse right in land would be bound by that right if it was legal, but not if it was equitable—and this had two consequences:

1. The more legal rights there were in land, the more difficult it was for a purchaser to know whether he or she was buying an estate free of adverse rights.

2. Because of the doctrine of notice, the more equitable rights there were, the more difficult it was to be certain of property rights. On the one hand, equitable rights could be lost if the legal estate in the land was bought by a bona fide purchaser for value without notice; on the other hand, a purchaser might be deemed to have constructive notice of equitable rights even though he or she did not, in fact, know of them. Neither situation was entirely fair or satisfactory.

The solution of the 1925 property legislation was to alter radically the system of legal and equitable interests in land. Some of the main outcomes of this are that:

- the range of legal rights that can exist in land was reduced to two estates and a limited number of interests under LPA 1925, s. 1, as we saw at the start of this chapter;

- provision was made for registration of interests in land, so that the effect of the doctrine of notice was reduced;

- a way was devised for some equitable interests to be 'lifted off' the land and transferred into the purchase price paid for the legal estate. This is known as 'overreaching' (see 2.5.3).

2.5.1 The two legal estates

The two legal estates are a fundamental provision of LPA 1925, s. 1, which we introduced at the beginning of the chapter. Now that we have looked at the history of the law, and have established what an estate is, what legal and equitable rights are, and why it mattered whether an interest in land was legal or equitable, we can look at the section in more depth.

 STATUTE

Law of Property Act 1925, s. 1(1)

The only estates in land which are capable of subsisting or of being conveyed or created at law are—

(a) An estate in fee simple absolute in possession;

(b) A term of years absolute.

▶ CROSS REFERENCE

For more on the fee simple absolute in possession, see Chapter 3.

For more on the term of years absolute, see Chapter 5.

The very first section of the LPA 1925 reduces the number of legal estates that can exist in land to only two. This is the meaning of the words 'capable of subsisting or of being conveyed or created at law'. The first legal estate is the **fee simple absolute in possession**, or freehold estate. The second is the **term of years absolute**, or leasehold estate.

> **fee simple absolute in possession** this refers to the legal freehold estate
>
> **term of years absolute** this refers to the leasehold estate

▶ CROSS REFERENCE

For more on these trusts, see Chapter 10.

Before 1926, there could also be equitable freehold estates in land, but this is no longer possible: former equitable estates are now equitable interests and can exist only as beneficial interests under a trust. Therefore fees tail, life interests, etc. are now equitable interests, rather than estates in land as they were formerly. The fee simple absolute in possession (the legal freehold) is held on trust to give effect to these lesser interests in equity.

2.5.1.1 Legal interests in land

Having reduced the number of legal estates to two, LPA 1925, s. 1, goes on to limit the number of **legal interests** that can exist in land.

> **legal interests**
> interests in land that can exist at common law, rather than in equity

 STATUTE

Law of Property Act 1925, s. 1(2)

The only interests or charges in or over land which are capable of subsisting or of being conveyed or created at law are—

(a) An easement, right, or privilege in or over land for an interest equivalent to an estate in fee simple absolute in possession or a term of years absolute;

(b) A rentcharge in possession issuing out of or charged on land being either perpetual or for a term of years absolute;

(c) A charge by way of legal mortgage;

(d) … and any other similar charge on land which is not created by an instrument;

(e) Rights of entry exercisable over or in respect of a legal term of years absolute, or annexed, for any purpose, to a legal rentcharge.

This subsection contains a list of interests in land that can exist at common law, rather than in equity. Some of these will be considered in later chapters of this book. For present purposes, it is important to note that this is only a short list of interests. Other interests in land were not abolished, but LPA 1925, s. 1(3) provides that, unless an interest in land falls within the list in LPA 1925 s. 1(2), it will be equitable rather than legal.

 STATUTE

Law of Property Act 1925, s. 1(3)

All other estates, interests, and charges in or over land take effect as equitable interests.

2.5.1.2 Summary

The combined effect of these provisions is to limit the number of legal estates and interests in land, and thus to limit the number and types of rights that will bind a purchaser without notice. This therefore carries out the first of the objectives of the 1925 property legislation.

Next, we will consider the second part of the reforms: the introduction of a system of registration.

2.5.2 Registration

The idea of **land registration** was not new in 1925. There had been a number of previous attempts to bring in systems of registering interests in land—particularly in densely populated areas, such as London. But the 1925 legislation was the first time that a compulsory, nationwide system of registration was introduced.

> **land registration**
> the system of registering certain legal estates and interests in land

It is important to grasp at the outset that the 1925 legislation introduced not one, but two systems of registration: one of these, registration of title, is intended to be permanent; the other, registration of land charges, is intended to be temporary, although it will continue to exist for some time to come. The differences between the two are summarized in Table 2.4.

Table 2.4 The two systems of land registration

Registration of title	The nationwide, compulsory system started in 1925 by the Land Registration Act 1925. The idea behind the system is that title to the land should be registered, and that the register should reflect all of the estates and interests affecting the land.	Land already included in this scheme is known as *registered land*
Registration of land charges	This is intended to be a temporary solution to the unfairness of the doctrine of notice until title to all land is registered. It enables certain categories of equitable interest in land to be entered on a register. Purchasers must inspect the register to see what equitable interests exist. Constructive and imputed notice does not apply to such interests. Owners of registered equitable interests can be sure that a transfer of the legal estate will not destroy their interests.	This type of registration applies only to land that is not yet registered land, known as *unregistered land*

THINKING POINT

Why do you think a temporary system of registration was necessary, as well as a permanent one?

The answer to this question is a practical one. It takes time to create a register of all of the titles to land in England and Wales. The authors of the legislation were aware of this and therefore decided that a partial reform applying to unregistered land was necessary as well. By April 2015, 85 per cent of the land area of England and Wales was registered, although well over 90 per cent of titles (over 24 million) are registered, because it is mainly owners of larger areas of land who have not yet registered their titles.

There is, therefore, a large area of unregistered land to which the temporary system of registration of land charges still applies.

2.5.2.1 Unregistered land

> **unregistered land**
> land to which the title has not yet been registered at the Land Registry. Title to such land has to be proven by documentary evidence, known as 'title deeds'.

The system of registration that was introduced for **unregistered land** was a partial reform only of the doctrine of notice: it applies only to certain equitable interests granted in unregistered land. The legislation is now contained in the Land Charges Act 1972. Not all equitable interests can be registered and those that cannot still rely on the old doctrine of notice.

Registrable interests

The categories of registrable interests are contained in Land Charges Act 1972, s. 2. A summary of these can be seen in Table 2.5.

Table 2.5 The categories of registrable interests

Category	Definition	Summary
Class A	'rent or other annuity or principal money … which is a charge on land … created pursuant to the application of some person under … an Act of Parliament'	These are charges on land in respect of certain statutory payments made—for example, by landlords to tenants in relation to improvements
Class B	'a charge on land (not being a local land charge) … created otherwise than pursuant to the application of any person'	These are charges created automatically by statute to ensure the repayment of costs or expenses—for example, the costs of legal aid should land be recovered or preserved by the case person'
Class C	'(i) puisne mortgage, (ii) limited owner's charge, (iii) a general equitable charge, (iv) an estate contract'	This is an important category of charges. A puisne (pronounced 'puny') mortgage is one that is not protected by deposit of title deeds. The usual way for a first legal mortgage of unregistered land to be protected is for the mortgagee (lender) to take physical possession of the documents proving title to the land. This will prevent the land being sold without the mortgagee's consent. A second or subsequent mortgagee (legal or equitable) cannot have the title deeds, however, because the first mortgagee already has them. Therefore, he or she can enter a charge on the land charges register to protect their interest in the land.
		A limited owner's charge is a charge to protect the repayment of money spent on the land by someone who has only a limited interest in it—for example, money spent by someone who has only a life interest under a settlement
		The general equitable charge is a sort of 'sweeping up' category, defined by reference to all of the things it is not—see Land Charges Act 1972, s. 2(4)(iii). It includes, for example, a charge on land that a vendor (seller) of the land has in respect of unpaid purchase money.

CROSS REFERENCE

For more on mortgages, see Chapter 13.

CROSS REFERENCE

For more on settlements, see Chapter 10.

(Continued)

Table 2.5 Continued

Category	Definition	Summary	
		An estate contract is defined as 'a contract by an estate owner … to convey or create a legal estate, including a contract conferring … a valid option to purchase, a right of pre-emption or any other like rights' under Land Charges Act 1972, s. 2(4)(iv). An option to purchase is a right that is granted to another person to buy the estate in land within a certain period of time. If the right is exercised, the estate owner is obliged to sell. A right of pre-emption is a right of 'first refusal': if the estate owner decides to sell, he or she must offer the land to the holder of the right of pre-emption first.	
Class D	'(i) an Inland Revenue charge, (ii) a restrictive covenant, (iii) an equitable easement'	An Inland Revenue charge is a charge on land registered by the Inland Revenue in relation to unpaid Inheritance Tax	**CROSS REFERENCE** For more on restrictive covenants, see Chapter 12.
		A restrictive covenant is an agreement contained in a deed that a landowner will refrain from doing something on his or her land (see Chapter 12). Such covenants may be enforceable between subsequent landowners, as well as between the persons who actually entered into the agreement—hence they are registrable as land charges.	
		An easement is a right for the benefit of one piece of land over another piece of land—for example, a right of way (see Chapter 11). If such a right is equitable (rather than legal), it must be registered as a land charge.	**CROSS REFERENCE** For more on easements, see Chapter 11.
Class E	An annuity created before 1 January 1926 and not registered in the register of annuities	These are old annuities and increasingly unlikely to be encountered	
Class F	A charge affecting land by virtue of the Family Law Act 1996, Pt IV	This is a charge in respect of a spouse's (or civil partner's) statutory right to occupy a matrimonial (or partnership) home of which he or she is not the owner	

This is a very long list of interests and you do not need, at this stage, to understand what they all mean. The important thing to note about these interests is that most of them are the kinds of interest in land that are likely to have been granted in return for money or money's worth—that is, they are commercial interests rather than 'family' interests.

So, for example, Class C land charges include estate contracts, which would include a contract to buy the land, either immediately or in the future (an option contract). Class D land charges include equitable easements, which would include rights of way and other rights over neighbouring land. The reason why these sorts of interest can be considered commercial is that they would usually be granted for money, or would increase the price that someone would pay for their land. It is therefore important that they are not destroyed when the land is sold.

'Family interests', on the other hand, are those types of interest that one would not expect to continue in relation to the land once it has been sold to someone else. For example, the family home may be subject to equitable interests in favour of family members who have paid for its purchase. These interests can be satisfied by a share of the purchase money once the house is sold; they do not need to continue to bind the land in the hands of a purchaser and therefore are not registrable under the Land Charges Act 1972.

Effect of registration

If the interest is one that can be registered under the Land Charges Act 1972, registration is both necessary and sufficient. The owner of the equitable interest must register it and, if that is done, the interest will be protected because registration is deemed to constitute actual notice to the purchaser of the legal estate under LPA 1925, s. 198(1).

 STATUTE

Law of Property Act 1925, s. 198(1)

The registration of any instrument or matter in any register kept under the Land Charges Act 1972 or any local land charges register shall be deemed to constitute actual notice of such instrument or matter, and of the fact of such registration, to all persons and for all purposes connected with the land affected, as from the date of registration or other prescribed date and for so long as the registration continues in force.

Because the effect of registration is to constitute actual notice, once an equitable interest is registered under the Land Charges Act 1972, it will be binding upon any subsequent owner of the land.

Consequences of failure to register

We have already stated that registration is both necessary and sufficient: if you *can* register the interest, then you *must* do so. The inevitable consequence of this is that, if you do not register it, your interest may well be lost if the land is sold to a new owner. Under Land Charges Act 1972, s. 4 if a registrable interest is not registered, it will be void (which means it will have no effect) as against:

- 'a purchaser of the land charged with it, or of any interest in such land' (Classes A, B, C(i), (ii), and (iii), and F);
- 'a purchaser for money or money's worth of the legal estate in the land charged' (Classes C(iv) and D).

Note that both of these apply to a purchaser. Someone who receives land as a gift or inheritance, for example, will be bound by all prior equitable interests, registered or not.

The legislation is clear in rejecting any 'conscience' element in registration, for fear of bringing back constructive notice by the back door. Even actual notice on the part of the purchaser is not sufficient to protect an unregistered interest.

 CASE CLOSE-UP

Midland Bank v. Green [1981] AC 513

This case concerned a family farm, originally owned by the father, Walter Green. He granted an option to purchase the farm, which was unregistered land, to his son, Geoffrey.

This option was an estate contract and therefore should have been registered as a Class C(iv) land charge—but Geoffrey failed to register it.

Walter fell out with Geoffrey and, intending to defeat the option, sold the land to his wife (Geoffrey's mother, Evelyn) for £500. The farm was worth £40,000 at that time.

The question arose whether this sale was valid to defeat the unregistered option. There was no doubt that the sale was a breach of contract by Walter. Equally, there was no doubt that Evelyn knew of the option. Under what is now the Land Charges Act 1972, s. 4(6), however, an unregistered estate contract is void against 'a purchaser for money or money's worth of the legal estate in the land charged'.

Two main arguments were put forward for Geoffrey:

1. that the word 'purchaser' should be interpreted as meaning purchaser 'in good faith';

2. that 'money or money's worth' should be interpreted to exclude nominal or inadequate consideration.

Lord Wilberforce (who gave the only substantive judgment) rejected both of these arguments, saying:

> The case is plain: the Act is clear and definite. Intended as it was to provide a simple and understandable system for the protection of title to land, it should not be read down or glossed: to do so would destroy the usefulness of the Act. Any temptation to remould the Act to meet the facts of the present case, on the supposition that it is a hard one and that justice requires it, is, for me at least, removed by the consideration that the Act itself provides a simple and effective protection for persons in Geoffrey's position—viz.—by registration.

It can be seen from this case that the House of Lords applied the Land Charges Act 1972 strictly, refusing to alter its plain meaning so as to bring it more into line with the equitable doctrine of notice. It is worth noting that Geoffrey was not left without remedy: he was awarded damages against his solicitors for negligence and against his father for breach of contract. Neither of these remedies, however, entitled him to enforce the option against his mother.

Problems with registration of land charges

Registrable equitable interests in unregistered land must be 'registered against the name of the estate owner whose estate is intended to be affected' under the Land Charges Act 1972, s. 3(1). Because the land itself is not registered, the only possible way for equitable interests to be registered is against the name of the estate owner. This means that a purchaser has to search the register for entries made against that name.

This has led to two problems, as follows:

1. The owner of the equitable interest who needs to protect it by registration may not know the full name of the estate owner, or may be mistaken about it. He or she may therefore register against the wrong name.

2. The purchaser may not know all of the possible names against which to search, because documents of title dating from as early as 1925 may have been lost in the meantime. Therefore the name of a previous owner may be unknown to the purchaser.

An example of the first problem—the incorrect name—is shown in the case of *Oak Co-operative Building Society v. Blackburn*.

🔍 CASE CLOSE-UP

Oak Co-operative Building Society v. Blackburn [1968] Ch 730

The estate owner in this case was Francis David Blackburn. He agreed to sell the house to a Mrs Caines, who moved in. The house was not legally transferred to her and so the agreement to buy the house was an estate contract, which was required to be registered as a Class C(iv) land charge. This was eventually done, against the name of *Frank* David Blackburn, a name by which Mr Blackburn was known in the neighbourhood.

Subsequently, Mr Blackburn mortgaged the property to the claimant building society. They made a search of the land charges register against the name Francis *Davis* Blackburn and did not find the registration of the estate contract. The question to be decided by the Court of Appeal was whether the building society was bound by the estate contract.

It was held that it was. The Court held that registration against a version of the estate owner's true name was effective against a purchaser who did not search at all, or who searched (as here) against an incorrect name. It would not, however, be effective against a purchaser who searched against the full, correct name (see *Diligent Finance Co. Ltd v. Alleyne* (1972) 23 P & CR 346).

▶ CROSS REFERENCE

For more on transfers of unregistered land, see Chapter 3.

title deeds

the documentary evidence that shows how land came to its present owner

In this case, the Court seems to have taken a practical view and to have tried to get the legislation to work as well as possible. Any system based on names, however, is going to give rise to these sorts of difficulty.

The second problem is one that is caused by the age of this partial system of registration of land charges. It has now been in place for over ninety years, during which time land may have changed hands many times. The main proof of title for unregistered land is the collection of **title deeds**— that is, conveyances and other documents showing how land came into the possession of the present owner.

These documents must go back at least fifteen years. Often, there will be documents going back further than this—but this is not always the case. There may be names against which land charges have been validly registered in the past, but against which the purchaser does not know to search.

➡ EXAMPLE

Bleak House, which is unregistered land, was conveyed to Anna in 1925. Since then, the transfers have been as follows.

1932 Anna transferred it to Ben.

1946 Ben transferred it to Chris, who granted an equitable right of way (easement) over Bleak House in favour of the house next door, Windy Corner. This equitable easement has been correctly registered against Chris's full name.

1958 Chris transferred Bleak House to Edie.

1965 Edie transferred Bleak House to Fatima.

1973 Fatima transferred the house to Gopal.

1989 Hari inherited the property from Gopal.

In 2015, Hari contracted to sell Bleak House to Ines. The land is still unregistered. To prove good title, Hari must produce a conveyance (transfer) going back at least fifteen years. This means that he must show how he inherited the property, and the conveyance to Gopal in 1973. These will give Ines the names of Fatima, Gopal, and Hari, and she can search against these names in the land charges register. But there is no guarantee that the conveyances from 1946 or 1958 will have been kept, so Ines may not be able to search against Chris's name. Therefore she will not discover the right of way, but will still be treated as if she had actual knowledge of it under LPA 1925, s. 198(1).

This problem has been addressed by statute, in the Law of Property Act 1969, which introduced a scheme of compensation to deal with undiscoverable land charges that are not within the actual knowledge of the purchaser.

 STATUTE

Law of Property Act 1969, s. 25 [Compensation in certain cases for loss due to undisclosed land charges]

(1) Where a purchaser of any estate or interest in land under a disposition to which this section applies has suffered loss by reason that the estate or interest is affected by a registered land charge, then if—

   (a) the date of completion was after the commencement of this Act; and

   (b) on that date the purchaser had no actual knowledge of the charge; and

   (c) the charge was registered against the name of an owner of an estate in the land who was not as owner of any such estate a party to any transaction, or concerned in any event, comprised in the relevant title;

   (d) the purchaser shall be entitled to compensation for the loss.

The purchaser remains bound, therefore, by the equitable interests that were correctly registered, but which they could not discover, but unless the purchaser actually knew about those interests when he or she bought the land, compensation will be paid. It is a partial solution, even if it is not as good a solution as would be ensuring that all registered interests can be discovered.

Both of these problems are examples of the intended temporary nature of registration of land charges when compared to the permanent system of registration of title.

2.5.2.2 Registered land

The nationwide, compulsory system of land registration was started in 1925 by the Land Registration Act 1925, although there had been previous systems in place, particularly in London. The idea behind the system is that title to all land should be registered, and that the register should reflect all of the estates and interests affecting the **registered land**.

> **registered land**
> land to which the title is registered with the Land Registry. Title to such land is guaranteed by the Land Registry and is proven by a search of the register.

The principles of registration

There are three main principles of registration of title, first set out by Theodore Ruoff, a former Chief Land Registrar, as follows:

1. **The mirror principle**

    The register should be a mirror of the estates and interests affecting the land.

2. **The curtain principle**

    The details of any trusts affecting the land should be kept off the title.

3. **The indemnity principle**

    An indemnity (compensation) is payable by the state if loss is caused by errors in the register.

> **mirror principle** the principle in registration of title that the register should be a mirror of the estates and interests affecting the land
>
> **curtain principle** the principle in registration of title that the details of any trusts affecting the land should be kept off the title
>
> **indemnity principle** an indemnity (compensation) is payable by the state if loss is caused by errors in the register

Registration of title is now governed by the Land Registration Act 2002 (LRA 2002), which replaced the Land Registration Act 1925 on 13 October 2003. The 2002 Act preserves the register of titles and continues the basic scheme of 1925, but introduced substantial amendments to the way in which the system works.

The register of title

The Land Registry keeps a register of all land in England and Wales. Each title is identified by number, and is related to a map reference and plan that is based on the Ordnance Survey Map, not to the name of the estate owner.

There are three parts to the register of each title:

▶ CROSS REFERENCE

For more on incorporeal hereditaments,
see Chapter 1.

1. **The property register**

    This contains a description of the land, including incorporeal hereditaments, such as easements over other land, restrictive covenants, etc., for the benefit of the land.

2. **The proprietorship register**

    This gives the names of the estate owner(s), the type of title, and any restrictions to which they are subject when dealing with their title.

3. **The charges register**

    This contains those things that are a charge or encumbrance on the land—that is, those things that do not benefit the land, but rather are a burden on it. Examples include mortgages and rights of way over the land (as opposed to those over other land for the benefit of this land).

> **property register** first part of the register of title, containing a description of the land by address and postcode, and including incorporeal hereditaments, such as easements over other land and restrictive covenants benefitting the land
>
> **proprietorship register** second part of the register of title giving the names of the registered proprietor, the type of title, and any restrictions to which the registered proprietor is subject when dealing with their title

charges register third part of the register of title, containing charges or encumbrances over land such as mortgages, easements, and restrictive covenants burdening the land

Form 2.1 shows an example of a register of title. At the top, you can see the title number, which is the Land Registry's unique reference number for that estate in land. The register is then divided into the three parts listed above.

Form 2.1a Example of a register of title

```
-------------- ---------------- ----------------------------------------------------------- -----------
--------
TITLE NUMBER : UG234567
A PROPERTY REGISTER
This register describes the land and estate comprised in the title.
-------------- ---------------- ----------------------------------------------------------- -----------

GREATER LONDON       LONDON BOROUGH    Ruxley

1. (23 November 1967) The Freehold land shown edged with red on the
plan of the above Title filed at the Registry and being 36 Hillendale
Road, Ruxhurst.

2. (23 November 1967) This property enjoys rights of drainage over
neighbouring properties.

END OF A REGISTER
-------------- ---------------- ----------------------------------------------------------- -----------

TITLE NUMBER : UG234567
B PROPRIETORSHIP REGISTER
This register specifies the class of title and identifies the owner.
It contains any entries that affect the right of disposal.
TITLE ABSOLUTE
-------------- ---------------- ----------------------------------------------------------- -----------

1. (25 March 1988) Proprietor: STANLEY CLIFFORD WENTWORTH and
PATRICIA ANNE WENTWORTH both of 36 Hillendale Road, Ruxhurst, London.


END OF B REGISTER
-------------- ---------------- ----------------------------------------------------------- -----------

TITLE NUMBER : UG234567
C CHARGES REGISTER
This register contains any charges and other matters that affect the
land.
-------------- ---------------- ----------------------------------------------------------- -----------

1. (23 November 1967) The land is subject to rights of drainage.


2. (23 November 1967) A Conveyance of the land in this title dated 31
July 1928 made between (1) J.W. Ellingham Limited (Vendor) and (2)
Albert Edward Gales (Purchaser) contains covenants details of which
are set out in the schedule of restrictive covenants hereto.

3. (25 March 1988) REGISTERED CHARGE dated 1 June 1988 to secure the
monies including the further advances therein mentioned.

PROPRIETOR of Charge dated 1 June 1999 Barnebridge Building Society
of Barnebridge House, Crown Street, Barnebridge BR2 9QT.
```

Form 2.1b Example of a register of title (continued)

TITLE NUMBER : UG234567
SCHEDULE OF RESTRICTIVE COVENANTS

The following are details of the covenants contained in the
Conveyance dated 31 July 1928 referred to in the Charges Register:-

1. No house or other building shall be erected on the land except in
accordance with these stipulations;

2. One house only of the cost of at least Five hundred pounds and in
all respects according to front elevations to be approved of by the
Vendor or the surveyor of the Vendor shall be erected on the land and
for the purposes of this stipulation the cost of every house shall be
taken to be the net first cost thereof in labour and materials alone
(exclusive of ornamental fittings) to be estimated by the surveyor
for the time being of the Vendor at the lowest current prices.

3. No hoarding shall be erected or placed on the land for
advertisements and no hut shed caravan house on wheels or other like
erection movable or otherwise intended or adapted or capable of
adaption for use as a dwelling or sleeping apartment shall be erected
or placed or be allowed to be or remain on the land.

4. No road or way shall be made or permitted across the land hereby
conveyed for access to or regress from any adjoining lands and
premises.

END OF REGISTER
NOTE: The date at the beginning of an entry is the date on which the
entry was made in the Register.

The first part, the property register, gives the address of the land (36 Hillendale Road, Ruxhurst) and refers to a plan filed at the Registry. It also states that the land is freehold land. The property register then lists an easement that exists for the benefit of this land—that is, rights of drainage over neighbouring properties. The easement, being an incorporeal hereditament, forms part of the definition of the land in this title.

The second part, the proprietorship register, gives the names of the proprietors (owners) of the estate in land—namely, Stanley and Patricia Wentworth. There are no restrictions entered on the proprietorship register limiting their power to deal with the title.

The third part, the charges register, contains any encumbrances on the land:

> **CROSS REFERENCE**
>
> For more on easements, see Chapter 11.
>
> For more on restrictive covenants, see Chapter 12.
>
> For more on mortgages, see Chapter 13.

1. The first entry in this section concerns an easement—namely, rights of drainage. Read in combination with the similar entry in the property register, it looks as though the drains for this property and neighbouring ones run under a number of properties. Each of the properties carries with it a right to use all of the drains, not only the bit that runs under its own land.

2. The second entry refers to restrictive covenants into which a previous owner of the land entered. These covenants are listed in a schedule at the end of the register, and include restrictions on the type and number of houses that may be built on the land. Such restrictive covenants may still be enforceable against the present proprietors.

3. The third entry is a charge, or mortgage over the land, and the proprietor of the charge (the lender)—in this case, the Barnebridge Building Society—is shown below it.

Classes of title

The Land Registry will assign a particular 'class' to each title. For freehold land, there are three classes; for leasehold land, along with absolute leasehold, possessory leasehold, and qualified leasehold, there is a fourth class, 'good leasehold' (see Table 2.6).

Table 2.6 Land Registry classes of title

Class of title	Summary
Absolute freehold/ absolute leasehold	The most usual class of title. This means that the Land Registry is satisfied with the title.
Possessory freehold/ possessory leasehold	This class of title is granted to squatters who have been on the property long enough to claim the land and to anyone else with no documentary proof of title. It is vulnerable to someone able to prove better title.
Qualified freehold/ qualified leasehold	This class of title is very rare and means that the Registry is not completely satisfied with respect to one aspect of the title.
Good leasehold	This class of title means that the Registry is satisfied with the leasehold title, but not necessarily with the estate out of which it has been granted—usually because that estate is not yet registered. In practice, good leasehold is acceptable to purchasers.

If you look back at Form 2.1, you will see that this estate has been given 'Title Absolute' (look near the top of the proprietorship register).

First registration

There was no attempt in 1925 to force everybody to register their land immediately—to do so would have overloaded the system and left the Land Registry unable to cope. Instead, areas of the country were made areas of 'compulsory registration', which meant that any land that was the subject of a 'triggering event', such as a sale, was subject to **first registration of title**. The areas of compulsory registration began with major cities, because there are more separate pieces of land in urban areas.

Eventually, in 1990, the whole of England and Wales was made an area of compulsory registration. In addition, the number of triggering events was increased by subsequent legislation. These are now set out in LRA 2002, s. 4.

This section requires the first registration of:

- any type of transfer of a 'qualifying estate', whether by sale, gift, inheritance, court order, etc.;
- the grant out of a qualifying estate of leases of more than seven years, plus certain other leases;
- the creation of a protected first legal mortgage of a qualifying estate.

Under LRA 2002, s. 4(2) a 'qualifying estate' is a fee simple absolute in possession (the freehold) or a leasehold estate that has more than seven years to run.

LRA 2002, s. 4 gives the Lord Chancellor power to extend the list of relevant events that will trigger registration. The duty to apply for registration is dealt with in LRA 2002, s. 6, and, broadly speaking,

> **first registration of title**
>
> the first time that title to an estate in land is registered at the Land Registry and at which point it therefore changes from unregistered land to registered land

the duty is on the responsible estate owner—the person to whom the estate is transferred when registration is triggered. The estate must be registered within two months of the date on which the relevant (triggering) event occurs. Failure to do so will result in the transfer failing to operate at law, which means that the legal estate will stay with the transferor, or that only an equitable lease or mortgage will have been granted.

 STATUTE

Land Registration Act 2002, s. 7 [Effect of non-compliance with section 6]

(1) If the requirement of registration is not complied with, the transfer, grant or creation becomes void as regards the transfer, grant or creation of a legal estate.

(2) On the application of subsection (1)—

   (a) in a case falling within section 4(1)(a) or (b), the title to the legal estate reverts to the transferor who holds it on a bare trust for the transferee, and

   (b) in a case falling within section 4(1)(c) to (g), the grant or creation has effect as a contract made for valuable consideration to grant or create the legal estate concerned.

   …

▶ CROSS REFERENCE

For more on equitable leases, see Chapter 5.

As you can see from LRA 2002, s. 7(2)(a), this will leave the legal title with the transferor of the estate and he or she will hold it on trust for the transferee. This means that the transferor of the estate will continue to hold the legal title to the land and that the transferee will have only an equitable interest. Any expenses of retransferring the legal estate will fall on the transferee.

If a legal lease or charge was intended, but fails because it is not registered, the transfer operates as if it were a contract to create that interest. This will also result in the transferee having only an equitable interest in the land. The interests will be equitable rather than legal, so they may be unenforceable against a subsequent purchaser of a legal estate in the land. It is therefore essential to register title as required by the Act.

The classification of interests that may be registered

There are three main classes of interest in registered land, as follows:

1. registrable dispositions;
2. interests protected by notice or restriction;
3. overriding interests.

(Note that the LRA 2002 refers to this last class as 'interests which override'—but the older term 'overriding interests' is in common use.)

- **Registrable dispositions**

    These are the most important interests in registered land. They consist of a number of interests, of which the transfer or creation of the following are most important:

    - a fee simple absolute in possession;
    - a lease exceeding seven years and certain other leases;
    - the creation of a legal mortgage of such an estate;
    - the express creation of legal easements, profits, and rentcharges out of such an estate, under LRA 2002, s. 27.

This list clearly has a great deal in common with the list of relevant events in LRA 2002, s. 4, which is not surprising. Estates and interests that trigger first registration will be registrable dispositions once title to the estate is registered. Again, in a similar way to first registration, a registrable disposition must be registered or it will not take effect at common law—that is, it will remain equitable.

 STATUTE

Land Registration Act 2002, s. 27 [Dispositions required to be registered]

(1) If a disposition of a registered estate or registered charge is required to be completed by registration, it does not operate at law until the relevant registration requirements are met.

...

It is therefore very important to ensure that any registrable disposition of registered land is correctly registered. The procedure for registration is set out in LRA 2002, Sch. 2, and the Land Registration Rules 2003, SI 2003/1417 (LRR).

- **Interests protected by notice or restriction**

  Most interests that are not registrable dispositions need to be entered on the charges register or proprietorship register as either notices or restrictions.

  There are two types of notice: unilateral and agreed. Unilateral notices are those entered without the consent of the registered proprietor. Agreed notices are entered, as their name suggests, by agreement with the registered proprietor. Notices can be entered either unilaterally or by agreement with the proprietor in respect of 'the burden of an interest affecting a registered estate or charge'—LRA 2002, s. 32(1).

  Certain interests are excluded from entry as a notice by LRA 2002, s. 33, and these include interests under trusts of land, leases for three years or less, and restrictive covenants between lessors and lessees affecting only the leased property.

 THINKING POINT

Consider the example register in Form 2.1. What notices can you see?

The types of interest that are usually protected by entry of a notice include:

- legal leases for over three years (but not over seven, because longer leases are registrable dispositions);
- equitable leases;
- estate contracts;
- equitable easements and profits à prendre;
- equitable mortgages and charges;
- restrictive covenants in freehold land.

  If you look at the charges register, there are three entries. Entries (1) and (3) concern, respectively, an easement of drainage and a legal charge (mortgage), both of which are registrable dispositions and must therefore be completed by registration under LRA 2002, s. 27. Under LRA 2002, s. 38, however, the registrar must also note them on the charges register of the estate affected.

  Entry (2), however, is a 'noted interest'. It gives notice of restrictive covenants which affect this estate. The details of the covenants are contained in the schedule at the end of the register. Note that restrictive covenants are quite different to 'restrictions', despite the similar name.

  There are no restrictions on this register. If there were, they would be in the proprietorship register.

Under LRA 2002, s. 40(1) a restriction regulates dealings with the estate by limiting the registration of dispositions.

 STATUTE

Land Registration Act 2002, s. 40 [Nature]

(1) A restriction is an entry in the register regulating the circumstances in which a disposition of a registered estate or charge may be the subject of an entry in the register.

...

A restriction may completely forbid a certain disposition, or may impose conditions on it. A very common restriction is one that requires money to be paid to two trustees if land is held on trust. This is a restriction that will be entered automatically by the registrar under LRA 2002, s. 44. The registrar may enter other restrictions at his discretion, to protect a right or claim, or to prevent invalidity or unlawfulness—LRA 2002, s. 42.

Interests protected by notice or restriction are sometimes referred to as 'minor interests', because this was the term used in the Land Registration Act 1925.

- **Overriding interests**

overriding interests
certain rights and interests in land that need not be protected by registration, but which will bind the proprietor and any subsequent purchaser unless overreached

Overriding interests are interests in registered land that do not have to be registered, but which are binding on a purchaser of the land. There are two categories of overriding interest: those that override first registration (under LRA 2002, Sch. 1) and those that override registered dispositions (under LRA 2002, Sch. 3). Both Schedules contain a similar list of interests, but there are more restrictions on the scope of those interests in Sch. 3.

The interests include:

- leasehold estates of seven years or shorter;
- interests of persons in actual occupation of land;
- some easements and profits à prendre;
- customary and public rights;
- local land charges;
- mines and minerals;
- certain other miscellaneous rights.

CROSS REFERENCE

For more on interests in the family home, see Chapter 9.

Overriding interests are an obvious breach of the 'mirror principle' of land registration, because they make it impossible for the register to be a true reflection of all of the interests in the land. Despite this, they were not abolished by the LRA 2002 and the Law Commission explained the reason for their retention as follows:

> Most overriding interests do appear to have one shared characteristic, however, that is related to the orthodox explanation of them, namely that it is unreasonable to expect the person who has the benefit of the right to register it as a means of securing its protection.

(Law Commission/HM Land Registry, 1998)

CROSS REFERENCE

For more on rights of way, see Chapter 11.

The Law Commission, in conjunction with the Land Registry, identified a number of categories of overriding interest.

1. **Rights that were created informally, or the origin of which is obscure**

These would include informal arrangements under which, for example, a boyfriend moves in with his girlfriend and pays money towards the purchase of their home, without being registered as having any interest in it.

2. **Rights that had overriding status prior to 1926**

   This category relates mostly to ancient rights that can no longer be created, but which can continue in existence, such as the liability to pay for repairs to sea walls.

3. **Incorporeal rights that were in existence at the time of first registration, but which were not registered**

   This would include, for example, such rights as legal rights of way.

4. **Rights that it would be inconvenient or pointless to register**

   This category might include short leases, for example.

5. **Rights that are otherwise protected**

   This category would include, for example, rights such as local land charges, which have their own register.

The LRA 2002 sought to cut down the number of overriding interests—particularly those that affect registered dispositions—but it was agreed that they could not be done away with altogether, because those who create rights in land informally, for example, are unlikely to think about registration. In the end, the law has to balance justice with certainty.

The effect of registration of title

Land registration is a complex system and it cannot be explained in one short attempt. Instead, having introduced the subject, we will look at it again in more depth in Chapter 4. Also, and very importantly, this book will deal with registration in each chapter, as the interests to be registered are covered. We hope that this will enable you to understand registration in context, rather than as an academic set of rules. Registration really makes very little sense until you understand what you are trying to register, and why. So remember, you should keep thinking about registration throughout the course, rather than trying to learn it in its entirety, as a topic right at the beginning.

2.5.3 Lifting equitable interests off the land: overreaching

The last of the three main principles of the 1925 property legislation was to establish a method of selling land free from the 'non-commercial' or 'family' equitable interests that existed within it. The method devised for doing this is called **overreaching** and is dealt with in LPA 1925, s. 2.

overreaching
the process by which interests in land are converted into corresponding interests in money arising from the sale of the land

 STATUTE

Law of Property Act 1925, s. 2 [Conveyances overreaching certain equitable interests and powers]

A conveyance to a purchaser of a legal estate in land shall overreach any equitable interest or power affecting that estate, whether or not he has notice thereof, if—

(i) the conveyance is made under the powers conferred by the Settled Land Act 1925 … ;

(ii) the conveyance is made by trustees [of land] and the equitable interest or power is at the date of the conveyance capable of being overreached by such trustees under the provisions of sub-section (2) of this section or independently of that sub-section, and [the requirements of section 27 of this Act respecting the payment of capital money arising on such a conveyance] are complied with;

(iii) the conveyance is made by a mortgagee or personal representative in the exercise of his paramount powers, and the equitable interest or power is capable of being

> overreached by such conveyance, and any capital money arising from the transaction is paid to the mortgagee or personal representative;
>
> **(iv)** the conveyance is made under an order of the court and the equitable interest or power is bound by such order, and any capital money arising from the transaction is paid into, or in accordance with the order of, the court.

▶ CROSS REFERENCE
To find out what occurs if money is not paid to two trustees, see Chapter 7.

Overreaching does not apply to 'commercial' interests, such as those registrable under the Land Charges Act 1972—see LPA 1925, s. 2(3)–(5).

This provision allows trustees of land, for example, to sell that land free from the interests of the beneficiaries. It is important that any provisions are complied with—particularly the provision of LPA 1925, s. 27 that any capital money is paid to two trustees.

▶ CROSS REFERENCE
Overreaching is considered in more detail in Chapter 7.

The effect of overreaching is that the equitable interests no longer exist in the land itself, but in the purchase money that has been paid for it. In other words, the equitable interests are lifted off the land and transferred into the money. Instead of owning an interest in land, the beneficiary owns an interest in money. This makes it much easier to sell the land, because the purchaser has a simple way of ensuring that it can be bought free from 'family'-type interests.

2.6 Conclusion

Figure 2.3 shows how legal and equitable rights in land have worked since 1925. Land can now be divided into land to which title is registered (registered land) and land to which it is not yet registered (unregistered land).

Figure 2.3 Legal and equitable rights since 1925

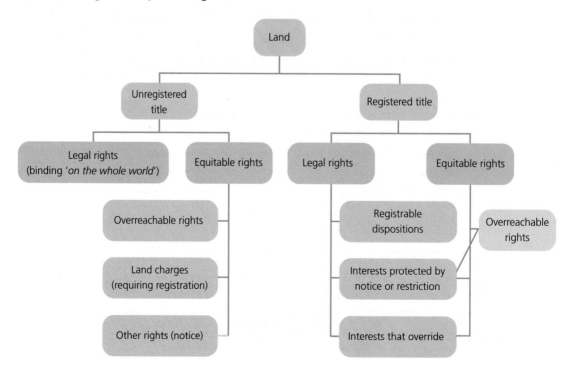

Within unregistered land, legal rights bind 'the whole world', without need for registration (except for puisne mortgages—see Table 2.5). Equitable interests are divided into three groups:

- overreachable rights, which are not registered and which will not bind a purchaser as long as he or she complies with the overreaching provisions;
- registrable rights, which must be registered under the Land Charges Act 1972 against the name of the estate owner whose estate is intended to be affected;
- equitable interests, which do not fit into either category and which depend upon the doctrine of notice for their enforceability against a purchaser.

Within registered land, legal rights do need to be registered. Some of them—the most important, such as the two legal estates—will be registrable dispositions. Others will be noted interests—such as a legal lease for a term of four years; others will be overriding interests—such as informally created legal easements. Equitable interests will never be registrable dispositions, but may be noted interests or overriding interests (and some interests are capable of being in either category). Only equitable interests can be overreached. Overreachable interests may appear on the register as restrictions or notices, but this will not prevent them from being overreached. Even potentially overriding interests are capable of being overreached—see *City of London Building Society v. Flegg* [1988] AC 54.

It can be seen, then, that the scheme for registration of title is far more comprehensive and therefore more complex than that for unregistered land—but the rules will become clearer in the subsequent chapters, in which they will be explained in context.

Summary

1. Land law has ancient origins and some of those ancient concepts—such as estates— survive into the modern day.

2. Land law has been influenced by both common law and equity, with the development of the trust and the mortgage being particularly important features introduced by equity.

3. Legal and equitable estates and interests differed in their effects on purchasers of the land, because common law acts *in rem* and equity *in personam*. This gave rise to the doctrine of notice.

4. Problems with the increasing numbers of estates in land and with the doctrine of notice eventually led to the 1925 property legislation, a series of Acts of Parliament that reformed the way in which land law worked.

5. There are now two legal estates in land under LPA 1925, s. 1(1): the fee simple absolute in possession (freehold) and the term of years absolute (leasehold).

6. There are a limited number of legal interests in land under LPA 1925, s. 1(2), which include easements, profits à prendre, and mortgages.

7. All other interests in land exist in equity only—LPA 1925, s. 1(3).

8. The LPA 1925 introduced compulsory registration of title and there are now two systems: registered land and unregistered land.

9. Unregistered land is governed by the Land Charges Act 1972 and is a system of partial registration of certain equitable interests against the name of the estate owner.

10. Registered land is a comprehensive system of registration of titles to land. It is based on maps and title numbers. It is hoped that, eventually, all titles to land will be registered.

The bigger picture

- This chapter is the theoretical structure of land law. You can find out more about how land law fits together under the system of registration of title by looking at Chapter 14, and in particular 14.6. See also Chapter 15, 15.4 for ideas on how to answer questions on the areas covered by this chapter.

- If you are really interested in the history of land law, a good starting point is A. W. B. Simpson (1961) *An Introduction to the History of Land Law*, Oxford: Oxford University Press. For later history, see J. Stuart Anderson (1992) *Lawyers and the Making of English Land Law 1832–1940*, Oxford: Oxford University Press.

- There are other suggestions in the 'Further reading' section, and more on the *Mabo v. Queensland* case on the Online Resource Centre.

? Questions

Self-test questions

1. From what historical event did the doctrines of tenure and estate originate? How important are they in the modern law?

2. What were the main differences between legal and equitable interests in land before 1925?

3. Which estates in land can now exist 'at law'? What has happened to the other former estates?

4. What is the difference between 'registered' and 'unregistered' land?

5. How are equitable interests protected in unregistered land?

6. Define the following:

    (a) registrable disposition;

    (b) notice (in registered land);

    (c) restriction;

    (d) overriding interest.

Exam question

1. What were the main objectives of the 1925 property legislation?

For suggested approaches to answering these questions visit the Online Resource Centre.

Further reading

Bright, S. and Dewar, J. (eds) (1998) *Land Law Themes and Perspectives*, Oxford: Oxford University Press, chs 1, 4, and 11
Chapter 1 discusses the idea of property in land and explains the abstract nature of English property law concepts. You might find it useful if you want to understand different theoretical models of property ownership.
Chapter 4 deals with the thinking behind the 1925 property legislation.
Chapter 11 deals with Australian indigenous land rights.

Butt, P., 'Native land rights in Australia: the Mabo case' [1995] Conv 33
This article deals with the *Mabo* case and Australian indigenous land rights.

Gardner, S. and MacKenzie, E. (2012) *An Introduction to Land Law* (3rd edn), Oxford: Hart, chs 1–3
These chapters give a brief, but illuminating, theoretical explanation of rights *in rem*, ownership, and registration, as well as looking at the human rights aspect of land law.

Law Commission/HM Land Registry (1998) Land Registration for the Twenty-First Century: A Consultative Document, Law Com No. 254, available online at http://www.lawcom.gov.uk/project/land-registration-for-the-21st-century/#land-registration-for-the-21st-century- consultation.
This report sets out the reasons behind the reform of the law in the LRA 2002.

McFarlane, B. (2008) *The Structure of Property Law*, Oxford: Hart, Part 1
This book explains the tensions behind land law and how the law is structured to deal with those tensions.

Registering land or property with Land Registry
https://www.gov.uk/registering-land-or-property-with-land-registry.
This is a simple guide to the basics of registration of title.

 Online Resource Centre

www.oxfordtextbooks.co.uk/orc/clarke_directions5e/

For more advice relating to this chapter, including self-test questions and an interactive glossary, visit the Online Resource Centre.

PART 2
LEGAL ESTATES

3

The freehold estate

Introduction

In the last chapter, we saw that the 1925 property legislation made important changes to land law. One of the most fundamental was the reduction of the number of legal estates in land to just two:

- the fee simple absolute in possession (freehold estate);
- the term of years absolute (leasehold estate).

In this chapter, we will be looking at the fee simple absolute in possession, which is the technical name for the freehold estate.

3.1 The fee simple absolute in possession

In order to understand more fully the nature of the legal freehold, we have to consider each of the terms that make up its legal definition: the 'fee simple absolute in possession'. This is a very technical phrase, but unless an estate satisfies each part of it, the estate cannot be a legal freehold, but must instead be an equitable interest in land.

3.1.1 **Fee simple**

> **fee**
>
> the estate is inheritable, meaning that it can be left in a will after someone dies

A **fee** is an inheritable estate which can pass from one generation to another, unlike a life interest, which ends on the death of the owner. Potentially, therefore the freehold estate can last forever, because it lasts until the owner for the time being dies without leaving an **heir**.

In modern times, **fee simple** means that the estate continues for as long as there is anyone to inherit it, whether by will, or upon an intestacy (when someone dies without leaving a will) under the Administration of Estates Act 1925. If there is no will and no one to inherit under that Act, the estate will go back to the Crown.

> **heir**
>
> originally, the person entitled to inherit freehold land (usually the eldest son); now someone who inherits property under a will

Other fees do exist—in particular, the **fee tail**. They cannot nowadays be legal estates in land, but can exist as equitable interests only.

> **fee tail** an estate that is inheritable for as long as there are lineal descendants of the owner

3.1.2 **Absolute**

> **fee simple**
>
> an estate that is inheritable for as long as there are general heirs of the owner

The word **absolute** means that the fee simple must belong to the owner outright, without the possibility of being brought to an end (other than on the failure of heirs). In other words, the estate must not be limited in any way. There are two types of fee simple that are not absolute: determinable fees and conditional fees.

> **absolute**
>
> complete; unconditional; not qualified

3.1.2.1 **Determinable**

The **determinable fee simple** is an estate that might last forever, but which may be cut short by a specified but unpredictable event.

CROSS REFERENCE
See Chapter 2, especially Table 2.2.

> **determinable fee simple** an estate that may last forever, but which may be cut short by a specified but unpredictable event

 EXAMPLE

Abishek may transfer his house to Biljana on the following terms: '... in fee simple until she passes her land law exam'.

 THINKING POINT

If the grant had been made to Biljana 'until she dies', would that also be a determinable fee?

The event must be unpredictable: that is, it must not be certain to happen. Although we hope Biljana will pass her land law exam, it is not certain. Unfortunately, death is a certain event for all of us, including Biljana, at some point. This grant would have created a life interest, which is something very different.

3.1.2.2 Conditional

A **conditional fee simple** is an estate that might last forever, but which may be brought to an end on the satisfaction of a **condition subsequent** —that is, a conditional event that may occur after the estate has been created.

 EXAMPLE

Abishek may transfer his house to Biljana on the following terms: ' ... in fee simple on condition that she does not pass an exam in land law'.

Again, the occurrence of the conditional event must be unpredictable.

3.1.2.3 Differences between determinable and conditional fees

As you will note from the two examples, a similar result can be achieved by a determinable fee and a conditional fee, which raises the question of why we should bother distinguishing between them. The answer is that the two estates actually have different legal effects. The law regards the coming to an end of the two estates differently: while a determinable fee comes naturally to an end as soon as the determining event happens, a conditional fee potentially lasts forever and is cut short only if the condition is satisfied—that is, if the conditional event occurs. In practice, this is shown by the difference in wording—examples of which are shown in Table 3.1.

Table 3.1 Differences in wording between determinable and conditional fees

Words that indicate a determinable fee	Words that indicate a conditional fee
while	provided that
during	on condition that
as long as	but if
until	if it happen that

The first legal difference is that a determinable fee comes to an end immediately and automatically when the determining event occurs.

 EXAMPLE

Abishek transferred his house to Biljana 'in fee simple until she passes her land law exam'. As soon as Biljana passes her land law exam, her estate in the house will come to an end. Abishek need not take any action to end it.

Conditional fees, on the other hand, give the grantor (the person who transferred the estate to the owner of the conditional fee) the right to enter and bring the estate to an end when the event occurs.

EXAMPLE

Abishek transferred his house to Biljana 'in fee simple on condition that she does not pass an exam in land law'. When Biljana passes her land law exam, Abishek (the grantor of the estate) has a right to put an end to Biljana's estate in the land. If he does not do so, however, the estate will continue.

---

forfeiture

the bringing to an end of an estate as the consequence of an offence or a breach of an undertaking

---

Because a conditional fee contains this right to **forfeiture** (bringing the estate to an end), the courts have construed such conditions strictly. It must be possible to say with certainty when such a condition has been breached, so vague conditions will be struck out. In addition, the courts have struck down certain conditions if they make it impossible for land to be transferred, or if they are against public policy. In general, conditions that wholly prohibit marriage, or which encourage illegal or immoral behaviour, have been struck out. Conditions forbidding marriage to certain classes of persons, however, or forbidding a person from following certain religions, have been upheld.

 CASE CLOSE-UP

Blathwayt v. Lord Cawley [1975] 3 All ER 625

In this case, a condition in the settlement stated:

> if any person who under the trusts hereof shall become entitled ... to the possession of [the settled property] shall ... be or become a Roman Catholic ... the estate hereby limited to him shall cease and determine and be utterly void.

This condition was held not to be void as against public policy. Lord Wilberforce agreed that public policy must move with the times, but said:

> Discrimination is not the same thing as choice: it operates over a larger and less personal area, and neither by express provision nor by implication has private selection yet become a matter of public policy.

It is possible that the provisions seen in *Blathwayt v. Lord Cawley* would now be incompatible with the beneficiary's human rights—in this case, the 'right to freedom of thought, conscience and religion' under the European Convention on Human Rights (ECHR), Art. 9. Lord Wilberforce was referred to the ECHR in the *Blathwayt* case, but declined to apply its standards to a will taking effect in 1936 (which was before the ECHR was drafted). Since the enactment of the Human Rights Act 1998, which incorporates the ECHR into domestic law, the courts might be inclined to take a different view.

A second legal difference between determinable fees and conditional fees is that conditional fees are capable of being legal estates, whereas determinable fees are always equitable interests only. The reason for this distinction is the Law of Property Act 1925 (LPA 1925), s. 7, which was amended for historical reasons that are not relevant today.

 STATUTE

Law of Property Act 1925, s. 7 [Saving of certain legal estates and statutory powers]

A fee simple which, by virtue of the Lands Clauses Acts, ... or any similar statute, is liable to be divested, is for the purposes of this Act a fee simple absolute, and remains liable to be divested as if this Act had not been passed, [and a fee simple subject to a legal or equitable right of entry or re-entry is for the purposes of this Act a fee simple absolute].

As a consequence of the amendment in the square brackets in this section, most conditional fees—as long as they contain a legal or equitable **right of re-entry**, which almost all do—are treated as fees simple absolute and are therefore capable of being legal estates, rather than as equitable interests.

The situation is consequently as follows:

* the fee simple absolute can be a legal estate;
* the determinable fee simple can only ever be an equitable interest;
* the conditional fee simple can be a legal estate under LPA 1925, s. 7(1) if it is subject to a right of re-entry. Otherwise, it will be an equitable interest.

> **right of re-entry**
> a legal or equitable right to resume possession of land, here as the result of forfeiture

3.1.3 **In possession**

The final requirement for a legal freehold is that the fee simple absolute must be **in possession**. This means that the estate must confer upon its owner the immediate right to enjoy the land, or the rents and profits of the land, from the date on which the estate is granted—LPA 1925, s. 205(1)(xix).

The owner may be in possession either by occupying the property or by receiving the rents and profits from it.

> **in possession**
> the estate must confer upon its owner the immediate right to enjoy the land, or the rents and profits of the land, from the date of the grant

 EXAMPLE

Peter owns a fee simple absolute in Mulberry House. He works abroad and therefore does not live in his house, which is leased to Jane.

Peter is in receipt of the rent from Mulberry House paid by Jane. This means that his fee simple absolute is 'in possession' and is a legal freehold estate. Jane has a leasehold estate in Mulberry House.

There are two types of estate that are not in possession: estates in remainder and estates in reversion.

3.1.3.1 **In remainder**

An **estate in remainder** is an interest that gives its owner the present right to future enjoyment of that estate. This is best explained by looking at an example.

> **estate in remainder**
> an interest that gives its owner the present right to future enjoyment

 EXAMPLE

Peter grants Mulberry House 'to Abigail for life, remainder to Belinda in fee simple absolute'.

Abigail has a life interest in the house, which is in possession—that is, she can enjoy the land now. Even if Mulberry House is still leased to Jane, as in the earlier example, Abigail is entitled to the rents and profits, so her life estate is in possession.

Belinda has a fee simple absolute, but it is not in possession. It will fall into possession when Abigail dies. She has a fee simple absolute in remainder.

Notice that neither Abigail nor Belinda has a legal estate—that is, a fee simple absolute in possession—in Mulberry House. Abigail does not have a fee at all, because she has only a life

interest, which can only be equitable. Belinda has a fee simple absolute, but not in possession: it is in remainder and is therefore an equitable interest.

In this situation, a trust of land will have been created. The legal freehold (fee simple absolute
in possession) will be held by trustees to give effect to Peter's dispositions.

> **vested remainder**
>
> the present right to a
> future interest

In the example, Belinda's fee simple in remainder is said to be a **vested remainder**. This means
that Belinda is certain to get Mulberry House at some point in the future, because Abigail is certain
to die. Even if Abigail were to live longer than Belinda, she would still die at some time, and then
Belinda's successors—the persons to whom she has left her equitable fee simple in Mulberry House
after her death—will be entitled in possession.

The opposite of a vested remainder is a **contingent remainder**. This is a future interest which may
or may not come into being, depending upon the fulfilment of a **condition precedent** —that
is, the occurrence of some specified event before the estate comes into being, as in the following
example.

> **contingent remainder** a future interest that can only come into being on meeting a condition
> precedent
>
> **condition precedent** a condition that must be met before the estate comes into being

---

 EXAMPLE

Peter grants Mulberry House 'to Abigail for life, remainder to Belinda in fee simple provided
that she survives Abigail'.

Abigail has a life interest in possession in Mulberry House. Belinda has a fee simple absolute
in remainder, but only if she lives longer than Abigail. The phrase *'provided that she survives
Abigail'* is a condition precedent. If Belinda dies first, she (or her successors) will not be entitled
to Mulberry House. Instead, unless there are other remainders, Mulberry House will revert to
Peter (see 3.1.3.2). If Abigail dies first, Belinda becomes entitled to the fee simple absolute,
which will then become a legal estate vested in possession.

Both vested and contingent remainders are equitable interests under the 1925 property legislation. There are rules against contingent remainders vesting after too long a lapse of time and thus
tying up the land too far into the future: rules against remoteness of vesting and the rule against
perpetuities. The details of these rules are, however, outside the scope of this book.

> **estate in reversion**
>
> an interest that is
> retained by the grantor,
> because the fee simple
> estate in the land has not
> been transferred
> to anyone

3.1.3.2 In reversion

An **estate in reversion** is an interest that is retained by its owner (the grantor), because the fee
simple estate has not been transferred to anyone else. There was an example of an estate in reversion in the example in 3.1.3.1, in which Mulberry House reverted to Peter. Another example of an
estate in reversion is as follows:

> **EXAMPLE**
>
> Peter grants Mulberry House 'to Abigail for life'.
>
> Abigail has a life interest in possession in the house. But Peter has not disposed of the fee simple in the house: once Abigail's interest comes to an end on her death, there is no further grant of the house to someone else. Therefore, Peter has a fee simple absolute in reversion in Mulberry House, which is an equitable interest. When Abigail dies, Peter's fee simple absolute will fall into possession.

An estate in reversion arises by operation of law. It is not the same as the 'possibility of reverter' that occurs when there is a determinable fee simple, or the right of re-entry that accompanies a conditional fee simple. An estate in reversion is always a vested interest, because it is any part of the full legal fee simple absolute that the grantor has not transferred and which therefore remains with them. Estates in reversion are always equitable interests.

3.1.4 Summary

In order, therefore, to have a legal freehold, it must be shown that the estate meets all the parts of the description 'fee simple absolute in possession'. It might be useful to think of each of the terms as a hurdle that must be cleared before the estate owner can reach the goal of a legal freehold. If any of the hurdles is 'knocked down'—for example, if it is a life estate only and therefore not a 'fee', or if it is in remainder and therefore not 'in possession'—then the estate can exist in equity only.

It is also important to remember that a legal freehold must exist in each piece of land, unless it is held outright by the Crown. If no individual appears to hold the fee simple absolute in possession, then, since 1925, either a settlement or a trust must have arisen.

Since 1997, the fee simple absolute in possession that is not vested in a single person will, in the vast majority of cases, be held by trustees as a trust of land.

Even if the estate owner does have a fee simple absolute in possession, he or she still may not hold a legal estate if the correct formalities for creation or transfer of the estate have not been observed.

CROSS REFERENCE
For more on subinfeudation and Quia Emptores, see Chapter 2.

CROSS REFERENCE
For more on settlements and trusts, see Chapter 10.

CROSS REFERENCE
For more on joint owners and trusts of land, see Chapter 8.

3.2 The creation of a legal freehold

The creation of a legal freehold is not possible except by the Crown. This is because other freehold owners are no longer able to create new freeholds out of their own freeholds by subinfeudation, which was outlawed by Quia Emptores in 1290.

The Crown can grant freeholds to others out of Crown land and these will then constitute new fees simple absolute in possession, which will have to be registered at the Land Registry as a new estate in land (first registration of title).

Since the Land Registration Act 2002 (LRA 2002) came into force, the Crown can also grant itself freeholds—something that was impossible at common law. This means that the Crown can register those freeholds at the Land Registry.

CROSS REFERENCE
For more on subinfeudation and Quia Emptores, see Chapter 2.

CROSS REFERENCE
For more on first registration, see Chapter 4.

3.3 Transfer of the legal freehold

Although freehold owners cannot create new freeholds, they are generally free to transfer all, or part, of the freehold that they own to someone else. If that freehold is in unregistered land, the owner has wide powers under which to deal with it at common law, as preserved by LPA 1925, s. 1(4). If the freehold is in registered land, the registered proprietor has wide powers of disposal under LRA 2002, s. 23.

 STATUTE

Land Registration Act 2002, s. 23 [Owner's powers]

Owner's powers in relation to a registered estate consist of—power to make a disposition of any kind permitted by the general law in relation to an interest of that description, other than a mortgage by demise or sub-demise, and power to charge the estate at law with the payment of money… .

> **CROSS REFERENCE**
>
> For more on mortgages, see Chapter 13.

Subsection (1)(a) means that the owner can make any kind of disposal of the land—for example, selling it, leasing it, etc.—other than creating a mortgage of it by the old-fashioned method known as 'demise', or 'sub-demise'. Subsection (1)(b) allows a mortgage to be granted by way of a charge over the land. This has, for years, been the way in which land is mortgaged, so the LRA 2002 was simply tidying up the law to reflect modern practice.

> **CROSS REFERENCE**
>
> For more on sole owners and trusts of land, see Chapter 7.
>
> For more on the rights of the sole owner of land, see Chapter 7.

In some cases these wide powers may be limited in some way—for example, if the owner is a trustee. If the land is unregistered, the limitation may be apparent from the terms of the convey-ance, or may be registrable as a land charge, or may depend on the doctrine of notice. In the case of registered land, the notice is given by placing a restriction in the proprietorship register. Some restrictions must be placed there by the Chief Land Registrar; others are voluntary and the regis-tered proprietor must apply for them to be entered—LRA 2002, s. 42.

Although the owner of the freehold is generally free to transfer his or her land, English law has always required a certain element of formality in transfers of land. Reasons for this include deterring fraudulent transactions and helping to ensure certainty of ownership. Nowadays, that formality is satisfied in the requirements for formal documentation and in the requirements for registration.

In explaining the formalities needed to transfer estates in land, it is helpful to set out the four main steps in the process of buying and selling land, or **conveyancing**, as it is generally called:

> **conveyancing**
>
> the process of transferring a legal estate in land from one person to another

1. negotiation and agreement;
2. formation of the contract and exchange of contracts;
3. transfer or conveyance of the legal estate;
4. registration.

3.3.1 Negotiation and agreement

At this first stage, the purchaser (buyer) will look at the property and decide, in principle, to buy it. This results in an agreement to buy the land 'subject to contract'. This is not a legally binding agreement: either party is free to withdraw. During this stage, the purchaser will usually arrange a loan with which to pay for the property, unless he or she is lucky enough to be wealthy enough not to need one. The loan will usually be secured by the grant of a **mortgage** by the purchaser over the land. This is often called 'arranging a mortgage', but you should note that the mortgage, or charge, is properly the name of the security for the loan. It is not the bank or other lender who grants the mortgage, but rather the purchaser, in return for the loan. Of course, the purchaser does not own the land at the time of the arrangement to borrow the money, but agrees to grant a mortgage as soon as he or she becomes the owner. The paperwork for the mortgage and the purchase will later be sent to the Land Registry together.

The purchaser will usually have one of three types of survey, or report, completed in order to establish the condition of the property:

- A full structural survey

  This is the most expensive of the surveys, because it is most detailed. It is most appropriate for older properties, or if the buyer has concerns about the house.

- A home condition report

  This is not as detailed as a full structural survey, but should discover any major defects in the property and many minor ones as well.

- A valuation report

  This type of report is not very detailed, because the surveyor is concerned only with establishing that the house is worth the amount of money for which the vendor (seller of the property) is asking.

If a mortgage is to be granted in return for a loan, a valuation survey will be a requirement of the lender. Following completion of the survey, there may be further negotiations on price, either as a result of defects found in the survey, or because the value of land is rising or falling at the time of the negotiations.

Sometimes, at this stage, a vendor will threaten to pull out of an agreement because he has received a higher offer—referred to as **gazumping**, or sometimes the purchaser may refuse to proceed unless the vendor accepts a lower price—sometimes called **gazundering**, or the vendor may pull out of selling altogether because of uncertainty and a lack of available properties to buy—referred to as **gazanging**. This stage of the house-buying process is often very stressful, because the purchaser will be incurring costs in arranging loans and having surveys carried out, as well as paying a solicitor or licensed conveyancer for the early stages of conveyancing (such as proof of title and local authority searches). If the transaction does not eventually go ahead, those costs will be wasted.

> **mortgage**
> properly, the name for the charge over land that is the security for the loan granted by a bank to the purchaser of the land, rather than the name for the loan itself

❯ CROSS REFERENCE

For more on mortgages, see Chapter 13.

> **gazumping** the process of a third party offering, or the vendor accepting, a higher offer on a property on which a sale price has already been agreed, but for which agreement no binding contract is yet in place
>
> **gazundering** the process of the purchaser demanding a lower price on a property after a sale price has already been agreed, but for which agreement no binding contract is yet in place
>
> **gazanging** the vendor pulling out of the sale altogether at the last moment

It is often the case that the vendor is a purchaser as well, because many house-buying transactions take place in chains—that is, there are a number of transactions that are dependent on each other.

EXAMPLE

Ben and Belinda live in a small house. They want to move into a larger house. They look at Callum's house and offer to buy it.

Ben and Belinda however, cannot, afford to own both their present house and Callum's house at the same time. They must find someone to buy their house before they can formally agree to buy Callum's house.

Ali is looking for a small house to buy as his first home. He looks at Ben and Belinda's house, and agrees to buy it.

Ali, Ben and Belinda, and Callum are all part of a 'chain' of transactions:

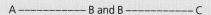

A ———————— B and B ———————— C

If any of the parties change their minds, or if something goes wrong, all of the purchases and sales come to a stop, and may 'fall through'.

Clearly, this chain could be even longer. Callum may be moving to a new house as well—say, Diljot's house—in which case, his purchase is also part of the chain, as might be Diljot's purchase:

A ——————— B and B ——————— C ——————— D ——————?

All chains are only as strong as their weakest link, so the longer the chain, the greater the chance of a breakdown.

In 2007 it was estimated that 28 per cent of property transactions failed after terms have been agreed and that over £350m each year was wasted in costs of purchases and sales that did not go ahead. The then government tried to address the issue of wasted costs by introducing Home Information Packs (HIPs) which contained important information about the property for sale and which could be relied upon by any purchaser without the costs of searches, etc. being repeatedly incurred. However, HIPs did not lead to a dramatic reduction in wasted costs, and were unpopular with those selling homes as they cost up to several hundred pounds. They were suspended from 21 May 2010 and abolished in 2012. All that is now required is an Energy Performance Certificate.

3.3.2 **Formation of the contract and exchange of contracts**

Once the parties have agreed terms, they can enter into a formal contract for the sale and purchase of the land. The agreement is not legally binding until both parties have entered into a formal contract. Contracts for the sale of land are required to be made in writing incorporating all of the terms of the agreement, under Law of Property (Miscellaneous Provisions) Act 1989 (LP(MP)A 1989), s. 2.

 STATUTE

Law of Property (Miscellaneous Provisions) Act 1989, s. 2 [Contracts for sale etc. of land to be made by signed writing]

(1) A contract for the sale or other disposition of an interest in land can only be made in writing and only by incorporating all the terms which the parties have expressly agreed in one document or, where contracts are exchanged, in each.

(2) The terms may be incorporated in a document either by being set out in it or by reference to some other document.

(3) The document incorporating the terms or, where contracts are exchanged, one of the documents incorporating them (but not necessarily the same one) must be signed by or on behalf of each party to the contract.

...

(5) This section does not apply in relation to—

(a) a contract to grant such a lease as is mentioned in section 54(2) of the Law of Property Act 1925 (short leases);

(b) a contract made in the course of a public auction; or

[(c) a contract regulated under the Financial Services and Markets Act 2000, other than a regulated mortgage contract [, a regulated home reversion plan, a regulated home purchase plan, or a regulated sale and rent back agreement];]

and nothing in this section affects the creation or operation of resulting, implied, or constructive trusts.

...

Before this section came into force, contracts for the sale of land were governed by LPA 1925, s. 40. This required the contract to be *evidenced in writing*, which meant that an oral contract could be given validity by a later written memorandum. This is no longer possible. It also provided an exception for transactions of which there had been *part performance*—most typically, situations in which the purchaser was allowed to move into the premises before the conveyance. However, any act of part performance could make the contract enforceable, provided the act was *directly referable* to the contract. LPA 1925, s. 40 no longer applies, but it is useful to be aware of it when reading older cases.

> **CROSS REFERENCE**
>
> For more on implied, resulting, and constructive trusts, see Chapter 10.

It is still possible for an informal agreement to take effect if it can be shown that it has given rise to a resulting, implied, or constructive trust, because LP(MP)A 1989, s. 2(5) specifically provides that the section is not to affect the creation or operation of such trusts. It is this exception which has led to most case law. In particular, there has been debate about whether proprietary estoppel can be used to save an informal transaction that does not comply with this section, although it is not specifically mentioned in s. 2(5). *Yaxley v. Gotts* [2000] Ch 162 seemed to indicate that this was possible, by finding that the proprietary estoppel gave rise to a constructive trust. However, a claimant who fails to enter into a formal agreement, particularly in a commercial situation, will not always succeed.

🔍 CASE CLOSE-UP

Cobbe v. Yeoman's Row Management Ltd [2008] UKHL 55

The claimant was a property developer who spent large sums of money in obtaining planning permission for the development of property belonging to the defendant. He was relying on an 'in principle' oral agreement that he could buy the property from the defendant, develop it, and then they would both get further sums from the sale of the units developed. However, once planning permission had been granted, the defendant went back on his agreement and refused to sell the property to the claimant after all. Since there was no written contract complying with LP(MP)A 1989, s. 2(1), no claim could be brought to enforce the contract.

> Therefore, the claimant brought an action claiming that there was a proprietary estoppel in his favour, or that alternatively there was a constructive trust, both of which would have given him a proprietary interest in the property. He also made claims based on restitution and unjust enrichment, as well as a claim to a *quantum meruit*.
>
> The House of Lords, reversing the Court of Appeal ([2006] EWCA Civ 1139), held that there were no grounds for holding that there was either a proprietary estoppel or a constructive trust. There was no proprietary estoppel because there was no certain interest in land that it was expected would be transferred; there were to be further negotiations on the exact terms of the agreement. The claimant, an experienced property developer, knew that the agreement was binding 'in honour' only. There was no constructive trust because the defendant withdrawing unconscionably from the agreement was not enough to found such a trust. The property had been owned by the defendant long before the agreement was reached.
>
> The claimant was entitled to damages based on unjust enrichment and *quantum meruit* for the sums he had spent, but not to an interest in the property.

> **CROSS REFERENCE**
>
> For more on proprietary estoppel, see Chapters 6 and 9.
>
> See the Online Resource Centre 'Advanced Topics' for more detail on the interpretation of LP(MP)A 1989, s. 2.

Whittaker v Kinnear [2011] EWHC 1479 (QB) has also held that proprietary estoppel in cases relating to land has not been abolished by the LP(MP)A 1989.

In practice, the Law Society's Standard Conditions of Sale are normally used as the terms of the contract. It is common practice for each party to sign a separate copy of the contract, each of which is then 'exchanged'—often by agreement over the telephone, rather than physically—when both parties are ready to proceed. Once contracts have been exchanged, the parties are bound to carry out the transaction. If one party backs out, he or she will be in breach of contract. The most usual remedy for breach of a contract to sell land is **specific performance** —that is, the court will order the transfer of the land from the vendor to the purchaser.

> **specific performance**
>
> a remedy for breach of contract that demands the fulfilment of obligations under the contract

The availability of specific performance as a remedy leads to an important consequence for the vendor and purchaser: after contracts are exchanged, the property belongs to the purchaser in equity. In other words, after exchange, a trust is imposed upon the vendor to hold the property in trust for the purchaser. One important consequence of this is that the purchaser must insure the property from the moment of exchange.

3.3.3 **Transfer or conveyance of the legal estate**

3.3.3.1 **Proof of title**

After contracts have been exchanged, the purchaser's solicitor will conduct searches to establish that the vendor has title to the land and to establish what encumbrances—third-party rights, such as rights of way, restrictive covenants, etc.—exist on the land.

The requirement to prove title will be met in different ways depending upon whether the land is registered or unregistered.

Registered land

If the land is registered, the proof of title lies in the Land Registry entry for that land. The registered proprietor has the power to transfer the land, unless there are restrictions entered on the proprietorship register. Entry as the registered proprietor is conclusive proof of ownership of the legal estate in the land.

> **CROSS REFERENCE**
>
> For more on overriding interests, see Chapters 2 and 4.

The purchaser should also inspect the land itself, however, not least to see if there are any potential overriding interests, which are binding on purchasers without being registered.

Unregistered land

If land is unregistered, there is, of course, no Land Registry entry to consult. Instead, the vendor must provide a documentary root of title going back at least fifteen years—Law of Property Act 1969, s. 23. This root of title is likely to be a conveyance to the present owner of the property. Older conveyances may be handwritten.

An example of the beginning of an old conveyance is shown in Figure 3.1. (The original is five pages long.)

The purchaser will also have to search the land charges register for registered land charges, and be aware that other legal and equitable interests in the land may exist. He or she can most easily find out about them by inspecting the land itself.

> **CROSS REFERENCE**
> For more on legal and equitable interests, see Chapter 2.

> **CROSS REFERENCE**
> Figure 3.1 is the original conveyance of the piece of land considered in Chapter 2, Form 2.1.

Figure 3.1 An old-fashioned conveyance

3.3.3.2 The requirement for a deed

The main requirement for formality in transferring land in modern times is that a legal estate in land must be transferred by **deed**.

> **deed**
> a formal document that makes it clear, on its face, that it is intended to be a deed and which is executed as a deed

 STATUTE

Law of Property (Miscellaneous Provisions) Act 1989 [as amended by the Regulatory Reform (Execution of Deeds and Documents) Order 2005], s. 1 [Deeds and their execution]

...

(2) An instrument shall not be a deed unless—

   (a) it makes it clear on its face that it is intended to be a deed by the person making it or, as the case may be, by the parties to it (whether by describing itself as a deed or expressing itself to be executed or signed as a deed or otherwise); and

> **(b)** it is validly executed as a deed—
>
> > **(i)** by that person or a person authorised to execute it in the name or on behalf of that person, or
> >
> > **(ii)** by one or more of those parties or a person authorised to execute it in the name or on behalf of one or more of those parties.
>
> **(2A)** For the purposes of subsection (2)(a) above, an instrument shall not be taken to make it clear on its face that it is intended to be a deed merely because it is executed under seal.
>
> **(3)** An instrument is validly executed as a deed by an individual if, and only if—
>
> > **(a)** it is signed—
> >
> > > **(i)** by him in the presence of a witness who attests the signature; or
> > >
> > > **(ii)** at his direction and in his presence and the presence of two witnesses who each attest the signature; and
> >
> > **(b)** it is delivered as a deed …
>
> …

These requirements are set out in LP(MP)A 1989, s. 1, which replaced the old common law requirement from 1 January 1990. Before that time, a deed had to be 'signed, sealed and delivered'.

As you can see from LP(MP)A 1989, s. 1(2A), the execution of a document under seal is no longer enough to show that it is a deed. It must comply with the new provisions. The requirement for a seal had become largely obsolete since sealing wax and seal rings fell out of use, and it was replaced by the requirement for attestation (witnessing) by the required number of witnesses.

The modern requirements for a deed can thus be summarized as in Table 3.2.

The requirement to use a deed is set out in LPA 1925, s. 52.

Table 3.2 The requirements for a valid deed

Requirement	Details
Declares on its face that it is a deed	Either by: (i) 'describing itself as a deed'—usually by the document beginning 'this deed'; (ii) expressing itself to be 'signed or executed as a deed'—usually by words such as 'executed as a deed' at the end of the document; or (iii) otherwise—that is, anything else that makes it clear it is a deed—see *HSBC Trust v. Quinn* [2007] EWHC 1543 (Ch)
Signed	Either: (i) by the party making the deed; or (ii) at his or her direction and in his or her presence—that is, by someone other than the vendor, if he or she is too ill to sign the deed, or cannot write
Attested (witnessed)	If signed by the maker of the deed, by one witness who must be present when the deed is signed. If signed at his or her direction, by two witnesses, who must be present when the deed is signed.
Delivered	This used to mean physical delivery to the other party to the transaction, but nowadays means that the deed is irreversible. The fact that the deed is to be delivered is usually stated at the end of the document, just above the signature.

STATUTE

Law of Property Act 1925, s. 52 [Conveyances to be by deed]

(1) All conveyances of land or of any interest therein are void for the purpose of conveying or creating a legal estate unless made by deed.

…

Under LPA 1925, s. 205(1)(ii), 'conveyance' includes a mortgage, a charge, and a lease, as well as a straightforward transfer of the land.

There are a number of exceptions to this requirement in s. 52(2), some of which will be encountered later in this book. Since this chapter deals with express transfers of the legal freehold, s. 52(1) applies and a deed must be used.

Nowadays, the document used to transfer the land is invariably the Land Registry form, TR1 (see Form 3.1). This is used for both registered and unregistered land, because it contains the right information to enable the estate to be correctly registered after transfer. All transfers of the legal freehold must be registered (see 3.3.4).

The information required for the transfer can be seen in the form.

Box 1 deals with the title number of the property. If the property were unregistered land, this box would be left blank and a title number would be assigned by the Land Registry when the land is registered.

Box 2 describes the property. Because it is already registered and will be identifiable on a plan filed at the Registry, only the address need be given. If it were unregistered land, it would have to be described in such a way as to be identifiable. This would usually be by reference to the description in one of the documents relied upon as a good root of title.

EXAMPLE

When 36 Hillendale Road was transferred to Stanley and Patricia Wentworth, the description given was: '… the land comprised in a Conveyance dated the 31st day of July 1928 made between J. W. Ellingham Limited of the one part and Albert Edward Gales of the other part'.

The conveyance referred to is that in Figure 3.1.

Box 4 gives the name of the transferor. In this case, there are two transferors: Stanley and Patricia Wentworth. They are the vendors in this case.

In Box 5, Sandra Clarke and Sarah Greer are named as the transferees (the purchasers in this case).

Box 6 requires an address for service. It is important to make sure that the Land Registry has at least one up-to-date address for the service of any notices or other communications to do with the land. Here, the transferees have given the address of the property itself, so they probably intend to live there. If they had bought the property to let out to tenants, for example, they would have given an alternative address. It is also possible to add an email address.

Box 7 contains the words that actually carry out the transfer of the land: 'The transferor transfers the Property to the Transferee.'

CROSS REFERENCE

For more on joint tenants and tenants in common, see Chapter 8.

Box 8 deals with the consideration paid for the transfer. Note that there need not be any consideration: the deed itself 'imparts consideration' and can be sued upon even if no consideration is paid—but it is usual for some consideration to be paid.

Box 9 deals with the title guarantee. This is a conveyancing matter that is beyond the scope of this book.

Box 10 contains a declaration of trust, to set out whether the transferees are to hold the property as joint tenants or as tenants in common in equal shares.

Box 11 can be used to write in any special agreements the parties have made.

EXAMPLE

If Mr and Mrs Wentworth want Sandra and Sarah to promise not to build any further buildings on the land, this agreement or 'covenant' could be recorded in Box 11 on the transfer form. The Land Registry would then be able to enter the covenant in the charges register of the title.

In the last box on the form, there is space to execute the form as a deed. The formalities referred to earlier must be observed. Thus, in this case, the transferors must sign the document in the presence of a witness, who must attest the signature. If Sandra and Sarah have made any promises—for example, the covenant mentioned in the example—they must execute the deed as well.

Form TR1 will be sent to the Land Registry along with any other relevant documents—such as the old conveyance if the land is to be registered for the first time—and any documents relating to a mortgage being granted by Sandra and Sarah over the land.

3.3.4 **Registration**

CROSS REFERENCE

For an introductory discussion of land registration, see Chapter 2.

After the transfer of the freehold estate has taken place, it must be completed by registration at the Land Registry.

3.3.4.1 **First registration of title**

LRA 2002, s. 4(1) requires the registration of the transfer of a 'qualifying estate'. Under subsection s. 4(2) *a qualifying estate is an unregistered legal estate in land which is—(a) a freehold estate in land ...*', so the transfer of an unregistered freehold estate in land will be an event that triggers registration of land that has not previously been registered.

The Land Registrar will inspect all of the documents sent in with the application for first registration and register the purchaser with one of the possible grades of title:

- absolute;
- qualified;
- possessory.

Of these, absolute title is by far the most common and it is that which we shall consider.

A person will be registered with absolute title 'if the registrar is of the opinion that the person's title to the estate is such as a willing buyer could properly be advised by a competent professional adviser to accept'—LRA 2002, s. 9(2).

The effect of first registration is set out in LRA 2002, s. 11.

Form 3.1 Land Registry transfer form TR1

© Crown copyright

Land Registry
Transfer of whole of registered title(s)

TR1

If you need more room than is provided for in a panel, and your software allows, you can expand any panel in the form. Alternatively use continuation sheet CS and attach it to this form.

Leave blank if not yet registered.	1 Title number(s) of the property: UG23456
Insert address including postcode (if any) or other description of the property, for example 'land adjoining 2 Acacia Avenue'.	2 Property: 36 Hillendale Road, Ruxhurst, London, RU1 3BW
	3 Date: 05/08/2009
Give full name(s).	4 Transferor: Stanley Clifford Wentworth and Patricia Anne Wentworth both of 36 Hillendale Road Ruxhurst, London RU1 3BW
Complete as appropriate where the transferor is a company.	 For UK incorporated companies/LLPs Registered number of company or limited liability partnership including any prefix: For overseas companies (a) Territory of incorporation: (b) Registered number in England and Wales including any prefix:
Give full name(s).	5 Transferee for entry in the register: Sandra Clarke and Sarah Greer both of 12 Brixton Road Greenwich London SE9 1 LS
Complete as appropriate where the transferee is a company. Also, for an overseas company, unless an arrangement with Land Registry exists, lodge either a certificate in Form 7 in Schedule 3 to the Land Registration Rules 2003 or a certified copy of the constitution in English or Welsh, or other evidence permitted by rule 183 of the Land Registration Rules 2003.	For UK incorporated companies/LLPs Registered number of company or limited liability partnership including any prefix: For overseas companies (a) Territory of incorporation: (b) Registered number in England and Wales including any prefix:
Each transferee may give up to three addresses for service, one of which must be a postal address whether or not in the UK (including the postcode, if any). The others can be any combination of a postal address, a UK DX box number or an electronic address.	6 Transferee's intended address(es) for service for entry in the register: 36 Hillendale Road, Ruxhurst, London RU1 3BW
	7 The transferor transfers the property to the transferee

Form 3.1 Continued

Place 'X' in the appropriate box. State the currency unit if other than sterling. If none of the boxes apply, insert an appropriate memorandum in panel 11.	**8 Consideration** ☐ The transferor has received from the transferee for the property the following sum (in words and figures): ☐ The transfer is not for money or anything that has a monetary value ☐ Insert other receipt as appropriate:
Place 'X' in any box that applies. Add any modifications.	**9 The transferor transfers with** ☐ full title guarantee ☐ limited title guarantee
Where the transferee is more than one person, place 'X' in the appropriate box. Complete as necessary.	**10 Declaration of trust. The transferee is more than one person and** ☐ they are to hold the property on trust for themselves as joint tenants ☐ they are to hold the property on trust for themselves as tenants in common in equal shares ☐ they are to hold the property on trust:
Insert here any required or permitted statement, certificate or application and any agreed covenants, declarations and so on.	**11 Additional provisions**
The transferor must execute this transfer as a deed using the space opposite. If there is more than one transferor, all must execute. Forms of execution are given in Schedule 9 to the Land Registration Rules 2003. If the transfer contains transferee's covenants or declarations or contains an application by the transferee (such as for a restriction), it must also be executed by the transferee.	**12 Execution**

WARNING
If you dishonestly enter information or make a statement that you know is, or might be, untrue or misleading, and intend by doing so to make a gain for yourself or another person, or to cause loss or the risk of loss to another person, you may commit the offence of fraud under section 1 of the Fraud Act 2006, the maximum penalty for which is 10 years' imprisonment or an unlimited fine, or both.

Failure to complete this form with proper care may result in a loss of protection under the Land Registration Act 2002 if, as a result, a mistake is made in the register.

Under section 66 of the Land Registration Act 2002 most documents (including this form) kept by the registrar relating to an application to the registrar or referred to in the register are open to public inspection and copying. If you believe a document contains prejudicial information, you may apply for that part of the document to be made exempt using Form EX1, under rule 136 of the Land Registration Rules 2003.

© Crown copyright (ref: LR/HO) 07/08

STATUTE

Land Registration Act 2002, s. 11 [Freehold estates]

(1) This section is concerned with the registration of a person under this Chapter as the proprietor of a freehold estate.

(2) Registration with absolute title has the effect described in subsections (3) to (5).

(3) The estate is vested in the proprietor together with all interests subsisting for the benefit of the estate.

(4) The estate is vested in the proprietor subject only to the following interests affecting the estate at the time of registration—

   (a) interests which are the subject of an entry in the register in relation to the estate,

   (b) unregistered interests which fall within any of the paragraphs of Schedule 1, and

   (c) interests acquired under the Limitation Act 1980 (c. 58) of which the proprietor has notice.

(5) If the proprietor is not entitled to the estate for his own benefit, or not entitled solely for his own benefit, then, as between himself and the persons beneficially entitled to the estate, the estate is vested in him subject to such of their interests as he has notice of.

...

The proprietor is now the owner of the freehold estate, together with all interests subsisting for its benefit, but subject to the interests listed in the section affecting the estate at the time of registration, as summarized in Table 3.3.

It is the duty of the transferee to apply for first registration—LRA 2002, s. 6. If registration does not take place within two months of the transfer, the title to the legal estate reverts to the transferor, who holds it on a bare trust for the transferee. In other words, in this situation, the transferee is no longer the legal owner of the estate; instead, he or she has only an equitable interest in it and the transferor holds the legal estate on trust—LRA 2002, s. 7. Any costs of sorting out a transaction that has not been registered properly will have to be paid by the transferee—LRA 2002, s. 8.

Table 3.3 Interests that affect the first registered proprietor

Section	Interest	Effect
LRA 2002, s. 11(4)(a)	Interests that are the subject of an entry in the register in relation to the estate	This means rights that the registrar enters onto the register—that is, mortgages and any interests protected by notices or restrictions in the register
LRA 2002, s. 11(4)(b)	Unregistered interests that fall within any of the paragraphs of Sch. 1	These are overriding interests—that is, interests that are binding on a transferee without being registered—and include short leaseholds, interests of those who are in 'actual occupation' of the land, unregistered easements and profits, local land charges, and certain other rights

(Continued)

Table 3.3 Continued

Section	Interest	Effect
LRA 2002, s. 11(4)(c)	Interests acquired under the Limitation Act 1980 (c. 58) of which the proprietor has notice	These are rights of persons who have adversely possessed land and of whom the new registered proprietor has notice. This section is unlikely to apply to many cases.
LRA 2002, s. 11(5)	If the proprietor is not entitled to the estate for his or her own benefit, or not entitled solely for his or her own benefit, then, as between the proprietor and the persons beneficially entitled to the estate, the estate is vested in the proprietor subject to such of their interests of which he or she has notice	This deals with situations in which the proprietor is holding the estate as a trustee. The estate is vested in the proprietor, subject to the rights of the beneficiaries.

3.3.4.2 Registrable dispositions

registrable disposition

a transfer of an estate or interest in registered land that is to be registered in the name of the new proprietor

If a transfer of land that is already registered is made, the transfer is a **registrable disposition** that must be completed by registration—LRA 2002, s. 27(2)(a).

Until it is registered, the transfer has no effect at law, so the transferee does not become the legal owner until the moment at which the transfer is registered. This means that the transferor remains as the registered proprietor during the time it takes the Land Registry to process the application for registration.

In theory, the transferor could continue to deal with the land, creating new interests in it, such as easements or leases. In practice, if the transferor were to do so, it would be a breach of contract and of trust, because the land belongs in equity to the transferee. The transferee would, however, be bound by those dispositions under the terms of LRA 2002, s. 28.

registration gap

the period of time between the date of the transfer of property and the date of land registration

The time between the date of the transfer and the date of registration is known as the **registration gap**. It is accepted as a weakness of the land registration system and provisions to eliminate the registration gap were introduced by the LRA 2002. These provisions provide for a system of electronic conveyancing but have not been brought into force (see 3.4).

The effect of registering the transfer of the freehold estate is set out in LRA 2002, s. 29.

 STATUTE

Land Registration Act 2002, s. 29 [Effect of registered dispositions: estates]

(1) If a registrable disposition of a registered estate is made for valuable consideration, completion of the disposition by registration has the effect of postponing to the interest under the disposition any interest affecting the estate immediately before the disposition whose priority is not protected at the time of registration.

(2) For the purposes of subsection (1), the priority of an interest is protected—in any case, if the interest—

(i) is a registered charge or the subject of a notice in the register,

(ii) falls within any of the paragraphs of Schedule 3, or

(iii) appears from the register to be excepted from the effect of registration,

...

The section uses the terms **priority** and **postponement**. In terms that we have used previously, if an interest in the land *is binding* on the new registered proprietor, it is said to have priority; if it *is not binding* on the new registered proprietor, it is said to have been postponed to his or her estate.

> **priority**
> when an interest in land is binding on its new registered proprietor

Notice that the section applies only to a disposition made 'for valuable consideration'. Transfers by way of gift, for example, do not give the new registered proprietor priority over any previously created interest in the land, registered or not—LRA 2002, s. 28. Transfers by way of sale, on the other hand, give the new registered proprietor priority over 'any interest affecting the estate immediately before the disposition whose priority is not protected at the time of the disposition'—that is, any interest in the land that was not protected in one of the ways listed in s. 29(2) will not be binding on the new proprietor.

> **postponement**
> when an interest in land is not binding on its new registered proprietor

The ways in which the priority of an interest can be protected (so that the interest remains binding on the new proprietor) can be summarized as in Table 3.4.

Table 3.4 Interests that have priority over a purchaser of registered land

Section	Definition	Summary
LRA 2002, s. 29(2)(a)(i)	'is a registered charge'	This means a correctly registered mortgage
LRA 2002, s. 29(2)(a)(i)	'or the subject of a notice in the register'	This means interests that are protected on the register by the entry of a notice in the charges register
LRA 2002, s. 29(2)(a)(ii)	'falls within any of the paragraphs of Schedule 3'	This means that it is an overriding interest, which is binding without the need for registration. These include short leaseholds, certain interests of persons in actual occupation of the land, certain legal easements, local land charges, and a number of other rights listed in LRA 2002, Sch. 3.
LRA 2002, s. 29(2) (a)(iii)	'appears from the register to be excepted from the effect of registration'	This will apply only if the estate was registered with a grade of title other than absolute—that is, as either qualified or possessory title

Therefore, if the interest in the land was created before the sale of the property, but was not protected by an entry on the register and is not an overriding interest, then a purchaser of the freehold estate will 'take' (ie acquire title) free from it.

Figure 3.2 illustrates the effect of LRA 2002, s. 29.

3.4 Electronic conveyancing (e-conveyancing)

> **electronic conveyancing, or e-conveyancing**
> the transfer of land by electronic, rather than paper-based, means

LRA 2002, Pt 8 (ss. 91–95), introduced provisions for a move to **electronic conveyancing or e-conveyancing**. This part of the Act has not been brought into force, however, and in July 2011 the Land Registry announced the suspension of further development of e-charges and e-transfers following a consultation exercise.

Figure 3.2 The effects of registration

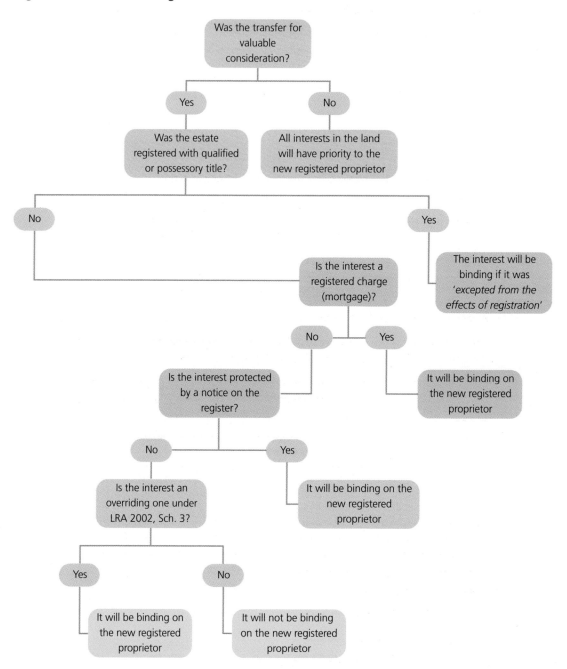

There would be a number of advantages to electronic conveyancing. Firstly, it would do away with the registration gap problem (see 3.3.4.2). Instead of having to execute a transfer of the estate and then send off the paperwork to the Land Registry, the parties would be able to go online to execute the transfer and the registration simultaneously. There would, then, be no 'gap' during which the vendor (who remains the registered proprietor for some time after the transfer in the present system) can create any interests or, indeed, during which any interests at all can arise in any way. Secondly, it would eventually become impossible for any interest in registered land—other than an overriding interest—to be created except by registration. This would mean that all interests would be automatically registered as they were created.

It was also intended that the Land Registry should manage 'chains' of transactions by electronic means, which would help to speed up the process of buying and selling property.

The Law Commission is currently undertaking a review of land registration, which includes e-conveyancing. A report is expected in late 2017.

Summary

1. The legal freehold is technically called the fee simple absolute in possession. Any other type of freehold estate cannot be legal, but takes effect as an equitable interest in land.

2. As well as being a fee simple absolute in possession, the legal freehold must be transferred using the appropriate formalities, otherwise—at best—only an equitable interest in land will be transferred.

3. A contract for the sale or other disposition of a legal freehold must be made in writing and must incorporate all the terms of the contract—LP(MP)A 1989, s. 2.

4. A conveyance of a legal freehold must be made by deed—LPA 1925, s. 52.

5. The conveyance of a legal freehold must be completed by registration, whether or not the land was registered before the transfer—LRA 2002, ss. 4 and 27(2).

6. LRA 2002, Pt 8 made provision for electronic conveyancing, which was not implemented, but there are some signs that e-conveyancing may become a reality in the not too distant future.

The bigger picture

- If you want to know more about registers of title, look at Chapter 14, especially 14.1. For possible exam questions on this area, see Chapter 15, 15.5. If you need more detailed information on the formation of a contract for the sale of land under LP(MP)A 1989, s. 2, please see the Online Resource Centre under 'Advanced topics', chapter 3.
- More information on registration can be found in Chapters 2 and 4.
- If you need more information for coursework, see the cases listed below.

Absolute, determinable, and conditional fees

Blanchfield v. AG of Trinidad and Tobago [2002] UKPC 1

Fraser v. Canterbury Diocesan Board of Finance (No. 2) [2005] UKHL 65

Re Da Costa [1912] 1 Ch 337

Re Leach [1912] 2 Ch 422

Re Moore (1888) 39 Ch D 116

Re Tepper's Will Trust [1987] Ch 358

Walsingham's Case (1573) 2 Plowd. 547

? Questions

Self-test questions

1. Anna is the registered proprietor of Green Cottage. She grants Barry a life interest in Green Cottage. Will this estate be legal or equitable?

2. Anna grants Barry a life interest in Green Cottage, with remainder in fee simple to Cassie. Will Cassie have a legal estate in Green Cottage:

   (a) before Barry's death?

   (b) after Barry's death?

3. Donald transfers his house to Edwin 'until he qualifies as a barrister'. What kind of estate will this be? Is it legal or equitable?

4. Look back at Question 1: when Barry dies, who will be the owner of Green Cottage?

5. Gary wants to buy Frank's house. They have entered into an agreement 'subject to contract'. What rights does this give Gary over Frank's house?

6. Frank has entered into a written contract to sell his house to Gary. What interest, if any, does Gary have in Frank's house?

Exam questions

1. Frank executes a deed transferring his house, which is unregistered land, to Gary. What interest does Gary have in the house? What difference would it make to your answer if the house had been registered land at the time of the transfer?

2. What is meant by the 'registration gap'? How could the problem of the registration gap be resolved?

@ For suggested approaches to answering these questions visit the Online Resource Centre.

☰ Further reading

On Crown Land

Law Commission/HM Land Registry (2001) *Land Registration for the Twenty-First Century: A Conveyancing Revolution*, Law Com No. 271, available online at http://www.lawcom.gov.uk/project/land-registration-for-the-21st-century/, paras 2.7, 11.5–11.19 This Law Commission/HM Land Registry report introduced the LRA 2002. You can see here details of provisions about Crown land.

ON LP(MP)A 1989, S. 2

Chambers, K., 'Property supplement: Yeoman's scope' (2008) 158 NLJ 1629

Pawlowski, M., 'Oral Agreements: estoppel, constructive trusts and restitution' (2008) 12 L and T Rev 163

These two articles discuss the effect of *Cobbe v. Yeoman's Row Management Ltd* [2008] UKHL 55.

On Electronic Conveyancing

Hatfield, E., The e-conveyancing re-revolution [2015] 2 Conv 148–51

This article discusses renewed initiatives to introduce e-conveyancing and compares progress here with that in other common law jurisdictions.

https://www.gov.uk/government/organisations/land-registry

This is the website of the Land Registry. It features publications explaining land registration and you can look at the forms required to register land.

Law Commission (2001) Law Com No. 271, paras 2.41ff

These paragraphs offer the Law Commission's rationale for the introduction of electronic conveyancing.

Law Commission Project on Land Registration

Details of the current project, which includes e-conveyancing, are to be found at http://www.lawcom.gov.uk/project/land-registration/.

Online Resource Centre

www.oxfordtextbooks.co.uk/orc/clarke_directions5e/

For more advice relating to this chapter, including self-test questions and an interactive glossary, visit the Online Resource Centre.

4

Registration of title

☐ **LEARNING OBJECTIVES**

After reading this chapter, you will be able to:

● appreciate the main features of the system of registration of title to land;

● distinguish between first registration of title and registrable dispositions;

● understand substantive registration, interests protected by notice, and overriding interests;

● understand what is meant by alteration and rectification of the register;

● know when an indemnity will be payable as the result of a mistake in the register.

Introduction

You may be wondering why we have devoted another whole chapter to registered land, more accurately called registration of title, because we have already introduced you to it in some detail in the first three chapters. There are a number of very good reasons for this.

1. Registration of title now runs through the whole of land law. It affects the validity of estates and interests in land, and their enforceability against others. This alone means that it merits a whole chapter to itself.

2. It should be easier for you to answer questions about land registration if you can find the law all in one chapter, even if that chapter sometimes refers you to other chapters for more detail.

3. There are areas of land registration law that do not fit neatly into the first three chapters, but which you need to know. These areas are addressed in this chapter.

Having said all of this, the disadvantage to explaining land registration in more detail so early in the book is that, as yet, you have not had a chance really to understand the interests in land that need to be registered. This inevitably makes it more difficult to explain clearly what is being registered and why. What we suggest is that, after reading through this chapter, you dip into it again later in your land law course and use it to fill in any gaps in your understanding.

4.1 The legislative framework

The current system of registration of title was introduced by the Land Registration Act 1925. It was part of a series of reforms of land law made by the **1925 property legislation**.

▶ CROSS REFERENCE

For more on the 1925 property legislation, see Chapter 2.

> **1925 property legislation** a series of Acts of Parliament that came into effect on 1 January 1926. These Acts consolidated earlier piecemeal changes in the law—particularly from 1922–24—and brought them all together as a body of law, which made substantial changes to the common law of property

The system of registration of title worked well, although it was acknowledged that the legislation was far from perfect. In 1998, the Law Commission and the Land Registry published a joint consultative document which stated:

> The present legislation is widely acknowledged to be both badly drafted and lacking in clarity. It is also very complicated. Not only are there 148 sections of the Act, but there are several hundred rules made under it. There is no clear division between what is found in the Act and what is found in the rules. The land registration system has been made to work very effectively, but this has often been in spite of rather than because of its legislative structure.
>
> (Law Commission/HM Land Registry, 1998)

It was therefore decided that the legislation would be updated and, in 2001, a second Law Commission report was published, to which was attached a draft Bill. This Bill eventually became the Land Registration Act 2002 (LRA 2002).

The LRA 2002 did not simply tidy up the legislation relating to land registration; it also changed some aspects of the law. Its stated objectives included the introduction of electronic conveyancing and making fundamental changes to the law of registration of title. The second Law Commission report stated:

> The fundamental objective of the [LRA 2002] is that, under the system of electronic dealing with land that it seeks to create, the register should be a complete and accurate reflection of the state of the title of the land at any given time, so that it is possible to investigate title to land on line, with the absolute minimum of additional enquiries and inspections.
>
> (Law Commission, 2001, para. 1.5)

So, the aim of registration of title is to enable a purchaser to make fewer enquiries about, and inspections of, the land than was formerly the case with unregistered title. The LRA 2002 is now itself the subject of a project by the Law Commission, which is looking in particular at rectification and alteration of the register, the guarantee of title, and the impact of fraud. It will also consider electronic conveyancing. It is due to report in late 2017.

4.2 The register

LRA 2002, s. 1 provides that 'there is to continue to be a register of title kept by the registrar', and goes on to provide for the making of rules about the keeping of the register. These rules take form in the Land Registration Rules 2003, SI 2003/1417 (LRR 2003), which have subsequently been amended, most recently in 2011.

The Chief Land Registrar, who is also the chief executive of the Land Registry, officially keeps the register. Registration is carried out by staff appointed by the registrar, and those staff are located both at the head office in Croydon, London and at land registry offices, which deal with the registration of title in designated areas.

The registrar may refer any disputes about land registration to the Land Registration division of the Property Chamber First-tier tribunal, which may avoid the need for the parties to go to court.

LRA 2002, s. 2 sets out the scope of title registration.

 STATUTE

Land Registration Act 2002, s. 2 [Scope of title registration]

This Act makes provision about the registration of title to—

    (a) unregistered legal estates which are interests of any of the following kinds—

        (i) an estate in land,

        (ii) a rentcharge,

        (iii) a franchise,

        (iv) a profit à prendre in gross, and

        (v) any other interest or charge which subsists for the benefit of, or is a charge on, an interest the title to which is registered; and

    (b) interests capable of subsisting at law which are created by a disposition of an interest the title to which is registered.

 THINKING POINT

Look carefully at LRA 2002, s. 2, above. What is the difference between subsections (a)(i)–(iv) and subsections (a)(v) and (b)? You may find it helpful to look back at Chapter 2.

Subsections (a)(i)–(iv) deal with estates or interests in land that have not yet been registered (unregistered land). Subsections (a)(v) and (b) deal with interests in and dispositions of registered land.

Interests in land that can be registered with their own title are listed as follows.

    1. Estates in land

        You will remember from LPA 1925, s. 1(1) that there are only two legal estates in land: the freehold and the leasehold.

CROSS REFERENCE

For the meaning of a bare trust, see Chapter 7.

        The owner of a freehold estate in land may apply to be registered as owner of that estate. A person who is entitled to have a freehold estate vested in him or her by reason of a bare trust may also apply to be registered as owner of that estate.

        Not all leasehold estates may be registered with their own title. This is because short leases, such as typical residential shorthold tenancies that last six months, would be quite inconvenient to register, from both the Registry's and the tenant's point of view.

        The following types of lease can be registered with their own title:

CROSS REFERENCE

For more on leases, see Chapter 5.

        • leases that, at date of grant, transfer, or creation, have more than seven years to run;

        • leases that take effect more than three months after the date of the grant (sometimes called 'reversionary leases');

- leases with a discontinuous right to possession ('timeshare leases');
- property subject to the 'right to buy' provisions of Housing Act 1985.

2. A rentcharge

   A **rentcharge** is a charge for the payment of money over freehold land. Very few new rentcharges can be created and most existing rentcharges are being phased out under the Rentcharges Act 1977.

3. A franchise

   A **franchise** is the exclusive right to do something on certain land—for example, to hold a market—and most of these are very ancient in origin.

4. A profit à prendre in gross

   A **profit à prendre** is the right to take something from land—for example, firewood—and if it is 'in gross', the benefit of the profit is not attached to any land. It can therefore be registered in its own right.

The rest of the section deals with interests in land to which the title has already been registered. Any interest or charge that either benefits registered land or that is a burden over registered land is subject to the registration provisions. In addition, any disposition of registered land, such as granting a lease of it or selling the freehold to someone else, is subject to the registration provisions. We use the term 'subject to the registration provisions', because some interests, known as overriding interests (see 4.4.6), do not need to be registered.

The key point to remember throughout your whole study of land law is that registration must be considered whenever anything happens to registered land: once land is registered, registration affects every interest in it.

> **rentcharge**
> a charge for the payment of money that is held over freehold land

> **franchise**
> a right, conferred by the Crown on a subject, to do something specific on certain land, eg hold a market

> **profit à prendre**
> the right to take natural produce from another person's land

> ▶ **CROSS REFERENCE**
> For more on profits à prendre, see Chapter 11.

4.3 Crown land

As noted earlier, estates in land can be registered—but you will remember that the Crown, uniquely, can own land outright, rather than owning an estate in the land. Indeed, at common law, the Crown could not grant itself an estate at all: it would be like someone being both landlord and tenant—the Crown cannot 'hold' the land of itself. Nonetheless, the Crown wished to be able to register its land, partly because registration now gives better protection against land being taken by squatters.

LRA 2002, s. 75 gives the Crown power to grant itself a freehold estate out of desmesne land. The Crown can also register a **caution against first registration** of desmesne land—LRA 2002, s. 81. This is an entry made on the register, which means that the Crown will be notified if anyone else tries to register desmesne land—a situation that might arise if someone were claiming adverse possession of that land. This notification would allow the Crown to object to the registration.

> **caution against first registration** a notice lodged with the Land Registry by any person claiming to have ownership of, or an interest in, unregistered land that obliges the Registry to notify that person of any application for first registration of title to that land

LRA 2002, s. 82 allows an estate that has escheated to the Crown to remain on the register until disposed of by the Crown. This is more convenient than the estate ceasing to exist and then a new estate having to be created by the Crown when the land is disposed of to a new owner.

> ▶ **CROSS REFERENCE**
> For more on squatters and adverse possession, see Chapter 6.

> ▶ **CROSS REFERENCE**
> For the meaning of desmesne land, see Chapter 2.

> ▶ **CROSS REFERENCE**
> For the meaning of escheat, see Chapter 2.

4.4 First registration of title

In this section, we are considering land that is unregistered at the time of a sale, or other relevant event, and which therefore becomes subject to registration on the happening of that event.

CROSS REFERENCE

For a refresher on first registration of title, before reading further, see Chapter 2, 2.5.2.2.

The whole of England and Wales has been an area of compulsory registration since December 1990, which means that all relevant events—such as a sale or first mortgage of land—will trigger registration.

The relevant events which trigger registration were extended by the Land Registration Act 1997 and continued by LRA 2002, s. 4(1). LRA 2002, s. 6 imposes a duty to register on any of the relevant events. It is the transferee who is generally obliged to register.

The effects of failing to register as required are set out in LRA 2002, s. 7. A legal estate that has not been registered within the required time period 'becomes void as regards the transfer, grant or creation of a legal estate'. This is quite significant for the transferee: until his or her title is registered, he or she will not actually be the legal owner of the land. The transferee will also have to foot the bill of any costs of putting this right and is in danger of losing priority over a subsequent purchaser of the land. This would mean that his or her (unregistered) interest would not be binding on somebody who had subsequently bought an interest in the same land.

4.4.1 Cautions against first registration

Someone who claims an interest in land that is as yet unregistered can lodge a caution against first registration—LRA 2002, s. 15. This means that the Land Registry will let them know if there is any attempt to register the land, giving them a chance to object to the registration.

> **EXAMPLE**
>
> Bert holds legal title to unregistered land and Anna has a beneficial interest in it under a trust of land. Anna can lodge a caution against first registration against that land, so that she will be notified if Bert applies to register it. That way, she can make sure that any appropriate register entries are made to protect her interest.

CROSS REFERENCE

For more on adverse possession, see Chapter 6.

For more on classes of title, see Chapter 2, 2.5.2.2, Table 2.6.

However, someone who claims to be the owner of a freehold estate or a leasehold estate of which more than seven years are left to run cannot lodge a caution against first registration. Instead, the owner should voluntarily register that estate in the land. This is because lodging a caution should not be used as a substitute for first registration of title to the land. This provision also means that a person claiming to be in adverse possession of unregistered land cannot lodge a caution against first registration, as they will be claiming a freehold or leasehold estate in the land: *Turner v. Chief Land Registrar* [2013] EWHC 1382 (Ch).

4.4.2 Classes of title

The registrar will assign a particular class to each title. The effect of each class of title is set out in LRA 2002, s. 11 [Freeholds], and LRA 2002, s. 12 [Leaseholds].

The vast majority of titles are absolute freehold, absolute leasehold, or good leasehold.

4.4.3 **The effect of registration with absolute title**

Because most titles are absolute, we will concentrate on the legal effect of registration with absolute title.

> CROSS REFERENCE

For more detail on the interests postponed to first registration, see Chapter 3, 3.3.4.1, Table 3.3.

STATUTE

Land Registration Act 2002, s. 11 [Freehold estates]

(1) This section is concerned with the registration of a person under this Chapter as the proprietor of a freehold estate.

(2) Registration with absolute title has the effect described in subsections (3) to (5).

(3) The estate is vested in the proprietor together with all interests subsisting for the benefit of the estate.

(4) The estate is vested in the proprietor subject only to the following interests affecting the estate at the time of registration—

   (a) interests which are the subject of an entry in the register in relation to the estate,

   (b) unregistered interests which fall within any of the paragraphs of Schedule 1, and

   (c) interests acquired under the Limitation Act 1980 (c. 58) of which the proprietor has notice.

(5) If the proprietor is not entitled to the estate for his own benefit, or not entitled solely for his own benefit, then, as between himself and the persons beneficially entitled to the estate, the estate is vested in him subject to such of their interests as he has notice of.

...

LRA 2002, s. 12 contains similar provisions in relation to absolute leasehold title, except that registration is also subject to the terms of the lease—particularly covenants.

> CROSS REFERENCE

For more on leasehold title, see Chapter 5.

This provision makes the registered proprietor the legal owner of the estate, whatever the circumstances of the transfer of the land to him or her. This changes the common law position that no-one can give good title to an estate that he or she does not own.

EXAMPLE

To take an extreme example, if you were to try to sell the Houses of Parliament to a gullible tourist, he or she would not become the owner of it, because you have no title to the Houses of Parliament that you can sell!

But a gullible tourist who is then *registered* as the proprietor of the Houses of Parliament *would* become their legal owner, because of LRA 2002, ss. 11 and 58.

You can see a rather more realistic example of this in the case of *Re 139 Deptford High Street*.

CASE CLOSE-UP

Re 139 Deptford High Street [1951] Ch 884

The vendor transferred a shop to the purchaser, together with an annexe. In fact, the annexe did not belong to the vendor, but to someone else. The purchaser was registered as first registered proprietor of the property, including the annexe. Naturally, the true owner of the annexe, once he found out, was keen to get the register altered to correct the mistake.

It was clear that the registered proprietor was the legal owner of the annexe, even though the vendors did not have power to transfer it to him, because they did not own it. If it had not been for registration, he would not have been the owner.

The register was rectified (altered) to exclude the annexe from the registered title.

(See 4.6 for more on alteration, rectification, and indemnity.)

Re Deptford High Street was decided under the Land Registration Act 1925—but the fact that registration makes the registered proprietor the legal owner of the land is even clearer under LRA 2002, s. 58.

STATUTE

Land Registration Act 2002, s. 58 [Conclusiveness]

(1) If, on the entry of a person in the register as the proprietor of a legal estate, the legal estate would not otherwise be vested in him, it shall be deemed to be vested in him as a result of the registration.

...

▶ CROSS REFERENCE

For more on interests affecting the sole ownership of land, see Chapter 7.

Notice that s. 58 mentions only the legal estate. We noted earlier in the book, however, that the owner of a legal estate need not necessarily be the owner in equity: he or she may be a trustee for someone else, for example. This point is dealt with in LRA 2002, s. 11(5), which states that 'as between himself and the persons beneficially entitled to the estate, the estate is vested in [the registered proprietor] subject to such of their interests as he has notice of'. So, if the registered proprietor knows the estate is held on trust for someone, that person will still be able to assert the equitable rights of a beneficiary.

▶ CROSS REFERENCE

For more details on adverse possession, see Chapter 6.

▶ CROSS REFERENCE

For more on interests gained by squatters, see Chapter 6.

LRA 2002, s. 58 can have strange effects. For example, in *Parshall v. Hackney* [2013] EWCA (Civ) 240, the defendant was wrongly registered as the proprietor of a small piece of land which really belonged to the claimant. The defendant had in fact been in adverse possession of it for some time, but it was held by the Court of Appeal that a person registered as a proprietor of land cannot claim adverse possession, even if registered as proprietor by mistake, and is open to a claim for rectification of the register.

The registered proprietor is therefore the legal owner of the estate, and is subject only to:

- interests discoverable from looking at the register—LRA 2002, s. 11(4)(a);
- interests that override first registration—that is, the overriding interests contained in LRA 2002, Sch. 1—LRA 2002, s. 11(4)(b);
- interests gained by squatters under the Limitation Act 1980 of which the proprietor has notice—LRA 2002, s. 11(4)(c).

4.4.4 Interests protected by notice on the register

As you can see from LRA 2002, s. 11(4)(a), the registered proprietor is subject to any entries that are protected in the register. Some interests are protected by **notice** on the register.

STATUTE

Land Registration Act 2002, s. 32 [Nature and effect]

(1) A notice is an entry in the register in respect of the burden of an interest affecting a registered estate or charge.

(2) The entry of a notice is to be made in relation to the registered estate or charge affected by the interest concerned.

(3) The fact that an interest is the subject of a notice does not necessarily mean that the interest is valid, but does mean that the priority of the interest, if valid, is protected for the purposes of sections 29 and 30.

> **notice**
> an entry against a registered title lodged by a person with a specified interest in the land

Notices are entered on the charges register section of the register of title. The effect of entering a notice is very different from that of registering title—LRA 2002, s. 32(3). The registrar does not guarantee that the interest is valid, unlike registered estates or charges, but it is vital to register the interest, because registration by notice protects the priority of valid interests. In other words, if a valid interest is registered by notice, it will be binding on a purchaser of the land; if it is not registered, it will not be binding on a purchaser.

> ❯❯ CROSS REFERENCE
> For more on the binding nature of registered interests, see Chapter 2.

The LRA 2002 does not set out what interests can be registered as notices, but s. 33 sets out those that cannot.

STATUTE

Land Registration Act 2002, s. 33 [Excluded interests]

No notice may be entered in the register in respect of any of the following—

(a) an interest under—

   (i) a trust of land, or

   (ii) a settlement under the Settled Land Act 1925 (c. 18),

(b) a leasehold estate in land which—

   (i) is granted for a term of years of three years or less from the date of the grant, and

   (ii) is not required to be registered,

[(ba) an interest under a relevant social housing tenancy,]

(c) a restrictive covenant made between a lessor and lessee, so far as relating to the demised premises,

(d) an interest which is capable of being registered under the Commons Registration Act 1965 (c. 64) [Part 1 of the Commons Act 2006], and

(e) an interest in any coal or coal mine, the rights attached to any such interest and the rights of any person under section 38, 49 or 51 of the Coal Industry Act 1994 (c. 21).

CROSS REFERENCE

For a list of the types of interest that are usually protected by the entry of a notice, see Chapter 2.

The section specifies that interests under trusts cannot be registered by notice. They will appear only as restrictions on the proprietorship register (see 4.4.5). Other excluded interests include most leases of three years or less—unless they are discontinuous, or reversionary leases (see 4.2). Restrictive covenants in leases are not registrable, because they apply only between the landlord and the tenant.

The interests in subsections (d) and (e) have their own special registers.

There are two types of notice: an **agreed notice** and a **unilateral notice** —LRA 2002, s. 34.

> **agreed notice** a notice on registered land that is either requested or agreed to by the proprietor, or the validity of which satisfies the registrar
>
> **unilateral notice** a notice on registered land to which the proprietor will not agree, which consequently represents a disputed interest

📖 STATUTE

Land Registration Act 2002, s. 34 [Entry on application]

(1) A person who claims to be entitled to the benefit of an interest affecting a registered estate or charge may, if the interest is not excluded by section 33, apply to the registrar for the entry in the register of a notice in respect of the interest.

(2) Subject to rules, an application under this section may be for—

    (a) an agreed notice, or

    (b) a unilateral notice.

(3) The registrar may only approve an application for an agreed notice if—

    (a) the applicant is the relevant registered proprietor, or a person entitled to be registered as such proprietor,

    (b) the relevant registered proprietor, or a person entitled to be registered as such proprietor, consents to the entry of the notice, or

    (c) the registrar is satisfied as to the validity of the applicant's claim.

In subsection (3), references to the relevant registered proprietor are to the proprietor of the registered estate or charge affected by the interest to which the application relates.

Agreed notices must satisfy one of the conditions in LRA 2002, s. 34(3). That means that the proprietor asks for the notice to be entered, that the proprietor agrees to the notice, or that the registrar is satisfied by the claim giving rise to the notice. This third condition means that agreed notices can be entered even if the registered proprietor objects, provided that the registrar is satisfied that the interest is valid.

EXAMPLE

If an access order has been granted to someone under the Access to Neighbouring Land Act 1992, that right will be registered as an agreed notice, even if the registered proprietor of that land objects.

This is because, despite the proprietor's objection, the Land Registry would be satisfied as to the validity of the notice.

If an agreed notice cannot be entered, a unilateral notice may be entered instead—LRA 2002, s. 35.

STATUTE

Land Registration Act 2002, s. 35 [Unilateral notices]

(1) If the registrar enters a notice in the register in pursuance of an application under section 34(2)(b) ('a unilateral notice'), he must give notice of the entry to—

    (a) the proprietor of the registered estate or charge to which it relates, and

    (b) such other persons as rules may provide.

(2) A unilateral notice must—

    (a) indicate that it is such a notice, and

    (b) identify who is the beneficiary of the notice.

(3) The person shown in the register as the beneficiary of a unilateral notice, or such other person as rules may provide, may apply to the registrar for the removal of the notice from the register.

Because the registrar does not have to be satisfied that the interest claimed is genuine, there is potential for people to enter unilateral notices for hostile reasons. This might cause a registered proprietor who is trying to sell the land considerable difficulties, because many purchasers will be put off by the very existence of a unilateral notice on the basis that it indicates disagreement over rights in the land.

For this reason, the registered proprietor and others interested in the land are informed about the unilateral notice by the registrar. The registered proprietor can then apply for its cancellation. If the beneficiary of the unilateral notice opposes the cancellation, the matter will be referred to the Land Registration division of the Property Chamber First-tier tribunal, which may uphold the notice—turning it into an agreed notice, or ordering registration of the interest in some more appropriate way—or order its cancellation. If the beneficiary of the notice has acted without reasonable cause, the registered proprietor can bring an action against that beneficiary in tort and claim damages for breach of statutory duty.

4.4.5 Interests protected on the register by the entry of a restriction

Restrictions are entries that are placed on the proprietorship part of the register and they restrict the right of the registered proprietor to deal with his or her land. Restrictions are most often used to protect 'family'-type interests, many of which will be overreached on the sale of the land.

> **CROSS REFERENCE**
> For the meaning of overreaching, see Chapter 2, 2.5.3.

restriction a limitation on the right of a registered proprietor to deal with the land or charge in a registered title

STATUTE

Land Registration Act 2002, s. 40 [Nature]

(1) A restriction is an entry in the register regulating the circumstances in which a disposition of a registered estate or charge may be the subject of an entry in the register.

(2) A restriction may, in particular—

    (a) prohibit the making of an entry in respect of any disposition, or a disposition of a kind specified in the restriction;

    (b) prohibit the making of an entry—

        (i) indefinitely,

        (ii) for a period specified in the restriction, or

        (iii) until the occurrence of an event so specified.

(3) Without prejudice to the generality of subsection (2)(b)(iii), the events which may be specified include—

    (a) the giving of notice,

    (b) the obtaining of consent, and

    (c) the making of an order by the court or registrar.

The entry of a restriction is to be made in relation to the registered estate or charge to which it relates.

The purpose of a restriction is to ensure that certain conditions are complied with on the transfer of land, because 'no entry in respect of a disposition to which the restriction applies may be made in the register otherwise than in accordance with the terms of the restriction'—LRA 2002, s. 41(1). This means that, if, for example, the consent of a certain person is required for the sale of the property, no transfer can be registered without that consent.

Some restrictions will be entered automatically by the registrar under LRA 2002, s. 44.

STATUTE

CROSS REFERENCE

For more on the types of restrictions entered in cases of co-ownership, see Chapter 8.

Land Registration Act 2002, s. 44 [Obligatory restrictions]

(1) If the registrar enters two or more persons in the register as the proprietor of a registered estate in land, he must also enter in the register such restrictions as rules may provide for the purpose of securing that interests which are capable of being overreached on a disposition of the estate are overreached. …

Other restrictions may be entered if the registered proprietor applies for them to be entered, or consents to them being entered, or if the person applying for the restriction 'otherwise has a sufficient interest in the making of the entry'—LRA 2002, s. 43(1).

As with notices, if a person applies for a restriction to be entered without reasonable cause, the registered proprietor will be able to sue in tort for any loss caused.

4.4.6 Interests that override first registration

CROSS REFERENCE

For a definition of overriding interests, see Chapter 2.

Overriding interests are interests that do not need to be registered, but which are nevertheless binding on a purchaser of the estate. This is quite a tricky concept—particularly when we have just stated that the purpose of land registration is that as much information about the land as possible should be recorded on the register.

The statute divides overriding interests into those that override the first registration of land—that is, when unregistered land becomes registered land—and those that override subsequent registrable dispositions of land, for example, when registered land is sold.

Those interests that override first registration of land are set out in LRA 2002, Sch. 1 and include:

- leases;
- persons in actual occupation;
- easements and profits;
- customary and public rights;
- local land charges;
- mineral rights;
- (other miscellaneous rights).

4.4.6.1 Leases

 STATUTE

Land Registration Act 2002, Sch. 1, para. 1 [Leasehold estates in land]

A leasehold estate in land granted for a term not exceeding seven years from the date of the grant, except for a lease the grant of which falls within section 4(1) (d), (e) or (f).

LRA 2002, Sch. 1, para. 1 provides that short leases are overriding interests. Longer leases (those over seven years) are registrable interests, but shorter leases are not, other than those that are reversionary (see 4.2) and certain local authority leases. Shorter leases are protected by being overriding interests. Similar provision is made for relevant social housing tenancies by Sch. 1, para. 1A. These paragraphs apply only to legal leases, because the term used is 'leasehold estate'. A tenant under an equitable lease who actually lives in the property, however, is likely to have an overriding interest under LRA 2002, Sch. 1, para. 2 as a 'person in actual occupation' of the land.

4.4.6.2 Persons in actual occupation

 STATUTE

Land Registration Act 2002, Sch. 1, para. 2 [Interests of persons in actual occupation]

An interest belonging to a person in actual occupation, so far as relating to land of which he is in actual occupation, except for an interest under a settlement under the Settled Land Act 1925 (c. 18).

LRA 2002, Sch. 1, para. 2 provides that the interests of persons who are in actual occupation of the land are overriding interests. This is a very important category: it is intended to protect those who live on the land, or who are otherwise in actual occupation of it.

The first, very important, point to grasp is that being in actual occupation is not itself enough to give someone an overriding interest in land: a person must have an interest in land to start with, which is then coupled with his or her actual occupation, to create an overriding interest.

> **EXAMPLE**
>
> 1. Clare has just moved in with her boyfriend, Don. She has not paid any money towards the house and Don has not made her any promises about ownership.
>
> Clare will not have an overriding interest in Don's house. Although she is living there and is in actual occupation, she does not have an interest in the house.
>
> 2. Eddie has just helped his girlfriend, Fiona, to buy a house. He has paid part of the deposit and has agreed to help her with mortgage payments. Fiona has told him that he should think of himself as part-owner, but Eddie does not want to put his name on the register in case his ex-wife finds out he has more money than he has declared.
>
> Eddie may well have an overriding interest in the house. His payment of part of the deposit, and the agreement between him and Fiona, may have created either a resulting or constructive trust in his favour, which gives him an interest in the house. As long as he lives in the house, he will have both an interest plus actual occupation, which amounts to an overriding interest.

In other words:

$$\text{interest in land} + \text{actual occupation} = \text{overriding interest}$$

Interests in land capable of overriding

> **CROSS REFERENCE**
>
> For more on *National Provincial Bank v. Ainsworth* and proprietary rights, see Chapter 1.

It is quite clear that the interest in land must be a proprietary right that can bind third parties: if it is not, then the fact of actual occupation will not make it binding on purchasers.

For example, in *National Provincial Bank v. Ainsworth* [1965] AC 1175, the right of a wife to stay in her husband's house after he had left her (the deserted wife's equity) was held not to be a proprietary right and so could not be an overriding interest. The modern statutory equivalent—the spouse's or civil partner's statutory right of occupation—is also incapable of being an overriding interest—Family Law Act 1996, s. 31(1)(b).

> **CROSS REFERENCE**
>
> For more on successive interests in land, see Chapter 8.

In addition, if you look back at LRA 2002, Sch. 1, para. 2, you will see that interests under the Settled Land Act 1925 are incapable of being overriding interests. These are successive interests in land, under old law.

> **Q** **CASE CLOSE-UP**

> **CROSS REFERENCE**
>
> For more on this this case see Chapter 7.

Scott v. Southern Pacific Mortgages Ltd (Re Northern Property Buyers litigation) [2015] AC 385; [2014] UKSC 52

The Supreme Court reiterated that an overriding interest can be founded only on a proprietary right. Mrs Scott had sold her home to a purchaser, relying on a promise that the house would be leased back to her for as long as she wanted to live there. Unknown to her, the purchaser really intended to grant a legal mortgage over the property to SPM and pocket the money. The house was registered in the purchaser's name at the same time as the mortgage granted to SPM, and a short-term lease in breach of the mortgage conditions was granted to Mrs Scott.

The purchaser duly defaulted on the loan repayments, and SPM sought possession of the house. The Supreme Court held that the promise to grant a lease did not take priority over the charge by way of legal mortgage because it was not a proprietary right.

Many different types of proprietary rights can be sufficient for actual occupation to turn them into overriding interests. In *Swift 1st Ltd v. Chief Land Registrar* [2015] EWCA Civ 330, for example, it was held that the right to rectify the register (see 4.6.1) was an interest capable of being an overriding interest.

Most cases on this area of the law, however, concern rights under resulting or constructive trusts of land and it is clear that these rights, even though they are potentially overreachable, can be overriding interests—*Williams & Glyn's v. Boland* [1981] AC 487. Rights that have actually been overreached, however, are no longer interests in land and cannot be overriding—*City of London Building Society v. Flegg* [1988] AC 54.

⟩ CROSS REFERENCE

For more on the overreaching of overriding interests, see Chapter 2 and Chapter 7.

⟩ CROSS REFERENCE

For more on *Williams & Glyn's v. Boland* and *City of London Building Society v. Flegg*, see Chapter 7.

Actual occupation

As we have already stated, actual occupation without an interest in the land does not give rise to an overriding interest under LRA 2002, Sch. 1, para. 2. The reverse is also true: an interest without actual occupation does not give rise to an overriding interest either. It is important, therefore, to know what is meant by 'actual occupation'.

🔍 CASE CLOSE-UP

Williams & Glyn's Bank plc v. Boland [1981] AC 487

The question had to be decided whether two wives were in actual occupation of their matrimonial homes.

It was argued in favour of the bank that their occupation was merely as a '*shadow*' of their husbands' occupation, or alternatively, that their occupation was not adverse to their husbands and therefore did not amount to actual occupation.

Fortunately, the House of Lords did not accept these arguments. As Lord Wilberforce said, at 504:

> Were the wives here in 'actual occupation'? These words are ordinary words of plain English, and should, in my opinion, be interpreted as such.

He went on to hold that their ordinary living in the house was indeed actual occupation.

If the property is a dwelling house, actual occupation has been found in cases in which a person supervises builders—*Lloyds Bank plc v. Rosset* [1989] Ch 350 (although the case was eventually reversed on the grounds that Mrs Rosset did not have an interest in the house—[1991] AC 107).

⟩ CROSS REFERENCE

For more on *Lloyds Bank plc v. Rosset*, see Chapter 9.

If a person is temporarily absent from a house, but usually lives there, this will not prevent that person from being in 'actual occupation' while he or she is away.

🔍 CASE CLOSE-UP

Chhokar v. Chhokar [1984] FLR 313

A wife who had an interest in the family home went into hospital to have a baby. During that time, her husband sold their house at an under-value and left the country with the money.

The Court of Appeal accepted that the wife had an overriding interest in the house; her absence in hospital did not mean that she ceased to be in actual occupation.

Similarly, in *Link Lending Ltd v. Bustard* [2010] EWCA Civ 424, a person who was detained in hospital under the Mental Health Act 1983, but who made regular visits home and who always intended to return there, was held to be in actual occupation of her home.

On the other hand, temporary presence in a house is unlikely to constitute actual occupation: it must be more permanent.

 CASE CLOSE-UP

Abbey National Building Society v. Cann [1991] 1 AC 56

A mother tried to claim an overriding interest in her son's house. She needed to prove actual occupation on the day she moved into the house. In fact, she was abroad on that day, but her son and husband moved her property into the house.

It was held by the House of Lords that this did *not* amount to actual occupation. Lord Oliver said that actual occupation did not have to involve physical presence and that a caretaker, for example, could occupy the property on behalf of his employer, but it had to '*involve some degree of permanence and continuity which would rule out mere fleeting presence*' (at 93). Measuring up for curtains or planning decorations before moving in would not amount to actual occupation.

If the property is not a dwelling house, actual occupation can be shown by a number of means. In *Kling v. Keston Properties Ltd* (1989) 49 P & CR 212, the parking of a car in a lock-up garage was held to be actual occupation. However, in *Chaudhary v. Yavuz* [2011] EWCA Civ 1314; [2013] Ch 249 (CA (Civ)) (see 4.5.1), tenants walking up and down a staircase built on neighbouring land was not enough to show actual occupation of that land.

▶ CROSS REFERENCE

For more on actual occupation, see Chapter 7.

If the actual occupation does not extend to the whole of the property, the overriding interest applies to only that part actually occupied 'so far as relating to land of which he is in actual occupa-tion'—LRA 2002, Sch. 1, para. 2. This wording reversed the previous law under Land Registration Act 1925, s. 70(1)(g), as decided in *Wallcite Ltd v. Ferrishurst Ltd* [1999] 1 All ER 977. In that case, a person who had rights in both offices and a garage was held to have an overriding interest in both, despite the fact that only the offices were occupied. Under LRA 2002, this would no longer be the case.

4.4.6.3 Easements and profits

 STATUTE

Land Registration Act 2002, Sch. 1, para. 3 [Easements and profits à prendre]

3   A legal easement or profit à prendre.

▶ CROSS REFERENCE

For more on, and the meanings of, easements and profits, see Chapter 11.

A legal easement or profit à prendre will override first registration of land. Note that this will not apply to equitable easements or profits.

4.4.6.4 Customary and public rights

STATUTE

Land Registration Act 2002, Sch. 1, paras 4–5 [Customary and public rights]

4   A customary right.

5   A public right.

Customary and public rights are enjoyed by the public or some group of people. An example would be the rights of way over a public footpath. These rights are overriding.

⟩ CROSS REFERENCE

For more on customary and public rights, see Chapter 11.

4.4.6.5 Local land charges

STATUTE

Land Registration Act 2002, Sch. 1, para. 6 [Local land charges]

6   A local land charge.

Local land charges are registered on an independent register that used to be kept by all local authorities within England and Wales, but which has now been transferred to the Land Registry by the Infrastructure Act 2015, s. 34. They contain such matters as tree preservation orders, outstanding liability for any charges levied by local authorities, etc. Local land charges are overriding interests.

4.4.6.6 Mineral rights

STATUTE

Land Registration Act 2002, Sch. 1, paras 7–9 [Mines and minerals]

7   An interest in any coal or coal mine, the rights attached to any such interest and the rights of any person under section 38, 49 or 51 of the Coal Industry Act 1994 (c. 21).

8   In the case of land to which title was registered before 1898, rights to mines and minerals (and incidental rights) created before 1898.

9   In the case of land to which title was registered between 1898 and 1925 inclusive, rights to mines and minerals (and incidental rights) created before the date of registration of the title.

These are mineral rights dating from before 1925 which are not recorded anywhere and which are therefore protected as overriding interests.

4.4.6.7 Miscellaneous rights

There were a number of rights of ancient origin listed in LRA 2002, Sch. 1, paras 10–16 (now repealed) which remained as overriding interests for ten years after the LRA 2002 came into force.

This was to allow those who owned them time to register them. They included franchises, manorial rights, and the liability to repair sea walls and church chancels.

They ceased to be overriding on 13 October 2013 and if owners of such interests have not registered them, they will be unenforceable following any registered dispositions after that date.

4.5 Registrable dispositions

 CROSS REFERENCE

For the meaning of registrable disposition, see Chapter 3.

Once land is registered, any dealing with it must take registration into account. This section therefore looks at the law that applies to land that is already registered. As we have seen, LRA 2002, s. 23, sets out the registered proprietor's powers to deal with the estate. Major dealings with registered land are registrable dispositions—that is, dealings that must be registered if they are to take effect at law.

📖 STATUTE

Land Registration Act 2002, s. 27 [Dispositions required to be registered]

If a disposition of a registered estate or registered charge is required to be completed by registration, it does not operate at law until the relevant registration requirements are met.

In the case of a registered estate, the following are the dispositions which are required to be completed by registration—

    (a) a transfer,

    (b) where the registered estate is an estate in land, the grant of a term of years absolute—

        (i) for a term of more than seven years from the date of the grant,

        (ii) to take effect in possession after the end of the period of three months beginning with the date of the grant,

        (iii) under which the right to possession is discontinuous,

        (iv) in pursuance of Part 5 of the Housing Act 1985 (c. 68) (the right to buy), or

        (v) in circumstances where section 171A of that Act applies (disposal by landlord which leads to a person no longer being a secure tenant),

    (c) where the registered estate is a franchise or manor, the grant of a lease,

    (d) the express grant or reservation of an interest of a kind falling within section 1(2)(a) of the Law of Property Act 1925 (c. 20), other than one which is capable of being registered under the Commons Registration Act 1965 (c. 64) [Part 1 of the Commons Act 2006],

    (e) the express grant or reservation of an interest of a kind falling within section 1(2)(b) or (e) of the Law of Property Act 1925, and

    (f) the grant of a legal charge.

    ...

CROSS REFERENCE

For more details on LRA 2002, s. 29, see Chapter 3, 3.3.4.2.

LRA 2002, s. 27, sets out the dealings with registered land that are registrable dispositions and which must therefore be completed by registration if they are to take effect at law. As you can see, they include a transfer of the estate, the grant of leases of over seven years (plus certain other leases, including reversionary leases and timeshare leases), and the grant of interests falling under LPA 1925, s. 1(2), which, you should remember, is the section listing those interests in land that can be legal, rather than equitable. Such interests include legal easements and profits, legal rent-charges, and legal charges, or mortgages (see 4.2).

The effect of registering a registrable disposition is set out in LRA 2002, s. 29, which essentially means that the registered proprietor takes their estate or interest in the land subject only to existing registered charges, interests protected by a notice on the register, and overriding interests.

The precise details of how to register each interest can be found in LRA 2002, Sch. 2.

4.5.1 The protection of those who are registered as a result of a registrable disposition

When there has been a registrable disposition of land and it has been correctly registered, the **disponee** is protected by LRA 2002, s. 26.

> **disponee**
> the person to whom a registrable disposition is made

 STATUTE

Land Registration Act 2002, s. 26 [Protection of disponees]

(1) Subject to subsection (2), a person's right to exercise owner's powers in relation to a registered estate or charge is to be taken to be free from any limitation affecting the validity of a disposition.

(2) Subsection (1) does not apply to a limitation—reflected by an entry in the register, or imposed by, or under, this Act.

This section has effect only for the purpose of preventing the title of a disponee being questioned (and so does not affect the lawfulness of a disposition).

Once registered as a result of a registered disposition, the new proprietor is entitled to exercise owner's powers in respect of the estate 'free from any limitation affecting the validity of the disposition', unless that limitation is reflected by an entry in the register or imposed under the LRA 2002. This means that the new proprietor is treated as correctly registered, subject only to entries in the register and other statutory limitations.

Under LRA 2002, s. 26(3), however, if the disposition was actually unlawful in some way, its registration does not make it lawful. This is a complicated concept and you may understand it better if you think about an example.

 EXAMPLE

Davan and Emma are the registered proprietors of Hillcrest Farm. They hold the land on trust for themselves for life and then for their nephew, Freddy, absolutely. The terms of the trust state that Freddy's consent is needed for any sale of Hillcrest Farm—but there is no restriction in the proprietorship register preventing a sale from taking place without Freddy's consent.

Davan and Emma sell the land to their friend, Govan, without getting Freddy's consent. He is devastated and wants to get Hillcrest Farm back.

> LRA 2002, s. 26, means that Govan's title is protected because, although the sale was unlawful (it was in breach of trust), that invalidity was not reflected by an entry in the register—there was no restriction entered and it was not affected by any provision in LRA 2002.
>
> Section 26 does *not* actually make the sale itself lawful, however: Davan and Emma can be sued for breach of trust, and they will be liable in damages. In addition, if Freddy can show that Govan knew about the trust, he may be held liable in equity to Freddy for knowing receipt of trust property.

It can be argued that, in the example above, because the new registered proprietor can still be held personally liable, the protection given by LRA 2002, s. 26, is not as good as it first appears to be. The registered proprietor may well feel unprotected by the legislation.

4.5.1.1 Forged dispositions

The protection of disponees under a disposition of the land that turns out to have been a forgery has been a controversial matter. Under the old law, LRA 1925, in the case of *Malory Enterprises Ltd v. Cheshire Homes (UK) Ltd* [2002] EWCA Civ 151, the Court of Appeal held that a transfer of registered land that was a forgery (it was executed by someone pretending to be the registered proprietor) gave the transferee a legal title to the land, but not the equitable title. This case was followed in *Fitzwilliam v. Richall Holding Services* [2013] EWHC 86 (Ch), a similar case under LRA 2002. This meant that the innocent transferee under a forged transfer did not have the protection of LRA 2002, s. 26.

It was also unclear whether the transferee could get an indemnity (compensation) from the Land Registry when the land was transferred back to the true owner because the Court in *Malory Enterprises* held that a forged transfer is not a 'disposition'.

However, a recent case has changed this:

🔍 CASE CLOSE-UP

Swift 1st Ltd v. Chief Land Registrar [2015] EWCA Civ 330

Mrs R was the registered proprietor of a house which was her home at all material times. In 2006, someone took out a loan from Swift 1st Ltd, the appellants, and created a forged charge (mortgage) over Mrs R's house as security. The charge was registered on Mrs R's register of title. When the loan was not paid back, the appellants sought to repossess Mrs R's house. She, of course, argued that since the charge was a forgery, she was not liable to pay, and that her right to have the register rectified plus her actual occupation was an overriding interest in her home.

The appellants accepted this, but argued for an indemnity from the Land Registry, as they were innocent disponees who had suffered a loss.

The Court of Appeal decided that *Malory* had been decided *per incuriam*, and that they were therefore at liberty to depart from it. A transfer under a forged disposition conveys both the legal and equitable interest in the property to the innocent disponee, who is entitled to an indemnity under LRA 2002, Sch. 8, para. 1(2)(b).

4.5.1.2 What happens if the purchaser actually knows about an unregistered interest?

⟩ CROSS REFERENCE

For more on *Midland Bank v. Green*, see Chapter 2.

One possible disadvantage of systems of registration is that they enable unscrupulous people, who know that an interest is not registered, to take advantage of that fact. We have seen an example of exactly this sort of thing happening in a case concerning the registration of land charges in unregistered land—*Midland Bank v. Green* [1981] AC 513. (Note that this is not a case concerning registered land, but that we are using it as an example here because its facts illustrate the kind of dilemma to which we are referring.)

In that case, a father knew that his son's option to buy the family farm was not registered under the Land Charges Act 1972 and, after falling out with his son, the father sold the property at a fraction of its true price to his wife. She knew all about the option, but was held by the House of Lords not to be bound by it, because it was unregistered.

What would the situation be if someone were to undertake the same action in relation to registered land? Would the court stand by and let them do it, or would it apply equitable principles such as 'equity will not allow a statute to be used as an instrument of fraud'?

Under LRA 1925, there was a much-criticized decision in *Peffer v. Rigg* [1977] 1 WLR 285 that seemed to mean that a purchaser who had knowledge of an unregistered interest could be bound by it.

 CASE CLOSE-UP

Peffer v. Rigg **[1977] 1 WLR 285**

Two brothers-in-law bought a house for their mother-in-law to live in. It was registered in Mr Rigg's sole name, but it was actually held on trust by him for himself and Mr Peffer.

No restriction was entered on the register, so Mr Peffer's equitable interest was unregistered. Later, as part of a divorce settlement, Mr Rigg transferred the house to his wife for the sum of £1.

Clearly, this transfer was in breach of trust and Mr Rigg was liable to Mr Peffer for half the value of the house. The question was, however, whether Mrs Rigg held the house on trust for Mr Peffer, because she knew all about his equitable interest in the house.

Graham J held that Mrs Rigg was a trustee for Mr Peffer. The transfer to Mrs Rigg in circumstances under which she knew of the breach of trust gave rise to a constructive trust in favour of Mr Peffer.

A constructive trust is one that arises because equity imposes it on someone who has acted improperly.

There are other cases in which a constructive trust has been imposed on a purchaser who has behaved improperly.

 CASE CLOSE-UP

Jones v. Lipman **[1962] 1 WLR 832**

The defendant had entered into a contract to sell his land to the claimant. He changed his mind and, to escape the contract, transferred the land instead to a company over which he had control. The agreement to sell the land to the claimant was not registered by notice.

Russell J ordered the company to sell the land to the claimant at the agreed price. As the judge, very colourfully, said:

> The defendant company is the creature of the first defendant, a device and a sham, a mask which he holds before his face in an attempt to avoid recognition by the eye of equity.

In a slightly different set of circumstances, the case of *Lyus v. Prowsa Developments* [1982] 1 WLR 832 recognized that an unregistered contract can be enforced against a purchaser of the land.

 CASE CLOSE-UP

Lyus v. Prowsa Developments [1982] 1 WLR 832

The claimants had agreed to buy a plot of land from a building company, with a house built on it to their specifications. They had paid a deposit, but when the house was only part-built, the company became insolvent and a bank became entitled to sell the land as mortgagees.

The bank sold the land to Prowsa Developments subject to, and with the benefit of, the contract to complete the house and sell it to the claimants. Prowsa promised to honour the contract, but failed to do so. The contract was not registered.

Dillon J held that Prowsa was subject to a constructive trust. It not only knew of the contract, but also had expressly agreed to honour it.

The main criticism of these cases, especially of *Peffer v. Rigg*, is that they come close to saying that it is fraud for a purchaser of land to rely on the provisions of an Act of Parliament to escape liability. LRA 2002, s. 26 provides that a disponee can assume that the registered proprietor is free to sell the land without any restrictions unless they are registered, or imposed under the Act—such as overriding interests. If, in fact, a purchaser will be made liable personally as a constructive trustee, this seems to do away with the protection in the Act.

This was considered at para. 4.11 in the Law Commission report (2001) that introduced the LRA 2002, and it was accepted that a disponee might be personally liable under a constructive trust. However, it appears that knowledge alone will not be held sufficient to impose such a trust, but that other considerations must be present, such as the obvious sham in *Jones v. Lipman* or the express promise in *Lyus v. Prowsa Developments*. This seems to be confirmed by *Chaudhary v. Yavuz*, decided under LRA 2002.

 CASE CLOSE-UP

Chaudhary v. Yavuz [2011] EWCA Civ 1314; [2013] Ch 249 (CA (Civ Div))

This concerned a first floor flat which was accessible only by using an exterior staircase and balcony situated on the neighbouring defendant's land. The staircase had been built by the claimant in 2006, and had been of advantage to both the claimant and his then neighbour, as it allowed the neighbour to demolish an old internal staircase on his own property. However, no right of way was registered by the claimant over the new staircase. When the neighbour's property was sold to the defendant, he demolished the exterior staircase and balcony, rendering the flat inaccessible. The claimant tried to claim that the defendant was bound by his unregistered equitable right of way, as the staircase was plainly visible, and the standard conditions of sale include a term rendering the property subject to incumbrances 'discoverable by inspection of the property before the contract'.

The Court of Appeal did not accept this argument. The defendant had entered into no specific agreement to honour the right of way. Therefore, in the absence of registration, he was not bound by it.

The Court also rejected an argument that the claimant was in actual occupation of the staircase because the tenants had been walking up and down it. This was not sufficient to show occupation, but only use of the staircase as a right of way—which was, as explained earlier, unregistered and unenforceable.

4.5.2 Interests that override registered dispositions

Earlier in this chapter (see 4.4.6), we looked at interests that override first registration. There is a similar list of interests that override registered dispositions and this is contained in LRA 2002, Sch. 3.

In many respects, the list in Sch. 3 is the same as that in Sch. 1—but there are two big differences:

- interests of persons in actual occupation—LRA 2002, Sch. 3, para. 2;
- easements and profits à prendre—LRA 2002, Sch. 3, para. 3.

In each case, the Sch. 3 paragraph is much longer than that of Sch. 1 and cuts down the number of interests that will count as overriding interests.

4.5.2.1 Interests of persons in actual occupation

 STATUTE

Land Registration Act 2002, Sch. 3, para. 2 [Interests of persons in actual occupation]

An interest belonging at the time of the disposition to a person in actual occupation, so far as relating to land of which he is in actual occupation, except for—

(a) an interest under a settlement under the Settled Land Act 1925 (c. 18);

(b) an interest of a person of whom inquiry was made before the disposition and who failed to disclose the right when he could reasonably have been expected to do so;

(c) an interest—

(i) which belongs to a person whose occupation would not have been obvious on a reasonably careful inspection of the land at the time of the disposition, and

(ii) of which the person to whom the disposition is made does not have actual knowledge at that time;

(d) a leasehold estate in land granted to take effect in possession after the end of the period of three months beginning with the date of the grant and which has not taken effect in possession at the time of the disposition.

If you compare this paragraph with the equivalent one under LRA 2002, Sch. 1, you will see that it is much longer and more complex. Certain things do remain the same—the meaning of actual occupation is the same, as is the fact that the overriding interest extends only to the land actually occupied.

It is also vitally important to show that the person claiming the right in the land has a valid proprietary interest in it. Remember that:

interest in land + actual occupation = overriding interest

The differences lie in the number of situations that are excluded from the paragraph—a person is not in actual occupation if:

- the interest claimed is an interest under the Settled Land Act 1925 (this was also in LRA 2002, Sch. 1);
- he or she did not tell the purchaser about his or her interest in the land when asked about it and 'could reasonably have been expected to do so';

CROSS REFERENCE

This provision is considered in more detail in Chapter 7.

- the interest is one that would not have been obvious on a 'reasonably careful inspection' of the land at the time of the disposition unless the purchaser actually knew of the interest;
- it is an interest under a reversionary lease.

This paragraph is evidence of the policy in the LRA 2002 to reduce the number of overriding interests. It raises certain questions, including when it will be reasonable for a person to disclose his or her interest in the land and what is meant by a 'reasonably careful inspection' of the land. In *Thomas v. Clydesdale Bank plc* [2010] EWHC 2755 (QB) it was held that 'it is the visible signs of occupation which have to be obvious on inspection' (per Ramsey J at [40]). Additionally, the judge held that the 'actual knowledge' required in Sch. 3, para. 2(c)(ii) is 'actual knowledge of the facts giving rise to the interest' rather than actual knowledge of the interest itself.

4.5.2.2 Easements and profits

> **STATUTE**
>
> **Land Registration Act 2002, Sch. 3, para. 3 [Easements and profits à prendre]**
>
> (1) A legal easement or profit à prendre, except for an easement, or a profit à prendre which is not registered under the Commons Registration Act 1965 (c. 64) [Part 1 of the Commons Act 2006], which at the time of the disposition—
>
>   (a) is not within the actual knowledge of the person to whom the disposition is made, and
>
>   (b) would not have been obvious on a reasonably careful inspection of the land over which the easement or profit is exercisable.
>
> (2) The exception in sub-paragraph (1) does not apply if the person entitled to the easement or profit proves that it has been exercised in the period of one year ending with the day of the disposition.

CROSS REFERENCE

For more on easements and profits, generally, and for more detailed discussion of LRA 2002, Sch. 3, para. 3, in particular, see Chapter 11.

LRA 2002, Sch. 3, para. 3 excludes a number of legal easements and profits from the category of overriding interests.

A legal easement or profit will override a registered disposition only if:

- the purchaser actually knows of it; or
- it is obvious on a reasonably careful inspection of the land over which the easement or profit is exercisable; or
- it has been exercised within the period of one year before the disposition.

This paragraph is also intended to cut down the number of legal easements and profits that do not appear on the register, in line with the policy of the LRA 2002 of reducing the number of overriding interests.

4.5.3 Electronic conveyancing (e-conveyancing)

Electronic conveyancing was originally intended to be a major part of the updating of registration of title by the LRA 2002. As you may remember from Chapter 3, however, the Land Registry has put the plans for electronic transfers and charges on hold.

One major advantage of electronic conveyancing was to be the elimination of the registration gap—that is, the period of time between a person having the land transferred to them and their being registered as the proprietor. If there is a registrable disposition, the legal estate does not pass until registration takes effect and, in the meantime, there can be dealings with the legal title by the previous owner, who remains the registered proprietor. Such dispositions will often not be binding on the purchaser, under LRA 2002, s. 29(1), because they will have arisen at a later time than did the transfer to the purchaser.

If an overriding interest is created before the estate is registered, however, it will be binding on the registered proprietor—and this is what happened in *Barclays Bank plc v. Zaroovabli* [1997] Ch 321, in which a lease was binding on a mortgagee who had not yet registered the mortgage.

There have also been cases in which a purchaser has tried to exercise the rights of a registered proprietor, but was unable to do so because he or she was not yet registered. In *Brown and Root Technology Ltd v. Sun Alliance and London Assurance Co. Ltd* [2001] Ch 733, for example, the purchaser of a leasehold estate tried to give notice to bring the lease to an end, but could not do so for this reason.

> **CROSS REFERENCE**
> For more on electronic conveyancing, see Chapter 3.

4.6 Alteration of the register

One of the three principles of registration of title is the **indemnity principle**. This means that the state guarantees registered title and that a registered proprietor should feel secure in the knowledge that he or she is the true owner of the land, and that interests in it are correctly reflected in the register. This does not, however, mean that the register is absolutely free from mistakes or that those mistakes cannot be put right.

> **CROSS REFERENCE**
> For a reminder of the three principles of registration of title, see Chapter 2.

> **indemnity principle** an indemnity (compensation) is payable by the state if loss is caused by errors in the register

Provisions for altering the register are contained in LRA 2002, s. 65 and Sch. 4.

4.6.1 Introduction

STATUTE

Land Registration Act 2002, Sch. 4, para. 1 [Introductory]

In this Schedule, references to rectification, in relation to alteration of the register, are to alteration which—

(a) involves the correction of a mistake, and

(b) prejudicially affects the title of a registered proprietor.

Under LRA 2002, there are two kinds of changes to the register:

- Alteration

An **alteration** is any change to the register.

- Rectification

A **rectification** is an alteration to the register that prejudicially affects the title of the registered proprietor and which is made to correct a mistake. This means that, when the mistake is corrected on the register, it may make the land less valuable, for example, or remove some of the land from the register.

Not surprisingly, rectification is subject to stricter rules than are other alterations.

> **alteration**
> any change to the register

> **rectification**
> a change to the register that is made to correct a mistake and which prejudicially affects the title of the registered proprietor

4.6.2 **Who can alter the register?**

Any person may apply for alteration of the register; they need not have an estate or interest in the land to have standing to do so: *Paton v. Todd* [2012] EWHC 1248 (Ch).

The register can be altered either by the court or by the registrar. The powers of the court are set out in LRA 2002, Sch. 4, para. 2(1).

📖 STATUTE

Land Registration Act 2002, Sch. 4, para. 2 [Alteration pursuant to a court order]

(1) The court may make an order for alteration of the register for the purpose of—

    (a) correcting a mistake,

    (b) bringing the register up to date, or

    (c) giving effect to any estate, right or interest excepted from the effect of registration.

…

The powers of the registrar are set out in LRA 2002, Sch. 4, para. 5, and are the same as those of the court, except that the registrar also has power to remove superfluous (unneeded) entries from the register.

4.6.3 **The grounds for altering the register**

4.6.3.1 **Correcting a mistake**

There are a number of cases that illustrate the kinds of mistake that may occur in transferring land. For example, the same piece of land may be transferred to two different people: generally, this means that the later transfer is a mistake, but if it is registered first, the registered proprietor will become the legal owner. This happened in the case of *Re 139 Deptford High Street* [1951] Ch 884, in which the register was altered to give the land back to the rightful owner. But if the registered proprietor is in possession of the land, this will be a rectification and may not be granted—see, for example, *Epps v. Esso Petroleum* [1973] 1 WLR 1071.

Alternatively, there may be an entry on the register that should not be there. In *Re Dances Way, West Town, Hayling Island* [1962] Ch 490, an easement was mistakenly entered on the register. This entry could be removed.

Transfers of land obtained by fraud may also be reversed under this heading. In *Baxter v. Mannion* [2011] EWCA Civ 120, it was held that Sch. 4, paras 1 and 5 could be used to restore land to its rightful owner after a claim for adverse possession had wrongly been allowed. No distinction was to be drawn between fraud and a mistake induced by a wrong application, because in both cases false information had been given to the registrar.

》 CROSS REFERENCE

For adverse possession, including more on this case, see Chapter 6.

Rectification may change the priority of interests on the register.

 CASE CLOSE-UP

Gold Harp Properties Ltd v. MacLeod [2014] EWCA Civ 1084 (CA (Civ))

In this case the top floor of a building was held on long leases by the respondents. The freehold owners, the Ralphs, engineered a scheme to forfeit the leases then create new leases ultimately in favour of the appellants, Gold Harp Ltd, a company owned and controlled by them. They got the forfeited leases removed from the Register of Title and registered the new lease in favour of Gold Harp. The Court held that the forfeiture had been defective, and that the old leases should not have been removed from the register. The appellants sought alteration of the register under LRA 2002, Sch. 4. They wanted the registers of title of their leases reinstated, and those leases noted on the freehold title. The problem was that the new lease to Gold Harp had now been registered, and might therefore have priority over their leases. LRA, s. 29 gives priority to a registered disposition except where prior interests are registered or overriding. Neither applied here.

It was held by the Court of Appeal that the rectification did change the priorities of the interests, and that the old leases took priority over Gold Harp's lease. The Court held that the case fell within LRA 2002, Sch. 4, para. 8:

> The powers under this Schedule to alter the register, so far as relating to rectification, extend to changing for the future the priority of any interest affecting the registered estate or charge concerned.

4.6.3.2 Bringing the register up to date

Bringing the register up to date involves adding or removing an entry, because the situation has changed or because a right has been established. For example, if someone has established an easement of light by prescription, that should be registered.

This provision also allows the register to be altered if, for example, a transfer which is voidable for fraud is avoided. For example, in *Norwich and Peterborough Building Society v. Steed* [1993] Ch 116, the transfer was effected by the misuse of a **power of attorney** and the original owner was reinstated.

》 CROSS REFERENCE

For easements, generally, and for the meaning of establishing an easement by prescription, in particular, see Chapter 11.

power of attorney
a formal instrument by which one person empowers another to act on his or her behalf

4.6.3.3 Giving effect to any estate, right, or interest excepted from the effect of registration

The giving of effect to any estate, right, or interest exception from the effect of registration is to do with estates registered with possessory or qualified title, and is beyond the scope of this book.

4.6.3.4 Removal of superfluous entries

Removing superfluous entries simply means removing entries that are no longer required, such as a notice about an option that has expired. There is, of course, bound to be some overlap between this ground and that of bringing the register up to date.

4.6.4 Restrictions on altering the register: rectification against a proprietor in possession

Where either the courts or the registrar wish to alter the register, a proprietor in possession has additional protection under LRA 2002, Sch. 4, para. 3.

 STATUTE

Land Registration Act 2002, Sch. 4, para. 3

...

(2) If alteration affects the title of the proprietor of a registered estate in land, no order may be made under paragraph 2 without the proprietor's consent in relation to land in his possession unless—

(a) he has by fraud or lack of proper care caused or substantially contributed to the mistake, or

(b) it would for any other reason be unjust for the alteration not to be made.

...

(4) In sub-paragraph (2), the reference to the title of the proprietor of a registered estate in land includes his title to any registered estate which subsists for the benefit of the estate in land.

Firstly, we need to know what is meant by a 'proprietor in possession'. This is defined in LRA 2002, s. 131.

 STATUTE

Land Registration Act 2002, s. 131 ['Proprietor in possession']

(1) For the purposes of this Act, land is in the possession of the proprietor of a registered estate in land if it is physically in his possession, or in that of a person who is entitled to be registered as the proprietor of the registered estate.

(2) In the case of the following relationships, land which is (or is treated as being) in the possession of the second-mentioned person is to be treated for the purposes of subsection (1) as in the possession of the first-mentioned person—

(a) landlord and tenant;

(b) mortgagor and mortgagee;

(c) licensor and licensee;

(d) trustee and beneficiary.

...

You can see from this section that a proprietor is in possession if either:

- he or she is physically in possession of the land;
- the land is in the possession of someone entitled to be registered as proprietor (such as a trustee in bankruptcy, for example);
- it is one of the special relationships in s. 131(2).

LRA 2002, s. 131(2), says, for example, that land in the possession of a tenant is treated as being in the possession of the landlord. This means that the proprietor would still be treated as being in possession if the property was let to tenants. A squatter on land is not treated as being in possession for this purpose—LRA 2002, s. 131(3).

So, once the court or the registrar has established that the alteration of the register is going to affect the title of the registered proprietor prejudicially and that he or she is a proprietor in possession, rectification of the register can be ordered only if:

- the proprietor in possession either caused the mistake or substantially contributed to it by fraud or lack of proper care;
- it would, for any other reason, be unjust for the alteration not to be made.

Fraud or lack of proper care goes beyond submitting a transfer for registration that turns out not to be accurate. In this case, the land may be wrongly described and the buyer simply may not know this. This is a change from the previous law, because older cases, such as *Re 139 Deptford High Street* (see 4.6.3.1), had found that proprietors who put forward an inaccurate conveyance for registration were guilty of contributing to the mistake, even where they were acting completely innocently. Someone who gains possession of land by fraud, however, would clearly not be entitled to argue that he or she should keep it.

Most of the cases have been on the second ground: that of it being unjust not to rectify the register.

 CASE CLOSE-UP

Kingsalton Ltd v. Thames Water [2001] EWCA Civ 20

In this case, a registered proprietor was in possession of a disputed strip of land that had been erroneously conveyed twice.

Rectification was not ordered, but instead an indemnity was paid to the person who should have been the owner (see later for when an indemnity will be paid).

An argument based on human rights was rejected in this case; rectification was held not to be a deprivation of property under the European Convention on Human Rights (ECHR), Protocol 1, Art. 1, because it was a proportionate measure to enhance the security of land, and compensation in the form of an indemnity was paid.

If the registered proprietor has full knowledge of the other party's interest, the register may be rectified, even though the proprietor is in possession.

 CASE CLOSE-UP

Horrill v. Cooper (1998) 1 P & CR 293

Because of a mix-up, a restrictive covenant was not entered on the register. In fact, the registered proprietor in possession knew all about the mix-up and had paid less for the land because of it.

It was held that it was unjust not to rectify the register to give effect to the covenant.

A similar situation occurred in the complicated case of *Sainsbury's Supermarkets v. Olympia Homes Ltd* [2005] EWHC 1235 (Ch). Rectification was ordered to give effect to an unregistered option. The registered proprietor had been registered by mistake and all of the parties had proceeded on the basis that the option was valid; the prices agreed between the parties reflected this. Under these circumstances, it would have been unjust not to rectify.

These two cases show that the courts will look at the parties' behaviour—for example, in terms of agreements about the price of the land—and will use their discretion under this provision to avoid unjust enrichment.

In *Baxter v. Mannion* (see 4.6.3.1) it was unjust not to rectify the register against the new proprietor in possession because he had wrongly claimed to have fulfilled the conditions for adverse possession.

In *Parshall v. Hackney* [2013] EWCA (Civ) 240, it was unjust not to rectify the register where a series of mistakes by the land registry had moved a slip of land from one title to another, even though the (mistakenly) registered proprietor was using the land for parking.

An example of a case in which the discretion was not exercised is *London Borough of Hounslow v. Hare* (1990) 24 HLR 9.

 CASE CLOSE-UP

London Borough of Hounslow v. Hare (1990) 24 HLR 9

In this case, the registered proprietor in possession had exercised her right to buy her council house. It turned out that she should not have had a right to buy, so the sale was *ultra vires* (beyond the powers of) the council.

The court would not rectify the register because the house was Hare's home.

This case shows why the legislation takes the rights of registered proprietors in possession so seriously.

4.6.5 **Indemnity**

LRA 2002, Sch. 8, provides the rules as to when the Land Registry will pay an indemnity (compensation) to someone suffering loss as a result of a mistake in the register. This right to an indemnity is at the heart of the system of land registration: it is a 'state-guaranteed' system. Those dealing with land are entitled to rely on the register of title and, if the register is wrong, there is a presumption that compensation will be payable. In the past few years, there has been increasing concern about fraudsters using the open land register to 'steal' land or obtain money by fraudulently mortgaging land they do not own. The Land Registry removed certain documents, such as mortgage deeds, from online availability so that signatures cannot be copied and it requires conveyancers to certify the identity of those involved in transactions. If parties are acting in person, they must provide evidence of identity. These requirements came into effect in November 2008. In 2014–15 the Land Registry paid out £5.2m in compensation for losses caused by fraud, less than in previous years.

LRA 2002, Sch. 8, para. 1 sets out when an indemnity will be payable.

4.6.5.1 Loss caused by rectification

> **CASE CLOSE-UP**
>
> **Land Registration Act 2002, Sch. 8, para. 1 [Entitlement]**
>
> **(1)** A person is entitled to be indemnified by the registrar if he suffers loss by reason of—
>
> rectification of the register,
>
> ...
>
> **(2)** For the purposes of sub-paragraph (13)(a)—
>
> **(a)** any person who suffers loss by reason of the change of title under section 62 is to be regarded as having suffered loss by reason of rectification of the register, and
>
> **(b)** the proprietor of a registered estate or charge claiming in good faith under a forged disposition is, where the register is rectified, to be regarded as having suffered loss by reason of such rectification as if the disposition had not been forged.
>
> ...

It is very important to note that it is essential that the loss is caused by *rectification*, not by any other type of alteration of the register. Remember, rectification is an alteration to the register that prejudicially affects the title of the registered proprietor and which is made to correct a mistake. Some changes to the register may appear to affect the title of the registered proprietor prejudicially, but may not, in fact, do so.

The classic case of this is if the register is altered to give effect to an overriding interest.

> **CASE CLOSE-UP**
>
> **Re Chowood's Registered Land** [1933] Ch 574
>
> In this case, no indemnity was payable when the register was altered so as to give effect to the rights of a squatter who had gained title to part of the land.
>
> The rights of the squatter under the law at that time amounted to an overriding interest, which was always binding on the registered proprietor, whether he knew about it or not. He had not suffered any loss, so could not claim an indemnity.

Therefore, not everyone who feels they have suffered a loss will get compensation. This rule makes perfect sense within the scheme of registration, however, because every registered proprietor takes the land subject to any overriding interests subsisting in it at the date of registration, even if they do not always know about them.

The claimant in *Baxter v. Mannion* (discussed earlier) did not receive an indemnity, as the effect of the decision was that he had never been entitled to the land at all, so no loss was caused by the rectification.

LRA 2002, Sch. 8, para. 1(2)(b) provides that proprietors claiming under a forged disposition should be able to claim indemnity in the same way as if the disposition had not been forged. This was considered in *Swift 1st Ltd v. Chief Land Registrar* [2015] EWCA Civ 330 (see 4.5.1.1) and an indemnity was given.

4.6.5.2 **Loss caused by a decision not to rectify**

> **STATUTE**
>
> ---
>
> **Land Registration Act 2002, Sch. 8, para. 1 [Entitlement]**
>
> **(1)** A person is entitled to be indemnified by the registrar if he suffers loss by reason of—
>
> …
>
> **(b)** a mistake whose correction would involve rectification of the register,
>
> …

An indemnity may also be payable if a mistake is not rectified. This is more likely under the modern law, because there is a presumption against rectifying against a proprietor in possession and a less strict definition of what constitutes contributing to a mistake.

4.6.5.3 **Losses caused by other types of mistake**

> **STATUTE**
>
> ---
>
> **Land Registration Act 2002, Sch. 8, para. 1 [Entitlement]**
>
> **(1)** A person is entitled to be indemnified by the registrar if he suffers loss by reason of—
>
> …
>
> **(a)** a mistake in an official search,
>
> **(b)** a mistake in an official copy,
>
> **(c)** a mistake in a document kept by the registrar which is not an original and is referred to in the register,
>
> **(d)** the loss or destruction of a document lodged at the registry for inspection or safe custody,
>
> **(e)** a mistake in the cautions register, or
>
> **(f)** failure by the registrar to perform his duty under section 50.
>
> …

LRA 2002, Sch. 8, para. 1 goes on to list a number of further types of mistake that are not caused by rectification, in respect of which indemnity can be claimed. Remember that the person claiming the indemnity must show a loss caused by the error before a claim can be made.

4.6.5.4 **Fraud or lack of proper care**

> **STATUTE**
>
> ---
>
> **Land Registration Act 2002, Sch. 8, para. 5 [Claimant's fraud or lack of care]**
>
> **(1)** No indemnity is payable under this Schedule on account of any loss suffered by a claimant—
>
> **(a)** wholly or partly as a result of his own fraud, or
>
> **(b)** wholly as a result of his own lack of proper care.

> (2) Where any loss is suffered by a claimant partly as a result of his own lack of proper care, any indemnity payable to him is to be reduced to such extent as is fair having regard to his share in the responsibility for the loss.
>
> ...

Under LRA 2002, Sch. 8, para. 5, if someone causes his or her own loss by fraud, he or she is not entitled to an indemnity in relation to that loss. Even if the fraud were to be only partly the cause of the loss, no indemnity would be payable.

If lack of proper care is the whole cause of the loss, then, similarly, no indemnity is payable; if the loss is only partly caused by lack of proper care, however, then a reduced indemnity will be payable. This is very like the principle of contributory negligence in the law of torts. So, for example, if the person suffering the loss did not check the details of the transaction carefully, or did not check on the identity of the person claiming to transfer the land, he or she may be held partly liable for his or her own loss.

4.6.5.5 The amount of indemnity payable

Indemnity is intended to compensate the person who has suffered the loss. Both losses that arise as a direct result of the mistake—such as the value of the land lost if the register is rectified—and any consequential losses—such as the costs of a sale falling through because of a mistake on the register—may be claimed.

Where an estate, interest, or charge over land has been lost, LRA 2002, Sch. 8, para. 6 sets out the rules for valuation of that interest.

 STATUTE

Land Registration Act 2002, Sch. 8, para. 6 [Valuation of estates etc.]

Where an indemnity is payable in respect of the loss of an estate, interest or charge, the value of the estate, interest or charge for the purposes of the indemnity is to be regarded as not exceeding—

(a) in the case of an indemnity under paragraph 1(1)(a), its value immediately before rectification of the register (but as if there were to be no rectification), and

(b) in the case of an indemnity under paragraph 1(1)(b), its value at the time when the mistake which caused the loss was made.

As you can see, there are two different ways of valuing the indemnity payable: one in which rectification is ordered and one in which it is not:

- If rectification is ordered, the amount payable is the market value of the estate, interest, or charge at the moment before rectification was ordered—that is, at current market value.
- If rectification is not ordered, the amount payable is the value of the estate, interest, or charge at the time at which the mistake was made—that is, its value at some time in the past. Because land usually rises in value over time, this will usually be a lesser amount.

This disparity in the two valuations was raised in *Kingsalton Ltd v. Thames Water*, but held not to be in breach of the ECHR.

Summary

1. Land registration is a national system, first introduced in 1925 and now regulated by the Land Registration Act 2002.

2. Different provisions of the Act apply to first registration of land and to registrable dispositions.

3. A person registered as the first proprietor of the land owns the legal estate, even if the person transferring the land to him or her did not have power to do so.

4. The first registered proprietor takes the land subject to entries in the register, interests that override first registration, and rights obtained by adverse possession.

5. Once land is registered, any dealing with it will be subject to registration provisions. Such dealings may be registrable dispositions, registrable by notice or restriction, or interests that override registered dispositions.

6. Someone registered as the result of a registrable disposition—that is, a disponee—is entitled to assume that the seller had power to deal with the land, unless there was a restriction on his or her powers or an overriding interest. The disponee may be held personally liable, however, if he or she assists in a breach of trust by the registered proprietor.

7. Mistakes in the register may be corrected. This is known as an 'alteration', or, if it adversely affects the registered proprietor, a 'rectification' of the register.

8. An indemnity (compensation) may be payable as the result of a claim for rectification.

The bigger picture

- If you want to see how this area of land law fits into the rest of your studies, you can look at Chapter 14. That whole chapter revolves around the understanding of a register of title. Use it to practise identifying the various interests in land. You might also find it helpful to look at the registration sections in other chapters, such as Chapter 11, 11.5 on the registration of easements; Chapter 12, 12.5.2.4 on the registration of covenants; Chapter 13, 13.5 on priorities of mortgages. Chapter 7, 7.3 contains vital information on the effect of land registration on co-ownership, and there is a lot of material here about overriding interests, particularly rights of persons in actual occupation of the land.

- Additional cases you may wish to look at on the interpretation of LRA 2002 include:

  Blemain Finance Ltd v. Goulding [2013] EWCA Civ 1630; [2014] 1 P & CR DG16 (CA (Civ Div))

  Walker v. Burton [2013] EWCA Civ 1228; [2014] 1 P & CR 9 (CA (Civ Div))

  Cherry Tree Investments Ltd v. Landmain Ltd [2012] EWCA Civ 736; [2013] Ch 305 (CA (Civ Div))

  Gelley v. Shephard [2013] EWCA Civ 1172; [2014] 1 P & CR DG5 (CA (Civ Div))

- The most authoritative work on land registration is *Ruoff and Roper on the Law and Practice of Registered Conveyancing* (London: Sweet & Maxwell), which you may find in your library or as part of a Westlaw subscription. Alternatively, Harpum, C. and Bignall, J. (2002) *Registered Land: The New Law*, Bristol: Jordan Publishing Ltd is a very comprehensive guide to registration under the LRA 2002, but it is rather technical.

? Questions

Self-test questions

1. Adam is the owner of unregistered freehold land. He transfers it to Bert. Is Bert obliged to register his title to the land? What will happen if he does not do so?

2. Catherine has a legal easement over the land that is now Bert's. There is no mention of the easement on Bert's new register of title. Is Bert bound by the easement?

3. Bert sells his registered estate to Dolly. Catherine still has not registered her legal easement. Is Dolly bound by it?

4. If Dolly is bound by Catherine's easement:

    (a) is Catherine entitled to ask for the register to be altered to show her easement?

    (b) is Dolly entitled to an indemnity if the value of her land with the easement over it is less than it would be without such a burden?

Exam questions

1. 'Because [overriding interests] subsist and operate outside the register, they are an inevitable source of tension within the land registration system. In making proposals for reform there is often a difficult balance to be struck between, on the one hand, the desire to achieve a fair result in individual cases, and on the other, the goal of making conveyancing simpler, quicker and cheaper, which is the justification for title registration.'
(*Law Commission, Land Registration for the 21st Century, Consultative Document*).
Discuss.

2. In 2015, Gerry bought a plot of land from Veronica. It consisted of a small farm and out-buildings with some scrubland. Title to it had not previously been registered, so Gerry applied for and received registration as proprietor with absolute title. Unfortunately, the conveyance of the land mistakenly included a small barn belonging to Tom. Gerry has also discovered that several surrounding landowners have rights to water their animals at the stream running through his land, and there are two rights of way crossing it. This means that it will be difficult to turn the land into a development of holiday cottages, which is what Tom intended. Tom wishes he had never bought the land at all.

    Advise Tom and Gerry.

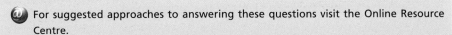 For suggested approaches to answering these questions visit the Online Resource Centre.

≡ Further reading

Bogusz, B., 'Defining the scope of actual occupation under the LRA 2002: some recent judicial clarification' [2011] Conv 268
This is an article on the interpretation of LRA 2002, Sch. 3, para. 2 (rights of persons in actual occupation) case law.

Dixon, M., 'Rectification and priority: further skirmishes in the land registration war' (2015) 131(Apr) LQR 207–13
This examines the decision in *Gold Harp Properties v. MacLeod* [2014] EWCA Civ 1084.

Griffiths, G., 'An important question of principle—reality and rectification in registered land' [2011] Conv 331
This case note discusses the case of *Baxter v. Mannion* [2011] EWCA Civ 120.

Hopkins, N., 'Priorities and sale and lease back: a wrong question, much ado about nothing and a story of tails and dogs' [2015] 3 Conv 245–53
This discusses *North East Property Buyers Litigation, Re* [2014] UKSC 52; [2015] AC 385 (SC).

Law Commission/HM Land Registry (1998) *Land Registration for the Twenty-First Century: A Consultative Document*, Law Com No. 254, available online at http://www.lawcom.gov.uk/wp-content/uploads/2015/04/lc254.pdf.

Law Commission/HM Land Registry (2001) *Land Registration for the Twenty-First Century: A Conveyancing Revolution*, Law Com No. 271, available online at http://www.lawcom.gov.uk/wp-content/uploads/2015/04/Lc271.pdf.
These two Law Commission/HM Land Registry reports set out the reasons for the reform of the law in the LRA 2002.

Current Law Commission review of land registration: http://www.lawcom.gov.uk/project/land-registration/.
The Land Registry publishes online a number of very helpful practitioners' guides to many aspects of registration. They can be found at https://www.gov.uk/topic/land-registration/practice-guides.

Lees, E., Registration make-believe and forgery—*Swift 1st Ltd v. Chief Land Registrar* (2015) 131(Oct) LQR 515–19
This article discusses the problems caused by forgery in land registration.

McFarlane, B., 'Eastenders, Neighbours and Upstairs Downstairs: Chaudhary v Yavuz' [2013] 1 Conv 74
This is a case note on *Chaudhary v. Yavuz* [2011] EWCA Civ 1314.

Willams, P., 'When the experts get it wrong' [2014] 5 Conv 369–74
This short article examines a number of difficulties which have arisen with LRA 2002.

 ## Online Resource Centre

www.oxfordtextbooks.co.uk/orc/clarke_directions5e/

For more advice relating to this chapter, including self-test questions and an interactive glossary, visit the Online Resource Centre.

5 Leases

By the end of this chapter, you will be able to:

- explain what is meant by a 'leasehold estate in land';
- identify the essential requirements of a lease;
- distinguish between a lease and a licence;
- understand how a lease is created and explain the necessary formalities;
- identify some of the usual covenants contained in a lease;
- offer a general overview of the enforceability of leasehold covenants.

Introduction

We have already looked at freehold estates in land (see Chapter 3) and we have seen that they are for an indefinite duration. The other estate in land is the leasehold estate—more commonly referred to as simply a 'lease'. A lease is a more limited estate in land than a freehold, because it is only granted for a specified period of time. In practice, this period can be very short, or very long indeed: sometimes, even thousands of years. You will probably already be quite familiar with some of the aspects of a lease, perhaps through renting accommodation while at university or through buying a leasehold flat. There is a very specific set of sometimes quite complicated legal principles and rules that apply to the leasehold estate, and, in this chapter, we will disentangle them.

5.1 Frequently used terms

Before we start looking at what it means to have a leasehold estate in land, we will have a quick look at some of the most frequently used terms in this area of law. Each of these will be explained in more detail as we go through the chapter, but, at this stage, it will help you to have some understanding of their meaning.

term of years absolute this refers to the leasehold estate

lease or tenancy any such term refers to a lease: shorter leases tend to be called tenancies, longer leases tend to be referred to as leases—but often, for all practical purposes, the terms are used interchangeably

landlord or lessor the person granting the lease, which is sometimes described as 'letting' the property

tenant or lessee the person to whom the lease is granted

reversion the interest that the landlord retains in the land after the lease has finished

5.2 Leases in practice: some examples

We will shortly be looking at the legal meaning of a lease, but first, it might be helpful simply to understand how a lease works in practice. Leases can be granted in respect of residential, commercial, and agricultural property—but, for the rest of this chapter, we will concentrate on residential leases. These are the sorts of lease with which you may well already be familiar.

 EXAMPLE

Alex owns a freehold house in London. One day, his employer tells Alex that he is going to be working in New York for two years. Rather than sell his house or leave it empty, Alex decides to let the property: he will rent it out while he is away. He grants a two-year lease to Rav, in return for a monthly rent.

Both parties sign a lease agreement, under which they promise to do various things. Rav agrees to pay rent and not to wreck Alex's house; Alex agrees that Rav can live in the premises without interruption and disturbance, and to keep the house in good repair while Rav is living there.

At the end of two years, Rav moves out and Alex moves back in. Rav's interest in the land has ended with the end of the lease.

Their relationship might be illustrated as in Figure 5.1.

Figure 5.1 The landlord–tenant relationship

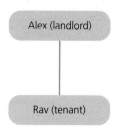

Sometimes, the situation can get more complicated.

 EXAMPLE

Yasmeen owns a freehold house in London. She grants a 25-year lease of the property to Davina. The lease agreement contains a clause allowing Davina to 'sublet' the property with Yasmeen's consent. This means that, if she chooses, Davina can rent the property out to somebody else. She decides to sublet to Pete. She can only sublet the property for a period shorter than her own interest in the land. (This is common sense—she cannot grant a sublease of thirty years if she herself only has an interest in the land for twenty-five years.) She lets the property to Pete.

The relationship of the parties might be illustrated as in Figure 5.2.

These two examples will give you some idea of how a lease works in everyday situations.

Figure 5.2 The landlord–tenant–subtenant relationship

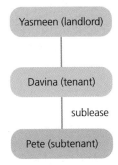

Legally, however, the nature of a lease is quite tricky. On the one hand, it is a contract, as we have seen, because essentially the parties promise each other that they will do, or will not do, certain things; on the other hand, because a lease confers an estate in the land, it gives the tenant a proprietary interest in the land itself—which is why, in our last example, Davina is able to sublet the property. Part of the legal difficulty inherent to leases lies in this dual character: the lease has one foot in contract law and the other in land law.

5.3 Statutory protection

Over the years, the law has provided statutory protection for the tenant, to reduce bad practice by landlords. The kind of protection given to the tenant partly depends on the kind of lease that he or she holds. Detailed consideration of the statutory protection is outside the scope of this book, but we will mention it when we start to examine the essential characteristics of a lease—partly because most of the cases arose in situations in which landlords were trying to avoid their statutory obligations!

5.3.1 Definition of a lease

The statutory definition of a lease under Law of Property Act 1925 (LPA 1925), s. 205(xxvii) is a good starting point at which to begin our exploration of leases.

STATUTE

Law of Property Act 1925, s. 205(xxvii)

'Term of years absolute' means a term of years (taking effect either in possession or in reversion whether or not at a rent) … liable to determination by notice … and … includes a term for less than a year, or for a year or years and a fraction of a year or from year to year;

We have attempted to pick out the most important points in the subsection, because the whole definition is lengthy and somewhat circular.

We can, however, identify some useful information.

> **in possession**
> immediately

The phrase 'term of years' refers to the fact that the lease is granted for a period of time. It can begin immediately (**in possession**) or in the future (**in reversion**), although not more than twenty-one years in the future—LPA 1925, s. 149(3).

> **in reversion**
> at some point in
> the future

 THINKING POINT

Look at Form 5.1, the sample tenancy agreement.

Try to identify the names of the parties and the length of the lease. Read through the covenants contained within it. It may be helpful to refer back to it as you read through this chapter and then to have a final look at it when you have finished the chapter.

> **determined**
> ended; terminated

It can be ended (**determined**) by one of the parties giving notice.

The duration can be for any length of time, provided that it is certain. It can be for a fixed period, which can be a fraction of a year, less than a year, a year, or more than a year. The lease can also operate as a periodic tenancy (see 5.3.2.2), which may run from year to year.

We will look a little further at these different types of lease and how they are created, and then we will think about the essential elements that are present in every kind of lease.

5.3.2 Types of lease

5.3.2.1 Fixed-term lease

> **fixed-term lease**
> a lease that is entered
> into for a fixed period
> of time

The **fixed-term lease** is probably the most common kind of lease. You may well have seen it in practice, if you have rented accommodation yourself. It simply means a lease for a fixed period of time, which can be for as long as the parties want it to be. If you buy a leasehold flat, the lease will often be for over 100 years; if you rent a student flat, it may be for a period of six months or for the duration of the academic year.

The key ingredient with fixed-term leases is that the period is fixed and certain at the time of creation. The lease cannot continue indefinitely.

5.3.2.2 Periodic tenancy

> **periodic tenancy**
> a lease or tenancy in
> which rent is payable at
> fixed intervals and which
> continues indefinitely
> from one rent period to
> the next, until being
> terminated by notice

A **periodic tenancy** may last indefinitely: it is a lease that runs from week to week, from month to month, or from year to year. It can arise by the express agreement of the parties, or by implication, should a tenant move into the property with the permission of the landlord and pay rent, which the landlord accepts.

Effectively, the periodic tenancy is being renewed at the end of each term—that is, at the end of each period for which rent is paid—which prevents the term from being uncertain. So, for example, if the tenancy agreement stipulates a weekly rent, it will be a weekly periodic tenancy; if the payment term is monthly, it will be a monthly periodic tenancy, etc. Even if the tenant actually makes the payment on a different basis, the agreement will set the length of the term.

The term is important in a periodic tenancy because the length of its term determines the notice period should either side wish to terminate the lease. The notice period required to end the tenancy is usually equivalent to a single payment term. The only exception to this is that the termination of an annual tenancy will only require six months' notice.

5.3.2.3 Tenancy at will

The **tenancy at will** is an odd type of tenancy that is seldom seen nowadays, except sometimes in transitional periods—for example, between the end of one lease and the start of another. It is odd because the interest that it confers on the tenant is neither a lease nor a licence, but something in between.

It is essentially a personal agreement between the parties—*Wheeler v. Mercer* [1957] AC 426. The tenant at will has no proprietary interest in the land, so he or she cannot, for example, assign any interest in the property to someone else. The tenant at will can, however, continue to live in the property until either he or she, or the landlord, decides that the arrangement is to end, or until the death of one of the parties. There is no need for either side to give notice, which makes the whole situation rather precarious.

Tenancies at will often arise when a more formal arrangement has come to an end, or if the parties are negotiating the terms for a formal lease, but the tenant moves into the property before the negotiations are finalized.

> **tenancy at will**
> a lease or tenancy, which usually arises by implication, that can be terminated by the landlord or tenant at any time

5.3.2.4 Tenancy at sufferance

The **tenancy at sufferance** arises when a tenant stays on in a property after the end of a fixed-term lease. Unlike a tenancy at will, the landlord does not explicitly consent to this, but he does tolerate—that is, 'suffer'—it.

Under the tenancy at sufferance, while the tenant's initial occupation of the premises was lawful, after the end of the fixed-term tenancy, he or she can be removed at any moment. This is not, then, a very comfortable situation for the tenant!

> **tenancy at sufferance**
> a lease or tenancy that arises when a tenant stays on in a property after a lease is ended, but to which occupation the landlord has not indicated agreement or otherwise

5.3.2.5 Tenancy by estoppel

The **tenancy by estoppel** arises if the person granting the lease does not, in fact, have any estate in the land from which it is possible to make that grant. Despite his or her lack of title, if the agreement reflects all of the essential characteristics of a lease (see 5.5), the court will 'estop'—that is, prevent—the landlord from denying the existence of the lease.

An example may make this clearer.

> **tenancy by estoppel**
> a lease or tenancy that exists despite the fact that the person who granted it had no right to do so

 EXAMPLE

George is in the process of buying a house. Before the purchase is completed, he grants a lease of the property to Nick. Technically, at this stage, George does not have any estate in the land that he is purchasing. But if the agreement confers exclusive possession for a term on Nick, George will be estopped (prevented) from denying the tenancy, because of his lack of title. It will be a tenancy by estoppel.

> Note, too, that after completion of the purchase, once George becomes the legal owner of the property, the tenancy by estoppel is automatically converted into a 'proper' tenancy. This is known as 'feeding the estoppel'.

CROSS REFERENCE

For more on adverse possession, look at Chapter 6

Mitchell v. Watkinson [2014] EWCA Civ 1472 concerned a tenancy by estoppel, where a father entered into a tenancy with a cricket club after he had gifted the relevant land to his son. The implications of this and subsequent events led to a successful claim by the cricket club that they were in adverse possession of the land many years later.

5.4 Creation of a lease

A lease may exist in law—that is, it may be a **legal lease**—or in equity—that is, it may be an **equitable lease**.

> **legal lease** a lease that creates an estate in land for a term of years absolute and with certain formalities
>
> **equitable lease** a lease that grants an interest in land on terms that correspond to those of a legal lease, but without completion of the legal formalities

5.4.1 **Legal leases**

STATUTE

Law of Property Act 1925, s. 52(1)

All conveyances of land or of any interest therein are void for the purpose of conveying or creating a legal estate unless made by deed.

CROSS REFERENCE

For more on deeds, see Chapter 3.

Under LPA 1925, s. 52(1), to create a legal lease, as with any legal estate in land, the parties must execute a deed, with all of the formalities that this requires.

5.4.1.1 **Leases of three years or less**

There are some exceptions, however, to this requirement. LPA 1925, s. 52(2)(d) makes an exception for 'leases or tenancies … not required to be made in writing'.

> **premium (or fine)**
> a sum that is sometimes charged by a landlord as the 'price' of granting a lease, which is usually seen in commercial or long leases

According to LPA 1925, s. 54(2), leases granted for a period of three years or less, taking effect in possession, with no **premium (or fine)**, and at **market value** do not need to be in writing. Such leases can, then, be legal leases, despite the lack of a deed, or even if made orally by agreement between the parties.

> **market value**
> a full rent at current economic rates

For all other leases, if they are to be legal leases, a deed must be executed. If this is not done, the lease will take effect only as an equitable lease for the period stated, or alternatively as a legal periodic tenancy if the tenant moves in and starts paying rent. For example, in *Hutchison v. B&DF Ltd* [2008] EWHC 2286 (Ch), the defendants were allowed into possession of business premises although the lease documents had not been signed. It was held that the oral agreements for leases of less than three years were valid legal leases, and that an oral agreement for a lease of five years took effect as a periodic tenancy.

5.4.1.2 Registration

Generally, interests in land will only take effect as legal interests once they have been registered—
LRA 2002, ss. 4(1) and 27(1). Leases are no exception to this rule, although there are some additional
considerations to bear in mind.

Not all leases need to be registered in order to be legal leases. LRA 2002, ss. 4(2)(b) and 27(2)(b)
state that only leases of over seven years in duration must be registered. Most leases for durations
of up to seven years can still take effect as legal leases even without registration, provided that the
necessary formal requirements have been carried out, as they are overriding interests (see Table 5.1).

Parliament has left open the possibility that, in the future, it may vary the requirement to register only
leases exceeding seven years in duration—LRA 2002, s. 118(1)(b). It seems likely that this may one day
be extended to become a requirement for all leases of over three years. Under the old LRA 1925, only
leases of over twenty-one years had to be registered, but this was widely considered to be insufficient.

Finally, a number of particular kinds of lease must be registered to take effect as legal leases even if
they are for less than seven years. The most important of these is a lease that 'takes effect in possession after the end of the period of three months beginning with the date of the grant'—effectively, a
lease that does not start immediately—and a lease 'under which the right to possession is discontinuous'—for example, a timeshare. These and the other exceptions can be found in LRA 2002, s. 27(2)(b).

If registration is required and not complied with, the lease will take effect only as an equitable lease.

Remember that each leasehold estate is registered independently, with its own title number. This
can mean that one piece of land has a number of different entries in the Land Register.

> **CROSS REFERENCE**
>
> For more on the registration
> of legal interests, see
> Chapter 3.

 EXAMPLE

Matthew owns the freehold title to The Grange, a large Victorian property, which is registered land. He decides to divide it up into three flats, and grants two 120-year leases to Greg
and Will. He decides to keep one of the flats for himself and rents it out to Tim for a year.

How many separate titles would be registered at the Land Registry?

Three separate titles would appear on the register for the property. Matthew's freehold title
would obviously be registered, as would Greg and Will's long leases (they exceed seven years).
Tim's lease would not be registered, because it is for less than three years.

5.4.1.3 Summary

We therefore have slightly different requirements for leases of different durations, which are
summarized in Table 5.1.

> **CROSS REFERENCE**
>
> For more on the registration
> of leases, see Chapter 4.

Table 5.1 The requirements for a legal lease

Duration of lease	Formalities (legal lease)	Registration
Three years or less (including periodic tenancies)	Can be oral, or by contract, with no need for a deed	Not yet required—they take effect as overriding interests
Between three and seven years	Deed necessary	Not yet required—they take effect as overriding interests
Over seven years	Deed necessary	Required

Failure to comply with the formalities and registration (where necessary) will result in the creation of an equitable lease for the term specified, or a legal periodic tenancy if the tenant has moved in and is paying rent. Since a periodic tenancy is less than three years (it takes effect from year to year or month to month), this takes effect as an overriding interest.

5.4.2 **Equitable leases**

As we have just seen, many equitable leases arise by accident, as a result of failure to comply with the statutory requirements to create a legal lease. Sometimes, the parties will draft a contract for this lease, but will not get around to executing it as a deed. If it is the kind of lease that needs to be made by deed and a deed is not prepared, then the lease will exist only as an equitable lease.

 CASE CLOSE-UP

Walsh v. Lonsdale (1820) 21 Ch D 9

The landlord tried to grant a seven-year lease of a mill to the tenant. One of the terms of the agreement was that the rent was payable in advance, which meant, in this case, at the start of each year. No deed was executed.

The tenant moved into the mill. He paid his rent in arrears (at the end of the year). A few years later, the landlord claimed that the tenant was behind with his rent and insisted that the agreement was for payment of rent in advance.

The tenant argued that the lease agreement had never been executed as a deed and so was not effective. He said that, because he had been paying and the landlord had been accepting rent, a periodic tenancy had arisen (see earlier) and one of the terms of this tenancy was payment of rent in arrears.

The Court of Appeal said that, in the absence of a deed, an equitable lease had arisen. Underlying the Court's decision was the equitable maxim 'equity treats that as done that which ought to be done'. Under the circumstances of the lease contract, the Court would have awarded an order for specific performance, which means that it would have ordered each of the parties to comply with its side of the contract. Equity would therefore treat the agreement as though it had been properly made: it would consider it to be an equitable lease, made on the same terms as originally agreed. The tenant had to pay his rent in advance.

Remember that, for an equitable lease, there must first be a valid contract for the grant of a lease. For leases created after 26 September 1989, this means complying with Law of Property (Miscellaneous Provisions) Act 1989 (LP(MP)A 1989), s. 2(1).

 STATUTE

Law of Property (Miscellaneous Provisions) Act 1989, s. 2(1)

A contract for the sale or other disposition of an interest in land can only be made in writing and only by incorporating all the terms which the parties have expressly agreed in one document, or, where contracts are exchanged, in each.

The contract must also be one for which the court would award specific performance. Specific performance is a discretionary remedy and its grant depends on a number of factors. For example, the court may not award such a remedy if the party asking for the remedy is in breach of covenant.

Although it might seem, looking at *Walsh v. Lonsdale*, that an equitable lease is effectively the same as a legal lease, do not be deceived. All equitable interests are more vulnerable to third parties than are their legal counterparts and there may also be issues when looking at the enforceability of leasehold covenants in equitable leases, because there will be no privity of estate (see 5.7.1).

> **CROSS REFERENCE**
For the meaning of specific performance, see Chapter 3.

5.5 Essential characteristics of a lease

In order to identify the characteristics that are common to all leases, we must turn to the leading case of *Street v. Mountford* [1985] AC 809.

Remember throughout that the context for this case, and for many of the cases to which we refer in the subsequent discussion, is that the landlord was trying to avoid the appearance of a lease. If he were found to have granted the tenant a lease, the tenant would be protected by statute— particularly, at that time, the Rent Act 1977, which regulated the rent (among other things). If the landlord had created only a **licence**, then the tenant would have no statutory protection.

In all of these cases, the landlords dressed the lease agreements up as 'licence agreements'. In order to work out whether the agreement was a lease or a licence, it was necessary for the courts to consider the elements that are both essential and common to every lease, but not to the grant of a licence.

licence
a personal arrangement between licensor and licensee under which the licensee may occupy the licensor's property for a specified purpose

 CASE CLOSE-UP

Street v. Mountford [1985] AC 809

Mr Street and Mrs Mountford entered into an agreement whereby Mr Street agreed to allow Mr and Mrs Mountford to occupy furnished rooms for a rent of £37 per week. The agreement was headed 'Licence Agreement' and included a clause stating that Mrs Mountford accepted that the agreement did not confer on her the protection of the Rent Act 1977.

Some time later, Mrs Mountford attempted to invoke the protection of the Rent Act 1977 in respect of a fair rent. Mr Street argued that, because she only had a licence rather than a tenancy, she could not do this. Eventually, the matter worked its way up to the House of Lords, where their Lordships had to decide whether the agreement was, in reality, a tenancy, or a licence, as it was described.

Lord Templeman, firstly, drew the traditional distinction between a lease and a licence. With a lease, the tenant had an estate in the land: she had the right of exclusive possession of the premises and could exclude all others from the property—even the landlord. With a licence, the licensee had no such rights, because she was given no estate in the land. A licensee was allowed occupation of the premises only by permission of the landlord. The essential elements of a lease, according to Lord Templeman, were 'exclusive possession for a term at a rent' (see 5.5.2 for more discussion about whether a rent is necessary).

In deciding that the agreement was a tenancy, despite its appearance, Lord Templeman looked at the factual matrix of the case: whatever the agreement called itself, if the effect of it was to confer exclusive possession of the premises for a term at a rent, then it was a tenancy.

We will now look at each of the three elements identified in *Street v. Mountford*—that is, certain term, rent, and exclusive possession—in turn.

5.5.1 **Certain term**

certain term

a period that has a specified beginning and end

Although a lease can be for any duration, to be valid, it must have a **certain term** —that is, a certain beginning and a certain end. It can be a fixed term or a periodic term (see 5.3.2.1 and 5.3.2.2).

This does not mean, however, that the lease must continue for the full term. Many commercial leases, in particular, have **break clauses**, which allow the parties to end the lease at various intervals during the term. For example, a 21-year lease may have a seven-year break clause allowing the lease to be ended after seven or fourteen years. What matters is that the lease cannot be indefinite, because one of the essential characteristics of a leasehold estate is that it is for a period of time.

break clause

a clause that allows the parties to bring a lease to an end at various specified points in advance of the lease's end

> ### Q | CASE CLOSE-UP
>
> *Lace v. Chantler* [1944] KB 368
>
> The tenant was granted a tenancy of a house 'for the duration of the war'.
>
> The court held that this was not a valid fixed lease: the term granted had to be certain from the outset and 'the duration of the war' was not certain.
>
> The decision had a significant impact on many wartime leases and led to the passing of the Validation of War Time Leases Act 1944, which converted all such agreements into ten-year leases, determinable by one month's notice if the war ended before then.

This requirement was affirmed in *Prudential Assurance Co Ltd v. London Residuary Body* [1992] 3 WLR 279.

> ### Q | CASE CLOSE-UP
>
> *Prudential Assurance Co. Ltd v. London Residuary Body* [1992] 3 WLR 279
>
> The (then) London County Council purchased a strip of land, situated alongside a road, and then rented it back to its original owner. The rent was £30 per annum and the lease was said to continue until the Council needed the land back in order to widen the road. The road was never widened and, some sixty years on, the tenants had a very good deal, because they continued to pay rent at £30 p.a. The matter went to court, with the House of Lords deciding that the original lease was invalid, because the term was not certain, following *Lace v. Chantler.*
>
> Interestingly, however, the House of Lords found that there was in existence a yearly periodic tenancy, because the tenant had paid and the landlord accepted rent on an annual basis (see earlier). This yearly periodic tenancy could be determined by six months' notice.

A rather surprising decision was made by the Supreme Court in the following case where there was potential uncertainty of term in respect of social housing:

CASE CLOSE-UP

Berrisford v. Mexfield Housing Co-operative [2011] UKSC 52

The claimant had been granted an 'occupancy agreement' which entitled him to live in the property 'from month to month until determined'. The agreement could be ended by the claimant on one month's written notice, but could be determined by the defendants only in four specified circumstances, none of which had occurred.

The defendant housing co-operative served one month's notice on the claimant. They argued that the agreement was to be interpreted as a tenancy from month to month, because any agreement to end it on specified grounds only would make it uncertain, as in the _Prudential Assurance_ case.

The Supreme Court held that such an agreement, if entered into before 1925, would have been interpreted as a 'lease for life'. These are converted into ninety-year tenancies by LPA 1925, s. 149(6). Therefore the claimant had a lease for ninety years, subject only to determination on the four grounds agreed.

This is rather surprising, as the courts do not seem to have used this section before in such a way. The Court did give weight to the nature of the property—social housing—and held that certainty of tenure must have been intended.

Berrisford v. Mexfield Housing Co-operative was recently distinguished by the High Court in _Southward Housing Co-operative Ltd v. Walker_ [2015] EWHC 1615 (Ch). In this case, the defendants were joint tenants of a property owned by a housing co-operative. The agreement specified that the tenancy could only be terminated if certain conditions occurred, one of which was rent arrears. The housing co-operative duly sought possession when the tenants went into rent arrears, but the tenants claimed that the fact that notice to quit could only be served on restricted conditions meant that the lease was for an uncertain term. They argued that, following _Berrisford_, this meant that they had a ninety-year lease under LPA 1925, s. 149(6). However, the court decided that although the term was uncertain, it did not give rise to a ninety-year lease. In this case, it was clear that the parties had not intended to create a lease for life. Instead, the agreement should be construed as a contractual licence, which was brought to an end by the notice to quit. This is an interesting development, not least because it demonstrates the importance that the court attaches to the intention of the parties in reaching its decision.

Note, finally, that although we have said that the beginning of the term must be certain, the lease does not need to be expressed as starting on a particular date. It has been held that an agreement to grant a lease based on an uncertain event—for example, the outbreak of war—is sufficiently certain—_Swift v. MacBean_ [1942] KB 375.

5.5.2 **Rent**

Although Lord Templeman, in _Street v. Mountford_, implied that rent is an essential requirement for a valid lease, the courts have subsequently decided that this is not the case—_Ashburn Anstalt v. Arnold_ [1989] Ch 1.

THINKING POINT

Can you think why this might be? Have a look again at the statutory definition of a lease at 5.3.1.

The definition clearly states 'whether or not at a rent': the courts could not fly in the face of statute.

Despite this undoubtedly correct judicial reasoning, it seems that payment of rent is likely to be evidence at least indicative of the existence of a lease, even if it is not conclusive.

5.5.3 Exclusive possession

exclusive possession

possession of a property to the exclusion of all others, including the landlord

A person occupying residential property with the permission of the owner will either be a tenant or a licensee, depending on whether or not he or she has **exclusive possession** of the premises.

The concept of exclusive possession is central to the grant of a lease. It means essentially that the tenant can exclude anyone else from the premises, even the landlord. The landlord who reserves the right to enter the property to maintain it from time to time does not negate exclusive possession—*Street v. Mountford*—nor does it matter that the landlord keeps a set of keys—*Aslan v. Murphy* [1990] 1 WLR 767.

It is, however, a concept with which the courts have sometimes struggled, as we shall see. It means that the tenant can effectively control the property: he or she has the right to decide who comes into it and who he or she wants to keep out.

exclusive occupation

sole occupation of all, or part, of a property

This can be contrasted with the right of a licensee. A licensee occupies the property only by permission of its owner: the licensee has no proprietary right in the property itself. He or she may have **exclusive occupation** of it, but this is different from exclusive possession. The licensee's interest will not be binding on third parties, unlike the interest of a tenant in the land—*Ashburn Anstalt v. Arnold*. All exclusive occupation means is that the occupier has sole or exclusive use of the property, or part of it.

In the 1970s, 1980s, and early 1990s, there was a succession of cases in which the courts grappled with the concept of exclusive possession. In most of these cases, the landlord wanted to avoid creating a lease, because that would confer statutory protection on the tenant. The best way in which to avoid the court construing an agreement as a lease was to ensure that the agreement did not confer the right of exclusive possession on the occupier—and landlords went to extreme lengths to avoid the appearance of exclusive possession, as we shall see!

Our starting point will be a case before *Street v. Mountford* which marked a high point for landlords, although the courts soon redressed the balance between landlord and tenant.

 CASE CLOSE-UP

Somma v. Hazelhurst [1978] 1 WLR 1014

A young unmarried couple wanted to rent a bedsit to share together. They each entered into a separate agreement with the owner of the property. The unusual agreement stated that the owner could, if she wished, move in with the couple—or even move a stranger in with them!

Let us pause for a moment here.

 THINKING POINT

Why do you think that the agreement contained these odd suggestions?

The owner was trying to avoid conferring exclusive possession on the occupiers. If they were found to have exclusive possession, the agreement would have been a lease and the Rent Acts would have protected the tenants.

 CASE CLOSE-UP

Somma v. Hazelhurst [1978] 1 WLR 1014

The court found that there was only a licence agreement. Exclusive possession had not been conferred on the occupiers.

When *Street v. Mountford* was decided a number of years later, the court criticized the decision in *Somma v. Hazelhurst*. Although the starting point for determining whether a lease or licence exists is always the agreement itself, Lord Templeman warned that the courts would be careful to detect 'sham devices and artificial transactions' inserted into the agreement to prevent the grant of exclusive possession. The clause in *Somma v. Hazelhurst* allowing the owner to move in with the occupiers was clearly such a sham.

Subsequent to *Street v. Mountford*, the court would look at the whole factual matrix of the situation and examine the substance of what was actually happening at the premises, in order to decide whether exclusive possession had, in fact, been conferred. This was applied many times by the courts in the years after *Street v. Mountford*.

 CASE CLOSE-UP

Aslan v. Murphy [1990] 1 WLR 767
Crancour Ltd v. Da Silvesa [1986] 1 EGLR 80

In both of these cases, the owner had inserted a clause apparently requiring the occupier to vacate the premises for an hour and a half each day. In *Aslan v. Murphy*, there was a further clause that the occupier might be required to share the room (measuring 4 ft 3 in x 12 ft 6 in) with another person.

The court found, in both cases, that these were sham clauses, designed to negate the grant of exclusive possession. When the court looked at what was actually happening at the premises, it found that the occupiers, as a matter of fact, had exclusive possession and thus both had a lease rather than a licence.

Street v. Mountford said that the title and wording of the agreement (in terms of lease or licence) was not relevant in deciding whether the document conferred a lease or a licence. In *National Car Parks Ltd v. Trinity Development Co. (Banbury) Ltd* [2001] EWCA Civ 1686, however, the Court of Appeal said that the title and wording should be used as a pointer by the courts when ascertaining the nature of the agreement. This decision reflects the fact that, sometimes, the parties do genuinely intend only to confer a licence and that the real intention of the parties should be considered by the courts.

5.5.4 Lodgers

In *Street v. Mountford*, Lord Templeman made it clear that, should someone be a lodger, he or she will be a licensee rather than a tenant. An example of a lodger might be a student renting a room in a family house during term time. Clearly, in this situation, the lodger cannot exclude the homeowner from his or her own home. Lord Templeman said (at 818) that a 'lodger is entitled to live in the premises but cannot call the place his own'.

5.5.5 Multiple occupiers

Some interesting issues arise in circumstances under which a number of people share the same premises.

There are a number of possibilities with shared property:

- the occupiers may be joint tenants of the whole property and so may have a lease together;
- the occupiers might be tenants of a particular part of the property, such as their own bedrooms;
- the occupiers may simply be licensees.

CROSS REFERENCE

For more on survivorship, see Chapter 8.

Whether the occupiers are deemed to have been granted a lease or a licence will depend on the circumstances of their sharing arrangements.

Q | CASE CLOSE-UP

AG Securities v. Vaughan [1990] 1 AC 417

This case was heard at the same time as *Antonaides v. Villiers* [1990] 1 AC 417. The two cases make an interesting contrast.

Four people moved into a four-bedroom flat. Each signed a separate 'licence' agreement with the owner, which allowed him or her to occupy the flat with the other licensees. It also expressly negated any right to exclusive possession. The agreements were all made at different times; some were for differing rents and for different periods. Each of the occupiers had replaced other occupiers when vacancies occurred over a three-year period.

The House of Lords decided that the occupiers were licensees. The four unities required for a joint tenancy (time, interest, possession, title) were not present.

Lord Templeman explained that, if the occupiers had been joint tenants and one of them had died, the remaining three occupiers would have been entitled to exclusive possession of the flat (by the operation of survivorship).

In this situation, however, it was clear that, if one of the occupiers had died, the owner of the property would have had the right to replace him and the existing occupiers could not have prevented him from doing this. They did not, therefore, have exclusive possession of the property and so had a licence.

Compare this with the case of *Antonaides v. Villiers*.

Q | CASE CLOSE-UP

Antonaides v. Villiers [1990] 1 AC 417

A couple lived together in a one-bedroom flat, by themselves. They had each signed a separate 'licence' agreement and had each agreed to pay half the rent. The agreement provided that the owner could move into the accommodation at any time or even arrange for someone else to do so!

The House of Lords decided that this was a lease. The couple had a joint tenancy of the flat. The agreements, although made separately, were interdependent: neither would have signed without the other. The couple had exclusive possession of the property and the clause suggesting that someone else could move in with them was a sham.

5.5.6 Business premises

Exclusive possession is also relevant in deciding whether an occupier holds business premises on a lease or licence—*Shell-Mex and BP Ltd v. Manchester Garages Ltd* [1971] 1 All ER 841.

5.5.7 Exceptional cases

There are some situations in which, even though all of the essential characteristics of a lease are present, a lease will not exist. Lord Templeman, in *Street v. Mountford*, identified three different categories of case in which this would happen:

1. those in which there is no intention to create a legal relationship;
2. those in which there is only a service occupancy;
3. those in which the landlord had no power to grant a tenancy.

5.5.7.1 No intention to create a legal relationship

When the parties enter into a lease, they are entering into a binding contract, intending to be bound by it. Lord Templeman recognized that there may be occasions—particularly in a family context—on which the parties may unintentionally create a lease by satisfying the essential elements. For example, in *Cobb v. Lane* [1952] 1 All ER 1199, a woman allowed her brother to live in her bungalow rent free. This was held to be a licence, rather than a lease, because the woman had no intention to create legal relations: she was simply helping out her brother.

This exception also stretches to acts of friendship or generosity. In *Booker v. Palmer* [1942] 2 All ER 674, a wartime case, evacuees whose home had been bombed were allowed to live in a cottage as a favour. They later claimed (rather ungratefully!) that they had a lease, but the Court of Appeal held that there had been no intention to create legal relations and so there was no lease.

5.5.7.2 Service occupancy

There will also be no tenancy if the occupier is living in the premises because he or she is required to do so for his or her job. For example, a school caretaker will often live in the grounds of a school, so that he or she can be on site when needed to repair and maintain the school property. In these circumstances, the caretaker will be a licensee.

The test to establish whether someone has a service occupancy is to ask whether he or she is 'genuinely required to occupy the premises for the better performance of his duties'—*per* Woolf LJ in *Norris v. Checksfield* [1991] 1 WLR 1241. If he or she is living on the premises simply for convenience, or as some kind of fringe benefit, then the agreement may well result in a tenancy being created.

5.5.7.3 No power to grant a tenancy

It has long been thought that a person cannot grant a lease if he or she does not have either a freehold or leasehold interest in the land. This seems to be common sense: if someone only has a licence to occupy a property, how could they possibly grant another person a lease, which would be a greater estate in the land than their own?

This sensible supposition has been shaken slightly by a House of Lords' decision that has had both academics and property lawyers scratching their heads in disbelief.

The following unusual case needs to be considered on its own, before we think about whether it changes anything that we have already said about leases.

🔍 CASE CLOSE-UP

Bruton v. London and Quadrant Housing Trust [2000] 1 AC 406

London and Quadrant Housing Trust (LQHT) was a charitable organization that provided accommodation for the homeless. For this reason, Lambeth Borough Council gave LQHT a licence to use a block of flats that Lambeth owned. In the agreement between LQHT and Lambeth, it was made clear that no proprietary interest was to be conferred on LQHT. Indeed, it would have been *ultra vires* for Lambeth to make such a grant. The housing was to be used to provide temporary accommodation for the homeless.

As part of this worthy scheme, LQHT offered Mr Bruton a flat, under a weekly licence agreement.

The case came to court because Mr Bruton claimed that LQHT was in breach of a repairing obligation under Landlord and Tenant Act 1985, s. 11. LQHT maintained that, because there was no lease, it was not liable under this section. The Court then had to decide whether Mr Bruton had been granted a lease or a licence.

The Court of Appeal had no difficulty in deciding that Mr Bruton was a licensee.

The House of Lords, however, disagreed. Lord Hoffmann decided that the agreement had all the necessary hallmarks of a tenancy, according to *Street v. Mountford*—that is, exclusive possession for a term at a rent. He also held that, although LQHT had no estate from which to grant a lease, the term 'lease' described the relationship between the parties and did not need to grant a proprietary right or interest in the land.

This is a very strange judgment. If a lease does not have to confer a proprietary right, but is only a contract between the parties, then it starts to look very much like a licence—in which case, are tenants under such contractual leases afforded the statutory protection that tenants under conventional (proprietary) leases enjoy?

▶ CROSS REFERENCE

For help in incorporating *Bruton* into an exam question on this topic, see Chapter 15.

In *Bruton*, the implications for the charity providing housing for the homeless are significant: LQHT was suddenly burdened with a duty to repair, despite the fact that it had no proprietary interest in the property!

We suggest that, although you should think about (and hopefully read) the case of *Bruton*—it is, after all, still good law and has not yet been overruled—you should concentrate your efforts on grasping the conventional *Street v. Mountford* principles.

5.6 Leasehold covenants

leasehold covenant

a clause in a lease, specifying certain obligations on the part of either party

As we have already recognized, a lease is essentially a contract between landlord and tenant. As with any contract, the parties can agree to include any term or clause that they choose. The clauses in a lease are referred to as 'covenants'—but a **leasehold covenant** should not be confused with a freehold covenant.

The phrase 'leasehold covenants' simply refers to the terms included in the lease. These can be expressly stated in the agreement (**express covenants**) or implied by law into the agreement (**implied covenants**). They can be separated into the duties imposed on the landlord (**landlord's covenants**) and the duties imposed upon the tenant (**tenant's covenants**).

CROSS REFERENCE

For more on freehold covenants, see Chapter 12.

---

express covenants terms that are expressly stated in a lease

implied covenants terms that are implied into a lease by law

landlord's covenants clauses in a lease specifying the obligations of the landlord under the lease

tenant's covenants clauses in a lease specifying the obligations of the tenant under the lease

---

We will look firstly at some of the usual covenants, and then we will consider briefly the slightly tricky question about whether leasehold covenants can bind landlords and tenants who acquire their title from the original contracting parties.

5.6.1 The landlord's covenants

5.6.1.1 Quiet enjoyment

The lease agreement will usually contain a term entitling the tenant to 'quiet enjoyment' of the leased premises. If no such express provision is made, then the law will imply such a term into the lease.

'Quiet enjoyment' implies fundamentally that the landlord should allow the tenant to enjoy his or her occupation of the premises without disturbance from the landlord, or their agent, or anyone else claiming title from the landlord (for example, another of their tenants)—*Sanderson v. Berwick-upon-Tweed Corporation* (1884) 13 QBD 547.

Many of the cases involving the breach of this covenant arise in circumstances under which the landlord is trying to evict the tenant from the premises, so the actions taken by the landlord are often somewhat extreme. For example, in *Lavender v. Betts* [1942] 2 All ER 72, the court (not unreasonably) decided that, by removing the doors and windows from the leased premises, the landlord had breached the covenant to quiet enjoyment. Intimidation or threatening behaviour towards the tenant can also breach this covenant—*Kenny v. Preen* [1963] 1 QB 499—and it can also breach statutory protection that is in place for the tenant under Protection from Eviction Act 1977, s. 1(3).

These are quite obvious forms of interference. However, the House of Lords has held that, for a breach to occur, there need not always be direct, physical interference: it potentially includes anything that might interfere with a tenant's occupation of his or her property, such as 'regular excessive noise'—*Southwark Borough Council v. Mills* [1999] 4 All ER 449, 455.

The tenant's right to quiet enjoyment is prospective, which means that it arises from the date on which the tenancy began. This means that, if the breach of covenant is caused by a condition that existed before his or her tenancy began, the tenant will have no redress against the landlord.

🔍 CASE CLOSE-UP

Southwark Borough Council v. Mills [1999] 4 All ER 449

The House of Lords considered a conjoined appeal from two tenants of local authorities who were living in old buildings with no soundproofing. The women complained that they could hear excessive noise from the flats around them. These flats were occupied by other council tenants (who therefore claimed their title from the local authority landlords).

The noise was simply the noise of everyday living, but because of the structure of the flats, it really bothered the women who had to suffer it. The women argued that this was a breach of the covenant to quiet enjoyment of their property.

The House of Lords, firstly, reviewed the history of the covenant and Lord Millett explained (at 467) that there would be a breach where:

> the landlord or someone claiming under him does anything that substantially interferes with the tenant's title or possession of the demised premises, or with his ordinary and lawful enjoyment of the demised premises.

In this case, however, there had been no breach of covenant. The covenant was prospective, which meant that it only took effect from the start of the tenancy: '[t]*he covenant does not apply to things done before the grant of the tenancy, even though they may have continuing consequences for the tenant*' (*per* Lord Hoffmann at 455). Unfortunately for the tenants, the problems arising from lack of soundproofing had existed for many years before their tenancy commenced. They had no remedy against their landlords.

The tenant's remedies for breach of this covenant may be an injunction, to stop the landlord from committing further breaches, or damages, to compensate the tenant for any loss suffered.

5.6.1.2 Non-derogation from grant

The somewhat grand-sounding covenant of 'non-derogation from grant' simply means that, having granted the tenancy, the landlord cannot then undermine it in any way. It is implied into the lease agreement.

In *Southwark Borough Council v. Mills*, Lord Millett said that the covenants of non-derogation from grant and of quiet enjoyment were in effect, very similar: '[t]he principle is the same in each case: a man may not give with one hand and take away with the other'.

CASE CLOSE-UP

Harmer v. Jumbil (Nigeria) Tin Areas Ltd [1920] All ER 113

The landlord granted a lease expressly allowing the tenant to use the land to store explosives. In order to do this, the tenant had to obtain a licence under the Explosives Act 1875, which imposed certain restrictions on him. The landlord was aware that some restrictions would be necessary. The landlord retained land adjoining the tenant's property. The licence provided that, if buildings were erected on the landlord's land within a specified distance of the tenant's property, the licence would be withdrawn.

Some years later, the landlord granted a lease of the adjoining land to another tenant. This tenant built in the restricted area and also began reopening old mine shafts—not altogether wise, given the explosives stored next door!

The first tenant brought an action to stop the mining works and remove the buildings, claiming that this amounted to a derogation of the landlord's grant.

The Court of Appeal agreed that the landlord had effectively breached his covenant. If the buildings were allowed to remain, the licence would be withdrawn and the effect, according to Younger LJ, would be to '*completely sterilize the property in his tenant's hands*'.

To be in breach of this covenant, the landlord must have known at the time of the grant what the tenant intended to do with the land—*Robinson v. Kilvert* (1889) 41 Ch 88.

If the tenant establishes a breach, he or she may obtain an injunction, stopping the landlord breaching the covenant, and/or damages, to compensate the tenant for the loss suffered.

5.6.1.3 Covenant to repair

As you might expect, the landlord will also be subject to certain obligations to maintain the leased premises. Both the common law and statute imply a number of covenants to repair into the lease.

At common law

- Fitness for human habitation

    If the property is let with furniture already in it—that is, if it is furnished—then the law implies a covenant that it is let 'fit for human habitation'. This basically means that it must be suitable for people to live in. Usually, it is fairly easy to work out when a property is *not* fit for human habitation:

    > The meaning of the phrase must vary with the circumstances to which it is applied. In the case of unclean furniture or defective drains or a nuisance by vermin the matter is not, as a rule, one of difficulty. The eye or the nostrils can detect the fault and measure its extent.

    > (*Collins v. Hopkins* [1923] 2 KB 617, 620–1, *per* McCardie J)

    Note, however, that the covenant only says that the property must be fit for human habitation at the beginning of the tenancy: there is no continuing obligation *during* the tenancy—*Sarson v. Roberts* [1895] 2 QB 395.

    The covenant does not apply to unfurnished premises.

- Maintenance of means of access

    A covenant for the 'maintenance of means of access' would apply if a landlord were to own a building divided into a number of rented units—perhaps a block of flats. In this situation, the law will imply a covenant for the landlord to take reasonable steps to keep the 'common parts' of the building in good repair—*Liverpool City Council v. Irwin* [1977] AC 239. The common parts are those parts of the building used by all the tenants—for example, staircases and landings, or corridors between the individual flats.

- Correlative obligations

    Sometimes, in order to make the lease work sensibly, the law will imply a correlative obligation on the landlord. This might be necessary, for example, if the lease expressly imposes a duty on the tenant to repair the *inside* of the leased premises, but does not mention who is responsible for maintaining the *outside* of the premises—*Barrett v. Lounova* [1989] 1 All ER 351. The court would recognize that somebody must be responsible for maintaining the exterior of the premises—otherwise the building might eventually fall down! In these circumstances, then, it may well impose a duty on the landlord to repair the outside, because this would be matched by—that is, it would 'correlate' to—the duty of the tenant to maintain the inside.

Under statute

- Fitness for human habitation

    In a number of exceptional cases, Landlord and Tenant Act 1985 (LTA 1985), s. 8, imposes a statutory duty on the landlord to keep the property fit for human habitation *during* the tenancy. This only applies to low-rent properties—that is, a tenancy granted after 6 July 1957, for a rent not exceeding £80 p.a. in London and £57 p.a. elsewhere in the country. Those of you paying rent will appreciate how few tenancies will actually meet these criteria!

- Repairing obligations

  LTA 1985, s. 13(1) also imposes repairing obligations on landlords if the lease is for a dwelling house and was granted after 24 October 1961 for less than seven years. Under LTA 1985, s. 11, the landlord has to keep the structure and exterior of the building in repair, as well as the various installations in the house that provide the tenant with gas, electricity, and water. The court will take into account the age and character of the property, and its locality, when considering the extent of the landlord's obligation to repair—LTA 1985, s. 11(3).

If the landlord has breached any of the repairing covenants, the tenant may be able to obtain an order for specific performance, to ensure that the necessary repairs are done. If the tenant, in desperation, has completed the repairs him- or herself, he or she may be entitled to offset the cost of those repairs against future rent payments. The tenant may also be able to recover damages.

Q | CASE CLOSE-UP

Edwards v. Kumarasamy [2015] EWCA Civ 20

In *Edwards v. Kumarasamy* the Court of Appeal considered the extent of a landlord's liability for a defect outside the rented premises. In this case the landlord, Mr Kumarasamy, held a long lease from the freeholder of a second-floor flat. He granted an assured shorthold tenancy to his own tenant, Mr Edwards. When taking some rubbish out, Mr Edwards tripped and injured himself on a defective paving stone which led to the communal bins and car park. He sued Mr Kumarasamy for damages, on the grounds that Mr Kumarsamy had breached his covenant to keep the premises in good repair.

Section 11, LTA 1985 provides that, in addition to the landlord's duty to maintain the structure and exterior of the building, he or she must also keep in good repair any area in which he or she (the landlord) holds an estate or interest. Although Mr Kumarasamy did not own the relevant area—that was owned by the freeholder—he did have a legal easement over it, which permitted him (and therefore his tenant, Mr Edwards) to walk across it. The Court of Appeal said that this meant that Mr Kumarasamy did have an obligation to maintain this area in good repair.

Before this case, case law suggested that the landlord had to be notified that an area had fallen into disrepair before he became liable. There was also a clause in the head lease (between Mr Kumarasamy and the freeholder) that provided that notice of a defect was necessary, so that the freeholder had the opportunity to remedy the defect, before the freeholder was liable. Mr Edwards had not notified Mr Kumarasamy of the defect, and Mr Kumarasamy had not notified the freeholder of the defect.

However, in this case, the Court of Appeal said that the area was external to the property and therefore accessible and visible to the landlord—he should have ensured that it was kept in good repair. It was not necessary for the tenant to give notice of the defect to the landlord in order for the landlord to become liable for any breach. This decision has caused some concern to landlords who suddenly seem to have a more onerous obligation in respect of repair to the exterior of the rented property. The case has been appealed to the Supreme Court, so we will wait to see whether this is confirmed.

5.6.2 **The tenant's covenants**

5.6.2.1 **Rent**

Although we have seen that a tenant does not have to pay rent for a lease to exist (see 5.5.2), in the vast majority of cases, an express term requiring payment of rent will be contained in the lease agreement. The agreement will usually state how much rent is to be paid, when it is due, and whether it is to be paid in advance or in arrears.

THINKING POINT

Carl moved into a rented flat on 1 October 2007. His rent is £350 per month in advance. When will October's rent payment be due?

It is due on 1 October—that is, in advance of the coming month.

THINKING POINT

What if Carl's lease had said that his rent was due monthly in arrears?

If the rent were due in arrears, his rent would be due on 31 October—at the end of the month during which he had occupied the property.

Sometimes—particularly in longer leases—the lease will also contain a clause allowing the landlord to review and raise the rent at certain intervals. Different types of tenancy have different levels of protection in terms of the landlord charging a fair rent. Interesting though the statutory framework of such protection is, however, its consideration is outside the scope of this book.

5.6.2.2 Repair

Unlike the landlord, the tenant will not be subject to any implied obligation to repair the leased premises. In practice, the lease usually includes a clause requiring the tenant to keep the premises in 'good tenantable repair' or something similar. Most landlords accept that everyday wear and tear is inevitable. The court will interpret the tenant's repairing obligation in the context of the particular premises—*Brew Brothers Ltd v. Snax (Ross) Ltd* [1970] 1 QB 612—for example, taking its age and character into account.

5.6.2.3 Waste

Lease agreements will often contain a clause prohibiting a tenant from committing **waste**. An obligation is also implied into the agreement.

In this context, the term 'waste' has nothing to do with rubbish: it simply means that the tenant cannot do, or fail to do, anything that would result in the premises being permanently changed in any way. **Voluntary waste** involves the positive act of the tenant changing the nature of the premises. **Permissive waste** occurs if the tenant fails to do something and if that omission leads to a permanent change to the property. This might include, for example, failing to clear out a ditch, resulting in the foundations of the property rotting through—*Powys v. Belgrave* (1854).

> **waste**
> any permanent alteration of tenanted property that is caused by the tenant's action or neglect

> **voluntary waste** waste that is caused by a voluntary action of the tenant
>
> **permissive waste** waste that is caused by the tenant's neglect

In either case, the tenant is under an implied obligation to use the premises in a 'tenant-like' manner. He or she must, in the words of Lord Denning in *Warren v. Keen* [1953] 2 All ER 1118, 'do the little jobs about the place which a reasonable tenant would do'.

5.6.2.4 **Assignment or subletting**

assignment

the transfer of the whole of the remainder of the term of a lease

Assignment occurs if the tenant transfers the whole of his or her remaining interest in the property to someone else (the assignee).

EXAMPLE

If Leanne has a fifteen-year lease on a property and, after five years, she transfers the lease for the whole of the remaining ten years to Tracy, she has assigned her interest. This relationship might be illustrated as in Figure 5.3.

Figure 5.3 The landlord–tenant–assignee relationship

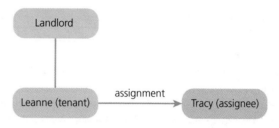

Subletting, meanwhile, occurs if the tenant grants a lease to someone else for a lesser period than his or her own.

subletting the granting of a sublease by someone who is himself or herself a tenant, for a period shorter than that of his or her own (head) lease

EXAMPLE

Liam has a ten-year lease on the property and he grants a sublease for five years to Debbie. This is a sublease because, at the end of the five years, Liam still has an interest in the property.

This relationship might be illustrated as in Figure 5.4.

Figure 5.4 The landlord–tenant–subtenant relationship

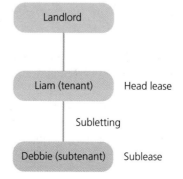

There is often a clause in the lease agreement prohibiting the tenant from assigning or subletting the property to someone else. The reason for this is that most landlords like to know who their tenants are, and to make sure that they are responsible and trustworthy. Sometimes, rather than forbidding the tenant to sublet, the lease will permit it, provided that the tenant obtains the consent of the landlord.

5.6.2.5 Breach of the tenant's covenants

If the tenant breaches one of the covenants in the lease, the landlord has various remedies against him or her.

Under certain circumstances, the landlord can forfeit the lease. This means that he or she can decide that the lease is at an end before the end of the term and re-enter the premises. This is obviously an extreme remedy and, in a legal lease, the right of re-entry and forfeiture must be expressly stated: it will not be implied. The exercise of the landlord's right of forfeiture is strictly controlled by statute and the courts.

> **CROSS REFERENCE**
> For more on forfeiture, see Chapter 3.

Less draconian alternatives for the landlord include damages for breach of covenant (other than a covenant for payment of rent) and/or an injunction or order of specific performance.

At present, the landlord can resort to the ancient remedy of **distress**, which allows him or her to enter the premises and seize the tenant's goods to the value of the outstanding rent. This remedy dates back to the Norman Conquest and some of the legal principles are wonderfully quaint, bringing to mind old black-and-white films of the wicked landlord casting out the poor family from the premises into the night, with no mercy. The Tribunals, Courts and Enforcement Act 2007 contained provisions to abolish the remedy of distress and create a statutory recovery scheme for arrears in respect of commercial premises. One of the parts of this Act established a new scheme called Commercial Rent Arrears Recovery (CRAR). This came into force in 2014. Note though that CRAR only applies to commercial premises, and not to those properties either let or occupied as a dwelling (ie residential property).

> **distress**
> the seizure of goods as security for the performance of an obligation

5.7 Assignment and the running of covenants

We have seen that leasehold covenants are essentially clauses in a contract (a deed) between landlord and tenant. If either side breaches a covenant, then the wronged party can bring proceedings to remedy the breach. The original parties have **privity of contract**.

Problems may arise, however, when either the landlord assigns his or her reversion, or the tenant assigns his or her lease. Remember that 999-year leases are not uncommon: there may be many assignments over the course of a millennium! Suddenly, the parties to the contract are different: what we need to establish is whether the new parties are still bound by the terms of the original agreement.

> **privity of contract**
> the relationship that exists between parties to a contract that allows each to sue, or be sued, under the contract

We will work through an example in stages, to illustrate the process of assignment and to help you to appreciate its implications. We will then look at the law relating to the enforceability of leasehold covenants: firstly, for leases created after 1995 and, then, for those arising before 1996. The reason for this is that the Landlord and Tenant (Covenants) Act 1995 (LTCA 1995) introduced a new statutory regime to simplify the rules about enforceability of leasehold covenants. It only applies to new leases, which means, in broad terms, those created after 31 December 1995—LTCA 1995, s. 1(1).

> **CROSS REFERENCE**
> For more on freehold covenants, see Chapter 12.

Remember throughout that leasehold covenants operate under different rules from those of freehold covenants.

Thankfully, leasehold covenants are now (relatively) straightforward. The following represents an overview of this substantial topic—but, should you need a more detailed consideration of the subject, please consult the further reading that is listed at the end of the chapter.

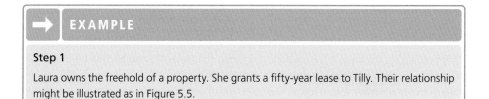

> ### ➡ EXAMPLE
>
> **Step 1**
>
> Laura owns the freehold of a property. She grants a fifty-year lease to Tilly. Their relationship might be illustrated as in Figure 5.5.

Figure 5.5 Laura grants a fifty-year lease to Tilly

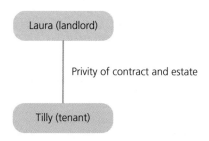

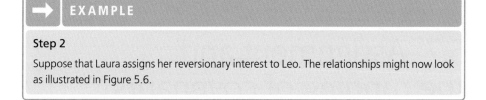

> ### ➡ EXAMPLE
>
> **Step 2**
>
> Suppose that Laura assigns her reversionary interest to Leo. The relationships might now look as illustrated in Figure 5.6.

Figure 5.6 Laura assigns her reversionary interest to Leo

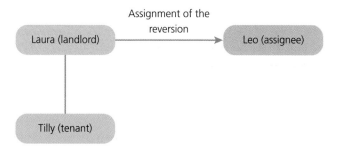

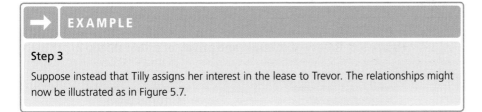

Step 3

Suppose instead that Tilly assigns her interest in the lease to Trevor. The relationships might now be illustrated as in Figure 5.7.

Figure 5.7 Tilly assigns her interest in the lease to Trevor

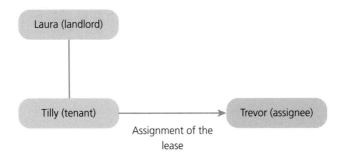

5.7.1 Step 1: Laura and Tilly

Between Laura and Tilly there is privity of contract, meaning that, if either party breaches a covenant, the wronged party can sue. There is also **privity of estate**. Privity of estate again refers to a relationship between the parties, but this time it relates to the nature of the relationship between landlord and tenant. Both parties have an estate in the land: Laura has a freehold estate and she has granted Tilly a leasehold estate. Between any landlord and any tenant there will always be privity of estate, as we shall see.

> **privity of estate**
> the relationship that exists between landlord and tenant under the same lease that allows each to enforce his or her obligations against the other

5.7.2 Step 2: Laura assigns the reversion to Leo

Here, privity of contract only exists between Laura and Tilly: Leo was not a party to the original contract (Figure 5.8).

THINKING POINT

Who now has privity of estate?

Leo and Tilly: they are in a landlord–tenant relationship.

See Figure 5.8 for an illustration of the relationship as it now stands.

Figure 5.8 Privity of contract and privity of estate at Step 2

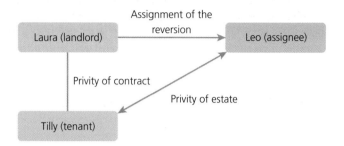

5.7.3 Step 3: Tilly assigns her lease to Trevor

Once again, at this step, privity of contract exists only between Laura and Tilly. There is no privity of contract between Laura and Trevor. There is, however, privity of estate between Laura and Trevor, because they are in a landlord–tenant relationship.

The relationships as they now stand are illustrated in Figure 5.9.

Figure 5.9 Privity of contract and privity of estate at Step 3

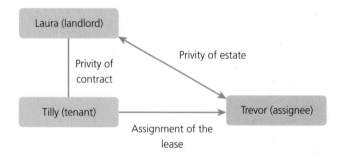

You will have noticed by now that the main difficulty, after the reversion or lease has been transferred, is that privity of contract continues to exist between the original parties. It is not destroyed by the transfer; neither does the transfer create any privity of contract between the new parties. This means that, without the legal mechanisms we are to discuss next, the old parties would remain forever liable for any breaches of covenant by the new parties and the new parties would be unable to sue for any breach of covenant.

We will now consider the legal positions of the parties after Steps 2 and 3.

5.7.4 After Step 2: assignment of the reversion

5.7.4.1 Leases granted after 1995

In our example, Laura assigns the reversion to Leo. LTCA 1995, s. 3(1), first annexes the leasehold covenants to the land itself, which has the effect of transferring to the new landlord the covenants in the original lease, unless those covenants are personal in nature.

In our example, if the lease were to have been granted after 1995, Leo would then automatically be bound by the landlord's covenants in the lease and would have the benefit of the tenant's (Tilly's) covenants. This right only arises from the date of transfer of the reversion. So for example, if Tilly were to owe Laura rent, Leo would not be able to sue her to recover it, because the breach of covenant took place before Leo acquired his interest in the land.

So far so good—but the other problem with leasehold covenants is that, as we have seen, privity of contract continues to exist between the original parties. In our example, this would mean that, if Leo were to breach his landlord's covenant to repair, Tilly could sue Laura if Leo were to refuse to comply!

LTCA 1995, s. 6(2), offers landlords in Laura's position an escape from this continuing obligation. Under this subsection, the original landlord can, with the permission of the tenant, be released from the covenants, and, once released, he or she is free from both burden and benefits. The landlord is also released if the tenant simply fails to respond to the landlord's request for release— LTCA 1995, s. 8(2)(a).

 EXAMPLE

Laura and Tilly's lease was created in 1997. In 2000, Laura assigns her reversion to Leo. In accordance with LTCA 1995, s. 8(1) Laura writes to her tenant, Tilly, to serve notice of the transfer of the reversion and to ask for permission to be released from the covenant. Tilly does not respond to the notice.

Four weeks after the date on which the notice was served and with no response from Tilly, Laura is automatically released from the covenants under LTCA 1995, s. 8(2)(a).

Some time later, Leo breaches his covenant to repair. Because of the LTCA 1995 provisions, Tilly has no redress at all from Laura—she must pursue only Leo for a remedy. Without the provisions, she would have been able to pursue both Leo and Laura.

5.7.4.2 Leases granted before 1996

As we have seen, there is privity of estate between the original tenant, Tilly, and the new landlord, Leo. LPA 1925, ss. 141(1) and 142(1) transfer the benefit and burden of the original covenants from the original to the new landlord—but they only appear to transfer those covenants that 'touch and concern' the land. The meaning of this phrase was the main difficulty under the old law, for leases granted before 1996.

The other difficulty was that the original landlord—Laura—remained liable to the original tenant— Tilly—for any breaches of covenant by the new landlord—Leo. This meant that, in order to protect him- or herself, the original landlord had to obtain an indemnity from the new landlord, which would allow the original landlord to recover from the new landlord any money paid to the tenant if the original landlord were to be sued.

This is not always as useful as it sounds, as the following example demonstrates.

 EXAMPLE

Imagine the same parties as in the previous example, but that, this time, the lease was created before 1996.

Laura transfers the reversion to Leo, with an indemnity clause. Leo breaches his covenant to repair. Tilly discovers that Leo has become insolvent. She decides to sue Laura instead. Laura is forced to pay the cost of repairs. She tries to rely on her indemnity to recover the cost of this from Leo. What do you think will be the problem?

The problem is that Leo will not be able to repay Laura: she will have to bear the cost herself.

5.7.5 After Step 3: assignment of the tenancy

5.7.5.1 Leases granted after 1995

In our example, the original tenant, Tilly, transfers the tenancy to Trevor. If the lease were to have been granted after 1995, Trevor would have privity of estate, but not privity of contract with the landlord, Laura. Tilly would still have privity of contract with Laura.

On assignment, however, LTCA 1995, s. 5 automatically releases the original tenant from the covenants of the lease. This means that, on assignment, Tilly can walk away from the property with no fear of liability for Trevor's breaches and no right to sue Laura for any of her future breaches under the lease.

 EXAMPLE

Laura and Tilly's lease is created in 1997. In 2000, Tilly assigns her interest to Trevor. Some years later, Trevor does not pay his rent.

LTCA 1995, s. 5 operates to release Tilly from all of the covenants of the lease. Laura cannot sue Tilly for Trevor's unpaid rent.

5.7.5.2 Leases granted before 1996

If the lease were to have been granted before 1996, however, Trevor would have privity of estate with the landlord, Laura. This means that he would be able to sue, or be sued, if either party committed any breaches of covenants that 'touch and concern' the land. There would, however, still be privity of contract between Tilly and Laura, the original parties to the lease.

An example will show what this might mean to Tilly.

 EXAMPLE

Laura and Tilly's lease is granted in 1990. In 2000, Tilly transfers the tenancy to Trevor. Some years later, Trevor does not pay his rent.

In this case, because there is privity of contract between Tilly and Laura, Laura can sue Tilly for Trevor's unpaid rent.

Once again, the original tenant can obtain an indemnity, but this will serve little purpose if the new tenant is insolvent. The law before LTCA 1995 obviously exposed the original tenant to great financial risks, because he or she might be sued for a breach occurring many years after assignment.

5.8 Putting it all together

Before we finish thinking about leases, it might be useful actually to look at a real tenancy agreement and to see how it all fits together. The sample agreement in Form 5.1 is one that is actually

Form 5.1 A tenancy agreement

Reproduced for educational purposes only by kind permission of Oyez Professional Services Limited.

TENANCY AGREEMENT

DATE 17th September 2007

PARTIES 1. **THE** Landlord BRIAN SMITH

2. **THE** Tenant TREVOR HOOD

PROPERTY Flat 4, The Warren
Maryfield,
Greenfordshire

And any fixtures and land held with the Property

TERM A fixed term of 10(ten) year(s)
from 17 September 2007 (start date)
until 16 September 2017 (end date)
And thereafter from month to month
(e.g., month to month)

RENT £ 1,000 per month (period)

PAYABLE in advance by equal monthly payments on the 17th
day of each month

FIRST PAYMENT to be made on 17 September 2007 (date)

1. **THE** Landlord lets the Property to the Tenant for the Term at the Rent payable as set out above.

2. **THE** Tenant agrees with the Landlord -

(1) To pay the Rent as set out above

(2) (a) To pay any council tax which the Tenant is obliged to pay under the Local Government Finance Act 1992 or any regulations under that Act

(b) To pay to the Landlord the amount of any council tax which, while the tenancy continues, the Landlord becomes obliged to pay under that Act or those regulations for any part of the period of the tenancy because the Tenant ceases to live at the Property

(c) To pay all other charges of any kind which are now or later come to be charged to the occupier of the Property as such by any body acting under statutory authority in making such a charge

(3) To pay for all gas, electricity, water and sewerage services supplied to the Property during the tenancy and to pay all charges for the use of any telephone at the Property during the tenancy. Where necessary, the sums demanded by the service provider will be apportioned according to the duration of the tenancy. The sums covered by this clause include standing charges or other similar charges and VAT as well as charges for actual consumption

(4) To keep the interior of the Property, the internal decorations and the fixtures, fittings and appliances in the Property in good repair and condition (except for damage caused by accidental fire and except for anything which the Landlord is liable to repair under this Agreement or by law). This clause does not oblige the Tenant to put the Property into better repair than it was in at the beginning of the tenancy

(5)   To allow the Landlord or anyone with the Landlord's written authority to enter the Property at reasonable times of the day to inspect its condition and state of repair, if the Landlord has given 24 hours' written notice beforehand

(6)   To use the Property as   residential only

(7)   Not to alter or add to the Property or do or allow anyone else to do anything on the Property which the Tenant might reasonably foresee would increase the risk of fire

(8)   Not to do or allow anyone else to do anything on the Property which may be a nuisance to, or cause damage or annoyance to, the tenants or occupiers of any adjoining premises

(9)   Not to assign or sublet the Property and not to part with possession of the Property in any other way without the Landlord's consent (but the Landlord will not unreasonably refuse or delay dealing with a request for consent to an assignment or subletting). If the Property is not residential property and the Landlord agrees that the Tenant may assign it, the Landlord's agreement may be given subject to the condition that the Tenant will enter into an authorised guarantee agreement within the meaning of the Landlord and Tenant (Covenants) Act 1995

(10)   To give the Landlord a copy of any notice given under the Party Wall etc. Act 1996 within seven days of receiving it and not to do anything as a result of the notice unless required to do so by the Landlord

(11)   At the end of the Term or earlier if the tenancy comes to an end more quickly to deliver the Property up to the Landlord in the condition it should be in if the Tenant has performed the Tenant's obligations under this Agreement

(12)   During the last twenty-eight days of the tenancy to allow the Landlord or the Landlord's agents to put up a notice that the Property is to be let and to enter and view the Property with prospective tenants at reasonable times of the day if the Landlord has given 24 hours' written notice beforehand.

3.   **IF** the Tenant -

(1)   is at least fourteen days late in paying the Rent or any part of it, whether or not the Rent has been formally demanded, or

(2)   has broken any of the terms of this Agreement

then, subject to any statutory provisions, the Landlord may recover possession of the Property and the tenancy will come to an end. Any other rights or remedies the Landlord may have will remain in force.

(**Note:** If the Property is residential, the Landlord may not be able to recover possession without an order of the court under the Housing Act 1988. Except in certain cases set out in the Act of substantial arrears of rent, the court has a discretion whether or not to make an order and is likely to take account of whether unpaid rent has later been paid or a breach of the terms of the tenancy has been made good

Note: This clause does not affect any rights of the Tenant under the Protection from Eviction Act 1977.)

4. **THE** Landlord agrees with the Tenant that the Tenant has the right to possess and enjoy the Property during the tenancy without any interruption from the Landlord or any person claiming through or in trust for the Landlord. But:

    (1) this clause does not limit any of the rights under this Agreement which the Tenant has agreed to allow the Landlord to exercise;

    (2) this clause does not prevent the Landlord from taking lawful steps to enforce his rights against the Tenant if the Tenant breaks any of the terms of this Agreement.

5. **IF** section 11 of the Landlord and Tenant Act 1985 applies to the tenancy, the Tenant's obligations are subject to the effect of that section.

    (Note: As a general rule, section 11 applies to tenancies of a dwelling-house for a term of less than seven years. It requires the landlord to keep in repair the structure and exterior of the dwelling-house including drains, gutters and external pipes; and to keep in repair and proper working order the installations for the supply of water, gas and electricity, for sanitation (including basins, sinks, baths and sanitary conveniences) and for space heating and heating water. The landlord is not obliged to repair until the tenant has given notice of the defect, and the tenant is obliged to take proper care of the Property and to do small jobs which a reasonable tenant would do.)

6. **IF** the Property is damaged to such an extent that the Tenant cannot live in it, the Rent will cease to be payable until the Property is rebuilt or repaired so that the Tenant can live there again unless

    (1) the cause of the damage is something which the Tenant did or failed to do as a result of which the Landlord's insurance policy relating to the Property has become void; and

    (2) the Landlord had given the Tenant notice of what the policy required.

    Any dispute about whether this clause applies must be submitted to arbitration under Part I of the Arbitration Act 1996 if both parties agree to that in writing after the dispute has arisen.

7. **WHERE** the context permits -

    (1) "The Landlord" includes the successors to the original landlord

    (2) "The Tenant" includes the successors to the original tenant

    (3) "The Property" includes any part of the Property.

NOTICE OF LANDLORD'S ADDRESS

The Landlord notifies the Tenant that the Tenant may serve notices (including notices in proceedings) on the Landlord at the following address:

> Flat 1, The Warren
> Maryfield,
> Greenfordshire

(This notice is given under section 48 of the Landlord and Tenant Act 1987, if applicable. The address must be in England or Wales.)

AS WITNESS the hands of the parties on the date specified above

SIGNED by the above-named   AS A DEED

    BRIAN JONES

(the Landlord) in the presence of

Paul Southvale,
Flat 2, The Warren

SIGNED by the above-named   AS A DEED

    TREVOR HOOD

(the Tenant) in the presence of

Fenella Southvale,
Flat 2, The Warren

AGREE1/3

DATED 17th September 2007
_____

BRIAN JONES

and

TREVOR HOOD

_____

Tenancy Agreement
for letting

Rent £ 1,000 per month
_____

©2002, 2007 Oyez 7 Spa Road, London SE16 3QQ   2007 Edition
3.2007

Agreement 1   5004017

AGREE1/4

used in practice. Read right through it and try to identify the various parts of the lease that we have discussed in this chapter. (The thinking points will help to guide you through it step by step.)

THINKING POINT

What kind of a document is this?

This is clearly a tenancy agreement—a contract between the parties, Brian Smith and Trevor Hood. Remember that the terms 'lease' and 'tenancy' are often used interchangeably. If the property being let is residential, it is usually called a tenancy, as in this case. The term 'lease' is more often used in commercial agreements. It is also a deed: it is a formal document that is independently witnessed and signed as a deed.

THINKING POINT

Who is the landlord?

Who is the tenant?

The landlord is Brian Smith and the tenant is Trevor Hood. The names and addresses of the parties are referred to as the 'preliminaries', contained in the 'premises' part of the agreement.

THINKING POINT

Which property is Brian letting to Trevor?

Brian is letting Flat 4, The Warren, to Trevor.

THINKING POINT

What is the term of the tenancy—that is for how long is the tenancy to be held?

The tenancy is for a term of ten years. The term is fixed, in that it has a certain start date and a certain end date. Note that, after the tenancy has come to an end, there is a provision for a monthly periodic tenancy. Remember that certainty of term is one of the essential requirements of a tenancy (see 5.5.1).

THINKING POINT

How much is the rent and when is it payable?

The rent is £1,000 per month, payable in advance—that is, at the beginning of each payment period—on the 17th of every month.

THINKING POINT

Can you see the tenant's covenants?

The tenant's covenants (see 5.6.2) begin at clause 2: 'THE tenant agrees with the landlord …'

These covenants are fairly standard. They include provision that the tenant (Trevor) will pay rent (clause 2(1)), Council Tax (clause 2(2)(a)), gas and electricity bills (clause 2(3)), etc. They also provide that Trevor will keep the interior of the property in good condition, but that he does not have to leave the property in a better condition at the end of the tenancy than that in which it was at the beginning (clause 2(4)).

The tenant's covenants also include giving the landlord permission to enter and inspect the premises at reasonable times, and with appropriate notice (clause 2(5)).

There are also some things that Trevor cannot do with the property. For example, he cannot sublet it—that is, let it out to another tenant—without the landlord's permission (clause 2(9)), nor can he do anything that may be a nuisance to his neighbours (clause 2(8)).

In this tenancy, the covenants are contained in the body of the agreement. Sometimes—particularly in more complicated, or commercial, tenancies—the covenants are set out in schedules that are attached to the tenancy.

THINKING POINT

Can you see the landlord's covenants?

The landlord's covenants (see 5.6.1) begin at clause 4: 'THE Landlord agrees with the tenant …'

These covenants are fairly short in this tenancy agreement, but include the provision that the tenant may enjoy the property with quiet enjoyment—that is, without interruption (disturbance) from the landlord. The tenancy also confers exclusive possession of the tenanted premises on Trevor—another essential element of a tenancy (see 5.5.3).

Remember as well that the law implies certain covenants into a tenancy agreement (see 5.6).

THINKING POINT

Is there anything in the tenancy that provides for what will happen if the tenant breaches a covenant—for example, if Trevor does not pay his rent?

Clause 3 says that, if Trevor is at least fourteen days late with his rent or breaks any of the other covenants, then Brian can repossess the property and the tenancy will come to an end. This is called a forfeiture clause.

THINKING POINT

Does this tenancy need to be registered?

Because this is a tenancy for more than seven years, it must be registered whether or not the land-lord's estate is registered—LRA 2002, ss. 4(2)(b) and 27(2)(b). Once it has been registered and because it has been made by deed, it will be a legal tenancy, complying with LPA 1925, s. 52(1).

5.9 Ending a lease

Once the lease has ended, the tenant ceases to have any interest in the leased property: it reverts back to the landlord in its entirety. If the tenant stays on in the property without the landlord's permission, the landlord can take legal steps to remove the ex-tenant from the property.

Some fixed-period leases simply end with the passing of time. When the period for which the lease has been granted reaches an end, it automatically terminates. Many leases, however, require notice to be given, in accordance with the terms of the lease agreement. This is true of private, residential leases, which are now fairly heavily regulated by statute.

We have also seen that, if a fixed lease ends and the tenant stays on with the landlord's permission, a periodic tenancy is created. This continues until one or the other side gives notice that he or she intends to terminate the tenancy. As discussed at 5.3.2.2, the notice period will be defined by the intervals at which rent has been agreed to be paid.

The tenant can bring the lease to an end either by express or implied **surrender**, which effectively means that he gives the property back to the landlord. The tenant usually achieves this by vacating the property and the landlord has to accept the surrender.

> **surrender**
> the giving up of a tenant's interest in a property to his or her landlord, which might be in the form of a deed (express) or as a consequence of the actions of both parties (implied)

Finally, remembering that a lease has its roots in contract law, it appears that a lease may also be terminated according to contractual principles. This can be achieved by **repudiation** of the lease agreement—that is, if one of the fundamental terms of the contract is to be breached. In *Hussein v. Mehlman* [1992] 2 EGLR 87, the court held that a landlord's continuing breach of his covenant to repair the premises allowed the tenant to repudiate the contract.

> **repudiation** an indication that a breach of contract will occur in the future, leading to the end of that contract

It also appears that a lease can be terminated by the doctrine of **frustration** —[1981] AC 675.

> **frustration** the termination of a contract as a result of an event that renders its performance impossible or illegal, or otherwise prevents its fulfilment

5.10 Commonhold

Commonhold is a relatively new development in land law. It is aimed at those people who own long leases of properties in a building in which there are a number of such leasehold properties, such as an old house that is subdivided into flats, which are held on long leases, or a block of leasehold flats or offices.

> **commonhold**
> a way of owning property that features shared areas, for which ownership needs to remain in central ownership and maintenance

Before the Commonhold and Leasehold Reform Act 2002 (CLRA 2002), the leaseholders of the individual units of property had no choice other than to pay ground rent to the freeholder who still owned the property as a whole. They would also have to pay a service charge to repair and maintain the property, but often would have little say in how their money was spent.

The legislation gives leaseholders in this situation the opportunity to obtain the freehold of their individual property and, collectively, to buy the freehold of the property as a whole. This gives them the opportunity to have a say in how the common parts of the property are maintained and so gives them more control over how their money is spent.

We will now look at the legislative detail of the scheme.

CLRA 2002, s. 1(1) sets out three requirements that must be met for the land to be commonhold.

 STATUTE

Commonhold and Leasehold Reform Act 2002, s. 1(1)

Land is commonhold land if—

(a) the freehold estate in the land is registered as a freehold estate in commonhold land

(b) the land is specified in the memorandum of association of a commonhold association as the land in relation to which the association is to exercise functions, and

(c) a commonhold community statement makes provision for rights and duties of the commonhold association and unit-holders (whether or not the statement has come into force).

commonhold association

the formal body that commonhold leaseholders must establish to manage the common parts of the property so held

The land, as a whole, must therefore be registered land. The leaseholders then need to set up a **commonhold association**.

This is effectively the group that will manage the common parts of the property. It operates as a management company and must be formally set up, which means that it must be limited by guarantee and registered at Companies House—CLRA 2002, s. 34.

This company is responsible for establishing a reserve fund to maintain the property. To do this, the individual leaseholders will pay service charges, much as they did before—but now they will have more control over how their money is spent. The association must also produce a commonhold community statement, the form of which is governed by CLRA 2002, s. 31. It must fundamentally define the land to be managed by the association, and set out its rights and duties.

If the leaseholders comply with these requirements, they can apply to the Land Registrar to register their commonhold as 'a freehold estate in commonhold land'—CLRA 2002, s. 2(1). In order to register the title, the leaseholders must obtain the consent of the registered proprietor of the freehold of the land (or part of it), the registered proprietors of any leaseholds of over twenty-one years in length, anyone with a charge over the land (so, for example, a mortgagee), and other classes of person that may be prescribed.

If all of the necessary formal requirements have been carried out, the commonhold estate will be registered, both in its own right and on the register entries of the individual proprietors of the property.

As you will see in Chapter 12, there are difficulties involved in enforcing freehold covenants on subsequent owners of land. One of the key advantages of the new scheme is that, when an individual property is sold, any of the rights and duties imposed on the original commonhold owner will be automatically transferred to the new commonhold owner, making life a lot easier for all involved.

Summary

1. A lease confers an estate in the land, for a certain period.

2. A lease is a hybrid of contract and proprietary interest.

3. A lease can be legal or equitable, depending on its method of creation.

4. There are various different types of lease, but they all share the same essential characteristics: that the tenant receives exclusive possession for a certain term.

5. Rent is not an essential element, although it is usually present and is indicative of a lease.

6. Even though all of the essential elements of a lease are present, it may still be a licence if there is no intention to create legal relations, or if there is a service occupancy, or—possibly—if the grantor lacks the estate to grant a lease.

7. Leases contain covenants, which impose various obligations on both landlord and tenant.

8. There are rules governing the enforcement of covenants for which the original landlord has assigned his reversionary interest or the original tenant has assigned his tenancy. The rules differ depending on whether the lease came into being before or from 1 January 1996.

9. A lease can be terminated by the passing of time, giving appropriate notice, surrender by the tenant, and the contractual principles of repudiation and frustration.

10. Commonhold is a new kind of landholding that allows owners of leasehold property to obtain the freehold of their individual property and (collectively) of the whole property.

11. Commonhold assists with the transfer of covenants to subsequent owners.

The bigger picture

- If you want to see how this area of land law fits into the rest of your studies, you can look at Chapter 14, especially 14.4.

- For some guidance on what sort of exam questions come up in this area, see Chapter 15, 15.7.

- The Mortgage Repossessions (Protection of Tenants etc.) Act 2010 offers some protection to the tenant in situations where a homeowner (mortgagor) has let the property to the tenant without the permission of the bank who is the mortgagee of the property, and the bank is trying to repossess the property.

- Read more about this at: http://www.communities.gov.uk/publications/housing/mortgagerepossessionguidance.

- Read more about mortgages in Chapter 13.

? Questions

Self-test questions

1. How is a valid legal lease created? What happens if the formal requirements are not carried out?

2. Sasha and Michael move into a one-bedroom flat together. They are a little concerned about two clauses in their 'licence agreement': that the owner of the property reserves the right to move in with them at any time and that they must vacate their premises between 10.30 a.m. and noon each day. Advise Sasha and Michael.

3. Halle has just moved into a new rented flat. She is a little confused about some of the clauses in the lease. Explain to Halle the meaning of the terms 'quiet enjoyment' and 'waste'. If she assigns her interest to Brendan, will he also be bound by the covenants?

Exam question

1. What are the essential characteristics of a lease? If all of these are present, will a lease always be created?

 For suggested approaches to answering these questions visit the Online Resource Centre.

≡ Further reading

Baker, A., 'Bruton, licensees in possession and a fiction of title' [2014] Conv 495
A thoughtful re-interpretation of *Bruton*, based on the premise that consensual possession is a root of title.

Bright, S., 'Avoiding tenancy legislation: sham and contracting out revisited' [2002] CLJ 146
A look at the courts' approach to the attempts of landlords to avoid creating tenancies.

Clarke, D., 'The enactment of commonhold: problems, principles and perspectives' [2002] Conv 349
An analysis of the CLRA 2002.

Lower, M., 'The Bruton Tenancy' [2010] Conv 38
This article looks at the idea of the non-proprietary lease, particularly in *Bruton* and its application in subsequent cases.

Smith, P., 'The purity of commonholds' [2004] Conv 194
This article examines the relationship between leases and commonholds.

Street v. Mountford **[1985] AC 809**
It really is worth reading this case in its entirety.

@ Online Resource Centre

www.oxfordtextbooks.co.uk/orc/clarke_directions5e/

For more advice relating to this chapter, including self-test questions and an interactive glossary, visit the Online Resource Centre.

6 Adverse possession

□ **LEARNING OBJECTIVES**

By the end of this chapter, you will be able to:

- explain what is meant by 'adverse possession';
- understand the rationale for adverse possession;
- distinguish between the old law and the new law in this area;
- understand the law under the Land Registration Act 2002.

Introduction

If you want to see how controversial and important the law on adverse possession has been in the recent past, you need look no further than the leading case in the area. In the case of *J. A. Pye (Oxford) Ltd and Others v. Graham and Another* [2002] UKHL 30 *(Pye v. Graham)*, the Grahams, who were farmers, had been using land belonging to a development company (Pye Ltd) to graze their cattle for many years. When Pye Ltd finally wanted to build on the land, the Grahams refused to leave. Pye Ltd sued them in the High Court, but lost, so they appealed to the Court of Appeal, and won. The Grahams then appealed to the House of Lords—and they won! The land, now worth some £10m, belonged to the Grahams, who had used it without paying rent for years, and who now owned it outright. Dismayed, Pye Ltd took its case to the European Court of Human Rights (*J. A. Pye v. United Kingdom,* Application No. 44302/02, 15 November 2005 *(Pye v. United Kingdom)*), where it was held that its human rights had been breached. This would not get Pye Ltd the land back, but it looked forward to compensation from the UK government. Unfortunately for Pye Ltd, the government appealed to the Grand Chamber, which reversed the previous decision (*J. A. Pye v. United Kingdom, Application No. 44302/02, 30 August 2007 (Pye v. United Kingdom)*). Pye Ltd, once the owner of a valuable piece of development land, was left with no land and no compensation—as well as a huge legal bill. How could such a case come about?

This remarkable (and expensive) litigation arose because of the law of adverse possession. This essentially deals with what most people refer to as 'squatters' rights'. It is about squatters taking possession of land without the consent of the owner, which may ultimately lead to the paper owner losing his or her estate to the squatter.

The whole concept of adverse possession seems very strange to most people. In effect, it makes lawful the 'stealing' of land by someone who has no documentary title to it. This raises the question of why the law should allow a squatter to claim ownership of land simply because he or she is in possession of it.

The situation described here is extreme: most adverse possession is on a smaller scale and, indeed, it is not always a hostile act. Small areas of land often 'move' between owners when boundary fences are replaced or realigned, and this may happen by mistake rather than by design. The rules of adverse possession are very old and were originally developed under the common law, but the current law can now be found mainly in the Limitation Act 1980 and the Land Registration Act 2002. In this chapter we will first have a look at why the law permits adverse possession and then look at the detailed rules. Because the law has changed recently, we will need to look at both the old and the new laws. Suffice to say, it has become more difficult to obtain property by adverse possession and, sadly for squatters like the Grahams, the days of acquiring valuable development land for nothing are probably over.

6.1 Reasons for allowing adverse possession

adverse possession

the possession of land by someone other than the registered proprietor or unregistered owner, without that proprietor or owner's consent

limitation period

statutory time limit after which no action to reclaim land under adverse possession can be started

squatter

a person in adverse possession of land

paper owner

the person who holds the documentary title—the 'papers'—to the land

One argument in favour of **adverse possession** is that there has to be a cut-off point in any legal action. You may remember from studying contract law that a person cannot sue on a contract after six years, because at that point the claim becomes stale. In the same way, there has to be some point at which a landowner is too late to claim land back from someone who has been in possession of it for a long time.

Most people would agree that, if someone has been peacefully in possession of a piece of land for many years, it would be too late for someone else to wave a piece of paper claiming title and get the land back. In fact, the **limitation period** for reclaiming land is currently usually twelve years for unregistered land and registered land adversely possessed before 13 October 2003 (see 6.9.2). For registered land adversely possessed after that date, there is no period of limitation as such (see 6.9.2), but the **squatter** may apply to be registered after ten years of adverse possession.

Another argument is that land is a finite resource. If a landowner has not even noticed for many years that someone else is occupying his or her land, why should that person not make better use of it? The squatter might even have wanted to ask permission to use the land, but may not have known for sure who the **paper owner** was. Adverse possession provides a way for abandoned land to be brought into economic use again.

Everybody has heard the maxim 'possession is nine-tenths of the law' and, traditionally, English land law has paid great attention to possession. Any person in peaceful possession of land is treated as having good title to it unless someone else can show a better title—*Harrow London Borough Council v. Qazi* [2003] UKHL 43, [2004] 1 AC 983.

> **➡ EXAMPLE**
>
> Arif has been squatting on land for five years. Barbara tries to evict him from the land, claiming that he has no right to be there, because he is not the registered owner.
>
> Barbara is not entitled to succeed unless she can show a better claim to the land than Arif: for example, if she is the registered proprietor, or if she inherited the land under the will of the

registered proprietor, or she has been granted a lease by the registered proprietor. Barbara may even win if she shows that she adversely possessed the land in the past, by possessing it for twelve years.

It is not enough, however, for Barbara simply to show that Arif himself has no title. He is entitled to stay there until someone with a better right to possession comes along.

This aspect of the common law is sometimes called **relativity of title**. The courts looked at all rights to land as relative and would declare the person with the best title to be entitled to the land.

Adverse possession also plays a vital role in relation to unregistered land, in that peaceful possession will eventually cure any defects in title to land. As there is no definitive proof of title in unregistered land, a good root of title going back at least fifteen years is accepted as proof. If the current owner and any predecessors can show peaceful possession for at least twelve years under that title, the law of adverse possession means that the title can be regarded as safe.

relativity of title

the doctrine that all rights to land are relative and that the person with the best title will be entitled to the land

> **CROSS REFERENCE**
For more on establishing title in unregistered land, see Chapter 2.

6.2 Arguments against allowing adverse possession

Despite the long-standing common law protection of possession, there are convincing arguments against adverse possession in modern times.

The vast majority of titles to land are now registered and it is the fact of registration that confers legal title upon the landowner. This makes any argument that is based on relativity of title less convincing, because the register guarantees title.

A squatter can easily look up the proprietor in the register, which is now available online, and negotiate to buy, or lease, apparently unwanted land. Only if the registered proprietor has disappeared without trace is there much justification for simply moving in, tempting though it might be to do so.

These concerns about adverse possession in modern times were well expressed by Lord Bingham in *Pye v. Graham*.

Q CASE CLOSE-UP

Pye v. Graham [2002] UKHL 30

This case (discussed in more detail at 6.5.2.1) concerned the Grahams, farmers who adversely possessed grazing land belonging to an investment company, Pye Ltd.

In giving judgment for the Grahams, Lord Bingham criticized the law of adverse possession as it applied to registered land. He pointed out that the Grahams had been using the land for many years without paying any rent and now had become the owners of very valuable land—worth £10m—without having paid a penny for it, or having to compensate the paper owner in any way.

This does seem unfair. In registered land, if there is no doubt about who actually owns the land, there seems to be very little justification for such a result.

There have also been concerns about squatters moving into empty property such as houses await-ing renovation, or the homes of persons who have died. It can take the paper owners of such properties time and trouble to evict squatters, and the property may be damaged.

6.3 Changes to the law

In their joint report of 1998, the Law Commission and the Land Registry recognized the concerns about the justice of acquiring land by adverse possession in modern times, particularly when that land is registered. The reasons for adverse possession are discussed at paras 10.1–10.19 of the report and it was concluded that the law of adverse possession as it applies to registered land should be reformed. This was a major change in policy, because previously the law relating to registered and unregistered land had been kept as similar as possible. The Land Registration Act 2002 (LRA 2002) changed com-pletely the way in which title to registered land can be acquired by adverse possession.

Even more recently, the Legal Aid, Sentencing and Punishment of Offenders Act 2012 (LASPOA 2012), s. 144 made squatting in residential property a criminal act. This has an effect on gaining title to such land by adverse possession, which we will look at later (see 6.7).

Table 6.1 represents a summary of the relevant dates and provisions.

Table 6.1 A summary of the law of adverse possession

Type of land	Completion of limitation period	Relevant law
Unregistered	Since 1980	Limitation Act 1980
Registered	By 12 October 2003	Limitation Act 1980 and LRA 1925, s.75
Registered	From 13 October 2003	LRA 2002
Registered and unregistered residential buildings	From 1 September 2012	LASPOA 2012, s.144

6.4 The main statutory provisions

6.4.1 The Limitation Act 1980

The Limitation Act 1980 (LA 1980) applies to unregistered land whatever the date of adverse possession; it also applies to registered land if the required period of adverse possession was com-pleted before 13 October 2003—the date on which LRA 2002 came into force.

The LA 1980 works by preventing the paper owner from bringing an action to recover the land once the limitation period has passed. The Act was applied to registered land by the Land Registration Act 1925 (LRA 1925), s. 75 (see 6.9.2).

The main limitation periods are detailed in Table 6.2.

After the end of the limitation period, the paper owner can no longer go to court to recover the land, which means that the squatter can no longer be evicted.

Table 6.2 The main limitation periods

Land	Length of adverse possession required	Authority
Most land	12 years from moment of adverse possession by squatter	LA 1980, s. 15
Land owned by Crown (see for example *Roberts v. Swangrove Estates* [2008] EWCA Civ 98)	30 years, but 60 years if the land is foreshore	LA 1980, Sch.1, para. 11
Land held by a tenant under a lease	12 years as against tenant, but a further 12 years as against freeholder when lease comes to an end	*Chung Ping Kwang v. Lam Island Co. Ltd* [1997] AC 38

Note that the time does not stop running even when the squatter transfers the land to someone else, or a different squatter comes into possession, as long as there is no gap between the periods of adverse possession.

 EXAMPLE

Carrie goes into adverse possession of Dave's house.

Four years later, Carrie transfers such rights as she has in the house to Egon. Nine years later, Dave brings an action to evict Egon.

He will be too late, because Egon can add his period of adverse possession to that of Carrie. Egon will be entitled to Dave's land.

The statutory provisions setting out what is required in order to prove adverse possession are set out in LA 1980, Sch. 1, which establishes the time at which the limitation period starts to run. These provisions are explained at 6.5.

 STATUTE

Limitation Act 1980, Sch. 1, para. 1

Where the person bringing an action to recover land, or some person through whom he claims, has been in possession of the land, and has while entitled to the land been dispossessed or discontinued his possession, the right of action shall be treated as having accrued on the date of the dispossession or discontinuance.

STATUTE

Limitation Act 1980, Sch. 1, para. 8(1)

No right of action to recover land shall be treated as accruing unless the land is in the posses-sion of some person in whose favour the period of limitation can run (referred to below in this paragraph as 'adverse possession'); and where under the preceding provisions of this Schedule any such right of action is treated as accruing on a certain date and no person is in adverse possession on that date, the right of action shall not be treated as accruing unless and until adverse possession is taken of the land.

Adverse possession under the LA 1980 extinguishes the title of the paper owner under s. 17.

 STATUTE

Limitation Act 1980, s. 17 [Extinction of title to land after expiration of time limit]

Subject to—

   (a) section 18 of this Act; and

   …

at the expiration of the period prescribed by this Act for any person to bring an action to recover land (including a redemption action) the title of that person to the land shall be extinguished.

This means that the squatter becomes the owner of the land, but with no conveyance of land by the paper owner to the squatter. (The full effects of this are explained at 6.8.)

6.4.2 The Land Registration Act 1925

The main purpose of LRA 1925, s. 75 was to apply the LA 1980 to registered land. It now applies only when the period of limitation was already complete before 13 October 2003—the date on which the LRA 2002 came into force.

Where title to the adversely possessed land was registered, the extinguishing effect of LA 1980, s. 17 presented some problems. The title of the paper owner could not simply vanish, because it was still on the register. Once adverse possession had been established, the squatter could apply to be registered as a proprietor; but what happened in the meantime, after the limitation period had been completed and before the squatter had been registered as proprietor? How were the conflicting titles of the registered proprietor and the squatter to be resolved?

The answer was provided by LRA 1925, s. 75.

 STATUTE

Land Registration Act 1925, s. 75 [Acquisition of title by possession]

   (1) The Limitation Acts shall apply to registered land in the same manner and to the same extent as those Acts apply to land not registered, except that where, if the land were not registered, the estate of the person registered as proprietor would be extinguished, such estate shall not be extinguished but shall be deemed to be held by the proprietor for the time being on trust for the person who, by virtue of the said Acts, has acquired title against any proprietor, but without prejudice to the estates and interests of any other person interested in the land whose estate or interest is not extinguished by those Acts.

(2) Any person claiming to have acquired a title under the Limitation Acts may apply to be registered as proprietor thereof.

...

As can be seen from this section, the paper owner's title was not extinguished, but was instead held on trust for the squatter. (The full effects of this are explained at 6.9.2.1.)

6.4.3 The Land Registration Act 2002

LRA 2002, ss. 96–98 apply to registered land when the limitation period under the LA 1980 has not been completed before 13 October 2003. In other words, unless there were twelve years of adverse possession before that date, the new law applies to registered land.

 STATUTE

Land Registration Act 2002, s. 96 [Disapplication of periods of limitation]

(1) No period of limitation under section 15 of the Limitation Act 1980 (c. 58) (time limits in relation to recovery of land) shall run against any person, other than a chargee, in relation to an estate in land or rentcharge the title to which is registered.

(2) No period of limitation under section 16 of that Act (time limits in relation to redemption of land) shall run against any person in relation to such an estate in land or rentcharge.

(3) Accordingly, section 17 of that Act (extinction of title on expiry of time limit) does not operate to extinguish the title of any person where, by virtue of this section, a period of limitation does not run against him.

The most fundamental change made by this section is that there is no longer an automatic barring of title by adverse possession. This means that adverse possession, of itself, does not bar the registered proprietor's title; instead, after being in adverse possession for ten years, the squatter can apply to be registered as the proprietor. Until such an application is made, the squatter has no rights in the land and can usually be evicted by the registered proprietor. (More details are set out at 6.9.1.2.)

6.4.4 The Legal Aid, Sentencing and Punishment of Offenders Act 2012

LASPOA 2012, s. 144 makes squatting in residential premises a criminal offence. This does not prevent the squatter from claiming adverse possession (*Best v. Chief Land Registrar* [2015] EWCA Civ 17) but naturally it will act as a deterrent. (For more details see 6.7.)

6.5 What does a squatter need to show to make a claim to the land?

No matter which set of legislation applies, there are certain points that must be established before a person can be said to be in adverse possession of someone else's land. They apply equally to registered and unregistered land and to both the old regime under the LA 1980 and the new regime under the LRA 2002—see LRA 2002, Sch. 6, para. 1.

6.5.1 Discontinuance or dispossession

Under LA 1980, Sch. 1, para. 1, time starts to run when the paper owner is dispossessed or when the paper owner discontinues his or her possession.

In most cases, there will be a **dispossession** rather than a **discontinuance**, because the courts accept that even very slight acts by the paper owner will negate any claim of discontinuance. For example, in *Powell v. MacFarlane* (1979) 38 P & CR 452, there was no discontinuance when the paper owner drove to the land and looked at it from a car.

> **dispossession** the act of being dispossessed—that is, of another person assuming ordinary possession of the land
>
> **discontinuance** the act of giving up possession, often an act of simply abandoning the land

Dispossession was defined by Slade J in *Powell v. MacFarlane*, as taking of possession from another without the other's licence or consent. Before 1833, dispossession had to be an 'ouster' by the squatter—an old word that means a forcible ejection of the true owner.

The modern law was clarified in *Pye v. Graham* (see 6.5.2.1), in which Lord Browne-Wilkinson said (at [38]) that there will be dispossession where the squatter 'assumes possession in the ordinary sense of the word'. Therefore, all that is required is that the squatter goes into ordinary possession of the land, because the paper owner cannot be in possession at the same time as the squatter. By definition, if the squatter is in possession, he or she must have dispossessed the paper owner.

6.5.2 Adverse possession

As well as there being a discontinuance or dispossession, another person (the squatter) must have gone into adverse possession—LA 1980, Sch. 1, para. 8(1). If the land simply remains unoccupied, the limitation period will not start to run.

It is therefore important to define adverse possession, so that both the start and end of the limitation period can be established. This is essential to knowing when title is extinguished under the LA 1980, or when the squatter is entitled to apply to be registered as proprietor under the LRA 2002.

LA 1980, Sch. 1, para. 1 defines adverse possession as when 'the land is in the possession of some person in whose favour the period of limitation can run'. Possession itself is not defined in the Act, but has been considered by case law. The leading case is the decision of the House of Lords in *Pye v. Graham*, in which Lord Browne-Wilkinson expressly approved the judgment of Slade J in *Powell v. MacFarlane* and adopted the definition of possession as set out in that case.

CASE CLOSE-UP

Powell v. MacFarlane (1979) 38 P & CR 452

The land in question was rough land bought originally to grow Christmas trees. The owner went abroad and, apart from occasional brief visits, did nothing with the land from 1956 to 1973.

The claimant, who was aged 14 at the time, started to use the land to graze his cow, go shooting, store trees prior to taking them to timber mills, and clearing and fencing work.

Slade J identified three main elements to adverse possession:

- the required degree of exclusive physical possession (occupation or control) of the land;
- an intention to possess the land to the exclusion of all others, including the paper owner, sometimes referred to as *animus possidendi*;
- an absence of consent by the paper owner (the paper owner did not give permission for the squatter to be on the land).

It was held that the claimant was not in adverse possession, because, although he had physical possession of the land without the consent of the owner, he lacked the *animus possidendi*—the necessary intention to possess.

Each of these three elements will now be considered in more depth.

6.5.2.1 Physical possession

Physical possession of land is a question of degree, and the necessary degree will be determined partly by the nature of the land.

physical possession
actual occupation or control of land

The degree of occupation and control that will be necessary to show possession of a residential property will be very different to that required to show possession of a tract of open moorland.

 CASE CLOSE-UP

Red House Farms (Thorndon) Ltd v. Catchpole [1977] 2 EGLR 125

The land in question was marshland. The only sensible use anyone could suggest for it was shooting over it. The defendant, Mrs Catchpole, used it for that purpose and, at all material times, the only access to the land in question was through her land.

This was held by the Court of Appeal to be a high enough degree of exclusive physical control.

CASE CLOSE-UP

Tecbild Ltd v. Chamberlain (1969) 20 P & CR 633

In contrast, allowing children to play on undeveloped land, and tethering and exercising ponies there, were held to be insufficient to establish adverse possession.

The Court of Appeal described them as 'trivial acts of trespass', which did not suffice for adverse possession.

In *Prudential Assurance v. Waterloo* (1999) 17 EG 131, the land in question was one face of a wall: decorating the wall, and attaching lights and an entryphone system established its possession.

In *Buckinghamshire County Council v. Moran* [1990] Ch 623 (see 6.5.2.2), the defendant incorporated into his garden a piece of land that had been acquired by the council for road widening. He maintained fences, locked gates, and cultivated the land. This was held by the Court of Appeal to be a sufficient degree of physical control to amount to possession.

Physical possession also means treating the land exactly as an owner would treat it. This was held in the leading case of *Pye v. Graham*.

🔍 CASE CLOSE-UP

Pye v. Graham [2002] UKHL 30

The grazing land in question had been bought by Pye Ltd, a property investment company. It did not have an immediate use for the land, which had been bought in the expectation that it could eventually be used for housing. In the meantime, Pye Ltd initially granted grazing licences to the Grahams, who farmed the adjoining land.

In December 1983, the last of these licences came to an end and was not renewed. The Grahams continued to graze cattle on the land.

The last contact between the Grahams and Pye Ltd. was in August 1984. From September 1984, the Grahams grazed cattle on the land, took crops of hay, manured the land, maintained hedges and ditches, and generally farmed the land as they had before. They had the only key to the gate, so Pye Ltd could not have obtained access without the Grahams' cooperation.

The House of Lords, reversing the Court of Appeal's decision, held that the Grahams *had* adversely possessed the land, so that Pye Ltd could not reclaim it when it started possession proceedings in April 1998.

Lord Browne-Wilkinson made it clear that there does not need to be any special type of possession to make it *'adverse'*. He said (at [36]):

> The question is simply whether the defendant squatter has dispossessed the paper owner by going into ordinary possession of the land for the requisite period without the consent of the owner.

Fencing is usually good evidence of physical control. In both *Pye v. Graham* and *Buckinghamshire County Council v. Moran*, the land was fenced off from others.

In *George Wimpey and Co. Ltd v. Sohn* [1967] Ch 487, Russell LJ said that it was in exceptional cases only that enclosure (fencing) of the land would not indicate adverse possession. In that particular case, it did not, because an easement to use the fenced land as a garden was established and that explained the fencing. If others are allowed to come and go freely through the land, there is unlikely to be the required degree of physical control—*Battersea v. Wandsworth* (2001) 19 EG 148. However, the land does not need to be fully enclosed; an unlocked gate will not be fatal to a claim of adverse possession if there is otherwise a sufficient degree of control: *Greenmanor Ltd v. Pilford* [2012] EWCA Civ 756.

Other actions that have been held to indicate exclusive physical control include controlling who may squat in a dwelling house, changing the locks, putting up 'no trespassing' signs, erecting buildings or fixtures on the land, and paying council tax. It is impossible to give a complete list: the important thing is to look for a sufficient degree of physical occupation and control, the nature of which will vary with the type of land in question.

6.5.2.2 Intention to possess (*animus possidendi*)

The squatter must have *animus possidendi:* intention to possess the land to the exclusion of all others, including the paper owner.

> *animus possidendi*
> an intention to possess the land to the exclusion of all others

---

Q | CASE CLOSE-UP

Powell v. MacFarlane (1979) 38 P & CR 452

Slade J described *animus possidendi* as follows (at 471):

> animus possidendi involves the intention, in one's own name and on one's own behalf, to exclude the world at large, including the owner with the paper title if he be not himself the possessor, so far as is reasonably practicable and so far as the processes of the law will allow.

The claimant was unable to establish the relevant intention to possess when he first entered the disputed land. He was only 14 years old at the time and Slade J found that he did not intend to possess the land, but simply to use it for grazing his family's cows. Such use may give rise to an easement or profit à prendre in the right circumstances, but it is not a sufficient intention for adverse possession.

> **CROSS REFERENCE**
> For more on easements and profits à prendre, see Chapter 11.

It is clear that intention is a separate requirement from that of physical control of the land. Lord Browne-Wilkinson reiterated this point in *Pye v. Graham*, at [40]. He compared someone staying overnight in a house, such as a friend looking after the house while the owner is away, with a squatter staying overnight at the house: both are in possession of the house, but the friend has the intention to take care of the house, not to take adverse possession of it.

Despite the fact that they are separate requirements, however, intention is proven primarily by what the squatter does on the land, rather than by what his or her intentions were declared to be. It is clear from the case law that evidence of exclusive physical control of land also goes to show evidence of intention to possess the land.

Q | CASE CLOSE-UP

Buckinghamshire County Council v. Moran [1990] 1 Ch 623

The claimant council was the paper owner of a strip of land bought many years before for road widening. The defendant's predecessor in title had incorporated the land into his garden in 1967 and the house was sold to the defendant with such rights as they had acquired over the extra land.

The defendant bought the house in 1971 and padlocked the gate leading from the road to the extra land, so that the access to the land was only though his garden. He cultivated the land, mowing the lawn, laying flowerbeds, etc.

In 1976, the council became aware of his use of the land and there was some correspondence, in which the defendant claimed the right to use the land until it was needed for widening and stated that he was consulting his lawyers. The council responded by saying that the defendant had no right to use the land, to which he replied claiming adverse possession. Nothing further happened until 1985, when the council began possession proceedings. The Court of Appeal held that this was too late, and that the land had been adversely possessed by the defendant.

The Court's reasons were that the defendant had acquired complete physical possession of the land and annexed it to his own land by October 1973. His actions unequivocally showed his intention to possess the land. The defendant had enclosed the land fully, so that access was only via his garden, and he had locked the gate that kept out everyone, including the council.

The Court also considered whether the required intention was to own the land, or simply to possess it as long as possible. They made it quite clear that intention to possess is required, not intention to own. As Slade LJ said (at 643), the required intention is 'an intention for the time being to possess the land to the exclusion of all other persons, including the owner with the paper title'.

It was also held that knowledge of the paper owner's future use of the land (in this case, the road widening) will not prevent the trespasser forming an intention to possess it.

 THINKING POINT

What do you think showed the defendant's intention to possess? What had he done to the land to indicate his intention?

As can be seen from the *Moran* case, the same acts that show physical possession often show intention to possess as well. For example, fencing is usually good evidence of intention to possess— but, if a different explanation for fencing can be found, it may negative that finding. In *Inglewood Investment Co. Ltd v. Baker* [2003] 2 P & CR 23, for example, it was found that the fence was to keep in sheep rather than to establish possession.

In *Pye v. Graham* the House of Lords considered whether the Grahams' willingness to have paid for a new grazing licence, if one had been offered, negated an intention to possess. It was held that it did not. This decision supports the fact that the squatter needs only to show an intention to keep possession for as long as the law allows. If the paper owner takes action within the limitation period, the squatter will have no option other than to pay for the use of the land, or to leave. In *Alston v. BOCM Pauls Ltd* [2008] EWHC 3310 (Ch), the squatter farmed the land in question. He did not think much about whether he had any right to be there, but he intended to stay there as long as he could and would not have left unless compelled to do so. This was held to be sufficient intention to possess.

6.5.2.3 Without consent

Possession cannot be adverse if the claimant is on the land with the consent of the landowner.

The Court of Appeal in *Parshall v. Hackney* [2013] EWCA Civ 240 held that a person who is the registered proprietor of land cannot maintain a claim for adverse possession of it, even if his registration as proprietor was made in error. This may be related to the idea that adverse possession must be 'adverse' in the sense of 'without consent'.

There are a number of particular situations in which people are on land with consent and the problem is usually to try to spot when that consent comes to an end, so that adverse possession can start.

Tenancies

⟩ CROSS REFERENCE

For more on leases and tenancies, see Chapter 5.

Anyone occupying land as a tenant cannot be in adverse possession. A tenant cannot adversely possess land that is the subject of the tenancy, because that would be to deny his or her landlord's title, which the tenant cannot do. Once the lease has ended, however, the tenant who stays in possession of the land can be in adverse possession of it.

In the case of an oral or implied periodic tenancy (one that has been created without writing, or one implied by law through the payment of rent) LA 1980, Sch. 1, para. 5(1) and (2) provides that time starts to run from the end of the first year or other period, or, if rent is received after that date, from the date of the last receipt of rent.

 EXAMPLE

Gerald moves into Hill House, which is owned by Jack. There is no written lease, but Gerald pays Jack £100 per month. Jack goes away on an extended holiday, so Gerald decides to stop paying the rent.

Clearly, while Gerald is paying rent to Jack, he is not in adverse possession of Hill House and the limitation period cannot start to run. Once Gerald stops paying rent, however, the limitation period will begin on the date of the last receipt of rent by Jack.

A former tenant who is given permission to stay on at the end of a tenancy will not be in adverse possession, because he or she has the consent of the landlord to be there.

Interestingly, however, if the tenant goes into possession of other land near to the leased land, whether it belongs to the landlord or someone else, there will be a presumption that the land is being acquired for the landlord, rather than for the tenant.

 CASE CLOSE-UP

London Borough of Tower Hamlets v. Barrett [2005] EWCA Civ 923

In this case, a piece of wasteland next to a pub was adversely possessed by the tenant of the pub.

It was held that the tenant acquired it on behalf of his landlord, the freeholder. The landlord transferred the freehold of the pub to the tenant and this operated to transfer the adversely possessed land as well. The council, the paper owner of the wasteland, was unable to reclaim it.

The presumption is rebuttable: if the land is a long way away from the demised (tenanted) land, it is more likely that the tenant will be held to have acquired it on his own behalf.

Trustees

A trustee cannot acquire title by adverse possession against a beneficiary—LA 1980, s. 22(2). This will also mean that one co-owner of property cannot acquire title against the other by adverse possession.

⏵ **CROSS REFERENCE**
For more on co-ownership, see Chapter 8.

Licences

It is quite clear that if someone is in possession of someone else's land with their permission, then their possession is not adverse. Such permission is referred to as a licence. There are a number of different situations in which a licence can arise.

⏵ **CROSS REFERENCE**
For a comparison of licences with leases, see Chapter 5.

Vendor and purchaser licences

The standard conditions of sale under which most land is sold provide that a purchaser who is allowed into possession before the transfer has taken place is there as a licensee of the vendor. Clearly, such a licensee cannot claim adverse possession against the vendor if the land is never transferred as intended. However, there are cases in which this term of the contract is absent or varied, and in these cases a different answer may be reached. See the Online Resource Centre for more details.

Express licences

CROSS REFERENCE

For more on licences, see Chapter 5.

An express licence is one that is deliberately created by a landowner in favour of some other person. Since licences are not proprietary interests and can be created without formality, it can be quite difficult to be sure when a licence has been granted and whether or not it has been revoked.

In *Pye v. Graham*, the Grahams originally occupied the land under a series of licences. These licences were in writing and were expressly limited to eleven months. It was therefore easy to establish that the last licence came to an end on a certain date and that possession after that date could be regarded as adverse. This, however, will not necessarily be the case if an open-ended licence is given.

 CASE CLOSE-UP

Trustees of Grantham Christian Fellowship v. Scouts Association [2005] EWHC 209 (Ch)

There were two pieces of adjoining land: one owned by the Scouts and one by a church. The church left its land undeveloped and granted a licence to the Scouts to use it, provided that they kept it tidy. The Scouts occupied it from 1959 until 2002, using it for recreation. They also built a rockery and a shed on it. There were changes in the Scout leaders during that time and the original licence was all but forgotten. When the Scouts tried to claim ownership of the land by adverse possession, however, Blackburne J held that the licence had never been revoked, so that their possession was never adverse.

The licence was not like the one in *Pye v. Graham*: it did not require the payment of rent and it did not have a fixed end date. Therefore, it could be held to be still in existence despite many years passing.

The grant of a licence means that the possession is not adverse, so the question arises whether the paper owner can unilaterally grant a licence to a squatter in order to prevent or stop the limitation period from running.

CASE CLOSE-UP

BP Properties v. Buckler [1987] 2 EGLR 168

A licence was granted without rent to a disabled woman who would not leave the property, essentially because BP had received very bad publicity after its attempts to evict the woman and her family from their home. She did not reply to the offer of licence, but continued to live in the house with her son. After her death, her son claimed the house by adverse possession.

It was held that Mrs Buckler had been a licensee, even though she had not formally accepted the licence. Dillon LJ held that Mrs Buckler should have replied to the letter, refusing the licence.

Therefore, the claim to adverse possession failed.

The decision in *BP Properties v. Buckler* is surprising, because it means that if a paper owner offers a squatter a licence, the onus is on the squatter to reject it in order to stay in adverse possession.

Implied licences

An implied licence is one which is not expressly granted, but which was implied by the law because the actions of the squatter were not inconsistent with the future plans of the owner: *Leigh v. Jack* (1879) 5 Ex D 264. It was held that uses of land that do not interfere, and are consistent, with the uses to which the paper owner wants to put the land are not acts of dispossession and do not provide evidence of discontinuance of possession by the paper owner.

For example, in *Wallis's Cayton Bay Holiday Camp v. Shell-Mex* [1975] QB 94, it was held that using land as part of the frontage to a holiday camp was by implied licence of the paper owner as it did not conflict with their future intended use of the land.

As you can appreciate, this would make it very difficult to claim adverse possession unless the squatter were to do something radical to the land, such as building on it.

This doctrine of implied licence was expressly overruled in LA 1980, Sch. 1, para. 8(4).

 STATUTE

Limitation Act 1980, Sch. 1, para. 8(4)

For the purpose of determining whether a person occupying any land is in adverse possession of the land it shall not be assumed by implication of law that his occupation is by permission of the person entitled to the land merely by virtue of the fact that his occupation is not inconsistent with the latter's present or future enjoyment of the land.

This provision shall not be taken as prejudicing a finding to the effect that a person's occupation of any land is by implied permission of the person entitled to the land in any case where such a finding is justified on the actual facts of the case.

In *Buckinghamshire County Council v. Moran* (see 6.5.2.2) the Court of Appeal held that the intentions of the future owner were irrelevant in deciding whether the squatter's possession of the land was adverse. The House of Lords further endorsed this decision in *Pye v. Graham*, in which the reasoning in *Leigh v. Jack* was expressly overruled and the future intentions of the paper owner were held to be irrelevant to adverse possession.

At this point, it seemed very clear that the doctrine of implied licence played no part in the law—but there were further developments, based on the Human Rights Act 1998 (HRA 1998), which brought this doctrine briefly back into play again, and which we discuss below.

6.6 Human rights

For a more detailed discussion of the law in this area, see the Online Resource Centre.

The brief revival of the doctrine of implied licence was directly due to the influence of human rights law on adverse possession and in particular European Convention on Human Rights (ECHR), Protocol 1, Art. 1.

STATUTE

European Convention on Human Rights, Protocol 1, Art. 1

Every natural or legal person is entitled to the peaceful enjoyment of his possessions except in the public interest and subject to the conditions provided for by law and by the general principles of international law.

The preceding provisions shall not, however, in any way impair the right of a State to enforce such laws as it deems necessary to control the use of property in accordance with the general interest or to secure the payment of taxes or other contributions or penalties.

The issue was raised before the House of Lords in *Pye v. Graham*, but because that case was decided before the HRA 1998 came into effect (2 October 2000), the House of Lords could not consider the point. When Pye Ltd eventually lost its land to the Grahams, however, it took its case to the European Court of Human Rights (ECtHR) in Strasbourg, to try to get compensation from the UK government for its loss. (That decision is discussed in later in this section.)

In the meantime, another adverse possession case was heard in the English courts after the HRA 1998 had come into force: *Beaulane Properties v. Palmer* [2005] EWHC 1071 (Ch), in which it was held that the law on adverse possession under the LA 1980 as it applied to registered land was contrary to ECHR, Protocol 1, Art. 1. Nicholas Strauss QC held that the correct course of action was to interpret the law so as to accord with human rights, as he had the power to do under HRA 1998, s. 3. After a careful consideration of the history of adverse possession, he concluded that he should reintroduce the idea of implied licence, by reading the LA 1980 as if Sch. 1, para. 8(4) had not been enacted. This essentially resurrected the rule in *Leigh v. Jack* for cases in which adverse possession of registered land occurred between 2 October 2000 (the date when the HRA 1998 came into force) and 12 October 2003 (after which the new law on adverse possession in the LRA 2002 became effective).

The first decision of the ECtHR in *Pye v. United Kingdom*, Application No. 44302/02, 15 November 2005 partially vindicated the decision of Nicholas Strauss QC in *Beaulane*, because the Court decided that the LA 1980 and LRA 1925, s. 75, were indeed incompatible with ECHR, Protocol 1, Art. 1.

However, the *Pye* case did not end there: the UK government referred it to the Grand Chamber of the ECtHR (*Pye v. United Kingdom*, Application No. 44302/02, 30 August 2007)—in effect, appealing the decision of the original Chamber. The Grand Chamber found, by a majority of ten judges to seven, that the law of adverse possession as it had applied in *Pye v. Graham* was *not* a breach of Protocol 1, Art. 1.

Since Pye Ltd eventually lost its case, it did not get any compensation and was faced with a huge bill for legal costs. However, the decision of the Grand Chamber could not and did not overrule the decision in *Beaulane Properties v. Palmer*. This left the law in a rather confused state, but this has since been effectively resolved by the Court of Appeal in the case of *Ofulue v. Bossert* [2008] EWCA Civ 7, [2008] 3 WLR 1253.

 CASE CLOSE-UP

***Ofulue v. Bossert* [2008] EWCA Civ 7, [2008] 3 WLR 1253**

The case concerned a house which was registered in the name of Mr Ofulue in 1976. He let the house to tenants, and moved to Nigeria. In 1981 the former tenants left and allowed the Bosserts into the property. At that time the property was in very poor condition. The Bosserts did a number of repairs and paid the rates, but did not pay any rent. The twelve-year limitation period was held by the trial judge to have ended in 1999, and was therefore before the HRA 1998 came into force. However, the Court of Appeal considered, *obiter dicta*, whether it should follow *Pye v. United Kingdom* and Arden LJ, in the only substantive judgment, held that the court was bound to do so. However, since the point was not strictly raised by the case, *Beaulane* was not expressly overruled.

(Note that the Court of Appeal's decision was upheld by the House of Lords at [2009] UKHL 16, after an appeal on a point not relevant to this discussion.)

It is expected that this will end claims that the operation of the law of adverse possession, as it applied to registered land before the LRA 2002 came into force, is in breach of human rights law. The doctrine of implied licences can once more be consigned to history, and this is reinforced by *Terence Chambers v. Havering LBC* [2011] EWCA Civ 1576, in which the doctrine in *Leigh v. Jack* was said to be 'heretical and wrong'.

6.7 Offence of squatting in a residential building

There is now a criminal offence of squatting in a residential building:

 STATUTE

Legal Aid, Sentencing and Punishment of Offenders Act 2012

144 Offence of squatting in a residential building

(1) A person commits an offence if—

    (a) the person is in a residential building as a trespasser having entered it as a trespasser,

    (b) the person knows or ought to know that he or she is a trespasser, and

    (c) the person is living in the building or intends to live there for any period.

(2) The offence is not committed by a person holding over after the end of a lease or licence (even if the person leaves and re-enters the building).

(3) For the purposes of this section—

    (a) 'building' includes any structure or part of a structure (including a temporary or moveable structure), and

    (b) a building is 'residential' if it is designed or adapted, before the time of entry, for use as a place to live.

(4) For the purposes of this section the fact that a person derives title from a trespasser, or has the permission of a trespasser, does not prevent the person from being a trespasser.

...

(7) For the purposes of subsection (1)(a) it is irrelevant whether the person entered the building as a trespasser before or after the commencement of this section.

This provision has the effect of criminalizing the act of entering into a residential building as a trespasser and living there or intending to live there for any period. The offence is committed whether the entry as a trespasser occurs before or after 1 September 2012 when the section came into force.

The Land Registry at first took the view that a breach of this section prevented the acquisition of a dwelling house by adverse possession. However, the Court of Appeal in *Best v. Land Chief Registrar* [2015] EWCA Civ 17 held that it does not have this effect. The squatter may be committing an offence but can still gain title by adverse possession.

6.8 Stopping the clock

There are a number of ways in which the limitation period can be stopped from running. If that happens, the squatter will have to start the period again from the beginning.

6.8.1 Successful action for possession within limitation period

Clearly, the most obvious way of stopping the clock is to bring a successful action for possession before the period of twelve years is up or, in the case of the new regime under the LRA 2002, before the squatter has applied for registration following at least ten years of possession.

It is essential to bring an action for possession promptly. In *Buckinghamshire County Council v. Moran* [1990] 1 Ch 623, for example, the council became aware of the annexation of its land by Mr Moran in 1976, but it did not begin possession proceedings until 1985, at which point it was too late and the council lost the land.

The proceedings must be commenced, by the service of a writ, before the twelve years have passed, and must be pursued to a conclusion—in *Ofulue v. Bossert* the original possession proceedings were discontinued and therefore did not stop time running.

6.8.2 Regaining physical possession

If the paper owner regains physical possession of the land, this will interrupt the period of adverse possession. However, the action taken must be such as to deprive the squatter of physical possession in a meaningful way: *Zarb v. Parry* [2012] 1 WLR 1240. Simply going onto the land and declaring you are taking possession, or putting up a notice, or planting a flagpole, were said not to be effective.

6.8.3 Acknowledgement of the paper owner's title by the squatter

A formal acknowledgement of the paper owner's title by the squatter will stop time running—LA 1980, s. 29. This acknowledgement must be in writing and signed by the person making it—LA 1980, s. 30—so a mere oral acknowledgement will not be sufficient.

Q | CASE CLOSE-UP

Archangel v. Lambeth (2000) EGCS 148

A letter signed by the squatter referring to the disputed land as *'Lambeth's property'* was held to have stopped time running.

CASE CLOSE-UP

Bigden v. Lambeth (2000) ECGS 147

A petition addressed to the council against the sale of the block of flats in question to a housing association was held to be a sufficient acknowledgement of title; the case provides a good example of an implicit acknowledgement of title. The squatters did not specifically state that the property belonged to Lambeth, but they did not question the power of the council to sell the property or to assert a better title to it.

Other kinds of implicit acknowledgement of title include offering to buy or to rent the land from the paper owner.

In *Colchester Borough Council v. Smith* [1992] Ch 421, an agreement to rent the land (a garden allotment) seems to have occurred after the limitation period had expired. It was held, nevertheless, to be an effective acknowledgement of title, because it was a bona fide compromise of the dispute over the ownership of the land, and the defendant was therefore estopped from going behind it and reopening the original dispute.

In *London Borough of Tower Hamlets v. Barrett* [2005] EWCA Civ 923, it was held that acknowledgement of title by the landlord will not prevent a tenant from acquiring land by adverse possession. This seems rather odd, in view of the fact that the tenant is generally deemed to have acquired the land on behalf of his or her landlord (see 6.5.2.3).

It is important to remember that the squatter does not have to believe that he or she is the true owner of the land. As we saw in *Pye v. Graham*, the Grahams did not think of themselves as owners of the grazing land and would have paid rent if they had been asked for it. However, no such agreement was actually entered into after the last licence expired, and this willingness to pay rent was not a formal acknowledgement of title and did not bar them from successfully claiming adverse possession.

6.8.4 Payment of rent by the squatter

As we saw earlier, if the squatter pays rent, he or she cannot be in adverse possession—LA 1980, ss. 29–30.

6.8.5 The grant of a licence

As discussed earlier, a squatter who is on the land by permission of the paper owner cannot be in adverse possession. In *BP Properties v. Buckler* [1987] 2 EGLR 168, the unilateral grant of a licence by the paper owner that was not acknowledged by the squatter was held to be effective in stopping time running. It therefore seems that the paper owner might write to the squatter granting a licence and that, if the letter were ignored, the licence would be valid and time would stop running. This seems very strange, because any acknowledgement of title must be in writing (see 6.8.3), so it is unclear why silence should be enough to constitute acceptance of a licence to occupy.

6.8.6 Letter threatening action

In *Buckinghamshire County Council v. Moran*, letters demanding the land back were held to be ineffective to stop time running, although earlier cases such as *Wallis's Cayton Bay Holiday Camp v. Shell-Mex* had suggested to the contrary. Since *Buckinghamshire County Council v. Moran* was approved in *Pye v. Graham*, the true law appears to be that letters by themselves are ineffective to stop time running; the paper owner must also bring possession proceedings.

6.8.7 Fraud, concealment, or mistake

LA 1980, s. 32, provides that the running of the limitation period will be postponed if the action is based upon the fraud of the defendant, if any fact relevant to the claimant's right of action has been concealed by the defendant, or if the action is based upon a mistake. The limitation period does not begin until the fraud, concealment, or mistake has been discovered, or could, with reasonable diligence, have been discovered.

6.9 The effect of adverse possession

Adverse possession under the LA 1980 extinguishes the title of paper owner, as we saw at 6.4.1. This means that the squatter now becomes the owner of the land.

Because the title of the previous owner ceases to exist under LA 1980, s. 17, there should be no possibility of the previous title to the land being revived, even if there is a subsequent acknowledgement of title by the squatter. As we saw at 6.8.3, however, in *Colchester Borough Council v. Smith* [1992] Ch 421 such an acknowledgement was held to be effective as a genuine compromise of a dispute about the land.

There is no conveyance of land to the squatter. The squatter takes the land subject to all proprietary obligations, even if they are unregistered, because he or she is not a purchaser—*Re Nisbet and Potts' Contract* (1906) 1 Ch 386. The squatter's title will not, however, be subject to a mortgage taken out after adverse possession commenced; but if the mortgage was taken out before adverse possession commenced, the squatter will be bound by it, unless no payments were made under the mortgage for the limitation period—LA 1980, s. 29(3).

6.9.1 Unregistered land

6.9.1.1 Freehold land

CROSS REFERENCE

For more on different classes of title, see Chapter 2.

For more on indemnities in registered land, see Chapter 4.

The squatter will have no paper title to the land. In order to sell the land, he or she would have to make a declaration of adverse possession in respect of it, because there would be no title deeds available. In practice, the squatter will register the land at the Land Registry with possessory title, which can be upgraded twelve years later to absolute title.

> **Q CASE CLOSE-UP**
>
> **Diep v. Land Registry** [2010] EWHC 3315 (Admin)
>
> The claimant challenged the decision of the Land Registrar to register land he had acquired by adverse possession with possessory title only. Mitting J upheld the registrar's decision, and the policy of the Land Registry, because an absolute title would give rise to a claim for indemnity if the paper owner turned up later and made a successful claim. Public funds were therefore at risk, so a cautious approach was wholly justified.

A possessory title can be sold, but a purchaser will expect to pay less for it. Usually, title insurance is taken out to compensate the purchaser if there is any subsequent challenge to the title.

6.9.1.2 Leasehold land

If there is adverse possession against a tenant, the squatter extinguishes the tenant's estate after twelve years; the landlord's estate is not extinguished until twelve years after the landlord has the right to possession against the tenant. In the meantime, the squatter has a freehold title (he or she never becomes a tenant of the landlord), but one that is liable to be determined by the landlord once they become entitled to possession.

EXAMPLE

Henry has been in adverse possession of a piece of unregistered land at the end of his garden for twelve years. He has discovered that Isabel owns the freehold of the land, but that the land has been leased to Jack until 2030.

Henry has extinguished Jack's title, because he has been in adverse possession for twelve years.

He will not extinguish Isabel's title until 2042 (twelve years after the lease ends).

The dispossessed tenant remains a tenant of the landlord, so the landlord can forfeit the lease for breach of covenant during its term. This will bring forward the landlord's right to eject the squatter. Therefore, it is in the squatter's interest to ensure that all of the covenants are complied with—otherwise the land may be reclaimed by the landlord.

The dispossessed tenant also remains in a contractual relationship with the landlord. This raises the question of whether he or she can deliberately bring an end to that contract by surrendering the lease to the landlord, thus bringing the tenant's estate to a premature end and entitling the landlord to possession. The landlord could then evict the squatter. This occurred in *Fairweather v. St Marylebone Property* [1963] AC 510, in which the House of Lords held by a majority that the tenant could surrender the lease and that the landlord was entitled to evict the squatter.

EXAMPLE

In the previous example, Jack might surrender his lease to Isabel. She could then evict Henry, because her freehold title has not been extinguished and will not be extinguished for twelve years.

6.9.2 Registered land

6.9.2.1 Periods of limitation completed by 12 October 2003

Freehold land

As we saw earlier, title to registered land cannot simply be extinguished. Therefore, some mechanism for applying the LA 1980 had to be found.

This was provided by LRA 1925, s. 75.

STATUTE

Land Registration Act 1925, s. 75 [Acquisition of title by possession]

(1) The Limitation Acts shall apply to registered land in the same manner and to the same extent as those Acts apply to land not registered, except that where, if the land were not registered, the estate of the person registered as proprietor would be extinguished, such estate shall not be extinguished but shall be deemed to be held by the proprietor for the time being on trust for the person who, by virtue of the said Acts, has acquired title against any proprietor, but without prejudice to the estates and interests of any other person interested in the land whose estate or interest is not extinguished by those Acts.

(2) Any person claiming to have acquired a title under the Limitation Acts may apply to be registered as proprietor thereof.

...

Instead of being extinguished, the squatter's title is held on trust by the registered proprietor. This is a rather odd trust, because the registered proprietor is obliged to act as trustee for someone who effectively may have 'stolen' the land. Until it is registered in the squatter's name, the registered proprietor (paper owner) continues to hold the legal title to the land, but the squatter has the beneficial (equitable) title.

This equitable title was originally protected as an overriding interest under LRA 1925, s. 70(1)(f), but is now protected as an overriding interest only if the squatter remains in actual occupation under LRA 2002, Sch. 3, para. 2.

The trust comes to an end when the squatter is registered as proprietor in place of the paper owner.

Leasehold land

The imposition of a trust under LRA 1925, s. 75(1) means that there were different results if a leasehold estate in registered land was adversely possessed. Because the dispossessed tenant held the land on trust for the squatter, he or she could not bring forward the landlord's right to evict the tenant by surrendering the lease, as can be done with unregistered land.

 CASE CLOSE-UP

Spectrum Investment Co. v. Holmes [1981] 1 WLR 221

In this case, the tenant tried to surrender the lease after the squatter had been registered with an absolute freehold title in respect of the tenant's estate.

It was held that, although this case was indistinguishable from *Fairweather v. St Marylebone Property* except that the land was registered, the tenant had no estate left to surrender.

Therefore, the squatter was entitled to keep the land until the lease expired.

That case expressly left open the position before the squatter is registered as proprietor—that is, the time during which the registered proprietor is holding on trust for the squatter. This point was raised in *Central London Estates v. Kato Kagaku* [1998] 4 All ER 948.

CASE CLOSE-UP

***Central London Estates v. Kato Kagaku* [1998] 4 All ER 948**

It was held that the same result applied where the squatter had not yet registered the adversely possessed leasehold estate. LRA 1925, s. 75 meant that the tenant held the leasehold estate on trust for the squatter.

When the tenant surrendered the lease to his landlord, the trusteeship passed to the landlord, so that it could not evict the squatter.

The result was that the squatter maintained valuable rights to a courtyard in central London, on which he was running a car park, until the end of the leasehold estate in 2028. The landlord could not evict the squatter until that date.

 EXAMPLE

Look back at the previous examples.

Suppose that Henry had completed twelve years of adverse possession of registered land before 12 October 2003. The land was leased to Jack until 2030. Jack would hold his estate on trust for Henry unless, and until, Henry was registered as proprietor.

Unlike the previous example, Jack cannot surrender the lease to Isabel either before, or after, Henry is registered as proprietor. Once Henry is registered, Jack has no estate to surrender; before Henry is registered, Jack holds on trust for him and cannot act in breach of trust. If he were to try to do so, Isabel would hold the land on trust for Henry until 2030.

These two cases clearly indicated that adverse possession could not work in exactly the same way in registered and unregistered land even before the reforms of 2002—and, in this way, they paved the way for the realization that different considerations apply to registered land.

6.9.2.2 Limitation periods completed from 13 October 2003

LRA 2002, ss. 96–98 applies to registered land for which the limitation period under the LA 1980 has not been completed before 13 October 2003.

The most fundamental difference between the LA 1980 rules and those under the LRA 2002 is that there is no longer an automatic barring of title by adverse possession. Under the LA 1980 rules, once the twelve years was up, the paper owner could not do anything about the squatter—it was too late!

Now, adverse possession alone does not bar the registered proprietor's title—LRA 2002, s. 96. Instead, after being in adverse possession for ten years, the squatter has the right to apply to the Land Registry to be registered as the proprietor of the land that he or she has adversely possessed. Note that the period has been reduced to ten years—but you would be wrong to think that this makes adverse possession under the LRA 2002 easier: the reverse is actually true.

The squatter has no rights in the land until an application to be registered is made, and can defend an action for possession only if one of the grounds in LRA 2002, Sch. 6, para. 5 (discussed later) can be made out. In the vast majority of cases, a squatter can be evicted however long he or she has been on the land.

The squatter must be in possession of the land when the application to be registered is made—that is, the ten years' adverse possession relied upon must immediately precede the date of the application.

EXAMPLE

1. Karen has been in adverse possession of a house for twelve years ending on 1 October 2013, and is still living there. The registered proprietor, Linda, can bring an action for possession against Karen and will succeed unless Karen can show one of the limited grounds in LRA 2002, Sch. 6, para. 5.

2. Manvir was in adverse possession of grazing land adjoining his garden for ten years ending in March 2010. Since then, however, he has stopped using the land. He cannot now make an application to be registered as proprietor, because he is not in possession of the land.

Note that it is for the Land Registry to determine initially whether someone is in adverse possession of the land under LRA 2002, not the courts: *Swan Housing Association v. Gill* [2012] EWHC 3129 (QB). It is only after the Land Registry has made its decision under the procedure outlined below that the court can consider the matter.

When the Land Registry receives the application, it will firstly decide if the squatter has an arguable case. If so, the Land Registry will notify certain people interested in the land:

- the registered proprietor;
- any registered chargee (mortgagee);
- if the estate is leasehold, the registered proprietor of any superior registered estate (for example, the freehold);
- certain other people interested in the land—LRA 2002, Sch. 6, paras 1 and 2.

These people have 65 days within which to object to the registration. As you can see, this is very different to the LA 1980, under which the registered proprietor got no warning at all that someone else was claiming the land.

▶ CROSS REFERENCE

For more on rectification and indemnity, see Chapter 4, 4.6.

If the registered proprietor does not respond at all, the land is presumed to have been abandoned and the squatter is entitled to be registered as the new proprietor. There is no provision to extend the time limits for replying, even in cases of hardship. However, a claim for rectification can be made if there are grounds for doing so.

CASE CLOSE-UP

Baxter v. Mannion [2011] EWCA Civ 120

It was held that a registered proprietor who did not object in time, but who had valid grounds for disproving adverse possession, could apply for rectification of the register. A person who did not have adequate grounds for claiming adverse possession was not entitled to be registered as registered proprietor of the land; this was implicit in LRA 2002, Sch. 6, para. 1. The registration had therefore been obtained by a mistake, which could be put right under LRA 2002, Sch. 4, paras 1 and 5.

If an objection is received in time, the squatter will not be registered as the proprietor unless the case falls within one of the exceptions in LRA 2002, Sch. 6, para. 5:

- if, under the principles of proprietary estoppel, it would be unconscionable for the registered proprietor to object to the squatter's application to be registered;

- if the squatter is otherwise entitled to the land;

- if the squatter is the owner of adjacent property and has been in adverse possession of the land in question under the mistaken, but reasonable belief, that he or she is its owner.

'Estoppel'

STATUTE

Land Registration Act 2002, Sch. 6, para. 5(2)

The first condition is that—

(a) it would be unconscionable because of an equity by estoppel for the registered proprietor to seek to dispossess the applicant, and

(b) the circumstances are such that the applicant ought to be registered as the proprietor.

This exception is clearly intended to deal with cases of **proprietary estoppel**. A proprietary estoppel arises where the owner has made assurances about the land, upon the strength of which assurances that claimant has relied and acted to his or her detriment.

> **CROSS REFERENCE**
>
> For more detail on proprietary estoppel, see Chapter 9.

proprietary estoppel a doctrine under which the courts can grant a remedy if a landowner has implicitly or explicitly led a claimant to act detrimentally under the belief that he or she would be granted rights in the land

There have been some objections to this provision, on the grounds that a person who moves into land under circumstances giving rise to a proprietary estoppel is unlikely to be in adverse possession. An estoppel is generally raised by the proprietor encouraging that person to move into the land, so he or she would be there by consent. It is probable that this provision is more likely to be used as a defence to possession proceedings than as the basis for a claim.

The Law Commission and Land Registry (2001, para. 14.42) suggest that the sorts of case that may fall under this exception are those in which the paper owner stands by while the squatter mistakenly builds on the land, or in which there is an informal purchase and sale, and the purchaser goes into possession. LRA 2002, Sch. 6, para. 5(2)(b)—'the circumstances are such that the applicant ought to be registered as the proprietor'—means that the Registry retains a discretion whether or not to register the squatter as proprietor, even if proprietary estoppel is made out.

'Otherwise entitled to the land'

STATUTE

Land Registration Act 2002, Sch. 6, para. 5(3)

The second condition is that the applicant is for some other reason entitled to be registered as the proprietor of the estate.

In the Law Commission/Land Registry report (2001), it was suggested at para. 14.43 that this exception is intended to deal with situations in which, for example, the squatter is entitled to the land as a beneficiary under the will or intestacy (death without leaving a will) of the previous registered proprietor, or in situations such as that in *Bridges v. Mees* [1957] Ch 475, in which the purchaser had gone into possession after paying the whole purchase price, but the land had not been transferred to him.

Boundary disputes

 STATUTE

Land Registration Act 2002, Sch. 6, para. 5(4)

The third condition is that—

   (a) the land to which the application relates is adjacent to land belonging to the applicant,

   (b) the exact line of the boundary between the two has not been determined under rules under section 60,

   (c) for at least ten years of the period of adverse possession ending on the date of the application, the applicant (or any predecessor in title) reasonably believed that the land to which the application relates belonged to him, and

   (d) the estate to which the application relates was registered more than one year prior to the date of the application.

This exception is intended to deal with genuine cases in which the boundary between two pieces of land is not fixed under Land Registration Rules 2003, SI 2003/1417, Part 10 (most boundaries are not) and the fence or other boundary line has been in its present position for at least the last ten years. If the applicant, or his or her predecessor in title, reasonably believed that the land on the wrong side of the paper boundary belonged to him or her, the applicant is entitled to be registered as proprietor of that land. This is most likely to occur when the fence or other boundary marker has always (or at least, for a long time) been in a different position from that on the filed plan. Essentially, it is better for the register to reflect the actual boundary on the ground than some theoretical boundary on a map.

The wording of the section does, however, mean that it will not apply if the applicant has moved the boundary deliberately, hoping to get more land, because it specifies that he or she must have reasonably believed that the land in question belonged to him or her.

 CASE CLOSE-UP

Zarb v. Parry [2012] 1 WLR 1240

The claimants (C) and defendants (D) owned adjoining land. C believed that the true boundary lay about 20m north of the established hedge, and in 2007 went on to that strip of land and began to remove fencing and plants in an attempt to take back the land by force. They were interrupted by D, who threatened to call the police.

In 2009, C made a legal claim for the boundary to be moved in their favour. D pleaded LRA 2002, Sch. 6(4). The trial judge held that C had the paper title to the strip of land, but that D had been in adverse possession of it for over ten years. The Court of Appeal upheld the decision.

It was held that the incident in 2007 had not been enough to interrupt D's possession of the land, as C did not themselves take exclusive possession of it—they were interrupted before they could do so.

It was also held that D's belief in the existing boundary was reasonable, as there was no dispute when they bought the land, and after the 2007 incident, a surveyor was employed by both parties who confirmed that the hedge was in the correct position. The CA indicated, however, that claims under this section need to be made 'promptly' or the belief of the adverse possessor may not remain reasonable.

In *IAM Group v. Chowdrey* [2012] EWCA Civ 505, it was held that the reasonable belief required is not that of a reasonably competent solicitor, but of the claimant himself. Knowledge that the paper owner disputed his title did not make that belief unreasonable in circumstances where he had occupied the disputed land since first moving into the property.

Rejected applications

If an objection is received to the application and the case does not fall within any of the exceptions outlined earlier, the squatter will not be registered as proprietor. The landowner, however, cannot sit back at that point and do nothing more. If an application for registration is refused, but the squatter remains in adverse possession for a further two years, a second application to be registered as proprietor can be made and the squatter will, this time, be registered as proprietor whether or not the registered proprietor objects—LRA 2002, Sch. 6, paras 6 and 7. The paper owner cannot ignore the squatter: action must be taken to either evict the squatter, or otherwise deal with the situation—perhaps by offering the squatter a lease or licence.

A comparison between the Limitation Act 1980 and the Land Registration Act 2002

The effect of adverse possession under the LRA 2002 is very different to that under the old law. Instead of operating negatively, by obliging the registered proprietor to hold the land in trust for the squatter, the LRA 2002 effectively transfers the paper owner's title to the squatter by registering the squatter in the paper owner's place. The squatter takes the paper owner's estate subject to any entries in the register that bound the paper owner, with the possible exception of registered charges. If the squatter is registered because there is no objection received, he or she will not be bound by any registered charge affecting the estate immediately before registration, because the chargee was notified of the application and did not object—LRA 2002, Sch. 6, para. 9(2). If, however, the squatter was registered because the case fell within one of the three exceptions, any registered charge will be binding—LRA 2002, Sch. 6, para. 9(4).

THINKING POINT

Think about the facts of *Pye v. Graham* under the new law. Would Pye Ltd have objected to an application by the Grahams to be registered as proprietors?

Pye Ltd would have objected. It still wanted the land and had not abandoned it, as its persistent attempts to get it back through the courts prove.

As the Grahams could not have made out any of the exceptions in LRA 2002, Sch. 6, para. 5, they would not have been registered as proprietors and Pye Ltd would not have lost land worth £10m.

6.10 How do I know which law applies?

Figure 6.1 is a flow chart which may be helpful in thinking about applying the law on adverse possession.

Figure 6.1 Adverse possession flowchart

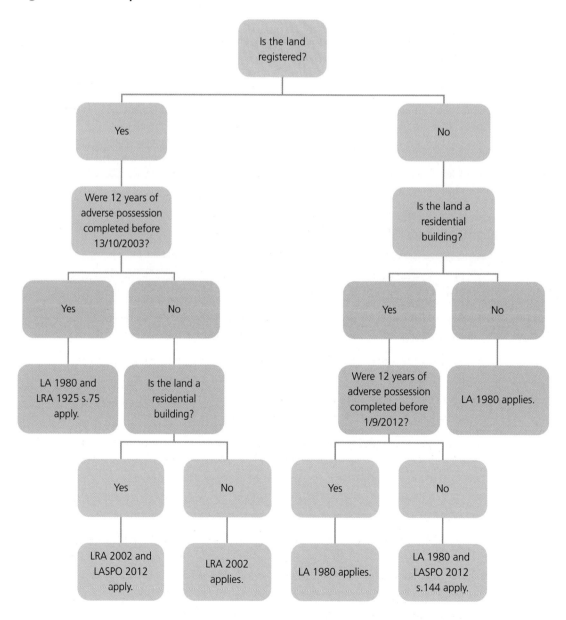

EXAMPLE

When you are looking at these examples, consider these three questions:

- Is the land registered or unregistered?
- If registered, on what date was the land adversely possessed?

1. Frances goes into adverse possession of Geraldine's unregistered land on 3 October 1994. She will be able to apply for the land to be registered in her name on 4 October 2006. Because the land is unregistered, the LA 1980 applies.

2. Harriet goes into adverse possession of Iris's registered land on 1 October 1988. She will be able to apply for registration as proprietor on 2 October 2000. Because this is before 1 October 2003, she will be subject to the LA 1980 and the LRA 1925. The land will now be held on trust for her by Iris until she is registered as proprietor.

3. Jack goes into adverse possession of Karen's registered land in November 1991. Twelve years' adverse possession is up in November 2003. Because this is after 13 October 2003, the new rules in the LRA 2002 apply. The rules in LRA 2002 apply. Karen will be notified, and what happens next depends upon her response.

 ## Summary

1. Adverse possession was originally justified as providing an end to disputes over the ownership of land, ensuring that abandoned land was utilized, and ensuring that the fact of possession and the legal title never got too far apart.

2. Some of these justifications are less convincing in relation to registered land.

3. The LA 1980 works by extinguishing the title of the paper owner after the limitation period (usually twelve years) has passed.

4. For the limitation period to begin, the paper owner must have discontinued possession, or been dispossessed, and the squatter must have gone into possession.

5. Possession means a sufficient degree of physical control and an intention to possess: see *Pye v. Graham*.

6. Possession is adverse if it is without the consent of the paper owner. Possession as a tenant or licensee will not be adverse to the paper owner.

7. There was considerable controversy over how adverse possession was affected by human rights law, but the current (and presumably final) position is that the law is not in breach of the ECHR.

8. The law on adverse possession for registered land was changed by the LRA 2002 for cases from 13 October 2003.

9. The new law makes it much harder to adversely possess registered land, because the paper owner is notified of any application by the squatter to be registered, and has a chance to object and then evict the squatter.

10. LASPOA 2012 applies from 1 September 2012 to criminalize squatting in residential buildings even if the entry as a trespasser was before that date.

The bigger picture

- This is an area of law which should be of diminishing importance as time goes by, since most land is registered and the new laws in the LRA 2002 and LASPOA 2012 make it much harder to claim adverse possession. However, there have been a number of recent cases, so the law on adverse possession is not yet in decline.

- If you want advice on answering examination questions on adverse possession, see Chapter 15, 15.8.

- For more detailed information on the human rights law decisions, see the Online Resource Centre.

- There are numerous additional cases on adverse possession, many of them quite old.

Consent

Hicks Development Ltd v. Chaplin [2007] EWHC 141 (Ch)

Sandhu v. Farooqui [2003] EWCA Civ 531

Smith v. Lawson (1997) 64 P & CR 239

General requirements

Markfield Investments v. Evans [2001] 1 WLR 1321

Mount Carmel Investments v. Peter Thurlow Ltd [1988] 1 WLR 1078

Ocean Estates v. Pinder [1969] 2 AC 19

Pavledes v. Ryesbridge Properties Ltd (1989) 58 P&CR 459

Seddon v. Smith (1877) 36 LT 168

Sze To Chun Keung v. Kung Kwok Wai David [1997] 1 WLR 1232

Treloar v. Nute [1976] 1 WLR 1295

? Questions

Self-test questions

1. Abu is aware of a strip of land adjoining the end of his garden. It appears to be unused. What should Abu do if he wishes to take adverse possession of the land? What must he show to prove adverse possession?

2. Abu receives a letter from the local council regarding the strip of land. The council claims to be the owner of the land, which it is planning to incorporate into a park in the future. What will be the effect of the letter if the council:

   (a) threatens to bring possession proceedings against Abu?

   (b) states that Abu may use the land by licence?

3. If Abu were a tenant of his land, to whom would the strip of land belong if he were to be successful in proving adverse possession?

4. If Abu were to be able to show a sufficient degree of adverse possession, how likely would he be to become the owner of the strip of land if his twelve years' adverse possession ended in November 2003 and the land was:

   (a) unregistered?

   (b) registered?

5. Suppose the council took no action while Abu lived in the house, but the strip of land was incorporated into the garden. Abu sold the house to Ben in 2006, not mentioning anything about the strip. In 2011, the council tried to evict Ben from the land. Ben sincerely believed that the land was part of the garden until the council wrote to him. Will Ben have any defence to possession proceedings?

Exam questions

1. Melody and Jasper met as students at the University of Woolwich in 2002. They were both short of funds, so they moved into an abandoned chalet sited behind a council block of flats. It had been left there after some building work, and was intended as a shelter for workmen, though it had a small kitchen and bathroom. The chalet was fairly basic and run down, but Melody and Jasper repaired it, insulated it, and had mains services connected. They have continued to live in it as they are struggling musicians who cannot afford a better home.

   Last week, a representative of the Woolwich Council appeared and told them that the land the chalet was standing on was registered in their name, and that the chalet belonged to them. They told Melody and Jasper that they were committing a criminal offence, and that they must leave immediately. Advise Melody and Jasper.

2. Is it still necessary for the law on adverse possession to apply to registered land?

 For suggested approaches to answering these questions visit the Online Resource Centre.

 ## Further reading

Brierley, A. R. H., 'Adverse possession: a case of death and regrettable resurrection' [1991] Conv 397
This article criticizes the decision in *Colchester Borough Council v. Smith* [1991] Ch 448 (Ch D).

Ex, L., 'What do we protect in land registration?' (2013) 129 (Oct) LQR 477
This is a case comment on *Parshall v. Hackney* [2013] EWCA Civ 240, [2013] 3 All ER 224.

Griffiths, G., 'An important question of principle—reality and rectification in registered land' [2011] ConvPL 331

Land Registry (2015) *Land Registry Practice Guide 4—Adverse possession of registered land*, available online at https://www.gov.uk/government/publications/adverse-possession-of-registered-land
This sets out the Land Registry procedure on adverse possession under the LRA 2002.

Land Registry (2015) *Land Registry Practice Guide 5—Adverse possession of (1) unregistered land (2) registered land where a right to be registered was acquired*

before 13 October 2003, available online at https://www.gov.uk/government/publications/adverse-possession-of-1-unregistered-land-and-2-registered-land

This sets out the law on applying under the old rules for registration of unregistered land that has been adversely possessed and registered land adversely possessed before the LRA 2002 came into force.

Law Commission/HM Land Registry (1998) *Land Registration for the Twenty-First Century: A Consultative Document*, Law Com No. 254, available online at http://www.lawcom.gov.uk/project/land-registration-for-the-21st-century/#land-registration-for-the-21st-century-consultation

See especially paras 10.1–10.19, which discuss the justification for adverse possession and go on to look at whether it should continue to exist in registered land.

Law Commission/HM Land Registry (2001) *Land Registration for the Twenty-First Century: A Conveyancing Revolution*, Law Com No. 271, available online at http://www.lawcom.gov.uk/wp-content/uploads/2015/04/Lc271.pdf

Part XIV contains a commentary on the provisions in the LRA 2002, and explains why they were introduced.

Murdoch, S., 'No trumping of reality' (2011) 1120 EG 111

These articles are about *Baxter v. Mannion* [2011] EWCA Civ 120.

Milne, P., 'Mistaken belief in adverse possession—mistaken interpretation?' [2010] 4 Conv 342

This is a comment on *IAM Group Plc v. Chowdrey* [2012] EWCA Civ 505 and the 'boundary dispute' exception.

Nield, S., 'Adverse possession and estoppel' [2004] Conv 137

This article discusses the exceptions under which a squatter may be registered under the new law in the LRA 2002. The article is quite technical, but contains interesting commentary on the estoppel exception, in particular.

'Residential squatting—the sting in the tail' (2015) 25(10) PLB 73–4

This discusses *Best v. Chief Land Registrar* [2015] EWCA Civ 17.

Woods, U., 'The English law on adverse possession: A tale of two systems' (2009) 38 (1) CLWR 27

This is an interesting article considering whether the role played by adverse possession in unregistered land could be replaced by marketable title legislation as commonly used in the USA.

 ## Online Resource Centre

www.oxfordtextbooks.co.uk/orc/clarke_directions5e/

For more advice relating to this chapter, including self-test questions and an interactive glossary, visit the Online Resource Centre.

PART 3

SOLE AND JOINT OWNERS OF LAND

7 The sole owner of land

☐ LEARNING OBJECTIVES

By the end of this chapter, you will be able to:

- identify the different combinations of legal and equitable ownership of land;
- recognize the potential pitfalls for a potential purchaser of property from a sole legal owner;
- appreciate the vulnerability of an equitable owner of land;
- discuss the legislative safety measures designed to reduce the risks that are faced by potential purchasers and equitable owners.

Introduction

We have already looked at the various different interests that can exist in a single piece of land and, more particularly, at the separation of the legal and equitable interests in land (see Chapter 2). In this chapter, we will start looking at what it means to be the 'owner' of a property. We will examine the meaning of the word 'owner' in land law and see what this title allows its holder to do with his or her land. In this chapter, we will concentrate on situations in which there is only one legal owner of the property—a 'sole' owner. This is not as straightforward a situation as it might at first seem, because there are often other people with interests in the land whom the owner must consider. In Chapter 8, we will look at 'co-ownership'—the situation in which more than one person owns the property.

7.1 Who is an 'owner' of land and what can he or she do with it?

The Land Registration Act 2002 (LRA 2002) offers some assistance in deciding who is an 'owner' of land. Although it does not provide a definition of the word, it does define what an 'owner' is permitted to do with his or her property—that is, the 'owner's powers'—and then explains who may exercise these powers.

 STATUTE

Land Registration Act 2002, s. 24 [Right to exercise owner's powers]

A person is entitled to exercise owner's powers in relation to a registered estate or charge if he is—

(a) the registered proprietor, or

(b) entitled to be registered as the proprietor.

▶ **CROSS REFERENCE**

For more on proof of title, see Chapter 3.

In registered land, then, whoever is entered into the proprietorship register as the registered proprietor of the property is deemed to have the authority to deal with the land as an owner. Remember that, in order to register his or her title, he or she will have demonstrated to the Land Registry that his or her title is good and that he or she is entitled to be registered as the owner of the land.

Subsection 24(b) refers to those who are 'entitled to be registered as the proprietor': this will be, for example, the **personal representatives** of someone who has died, and this includes both **executors** and **administrators**. This subsection allows the personal representatives to dispose of the land as though they owned it. Without this power, they would not be able to sell the land or transfer it to the deceased's heirs according to his or her will.

---

personal representatives those responsible for looking after the property of someone who has died, who might, for example, make sure that any bequests made in the deceased person's will are carried out

executors personal representatives named in the will

administrators personal representatives in cases of intestacy—that is, in which there is no will

---

The 'powers' of the owner to which this section refers are outlined in LRA 2002, s. 23.

 STATUTE

Land Registration Act 2002, s. 23(1)

Owner's powers in relation to a registered estate consist of:

(a) power to make a disposition of any kind permitted by the general law in relation to an interest of that description, other than a mortgage by demise or sub-demise, and

(b) power to charge the estate at law with the payment of money.

Initially, this may not seem to provide us with a very helpful explanation—but the important parts to understand for now are the first part of subsection (a) and the whole of subsection (b).

LRA 2002, s. 23(1)(a) tells us that the owner of land may dispose of his or her land in any way that the law permits. This will be different according to the kind of interest that the owner has in the land: the owner of freehold land, for example, can (in theory) do as he or she pleases with the land—whether that involves selling it, giving it away, or leaving it to someone under the terms of his or her will. The owner of leasehold land also has wide powers of disposal, although these will be more circumscribed.

CROSS REFERENCE

For more on the powers of the owner of leasehold land, see Chapter 5.

The only restriction placed by the Act on the owner is that he or she cannot grant a 'mortgage by demise or sub-demise', which is an obsolete form of mortgage no longer used in registered land. LRA 2002, s. 23(1)(b), meanwhile, allows the owner to grant a mortgage by way of a charge over the land. This is obviously a very important power, because most homes are bought with the help of money raised by the granting of a mortgage to a bank or building society.

CROSS REFERENCE

For more on mortgages, see Chapter 13.

7.2 The sole owner: three possibilities

When the land register shows that there is only one owner of land (also known as a **sole owner**), any would-be purchaser would be forgiven for thinking that a prospective purchase of the property will be straightforward—but he or she should be aware that this is not always the case.

> **sole owner**
> a person registered as the sole legal proprietor of land, who may or may not be the sole equitable owner

Even if the land register shows that there is only one registered proprietor, there may be other parties with interests in the property who must be considered when the land is bought and sold, as a result of one of the fundamental principles of land registration: the curtain principle.

CROSS REFERENCE

For more on the curtain principle, see Chapter 2.

The effect of the curtain principle is that equitable interests are kept off the land register—that is, they are hidden behind the 'curtain' of registration. As we will see, there are measures—such as overreaching—in place to protect both the purchaser from these hidden interests and the equitable owner from the prospective purchaser. As will become apparent, however, these protective measures do not always operate satisfactorily in situations in which there is one sole owner of land.

CROSS REFERENCE

For the meaning of overreaching, see Chapter 2.

There are essentially three alternative scenarios when the land register shows a sole registered proprietor of land, each of which reflects a different possibility in respect of the legal and equitable ownership of the land.

1. The registered proprietor is the sole legal and sole equitable owner of the land.
2. The registered proprietor is the sole legal owner, but he or she holds the equitable title on trust for someone else.
3. The registered proprietor is the sole legal owner, holding the equitable title on trust for him- or herself and (an)other equitable owner(s).

Before we consider each of these in turn, it is worth mentioning that in *Stack v. Dowden* [2007] UKHL 17, the House of Lords established a firm starting point for the court when looking at the equitable ownership of land. There is a presumption that the beneficial (equitable) interests in the land follow the registered legal interests in the land. It follows that, if the land is registered in the name of a sole owner, then the presumption is that the same person is the sole equitable owner. The presumption may, of course, be rebutted and it is for the person claiming that he or she has an equitable interest in the property to adduce evidence for the rebuttal.

CROSS REFERENCE

For more on *Stack v. Dowden*, see Chapter 9.

7.2.1 **Sole legal and sole equitable owner**

 CROSS REFERENCE

For more on trusts of land, see Chapter 10.

This is the simplest of the three possibilities. In this instance, the land register shows the whole picture in respect of interests in the land. The registered owner owns the legal title by him- or herself and is also the only equitable owner of the land. This means that there are no other unexpected interests lurking in the land of which a purchaser should be wary: the sole registered proprietor may dispose of the land exactly as he or she pleases.

Note that this is the only situation, in terms of land ownership, in which a trust of land does not come into being, because there is no separation of the legal and equitable ownership of the property.

> **➡ EXAMPLE**
>
> Bradley buys a house, for himself and in his own name. No one else contributes to the purchase price of the house, nor does anyone have any other equitable interest in it.
>
> The land holding in law and equity might be illustrated as in Figure 7.1.

Figure 7.1 Sole legal and sole equitable owner

7.2.2 **Sole legal owner, holding the equitable title on trust for someone else**

 CROSS REFERENCE

For more on properties held on trust, see Chapter 9.

In this scenario, the person named in the land register as registered proprietor looks as if he or she owns the land—indeed, he or she does own the legal title to the land—but, in reality, the person is simply holding it on trust for someone else—that is, the equitable owner.

> **➡ EXAMPLE**
>
> Tony is a property developer who does not want his ownership of the property to be made publicly known. (Remember that the land register is a public document.)
>
> To conceal his identity, he asks Cathy to hold the property on trust for him. He gives Cathy the money to purchase the property. This gives him an equitable interest in it. Cathy is the legal owner of the property—her name appears on the land register; Tony is the equitable owner—his name is not included on the land register.
>
> The land holding in law and equity might be illustrated as in Figure 7.2.

Figure 7.2 Sole legal owner, holding the equitable title on trust for someone else

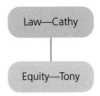

This type of trust is known as a **bare trust** —that is, the trustee holds property on trust for an adult beneficiary who is absolutely entitled to the property. This kind of trust is known as a **trust of land** and is governed by the Trusts of Land and Appointment of Trustees Act 1996 (TOLATA 1996).

> **bare trust** a trust under which the trustee has no obligation other than to hold property on trust for an adult beneficiary who is absolutely entitled to the property
>
> **trust of land** any trust of property that comprises or includes land

 STATUTE

Trusts of Land and Appointment of Trustees Act 1996, s. 1(1)(a)

'trust of land' means … any trust of property which consists of or includes land, …

 STATUTE

Trusts of Land and Appointment of Trustees Act 1996, s. 1(2)

The reference in subsection (1)(a) to a trust—

    (a) is to any description of trust (whether express, implied, resulting or constructive), including … a bare trust, and

…

Under TOLATA 1996, s. 6(1) the trustee is given 'all the powers of an absolute owner' in relation to the trust property—but, as we will see later in the book, the TOLATA 1996 also imposes a number of duties on the trustee in the exercise of these powers.

In the last example given, Tony deliberately intended to set up a trust. This kind of a trust can also be described as an **express trust** —that is, it arose because of the express intention of Tony (the **settlor**).

CROSS REFERENCE

For more on the provisions of TOLATA 1996, see Chapter 10.

> **express trust** a trust created by the express intention of the settlor
>
> **settlor** a person who creates a trust

For an express trust of land to be valid and enforceable by the beneficiary, the settlor must comply with certain formalities. Firstly, they must make their intention to set up a trust completely clear: they need not necessarily use special language—indeed, the settlor need not even use the word 'trust'—*Re Kayford* [1975] 1 WLR 279; they must, however, make it clear that they intend the trustee to hold the land on behalf of a beneficiary. This is not a particularly difficult requirement, especially given that solicitors arrange most express trusts of land.

Secondly, the settlor must comply with the requirements of Law of Property Act 1925 (LPA 1925), s. 53(1)(b).

 STATUTE

Law of Property Act 1925, s. 53(1)(b)

… a declaration of a trust respecting any land or any interest therein must be manifested and proved by some writing signed by some person who is able to declare such trust or by his will,

This requires the settlor to make sure that he or she evidences his or her intention in writing. The settlor may declare the trust orally, but he or she needs to provide proof of his or her intention in the form of some kind of written document, which contains the terms of the trust and which the settlor has signed. The document need not be formal and need not even be written at the same time as the trust is declared—*Rochefoucauld v. Boustead* [1897] 1 Ch 196. However, if the settlor does not comply with LPA 1925, s. 53(1)(b), the trust will be unenforceable in the courts by the beneficiary.

These formal requirements only relate to express trusts and not to trusts that arise more informally—that is, resulting and constructive trusts—as we shall see in due course.

7.2.3 Sole legal owner, holding for him- or herself and (an)other equitable owner(s)

In this situation, the person named in the land register as the registered proprietor of the land owns the legal title and also holds part of the equitable title. Concealed from a potential purchaser's knowledge is the fact that (an)other equitable owner(s) of the land also exist(s).

As you might expect, this situation is rather more complicated. In this situation, the sole legal owner is actually also a trustee of the land, holding the equitable title on behalf of him- or herself and (an)other equitable owner(s). The main difficulty with this kind of situation is that the trust will often have arisen informally, sometimes without the parties even realizing its existence.

 EXAMPLE

Ola buys a house and registers it in her name, but her partner, Ryan, contributes 25 per cent of the purchase price of the house. Although he is not registered as a legal owner, he nevertheless has acquired an equitable interest in the property. In this situation, Ola would be a trustee of the land, holding it on trust for herself and Ryan.

Their interests might be illustrated as in Figure 7.3.

Figure 7.3 Sole legal owner, holding for him- or herself and (an) other equitable owner(s)

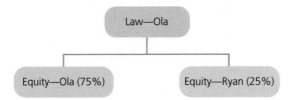

This kind of situation most often arises in the context of a family home, in which a resulting or constructive trust has arisen in respect of the property. In the last example given, Ryan's contribution to the purchase price of the property would mean that, at the very least, he had acquired an interest under a resulting trust.

The problem for Ryan is that his equitable interest is not protected on the face of the land register. He may not even know that he should take steps to protect his position. A prospective purchaser will not see from the land register that anyone other than Ola has an interest in the land—but Ryan's equitable interest is a proprietary interest, which means that, under certain circumstances, it will bind the purchaser, whether he or she knows about it or not.

This leaves both Ryan and the purchaser in a somewhat vulnerable position, as we shall now see.

> **CROSS REFERENCE**
>
> For more on trusts in the family home in general, and resulting trusts in particular, see Chapter 9.

> **→ EXAMPLE**
>
> Ola and Ryan's relationship breaks down, and Ola wants to sell the family home. Martin agrees to buy the property. Martin goes to have a look around the house. He sees male clothes and toiletries, and assumes that they belong to Ola's boyfriend, but does not ask her about them. He is very keen to buy the house.
>
> He looks at the land register, which shows that Ola is the sole registered proprietor of the property. There is no indication of Ryan's equitable interest in the property.

This situation obviously poses a number of potential difficulties, both for Ryan and for Martin. Before we consider these, however, think a little more about the entries on the land register.

> **💬 THINKING POINT**
>
> Why would Ryan's interest not appear on the land register?

One of the difficulties with this kind of informal arrangement is that Ryan may well be unaware of the kind of interest he has and so have taken no steps to protect it. In addition, remember that one of the fundamental principles of land registration is the 'curtain principle', under which equitable interests are kept off the face of the register.

As an equitable owner in the property whose interest is unprotected, Ryan is at risk, because Ola could, in theory, sell the property without his knowledge or consent. Martin is also at risk, because he could buy the land from Ola and then discover that he may be bound by Ryan's equitable interest, of which he was completely unaware. This is because Ryan's interest is potentially an overriding interest—that is, a special kind of equitable interest that may bind a purchaser even if not registered.

> **CROSS REFERENCE**
>
> For more on overriding interests, see Chapter 2.

7.3 Protection for equitable owners and purchasers

The law recognizes the potential dangers for equitable owners, such as Ryan, and purchasers, such as Martin, and has put in place a number of safeguards to protect them. The difficulty, however, is that the interests of equitable owners and potential purchasers are often in direct conflict with each other.

We will look at each of these safeguards in turn.

7.3.1 Protection primarily for the purchaser: overreaching

 CROSS REFERENCE

For more on the aims of the 1925 property legislation, see Chapter 2.

One of the primary objectives of the revolutionary property legislation of 1925 was to ensure that potential purchasers need only concern themselves with the legal title to land. This was to make the sale and purchase of property as easy and as quick to effect as possible.

In order to do this, the legislators needed to find a simple, but effective, way of ensuring that the purchaser need not worry about equitable interests in the land, while making sure that the equitable owners did not suffer undue hardship. They eventually came up with a very clever—if not entirely effective—mechanism called **overreaching**.

> **overreaching** the process by which interests in land are converted into corresponding interests in money arising from the sale of the land

Under overreaching, the purchaser takes the land free from any equitable interests, provided that he or she pays the purchase monies to at least two trustees (usually the legal owners). The equitable owners have a right to pursue the trustees to recover their share of the proceeds of sale.

The details of this overreaching mechanism can be found primarily in LPA 1925, ss. 2(1) and 27(1)–(2). A brief extract of these follows—but it may be helpful for you to read the sections in their entirety.

> 📖 **STATUTE**
>
> **Law of Property Act 1925 [as amended by Trusts of Land and Appointment of Trustees Act 1996, Sch. 3], s. 2(1)**
>
> A conveyance to a purchaser of a legal estate in land shall overreach any equitable interest or power affecting that estate, whether or not he has notice thereof, if—
>
>   …
>
> (ii) the conveyance is made by trustees of land and the equitable interest or power is at the date of the conveyance capable of being overreached by such trustees … and the [requirements of section 27 of this Act respecting the payment of capital money arising on such a conveyance] are complied with.

STATUTE

Law of Property Act 1925 [as amended by Trusts of Land and Appointment of Trustees Act 1996, Sch. 3], s. 27

(1) A purchaser of a legal estate from trustees of land shall not be concerned with the trusts affecting the land, and the net income of the land or the sale of proceeds of the land …

(2) … the proceeds of sale or other capital money shall not be paid to or applied by the direction of fewer than two persons as trustees, except where the trustee is a trust corporation …

Note too that 'purchaser' in this context includes a mortgagee.

What happens in practice is simple. A potential purchaser is protected as long as he or she pays the purchase money to two trustees. Once the purchaser has done so, he or she takes the land free of any equitable interests that may have existed in it. The equitable owner of the land from that point on has no further interest in the land, but does have an interest in the proceeds of sale. He or she must then pursue the trustees for his or her share.

CASE CLOSE-UP

City of London Building Society v. Flegg [1988] AC 54

Mr and Mrs Maxwell-Brown were the registered proprietors of a house. The house had been bought partly with the financial contribution of Mr and Mrs Flegg, who were Mrs Maxwell-Brown's parents. The intention was that both couples would share occupation of the property and this, indeed, happened. Because of their contribution to the purchase price under a resulting trust Mr and Mrs Flegg had an equitable interest in the property (just like Ryan, in our example given earlier).

The land holding might be illustrated as in Figure 7.4.

Unknown to Mr and Mrs Flegg, Mr and Mrs Maxwell-Brown granted a mortgage over the property to raise some cash. The Maxwell-Browns defaulted on their mortgage payments, and the building society tried to repossess the house in order to recover its money.

The key question was: had overreaching taken place? If it had, then Mr and Mrs Flegg's equitable interest in the property would be swept from the property itself and into the proceeds of sale, which Mr and Mrs Maxwell-Brown would hold on trust for them.

The House of Lords looked at the statutory formula for overreaching, summarized earlier in the extract from the Act, and decided that Mr and Mrs Flegg's interest had indeed been overreached. All that the purchaser had to do to trigger the overreaching mechanism was to pay the purchase money to two trustees. The building society had advanced the funds to the two trustees: Mr and Mrs Maxwell-Brown. The building society took free of any equitable interests and could repossess the property. Mr and Mrs Flegg no longer had any interest in the house, but did have an interest in the funds paid to the Maxwell-Browns.

Unfortunately for Mr and Mrs Flegg, Mr and Mrs Maxwell-Brown had already spent the money advanced to them!

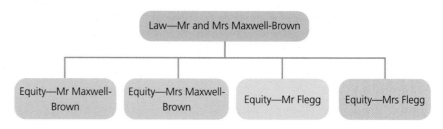

Figure 7.4 Legal and equitable interests in *City of London Building Society v. Flegg*

Flegg demonstrates how overreaching operates successfully in practice. How, then, does this help Martin, the purchaser in our example, or Ryan, our equitable owner?

Eagle-eyed readers will have spotted that LPA 1925, s. 27(2) says that overreaching will only be successful if the purchase money is paid to two or more trustees. In Ryan's case, there is only one trustee, Ola. If Martin were aware of Ryan's interest, he could insist that Ola appoint another trustee and pay the money to both of them, allowing him to take the property free of Ryan's interest. The problem with this solution is that, on the land register, there is no indication of Ryan's existence.

7.3.2 Protection for the equitable owner: restriction

▶ CROSS REFERENCE

For more on restrictions, see Chapter 2.

There is a means by which Ryan can warn a prospective purchaser, such as Martin, that there are equitable interests in the land that are not reflected on the land register. Because Ryan has an equitable interest under a trust of land he has 'sufficient interest' to apply for a restriction to be placed on Ola's Land Registry entry—LRA 2002, s. 43(1)(c) and Land Registration Rules 2003, SI 2003/1417 (LRR 2003), r. 93(a).

Ryan's restriction would be stated in the following terms:

> RESTRICTION: No disposition by a sole proprietor of the registered estate (except a trust corporation) under which capital money arises is to be registered unless authorised by an order of the court.

This is known as a restriction of Form A—that is, a restriction on dispositions by a sole proprietor—and may be found in LRR 2003, Sch. 4.

As soon as a prospective purchaser's solicitor sees this restriction, they will know that, to protect their client, they must insist upon appointing a second trustee of the land, and that the purchase monies must be paid to Ola and the second trustee together. When this is done, the purchaser, Martin, will be protected and need not worry about Ryan's interest. Ryan, meanwhile, will have to chase Ola for his 25 per cent share of the proceeds.

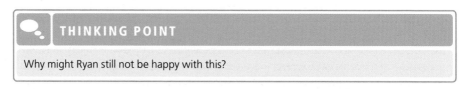

THINKING POINT

Why might Ryan still not be happy with this?

Although Ryan's interest has technically been protected, he may still not be happy with the result, because he no longer has any interest in the land and will have to leave his home, which he may not want to do. Additionally, he will have to find Ola and the second trustee, in order to ask for his share of the proceeds. This is not always as easy as it sounds—as you will see, case law has numerous examples of trustees disappearing after the sale!

The other main difficulty with protection by restriction is that many beneficiaries under a trust of land will neither know that they are indeed beneficiaries, nor that they need to protect their interest under a restriction. Similarly, a large number of sole registered proprietors, in the same situation as Ola, will not know that, legally, they have become trustees. As we have already said, these types of trust of land usually arise informally and in the context of family or romantic relationships, in which none of the parties ever imagine that they need legal protection from each other.

This brings us back to Ryan's situation: no steps have been taken to register a restriction and no second trustee has been appointed.

 EXAMPLE

Ryan has no idea that Ola is about to sell the property. Neither does he realize that he can protect his interest by entering a restriction. One day, he returns home from a short business trip to find his belongings in the street. His key no longer fits the front door. When he knocks at the door, Martin opens it and tells Ryan that he is the new legal owner of the property. Ola seems to have disappeared without trace.

We will leave poor Ryan on the doorstep for a moment while we think about how best we can help him.

7.3.3 Protection of beneficiaries under a trust of land: overriding interests

The 1925 draftsmen recognized that, just as protection for purchasers was required, so too was protection for equitable owners, such as Ryan. They decided that certain types of interest that could not be recorded on the face of the land register were so important that they could still bind the purchaser—even if the purchaser did not know of the existence of those interests at the time of purchase. These are called overriding interests.

For the purposes of this chapter, we will confine ourselves to looking at only one kind of overriding interest—that of an equitable owner in actual occupation of the land.

▶ CROSS REFERENCE

For more on overriding interests, see Chapter 4.

7.3.3.1 The old law: the Land Registration Act 1925

The concept of overriding interests was introduced in LRA 1925; the concept was preserved, with some changes, in the more recent LRA 2002. We will consider the old law first and then look at the changes made by the new Act.

 STATUTE

Land Registration Act 1925, s. 70(1)

All registered land shall, unless under the provisions of this Act the contrary is expressed on the register, be deemed to be subject to such of the following overriding interests as may be for the time being subsisting in reference thereto … (that is to say)—

…

(g) The rights of every person in actual occupation of the land or in receipts of the rents and profits thereof, save where enquiry is made of such person and the rights are not disclosed;

…

Essentially, for an interest to be overriding and so binding on a purchaser, the equitable owner must satisfy two criteria:

1. The equitable owner must be able to show that he or she has an equitable interest in the land. This might have arisen under an express, resulting, or constructive trust.

2. The equitable owner must prove that, at the time of the sale, he or she was in actual occupation of the land.

Although we need to consider the last of these in more detail, the requirements can be simply expressed as follows:

equitable interest + actual occupation = overriding interest

To demonstrate how this operates in practice, it will help to look at a case.

🔍 CASE CLOSE-UP

Williams and Glyn's Bank Ltd v. Boland [1981] AC 487

Mr and Mrs Boland purchased a property. The house was registered in the sole name of Mr Boland. Mrs Boland however, had made a substantial contribution to the acquisition of the property and so she had an equitable interest in it under a resulting trust.

The land holding might be illustrated as in Figure 7.5.

Unfortunately, at a later date, Mr Boland mortgaged the house to raise some money. Mrs Boland did not consent to or even, it appears, know of this transaction. The bank made no enquiries of Mrs Boland before lending the money. Mr Boland fell behind on mortgage repayments and, to recover its money, the bank tried to repossess the property. Mrs Boland claimed that her interest was binding on the bank because, although it did not appear on the land register, it was an overriding interest under LRA 1925, s. 70(1)(g).

She claimed that she had:

an equitable interest in the property + actual occupation of the property.

She said that this bound the bank.

The House of Lords agreed with her. Referring to both Mrs Boland and another wife, whose appeal was heard at the same time, Lord Wilberforce said (at 508):

> In my opinion, the wives' equitable interests, subsisting in reference to the land, were by the fact of occupation, made into overriding interests, and so protected by s. 70(1)(g).

Figure 7.5 Legal and equitable interests in *Williams and Glyn's Bank Ltd v. Boland*

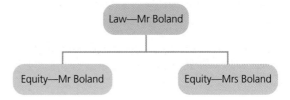

Actual occupation

One of the main discussions in *Boland* was the meaning of 'actual occupation'. No guidance was given in the LPA 1925. The question of whether or not somebody is in actual occupation is, as Lord Denning said when *Boland* passed through the Court of Appeal, a 'matter of fact, not a matter of law'—(at 322).

In the House of Lords, Lord Wilberforce decided that the words 'actual occupation' were 'ordinary words of plain English, and should … be interpreted as such' (at 504). He said that what was needed was a 'physical presence' in the property (at 505). In most cases, this is easily established—if the equitable owner is living at the property, then he or she will be in actual occupation of it.

In *Link Lending Ltd v. Bustard* [2010] EWCA Civ 424, Mummery LJ considered the reluctance of the courts to lay down a 'single legal test' for determining whether somebody is in actual occupation. He said that case law established various factors that the judge had to take into account, including: '[t]he degree of permanence and continuity of presence of the person concerned, the intentions and wishes of that person, the length of absence from the property and the reason for it and the nature of the property and personal circumstances of the person' (at 27).

Difficulties might arise when the equitable owner has not yet properly moved into the property—perhaps because of building works being undertaken prior to occupation—or when the equitable owner is temporarily away from the property. The courts however, have taken a sensible, realistic view of what constitutes actual occupation. In *Lloyds Bank v. Rosset* [1989] Ch 350, although Mrs Rosset did not live permanently at the premises, the Court of Appeal decided that she was in actual occupation. She stayed there regularly, and spent each day at the property supervising the builders' renovations and doing some redecoration herself. It should be noted, however, that Mrs Rosset's physical presence had a degree of permanence—the property was semi-derelict and required a great deal of work before it could be occupied. The case eventually went to the House of Lords—*Lloyds Bank v. Rosset* [1991] 1 AC 107—in which Mrs Rosset lost her claim to an equitable interest in the property. The Court of Appeal's comments on actual occupation are nevertheless still useful to us.

If the presence is more 'fleeting', then actual occupation will not be established. In *Abbey National v. Cann* [1991] 1 AC 56, going into a property to lay carpets and moving in a few pieces of furniture were not acts considered to constitute actual occupation.

> **CROSS REFERENCE**
> For more on *Rosset*, see Chapter 9.

Temporary absences

Temporary absences from a property will not undermine an equitable owner's actual occupation. In *Hoggett v. Hoggett* (1980) 39 P & CR 121, the Court of Appeal said (at 128) that '[g]oing to hospital for a few days could not be regarded as going out of occupation'; neither could going 'on a weekend visit to a friend, or … shopping for a few hours'.

 CASE CLOSE-UP

Chhokar v. Chhokar [1984] FLR 313

Mr and Mrs Chhokar lived together in their family home. Mr Chhokar was the sole legal owner, but Mrs Chhokar had an equitable interest in the property.

The land holding might be illustrated as in Figure 7.6.

One day, Mr Chhokar decided to sell the property, without Mrs Chhokar's knowledge, to a friend of his, Mr Parmar. He arranged for the sale to be completed when Mrs Chhokar was in hospital giving birth to their child!

When Mrs and Baby Chhokar arrived home, they discovered that the locks had been changed and the 'proud father' had fled to India with the proceeds of sale. Mrs Chhokar claimed that she had an overriding interest that was binding on Mr Parmar. The court decided that, although she was not living there when the sale to Mr Parmar was completed, some of her furniture was still there and, in the circumstances, she was still in actual occupation.

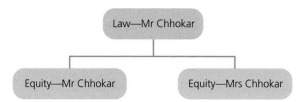

Figure 7.6 Legal and equitable interests in *Chhokar v. Chhokar*

Link Lending Ltd v. Bustard considered whether a mentally ill patient, Ms Bustard, was still in actual occupation of her home, even though she had been living away from it after being detained under the Mental Health Act 1983. The Court of Appeal decided that although she had not lived in the property for some time, Ms Bustard was still in actual occupation of it, because:

> it was her furnished home and the only place to which she genuinely wanted to return; she continued to visit the Property because she still considered it her home; those who had taken responsibility for her finances regularly paid the bills, such as the community charge, from her funds; she was in the process of making an application to the Mental Health Review Tribunal in order to be allowed to return home; and no-one took a final and irrevocable decision that she would not eventually be permitted to return home. (at 26)

Temporary absences (even if quite prolonged) will not, therefore, necessarily negate actual occupation, if other factors point to its existence.

Nature of the property

In *Thomas v. Clydesdale Bank* [2010] EWHC 2755 (QB) the property was owned by the male partner, but the expectation was that his girlfriend and her children would occupy the property with him. The house was in a state of disrepair, and the couple planned major renovations. In this case, the judge had to consider whether Ms Thomas, the female partner, had a 'realistic prospect' of establishing that she was in actual occupation of the property. In facts reminiscent of *Lloyds Bank v. Rosset*, Ms Thomas dealt with the builders on an almost daily basis, planning and supervising the renovations. Ramsey J said that in cases such as this, where the property was not yet suitable for habitation, the question of what constituted 'occupation' should be revised accordingly. He found that Ms Thomas was 'present at the property on a regular, almost daily basis' and that both parties had intended and wished for her to live there, after the renovation was complete: 'her presence was sufficient for the nature of the property in the course of renovation' (at para. 33). This raises the interesting question of whether the elements required to establish 'actual occupation' might vary with the nature of the property being occupied. In homes under renovation, such as this, it would not be reasonable to expect the claimant to be able to demonstrate a permanent physical presence in the usual sense of living at the property.

Timing

The need to prove an overriding interest most often arises when the sole legal owner of the property is trying to sell the property to someone else, without the equitable owner's consent. A difficulty in timing occurs here, because of the nature of land conveyancing in England and Wales.

When somebody buys a property, the process takes place in a number of stages. Following exchange of contracts, which makes the agreement binding on both parties, the sale is 'completed' by the payment of the monies owed. After this final stage, the new owner is able to move into the property. At this stage, however, you might be surprised to discover that the purchaser is not yet the legal owner of the property—he or she becomes such only when his or her title is registered at the Land Registry. The time between the completion of the sale and the registration of the new owner's title is called the registration gap.

In order to establish that he or she has an overriding interest, we know that the equitable owner has to establish both an equitable interest and that he or she is in actual occupation of the property. The registration gap, then, raises the issue of when that actual occupation must be established in order to bind the purchaser: is it at the date of completion or at registration of the new owner's interest?

The question was comprehensively considered in *Abbey National v. Cann*.

▶ **CROSS REFERENCE**

For more on the stages of conveyancing and the registration gap, see Chapter 2.

CASE CLOSE-UP

Abbey National v. Cann [1991] 1 AC 56

George Cann bought a house for his mother and stepfather. His mother contributed some of the purchase money for the property and so had an equitable interest under a resulting trust.

The land holding might be illustrated as in Figure 7.7.

The sale completed on 13 August. George raised some money by granting a mortgage and this charge was also executed on 13 August. George, however, was not registered as legal owner until 13 September and the charge on the property was registered at the same time. By the time that the charge was registered, Mrs Cann was living in the property.

George defaulted on his mortgage payments and the bank tried to repossess the property. Mrs Cann argued that she had an overriding interest, binding on the bank. She clearly had an equitable interest, but the issue became whether this was combined with the requisite actual occupation. This all turned on the relevant date for establishing actual occupation. If the relevant date was the date of completion, then Mrs Cann had not been in occupation and the bank took free of her interest. If the relevant date was the date of registration, then she had been in occupation and the bank was bound.

The House of Lords decided that the relevant date for establishing actual occupation was the date of completion. To decide otherwise would be to expose the purchaser to the possibility of being bound by overriding interests that he had no means of discovering and this would lead to a '*conveyancing absurdity*'.

However, although the relevant date for actual occupation was the date of completion, the relevant date for determining the existence of an overriding interest is the date of registration of the estate. *Cann* also raised the issue of whether there was a gap—a '*scintilla temporis*' between when the purchaser of a property acquired legal title to the land, and when she or he granted a charge over it to a mortgagee. The logic of this argument is that a purchaser can only grant a legal charge to a mortgagee if she or he actually holds the legal title, and so there must be a short gap between gaining legal title and granting a legal charge.

If there were such a gap, then in theory during this very short space of time, it was possible that an overriding interest could arise which would bind the mortgagee, or that an estoppel which had arisen before the purchaser acquired legal title to the property could be immediately 'fed' by the purchaser's acquisition of the legal title, and subsequently take priority over the mortgagee's interest in the property.

The House of Lords in *Cann* firmly established that there was no such gap: the relevant fact was that a purchaser acquiring a property with the assistance of a mortgage could only acquire the legal title with the funds that the mortgagee provided. Although there was often a physical gap between the registration of the purchaser's title and the registration of the legal charge, in reality the two events were indissolubly bound together, and the possibility of a *scintilla temporis* was nothing but a 'legal artifice'.

Figure 7.7 Legal and equitable interests in *Abbey National v. Cann*

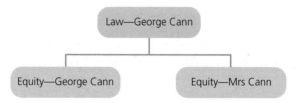

In *Scott v. Southern Pacific Mortgages* [2014] UKSC 52, this issue was raised again.

> ## 🔍 CASE CLOSE-UP
>
> ***Scott v. Southern Pacific Mortgages Ltd*** [2014] UKSC 52 *(Re North East Buyers Property Litigation)*
>
> This was a test case following a series of property transactions involving arrangements known as 'sale and rent back' deals. These usually involved home owners who had fallen into financial difficulties agreeing to sell their property to a buyer at a reduced price, in return for the promise that they could 'rent' their homes back after the sale of the property. These cases are now very rare, as it quickly became apparent that there were often problems with these arrangements, which were largely unregulated at the time. At the time that this case was heard in the Supreme Court, there were around ninety similar cases in the same geographical area involving around twenty lenders.
>
> Mrs Scott had agreed to a sale and rent back deal, whereby she sold her property to a purchaser on the understanding that she could continue to rent it back after the purchase; that she could do so for the rest of her life; that after her death the right would be transferred to her son; and that her son would receive a lump sum payment after an agreed period.
>
> After the sale, the purchaser granted Mrs Scott a two-year assured shorthold tenancy. Unfortunately, unknown to Mrs Scott, the purchaser had bought the house with the assistance of a mortgage, and had not informed the lender of any arrangements with Mrs Scott.
>
> The purchaser defaulted on the mortgage and the lender sought possession of the property.
>
> Mrs Scott argued that she had an overriding interest in the property which was binding on the lender. The Court was faced with the difficulty of deciding a case involving two innocent parties—Mrs Scott and the lender—neither of whom had been aware of the other's existence.
>
> The case raised some really interesting land law issues, and brings together some of the various points discussed earlier in this chapter. Firstly, Mrs Scott claimed that when contracts were exchanged on the property, she had acquired an equity in the property in addition to

► CROSS REFERENCE

For more on mortgages, see Chapter 13.

her freehold interest. (Don't forget that when exchange of a contract for the sale of land takes place in a conveyancing transaction, the seller still has the legal title, and the purchaser has the equitable title—only when the sale is registered does the legal title transfer to the purchaser.)

Secondly, she claimed that this equity was a proprietary right, because the purchaser had acquired a proprietary right to the property on exchange, and could therefore grant a proprietary right. Lastly, she claimed that this proprietary right combined with her actual occupation at the time of completion meant that she had an overriding interest which was binding on the lender.

The Court decided that the purchaser could not have conferred a proprietary right in the property on Mrs Scott, because the purchaser did not have legal title to the property at the time. Instead, the purchaser had conferred a personal right on Mrs Scott—a promise that she could continue to live in the property after the purchase. This could only be converted to a proprietary right if the promise (estoppel) was 'fed' by the purchaser's subsequent acquisition of the legal title in the property. At that point, the *Cann* principle would apply. In the absence of a *scintilla temporis*, there was no opportunity for Mrs Scott's interest to take priority over the lender's charge, as both the acquisition of the legal estate by the purchaser and the legal charge by the lender were 'indissolubly bound' and effectively took place in the same instant.

This decision has attracted some criticism from academic commentators, many of whom think that, although it was correctly decided, the reasons on which the decision was based were flawed.

The LRA 2002 confirms this decision (see 7.3.3.2).

Non-disclosure of an interest

To conclude our consideration of the old law under LPA 1925, s. 70(1)(g), we need to think about what happens if an equitable owner does not disclose his or her interest when asked to do so.

The section clearly says that, if an equitable interest and actual occupation are established, it will be binding on the purchaser 'save where enquiry is made of such person and the rights are not disclosed'. This means that, if a purchaser actually asks an equitable owner about his or her interest in the land and he or she deliberately conceals it, the purchaser will not be bound by the equitable owner's interest, even if the elements of the potentially overriding interest are made out.

7.3.3.2 The new law: the Land Registration Act 2002

 STATUTE

Land Registration Act 2002, Sch. 3, para. 2 [Interests of persons in actual occupation]

An interest belonging at the time of the disposition to a person in actual occupation, so far as relating to land of which he is in actual occupation, except for—

...

(b) an interest of a person of whom enquiry was made before the disposition and who failed to disclose the right when he could be reasonably expected to do so;

(c) an interest—

> (i) which belongs to a person whose occupation would not have been obvious on a reasonably careful inspection of the land at the time of disposition, and
>
> (ii) of which the person to whom the disposition is made does not have actual knowledge at that time;
>
> …
>
> (Note that LRA 2002, Sch. 1, deals with interests that override the first registration of land. LRA 2002, Sch. 1, para. 2, includes 'an interest belonging at the time of the disposition to a person in actual occupation'. LRA 2002, Sch. 3, refers to all subsequent dispositions of the land.)

⟩ CROSS REFERENCE

For more on overriding interests and dispositions, see Chapter 2.

On looking at LRA 2002, Sch. 3, para. 2 it becomes apparent that the new law basically repeats the old law under LPA 1925, s. 70(1)(g), with a few small, but important, additions.

In order to establish an overriding interest under that paragraph, one still needs to establish:

equitable interest + actual occupation.

The meaning of 'actual occupation' is not given in the LRA 2002 and so the old authorities, considered earlier, continue to apply.

The wording of LRA 2002, Sch. 3, para. 2 restricts the overriding interest to the part of the land that the equitable owner is actually occupying—something over which there was some confusion under the old law. In *Ferrishurst v. Wallcite* [1999] 1 All ER 977, the Court of Appeal held that, if a person had a right in relation to the whole of a piece of land, but was only in actual occupation of part of it, he or she would still have an overriding interest in respect of the whole of the land. Fortunately, LRA 2002, Sch. 3, now resolves this somewhat odd situation.

When will the interest not be overriding?

 STATUTE

Land Registration Act 2002, Sch. 3, para. 2 [Interests of persons in actual occupation]

An interest [will not be overriding where it is:]

…

(b) an interest of a person of whom enquiry was made before the disposition and who failed to disclose the right when he could be reasonably expected to do so;

…

LRA 2002, Sch. 3, para. 2(b) repeats the part of the old law relating to non-disclosure of the interest. Under the LRA 2002, if a potential purchaser asks an equitable owner about his or her interest in the land and the equitable owner does not disclose either his or her interest or the nature of his or her interest 'when he could be reasonably expected to do so', then the purchaser will take free of that interest.

In other words:

equitable interest + actual occupation + non-disclosure of that interest when asked
≠ overriding interest.

The courts' interpretation of when an equitable owner would 'be reasonably expected' to disclose his or her interest cannot be predicted, but it seems safe to assume that, as long as the purchaser asks the right questions of someone other than the legal owner living in the property, then he or she will continue to be protected. The difficulty, as discussed earlier, is that, due to the informality of family arrangements, equitable owners may not even realize that they have an equitable interest in the property: if somebody does not know that he or she has an equitable interest, could he or she be 'reasonably expected' to disclose it when asked by a potential purchaser? Often an equitable owner will only fully understand his or her rights following a visit to a solicitor after the legal owner has already sold the property!

 STATUTE

Land Registration Act 2002, Sch. 3, para. 2 [Interests of persons in actual occupation]

An interest [will not be overriding where it is:]

…

(c) an interest—

   (i) which belongs to a person whose occupation would not have been obvious on a reasonably careful inspection of the land at the time of disposition, and

   (ii) of which the person to whom the disposition is made does not have actual knowledge at that time;

…

Reading LRA 2002, Sch. 3, para. 2(c), it is tempting to conclude that the new Act has reintroduced the concept of notice to registered land. Certainly it appears that the purchaser must be much more careful when inspecting a property under the new Act.

Paragraph 2(c)(i) says that, if an interest was not obvious to the purchaser on a 'reasonably careful' inspection of the land, it will not be overriding. In most of the cases at which we have looked— for example, *Williams and Glyn's Bank v. Boland*—actual occupation would have been obvious, because the wife's possessions were apparent in the family home. However, as we know from cases such as *Chhokar v. Chhokar*, deceitful legal owners exist and they may deliberately conceal all evidence of actual occupation from a potential purchaser.

▶ CROSS REFERENCE
For more on the doctrine of notice, see Chapter 2.

This is what happened in an old case involving unregistered land: *Kingsnorth Trust Ltd v. Tizard* [1986] 2 All ER 54. In that case, following a separation, the husband obtained a substantial mortgage on the family home without the wife's knowledge or consent. The husband went to great lengths to conceal the wife's existence. He described himself as 'single' on his mortgage application form, arranged for the bank's surveyor to visit at a pre-arranged time at which his wife was not at the house, and apparently concealed all evidence of her presence there.

One of the issues in the case was whether the surveyor had carried out all of the inspections of the property that should reasonably have been made. Judge John Finlay QC expressed the following view of what could reasonably be expected (at 61):

> In his evidence [the surveyor] made it clear that he was suspicious; he was on the lookout for signs of female occupation; not the occupation of a wife, but that of a girlfriend. He found no such signs, but his evidence made it clear that he regarded it as his duty to look for them. He drew the line, however, at opening cupboards and drawers. [His] understanding of his duty to look for signs of occupation by anyone else accords with mine.

Tizard, then, provides us with a useful starting point: the purchaser need not 'open cup-boards and drawers', but must nevertheless be thorough when inspecting the property. In *Thomas v. Clydesdale Bank* [2010] EWHC 2755 (QB) Ramsey J helpfully addressed the issue of what might constitute a 'reasonable inspection' of the land. He said that 'the concept of inspection strongly suggests that what has to be obvious is the relevant visible signs of occupation upon which a person who asserts an interest by actual occupation relies'. He rejects the idea that the phrase implies either that the person inspecting should have any particular knowledge of another's occupation, or that there is any implied requirement on the person inspecting the property to make reasonable enquiries. He concludes (at 40): 'it is the visible signs of occupation which have to be obvious on inspection'. Useful though this judicial clarification is, it still does not provide any assistance to a potential purchaser in the case of an owner who has deliberately concealed the 'visible signs' of another's occupation at the property.

LRA 2002, Sch. 3, para. 2(c)(ii) also poses a potential problem in that it does not make clear whether the purchaser must have 'actual knowledge' of the equitable interest or the actual occupation in order to be bound by the interest. It seems sensible to assume that, if the potential purchaser actually knew that the person who occupied the property had an interest in the land and still went ahead with the purchase, he or she would be bound by this interest. This is confirmed by *Thomas v. Clydesdale Bank*, where the judge said (at 48 and 49):

> I consider that the question of actual knowledge under paragraph 2(c)(ii) has to be construed in the context of the type of interest which is being dealt with. Where an interest belongs to somebody in actual occupation, very often the scope and extent of that interest will depend on the legal analysis of a number of facts and will rarely be ascertainable from a legal document. In any event … even a legal document may be construed by lawyers for the Bank as not giving rise to an interest when in fact it does. In such circumstances it could be said that the Bank did not have actual knowledge of the interest. That would be contrary to common sense.
>
> In my judgment … the Bank has to have actual knowledge of the facts which give rise to the alleged interest. In this case, the Bank were aware that [the legal owner] had a new partner, that [that partner] was intending to contribute £100,000 to the Property and that the Property was intended to become the family home for the [legal owner] and his partner.

Matters such as the financial contribution to the purchase price of the property made by the person seeking to prove that he or she was in actual occupation and the intention of the parties in respect of the property are all relevant factors in establishing an overriding interest (equitable interest + actual occupation). If the purchaser is aware of such matters, then it appears from the judge's reasoning that he or she will be deemed to have actual knowledge under LRA 2002, Sch. 3, para. 2(c)(ii).

 EXAMPLE

Whatever happened to Ryan?

You will remember that we left Ryan at the front door of his former home, which Ola had sold to Martin. We are now armed with enough legal knowledge to advise him.

In order to establish that he has an overriding interest that is binding on Martin, Ryan must demonstrate two things. He must first show that he has an equitable interest in the property and then that he is in actual occupation of the property.

As we know:

equitable interest + actual occupation = overriding interest.

Ryan contributed to the purchase price of the property and so has an equitable interest under a resulting trust.

He also was actually living in the property—using Lord Wilberforce's 'ordinary words of plain English', he was in actual occupation of it. He was away on a short business trip, but, as we know from *Chhokar v. Chhokar*, temporary absences do not negate actual occupation.

Under the old law (LRA 1925, s. 70(1)(g)), Ryan would have established that he had an over-riding interest that was binding on Martin. Under the new law, although it is clear that he has established an overriding interest, we must double-check that it is not excluded under Sch. 3, paras 2(b) or 2(c):

- Did Martin ask Ryan about his interest in the property?
- If so, did Ryan fail to disclose it when he could reasonably be expected to have done so?

(There is no evidence that Martin ever asked Ryan about his interest in the property and so this exception does not apply.)

- Was Ryan's existence obvious from a reasonably careful inspection of the land?
- Did Martin have actual knowledge of his interest?

We are told that, when Martin went to look around the property, he saw male clothes and toiletries, but did not ask Ola about them. It would appear, then, that Ryan's existence was obvious from a reasonably careful inspection of the land. Martin should have made further enquiries and he failed to do so. Martin is bound by Ryan's equitable interest.

As we will see in later chapters, this means that Ryan may still have the right to occupy the property with Martin!

Recent developments

A recent decision by the Court of Appeal has some potential implications for the *Boland* principle, and although we will need to see what happens in the courts subsequently, it is an interesting situation to consider here briefly.

🔍 CASE CLOSE-UP

Credit & Mercantile Plc v. Kaymuu Ltd [2015] EWCA Civ 655

Mr Wishart and Mr Sami Mudurolgu ('Sami') had for some years undertaken joint business ventures, with no written agreement between them, but operating on a relationship based on trust. Mr Wishart wanted to buy a family home ('Dalhanna') using the proceeds of a joint business venture, and he asked Sami to deal with the purchase for him. He trusted his friend to the extent that he did not read the contract for the purchase of the property. Unknown to Mr Wishart, Sami purchased the property through his own company, Kaymuu Ltd.

Mr Wishart and his partner moved into the property. Unfortunately, after the couple moved into the property, Sami obtained a mortgage of £500,000 from Credit and Mercantile plc which was secured on the property. At a later date, Sami defaulted on the mortgage repayments and the lender sought possession of the property, eventually selling it to settle the outstanding mortgage debt.

> **CROSS REFERENCE**
> For more on mortgages, see Chapter 13.

Mr Wishart claimed that he was entitled to a share of the proceeds of sale, because he had an overriding interest in the property, under para. 2 of Sch. 3 of the LRA 2002, based on an equitable interest and actual occupation, which would have been obvious on a reasonably careful inspection of the land at the date that the mortgage was created.

Usually, as we have already seen in cases such as *Boland*, this combination of factors would have been binding on the lender. However, in this case, the Court found that by applying an old 'rule of law' called the *Brocklesby* principle, Mr Wishart did not have an overriding interest and the lender was therefore not bound.

The principle comes from a case called *Brocklesby v. Temperance Permanent Building Society* [1895] AC 173. It arises in a very specific set of circumstances where:

- the owner of an asset has given actual authority to another person (the agent) to deal with that asset in some way on his behalf; where
- the owner has given the agent the means of holding himself out to a purchaser or lender as the owner of the asset or having the full authority to deal with it; together with
- an omission by the owner to bring to the attention of a person dealing with the agent any limitation that exists as to the extent of the actual authority of the agent.

In these circumstances, the Court considered it fair that the lender should not be bound by the interests of a beneficial owner of the property, because the owner had effectively 'given the fraudster the means of committing the fraud'.

Mr Wishart had given Sami full authority to deal with the property on his behalf; he also supplied Sami with the means of holding himself out as the owner of the property and he 'omitted' to tell the lender the limitations of Sami's ability to deal with the property.

This is quite a difficult decision, not least because it is difficult to accuse Mr Wishart of an 'omission', given that he was completely unaware of Sami's actions, or even the existence of the lender!

The case may have wider implications for the *Boland* type claimant. Often, people are not even aware that they have an equitable interest in a property, and so may not realize that they need to act to protect their interest. Also, in a *Boland* scenario, the claimant has usually allowed a partner to take care of financial matters, and arguably each of the *Brocklesby* elements will be easily made out. In balancing the interests of two innocent parties—the equitable owner who is unaware of the legal owner's actions and the lender who has lent in good faith—the courts seem to be moving more consistently towards protecting the interests of the lender.

7.3.4 Overreaching tops overriding

As we saw at 7.3.1, if the purchase money is paid to two or more trustees, the interest of the equitable owner will be overreached—that is, it will disappear from the property and into the proceeds of sale. Once this has happened, the equitable owner will never again be able to claim that he or she has an overriding interest. This was established in *City of London Building Society v. Flegg* [1988] AC 54, and what it means, in practice, is that the interest of an equitable owner in actual occupation will only ever be overriding in situations in which there is one sole legal owner of land and the purchaser does not appoint a second trustee to receive the purchase money.

THINKING POINT

What might Martin have done to avoid being bound by Ryan's overriding interest?

He might have asked Ola to appoint a second trustee and insisted that he pay the purchase money to both. Ryan's interest in the property would then have disappeared and would only have existed in the proceeds of sale. Martin would have taken the house free of Ryan's interest.

 ## Summary

1. If the land register records a sole legal owner of property, there may be complications.

2. The sole legal owner may also be the sole equitable owner, in which case, no trust of land arises.

3. The sole legal owner may hold the land entirely on trust for someone else.

4. The sole legal owner may hold the land on trust for him- or herself and someone else. This causes the most potential difficulties.

5. The equitable owner can enter a restriction on the register to protect his or her interest.

6. If the equitable owner does not enter a restriction, he or she is at risk, as is a potential purchaser.

7. The equitable owner may have an overriding interest, which would bind the purchaser.

8. To establish an overriding interest, the equitable owner must establish an equitable interest and actual occupation.

9. The courts interpret 'actual occupation' in terms of 'ordinary words of plain English'.

10. To avoid an overriding interest, the purchaser can pay the purchase money to two or more trustees. This would overreach the equitable interests in the property.

11. The interest of the equitable owner would then be swept off the property and into the proceeds of sale.

 ## The bigger picture

- If you want to see how this area of land law fits into the rest of your studies, you can look at Chapter 14, especially 14.3.
- For some guidance on what sort of exam questions come up in this area, see Chapter 15, 15.9.
- For more judicial discussion on actual occupation, see the following cases:

Actual occupation

Stockholm Finance Ltd v. Garden Holdings Inc [1995] LTL (26 October 1995)

Thompson v. Foy [2009] EWHC 1076 (Ch)

? Questions

Self-test questions

1. Tajinder wants to buy a property. She looks on the land register and sees that the house is registered to Paul. Tajinder goes to look at the property. She meets Suli, who seems to be living there. She asks Suli whether she has any interest in the property. Suli does not seem to want to answer Tajinder's questions. She just says that the house 'is nothing to do with her'. Tajinder is very keen to buy the house, but is now a little worried about Suli. Advise Tajinder.

2. After Tajinder leaves, Suli becomes concerned that Paul is trying to sell the house. She contributed a considerable amount of money to the purchase price. She has been living there for the past three years, although her job as a pilot takes her on many trips away from home. She is due to go on a long-haul trip to China and she was intending to combine this with a three-month holiday, travelling around Asia. Now she feels anxious about what Paul might do when she goes away. Advise Suli.

Exam questions

1. Louise and Andy have been trying to buy their dream home by the seaside. They have realized that they simply cannot afford it by themselves, so they ask Ken and Doreen—Louise's parents—to help them. Ken and Doreen have plenty of money, so they agree to provide half of the money to buy the house. They make it clear that this is not a gift, and that they intend to live in the house with Louise and Andy. They say that they do not want their names put on the land register, however, because they do not want 'people to know [their] business'. The house is registered in the joint names of Louise and Andy. Both couples live in the property happily for a few years. One day, Louise and Andy decide to set up a dog-grooming business. Unknown to Ken and Doreen, they raise some funds by granting a mortgage over the seaside house. Unfortunately, they find that they have overestimated the demand for dog grooming by the seaside. They soon fall behind on their mortgage payments and the bank starts repossession proceedings. Advise Ken and Doreen.

 For suggested approaches to answering these questions visit the Online Resource Centre.

≡ Further reading

Bogusz, B., 'The relevance of "intentions and wishes" to determine actual occupation: a sea change in judicial thinking?' [2015] Conv 27
This article looks at how judges approach the question of determining actual occupation in the light of *Link Lending v. Bustard*.

Greer, S., 'As safe as houses?' (2015) 165(7669) NLJ 14

A longer analysis of *Credit & Mercantile plc v. Kaymuu Ltd* [2015] EWCA Civ 655.

https://www.gov.uk/government/organisations/land-registry

There are a lot of useful resources on this website, but look particularly at Practice Guide 15: overriding interests and their disclosure.

Law Commission/HM Land Registry (2001) Land Registration for the Twenty-First Century: A Conveyancing Revolution, Law Com No. 271, available online at http://www.lawcom.gov.uk/wp-content/uploads/2015/04/Lc271.pdf

Part VIII deals with overriding interests.

Owen, G., 'A new model for overreaching—some historical inspiration' [2015] Conv 226

A consideration of the history and future of the overreaching rules, including discussion of proposed reform in Northern Ireland.

Owen, G., 'A new paradigm for overreaching—some inspiration from Down Under' [2013] Conv 377

An interesting comparison of issues around the concept of overreaching in Australia and England and Wales.

Sparkes, P., 'Reserving a slice of cake' [2015] Conv 301

A comprehensive and critical analysis of *Scott v. Southern Pacific Mortgages* and its implications for the priority rules. Well worth reading for its detailed consideration of the earlier cases such as *Cann* and its review of s. 28 and s. 29 of the LRA 2002.

Tee, L., 'The rights of every person in equitable occupation: an enquiry into section 70(1)(g) of the Land Registration Act 1925' [1998] CLJ 328

This is an interesting analysis of the section.

 ## Online Resource Centre

www.oxfordtextbooks.co.uk/orc/clarke_directions5e

For more advice relating to this chapter, including self-test questions and an interactive glossary, visit the Online Resource Centre.

8 Joint owners of land (co-ownership)

LEARNING OBJECTIVES

By the end of this chapter, you will be able to:

- understand the difference between 'joint tenancy' and 'tenancy in common';
- identify the different methods of severing a joint tenancy in land;
- explain the practical legal implications of co-ownership of land.

Introduction

CROSS REFERENCE

It might help you to re-read Chapter 7 at this point. Make sure that you clearly understand the difference between legal and equitable title.

In the last chapter, we concentrated on situations in which land is owned by only one person, described as the 'sole' owner of land. In reality, land is often owned by more than one individual. The most common example of this is the situation in which a couple buys a house together as their family home. Both individuals are described as 'co-owning' the property, or as owning it 'jointly'. Groups of friends or family members may also pool their finances to buy a property together. These groups are also described as 'co-owners' of the land.

This very common form of ownership brings along its own unique set of legal implications. These are built on what you have already learnt about trusts of land. It is important to understand what it means to be a 'co-owner', and what rights and responsibilities are attached to this title.

In this chapter, we will look at 'express' co-ownership of land. This is the situation in which owners make a conscious decision to own land together. In the next chapter, we will consider a form of 'implied' co-ownership, which is the situation in which the law recognizes that co-ownership has arisen, even though this is sometimes far from the intention of the parties.

8.1 Types of co-ownership

Legally, co-owners are described as having a **concurrent interest** in the land. This means that each of the owners holds an interest at the same time as the others.

This can be contrasted with a **successive interest** in the land, which arises when one owner's interest in the land is followed by another owner's interest in the land. For example, one owner may be allowed to live in a property for the duration of his or her life and the property will then pass to another owner: this is not co-ownership, because both owners do not hold an interest in the property at the same time.

There are primarily two types of co-ownership:

- joint tenancy;
- tenancy in common.

It is worth mentioning at this point that the word 'tenant' in this context does not indicate a leasehold title. It is simply the term used to describe the nature of ownership in a co-owned property.

> **concurrent interest**
> the owners all hold an interest in the land at the same time

> **successive interest**
> one owner's interest in the land is followed by another owner's interest in the land

8.1.1 Joint tenancy

Joint tenancy means that all of the owners own all of the land together. There is no question of the individual owners being entitled to a specific share of the property: effectively, the owners hold the land as one single owner. Neither owner, unless he or she ends (severs) the joint tenancy, can unilaterally dispose of his or her interest in the land—for example, by selling it or leaving it by will. (Severance is discussed more fully at 8.6.)

> **joint tenancy**
> the legal or equitable co-ownership of land by persons who together own the whole of the land

> ➡ | **EXAMPLE**
>
> Jen and Bob have purchased a house as joint tenants. After a quarrel, Jen wants to sell her share to Aaron. Can she do this?
>
> Not without severing the joint tenancy. As joint tenants, Jen and Bob each own the *whole* of the house together. Jen does not have a 'share' as such to sell.

8.1.2 Tenancy in common

Tenancy in common means that each of the owners holds his or her individual share of the land: the share can be quantified and the owner can do as he or she pleases with it—for example, sell it, or give it away, or leave it to somebody else in a will.

Tenants in common are said to have an 'undivided share' in the land. This slightly confusing description means only that, although each tenant in common can quantify his or her own individual (intangible) proportionate share of the land, he or she cannot point to a specific (tangible) part of it and say 'that part is mine'. The land itself remains 'undivided', although each co-owner can say that he or she owns, for example, one-half of the property.

> **tenancy in common**
> the equitable co-ownership of land by persons in equal or unequal shares

> ➡ **EXAMPLE**
>
> Angelina, Billy, and Courtney have pooled their finances to buy a house together. They have decided to hold it as tenants in common. Angelina wants to sell her share to Brenda. Can she do this?
>
> Yes. As a tenant in common, Angelina can dispose of her share in any way she pleases.

8.2 Legal and equitable ownership

➤ **CROSS REFERENCE**

For more on the separation between legal and equitable ownership, see Chapter 7.

The other important distinction that you must remember is the separation between legal and equitable ownership.

In terms of co-ownership, the division between legal and equitable is made somewhat easier because, in law, co-owners can only ever hold the legal title to property as joint tenants. In equity, owners can hold property either as joint tenants or as tenants in common.

> ➡ **EXAMPLE**
>
> Suppose Amy and Brian are joint owners of land: they can hold it in one of two ways, which can be illustrated as in Figures 8.1 and 8.2.

Figure 8.1 Amy and Brian as joint tenants in law and equity

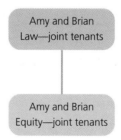

Figure 8.2 Amy and Brian as joint tenants in law and tenants in common in equity

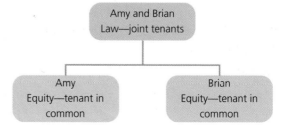

8.3 Joint tenancy

8.3.1 **Legal title**

As Figures 8.1 and 8.2 demonstrate, the only form of co-ownership now possible in terms of legal title is joint tenancy.

Before 1925, however, it was possible to hold the legal title in land as either joint tenants or tenants in common—and this caused a number of difficulties. Remember that tenants in common can act on their own share of the land at any time. They can sell it, or give it away, or leave it by will, for example. This caused serious problems if the owners of the land wanted to sell it, because, in order to do so, they had to obtain the consent of each and every one of the legal owners. Often, all of the legal owners could not be traced, or had themselves passed their title in the land on to other people.

To avoid such difficulties, the Law of Property Act 1925 (LPA 1925) simplified the position in respect of legal title in two ways. Firstly, it established that, at law, the co-owners had to hold as joint tenants.

STATUTE

Law of Property Act 1925, s. 1(6)

A legal estate in land is not capable of subsisting or being created in an undivided share in land …

Secondly, it restricted the number of legal owners to four.

STATUTE

Law of Property Act 1925, s. 34(2)

Where, after the commencement of this Act, land is expressed to be conveyed to any persons in undivided shares … the conveyance shall … operate as if the land had been expressed to be conveyed to the grantees, or if there are more than four grantees, to the first four named in the conveyance, as joint tenants in trust for the persons interested in the land.

This might sound very strange, but an example will demonstrate how this provision works in practice.

EXAMPLE

April, Bradley, Ceri, Dobir, and Evie have bought a house together. They have decided to hold it as tenants in common. Whose names will appear on the land register as the legal owners of the property?

April, Bradley, Ceri, and Dobir will all appear as the registered legal owners. This is because they are the first four named.

How does this affect Evie?

Evie will still be an equitable co-owner of the property. The four legal owners will hold the house on trust for themselves and Evie. As trustees, they have a legal responsibility towards

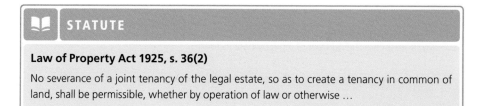

Evie that prevents them from acting inconsistently with her interests. If one of the four legal owners were to die, Evie could be added to the land register as a replacement (see Figure 8.3).

Figure 8.3 The legal and equitable co-ownership of five parties

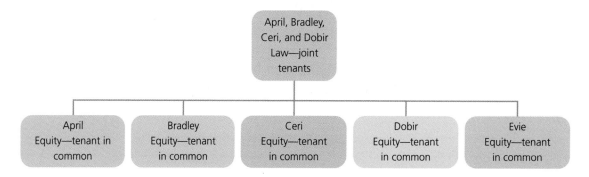

Remember that there is no limit to the potential number of equitable co-owners of the property.

It is not possible to sever the joint tenancy of a legal title.

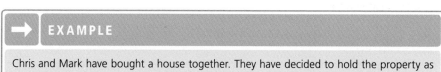

STATUTE

Law of Property Act 1925, s. 36(2)

No severance of a joint tenancy of the legal estate, so as to create a tenancy in common of land, shall be permissible, whether by operation of law or otherwise …

Severance of a joint tenancy of the equitable title is, however, possible, as we shall soon discover.

8.3.2 Equitable title

Many co-owners will want to hold the equitable title of their property as joint tenants. The reason for this is that, when land is held in this way, the right of survivorship (*ius accrescendi*) operates. This is probably the most important difference between joint tenancy and tenancy in common. It means that, if one of the joint tenants dies, the surviving tenant absorbs his or her interest in the property.

This is quite a difficult concept to explain. As we have already seen, if all of the joint tenants own the whole of the land together, they do not have shares or individual interests in the land as such. When one of them dies, he or she simply disappears from the joint tenancy and the other joint tenants remain. Perhaps an example will make this clearer.

EXAMPLE

Chris and Mark have bought a house together. They have decided to hold the property as joint tenants in equity.

The land holding might be illustrated as in Figure 8.4.

Chris has left her share of the property by will to her daughter, Sofia. When Chris dies, can Sofia inherit Chris's share?

No. As joint tenants, Chris and Mark both own the whole of the property, so Chris does not have a 'share' as such. When she dies, the principle of survivorship immediately operates and the remaining joint tenant, Mark, absorbs her interest. The land register will be altered to reflect the fact that she has died.

The landholding could then be illustrated as in Figure 8.5.

Figure 8.4 Chris and Mark as joint tenants in law and equity

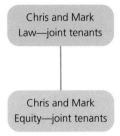

Figure 8.5 Mark as sole legal and equitable owner on the death of Chris

It is worth noting that a joint tenancy can never be severed in a will. We will discuss this further at 8.6.

8.3.2.1 Requirements for a joint tenancy in equity

In order for a joint tenancy in equity to exist, certain criteria must be satisfied—*A. G. Securities v. Vaughan* [1988] 3 WLR 1025.

These criteria are called the **four unities of joint tenancy** and are as follows:

1. unity of possession;
2. unity of interest;
3. unity of time;
4. unity of title.

To explore the four unities further, we will use an example.

> **four unities of joint tenancy**
>
> the four conditions that must be satisfied in order for a joint tenancy in equity to exist

> **➡ EXAMPLE**
>
> Ross and Rachel have bought the freehold of a house together and want to own it as joint tenants.
>
> In law, we have seen that they can only hold it as joint tenants, so there is no problem there. In order to hold it as joint tenants in equity, however, they must ensure that the four unities are present:
>
> - *Unity of possession* This means that both Ross and Rachel must be equally entitled to occupy and possess the whole of the house. Neither is prohibited from occupying, or restricted to occupying, any particular part of the property. In the example of Rachel and Ross, this unity is satisfied.
> - *Unity of interest* This means that both Ross and Rachel must hold the same interest in the property. This interest must be of the same nature and of the same duration. Rachel and Ross both own the freehold of the property, and so, once again, this unity is satisfied.
> - *Unity of time* This means that each tenant must acquire his or her title at the same time. Ross and Rachel bought the house together, and had it conveyed to them both at the same time, so this unity would be satisfied.
> - *Unity of title* This means that each of the tenants must acquire his or her title in the same way. Usually, this will mean that the title is transferred to them in the same document. Title to the property was transferred to Ross and Rachel in the same legal document or conveyance. This unity is also therefore satisfied.
>
> Ross and Rachel are therefore joint tenants both in law and in equity.
>
> We can illustrate the land holding of Ross and Rachel as in Figure 8.6.

Figure 8.6 Ross and Rachel as joint tenants in law and equity

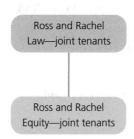

Ross and Rachel both own the whole of the land together.

8.4 Tenancy in common

8.4.1 **Legal title**

As we have already seen, the only form of co-ownership possible in terms of legal title is joint tenancy—LPA 1925, s. 1(6).

8.4.2 Equitable title

If the co-owners decide that they each want to retain their own 'share' of the property, they may decide to hold the equitable title as tenants in common. This means that each co-owner can dispose of his or her share of the property whenever and however he or she pleases, without the consent of the other co-owners. Most importantly, it also means that the principle of survivorship does not operate—that is, that when one of the co-owners dies, his or her share is not automatically vested in the remaining co-owners and he or she is free to leave it to whomever he or she chooses by will. Owners who are not romantically involved—perhaps friends who have bought a property together—often prefer this option.

8.4.2.1 Requirements for a tenancy in common in equity

The only requirement for a tenancy in common in equity is that the unity of possession must be satisfied. This means that each tenant in common must be entitled to occupy the whole of the property. It fits in with the idea of an 'undivided share' in the land: although a co-owner might only have contributed a quarter of the purchase price of the property and may thus only hold a quarter share of it, it would be difficult in practice if this were to mean that he or she were excluded from the remaining three-quarters of the property! As we have seen, the quantified share relates to the co-owner's share of the *value* of the property, rather than to a specific part of it.

Although the remaining three unities need not be present for a tenancy in common, in practice, they are sometimes satisfied.

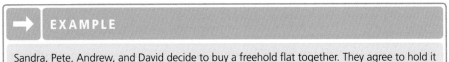

> **EXAMPLE**
>
> Sandra, Pete, Andrew, and David decide to buy a freehold flat together. They agree to hold it as tenants in common. The property is conveyed to them jointly on the same day. This would mean that the unity of time, the unity of interest, and the unity of title were all satisfied, as well as the unity of possession. But because they have decided to hold the property as tenants in common, then that is how they will hold the title in equity.

Again, thinking about this in terms of Figure 8.7 might be helpful.

Figure 8.7 Sandra, Pete, Andrew, and David as tenants in common in equity

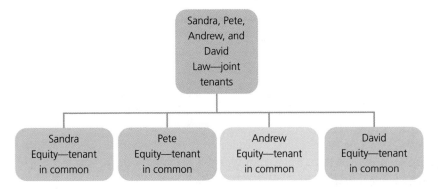

Note the difference between Figures 8.6 and 8.7. Remember that, in both cases, the co-owners have no choice but to hold the land as joint tenants in law—LPA 1925, s. 1(6). (Each owner being joined together in one box shows this.) In equity, however, each tenant in common has his or her own individual share and this is shown by separate boxes: each co-owner's share is his or hers to do with as he or she pleases.

8.5 Which is which? Identifying a joint tenancy or a tenancy in common

Now that we have explored the essential differences between a joint tenancy and a tenancy in common, it is important to establish how to identify each in practice (see Table 8.1).

Table 8.1 **Summary of the differences between a joint tenancy and a tenancy in common**

Joint tenancy	Tenancy in common
All of the joint tenants own the whole of the property together	Each of the tenants in common owns a quantifiable share of the property
Survivorship operates: following a joint tenant's death, the remaining joint tenants absorb his or her share into their own	Tenants in common can leave their share of the property by will
The four unities must all be present	Only the unity of possession must be present (the remaining three unities may or may not be present)

8.5.1 **Express declaration**

Of course, the starting point is that, when buying property, potential co-owners can decide how they intend jointly to hold the land and can expressly incorporate this into the conveyance at the outset. They can state that they wish to hold the property as joint tenants or as tenants in common. If they decide to be tenants in common, the solicitor conveying the property should ask them the proportion to be held by each co-owner. The document conveying the land to them will then refer to their chosen form of co-ownership.

 EXAMPLE

Ann and Barry purchase a house and decide that they wish to own it as joint tenants. The conveyance will indicate that the property is conveyed *'to Ann and Barry **jointly'** or 'to Ann and Barry, **on trust for themselves as joint tenants'.***

Jon and Vicky purchase a house and decide that they wish to own it as tenants in common, and that they will each own half of the property. The conveyance will indicate that the property is conveyed to *'Jon and Vicky **equally'*** or **'***to Jon and Vicky **in equal shares'.***

Remember that these are simply suggested wordings and the expressions most likely to be found in practice. Any words suggesting that each co-owner is entitled to an individual share of the property will indicate a tenancy in common. This is because, as we know, joint tenants do not have 'shares' as such.

The land register will also provide useful clues about the way in which the co-owners have decided to hold the land, as we will discover later at 8.7.

8.5.2 **General presumption**

In the absence of an express statement along the lines of those just suggested, there is a general presumption that, if land is conveyed to more than one owner, the owners will hold it in equity as joint tenants. This presumption has its origins in the old equitable maxim that 'equity follows the law'.

In law, as we know, co-owners can only hold the land as joint tenants. Applying the maxim, it follows that equity presumes the owners to hold the land as joint tenants in equity as well. This was confirmed in the case of *Stack v. Dowden* [2007] UKHL 17, in which Baroness Hale said that, where there were joint legal owners of a property, the starting point for the court was a presumption of joint beneficial ownership. Like any legal presumption, this can be rebutted by evidence (from the party claiming that the situation is different) which demonstrates that the parties intended to hold the property in different shares.

> **CROSS REFERENCE**
> For more on *Stack v. Dowden*, see Chapter 9.

Baroness Hale warned, however, that this was a task not to be lightly embarked upon and that the presumption would only be rebutted in unusual circumstances.

8.5.3 **Exceptions**

There are also certain sets of circumstances under which equity will be deemed *not* to follow the law and the court will presume the opposite—that is, that a tenancy in common was intended by the parties. All of these exceptions have the common feature that, in each, it would be unlikely that the parties would have intended the principle of survivorship to operate (as it does in a joint tenancy) and thus deprive them of disposing of their interest in the property as they wished.

The majority of the circumstances relate to commercial transactions, in which it is, of course, highly unlikely that one business partner would intend the other to acquire such a valuable windfall!

8.5.3.1 **Business partnerships**

If property is bought jointly for commercial purposes, there will be a presumption of a tenancy in common—*Malayan Credit v. Jack Chia–MPH Ltd* [1986] AC 549.

8.5.3.2 **Joint mortgagees**

If joint mortgagees lend money on the security of property, they are deemed to hold the property as tenants in common.

8.5.3.3 **Unequal contributions to purchase price**

Until *Stack v. Dowden*, if the co-owners each contributed different amounts to the purchase price of the property, the court presumed that they intended to hold the equitable title to the property as tenants in common. Now, however, the presumption has changed (see Chapter 9, 9.5.3.2).

EXAMPLE

Sam and Simon are two university friends. They decide to beat rising property prices and buy a house together. Of the £100,000 purchase price, Sam contributes £75,000 and Simon £25,000. Unfortunately, Sam dies suddenly.

What would the situation be if they had held the property as joint tenants in equity?

If the boys were joint tenants, on Sam's death, the *whole* of the property would belong to Simon. Sam's family would inherit nothing.

What would the situation be if they were tenants in common in equity?

If they were tenants in common, Sam's 75 per cent share of the property would pass to his heirs according to his will, or to his family on intestacy.

⟫ CROSS REFERENCE

For more on the family home, see Chapter 9.

Of course, there may be situations in which the co-owners contribute unequally—in some cases, one co-owner may pay the whole purchase price and the other nothing at all—but they will decide to hold the property as joint tenants. Usually, this happens within the context of a family home, where both co-owners want the survivor to be protected financially.

It is important to remember that these categories are not exhaustive. In *Malayan Credit v. Jack Chia–MPH Ltd*, Lord Brightman suggested that these categories were not '*rigidly circumscribed*' and that the court would look at the circumstances of the case in order to identify the intention of the parties in respect of their holding of the beneficial interest.

8.6 Severance

severance

the conversion of a joint tenancy in equity into a tenancy in common

As we have seen, the **severance** of a joint tenancy in law is not possible—LPA 1925, s. 36(2). A co-owner can, however, decide to sever his or her joint tenancy in equity at any time, provided that he or she does so in one of the following ways.

Severance converts the status of a co-owner from joint tenant to that of tenant in common. This means that he or she is now free to 'act on his own share'—that is, to sell it, give it away, or leave it by will to whomever he or she chooses. Survivorship no longer operates and so, on death, his or her share is passed according to his or her will or under the rules of intestacy. Only the co-owner who severs his or her joint tenancy becomes a tenant in common; the remaining owners (if there is more than one) continue to hold as joint tenants and only the severing owner's interest is affected.

 EXAMPLE

Emily, Jessica, and Hamish buy a property together. They decide to hold it as joint tenants (see Figure 8.8).

Figure 8.8 Emily, Jessica, and Hamish as joint tenants in law and equity

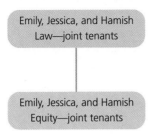

Emily, Jessica, and Hamish
Law—joint tenants

Emily, Jessica, and Hamish
Equity—joint tenants

 EXAMPLE

Jessica decides that she wants to travel the world. She wants to sell her share of the property, so she decides to sever her share and become a tenant in common.

Emily and Hamish continue to hold as joint tenants, but Jessica is now a tenant in common (see Figure 8.9).

Figure 8.9 Jessica as tenant in common in equity

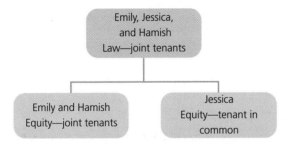

Emily, Jessica,
and Hamish
Law—joint tenants

Emily and Hamish
Equity—joint tenants

Jessica
Equity—tenant in
common

When a joint tenant severs the joint tenancy, he or she will take a share of the property that is proportionate to the number of joint tenants.

 EXAMPLE

In the previous example, there were originally three joint tenants. On severance, Jessica will take one-third of the property.

This is the case even if the original contributions to the purchase price were unequal. If co-owners decide that, although they have contributed unequal amounts to the purchase price of the property, they want to hold it as joint tenants, then there is no question, on severing the joint tenancy, that they will be able to revert to the proportion of their original contributions—*Goodman v. Gallant* [1986] Fam 106. The share each will take will depend on the number of joint tenants.

EXAMPLE

Margaret and Roman decide to buy a house together. The purchase price is £200,000. Margaret contributes £150,000 and Roman contributes £50,000. They decide that they will hold the house as joint tenants in equity.

Some years later, Margaret decides to sever the joint tenancy. Despite her original contribution of three-quarters of the purchase price, she will take only half of the value of the house as her share as a tenant in common.

Of course, the co-owners can agree among themselves the share that the severing tenant should take. But it should by now be apparent that, when considering purchasing a property with other people, it is essential to think carefully about the legal and financial implications of the choices to be made about co-ownership.

8.6.1 Means of severance

There are five principal means of severance, one of which is statutory and the remainder of which are rooted in case law.

8.6.1.1 Statutory severance: written notice

The simplest way to sever a joint tenancy is to serve a notice in writing on all of the joint tenants under LPA 1925, s. 36(2).

 STATUTE

Law of Property Act 1925, s. 36(2)

Where … any tenant desires to sever the joint tenancy in equity, he shall give to the other tenants a notice in writing of such desire …

This method of severance has the advantage of simplicity. The notice is entirely unilateral and does not require the consent of the remaining joint tenants. LPA 1925, s. 36(2) does not specify the form of the notice—only that it must be in writing; nor does it identify a mandatory means of service or delivery.

Case law has established certain other requirements, however, which are necessary for severance to be effective. Firstly, the intention to sever must be immediate, not planned for some future date—*Harris v. Goddard* [1982] 1 WLR 1203. The co-owner serving the notice of severance must intend it to take place from that moment on.

Secondly, there must be evidence that the notice has been delivered. This does not necessarily mean that it must have been read or even received by the other joint tenants.

 STATUTE

Law of Property Act 1925, s. 196(3)

This subsection provides that notice shall be sufficiently served if:

… it is left at the last-known place of abode or business in the UK of the … person to be served …

STATUTE

Law of Property Act 1925, s. 196(4)

This subsection provides that:

> ... notice ... shall also be sufficiently served if it is sent by post in a registered letter ... and if that letter is not returned through the post office undelivered ...

LPA 1925, s. 196(3)–(4) indicates that, provided the notice has been served by the means given in the subsections, it does not matter if the notice has not actually been received by the recipient. The case of *Kinch v. Bullard* [1998] 4 All ER 650 provides a practical demonstration of the court's interpretation of 'service'.

CASE CLOSE-UP

***Kinch v. Bullard* [1998] 4 All ER 650**

In this case, husband and wife were joint tenants, both in law and equity, of their family home. When the relationship broke down, the wife posted a notice of severance to her husband by first-class post. Unfortunately, the following day, her husband had a heart attack and was taken to hospital. The letter arrived, but the wife had changed her mind about severance and destroyed it. Following the death of the husband, the court held that delivery of the letter had effectively severed the joint tenancy, even though the husband had never been made aware of the intended severance.

This might seem a little harsh, but is consistent with the requirement that the intention to sever must be immediate.

THINKING POINT

Why do you think that the wife in *Kinch v. Bullard* had a sudden change of mind about severance after her husband's heart attack?

Because severance destroys the right of survivorship: if no severance had occurred, on her husband's death, the right of survivorship would operate and the wife would own the whole of the property. If severance had occurred before the husband's death, however, then the wife would own only her own share and her husband's share in the property would pass to whoever inherited his assets under his will or on intestacy.

Chadda v. Revenue and Customs Commissioners [2014] UKFTT 1061 (TC) was a case involving an inheritance tax dispute, which turned on whether or not severance had taken place before the husband's death. The parties had apparently signed a notice of severance, which had subsequently been lost by the solicitor and could not be found. The tribunal held that the question of whether written notice had been served was to be decided on the balance of probabilities. The evidence presented to them included the solicitor's and surviving relatives' unsurprisingly somewhat hazy recollections of what had happened over a decade before. The tribunal found that despite the lack of a copy of the written notice of severance, the joint tenancy had been severed by notice. Alternatively, the tribunal found that even if there was no valid written notice of severance, the joint tenancy had been severed by a mutual agreement—or—again alternatively—by the parties' mutual conduct. This case shows the potential overlap between the various possible means of severance.

8.6.1.2 **Other methods of severance**

Other methods of severance were identified in *Williams v. Hensman* (1861) 1 J & H 546, 557–8:

> A joint tenancy may be severed in three ways: in the first place, an act of any one of the persons interested operating upon his own share may create a severance as to that share … Secondly, a joint tenancy may be severed by mutual agreement. And, in the third place, there may be a severance by any course of dealing sufficient to intimate that the interests of all were mutually treated as constituting a tenancy in common …

Joint tenant 'operating on his own share'

This description is somewhat misleading, in that we have already decided that joint tenants do not own a 'share' of the land as such: all own the whole of the property. But it means that, if one of the joint tenants does something to indicate that he or she wishes to appropriate an individual share, rather than continue to own the whole with his or her fellow joint tenants, then that act will be taken as a desire to sever the joint tenancy.

The act is unilateral—that is, it does not require the agreement, or even the knowledge, of his or her fellow joint tenants—*Mortgage Corporation v. Shaire* [2001] Ch 743. It might involve something as straightforward as the severing tenant selling his or her interest in the land, or transferring it to a third party. Granting a mortgage on his or her share of the property would also constitute a severance—*First National Securities v. Hegarty* [1984] 1 All ER 139.

If a joint tenant becomes bankrupt, the joint tenancy is also severed. Clearly, this may well not be the joint tenant's intention, but the court's decision to declare the bankruptcy triggers a transfer of the joint tenant's interest to the trustee in bankruptcy. Although this is not a voluntary act by the joint tenant, severance nevertheless occurs.

Remember that the severance will only take effect in equity—LPA 1925, s. 36(2), which states that a joint tenancy cannot be severed in law. It must therefore comply with any relevant statutory provisions, such as LPA 1925, s. 53(1)(c), which requires that any disposition of an equitable interest must be in writing.

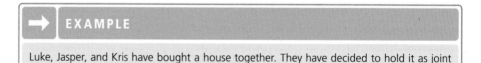

EXAMPLE

Luke, Jasper, and Kris have bought a house together. They have decided to hold it as joint tenants in both law and equity.

Their interests might be illustrated as in Figure 8.10.

Figure 8.10 Luke, Jasper, and Kris as joint tenants in law and equity

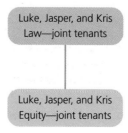

EXAMPLE

Kris has decided that he wishes to raise some money and sells his share of the property to Narissa (see Figure 8.11). How does this affect the interests of the remaining joint tenants?

Figure 8.11 Narissa is now a tenant in common in equity

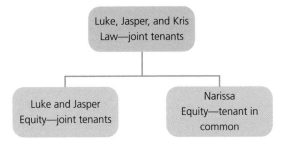

EXAMPLE

Nothing Kris can do—other than die—will sever the joint tenancy in law, so he will continue to hold the property as a joint tenant in law. But by selling his share, Kris has severed the joint tenancy in equity. He drops out of the picture and Narissa now holds his share as a tenant in common.

Note that Luke and Jasper will continue to hold the remaining part of the property as joint tenants, unless one of them severs the joint tenancy.

In order for his disposition to be effective, Kris must comply with LPA 1925, s. 53(1)(c), and ensure that the sale of property to Narissa is made in writing.

It is important to remember that severance cannot be effected by will. If a joint tenant leaves his or her 'share' to a third party in a will, it will not sever the joint tenancy. The reason for this is that, at the moment of death, the principle of survivorship operates and the interest of the deceased joint tenant immediately becomes absorbed into the interest of the remaining joint tenants. Leaving a share of property by will does not constitute a tenant operating on his or her own share.

Mutual agreement

Severance by mutual agreement is self-explanatory. It offers a flexible and less formal way for co-owners to sever their joint tenancy. All of the joint tenants must agree to sever and the agreement need not be in writing. Agreement can be express or implied—*Burgess v. Rawnsley* [1975] Ch 222.

The court will try to identify a clear intention that the parties intended to sever, although it will not necessarily need to see reference to 'severance', as such. The court will look in particular, for an indication that the parties no longer intend the principle of survivorship to operate. Evidence of this might include a mutual agreement that both joint tenants will leave each of their 'shares' of the property by will to a third party. Any agreement reached must relate to the *ownership* of the land, not just to its use or occupation.

The court will look at the evidence in order to establish that an agreement has actually been reached. If there is an express agreement to sever, the court will easily be able to find that the joint tenancy has been brought to an end; it is more difficult, however, when there is no evidence of an express agreement—although, even in this case, the court may decide on the facts that an implicit agreement has been made, which is sufficient to terminate the joint tenancy.

In many of these cases, there is an overlap between severance by mutual agreement and severance by a course of dealing between the parties.

 CASE CLOSE-UP

Burgess v. Rawnsley [1975] Ch 222

In this case, Mr Honick and Mrs Rawnsley met and bought a house together. Each paid half of the purchase price. They agreed to hold the house as joint tenants, both in law and equity. Following the breakdown of their friendship and Mrs Rawnsley's refusal to marry Mr Honick, the couple began negotiations to sell Mrs Rawnsley's share of the property to Mr Honick. Initially, the couple agreed on a price of £750 for her share, but Mrs Rawnsley subsequently demanded more money. Mr Honick died before any further progress was made in reaching an agreement. The issue then became whether the joint tenancy had been severed.

The court held that the agreement to settle at £750 was sufficient to sever the joint tenancy, although negotiations appeared to be continuing. Lord Denning said, however, that, even if an agreement had not been reached, there was sufficient indication of the parties' intention to sever by their mutual conduct in attempting to negotiate a price for the sale of Mrs Rawnsley's share. This decision illustrates the potential overlap between the various means of severance.

Mutual conduct or 'course of dealing'

In the absence of an obvious agreement to sever the joint tenancy, the court will also look at the conduct of the parties in order to identify whether there was, nonetheless, a mutual intention to effect severance. Sometimes, the conduct of the parties clearly demonstrates this: as in *Burgess v. Rawnsley*, for example, in which joint tenants negotiating the sale of one tenant's interest to the other indicated that both intended to sever the joint tenancy. But sometimes the conduct is less obvious: joint tenants making mutual wills leaving their 'share' of the co-owned property to a third party will also be construed as conduct evincing an intention to sever—*Re Wilford's Estate* (1879) 11 Ch D 267.

This is sometimes a more problematic decision for the court than a finding of mutual agreement, however, as *Burgess v. Rawnsley* itself demonstrates. In that case, although Lord Denning had no difficulty in identifying mutual conduct suggesting an intention to sever, Sir John Pennycuick suggested that, depending on the particular facts of the case, inconclusive negotiations may well not be sufficient to persuade the court that the parties had indeed formed an intention to sever. The difficulty is obvious: negotiations may be started and then dropped; words may be said in anger, with no real intention to trigger a significant legal implication. It may well not be sensible to treat inconclusive or preliminary negotiations as a manifestation of an intention to sever. The most important factor in all of these kinds of case, then, would seem to be the intention of the parties and the court will try to ascertain this from the facts of each particular case.

Two relatively recent cases highlight the difficulty for the court on occasions in identifying the means by which severance has taken place.

CASE CLOSE-UP

Quigley v. Masterson [2011] EWHC 2529 (Ch)

Mr Pilkington and his partner Mrs Masterson bought a house together as joint tenants in law and equity. Following the breakdown of their relationship, Mr Pilkington tried to sever the joint tenancy. His solicitors firstly sent a written notice of severance to Mrs Masterson's solicitors, and then sent a written notice to Mrs Masterson's place of work. Unfortunately, Mrs Masterson no longer retained her solicitors, and so they could not accept notice on her behalf. The notice sent to her work (which had her name misspelt) did not reach her.

Shortly afterwards, Mr Pilkington became unwell, and eventually the Court of Protection appointed his daughter, Mrs Quigley, as his deputy, which meant that she was responsible for his personal affairs. Plans were made to sell the house, with all parties assuming that Mr Pilkington and Mrs Masterson owned 50 per cent each. However, before any steps were taken to do this, Mr Pilkington died. The question then arose as to whether severance had occurred, and if so, by what means.

Firstly, neither notice was held to effect a severance under s. 36(2). It was not clear that the second notice had ever even been posted, and even if it had, the judge held that it did not satisfy the requirements of s. 196(3).

Mrs Quigley then argued that there was a mutual course of dealings, and that both parties had intended for severance to occur. The judge found that there was no such course of conduct, from the point at which Mrs Quigley took over as her father's deputy. On the contrary, she had done nothing to indicate that severance had been her intention.

However, the judge decided that severance had occurred by virtue of documents that Mrs Masterson had submitted to the Court of Protection, in which she accepted that she and Mr Pilkington each owned a 50 per cent share in the house. This constituted a notice under s. 36(2), and in the view of the judge: '*[r]ead in the context of the proceedings, it gave unambiguous notice of Mrs Masterson's present desire to sever the joint tenancy*' (at 33).

Further guidance in this area was provided by the then Master of the Rolls in *Davis v. Smith* [2011] EWCA Civ 1603.

 CASE CLOSE-UP

Davis v. Smith [2011] EWCA Civ 1603

Mr and Mrs Smith bought a property in joint names in 1989. When their marriage broke down in 2009, they were both advised by their solicitors to sever the beneficial joint tenancy, although neither had actually served a notice of severance on the other. During the process of their divorce proceedings, Mr and Mrs Smith's respective solicitors negotiated a division of the couple's assets, including the sale of the property, and shares in an endowment policy. Unfortunately, just before the divorce was finalized, Mrs Smith died unexpectedly. Mr Smith then claimed that although negotiations had been ongoing, the beneficial joint tenancy had not yet been severed.

THINKING POINT

Why would Mr Smith argue this?

Mr Smith would argue this because if the beneficial joint tenancy had not yet been severed, the principle of survivorship would operate, and Mr Smith would be entitled to the whole property.

 CASE CLOSE-UP

The judge at first instance held that severance had been effected, and Mr Smith appealed.

The Court of Appeal accepted that the proposal or even agreement to sell the property did not necessarily mean that the joint tenancy had been severed. Even if the house had been sold, a joint tenancy might continue into the proceeds of sale.

In this case though, there was a very clear understanding on both sides that the house would be sold, and the proceeds divided in agreed proportions between Mr and Mrs Smith. The couple had agreed that each would receive a proportion of the sale proceeds which would reflect the fact that Mr Smith had received more than Mrs Smith when their joint endowment policy had been sold some time earlier in the proceedings.

The Court also found it relevant that both parties had been legally advised and were conducting the negotiations on the basis of that advice. The fact that the policy had already been disposed of indicated that the division of assets which had been agreed upon was actually under way, and the sale of the house would have been the next phase of this process. The Court agreed that the beneficial joint tenancy had been severed.

Lord Neuberger also added some useful guidance on the relevance of the parties' intentions:

As in most cases involving arrangements between parties, whether contractual or otherwise, the court should concentrate on what passed between the parties by way of words or actions, and what was known to both parties. It should not normally consider what was in the mind of one of the parties, or what was communicated between one of the parties and his or her solicitor or other adviser.

What went on in a party's mind, what a party was advised, or what a party said to a third person is normally irrelevant to the issue of what the parties between them intended or understood. For the court to take into account such irrelevant material is normally positively dangerous (at 23 and 24).

Instead, he suggested, the Court should focus on 'what was known to, and, what passed between the parties, and what the parties actually did to the knowledge of each other' (at 24).

A final point to note is that the conduct of the parties should relate to the *ownership* of the property and not to its occupation. Perhaps surprisingly, if joint tenants physically divide the land between them, it will not indicate an intention to sever their joint tenancy.

 CASE CLOSE-UP

Greenfield v. Greenfield (1976) 38 P & CR 570

In this case, two brothers had purchased a house as joint tenants and had divided it into two flats: one in which each of them could live with his family. When one brother died, his wife claimed that the ownership of the flat in which they had lived had passed to her. Remember that, under a joint tenancy, the principle of survivorship means that the joint tenants—in this case, the brothers—both own the whole of the property. When one brother died, the whole of the property would therefore pass to the surviving brother. Only if the joint tenancy had been severed would the wife have acquired her late husband's share.

The court found that the joint tenancy had not been severed by the physical division of the property. Although the property had, indeed, been physically divided, this was to allow both families to have a separate home and was not an indication that the brothers wished to sever the joint tenancy. Once again, this case demonstrates the importance that the court places on identifying the intention of the co-owners.

Forfeiture

Forfeiture is probably the most sensational—but, thankfully, the least common—means of severance: if one co-owner unlawfully kills the other, the joint tenancy is deemed to have been severed. This is essentially on the grounds of public policy—that is, to prevent the murderer from benefiting from his or her crime.

 THINKING POINT

Without this rule, how would one joint tenant benefit from murdering his or her fellow joint tenant?

Remember that, when one of the joint tenants dies, the principle of survivorship kicks in and passes his or her interest to the remaining joint tenant. Clearly, the law would not want the murderer to benefit in this way from his or her crime, so it treats the act of murder as a severing event.

Once severance is deemed to have occurred, the murdered co-owner's share passes to his or her heirs under his or her will, or according to the rules of intestacy.

 EXAMPLE

Brenda and Bob buy a house together as joint tenants in law and equity.

Their interests might be illustrated as in Figure 8.12.

One day, many years later, Brenda murders Bob. This severs their joint tenancy in equity.

Their interests might now be illustrated as in Figure 8.13.

Figure 8.12 Brenda and Bob as joint tenants in law and equity

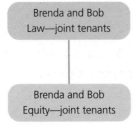

Figure 8.13 Brenda and Bob's heirs are now tenants in common in equity

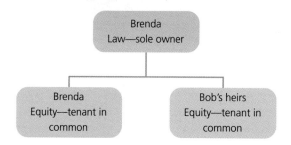

In cases other than murder—for example, manslaughter—the court is allowed some discretion to consider all of the circumstances of the case by means of Forfeiture Act 1982 (FA 1982), s. 2(1). FA 1982, s. 2(2) allows the court to consider matters such as the conduct both of the offender and victim, and any other material circumstances, in reaching its decision. This discretion has been exercised, for example, in cases in which the offender suffered domestic violence at the hands of the deceased—*Re K (Deceased)* [1986] Fam 180. In making a decision about whether or not to exercise its discretion, the court will consider not only the culpability of the offender and the conduct of the victim, but also the relative financial contributions of the parties to the purchase of the property (*Chadwick v. Collinson* [2014] EWHC 3055 (Ch)).

Q | CASE CLOSE-UP

Mack v. Lockwood [2009] EWHC 1524 (Ch)

Mr and Mrs Mack were initially joint tenants of their home. In 2004, Mr Mack severed the joint tenancy. In 2006, when he was 81 years old, Mr Mack killed his (much younger) wife, stabbing her around fifty-four times. There was evidence that the couple had had various arguments, but also that Mr Mack was suffering from a mental disorder, and he was eventually found guilty of the manslaughter of his wife. Mr Mack was the sole beneficiary of his late wife's will, which meant that her share of the family home would, under normal circumstances, pass to him.

The circumstances of the case meant that the rule of forfeiture operated to prevent the perpetrator (Mr Mack) benefitting from the victim's estate. However, in cases other than murder, as we have seen above, under FA 1982, s. 2, the court may mitigate the harshness of this rule, if it is not in the public interest to deprive the perpetrator of such benefit.

The Deputy Judge considered FA 1982, s. 2(2), which states that the court should not make such an order unless satisfied, given the conduct of the offender, the conduct of the deceased, and any other material circumstances, that the justice of the case required that the forfeiture rule should be modified. The 'paramount consideration' in deciding this was the extent to which the offender (Mr Mack) was to blame for his wife's death. Another consideration was the financial effect on other beneficiaries of a strict application of the rule.

The Deputy Judge concluded that Mr Mack's medical impairment did not significantly alter his responsibility for her death: he had intended to kill her. Mrs Mack had no history of violence towards her husband: this was not a domestic violence case. Neither would depriving Mr Mack of his late wife's interest in the house lead to unwelcome financial consequences: her share would pass to the couple's two sons, which it seemed likely that she would wish. For these reasons, it was not just for the court to disapply the forfeiture rule, and Mr Mack would not receive his late wife's share of the property.

8.7 Impact on the land register

Land owned by more than one owner can lead to problems for an unwary purchaser. When somebody buys a registered property, that person—or, more usually, his or her solicitor—will closely examine the land register in order to ascertain the true position in respect of the ownership of the land. One difficulty for potential purchasers is that, according to the 'curtain principle', details of equitable interests are kept off the face of the land register.

To protect the purchaser, the Land Registry under certain circumstances will make an entry in the register to restrict the proprietors' dealing with the land. In order to ascertain whether such a restriction is necessary, it must first obtain information about the way in which the co-owners intend to hold the land. As we have seen, when property is sold or transferred, the purchasers must complete a special form (TR1) to tell the Land Registry how the land is to be held.

The TR1 contains a section which asks co-owners to indicate whether:

- they are to hold the property on trust for themselves as joint tenants;
- they are to hold the property on trust for themselves as tenants in common in equal shares;
- they are to hold the property on trust: [indicate shares].

Depending on the answer indicated by the purchasers, the Land Registry will have to make slightly different entries in the register.

Unfortunately, as Baroness Hale pointed out in *Stack v. Dowden*, although form TR1 (introduced in 1998) is an improvement on the old Land Registry forms that did not ask about equitable interests at all, completing this part of form TR1 is still not mandatory. Baroness Hale expressed a fear that, given a highly competitive conveyancing market, solicitors often did not persuade their clients to complete it. If this part of the form were to be routinely completed by co-owners of land—or, indeed, were to be made mandatory—she suggested (at [52]) that '*the problem we now face would disappear*', because the equitable interests in the land would be decided and declared at the outset.

The starting point for the Land Registrar, when presented with co-ownership (and hence a trust of land), is that he or she must enter a restriction in the land register in the following terms:

> No disposition by a sole proprietor of the registered estate … under which capital money arises is to be registered unless authorised by an order of the court.

This is known as a 'Form A' restriction and the Land Registrar is obliged to do this under LRA 2002, s. 44(1), and LRR 2003, r. 95(2)(a).

> **CROSS REFERENCE**
> For more on the curtain principle, see Chapter 2.

> **CROSS REFERENCE**
> For more on restrictions, see Chapter 2. Take another look at Chapter 3, **Form 3.1**— the Land Registry transfer form TR1—before reading further.

> **STATUTE**
>
> **Land Registration Act 2002, s. 44 [Obligatory registrations]**
>
> (1) If the registrar enters two or more persons in the register as the proprietor of a registered estate in land, he must also enter in the register such restrictions as rules may provide for the purpose of securing that interests which are capable of being overreached on a disposition of the estate are overreached.
>
> …

▶ **CROSS REFERENCE**

For more on overreaching, see Chapter 7.

The purpose of the restriction is to comply with the overreaching provisions of LPA 1925, s. 27(2) (as amended by TOLATA 1996).

Essentially, the restriction warns any subsequent purchasers of the land that, to protect themselves, they must pay the purchase monies for the property to two trustees. By doing this, they trigger the overreaching provisions, and they then do not have to worry about unseen equitable interests in the land suddenly appearing and becoming binding on them.

However, depending on the co-owners' answers to the questions outlined earlier, it may not be necessary for the Land Registrar to enter the restriction, as we shall now see.

8.7.1 **Joint tenants**

If the co-owners intend to hold the land on trust for only themselves as joint tenants, then the Land Registrar does not need to enter a restriction on the register. The co-owners are able to deal with the land as they please and the potential purchaser is not threatened by the existence of undisclosed equitable interests, because, in this instance, the beneficiaries in equity are the joint tenants themselves.

In this case, the Land Registrar will simply enter the names of the joint tenants in the proprietorship register as proprietors of the legal estate in the land. (If there are more than four joint tenants, remember that only the first four will be included—see 8.3.1.) No other entry is necessary, because a subsequent purchaser of the property will be protected from any undetected beneficial interests by the presence of two or more trustees. Payment to both of these trustees means that any beneficial interests existing in the land are automatically overreached. The joint tenants—and indeed, because of the operation of survivorship, a remaining joint tenant—can give a valid receipt for capital monies provided to purchase the land.

8.7.2 **Tenants in common**

If the co-owners intend to hold the land as tenants in common, a restriction *must* be entered. This is because the existence of a tenancy in common may well mean that the ownership of the property in equity does not correspond to the ownership of the property in law, as it appears in the land register. Remember that a tenant in common can dispose of his or her share at any time and that another tenant in common will take his or her place. An example may explain the implication of this for would-be purchasers.

> **EXAMPLE**
>
> Asma and Richard buy a property together, and decide to hold it as tenants in common. They must, of course, hold it as joint tenants in law.
>
> Their interests might be illustrated as in Figure 8.14.

Figure 8.14 Asma and Richard as joint tenants in law and tenants in common in equity

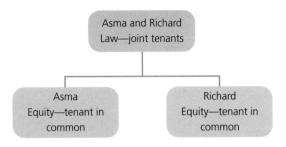

 EXAMPLE

In the land register, the names of Asma and Richard will be entered onto the proprietorship register as legal co-owners of the property. Because they intend to hold the land as tenants in common, the Land Registry will also enter a restriction in Form A (see earlier).

Some years later, Richard sells his interest to Colin.

The interests in the land might now be illustrated as in Figure 8.15.

Figure 8.15 Colin is now a tenant in common in equity

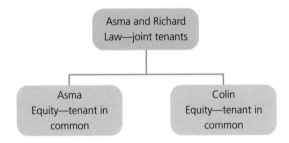

 EXAMPLE

The land register would not have changed at all. Asma and Richard are still the legal owners, because it is not possible to sever a joint tenancy in law. The would-be purchaser would have no idea that a new beneficiary—Colin—now had a valid (and binding) equitable interest in the property, because trusts are kept off the face of the register. The presence of the restriction would, however, alert the potential purchaser to the possibility that such changes may have occurred and to the necessity of paying the purchase money to two trustees. If the purchaser were to pay the money to two trustees, Colin's interest in the land would disappear and he would have instead an interest in the proceeds of sale. Colin would need to chase the trustees for his share of the money and, most importantly, he would have no claim on the purchaser at all.

8.7.3 **Severance**

If a joint tenant severs the joint tenancy, he or she must apply for a restriction to be entered on the land register—LRR 2003, r. 94(1). If severance has been effected by mutual agreement, this will be straightforward, but if the severance has taken place through a unilateral act—for example, by one joint tenant serving notice on another—then the severing joint tenant must send the Land Registry both a copy of the notice severing the joint tenancy and a signed certificate stating that this notice was served in accordance with LPA 1925, s. 36(2). The registrar will then complete the application without informing the other proprietors.

Once the restriction has been entered, however, the registrar will then inform all of the proprietors of a change in the register. They will then have an opportunity to object and to apply for alteration of the register if necessary.

An application must also be made if bankruptcy occurs, because this, of course, severs the joint tenancy. In this case, the trustee in bankruptcy may also apply for a restriction to be entered.

 ## Summary

1. Co-ownership of land brings with it a unique set of legal implications.

2. Co-owners can hold the land in equity either as joint tenants or as tenants in common.

3. The key characteristic of joint tenancy is that all of the owners own the whole of the land: it is not divided into quantifiable shares. On death, the principle of survivorship operates, whereby the interest of the deceased joint tenant is automatically absorbed by the remaining joint tenant(s).

4. Tenants in common, however, own a quantifiable share of the land.

5. Co-owners must decide how they wish to hold the land. For a joint tenancy to exist, however, the four unities must be present. These are the unities of possession, time, interest, and title. For a tenancy in common, only the unity of possession must be present.

6. Joint tenancies in equity can be severed to become tenancies in common.

7. Severance can occur in a number of ways: by notice (under LPA 1925, s. 36(2)); by mutual agreement; by a course of dealing; by a joint tenant operating on his or her own share (*Williams v. Hensman*).

8. Severance can also occur by forfeiture or bankruptcy.

9. Severance can never be effected by will, because, by then, survivorship has been triggered.

10. Co-ownership can also cause problems for unsuspecting purchasers of land.

11. If the co-owners are tenants in common, the Land Registrar will enter a restriction in the land register. This should also be entered if a joint tenancy is severed.

☐ The bigger picture

- If you want to see how this area of land law fits into the rest of your studies, you can look at Chapter 14, especially 14.3. For some guidance on what sort of exam questions come up in this area, see Chapter 15, 15.9.

- Reading cases in their entirety will always help you to further understand this area of law. Probably the most difficult part of severance lies in the analysis of mutual conduct. It is well worth reading *Burgess v. Rawnsley* [1975] Ch 222 and some of the later cases that seem to disagree with Lord Denning's analysis (such as *Gore & Snell v. Carpenter* (1990) 60 P & CR 456). The key seems to be that a common intention can be established: never an easy task in the circumstances that tend to give rise to these disputes.

- The more modern cases, such as *Quigley v. Masterson* [2011] EWHC 2529 (Ch) and *Davis v. Smith* [2011] EWCA 1603, are also worth looking at in more detail, as contemporary issues throw up new challenges for the courts.

? Questions

Self-test questions

1. Jac, Steve, and Sam are all friends from university. They decide to buy a house together. They have to decide whether they want to hold the land as joint tenants or tenants in common. Advise Jac, Steve, and Sam, giving your reasons.

2. They agree to be tenants in common. How would this be reflected on the land register? Why?

3. They agree to be joint tenants. How would this be reflected on the land register? Why?

Exam question

1. Mavis and Norris are the joint registered proprietors of Rose Cottage. They contributed equally to the purchase price. No restriction has been entered onto the register. One day, Mavis and Norris have a huge argument, and Mavis decides that she wants to leave her share of Rose Cottage to her sister, Rita. She writes a note, which she leaves for Norris on the mantelpiece, apologizing and stating her wish. Unfortunately, Norris has a heart attack and dies before he reads the note. When his will is read, Mavis is shocked to find that he has apparently left his share of Rose Cottage to Gail. Advise Mavis.

 For suggested approaches to answering these questions visit the Online Resource Centre.

Further reading

Conway, H., 'Joint tenancies, negotiations and consensual severance [2009] 1 Conv 67
This case comment considers an Australian case and uses it to determine the overlap (if any) between severance by mutual agreement and severance through a course of dealing.

Cooke, E., 'In the Wake of *Stack v Dowden*: the Tale of TR1' [2011] Fam Law 1142
This article discusses the Land Registry's TR1 form, which is still not compulsory.

The Land Registry provides a helpful Practice Guide on registration matters relating to Private Trusts of Land: https://www.gov.uk/government/publications/private-trusts-of-land/practice-guide-24-private-trusts-of-land
It also offers a helpful YouTube video which explains how to fill in a TR1 and what the various entries mean: https://www.youtube.com/watch?v=nlpPHDUAae4. It is very clear on the implications of joint tenancy and tenancy in common and how to complete the relevant section of the TR1 form.

Wilson, J., 'Tripping up on the TR1' [2006] Fam Law 305
This article reviews the background to the introduction of form TR1 by the Land Registry and comments on the problems that may arise in the future.

Online Resource Centre

www.oxfordtextbooks.co.uk/orc/clarke_directions5e/

For more advice relating to this chapter, including self-test questions and an interactive glossary, visit the Online Resource Centre.

9 Trusts and the family home

☐ LEARNING OBJECTIVES

By the end of this chapter, you will be able to:

- identify the requirements to establish an equitable interest under a resulting trust;
- recognize and discuss the elements required for a valid constructive trust;
- understand the different judicial approaches to situations in which there is a sole legal owner, or joint legal owners;
- understand the courts' approach to quantification of shares;
- appreciate the social context in which these issues are likely to arise.

Introduction

In Chapters 7 and 8, we have looked at the legal positions when a property is owned by a sole owner and when it is owned by more than one owner. We have considered the separation of legal and equitable title, and have talked a lot about 'equitable interests' in the land. In this chapter, we will think more about how those equitable interests come into being and we will then consider how the court might quantify the share of each equitable owner of the land.

Following the Supreme Court decision in *Jones v. Kernott* [2011] UKSC 53, there are now two very clear approaches for sole legal owner and joint legal owner cases. In joint legal owner cases, there is a presumption of joint beneficial ownership, giving rise to equal shares. This can be rebutted by the owner trying to prove otherwise. The court will then quantify each owner's share.

In sole legal owner cases, there is a two-step approach, which may be summarized as follows:

- Has X acquired an equitable interest in the property?

- If so, how much of the equitable interest does X own?

This two-stage approach in sole legal owner cases has recently been confirmed by the Court of Appeal in *Capehorn v. Harris* [2015] EWCA Civ 955. We will look firstly at how an equitable interest can be presumed or established, and then at the quantification of the shares in the family home.

9.1 Acquiring an equitable interest

9.1.1 Joint registered owner cases

Jones v. Kernott [2011] UKSC 53 confirmed that where the parties have registered the property in their joint names (and so hold as joint tenants in law), the presumption is that they also hold the property as joint tenants in equity. This can be rebutted by evidence either that the parties did not intend this at the time of purchasing the property, or that the parties' intentions later changed (see 9.5). This is more relevant for quantification of shares, and we will consider it in much more detail in 9.5.3. What it means in terms of establishing an equitable interest is that, in the case of joint registered owners, they are both presumed to have an equitable interest in the property, and need not worry about proving to the court that they have acquired one. In *Jones v. Kernott*, Lady Hale and Lord Walker said that this presumption was not based on the equitable maxim 'equity follows the law' (as *Stack v. Dowden* [2007] UKHL 17 seemed to suggest, see 9.5.3.2), but upon two overlapping reasons. Firstly, buying a home together, usually by means of a mortgage for which both parties are responsible, is a 'strong indication of emotional and economic commitment to a joint enterprise' (at 19). Secondly, there is a practical difficulty, given that the relationship may have lasted many years, in identifying the reality of the financial situation between the parties (at 22).

9.1.2 Sole legal owner cases

The situation is much more difficult where somebody is trying to claim that he or she has an equitable interest in a home owned by a sole legal owner, where the claimant's name is not included on the land register. In this situation, the Supreme Court confirmed in *Jones v. Kernott* that there is essentially a two-part process. The claimant must firstly establish to the satisfaction of the court that he or she has acquired an equitable interest in the property, and the court will then go on to quantify the parties' respective shares. In *Geary v. Rankine* [2012] EWCA Civ 555, Lewison LJ explains it thus: '*[i]n a single name case … the first issue is whether it was intended that the claimant should have any beneficial interest in the property at all. If that issue is determined in the claimant's favour, the second issue is what that interest is. There is no presumption of joint beneficial ownership*' (at 20).

We will look firstly at how a claimant can establish the acquisition of an equitable interest in the property. There are three ways in which this can happen:

- by means of an express trust;
- by means of a resulting trust;
- by means of a constructive trust.

We will consider each of these in turn.

9.2 Express trust

You will remember that the express trust arises at the express intention of the parties. For an express trust of land to be valid, it must meet the formal requirements of Law of Property Act 1925 (LPA 1925), s. 53(1)(b), which basically means that the parties must evidence their intention to create an express trust of land in writing.

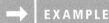

❯ CROSS REFERENCE

For more on the requirements of an express trust, see Chapter 7.

> **➡ EXAMPLE**
>
> Emily owns her own house. She is the sole legal and equitable owner. Her partner, Tom moves in with her and helps her to renovate the property completely. Emily decides that she would like Tom to have a share in the house as recognition for his hard work. She goes to her solicitor and arranges in writing to give Tom a 25 per cent equitable share in the property.
>
> The land holding might be illustrated as in Figure 9.1.
>
> This is a valid express trust, because Emily deliberately intended and created it. She has complied with the formal requirements of LPA 1925, s. 53(1)(b).

An express trust is relatively straightforward legally. Rather more complicated are the kinds of trust that arise informally: resulting and constructive trusts.

Figure 9.1 The express trust between Emily and Tom

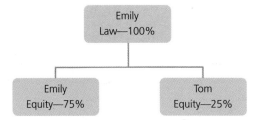

9.3 Resulting and constructive trusts in context

The real difficulty with **resulting and constructive trusts** is that they often arise without the knowledge of the parties. Parliament recognized this when it decided that the formalities required for the creation of valid express trusts of land were not required for the creation of valid resulting and constructive trusts.

resulting and constructive trusts
forms of implied trust that arise by operation of law

STATUTE

Law of Property Act 1925, s. 53(2)

This section does not affect the creation or operation of resulting, implied or constructive trusts.

For our purposes, we will concentrate on these trusts arising in relation to land. In order to demonstrate how easily they may arise, we will provide two alternative scenarios for Emily and Tom.

EXAMPLE

Resulting trust

Emily and Tom want to buy a house together. Emily contributes £70,000 towards the purchase price; Tom contributes £30,000. For various reasons, Tom does not want his name to appear on the land register, so Emily appears as the sole legal owner. Nevertheless, as a result of his contribution, Tom has an equitable interest in the house under a resulting trust.

The law holding might then be illustrated as in Figure 9.2.

Figure 9.2 The resulting trust between Emily and Tom

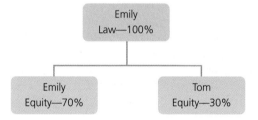

EXAMPLE

Constructive trust

Emily and Tom want to buy a house together. Emily pays for the house, but assures Tom that the house is to be owned by both of them. She tells him that she does not want to put his name on the land register with hers, because her father might discover that they live together. Tom agrees to this and so Emily appears on the land register as the sole legal owner. Believing himself to own half the house, Tom completely renovates it and landscapes the garden.

By doing this, as we shall see, it is likely that Tom will have acquired an equitable interest in the property under a constructive trust. The court would then decide on shares, but, based on the intention of the parties, it is likely to be illustrated as in Figure 9.3.

Figure 9.3 The constructive trust between Emily and Tom

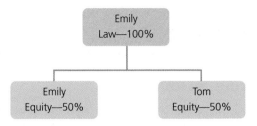

When reading cases in this area of law, do not be misled by judges who frequently refer to resulting and constructive trusts as though they were one and the same thing. Although both resulting and constructive trusts have the effect of creating an equitable interest in the property, the requirements for establishing each are different and, as you will see from the examples given earlier, the share awarded to the equitable owner often differs as well.

Before looking at each type of trust in detail, we will firstly examine why it may be necessary for an equitable owner to establish such an interest.

There are primarily two types of situation in which it becomes necessary to establish an interest under a resulting or constructive trust:

- the context of a family breakdown—that is, when an unmarried couple separate;
- when a third party—invariably a bank—is seeking to repossess a property that is owned by a sole legal owner, but which has more than one equitable owner.

9.3.1 **Family breakdowns**

When a married couple divorce, the court has wide powers under the Matrimonial Causes Act 1973 (MCA 1973) to divide the couple's property as it sees fit. It will take all kinds of matters into account when reaching this decision: the length of the marriage; the age of the parties; the needs of any children of the relationship, etc. Similar arrangements have been extended to same-sex couples who enter into a civil partnership under the Civil Partnership Act 2004.

Unfortunately, although many people who live together still believe that they become some sort of 'common-law' husband or wife, that status simply does not exist in English law. When an unmarried couple decide to live together—that is, to cohabit—and then separate, they do not have the same protection available to them that is available to those who are married or in civil partnerships. This means that, in order to acquire a share in the family home, a partner who is not registered as a co-proprietor of the property on the land register—often still the female partner—will need to prove that he or she has acquired an equitable interest in the property under a resulting or constructive trust.

If it seems remarkable to you that this is necessary in this day and age, you are not alone: despite huge pressure from family lawyers, the government is not yet willing to legislate to offer cohabiting couples the same protection as those who are married or in a civil partnership.

 THINKING POINT

Consider the constructive trust example of Emily and Tom. What would be the difficulty for Tom if the relationship were to break down?

In this example, Tom would not be named on the land register. In fact, he would have nothing in writing to indicate that the parties intended to share ownership of the property. They are not married and so Tom could not apply to the court for an order dividing the property fairly. The only way to establish his interest in the property would be to go to court and establish that he had an equitable interest under a constructive trust.

9.3.2 **Bank seeking possession**

The other situation in which it becomes important for an equitable owner to prove that he or she has an interest under a resulting or constructive trust is that in which a third-party bank or building society attempts to repossess the property.

To explain this situation, we will look at the facts of a case with which, by the end of this chapter, you will have become very familiar!

 CASE CLOSE-UP

Lloyds Bank plc v. Rosset [1991] 1 AC 107

Mr and Mrs Rosset bought an almost derelict farmhouse in which to make their family home. Mr Rosset purchased the house with money from a family trust fund, under which he was a beneficiary. The trustee of this trust fund refused to advance the money if the property was bought in joint names and so the house was registered in the sole name of Mr Rosset. He also funded the costs of the renovation work. Mrs Rosset did not make any direct financial contribution to the purchase price of the property, but she undertook considerable work in the house—supervising the builders and redecorating.

Unknown to Mrs Rosset, Mr Rosset raised some money to pay for the renovation work by means of a mortgage with Lloyds Bank. Unfortunately, he could not manage the repayments on this loan and the bank sought repossession of the property.

 THINKING POINT

Before we continue with the story, think about Mrs Rosset's options in these circumstances. Is there anything that she might have tried to establish that would be binding on the bank?

 CASE CLOSE-UP

Mrs Rosset's only real option was to try to establish that she had an overriding interest that was binding on the bank. She argued that she had such an interest under Land Registration Act 1925, s. 70(1)(g). If she could do this, then the bank would take subject to her interest and she would at least be able to recover some of the money sunk into the property.

Remember that what she needed to establish was:

equitable interest + actual occupation = overriding interest.

You will remember that, in order to establish actual occupation, it is necessary to demonstrate a *'physical presence'* on the land. The court had no difficulty in deciding that Mrs Rosset was in actual occupation, but this was no help to her if she did not have an equitable interest in the property—and in order to achieve this, she needed to prove that she had an interest under a constructive trust.

Let us leave Mrs Rosset there for a moment. It is enough for now for you to understand that this is a fairly typical situation in which there are a sole legal owner, other equitable owners, and a bank trying to repossess the property.

 THINKING POINT

Do any similar cases spring to mind? Think about those of Mrs Boland and Mrs Cann. How successful were they?

We will now look at resulting and constructive trusts in more detail.

9.4 Resulting trusts

9.4.1 Introduction

The term 'resulting' trust comes from the Latin *resultare*, which means 'to spring back'. A resulting trust can arise in a number of ways, but we will confine ourselves to resulting trusts that arise most frequently in relation to land.

The most important thing to remember is that a resulting trust arises from the presumed intention of the parties when they purchase their home. The recognition of a resulting trust by the court is its way of giving effect to what the court perceives to be the intention of the parties. This will become clearer as we continue thinking about resulting trusts.

9.4.2 Contribution to purchase price

By far the most important category of resulting trusts for our purposes are those arising when one party has made a contribution to the purchase price of the property. The way in which this works is quite simple.

 EXAMPLE

Lynne and Keith buy a house together. They are unmarried. Lynne contributes £70,000 and Keith contributes £30,000 to the purchase price of the property. Lynne is registered as the sole legal owner.

In equity, because of his contribution to the purchase price, Keith would have acquired an equitable interest under a resulting trust. Another way of saying this is that Lynne holds 30 per cent of the property on resulting trust for Keith.

The land holding might be illustrated as in Figure 9.4.

Figure 9.4 The resulting trust between Lynne and Keith

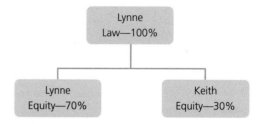

There is, then, a presumption that, if someone has contributed money to the purchase price of the property, he or she intended to keep the beneficial interest in that contribution for him- or herself—that is, there is a presumption that he or she did not intend to give that money away as a gift to the legal owner.

The authority for this presumption may be found in a very old case: *Dyer v. Dyer* (1788) 2 Cox 92.

CASE CLOSE-UP

Dyer v. Dyer (1788) 2 Cox 92, 93

The clear result of all the cases, without a single exception, is that the trust of a legal estate … whether taken in the names of the purchasers and others jointly, or in the names of others without that of the purchaser; whether in one name or several; whether jointly or successive, results to the man who advanced the purchase money.

To apply the Latin meaning of 'springing back', the equitable interest results—or 'springs back'—to the person who contributed to the purchase price of the property.

EXAMPLE

Exactly the same principles would apply if Keith were to have paid the *whole* of the purchase price of the property, but registered it in Lynne's sole name. Lynne would then hold the whole of the property on resulting trust for Keith.

The land holding would then be illustrated as in Figure 9.5.

Figure 9.5 The resulting trust between Lynne and Keith

9.4.3 Other kinds of contribution

The timing of the contribution is very important. The contribution must be made at the time that the house is purchased. This might include a contribution towards the initial deposit on the house. It might also include someone taking on a mortgage obligation in order to finance the purchase of the property.

9.4.3.1 Mortgage payments

> **EXAMPLE**
>
> Donny and Marie buy a house together. Donny contributes £75,000 in cash and Marie arranges a mortgage for her to pay the remaining £25,000. She pays the monthly mortgage instalments. Only Donny is registered as the legal owner.
>
> In this case, Donny will hold 25 per cent of the value of the property on resulting trust for Marie.

Similarly, if both parties agree *at the outset* to meet the mortgage commitments together, a resulting trust will arise—*Cowcher v. Cowcher* [1975] 1 WLR 425.

> **EXAMPLE**
>
> Richard and Karen buy a house together. Richard raises a mortgage of £100,000 to buy the property and is registered as the sole legal owner. At the time of purchase, however, he and Karen agree to divide the mortgage repayments equally between them, and each pays half every month.
>
> In this case, Richard would hold 50 per cent of the property on resulting trust for Karen.

The situation is different, however, when one party makes payments to the mortgage at some time *after* the house has been purchased.

> **EXAMPLE**
>
> Richard and Karen buy a house together. Richard raises a mortgage of £100,000 to buy the property and is registered as the sole legal owner. For a few years, Richard meets all of the mortgage repayments himself. After he is made redundant, however, Karen starts to contribute half of the mortgage payment.
>
> In this situation, because there was no agreement at the time of purchase, Karen's contributions would *not* give rise to an interest under a resulting trust.

This might seem a little unfair, but it was established in *Curley v. Parkes* [2004] EWCA Civ 1515.

9.4.3.2 Household expenses

Contributions to household expenses will not suffice to establish an interest under a resulting trust. This decision tends to impact rather more on female claimants than on male. Even today, more women stay at home, or work part-time in order to look after young children. Often, the male partner meets the mortgage commitments, and the female partner meets other expenses—for example, buying food and clothing. The following case, which illustrates this, will make you wonder whether equity as a body of law really does stand for justice and fairness!

CASE CLOSE-UP

Burns v. Burns [1984] Ch 317

Mr and Mrs Burns began living together in 1961. They lived in a house registered in the sole name of Mr Burns. They were not married, but Mrs Burns changed her name to his. The couple lived together for around nineteen years. Mr Burns paid the mortgage instalments; Mrs Burns looked after him and their children, and eventually returned to part-time work, after which she paid for some household expenses and household items, such as a washing machine.

Unfortunately, after the children had grown up, the relationship broke down and the parties ended up in court. Because they were unmarried, the MCA 1973 was of no assistance to Mrs Burns and so she had to try to establish that she had acquired an equitable interest in the family home by means of a resulting trust.

The Court of Appeal—while expressing some sympathy for Mrs Burns—decided that she did not have an interest by way of a resulting trust, because she had not made a direct financial contribution to the purchase price of the property. As we shall soon see, she also failed to establish the requirements to prove an interest under a constructive trust and so, after nearly twenty years of hard labour, she walked away from the relationship with nothing!

9.4.4 Rebutting the presumption

It is important to remember that, in all of the examples at which we have looked so far, the starting point is that a resulting trust is *presumed*. As with any legal presumption, it can, of course, be rebutted—by evidence that the person contributing the money to the purchase of the property did not intend to acquire any beneficial interest in the property, for example, but instead intended to make a gift, or a loan, to the legal owner.

EXAMPLE

Hamish is buying his first house. It costs £100,000. Sarah, Hamish's mother, decides to contribute £30,000, because Hamish has been such a wonderful son. She explains to Hamish that this is a gift and that she does not expect anything in return.

In this situation, the presumption of a resulting trust arises, because Sarah has made a contribution to the purchase price, but it is rebutted, because there is clear evidence that she intended it as a gift. Hamish is the sole legal and equitable owner of his home, and Sarah has no equitable interest in it.

9.4.4.1 Presumption of advancement

There is another, somewhat surprising, way of rebutting the presumption of a resulting trust. The **presumption of advancement**, as it is somewhat quaintly known, rebuts the presumption of a resulting trust and replaces it with another presumption—that in certain kinds of relationship the contributor did *not* intend to keep an equitable interest in the property for him- or herself. Rather, it is presumed that he or she intended to give the contribution as a gift to the person receiving it.

> **presumption of advancement** the presumption that, in certain types of relationship, a person who makes a transfer of or contribution to the purchase of a property held in the name of another is doing so for the benefit of that other

 EXAMPLE

Let us assume that Hamish is still intending to buy his house for £100,000. This time, his father, Iain, is to give him £30,000 towards it. There is no discussion about the nature of this contribution at the time that Iain gives the money to Hamish.

This time, although the presumption of a resulting trust would again arise, it would be rebutted immediately by the presumption of advancement. Father and child is one of those special relationships within which the presumption of advancement arises. Hamish would own both the legal and equitable title to the property, and Iain would retain no interest in the £30,000.

These kinds of relationship fall into two broad categories:

- father and child (but not mother and child);
- husband and wife (but not wife to husband).

It should be noted, however, that a contribution from anyone acting *in loco parentis* towards a child would fall into the presumption of advancement: the courts will presume that anyone who assumes the responsibility of providing for a child will be making a gift (advancement) to the child, rather than intending to keep an equitable interest in any property he or she transfers to that child.

> *in loco parentis*
> 'in place of a parent'

The presumption of advancement will be abolished when Equality Act 2010, s. 199 comes into force. This will only apply to acts occurring or gifts made after the section comes into force. The old law will continue to govern the period before this date.

9.5 Constructive trusts

9.5.1 Introduction

If a person cannot establish an equitable interest under a resulting trust—perhaps because he or she has not made a direct financial contribution to the purchase price of the property—then he or she may be able to claim an equitable interest under a constructive trust. The courts recognize constructive trusts in situations in which the parties have a common intention to share the equitable (also known as the 'beneficial') ownership of the property.

The underlying principle behind constructive trusts is that they arise when it would be 'unconscionable' for the legal owner to deny the other party a share in the equitable ownership of the property. What would be 'unconscionable' is sometimes difficult to define, however, and, in this area of law, the courts have preferred to identify specific sets of situations and circumstances under which a constructive trust would arise. In cases of this nature, the court is often dealing with the conflicting demands of ensuring that the law is certain and predictable, while trying to do justice to the parties in situations that are characterized by a lack of legal formality.

9.5.2 *Lloyds Bank plc v. Rosset*

We have already met Mrs Rosset at 9.3.2.

To defeat the bank's claim for repossession in *Lloyds Bank plc v. Rosset*, Mrs Rosset needed to establish that she had an overriding interest that was binding on the bank. In order to do this, she needed to show that, although the property was registered in Mr Rosset's sole name, she had an equitable interest in the property.

THINKING POINT

Could Mrs Rosset establish an equitable interest under a resulting trust?

No—she had not made a direct financial contribution to the purchase price of the property. The only way that she could prove her equitable interest was by means of a constructive trust.

In order to do this, Mrs Rosset had to rely on the principles established in cases such as *Gissing v. Gissing* [1971] AC 881. In this case, the House of Lords had to decide whether, after over thirty years of marriage, a wife had any interest in the family home that she had shared with her husband for all that time, but which was bought in her husband's sole name. Unfortunately for Mrs Gissing, the MCA 1973 had yet to be passed and she was forced to rely on trusts principles in order to establish an interest in the property.

In *Gissing*, the House of Lords laid down the principle that, in order to establish an interest in the family home under a constructive trust, two elements had to be proven:

1. There must have been evidence of some conduct on the part of the legal owner to indicate that he had led the claimant to understand that she was to have a share in the ownership of the property.

2. The claimant must have acted to her detriment on the strength of this belief.

The House of Lords decided that these requirements had not been met: Mrs Gissing had not made any direct financial contribution to the purchase price of the property. There had been no express discussions between the parties in relation to sharing the beneficial ownership of the property; neither was it possible for the court to infer from their conduct that they intended to share the beneficial ownership of the property. Unfortunately, Mrs Gissing was left with nothing.

Gissing was followed by a series of cases involving very similar situations, in which the courts tried to grapple with the difficulty of reconciling the competing requirements of ensuring legal certainty with doing justice to the parties.

In *Rosset*, however, the House of Lords reviewed the authorities in this area of law and attempted to lay down some basic legal guidelines to clarify the situation. Lord Bridge of Harwich said that a constructive trust would arise if the court could identify a common intention of the parties to share the equitable ownership of the property and if, on the basis of this common intention, the non-legal owner could establish that she had acted to her detriment. He went on to identify two possible means of establishing the requisite common intention:

- the court might find *express common intention*, which meant that there was evidence that the parties had actually expressed an intention to share the ownership of the property;

- the court might find *inferred common intention*, meaning that the court could infer a common intention based on the conduct of the parties.

In other words:

> express common intention + detriment = constructive trust

or:

> inferred common intention + detritment = constructive trust.

We will now look at each of these in turn.

9.5.2.1 **Express common intention**

As the words suggest, express common intention can be found in situations in which the parties expressly state their intention to share the equitable ownership of the property.

 CASE CLOSE-UP

Lloyds Bank plc v. Rosset [1991] 1 AC 107

Lord Bridge said (at 132):

> The first and fundamental question which must always be resolved is whether…there has at any time prior to acquisition, or exceptionally at some later date, been any agreement, arrangement or understanding reached between them that the property is to be shared beneficially. The finding of an agreement or arrangement to share in this sense can only, I think, be based on evidence of express discussions between the partners, however imperfectly remembered and however imprecise their terms may have been.

In *Lloyds Bank v. Rosset*, Lord Bridge said that the court must first look at whether the parties ever discussed beneficial ownership of the property between themselves. He recognized that this would often be difficult to prove—in some of the cases at which we have already looked, the property was bought over thirty years before the matter came to court!

Lord Bridge gave (at 133) some '*outstanding examples*' of cases involving express common intention. One of these was *Eves v. Eves* [1975] 1 WLR 1338, in which the male partner put the legal title of the house in his sole name, after telling his girlfriend that she was too young to appear as a legal owner. The second case was *Grant v. Edwards* [1986] Ch 638, in which the male partner, once again, put the legal title into his sole name—this time explaining to his girlfriend that putting the house into their joint names might impact on her divorce proceedings. In both of these cases, these discussions were held to be evidence of an express common intention to share the beneficial ownership of the property. Because each female partner had also acted to her detriment (see later), she was deemed to have acquired an equitable interest in the property under a constructive trust.

One of the key difficulties in trying to establish an express common intention is in adducing appropriate evidence of the discussions. Lord Bridge clearly recognized this, as did Waite LJ in *Midland Bank v. Cooke* [1995] 4 All ER 562, who referred (at 567) to:

> … the barrenness of the terrain in which the judges and district judges … are required to search for the small evidential nuggets on which issues as to the existence—or the proportions—of beneficial interest are liable to depend.

The parties must do their best to give an 'honest recollection' of any discussions and the court must try to make sense of them.

THINKING POINT

Does anything strike you as odd about these 'outstanding' examples of express common intention?

In both cases, the male partner was making excuses to avoid joint ownership of the property! The court found, however, that the fact that the discussion had occurred and that the male partner in both cases implied that the house—despite appearances—was to be owned by both parties were sufficient to provide evidence of an express common intention to share the beneficial ownership of the property. Under these circumstances, if the female partner had relied on this understanding and acted to her detriment, it would be unconscionable to allow the male partner to go back on his word.

In *Curran v. Collins* [2015] EWCA Civ 404, the Court of Appeal recognized the difficulty for appellate courts in overturning decisions of the courts of first instance where the judge had the advantage of seeing and listening to the parties give evidence. This causes particular difficulties in the 'excuse' cases—where one partner has given an excuse for not putting a property into joint names. The Court suggested that the first-instance decision is made by a thorough evaluation and interpretation of the facts in each case, and that the appeal court could only properly interfere if the judge had plainly got it wrong.

Detriment

Lord Bridge's other requirement was that, in reliance on this express common intention, the female partner had acted to her detriment or had '*significantly altered … her position*' (at 132). The kinds of activity that the court has held to be detrimental in express common intention cases vary greatly—but, in general, the threshold of 'detriment' is relatively low and need not be directly referable to the house itself.

In *Eves v. Eves* (affectionately known as the *Sledgehammer* case), Lord Denning was impressed at the female partner's efforts with a sledgehammer as she landscaped the garden and renovated the family home. This was clearly detriment, because he reasoned that she would not have undertaken such arduous physical tasks unless she had expected—or understood herself to own—a share of the property. Similarly, in *Grant v. Edwards*, the Court of Appeal decided that the female partner had acted to her detriment in paying substantial housekeeping expenses and looking after the children. It is important to remember that, although many different acts may well constitute detriment in express common intention cases, they must be fairly significant, rather than *de minimis*, or trifling.

de minimis
of the rule *de minimis non curat lex*, or 'the law does not take account of trifles'

Back to Mrs Rosset

In Mrs Rosset's case, there was nothing to suggest that she and her husband had discussed the ownership of the family home in this way. Like many couples, they had not directly considered it. There was clearly no express common intention to share ownership of the property and Lord Bridge decided that this meant that the court had to look at the second category of common intention cases.

9.5.2.2 Inferred common intention

In cases in which the court cannot find any evidence of express common intention, it may, in certain circumstances, infer a common intention from the conduct of the parties.

CASE CLOSE-UP

Lloyds Bank plc v. Rosset [1991] 1 AC 107

Lord Bridge said (at 132):

> In sharp contrast with this situation is the very different one where there is no evidence to support a finding of an agreement or arrangement to share, however reasonable it might have been for the parties to reach such an arrangement if they had applied their minds to the question, and where the court must rely entirely on the conduct of the parties both as the basis from which to infer a common intention to share the property beneficially and as the conduct relied on to give rise to a constructive trust. In this situation direct contributions to the purchase price by the partner who is not the legal owner, whether initially or by payment of mortgage instalments, will readily justify the inference necessary to the creation of a constructive trust. But, as I read the authorities, it is at least extremely doubtful whether anything less will do.

It is clear from Lord Bridge's speech in *Rosset* that, when he talks about the court inferring common intention from the conduct of the parties, he considers the relevant 'conduct' to be very specific. He appears to say that the *only* relevant conduct in this kind of situation is if the non-legal owner has made a *direct* financial contribution to the purchase price of the property: '*[I]t is at least extremely doubtful whether anything less will do.*'

 THINKING POINT

Can you see a problem here?

This is exactly what is needed in order to establish an interest under a resulting trust. Neither resulting trust principles nor either of the *Rosset* categories offers any hope for a claimant who has neither made a direct financial contribution, nor had express discussions about ownership of the property with his or her partner.

Detriment

If the non-legal owner has made a direct financial contribution to the purchase price, the requirement of detriment will automatically be satisfied, because the contributor will have acted to his or her detriment in actually making the payment.

Mrs Rosset again

But where does this leave Mrs Rosset? During her time at the family home, she had managed the renovation project, overseen the building work, decorated some of the rooms, and organized domestic arrangements, such as insurance and burglar alarms. She had not, however, made a direct financial contribution to the purchase price of the property.

Lord Bridge said that all of her hard work had been undertaken to enable the family to move into the property sooner and was '*irrespective of any expectation she might have of enjoying a beneficial interest in the property*'. This was not the kind of conduct on which the court could rely to infer a common intention—and so Mrs Rosset failed in her claim to acquire an equitable interest in the property.

9.5.2.3 **Problems with *Rosset***

Although the decision in *Rosset* went some way to clarifying the law by laying down clear guidelines, it left some very important questions unanswered. One of the main difficulties was that it did not consider whether *indirect* financial contributions could ever give rise to a constructive trust. Direct financial contributions include, for example, a contribution to the deposit paid for the property, or a cash payment to the purchase price, or payment of the mortgage instalments. But many couples, when they start to live together, make fairly arbitrary decisions about sharing the financial burdens of home ownership.

 EXAMPLE

Gillian and Neil decide to move in together. The house is registered in Gillian's sole name. They agree to share all expenses equally. To make this easier, Gillian pays for the mortgage and the telephone, while Neil pays for the council tax, gas, and electricity. This works out to almost equal payments. Gillian could not afford to pay the mortgage without Neil paying for the other household expenses.

Could Neil claim an interest in the property under a constructive trust, even though he had not contributed directly to the mortgage?

In *Rosset*, Lord Bridge did not address this situation specifically—but dicta from earlier cases, such as *Gissing*, suggest that there is no reason why this should not also give rise to an equitable interest under a resulting or constructive trust.

In that case, Lord Pearson refers to the often '*artificial*' search for an agreement as to beneficial ownership, given the informality of financial arrangements between the parties. He says (at 903) that, in identifying relevant 'contributions' in order to infer a common intention, the court is not:

> limited to those made directly in part payment of the price of the property or to those made at the time when the property is conveyed into the name of one of the spouses. For instance there can be a contribution if by arrangement between the spouses one of them by payment of the household expenses enables the other to pay the mortgage instalments.

In *Le Foe v. Le Foe* [2001] 2 FLR 970, after considering *Rosset, Gissing*, and *Burns*, the judge decided that indirect contributions (which allowed the other partner to pay the mortgage) *could* lead the court to infer a common intention to share the beneficial ownership of the property. If this were not the case, the judge reasoned, '*these cases would be decided by reference to mere acts of fortune, being the arbitrary allocation of financial responsibility between the parties*'. *Le Foe* was a first-instance decision, but it may indicate a more generous—and realistic—approach to such cases in the future.

In the significant decision of *Stack v. Dowden*, the House of Lords suggested, albeit obiter, that the law had '*moved on*' from *Rosset*. The House looked at the comments of Lord Bridge and, in particular, at his suggestion that it was '*at least extremely doubtful*' that anything less than a direct financial contribution to the purchase price of the property would allow the court to infer a common intention, and so establish an equitable interest in the property. Baroness Hale noted (at [63]) that these words '*had set that hurdle* [for claimants] *rather too high in certain respects*'. Lord Walker went further by suggesting (at [34]) that the House should move the law on '*a little more in the same direction*' by taking '*a wide view of what is capable of counting as a contribution towards the acquisition of a residence*'.

In *Jones v. Kernott* [2011] UKSC 53, although not commenting directly on *Rosset*, Lady Hale and Lord Walker confirmed that the approach in sole legal owner cases is still a two-stage process, firstly establishing the acquisition of a claimant's equitable interest and then quantifying the extent of that interest. In order to establish the acquisition of an equitable interest, the court must identify a common intention *'deduced objectively from [the parties'] conduct'* (at 52). See 9.5.3.3 for a closer examination of *Jones v. Kernott*.

Geary v. Rankine [2012] EWCA Civ 555 is one of the few significant sole legal owner cases post *Jones v. Kernott*, and the Court of Appeal followed the principle that *'the common intention has to be deduced objectively from* [the parties'] *conduct'* (at (20)). This a somewhat unusual case in that the property was an investment property rather than a family home, although both parties eventually lived in the property. It was also a very straightforward case, in many respects, as there was no evidence at all on which to base a common intention. In a second case, *CPS v. Piper* [2011] EWHC 3570 (Admin)—again with somewhat unusual facts—the judge again referred only to the *Jones v. Kernott* review of conduct in satisfying the first step in sole legal owner cases of establishing an equitable interest through a common intention. He also referred to the law having moved on from *Rosset*. What is interesting in both these cases is that the *Rosset* categories of common intention were not even considered, with the Court preferring a more fluid *Jones v. Kernott* review of conduct.

However, recently in *Re Ali* [2012] EWHC 2302 (Admin) and *Ullah v. Ullah* [2013] EWHC 2296 (Ch), both complicated cases involving a number of different properties most of which were in the name of a sole legal owner, the judges in each case reasserted the relevance of *Rosset* to the first stage, in establishing that the claimant has acquired an equitable interest, before moving on to apply the *Jones v. Kernott* conduct review to the second stage, that of quantifying the extent of that interest.

Some academic commentators are suggesting that *Rosset* has had its day, and some judges in the lower courts—most recently in *Bhura v. Bhura (No. 2)* [2014] EWHC 727—seem to be deciding cases on a *Jones v. Kernott* approach. However, a recent Court of Appeal decision has reminded us that, at least until the Supreme Court is faced with the challenge of a sole legal owner, *Rosset* type case, and decides differently, the two-stage approach should be followed in sole legal owner cases.

 CASE CLOSE-UP

***Capehorn v. Harris* [2015] EWCA Civ 955**

Ms Capehorn and Mr Harris began living together in 1983. Ms Capehorn worked in Mr Harris's frozen food business. In 1991, Mr Harris was declared bankrupt, and Ms Capehorn took over the business as a sole trader, and employed Mr Harris, who continued to be the dominant partner in the business. In 1993, Ms Capehorn purchased a property called Sunnyside Farm from her mother. She funded the purchase herself, and took on sole responsibility for a mortgage. The property was registered in her sole name.

In 2002, Ms Capehorn purchased another property (Beaumont Road), again in her sole name and also funded that by means of a mortgage in her own name, secured against her first property. Following the couple's separation, Mr Harris set up another company, in which Ms Capehorn had no interest. At some later date, the couple discussed their finances and Ms Capehorn agreed to transfer her shares in the frozen food business to Mr Harris's new company. In return, Mr Harris would continue to live at Sunnyside Farm (where the frozen food business was based) for a weekly rent. Eventually the relationship broke down completely. Mr Harris then tried to claim that he had a beneficial interest in Sunnyside Farm, and the court also had to decide the couple's respective interests in Beaumont Road and the business.

At first instance, the trial judge found that Mr Harris had no beneficial interest in Beaumont Road. She then found that there had never at any point been an understanding that Mr Harris should have a beneficial interest in Sunnyside Farm. However, she then suggested that Mr Harris's contribution to Ms Capehorn's business would allow her to impute to the parties an intention that Mr Harris would also acquire a beneficial interest in Sunnyside Farm. She awarded Mr Harris a share of 25 per cent of the property. The judge then went on to impute an intention that Ms Capehorn should be awarded a 35 per cent share in Mr Harris's business.

In a very short judgment by the Court of Appeal, Sales LJ explained that the trial judge had erred in her approach to the case. The correct approach in sole legal owner cases, such as this one, was a two-stage analysis: firstly, it was for the person claiming a beneficial interest to prove that there was an agreement between the parties that he was to have such an interest, even if there had been no agreement as to shares. Secondly, if such an agreement was established, if there had been no agreement as to shares, following *Stack v. Dowden* and *Jones v. Kernott*, the court may 'impute an intention that the person was to have a fair beneficial share in the asset and may assess the quantum of the fair share in the light of all of the circumstances' (at 16).

The trial judge had combined the two stages, and this was not correct: before moving to the second stage, the court must establish an actual agreement that the parties intended that the claimant acquire a beneficial interest in the property: '[a] court is not entitled to impute an intention to the parties at the first stage in the analysis' (at 17).

This is a welcome decision by the Court of Appeal, as it provides some much needed clarity in this area of law. The first-instance decision in this case was clearly wrong: even the parties themselves agreed that at least in respect of the shares in the business, there had never been any agreement that Ms Capehorn would have any beneficial interest in them.

For the moment, then, this constantly evolving area of law seems relatively settled. However, at the time of writing, an application has just been made for permission to appeal the sole legal owner decision of *Curran v. Collins* [2015] EWCA Civ 404 to the Supreme Court. This could well be the time for the legal issues in this area to be finally resolved. We will await any developments with great interest.

9.5.3 Shares

The starting point in determining shares, whether in a sole legal owner case or one involving joint owners, is always the intention of the parties: if there is evidence that the parties intended to share ownership in a certain proportion—perhaps 50/50—then the court will, of course, give effect to that intention. This is demonstrated by Lord Diplock's speech in *Gissing v. Gissing*.

> ### 🔍 CASE CLOSE-UP
>
> **Gissing v. Gissing [1971] AC 881**
>
> Lord Diplock said (at 908):
>
> > In such a case the court must first do its best to discover from the conduct of the spouses whether any inference can reasonably be drawn as to the probable common understanding about the amount of the share of the contributing spouse upon which each must have acted in doing what each did, even though that understanding was never expressly stated by one spouse to the other or even consciously formulated in words by either of them independently.

If there is no evidence of the parties' intentions, the court must try to quantify shares by a different means.

Jones v. Kernott has clarified the approach of the court in ascertaining shares in the property. Before looking at this in detail, it will be helpful to briefly look back at some of the key cases which fed into the Supreme Court's decision.

Before *Jones v. Kernott*, particularly in sole legal owner cases, there was a difference in the court's approach between quantifying interests under a resulting and a constructive trust. This can be seen in *Midland Bank v. Cooke*.

 CASE CLOSE-UP

Midland Bank v. Cooke [1995] 4 All ER 562

Mr and Mrs Cooke bought a house for £8,500. Of this, £6,540 was raised by way of mortgage, £1,100 as a wedding present to the couple by Mr Cooke's parents, and the remainder was provided by Mr Cooke. The house was registered in Mr Cooke's sole name and Mrs Cooke did not make any mortgage repayments, although she paid for household expenses. After some rather complicated financial juggling, the couple found themselves facing an action from the bank seeking to repossess the family home. Mrs Cooke claimed that, although she was not registered as a legal owner, she nonetheless had an equitable interest in the property.

At first instance, the judge found that Mrs Cooke had made a direct financial contribution to the purchase price of the property, in that she had contributed half of the joint wedding gift (£550 of the £1,100) from Mr Cooke's parents.

Calculating her equitable interest in mathematical proportion to her contribution, he said that she had acquired an interest of 6.74 per cent of the property.

The Court of Appeal, however, was able to find that, by reference to the inferred common intention of the parties (evidenced by Mrs Cooke's direct financial contribution), Mrs Cooke had acquired an interest of 50 per cent of the value of the property. Waite LJ said that, once a direct financial contribution had been made and in the absence of evidence of the parties' intentions as to shares, it was open to the court to look at the *'whole course of dealings'* of the parties.

In doing this, Waite LJ looked at more than just financial contributions (at 576):

> One could hardly have a clearer example of a couple who had agreed to share everything equally: the profits of his business while it prospered, and the risks of indebtedness suffered through its failure; the upbringing of their children; the rewards of her own career as a teacher; and, most relevantly, a home into which he had put his savings and to which she was to give over the years the benefit of the maintenance and improvement contribution. When to all that there is added the fact (still an important one) that this was a couple who had chosen to introduce into their relationship the additional commitment which marriage involves, the conclusion becomes inescapable that their presumed intention was to share the beneficial interest in the property in equal shares. I reach this result without the need to rely on any equitable maxim as to equality.

This 'broad brush' approach—which seems to allow the court to look at non-financial, as well as financial, contributions—was generally welcomed. Reading Waite LJ's judgment, it is apparent that he was careful to maintain that he had stayed within the court's professed remit, which was to give effect to the 'intention' of the parties—even when that intention was nowhere obvious to be found!

Two very important cases then moved the law on in an interesting direction.

9.5.3.1 *Oxley v. Hiscock*

The first, a Court of Appeal case ([2004] 3 WLR 715), seemingly swept away this somewhat artificial basis for quantification of the equitable interest in constructive trust cases and replaced it with the discretion of the court to decide what was 'fair' when quantifying the parties' beneficial interests.

🔍 CASE CLOSE-UP

Oxley v. Hiscock [2004] 3 WLR 715

The family home was registered in the name of Mr Hiscock, but had been acquired with the assistance of a direct financial contribution from Mrs Oxley. Mr Hiscock had contributed £60,700 of the £127,000 purchase price; Mrs Oxley, £36,300. The court treated both as contributing equally to the mortgage of £30,000. The relationship broke down and the house was sold. Mrs Oxley clearly had an equitable interest in the property, but the issue was how much of the property she owned: she claimed 50 per cent; Mr Hiscock argued that, in the absence of express discussions about shares, she should be restricted to an interest in proportion to her original contribution.

After reviewing the authorities, Chadwick LJ decided that none of the earlier approaches to quantification—including that of *Midland Bank v. Cooke*—was entirely satisfactory. Instead, he said that, in the absence of express discussions as to shares, it was the duty of the court to identify the share that it considered fair '*having regard to the whole course of dealing between them in relation to the property*' (at 246). This would include the financial arrangements made between the parties in respect of outgoings such as mortgage payments, council tax, utilities, housekeeping, insurance, and repairs.

Having considered this in relation to Mrs Oxley and Mr Hiscock's arrangements, he awarded 40 per cent to Mrs Oxley and 60 per cent to Mr Hiscock.

This approach promised a step forward for claimants who had contributed little financially to the property, but who had made a significant contribution in other ways. Chadwick LJ's use of the word '*include*' implies that the courts can look at conduct other than financial contributions. In *Oxley* itself, however, the Court restricted itself to considering financial contributions and awarded Mrs Oxley's share virtually in mathematical proportion to her financial contribution to the property.

Post-*Oxley* cases followed a similarly restrictive approach. Judges appear reluctant to explore the extent of their discretion. Indeed, in *Supperstone v. Hurst* [2005] EWHC 1309 (Ch), Michael Briggs QC commented (at [60]) that he did not:

> … consider that the ascertainment of the respective shares of co-owners of real property has yet, outside the confines of the court's special powers on divorce, reached the stage where it is truly a matter of discretion.

9.5.3.2 *Stack v. Dowden*

In the next case, Chadwick LJ in the Court of Appeal ([2005] EWCA Civ 857) had the opportunity to develop the principles that he had laid down in *Oxley*. As we will soon see, however, the House of Lords, while upholding the Court of Appeal's apportionment of the equitable interest between the parties, arrived at that conclusion by a different route, '*both in principle and on the facts*' ([95]).

CASE CLOSE-UP

Stack v. Dowden [2005] EWCA Civ 857 (Court of Appeal)

The facts

Mr Stack and Ms Dowden began their relationship in 1975, and started living together permanently in 1983. Originally, they lived in a house bought by Ms Dowden and registered in her sole name. They moved again, with their children, in 1993, to a property registered in joint names. Included on the land register was a declaration that the 'survivor can give a valid receipt for money arising on a disposition of the land'.

In addition, most of the money for the purchase came from Ms Dowden, although a mortgage for the balance was obtained in the names of both parties. The mortgage was soon after paid off with lump-sum payments from both Mr Stack and Ms Dowden.

The couple kept their finances almost entirely separate: the house was the only major asset in joint names. In 2002, the couple separated and Mr Stack moved out of the family home. He applied to the county court for an equal division of the property, which the judge awarded.

Ms Dowden appealed to the Court of Appeal.

We will look, firstly, at the Court of Appeal's analysis and then at that of the House of Lords. Remember, however, that it is the House of Lords' decision that represents the current law, although it now has to be read together with *Jones v. Kernott*.

▶ **CROSS REFERENCE**

For more on restriction, see Chapter 8.

CASE CLOSE-UP

Stack v. Dowden [2005] EWCA Civ 857 (Court of Appeal)

The Court of Appeal found that Mr Stack had an equitable interest in the family property by means of a common intention constructive trust. Once again, the Court had to quantify his share.

Chadwick LJ referred to the *Oxley* principle of fairness. He then addressed the 'whole course of dealing between the parties in relation to the property'. Once again, the only conduct he appears to have addressed is the contribution made by each party to the purchase price of the property (at 35):

> It is impossible, it seems to me, to reach the conclusion that it is fair, having regard to the whole course of dealing between the parties in relation to that property, that their beneficial shares should be equal. If the whole of the purchase price … other than the mortgage advance was provided by Miss Dowden from her own funds, that conclusion would fail to give proper weight to her financial contribution to the acquisition of the property.

He awarded Ms Dowden a 65 per cent share and Mr Stack a 35 per cent share of the property.

Although, in each of these cases, the outcome may well have been fair, it is striking that the share awarded was almost exactly in proportion to the initial direct financial contribution. This amounts to quantification on essentially resulting trust principles, despite *Oxley* appearing, at first reading, to offer more hope for those claimants whose financial contribution was small, but whose non-financial contribution was significant.

Q CASE CLOSE-UP

Stack v. Dowden [2007] UKHL 17 (House of Lords)

Although the House of Lords agreed with the Court of Appeal apportionment of the equitable interest between the parties, it arrived at its conclusion by a different route.

Starting point

The House first of all established a firm starting point for the courts in cases of this nature.

Essentially, the equitable interests in a property would be assumed to follow the legal interests. If there were a sole legal owner, the presumption would be that this person was also the sole equitable owner. If there were joint legal owners, the presumption would be that they were also joint beneficial owners. It would be for the person asserting that the equitable interests were different (in this case, Ms Dowden) to prove his or her case and to rebut the presumption.

Baroness Hale warned (at [68]) that rebutting the presumption was *'not a task to be lightly embarked on'* and would only succeed in *'unusual cases'*. The presumption will not be challengeable simply because the parties contributed unequally to the purchase price of the property.

Common intention

The task of the court is to search for the intention of the parties—but it cannot 'abandon that search in favour of the result which the court itself considers fair' (at [61]). The Court of Appeal's approach in *Oxley* and *Stack* is thus dismissed.

The House of Lords instead proposed a *'holistic'* approach to the quantification of shares. Baroness Hale stressed that, particularly in this area of law, cases will turn on their own facts. She did, however, provide a non-exhaustive list of factors that may be of relevance to the court, in addition to the obvious factor of the parties' respective financial contributions to the family home (at [69]):

- advice or discussions at the time of the transfer;
- the reason why a declaration for the receipt of capital monies was included on the land register;
- the purpose for which the home was acquired;
- how the purchase was financed;
- the nature of the parties' relationship;
- any children of the parties;
- how the couple arranged their finances;
- how the couple paid for the outgoings of the property and other household expenses;
- the parties' individual characters and personalities may also be relevant.

If the couple had acquired a joint mortgage, then the court should not be overly focused on exactly who had paid what: the inference drawn by the court should be that both of them intended to contribute as much as they could and that they would share the benefit equally.

Application

The House then applied the law as it had stated it to the facts of the instant case. Most significant were the facts that Ms Dowden had made a much greater financial contribution to the purchase price of the property and that, despite cohabiting for almost twenty years, the parties' financial arrangements (apart from the property) were almost entirely separate.

The House of Lords agreed with the 65/35 per cent division in favour of Ms Dowden.

Lord Neuberger, however, disagreed with the reasoning of the majority. He was very unwilling to interfere where Parliament had refused to act and said that changes in the law in this area should be implemented by Parliament. He suggested that, although it was appropriate (as the majority suggested) in cases in which the court was trying to infer a common intention to take into account all of the circumstances surrounding the couple's relationship, not all of the circumstances would be '*of primary or equal relevance to the issue*' (at [131]). He generally preferred the resulting trust approach, wherever possible, and said that he did not think it likely that the way in which the parties conducted their personal or day-to-day financial affairs after the purchase of the property should have any effect on the original beneficial interests in the property.

Stack v. Dowden appeared at the time to have clarified the law in this area, to some extent. It provided a straightforward starting point for the court and has indicated some of the factors that will be relevant in the court's search for the intention of the parties. In joint ownership cases, it allows for more flexibility in assessing the parties' respective shares, while not heading down the attractive, but rather unpredictable, road of judicial 'fairness'.

As some of the post-*Stack* cases show, however, the quantification of shares in this kind of situation remains a rather slippery business.

The difficulties in applying the *Stack* principles became apparent in the years following the decision. The only relatively straightforward application can be found in *Fowler v. Barron* [2008] EWCA Civ 377, a joint legal owner case where the court awarded equal shares in the property, despite the fact that the claimant had not made any financial contribution at all to the purchase price of the property (although she had, of course, contributed in other non-financial respects, during the course of the couple's seventeen-year relationship). The Court of Appeal decision in *Jones v. Kernott* followed a similar pattern of reasoning. However, the Supreme Court decision in *Jones v. Kernott* gave their Lordships the opportunity to develop and clarify their own thinking in *Stack*. We will look firstly at the case itself, and then work out some of the wider implications of it.

9.5.3.3 *Jones v. Kernott*

 CASE CLOSE-UP

Jones v. Kernott [2011] UKSC 53

In 1985, Ms Jones and Mr Kernott bought a house and registered it in their joint names. It was funded with a deposit paid for by Ms Jones, and the balance by a mortgage also in joint names. Over the years, the couple took out another loan to build an extension, and Mr Kernott did some of the building work on the extension. The couple also shared household expenses.

In 1993, Mr Kernott moved out of the family home following the breakdown of the couple's relationship. For the following fourteen and a half years, Ms Jones and the children lived in the house, and she paid all of the household expenses, with apparently little in the way of maintenance and support for the children by Mr Kernott.

At some point, after they had tried and failed to sell the jointly owned property, the couple cashed in a joint life assurance policy, to provide Mr Kernott with the money to pay for a deposit on his own home. He was able to pay the mortgage on his own property largely, it seems, because he did not contribute to his former home.

In 2006, Mr Kernott began trying to establish a share of the jointly owned property. Ms Jones then began proceedings in an attempt to resolve the situation, asking the court to either decide that she was the sole owner of the home that she occupied, or that she also had a beneficial interest in Mr Kernott's home, or that the couple jointly owned both properties.

At first instance, Ms Jones conceded that she had no interest in Mr Kernott's property. However, she argued that the couple's intentions in relation to ownership of the house that she occupied had changed over the years, despite their continuing joint registered ownership.

The judge agreed, and awarded Ms Jones 90 per cent of the first property, and Mr Kernott 10 per cent.

The Court of Appeal (by a majority) decided that the couple owned the property in equal shares as tenants in common. Part of the reason for this decision was that in the majority's view, there was no evidence that the parties' intentions had changed after their separation, and that the House of Lords' decision in *Stack v. Dowden* did not allow them to impute an intention of anything other than equal shares if there was no evidence of an express intention to the contrary and no conduct from which to infer an intention to the contrary.

The Supreme Court decision

The leading judgment was given by Lady Hale and Lord Walker, who welcomed the opportunity to clarify the principles outlined in *Stack*. The following guidance emerged, to be applied in all cases where the home is registered in joint names, the parties are jointly responsible for the mortgage, and no express declaration of the beneficial interests has been made:

1. The starting point is that there is a presumption of beneficial ownership as joint tenants.
2. That presumption can be rebutted by establishing that:
   (a) the parties had a common intention at the time of purchase that the beneficial ownership would be shared other than as joint tenants; or
   (b) the common intention in respect of beneficial ownership had later changed.
3. The common intention of the parties is to be deduced (inferred) by the court from the parties' conduct, using the *Stack* factors.
4. Where the court had established that the parties had not intended to share beneficial ownership from the outset, or where the parties' intentions had changed, but the court was not able to quantify the intended shares (either by looking at express declaration or by inference), the court could make a decision as to shares based on what the court considered fair, having regard to the 'whole course of dealing' of the parties in relation to the property. This approach had previously emerged in *Oxley v. Hiscock*.
5. This 'whole course of dealing' should be given a broad meaning, by consideration of similar factors as those used in ascertaining the parties' actual intentions: financial considerations are important but are only one of these factors.
6. Each case will turn on its own facts.

In this case, the parties had originally intended a joint beneficial ownership in equal shares, but the conduct of the parties indicated that this common intention had later changed. After separation, the couple had tried to sell the property and when that failed, cashed in a life insurance policy to allow Mr Kernott to buy his own home. The Court could infer from this conduct that the parties had intended that Mr Kernott's share of their joint property should crystallize then. From that point, the Court could infer that the parties intended that Ms Jones should be entitled to all of the capital gain from their former joint home, and Mr Kernott should enjoy the same in respect of his newly purchased home. On that basis, the Court upheld the decision of the judge of first instance, and awarded Ms Jones 90 per cent and Mr Kernott 10 per cent of the jointly owned property.

The Supreme Court has now established that in order to ascertain whether the presumption of joint equitable ownership has been rebutted, the court must look at the *Stack* factors to work out the common intention of the parties. Direct financial contribution is only one of these. It is disappointing, however, that some of the post-*Jones v. Kernott* cases demonstrate the lower courts' unwillingness to venture much beyond financial considerations. For example, in *Graham-York v. York* [2015] EWCA Civ 72, the Court attached little if any weight to the nature of the parties' relationship or the parties' individual personalities and characters—both of which potential factors were identified by Lady Hale in *Stack v. Dowden*. The Court appeared to dismiss evidence that the parties' relationship was dysfunctional, with the claimant (who was apparently suffering the symptoms of Asperger's and post-traumatic stress disorder) under the 'control' of her former partner. The trial judge found that the claimant would have handed over her earnings to the former partner had he demanded it, and the Court of Appeal accepted that it appeared that the claimant had 'endured years of abusive conduct by her partner'. Despite this, the Court of Appeal reminded itself that it could not perform redistributive justice between the parties and proceeded to make a decision largely based on the direct financial contribution of the parties. This appears to undermine the *Stack* direction to the courts to consider the 'whole course of dealing' of the parties.

In terms of quantifying shares in joint legal owner cases, the Supreme Court has now given the lower courts a very firm steer: if it is not possible to ascertain the parties' common intention as to shares, then the court itself can adopt an *Oxley* approach, based on fairness, and taking into account the 'whole course of dealing' between the parties. The relevant factors will again include the *Stack* factors.

Sole legal owner cases and *Jones v. Kernott*

The Supreme Court also made it clear that the court's approach should be different in sole legal owner cases. Here, the approach should be to firstly establish that the claimant has an equitable interest, then to quantify the appropriate share. That share should always be based on the common intention of the parties. See 9.5.2.3 for further discussion. Once that has been established, the court should go on to consider quantification of shares, again using common intention as its guiding principle. However, if the court was unable to identify a common intention as to shares, then it could use the same approach as for jointly owned cases: it could look at the 'whole course of dealing' of the parties and make a decision based on what was fair in the light of those dealings. This is an area which has been the subject of much academic debate in the years following *Jones v. Kernott*. Have a look at the further reading section for academic views which both support and reject a unified approach to these kinds of cases.

Resulting trusts and *Jones v. Kernott*

The Supreme Court held that the analysis of shares by means of a resulting trust no longer had a place in quantifying shares in a family home. This seems to suggest that shares will no longer be quantified in terms of mathematical proportion in relation to the financial contribution of each party. Instead, whether for sole or joint legal owner cases, in the absence of any common intention as to shares, the court will adopt the approach of fairness in relation to the whole course of dealing of the parties.

9.6 Other means of acquiring an equitable interest in the family home: proprietary estoppel

Another way of acquiring an interest in the family home is through the doctrine of proprietary estoppel. In cases judges often mention this doctrine in the same breath as resulting and constructive trusts—but you should remember that it has significant differences, which will be discussed here. Nonetheless, it is an important means of informally acquiring an equitable interest in land and so deserves a closer look.

9.6.1 Two-stage process

In order to acquire an interest in land by means of proprietary estoppel, it is necessary to go through two separate stages:

1. **The equity**

   The person claiming the interest must establish that an estoppel has actually arisen. (We will look in a moment in detail at how he or she does this.) This gives rise to an **equity**, which is different from an equitable interest: all it means is that the claimant has established the right to go to court and ask for a remedy, because he or she has suffered unconscionable behaviour at the hands of the legal owner.

2. **Satisfying the equity**

   The second stage of the process involves going to court and obtaining a remedy. This is known as **satisfying the equity**. As we shall see, the court has the discretion to order any remedy that it sees fit in the circumstances. Sometimes it may involve granting the claimant an interest in the land, but sometimes it does not. Until the court awards a remedy, the equity is described as **inchoate** —that is, the equity has not yet crystallized into a right.

> **equity**
> an equitable right or claim

> **satisfying the equity**
> the fulfilment of the equitable right or claim

> **inchoate**
> incomplete or unformed

9.6.1.1 Stage 1: the estoppel

In order to win the right to go to court, the claimant must prove that three specific requirements have been met—*Taylor Fashions Ltd v. Liverpool Victoria Trustees Co. Ltd* [1982] QB 133:

1. The claimant must prove that the legal owner of the property made an assurance to him or her that he or she already had, or would acquire, an interest in the land.

2. The claimant must have relied on this assurance.

3. The claimant must have acted to his or her detriment (or changed his or her position) in reliance on that assurance.

Rather simplistically, this can be summarized as:

$$assurance + reliance + detriment = proprietary\ estoppel\ equity.$$

A case example will help to explain how this works in practice.

CASE CLOSE-UP

Q

Inwards v. Baker [1965] 1 All ER 446

Mr Baker's son wanted to build himself a house. Mr Baker suggested that he build a bungalow on a piece of his land. He told his son that this would allow him to build a bigger property (assurance and representation). On the strength of his father's suggestion (reliance), the son spent a considerable sum of money (detriment), building his bungalow on his father's land and living there.

Unfortunately, when the father died, he left the land in his will (which had been written many years before the bungalow was built) to Inwards. Inwards then started proceedings in court to recover possession of the land (and bungalow). The son argued that he was estopped from doing so.

The Court of Appeal held that the son had an equitable right to occupy the land for life.

Although it is more convenient to think of each element as an individual requirement, in practice, they overlap considerably and you should bear this in mind as you read through the following sections.

Assurance

The legal owner of the property must have made some statement, or acted in such a way, as to lead the claimant to believe that he or she had, or would acquire, an interest in the land. This might be overt: for example, repeated assurances that the claimant would inherit the property—*Gillett v. Holt* [2001] Ch 210. The assurance or representation can also be passive: for example, a situation in which a legal owner watches the claimant build on land in the mistaken belief that he or she owns that land and yet the legal owner says nothing—*Ramsden v. Dyson* [1866] LR 1 HL 129. The representation need not be the sole inducement for the claimant doing as he or she does, as long as it is one of the inducements—*Wayling v. Jones* (1993) 69 P & CR 170.

Reliance

In order to succeed in a claim of proprietary estoppel, the claimant must have relied on the representation made. This means that he or she must have done something on the strength of the legal owner's assurance. Generally, the court in recent years has presumed reliance if an assurance and detriment has been proven—*Gillett v. Holt*. It is then for the legal owner to rebut that presumption and disprove reliance.

Detriment

If money has been spent by the claimant, the court will usually find that detriment has been proven—*Pascoe v. Turner* [1979] 1 WLR 431. The concept of detriment is, however, far wider than this, and can include the claimant caring for the legal owner and his or her family—*Greasely v. Cooke* [1980] 1 WLR 1306—or even giving up doing something that may have benefited the claimant. In *Gillett*, for example, the claimant had left school at the age of 16, at the suggestion of the legal owner, and so had foregone academic qualifications. This was held to be detriment by the court. In cases of relationship breakdown, the court must assess and evaluate the detriment over the whole course of the relationship and will also look at the benefits that both parties may have received (*Southwell v. Blackburn* [2014] EWCA Civ 1347).

9.6.1.2 **Stage 2: the remedy**

Once the elements have been established, it is the job of the court to provide an appropriate remedy to satisfy the claimant's equity. This is one of the major differences between the constructive trust and proprietary estoppel.

Once a constructive trust has been identified as having arisen, the claimant is automatically entitled to an equitable interest in the property. The court will determine the size of this share according to the guidelines we have already discussed (see 9.5.3). This equitable interest arises as soon as the elements required to establish the constructive trust have arisen (common intention and detriment).

With a proprietary estoppel claim, however, the court has the discretion to award any remedy that it sees fit in order to satisfy the claimant's equity. This may well mean that it awards the claimant an equitable interest in the property, but the remedy may also range from ordering the transfer of legal and equitable title to the claimant—as in *Pascoe v. Turner*—to deciding that justice has already been done to the claimant and so awarding nothing—*Sledmore v. Dalby* (1996) 72 P & CR 196.

This very wide discretion afforded to the court in deciding an appropriate remedy can lead to inconsistency of awards made by courts. The role of the judge is, of course, to review the facts of the case, apply the correct law, and '*weigh the material elements of advantage or disadvantage to those concerned*' in identifying the appropriate remedy to satisfy the equity (*Bradbury v. Taylor* [2012] EWCA Civ 1208 (at 52)). In recent cases, this has led to some substantial and perhaps excessive awards at first instance, with which the appellate courts are reluctant to interfere. In *Suggitt v. Suggitt* [2012] EWCA Civ 1140 Arden LJ suggests that there is no requirement for proportionality between the detriment suffered and the relief granted. Instead, she says that the appropriate test is whether the remedy is '*out of all proportion*' to the detriment suffered by the claimant (at 44). Unsurprisingly, perhaps, this very high hurdle is unlikely to be reached in most appeals, and in recent years a number of very generous decisions made by the lower courts have remained in place.

Finally, the remedy will take effect not from the date on which the elements of the estoppel were established, but from the date on which the court awards the remedy.

9.6.1.3 **Recent developments in the doctrine of proprietary estoppel**

In recent years, the clear lines of the three elements needed to establish a proprietary estoppel have become increasingly blurred. The courts have tended to discuss them under the broader concept of 'unconscionability', which, as we have seen in our discussion of constructive trusts (see 9.5.1), is not always an easy concept to grasp or define.

Two House of Lords cases have returned some much-needed clarification to this area of law, and it is worth considering them both in some detail.

In the first of these cases, *Cobbe v. Yeoman's Row Management Ltd* [2008] UKHL 55, Lord Walker divided proprietary estoppel cases into two broad categories—commercial cases, where the expectation of the parties was generally to acquire a contract, and domestic cases, where the expectation related to the acquisition of tangible property. All of the cases that we have looked at so far in 9.6.1 have related to domestic situations. *Cobbe* itself related to a contract for the development of land. It is therefore perhaps slightly out of place in a chapter devoted to trusts of the family home, yet it contains such important pronouncements on the doctrine of proprietary estoppel that it is well worth looking at it here.

 CASE CLOSE-UP

Cobbe v. Yeoman's Row Management Ltd [2008] UKHL 55

Mr Cobbe, an experienced property developer, entered into an agreement with the landowner, Mrs Lisle-Mainwaring (a director of Yeoman's Row Management Ltd), whereby he would, at his own expense, obtain planning permission to demolish the existing property on the land and build new houses on it.

They agreed that once planning permission had been granted, the land would be sold to Mr Cobbe for £12m: he would develop the property and pay Yeoman's Row a percentage of the profit, if it exceeded a certain amount.

However, the parties did not enter into a written contract, nor did they finalize all of the terms that would eventually need to be considered. Mr Cobbe obtained the planning permission but, unfortunately for him, Mrs Lisle-Mainwaring had already decided to renegotiate the agreement in order to increase her profits. The parties did not manage to reach a new agreement, and Mr Cobbe took the matter to court.

Initially, Mr Cobbe sued in contract, but soon realized that he would not succeed in this claim.

THINKING POINT

Why would Mr Cobbe not have succeeded in an action for breach of contract? Have a look back at Chapter 3 where we think about Law of Property (Miscellaneous Provisions) Act 1989 (LP(MP)A 1989), s. 2.

Under LP(MP)A 1989, s. 2, an interest in land can only be disposed of in writing, and here the parties had not entered into any written agreement. Mr Cobbe argued instead that he had an interest by means of proprietary estoppel or under a constructive trust. At first instance and in the Court of Appeal, it was decided that Mr Cobbe did have such an interest, although his means of acquiring it was discussed under the general term of 'unconscionability', and the court granted Mr Cobbe half of the increased value of the land due to the planning permission. The matter went to the House of Lords.

CASE CLOSE-UP

Cobbe v. Yeoman's Row Management Ltd [2008] UKHL 55

Lord Scott expressed concern that in reaching their decision, neither of the lower courts had identified 'any coherent formulation of the content of the estoppel' (at 17). Lord Scott said that in order for an estoppel to be established, the court had to work out firstly, what were the facts/law that the landowner was barred (estopped) from asserting. In this case, there was nothing to estop Mrs Lisle-Mainwaring from asserting her position. Both parties knew and accepted that the agreement that they had entered into was not legally binding, because it did not comply with LP(MP)A 1989, s. 2.

Secondly, the court had to identify Mr Cobbe's expectation—this had to be an expectation of a 'certain interest in land'. In this case, Mr Cobbe's expectation was that, after planning permission had been granted, the parties would negotiate further and eventually enter into a formal written contract. This was, for proprietary estoppel purposes, the 'wrong sort of expectation', in Lord Scott's opinion.

Lord Walker agreed. He said that proprietary estoppel cases in commercial situations were very different than those in domestic cases. In domestic cases, the claimant had an expectation to acquire an interest in tangible property. In commercial cases, the claimant often only expected to acquire a contract. Mr Cobbe was an experienced property developer, who knew that negotiations were incomplete and not legally binding. He had knowingly accepted a commercial risk (with potentially high rewards) in continuing with the application for planning permission. Proprietary estoppel was not *a sort of joker or wild card to be used whenever the court disapproves of the conduct of a litigant who seems to have the law on his side*' (at 46).

The House then looked at the issue of unconscionability. Lord Walker said that unconscionability did have a role to play in proprietary estoppel cases, whether commercial or domestic. He defined unconscionability (at 92) as: '*an objective value judgment on behaviour (regardless of the state of mind of the individual in question)*'.

He said that even if the three elements of proprietary estoppel had been made out, if the result did not '*shock the conscience of the court*', there may not be a proprietary estoppel. However, unconscionability alone, without the three elements, would not make out a proprietary estoppel. To decide otherwise would be a '*recipe for confusion*' (at 28).

Their Lordships decided that in this case, a proprietary estoppel was not made out, and Mr Cobbe was awarded £150,000 to compensate him for his time and effort in obtaining planning permission.

This decision is useful in that it clarifies the role of unconscionability in proprietary estoppel cases, whether domestic or commercial. The approach suggested in *Cobbe* is that the court:

- identifies the three elements of reliance, assurance, and detriment. If these are established then there is potentially at least a proprietary estoppel made out; then

- checks to see that the element of unconscionability is present. If the legal owner is not estopped from asserting his or her legal right, would the result be unconscionable? Would it 'shock the conscience of the court'?

If the result would not be unconscionable, then a proprietary estoppel may not have been made out. Importantly, *Cobbe* also establishes that unconscionability alone will *not* give rise to a proprietary estoppel.

The second of these important cases is set in the domestic context. The facts are interesting and rather unusual, and it raises some interesting points both on the element of assurance, and on the similarities between proprietary estoppel and constructive trusts.

🔍 CASE CLOSE-UP

Thorner v. Major [2009] UKHL 18

David Thorner had worked on a farm belonging to his uncle (Peter Thorner) for nearly thirty years. He had never been paid for his work. Both men were rather undemonstrative and Peter Thorner said very little. Peter had never directly promised David that he would inherit the farm, but he had made various rather indirect comments suggesting it. Peter had also written a will in which he left the farm to David, although he destroyed this (for reasons unrelated to David) shortly before his death. Peter died intestate, and David claimed that the farm belonged to him by means of a proprietary estoppel.

The judge at first instance found that all of the three elements of proprietary estoppel were present. The Court of Appeal disagreed, finding in particular that there had been no clear assurance from Peter that David would inherit the farm.

Their Lordships confirmed that in order to establish a proprietary estoppel, the court had to find a 'clear and unequivocal' assurance. However, in order to do this, the court had to look at the context of the relevant words and actions. As well as looking at the case contextually, the court had to examine it *'practically and sensibly'* (at 58). Their Lordships said that particularly in an unusual case such as this, appellate courts should be slow to disturb the findings of the judge at first instance, who had had the opportunity to hear the witnesses. Putting the facts in context, Peter and David Thorner were quiet and undemonstrative men, not given to great communication. Given the nature of the parties, their Lordships found that, despite the lack of clear verbal statements, an assurance was established.

This interesting and unusual case shows the courts taking a very pragmatic view of what constitutes an 'assurance'. The context in which the assurances were made (or in the case of *Thorner*, hardly made at all!) is very important. Courts will make a sensible and practical decision based on all the facts of the case. This has been confirmed in *Whittaker v. Kinnear* [2011] EWHC 1479 (QB).

9.6.2 Significance of the differences between constructive trusts and proprietary estoppel

You will have noticed that the requirements to establish a constructive trust or proprietary estoppel in this area of law are very similar. The elements required for an express common intention constructive trust are virtually identical to those for proprietary estoppel, where:

express discussions + detriment

is virtually the same as:

assurance + reliance + detriment.

The Court of Appeal in *Oxley v. Hiscock* (see 9.5.3.1) decided that, essentially, the two concepts had become identical. In *Thorner v. Major* (see 9.6.1.3), the House of Lords suggested that where representations related to an immediate acquisition of property, the appropriate mechanism should be proprietary estoppel, but where representations related to the future acquisition of property, the common intention constructive trust was the more appropriate remedy. Lord Scott also said that the facts in *Thorner* would give rise to a constructive trust.

THINKING POINT

Re-read the facts in *Thorner* at 9.6.1.3. Do you think that, as you understand it, the facts give rise to an express common intention constructive trust?

The difficulty with Lord Scott's assertion is that in *Thorner* there were no explicit express discussions at all! The estoppel was founded entirely upon rather indirect contextual comments. In constructive trust cases, such as *James v. Thomas* [2007] EWCA Civ 121, the court has been very reluctant to interpret any ambiguous statements as the expression of an intention to share beneficial ownership of the property. In addition, there is still a significant difference in effect between the court finding a constructive trust or proprietary estoppel. Lord Hope, in *Stack v. Dowden*, recognized this when he doubted (at [37]) that the two concepts could—or indeed should—be completely assimilated. When a claimant succeeds in establishing a claim under proprietary estoppel, he or she is unsure about the remedy that the court will decide to offer. Even if the claimant establishes that he or she has acquired an equity, the court may decide that the equity has been satisfied and decide not to award any remedy at all. As soon as the remedial outcome in a legal action becomes unpredictable, the claimant will always have to weigh up the potential costs of the proceedings with the likely result. The unpredictability of the remedy—even if the claimant 'wins'—may discourage him or her from bringing a claim at all.

With constructive trust cases, meanwhile, although there are the usual litigation risks, once the elements of the constructive trust have been established, the claimant is entitled to an equitable interest in the property. This is a proprietary right in the land and well worth having.

The timing of the remedy awarded is also significant. With a proprietary estoppel claim, the remedy begins at the date at which the court awards it; under a constructive trust, the equitable interest arises immediately when the events substantiating the requirements of common intention and detriment actually happen—and this could be many years before the case even comes to court. This timing difference may be very significant if third parties—for example, a bank providing a mortgage—have become involved with the property.

9.7 And finally, back to Mrs Burns

The main problem with all of these possible ways of acquiring an informal interest in land is that they apparently leave a whole population of claimants with no remedy. Remember Mrs Burns? (See 9.4.3.2.) Let us work through Mrs Burns' potential claims to see if, after nineteen years of hard labour at the kitchen sink, we can offer her an equitable interest in her family home.

In this chapter, we have identified the various means of acquiring an equitable interest in the property.

 THINKING POINT

Might Mrs Burns have relied on the MCA 1973 to assist her?

No—Mrs Burns was not married to Mr Burns. She had changed her name by deed poll to his. MCA 1973 will only assist married couples on divorce.

 THINKING POINT

Might Mrs Burns have claimed an interest under a resulting trust?

No—she had not made a direct financial contribution to the purchase price of the property. Contributions to household expenses will not give rise to a resulting trust.

 THINKING POINT

Might Mrs Burns have claimed an interest under a constructive trust? Were there any express discussions? Could the court infer a common intention?

No—the parties had not discussed the beneficial ownership of the property. She could not therefore establish an express common intention to share ownership. Under *Rosset*, the only relevant 'conduct' from which the court can infer a common intention is a direct financial contribution to the purchase price of the property—and Mrs Burns did not make such a contribution. Neither could she argue that she had made an indirect financial contribution, because there was no suggestion that the parties had arbitrarily decided to divide the financial expenses, nor was there any suggestion that her contribution allowed her partner to pay the mortgage.

THINKING POINT

Do *Stack v. Dowden* and *Jones v. Kernott* help Mrs Burns?

It would not seem so. The starting point in sole legal owner cases is that equity follows the law. Mrs Burns would have to rebut the presumption that Mr Burns, as the sole legal owner, was also the sole equitable owner. The court's task is still to find a common intention that the parties intended to share beneficial ownership of the property. It may help, however, in that the court must now look at the whole course of dealings between the parties in trying to find a common intention. This may possibly allow it to look at Mrs Burns' non-financial contributions. To confirm this, however, we need to see how the *Stack* and *Jones v. Kernott* principles are applied in the lower courts to sole legal owner cases in the years to come.

THINKING POINT

Would proprietary estoppel assist Mrs Burns?

No—there were never any assurances made to her by her partner (the legal owner) that she would acquire a share in the property. It seems that Mrs Burns—like many others today—simply assumed that she would have some interest in the home she had lived in and looked after for nearly twenty years. As the law stands, she would still walk away with nothing.

9.8 Law Commission— proposals for reform

The Law Commission is well aware of the problems faced by claimants such as Mrs Burns. It has produced a number of reports dealing with the issue (see the list of further reading at the end of the chapter). Many lawyers believe that the only way around the problem is to legislate, to provide cohabiting couples with the same, or similar, legal protection to that already given to married and registered same-sex couples.

Many Commonwealth countries already do this. Australia and New Zealand have both passed Acts that allow the court to order division of property between cohabiting couples in the event of their relationship breaking down. The UK Parliament has been much less willing to do this, because it fears that such an Act would undermine the institution of marriage.

In July 2007, the Law Commission published its Consultation Paper: *Cohabitation: The Financial Consequences of Relationship Breakdown*. In it, the Law Commission suggested a scheme that would apply to any cohabiting couples that satisfied eligibility requirements—either because they had a child together or had lived together for a minimum duration and had not opted out of the scheme by means of a written opt-out agreement and had made '*qualifying contributions to the relationship giving rise to certain enduring consequences at the point of separation*'.

Under the Law Commission's proposals, the applicant would have to show that the respondent retained a benefit, or that the applicant had a continuing economic disadvantage, as a result of contributions made to the relationship. The value of any award would depend on the extent of the retained benefit or continuing economic disadvantage.

This seems a workable solution to a complex problem, but let us return to Mrs Burns for a moment to make sure that it will work in practice.

 THINKING POINT

Would the Law Commission's proposals help Mrs Burns?

Yes—it is likely that they would!

Mr and Mrs Burns would satisfy either of the eligibility requirements: they have a child together and have also lived together for more than the minimum specified time period.

Mrs Burns would have to show that, during the cohabitation, she conferred a benefit on Mr Burns, or that she suffered an economic disadvantage as a result of the cohabitation. It is likely that she could prove both. For almost twenty years Mrs Burns provided cleaning, cooking, and childcare services. This allowed Mr Burns to pursue his own career, and saved him a lot of money in cleaning and childcare costs (and probably takeaways). She suffered her own economic disadvantage as well, by not building a career for herself away from the family home. This detriment would be continuing, because it is likely that when she returned to the job market after the separation, she would not be able to acquire a well-paid job—at least, not without retraining, which would cost her yet more money. This criterion appears to be fully satisfied.

The final hurdle for Mrs Burns is that she should not have opted out of the scheme. Provided that she and Mr Burns had not signed such an agreement, it is highly likely that, under the proposed scheme, Mrs Burns would acquire an interest in the family home.

Unfortunately for applicants such as Mrs Burns, however, in 2008 the government indicated that it would take no action to implement the Law Commission's proposals, although commending the report. In 2011, the Law Commission expressed the wish that its proposals might eventually be implemented by Parliament, given the prevalence of cohabiting couples and the increasing number of children being born to non-married parents.

More recently, the House of Lords has considered yet another Private Members' Bill as individuals recognize the need for urgent reform in this very important area of law. Lord Marks' Cohabitation Reform Bill suggests reform along the lines of the Law Commission's proposals, by allowing the court to make a financial settlement for separating cohabitees, with an opt-out option. The discussion of the Bill in the House of Lords followed predictable lines, with some members arguing that the Bill would undermine the institution of marriage, and that this should be a matter for the government to address. Unfortunately, at the time of writing, there is no indication that the government will prioritize reform in this area of law.

Summary

1. Interests in land can be acquired informally, as well as formally.

2. They can arise under a resulting or constructive trust, or through proprietary estoppel.

3. Establishing such an interest is important in situations in which the relationship of a cohabiting (unmarried) couple has broken down.

4. It will also be important for married couples, if the property is registered in the sole name of one of the partners and a third-party bank is seeking to repossess the property.

5. The approach in respect of properties owned by a sole legal owner and those owned by joint legal owners will be different.

6. In sole legal owner cases, the claimant must establish first that he or she has an equitable interest in the property. This will usually be under a resulting or constructive trust.

7. A constructive trust will arise in two situations:

   - if there has been express agreement to share the beneficial ownership of the property and the claimant has acted upon this to his or her detriment;

   - in the absence of express discussions, if the court can infer a common intention through the conduct of the parties (and detriment).

8. *Lloyds Bank plc v. Rosset* suggested that the only relevant conduct for the court's purposes is likely to be a direct financial contribution to the purchase price of the property.

9. *Stack v. Dowden* suggested that this set the '*hurdle rather too high*', and recent cases may suggest that the courts are moving towards a *Jones v. Kernott* review of conduct for establishing a common intention in relation to establishing the existence of an equitable interest in sole legal owner cases.

10. In joint legal owner cases, joint equitable ownership is presumed, but may be rebutted by a claimant proving a contrary common intention.

11. In terms of quantifying the equitable interest, in both sole and joint legal owner cases, following *Jones v. Kernott*, the court must first try to ascertain the common intention of the parties as to shares in the property. If it cannot do this, it can award what it considers to be fair, having regard to the whole course of dealing of the parties.

12. An equitable interest may be acquired through proprietary estoppel, but this is at the court's discretion and the claimant may be awarded a different remedy—or even no remedy at all.

13. A whole class of potential claimants—the 'Mrs Burns' claimant—is still left without a remedy.

 The bigger picture

- If you want to see how this area of land law fits into the rest of your studies, you can look at Chapter 14, especially 14.3. For some guidance on what sort of exam questions come up in this area, see Chapter 15, 15.9.

- One of the really interesting aspects of this area of law is the exploration of the need for reform. Read the Law Commission reports, especially the later one:
  - Law Commission (2002) *Sharing Homes: A Discussion Paper*, Law Com No. 278, available online at http://www.lawcom.gov.uk/wp-content/uploads/2015/04/lc278.pdf
  - Law Commission (2007) *Cohabitation: The Financial Consequences of Relationship Breakdown*, Law Com No.307, available online at https://www.gov.uk/government/uploads/system/uploads/attachment_data/file/228881/7182.pdf
- There have been some very interesting recent cases on proprietary estoppel, which have confirmed that entitlement to an easement can arise by proprietary estoppel (*Hoyl Group Ltd v. Cromer Town Council* [2015] EWCA Civ 782), and that proprietary estoppel may apply to intellectual property (*Motivate Publishing FZ LLC v. Hello Ltd* [2015] EWHC 1554 (Ch)). Although these are outside the scope of this chapter, they are well worth a read.

? Questions

Self-test questions

1. Carly and James want to buy a house together. James suggests to Carly that, because she is going through an unpleasant divorce, the house should be registered in James' sole name. Carly agrees. The couple move into the house and, while James is out at work, Carly completely landscapes the garden. She also redecorates a number of rooms. Some years later, their relationship breaks down. James tells Carly that, because her name is not on the land register and she has only contributed to household expenses, she has no interest in the house. Advise Carly.

2. Yasmeen and Bobby decide to buy a house together. The house is registered in Yasmeen's sole name. The house costs £100,000. Yasmeen contributes £75,000 and Bobby contributes £25,000. Bobby stays at home, and looks after the house and children, while Yasmeen goes to work. Some years later, their relationship breaks down. Advise Bobby.

Exam questions

1. Gemma and Tash, who are sisters, buy a house together. They register it in joint names. Tash pays 70 per cent of the purchase price of the property. The remaining 30 per cent is funded by a mortgage acquired in joint names. Other than the house, the sisters have completely separate financial affairs and have no other assets in joint names. After a few years, the girls decide to sell the house. Unfortunately, they do not agree as to how the proceeds should be divided. Tash claims that she is entitled to 70 per cent of the property, because that is what she originally contributed. Gemma says that they are either beneficial joint tenants or tenants in common with equal shares. Advise Gemma and Tash.

2. Sisco and Dylan have been living together for three years, in a house owned solely by Sisco. Although Sisco paid for most of the purchase price of the property, Dylan has taken a year off work to renovate it completely. He has also used his own money to build a small extension at the back of the house. Sisco and Dylan have now separated and Dylan is claiming a beneficial interest in the property. Advise Dylan.

@ **For suggested approaches to answering these questions visit the Online Resource Centre.**

Further reading

Etherton, T., 'Constructive trusts and proprietary estoppel: the search for clarity and principle' [2009] Conv 104
An analysis of the overlap between constructive trusts and proprietary estoppel post *Stack v. Dowden.*

Hess, E., 'The rights of cohabitants: when and how will the law be reformed?' [2009] Fam Law 405
An interesting comparison of suggested reforms in this area of law.

Jones v. Kernott [2011] UKSC 53
It is worth reading this case in its entirety.

Lees, K., '*Geary v Rankine*: money isn't everything' [2012] Conv 412
An interesting article which argues that the *Jones v. Kernott* principles can equally be applied to sole legal owner cases, and consequently that the *Rosset* principles have been relaxed.

Lloyds Bank plc v. Rosset [1991] 1 AC 107
It is worth reading this case in its entirety.

MacFarlane, B., and Sales, P., 'Promises, detriment and liability: lessons from proprietary estoppel' [2015] LQR 610
This article revists *Thorner v. Major* and considers the relationship between the doctrine of proprietary estoppel and the law of contract.

Mee, J., 'Proprietary estoppel and inheritance: enough is enough?' [2013] Conv 280
An interesting article which looks at the recent, rather generous approach of the lower courts to awarding remedies to claimants successfully claiming an interest in land by means of proprietary estoppel. The author calls for more guidance from appellate courts in the matter of remedies.

Pawlowski, M., 'Imputing a common intention in single ownership cases' (2015) 29(1) Tru LI 3
This article considers the difference between inferring and imputing a common intention, and compares the situation in the English courts with the Canadian approach of unjust enrichment.

Stack v. Dowden [2007] UKHL 17
It is worth reading this case in its entirety.

 Online Resource Centre

www.oxfordtextbooks.co.uk/orc/clarke_directions5e/

For more advice relating to this chapter, including self-test questions and an interactive glossary, visit the Online Resource Centre.

10 Trusts of land

□ **LEARNING OBJECTIVES**

By the end of this chapter, you will be able to:

● understand the statutory framework governing trusts of land;

● explain the functions and powers of the trustees of a trust of land;

● explain the rights of the beneficiaries under such a trust;

● outline the statutory procedure provided to resolve disputes arising from trusts of land.

Introduction

In Chapters 7, 8, and 9, we have looked at how trusts of land arise in practice. We have seen that there may be one sole legal owner, registered on the land register, and that this may conceal the existence of a trust of land. We have looked at co-ownership of land and the various ways in which co-owners can choose to hold land, as joint tenants and tenants in common. Finally, we have looked at how trusts of land come into being informally, through resulting and constructive trusts.

This chapter is the final piece of the trusts-of-land jigsaw puzzle. In this chapter, we will look at what the law requires of trustees of land and how it protects the beneficiaries of those trusts. We will also see that Parliament has provided a useful mechanism for resolving disputes in trusts of land, and we will examine how that works for both trustees and beneficiaries.

10.1 The Trusts of Land and Appointment of Trustees Act 1996

The Act on which we will be focusing in this chapter has the very grand title of the Trusts of Land and Appointment of Trustees Act 1996 (TOLATA 1996). This title, although rather wordy, efficiently describes the contents of the Act. It was eventually passed after a Law Commission Report in 1989 recommended that this area of law be reformed and it came into force on 1 January 1997. It is relatively simple and the lack of a significant volume of case law in the years following its implementation indicates that it is also generally well drafted.

We will look, firstly and very briefly, at why the Act was needed and, then and in more detail, at the provisions of the Act itself.

10.2 The need for the Trusts of Land and Appointment of Trustees Act 1996

Before the TOLATA 1996, all co-owned land was held on a **trust for sale**. As the name implies, trustees of such a trust had, first and foremost, a duty to *sell* the land—but, as we have already seen, in most cases of co-ownership, the trustees and beneficiaries are the same people, who have deliberately purchased their home not to sell it, but to live in it! It seems very odd, then, to impose on them an immediate duty to sell.

> **trust for sale** a trust under which the trustees were obliged to sell the property and hold the proceeds in trust for the beneficiaries

The trustees had other duties, of course, some of which were very similar to those found in the TOLATA 1996—including, for example, the duty to consult beneficiaries. They could also decide to postpone their power of sale, provided that all of the trustees agreed—but if one of the trustees changed his or her mind, the duty to sell would revive. This, together with the fact that the beneficiaries had no specific right to occupy the land, made the beneficiaries' existence somewhat uncomfortable.

The Law of Property Act 1925 (LPA 1925), s. 30 provided a mechanism whereby the beneficiaries of a trust for sale could apply to the court for a postponement of sale. The courts became extremely clever at finding ways around the trustees' duty to sell and preserving the beneficiaries' right to occupy the land. Under LPA 1925, s. 30, the court looked at all of the circumstances of the case in order to reach a decision. As we shall see, this dispute resolution mechanism was preserved in the TOLATA 1996 as s. 14 and the factors that the court must consider were preserved in s. 15. This means that much of the case law brought under LPA 1925, s. 30 remains relevant today.

The most significant change that the TOLATA 1996 introduced was that trusts for sale could no longer be created. Instead, all co-owned land is now held under a trust of land. There is, then, no longer an overriding duty on trustees to sell the land that they hold for beneficiaries.

We will now look in some detail at the Act itself. (For an overview of the Act, see Table 10.1.)

10.3 Trusts of land

TOLATA 1996, s. 1, defines a trust of land.

> **STATUTE**
>
> **Trusts of Land and Appointment of Trustees Act 1996, s. 1 [Meaning of 'trust of land']**
>
> (1) In this Act—
>
>   (a) 'trust of land' means ... any trust of property which consists of or includes land, and
>
>   (b) 'trustees of land' means trustees of a trust of land.
>
> (2) The reference in subsection (1)(a) to a trust—
>
>   (a) is to any description of trust (whether express, implied, resulting or constructive), including a trust for sale and a bare trust, and
>
>   (b) includes a trust created, or arising, before the commencement of this Act.
>
>   ...

The Act therefore covers every kind of trust for which the trust property includes land, whether that trust was created deliberately—that is, by the express intention of the parties—or arose informally—for example, by means of a resulting or constructive trust. As soon as such a trust comes into being, the trustees will be subject to the legal obligations imposed upon them by the TOLATA 1996 and the beneficiaries will enjoy the rights described in the Act.

We will look first at what this means for the trustees.

10.3.1 The trustees

10.3.1.1 Powers and duties of the trustees

The powers of the trustees under TOLATA 1996, s. 6, are considerable.

> **STATUTE**
>
> **Trusts of Land and Appointment of Trustees Act 1996, s. 6 [General powers of trustees]**
>
> For the purpose of exercising their functions as trustees, the trustees of land have in relation to the land subject to the trust all the powers of an absolute owner.
>
>   ...

▶ CROSS REFERENCE

For more on an owner's powers, see Chapter 3.

As you will remember, an owner's powers in relation to his or her land are extensive. He or she can, for example, sell it, grant a mortgage over it, or grant a lease of all or part of it.

The trustees of land have equally extensive powers, but they are, of course, constrained by the duty that they owe to the beneficiaries. They can only exercise their powers with the interests of the beneficiaries in mind.

STATUTE

Trusts of Land and Appointment of Trustees Act 1996, s. 6 [General powers of trustees]

...

(5) In exercising the powers conferred by this section trustees shall have regard to the rights of the beneficiaries.

...

The trustees are also subject to the usual fiduciary duties of trustees—TOLATA 1996, s. 6(6).

As well as exercising the rights of an absolute owner over the land subject to the trust, the trustees can also buy more land—perhaps as an investment or for occupation by a beneficiary. TOLATA 1996, s. 6(3) grants the trustees the power to do this in accordance with Trustee Act 2000 (TA 2000), s. 8.

TOLATA 1996, s. 6(2) also gives the trustees the right to convey the land to the beneficiaries, provided that the beneficiaries are adult, legally capable, and absolutely entitled to the land. The trustees can do this even if the beneficiaries do not ask them to do it. This power allows the trustees to end their responsibility and effectively to pass it on to the beneficiaries, who then take on the role of trustees. This is a statutory version of the common law rule in *Saunders v. Vautier* [1841] 4 Beav. 115.

Under TOLATA 1996, s. 7 the trustees have the specific power to partition the land, provided that they do so in accordance with the rights of the beneficiaries and with the consent of the beneficiaries. This may be useful in a situation in which the land might be partitioned in order to allow the beneficiaries to occupy different parts of it. If the beneficiaries do not agree to such partitioning, however, the trustees may well have to apply to the court for an order under TOLATA 1996, s. 14 or exercise their entitlement under TOLATA 1996, s. 13 to regulate occupation of the land by beneficiaries (see 10.3.2.1).

By power of attorney, trustees can delegate their powers to any adult beneficiary or beneficiaries who are entitled to an interest in possession of the land—TOLATA 1996, s. 9—but, in order to do this, all of the trustees must agree to it—TOLATA 1996, s. 9(3)—and any of the trustees can revoke it.

> **CROSS REFERENCE**
> For the meaning of power of attorney, see Chapter 4.

10.3.1.2 Restriction of the trustees' powers

TOLATA 1996, s. 8 allows the settlor to restrict the powers of the trustees under ss. 6 and 7 if he or she sees fit, and/or to impose a requirement that the trustees must obtain the consent of the beneficiaries before exercising their powers—TOLATA 1996, s. 8(2).

If the settlor requires the trustees to obtain the consent of the beneficiaries before, for example, exercising their power to sell the land, then TOLATA 1996, s. 10(1) provides that a purchaser of the land will be protected as long as at least two of the beneficiaries consented to its sale. This section is designed to protect the purchaser from potential legal action taken by angry beneficiaries; it does not relieve the trustees of their duty to obtain the consents required by the settlor. If the trustees sell the land without obtaining the requisite consents, they will still be acting in breach of trust and may be sued by the beneficiaries.

10.3.1.3 Consultation

Given that the powers of the trustees are potentially so sweeping, it is not surprising that the Act imposes some specific duties on the trustees to consult the beneficiaries before acting.

STATUTE

**Trusts of Land and Appointment of Trustees Act 1996, s. 11
[Consultation with beneficiaries]**

1   The trustees of land shall in the exercise of any function relating to land subject to the trust—

(a) so far as practicable, consult the beneficiaries of full age and beneficially entitled to an interest in possession in the land, and

(b) so far as consistent with the general interest of the trust, give effect to the wishes of those beneficiaries, or (in case of dispute) of the majority (according to the value of their combined interests).

…

The settlor can expressly exclude this requirement—TOLATA 1996, s. 11(2)(a). It also does not apply in some exceptional cases, the most important of which are in relation to trusts created in, or arising from, wills made before the commencement of the Act—TOLATA 1996, s. 11(2)(b).

Note the interesting wording at the beginning of this section—'*so far as practicable*'—and at the beginning of subsection (b)—'*so far as consistent with the general interest of the trust*'. Such general terms often lead to widespread litigation, although, in this instance, they have not. The terms simply seem to suggest that the trustees must make reasonable efforts both to consult with, and to give effect to the wishes of, the beneficiaries. There is, however, no absolute requirement that they do so.

10.3.2 **Rights of the beneficiaries**

10.3.2.1 **Occupation**

The beneficiaries have a number of specific rights under the Act. One of the most important of these is the right to occupy the property.

 STATUTE

Trusts of Land and Appointment of Trustees Act 1996, s. 12 [The right to occupy]

(1) A beneficiary who is beneficially entitled to an interest in possession in land subject to a trust of land is entitled by reason of his interest to occupy the land at any time if at that time—

(a) the purposes of the trust include making the land available for his occupation (or for the occupation of beneficiaries of a class of which he is a member or of beneficiaries in general), or

(b) the land is held by trustees so as to be so available.

(2) Subsection (1) does not confer on a beneficiary a right to occupy land if it is either unavailable or unsuitable for occupation by him.

(3) This section is subject to section 13.

> **CROSS REFERENCE**

It might help you to re-read Chapter 7 at this point.

If there is more than one beneficiary—for example, when the land is co-owned—then each beneficiary will have the same right to occupy the property. Note that the right to occupy only extends to beneficiaries with an interest in possession. This means that a beneficiary with an interest in remainder, which would follow only after the death of a beneficiary with a life interest, would not be immediately entitled to occupy the property.

 EXAMPLE

When Simon died, he left his house to his partner, Biddy, for life and, after her death, to Clive absolutely.

Under s. 12, Biddy would have the right to occupy the property. Clive would not be entitled to occupy the house, because he does not have an interest 'in possession'. His interest is 'in remainder': it takes effect only after Biddy's death.

TOLATA 1996, s. 12 looks relatively simple: it confers on the beneficiary the right to occupy the property, provided that one of the purposes of the trust is that he or she should do so, and that the land is *available* and *suitable* for that purpose. Usually, in everyday situations involving residential properties, the land will have been acquired with the intention that the beneficiaries occupy it. The issue then becomes whether the land is available and suitable.

'Unavailable' and 'unsuitable' are not defined in the Act, but the fact that there has been little litigation on the interpretation of these words may well mean that trustees, beneficiaries, and their lawyers are comfortable with a common-sense application of their meaning. *Medlycott v. Herbert* [2014] EWHC 4177 (Ch) established that if a property is let to a tenant at the date of the court hearing, then it is 'unavailable' for occupation by a beneficiary, even if the tenancy ends shortly afterwards (at 27). The case of *Chan Pui Chun v. Leung Kam Ho* [2002] EWCA Civ 1075 illustrates that, when the court is asked to make a decision as to whether a property is 'suitable' for occupation by a beneficiary, it will look not only at the physical features of the property itself, but also at the characteristics, circumstances, and needs of the particular beneficiary. It seems that the courts will usually be difficult to persuade of a property's unsuitability on the basis of size alone: *Medlycott v. Herbert* [2014] EWHC 4177 (Ch).

 CASE CLOSE-UP

***Chan Pui Chun v. Leung Kam Ho* [2002] EWCA Civ 1075**

This case concerned the ownership of a family home after the relationship between the parties, Miss Chan and Mr Leung, broke down. At first instance, the judge found that Miss Chan, a student, had a beneficial interest in the property under a constructive trust and ordered that she should be permitted to live in the property until such time as she finished her studies or decided to move out. At this point, the property was to be sold and the proceeds shared according to each party's beneficial entitlement.

The Court of Appeal agreed that Miss Chan had a beneficial interest in the property, which may entitle her, under TOLATA 1996, s. 12, to live in it. Jonathan Parker LJ then considered whether the property was '*suitable*' for her occupation under s. 12(2). He said (at [101]):

> There is no statutory definition or guidance as to what is meant by 'unsuitable' in this context, and it would be rash indeed to attempt an exhaustive definition or explanation of its meaning. In the context of the present case, it is, I think, enough to say that 'suitability' for this purpose must involve a consideration not only of the general nature and physical characteristics of the particular property but also a consideration of the personal characteristics, circumstances and requirements of the particular beneficiary. This much is, I think, clear from the fact that the statutory expression

> is not simply 'unsuitable for occupation' but 'unsuitable for occupation by him', that is to say by the particular beneficiary.
>
> He then went on to look at the characteristics of the property. The house was large, featuring four bedrooms, a swimming pool, and a fish pond (!). Mr Leung had argued that the house was too large for Miss Chan alone and that it was too expensive for her to maintain. The judge also took into consideration the fact that Miss Chan was only to continue in occupation until she finished her studies. Under these circumstances, the court felt that the property was perfectly suitable for her occupation.
>
> Jonathan Parker LJ added an aside that strikes a blow for justice in such cases (at [102]):
>
>> In any event, I would have taken some persuading that a property which was on any footing suitable for occupation by Miss Chan and Mr Leung whilst they lived together should be regarded as unsuitable for occupation by her alone once Mr Leung had left.

If the land subject to the trust is commercial property, it may well not meet the requirements for occupation in TOLATA 1996, s. 12. Firstly, such land is unlikely to be purchased for the purpose of providing accommodation for the beneficiaries; it will instead be bought for commercial purposes. Secondly, it may well not be available for occupation, because it will be in commercial use. Finally, given the nature of the property, it would probably be considered to be unsuitable for occupation by the beneficiaries and so they would have no right to occupy under that section.

10.3.2.2 Restriction/exclusion of occupation

TOLATA 1996, s. 12 is also subject to s. 13, which allows the trustees to restrict the occupation of beneficiaries under certain circumstances.

 STATUTE

Trusts of Land and Appointment of Trustees Act 1996, s. 13 [Exclusion and restriction of right to occupy]

(1) Where two or more beneficiaries are (or apart from this subsection would be) entitled under section 12 to occupy land, the trustees of land may exclude or restrict the entitlement of any one or more (but not all) of them.

(2) Trustees may not under subsection (1)—

    (a) unreasonably exclude any beneficiary's entitlement to occupy land, or

    (b) restrict any such entitlement to an unreasonable extent.

...

This allows the trustees to limit the entitlement of a beneficiary, or exclude him or her from occupation of the land. The wording of TOLATA 1996, s. 13(1) makes it clear that the trustees do not have the power to exclude all of the beneficiaries from the land; neither can they exclude a beneficiary who is already in occupation of the land, unless he or she gives his or her consent to the exclusion, or the court approves such an act—TOLATA 1996, s. 13(7). In restricting or excluding a beneficiary's right to occupy land, the trustees must behave reasonably and should take into account the matters outlined in s. 13(4). These matters include: the intentions of the creator(s) of the trust; the purpose for which the land is held; and the circumstances and wishes of each of the beneficiaries entitled to occupy the land.

The trustees may also impose conditions on the beneficiaries, provided that these are reasonable—TOLATA 1996, s. 13(3). For example, beneficiaries in occupation of the land may be required to pay any expenses or outgoings in respect of the land—s. 13(5)—or may be required to compensate beneficiaries who have been excluded from the land—TOLATA 1996, s. 13(6).

The difficulty with this section is that, in most disputes, the trustees and beneficiaries are the same people, and they may well find it difficult to reach agreement between themselves. The statute makes it clear that a beneficiary in occupation cannot be excluded from, or restricted on, the land without his or her consent and this is unlikely to be forthcoming. It is much more likely that, in such cases, the trustees will apply to the court for an order to exclude or restrict a beneficiary.

A good example of how this works is to be found in *Rodway v. Landy* [2001] EWCA Civ 471.

 CASE CLOSE-UP

***Rodway v. Landy* [2001] EWCA Civ 471**

Two doctors bought a property together, from which they ran a medical practice. The doctors owned it as joint tenants in law and as tenants in common in equal shares in equity. They were thus both trustees and beneficiaries of the land (see Figure 10.1).

Figure 10.1 Drs Rodway and Landy as joint tenants in law and tenants in common in equity

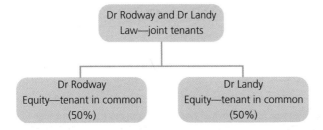

CASE CLOSE-UP

After a dispute between the doctors, Dr Rodway wanted to sell the property. Dr Landy did not want to sell: he wanted to partition the property into two practices. He could not rely on TOLATA 1996, s. 7 to do this, because that requires the consent of the beneficiaries and Dr Rodway refused to consent.

Dr Landy applied to the court under s. 14 (see 10.4) for an order under s. 13 restricting each of the doctors to a part of the property and excluding each of them from the other part. Remember that s. 13(7) allows the trustees to exercise their powers to restrict or exclude, even without the consent of the beneficiaries already in occupation, as long as the court approves.

The judge at first instance made the order as requested. Dr Rodway appealed. The Court of Appeal dismissed the appeal. The property lent itself to physical partitioning and each doctor could carry on his or her own practice in part of it. The court also held that it was not unreasonable to impose a condition on each beneficiary requiring him or her to contribute to the costs of adapting the property into two separate units.

The case of *Ellison v. Cleghorn* [2013] EWHC 5 (Ch) concerned the purchase of a piece of land by two friends, with a view to building a house each on the plot. The friends held the land as tenants in common, but without any formal agreement about the eventual division of the land. Unfortunately, the friends fell out over the location and construction of a double garage, and the relative sizes of their parts of the plot. One of them applied to the court for a sale of the property. The court decided that in these circumstances, the most appropriate action would be to order partition of the land, transferring each part of the partitioned land to the name of the appropriate individual. This is a slightly unusual case, in that the objective of the parties from the outset was to divide the land into two plots. Where this is the case, Briggs J suggested, *'partition is the direct and natural means of achieving that objective, with recourse to the court if the beneficiaries will not all consent'* (at 47).

10.4 Powers of the court

One of the most important parts of TOLATA 1996 is s. 14, which provides a mechanism for resolving disputes involving trusts of land.

CROSS REFERENCE

For more on mortgages, see Chapter 13.

Under s. 14(1) any trustee or person with an *'interest'* in the land can apply to the court for an order in respect of the land. Persons with an interest in the land will, of course, include beneficiaries and also the mortgagee (usually a bank or building society). The court may make an order in respect of any of the trustees' functions: it can even dispense with the need for the trustees to obtain the consent of the beneficiaries before exercising their powers—TOLATA 1996, s. 14(2)(a). The court can also make a declaration of the nature or extent of a person's interest in the land that is the subject of the trust: TOLATA 1996, s. 14(2)(b). This gives the court wide powers to intervene and sort out the problems that invariably arise in co-ownership of land.

The most common types of dispute will be between trustees and beneficiaries. As we have seen, the trustees and the beneficiaries are often the same people. When a relationship breaks down, one party might want to sell the land and the other may not want to. In this situation, in which the parties simply cannot reach an agreement, they can apply to the court under TOLATA 1996, s. 14 and the court will make a decision on their behalf. We have already looked at an example of an application under s. 14 in *Rodway v. Landy* (see 10.3.2.2).

TOLATA 1996, s. 14, may also be useful in other contexts—particularly if the owners of the property have fallen behind with mortgage repayments, or been made bankrupt and the creditors want the property to be sold in order to recover their money (see 10.5).

Finally, there may be disagreement among the trustees—or, indeed, the beneficiaries—that they are unable to resolve. TOLATA 1996, s. 14 allows them to ask the court to find a way forward in the dispute. A recent case shows that the courts may be creative in their approach to solving disputes between the beneficiaries.

CASE CLOSE-UP

Bagum v. Hafiz [2015] EWCA Civ 801

A mother (Mrs Bagum) and her two sons, Mr Hafiz and Mr Hai, owned a four-bedroomed property in Islington as tenants in common in three equal shares.

Following a dispute over the property, Mrs Bagum sought an order from the court under s. 14 of TOLATA that Mr Hai should be directed to sell his share of the property to Mr Hafiz. Mr Hai opposed the suggestion. At first instance, the judge held that she had no jurisdiction to make the order that Mrs Bagum sought, but that she could (and did) make an order which provided that the trustees sell the property, offering Mr Hafiz the first opportunity to purchase Mr Hai's share, at a valuation price determined by the court. If Mr Hafiz chose not to do this, then after six weeks the property should be offered for sale on the open market, when obviously all of the beneficial owners would have the opportunity to bid for it.

The Court of Appeal had two issues to consider: firstly, Mr Hai claimed that the judge did not have the power under TOLATA to make such an order; secondly, Mrs Bagum claimed that the judge did have the power to make the order that she had originally sought (ie to compel Mr Hai to sell his share to Mr Hafiz).

The Court of Appeal decided that the judge had correctly identified her powers under s. 14 and although the order that she had made was unusual, she was entitled to make it. The Court said that a judge could not direct a beneficiary to sell or transfer his or her beneficial interest to another beneficiary. However, the court had a 'substantially wider discretion, exercised upon the basis of wider considerations' than the trustees themselves (at 23). Whilst trustees were under a duty to act in the interests of the beneficiaries as a class, not preferring one beneficiary over another, the court was not so compelled. Provided it acted fairly and not capriciously, the court was not constrained by the rules of equity which bound trustees.

In this case, the judge had carefully considered the interests of the beneficiaries, including Mr Hai's wish that he should not be bought out of the property by his brother, and his anxiety that if this happened, he might not get the best price for his share. She had nonetheless identified that it was perfectly possible to get a sensible and accurate valuation of the property, given that there were a number of similar properties in the local area.

10.4.1 Factors that the court must consider

When making a decision under TOLATA 1996, s. 14, the court has a statutory duty to take into account the factors outlined in s. 15. This is not an exhaustive list of factors and other matters may well be relevant—*Bank of Ireland Home Mortgages Ltd v. Bell* [2001] FLR 805.

 STATUTE

Trusts of Land and Appointment of Trustees Act 1996, s. 15 [Matters relevant in determining applications]

(1) The matters to which the court is to have regard in determining an application for an order under section 14 include—

(a) the intentions of the person or persons (if any) who created the trust,

(b) the purposes for which the property subject to the trust of land is held,

(c) the welfare of any minor who occupies or might reasonably be expected to occupy any land subject to the trust as his home, and

(d) the interests of any secured creditor of any beneficiary.

...

(3) ... the matters to which the court is to have regard also include the circumstances and wishes of any beneficiaries of full age and entitled to an interest in possession in

property subject to the trust or (in case of dispute) of the majority (according to the value of their combined interests).

...

The Act does not indicate the relative importance of any of these factors: they are all to be taken into account when the court makes its decision.

We will consider each of the factors in turn.

10.4.1.1 Section 15(1)(a): intention

THINKING POINT

In what circumstances might the intention of the creator of the trust be useful to the court?

Under TOLATA 1996, s. 15(1)(a), the court must consider the intentions of the person(s) creating the trust. If a trust of land has been deliberately created, then there may well be a trust deed that sets out the terms of the trust, and, from this, the court may well be able to ascertain the intention of the settlor.

Think about the situation in which a beneficiary with an interest in remainder—that is, after the death of a beneficiary with a life interest—wants to sell the property. An example might help.

EXAMPLE

Bob has recently died. In his will, he set up a trust, leaving his home to his girlfriend, Susan, for life and then to his brother, Alan, in remainder. Both Susan and Alan have an equitable interest in the property: they are beneficiaries.

If Alan wants to sell the property and Susan does not, they can apply to the court under s. 14 for an order. The court will then look at the factors in s. 15, one of which is the intention of the creator of the trust. Susan could then adduce evidence as to Bob's intention that the trust was created to enable her to live in the property for the rest of her life. This may persuade the court not to make an order for the sale of the property.

In the majority of cases of co-ownership, however, the trust arises informally and so there will be no trust deed for the court to consider. The court will then try to infer the intention of the parties. There is obviously an overlap between the intention of the parties and the purpose of the trust—TOLATA 1996, s. 15(1)(b).

10.4.1.2 Section 15(1)(b): purpose

The court must consider the purpose for which the property subject to the trust is held. In many cases, the purpose will be to provide a family home. *Rodway v. Landy* established that the relevant purpose for consideration by the court is that subsisting at the time at which the court is considering the application—and this may not be the same as the purpose of the trust when the land was actually bought.

The court also takes into account the fact that the original purpose may be at an end. In the case of *Jones v. Challenger* [1961] 1 QB 176, which involved a couple who had divorced, the Court of Appeal decided that, although the purpose of the trust had originally been to hold and occupy the land as a family home, this had effectively ended and so an order for sale could be made.

Sometimes, the land is purchased for purposes other than providing a family home.

 CASE CLOSE-UP

Re Buchanan-Wollaston's Conveyance [1939] Ch 738

Four neighbours bought a piece of land by the seafront, close to properties that they already owned. The purpose of buying the land was to ensure that the land was not developed in a way that might cause the value of their own properties to fall. They bought the land as joint tenants and agreed only to sell the land if the majority of them agreed to the sale. When a dispute over selling the land arose, the court looked at the original purpose of buying the land. The court decided that this purpose was clear and continuing, and, for that reason, would not order a sale of the land if the majority of the owners were not in favour of selling it.

10.4.1.3 Section 15(1)(c): welfare of minors

If there are children occupying the property, or who might reasonably be expected to live there, the court will also consider their needs before making an order to sell the property. This may include not only the children of the owner of the property, but also, for example, grandchildren who live with their grandparents—*First National Bank v. Achampong* [2003] EWCA Civ 487.

The age of the children will be relevant: in *Bank of Home Mortgages v. Bell* [2001] 2 FLR 809, the welfare of a son who was almost 18 years old and living in the property was given little weight by the court.

The needs of the children may, however, be a consideration in a situation in which the owners of the property have separated and so the 'purpose' of the trust has come to an end (see 10.4.1.2). If this is the case, the children will still need a home in which to live and the court will balance this need with all of the other factors in TOLATA 1996, s. 15. In practice the court may well decide that the needs of the children—even those with disabilities which may make it preferable that they remain in the property—may be less significant than the needs of other parties with an interest in the property (see, for example *Begum v. Issa* (Leeds County Court, 5 November, 2014), and may only postpone a sale of the property for a short period of time.

10.4.1.4 Section 15(1)(d): interests of secured creditors

TOLATA 1996, s. 15 gives no indication of the weight that the court should attach to each of the four factors explicitly mentioned in the section and we have already established that other relevant matters may be brought before the court. Nevertheless, in recent years, the courts seem to have increasingly emphasized the importance of s. 15(1)(d).

Remember that anyone with an '*interest*' in the property can make an application to the court for an order for the sale of the property. A bank or building society that is a mortgagee has an interest in the property and, under TOLATA 1996, s. 14, can ask the court for an order for sale. The bank will only ever do this if the owner has fallen behind with mortgage repayments and if it appears as if the bank will not recover its money. Hence the small print: 'Your home is at risk if you do not keep up the repayments.'

> **CROSS REFERENCE**

For more on mortgages, see Chapter 13.

When a bank makes an application under s. 14, the court is again required to balance the various factors outlined in TOLATA 1996, s. 15. The court often has a difficult decision to make. On the one hand, the owners and their children need a place to live; on the other, the bank needs to recover its money. Under the law before TOLATA 1996, a similar exercise was undertaken under LPA 1925, s. 30. The courts made it clear, though, that the interests of the **secured creditor** would prevail unless there were exceptional circumstances—*Abbey National plc v. Moss* [1994] 26 HLR 249.

> **secured creditor** someone who has lent money to the owner of the property, and has 'secured' the loan on the property itself, meaning that, if the owner fails to meet the payments on the loan, the creditor can recover the money that it has lent by (usually) repossessing and selling the property

But one of the earliest significant TOLATA 1996 cases—*Mortgage Corporation v. Shaire* [2001] 4 All ER 380—decided that, under that Act, the courts had a much wider discretion when dealing with an application for an order of sale.

🔍 CASE CLOSE-UP

Mortgage Corporation v. Shaire [2001] 4 All ER 380

Mr and Mrs Shaire had bought a house together with the aid of a mortgage. After their divorce, Mrs Shaire agreed to buy out Mr Shaire's interest, and he agreed to transfer his share to his ex-wife and her new partner, Mr Fox. Mrs Shaire and Mr Fox took out a mortgage to help them to do this. Mrs Shaire owned 75 per cent of the equitable interest in the house and Mr Fox owned 25 per cent. Some years later, Mr Fox died.

Unfortunately, Mrs Shaire was destined once again to be unlucky in love. Unknown to her, the aptly named Mr Fox had taken out another two mortgages on the property, by forging Mrs Shaire's signature on the relevant documents. The second of the mortgagees applied to the court for the sale of the property to recover its money. (Note that, under the circumstances, it could only recover 25 per cent of this—that is, Mr Fox's share.)

Neuberger J considered the court's approach to TOLATA 1996, s. 15, and whether the old law relating to LPA 1925, s. 30 had any relevance to it. He concluded that s. 15 allowed the court a greater flexibility than the old law in the exercise of its discretion. Once the court had considered the factors in s. 15 (and any other relevant factors), it was for the court to decide how much weight it would give to each of the factors before reaching a decision. He added that s. 15(1)(d) did not automatically have any greater significance than s. 15(1)(c)—the welfare of children living in the house.

Having considered the factors—including the mortgagee's perfectly reasonable desire for its money and Mrs Shaire's equally reasonable desire to stay in the house—Neuberger J refused an order for sale and instead ordered that Mrs Shaire should effectively pay off the 25 per cent as a loan to the mortgagee. Only if she could not afford the payments should the property be sold.

This case would seem to indicate that the courts are, indeed, taking a more flexible approach to finding solutions in such situations. However, shortly after *Mortgage Corporation v. Shaire*, in *Bank of Ireland Home Mortgages v. Bell* [2001] FLR 805, Peter Gibson LJ described the interests of the secured creditor as a '*powerful consideration*' in weighing up the various factors in TOLATA 1996, s. 15.

This view was echoed in *First National Bank v. Achampong* (see 10.4.1.3), in which the Court of Appeal—after going through the same balancing exercise as that in *Bell*—ordered a sale. Blackburne J said (at [62] and [65]):

> The effect of refusing a sale is to condemn the bank to wait—possibly for many years—until Mrs Achampong should choose to sell before the bank can recover anything. In the meantime its debt continues to increase … I regard it as plain that an order for sale should be made. Prominent among the considerations which lead to that conclusion is that, unless an order for sale is made, the bank will be kept waiting indefinitely for any payment out of what is, for all practical purposes, its own share of the property.

In *Edwards v. Bank of Scotland* [2010] EWHC 652 (Ch), the Deputy Judge, having confirmed that the list of factors outlined in s. 15 was *'inclusive and not exclusive'* (at [25]) and that *'all relevant circumstances'* must be taken into account, then went on to begin his analysis by citing the passage in *Bell*, that the interest of the secured creditors was a *'powerful consideration'*. It would appear from these cases that, once again, the interest of the secured creditor will be given a somewhat heavier weighting when the court attempts to reconcile the competing needs and interests of the parties.

10.5 Bankruptcy

When somebody reaches a situation in which he or she cannot pay his or her debts—perhaps he or she has mortgage, credit card, and loan debts, for example, or business debts—that person can declare **bankruptcy**. In this instance, he or she will have declared voluntary bankruptcy—but the person can also be declared bankrupt by the court at the request of his or her creditors—that is, involuntary bankruptcy.

> **bankruptcy** a state under which a person has been judged by a court to be insolvent, involving the appointment of an administrator to distribute the bankrupt's assets among his or her creditors

The detailed procedure of bankruptcy is outside the scope of this book, but you need to know that, in these circumstances, a **trustee in bankruptcy** is appointed to try to recover as much money as possible for the creditors. Often, a bankrupt's biggest asset is his or her home. A trustee in bankruptcy is deemed to be an *'interested person'* and can apply to the court, under TOLATA 1996, s. 14, for an order to sell the bankrupt's property.

> **trustee in bankruptcy** a person in whom the property of a bankrupt is vested for the benefit of the bankrupt's creditors

When a trustee in bankruptcy applies for an order to sell under s. 14, the court has to take into account slightly different considerations. Instead of using the factors given in TOLATA 1996, s. 15, and discussed at 10.4.1, the court must refer to a different statute.

 STATUTE

Trusts of Land and Appointment of Trustees Act 1996, s. 15 [Matters relevant in determining applications]

...

> **(4)** This section does not apply to an application if section 335A of the Insolvency Act 1986 (which is inserted by Schedule 3 and relates to applications by a trustee of a bankrupt) applies to it.

The Insolvency Act 1986 (IA 1986), s. 335A sets out the various factors that the court must consider in deciding whether to make an order for sale.

 STATUTE

Insolvency Act 1986, s. 335A

...

(2) ... the court shall make such order as it thinks just and reasonable having regard to—

    (a) the interests of the bankrupt's creditors;

    (b) where the application is made in respect of land which includes a dwelling house which is or has been the home of the bankrupt or the bankrupt's spouse or former spouse—

        (i) the conduct of the spouse, civil partner, former spouse or former civil partner, so far as contributing to the bankruptcy,

        (ii) the needs and financial resources of the spouse, civil partner, former spouse or former civil partner; and

        (iii) the needs of any children; and

    (c) all the circumstances of the case, other than the needs of the bankrupt.

(3) Where such an application is made after the end of the period of one year...the court shall assume, unless the circumstances of the case are exceptional, that the interests of the bankrupt's creditors outweigh all other considerations.

You will notice that some of these are reasonably similar to TOLATA 1996, s. 15—for example, the needs of any children. There are, however, some fundamental differences between the two sections. The effect of s. 335A(3) is that if the trustee in bankruptcy applies for an order for sale after a year it will be granted by the court unless the bankrupt can prove that there are exceptional circumstances that mean that the order should not be granted. Most of the 'exceptional circumstances' cases involve ill health, such as serious life-threatening illness—*Re Bremner* [1999] 1 FLR 912—or chronic schizophrenia—*Nicholls v. Lan* [2006] EWHC 1255 (Ch). Less extreme instances of ill health, such as moderate depression, have been held to be not exceptional—*Ford v. Alexander* [2012] EWHC 266. *Foenander v. Allan* [2006] EWHC 2101 (Ch), which once promised a more flexible approach to exceptional circumstances, representing a move away from the medical cases, has not in fact given rise to more flexibility in subsequent cases. In any event, it should be remembered that even if the spouse can establish exceptional circumstances, it is not likely to defeat an order for sale completely, but will only postpone it for a relatively short period of time.

Everitt v. Budhram [2010] Ch 170 established that the word *'needs'* in s. 335A(2)(b) and (c) must be construed broadly, to include—potentially—emotional, psychological, or mental needs, and that it is not just restricted to financial needs. This means that in s. 335A(2)(b)(ii), the court may take into account the wider needs of the bankrupt's spouse or civil partner, but also means that in s. 335A(2)(c), any other 'needs' of the bankrupt—for example, in *Budhram*, the bankrupt's ill health—cannot be taken into consideration by the court.

In recent cases, the court has questioned the compatibility of this statutory test with the Human Rights Act 1998 (HRA 1998), and with the European Convention on Human Rights (ECHR), Protocol 1, Arts 1 and 8. In *Barca v. Mears* [2004] EWHC 2170 (Ch), Nicholas Strauss QC tentatively suggested that a shift in emphasis in the application of the test by the court might be required to ensure compatibility with the Act. However, it was held in *Nicholls v. Lan* [2006] EWHC 1255 (Ch) that the statutory test in IA 1986, s. 335A was not inconsistent with the rights of the homeowner: the duty of the court is to make an order that is fair and reasonable in the circumstances of the case. In *Ford v. Alexander* [2012] EWHC 266, Peter Smith J held once again that there was no incompatibility with ECHR, Art 8(2). The test in s. 335A was proportionate and ensured a balance between the rights of the bankrupt and the rights of the creditors.

10.6 The old law: prior to the Trusts of Land and Appointment of Trustees Act 1996

As we have seen, the TOLATA 1996 provides a much more sensible and realistic statutory framework for this kind of trust than that offered by the old trust for sale. The Act recognizes the significance of the purpose of the trust—usually to live in the property rather than to sell it—and the court, when deciding whether to make an order for sale, must take this into consideration. Beneficiaries are protected and trustees are given powers to enable them to provide workable solutions in the event of disputes.

10.6.1 The Settled Land Act 1925

The TOLATA 1996 (see Table 10.1) also provided that no **settlement** under the Settled Land Act 1925 (SLA 1925) could be made after 1 January 1997, although settlements made before that date continue to exist. These settlements relate to consecutive interests in land—for example, where land has been left to one person for their lifetime and then on their death, it is passed to another person. SLA 1925 settlements are outside the scope of this book, but if you are interested in them, consult some of the further reading listed at the end of the chapter.

> **CROSS REFERENCE**
> For the meaning of consecutive interests, see Chapter 8.

> **settlement** a disposition of land under which a trust is created designating beneficiaries and the terms on which they are to take the land

Table 10.1 An overview of the Trusts of Land and Appointment of Trustees Act 1996

Section(s)	Provision
1	Describes a 'trust of land'
2–5	Deal with the old law—settlements and trusts for sale becoming trusts of land
6–11	Deal with the powers and duties of trustees
12, 13	Deal with the rights of beneficiaries
14, 15	Provide a dispute resolution mechanism—governs applications to the court for an order and the factors that the court must consider. (Note: if a trustee in bankruptcy makes an application under s. 14, the court must look instead at IA 1986, s. 335A.)
16	Deals with the protection of purchasers
17	Deals with the proceeds of sale
18	Deals with personal representatives
19–21	Deal with the appointment and retirement of trustees

Summary

1. All trusts of land are now governed by the statutory framework set out in the TOLATA 1996.

2. The Act sets out the rights and responsibilities of trustees, and the rights of beneficiaries, under a trust of land.

3. Trustees have extensive powers over the land (s. 6(1)), but have a duty to act in the interests of the beneficiaries, to consult them, and to give effect to their wishes where possible (s. 11).

4. The beneficiaries (with an interest in possession) have a right to occupy the land (s. 12), although the trustees have the power, under certain circumstances, to restrict or exclude them from occupation (s. 13).

5. In cases of dispute over a trust of land, an interested party—which includes trustees, beneficiaries, mortgagees, and trustees in bankruptcy—can apply to the court for an order under s. 14.

6. In reaching its decision, the court will take into account the factors under s. 15, or, if the application is made by a trustee in bankruptcy, under IA 1986, s. 335A.

The bigger picture

- If you want to see how this area of land law fits into the rest of your studies, you can look at Chapter 14, especially 14.3.

- For some guidance on what sort of exam questions come up in this area, see Chapter 15, 15.9.

? Questions

Self-test questions

1. Some years ago, Rehana and Alan bought a house together as their family home. Unfortunately, their relationship has broken down. Rehana wants to sell the property, but Alan says that it makes more sense to separate it into two flats, one for each of them to occupy. Rehana comes home one day to find that the building work has started. Advise Alan and Rehana.

2. Amiel, Charlotte, and Jacob bought a flat together to share while they were at university. Now that they have well-paid jobs as lawyers, Amiel and Charlotte want to sell the flat. Jacob, who is an academic, wants to keep it. Advise Jacob as to how he can best resolve the dispute.

3. Charles died and left his house to his partner, Simon, for life, and then to his niece, Felicity, in remainder. Felicity wants to sell the property, but Simon insists that he wants to live there. Advise Felicity, particularly in relation to the factors that the court will consider if she applies to the court for an order for the sale of the property.

Exam questions

1. Julie and Mick bought a house together, but have fallen behind with their mortgage repayments. The bank wants to sell their home and has applied to the court under TOLATA 1996, s. 14. The couple have a three-year-old child who has a disability. Advise Julie and Mick.

2. Suppose that Mick has been made bankrupt. What will the court now consider? Would it make any difference if the house had been specially adapted to accommodate the child's disability? Advise Julie and Mick.

For suggested approaches to answering these questions visit the Online Resource Centre.

Further reading

Dixon, M., 'Trusts of land, bankruptcy and human rights' [2005] Conv 161
This article discusses *Barca v. Mears* and the implications of the HRA 1998 for IA 1986, s. 335A.

Ferris, G. and Bramley, E., 'The construction of sub-section 6(5) of the Trusts of Land and Appointment of Trustees Act 1996: When is a "right" not a "right"?' [2009] Conv 39
An interesting discussion of what TOLATA 1996, s. 6(5) might actually mean, in the context of TOLATA 1996, s. 15.

Gardner, S., 'Material relief between ex-cohabitants 1: liquidating beneficial interests other than by sale' [2014] Conv 95
This article looks at whether TOLATA 1996 may be of practical use to separating, unmarried cohabitants who do not wish to sell their property.

Greer, S., 'What's exceptional?' [2007] 157 NLJ 1374
This article offers a more detailed analysis of what constitutes 'exceptional circumstances' under IA 1986, s. 335A(3).

Hopkins, N., 'Regulating Trusts of the home: private law and social policy' [2009] 125(Apr) LQR 310
A very interesting discussion of how the regulation of trusts of the family home often conflicts with social policy objectives. This article has a useful perspective of both *Stack v. Dowden* and applications made by creditors.

Pascoe, S., 'Right to occupy under a trust of land: muddled legislative logic?' [2006] Conv 54
This is an interesting article on TOLATA 1996, ss. 12 and 13.

Pascoe, S., 'Section 15 of the Trusts of Land and Appointment of Trustees Act 1996: a change in the law?' [2000] Conv 315
This article compares TOLATA 1996, s. 15 with LPA 1925, s. 30.

 Online Resource Centre

www.oxfordtextbooks.co.uk/orc/clarke_directions5e/

For more advice relating to this chapter, including self-test questions and an interactive glossary, visit the Online Resource Centre.

PART 4

RIGHTS OVER LAND

11

Easements and profits

□ **LEARNING OBJECTIVES**

By the end of this chapter, you will be able to:

- recognize 'easements' and 'profits', and distinguish them from other rights over land;
- understand the nature of easements and profits;
- identify the different ways in which easements can be acquired;
- understand the remedies for interference with an easement or profit;
- identify how an easement can be extinguished.

Introduction

This chapter examines two of the most important rights that can be held by one person over land belonging to another person: easements and profits are rights that add to the value of the land they benefit, and without which modern living would scarcely be possible. Easements include, for example, rights of way, rights of drainage, and the right to run cables and pipes over (or under) land belonging to others. Profits à prendre include rights such as to take wood from land or to fish in a stream that belongs to someone else.

There has been a recent Law Commission report in this area of land law, *Making Land Work: Easements, Covenants and Profits à Prendre*, Law Com No. 327 (London: The Stationery Office 2011). This is discussed at 11.11.

11.1 Why are easements and profits important?

> **easement**
> a right enjoyed by the owner of land to a benefit from other land

If you look at any piece of land—a semi-detached house, for example—you will see numerous examples of **easements**. The drains that carry waste water away to the sewers might well be shared with neighbouring houses, meaning that an easement of drainage is needed; there may be a shared driveway, requiring a right of way for both houses; there may be rights of light to windows in the houses—the possibilities are endless!

Photo 11.1 Canal-side apartments
© Andy Green

To see this photo in more detail visit the Online Resource Centre.

 THINKING POINT

Look at Photo 11.1. What sorts of right might the owners of these canal-side apartments need?

The owners of the canal-side apartments in Photo 11.1 would need rights to run cables, pipes, etc. over other apartments, rights to access garages or storage, rights to use shared drains and gutters, rights of support, and maybe rights to moor boats.

> **profit à prendre**
> the right to take natural produce from another persons's land

Out in the country, there may be both easements and **profits à prendre**; the right to cut and remove grass from a field may be a valuable right for a farmer. Fishing rights, which are also profits à prendre, are often very valuable, and can be sold for large sums of money.

In this chapter, we will be concentrating on easements and will look at profits only at the end of the chapter, because, while the rules for profits and easements are quite similar, there is much more case law on easements.

There are two main steps in establishing whether an easement exists:

1. You must show that the right you are seeking is capable of being an easement: does it fit the definition of an easement?

2. You must show how the easement was acquired. It may have been expressly granted, but there are a number of other ways in which easements can arise, including the long-term exercise of a right that might be an easement.

We will begin by looking at the definition of an easement.

11.2 What is an easement?

The classic definition of an easement is given in *Halsbury's Laws of England*, 4th edn (London: LexisNexis), vol. 14, para. 1:

> An easement is a right annexed to land to utilize other land of different ownership in a particular manner (not involving the taking of any part of the natural produce of the land or of any part of its soil) or to prevent the owner of the other land from utilizing his land in a particular manner.

This definition sets out a number of the features of easements. Firstly, an easement is a right that is '*annexed to land*': it attaches to land, rather than being a personal right that anyone can exercise. It is not possible to be the owner of an easement without being the owner of land to which the easement is attached. For example, an easement of way involves two pieces of land: the land which can be reached by the right of way (known as the **dominant tenement**) and the land over which the path runs (known as the **servient tenement**). The requirement that there has to be a dominant tenement benefiting from an easement is sometimes expressed as the rule 'an easement cannot exist in gross'. (The words **in gross** in this expression mean 'not annexed to land'.)

Notice that the word 'tenement' means land, not a person. If the owners of the land are being discussed, they are referred to as the **dominant owner** and the **servient owner**, respectively. See Figure 11.1.

> **dominant tenement**
> a piece of land that benefits from an easement

> **servient tenement**
> a piece of land that bears the burden of an easement

> **in gross**
> not attached to land

> **dominant owner** the owner of the land that benefits from the easement
>
> **servient owner** the owner of the land that bears the burden of the easement

Secondly, the definition states that an easement is a right to utilize (use) land of different ownership in a particular manner. Most easements are positive rights, such as the right to walk or drive across the servient tenement. Negative easements can also exist, such as the right to support for a building, although there are fewer of them. This prevents the servient owner from pulling down his or her building if the dominant owner's building relies upon it for support. It is a negative right, because it stops the servient owner doing something that might otherwise have been done.

Note that the definition excludes rights that involve '*the taking of any part of the natural produce of the land or of any part of its soil*'—such rights are not easements, but profits à prendre (see 11.10).

> ➡ **EXAMPLE**
>
> Amy and Bradley are neighbours. Amy's house, Resthaven, adjoins the road and Bradley has a right of way over the path leading to the road from his land, Peacemore, over Amy's land.

So which is the dominant and which is the servient tenement?

- Peacemore is the dominant tenement: it has the benefit of the right of way.
- Resthaven is the servient tenement: it bears the burden of the right of way.

Bradley is the dominant owner, because he is able to use the right of way, and Amy is the servient owner, because she has to let Bradley walk across her land (see Figure 11.1).

Figure 11.1 Resthaven and Peacemore

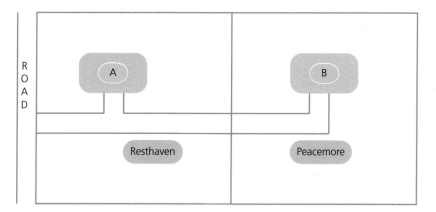

The leading case on the nature of easements is *Re Ellenborough Park* [1955] 3 All ER 667.

🔍 | CASE CLOSE-UP

Re Ellenborough Park [1955] 3 All ER 667

The Court of Appeal had to consider a right for the owners of certain houses to use a nearby park (or garden).

It was held that the right to use the park could exist as an easement. In reaching their decision, the judges of the Court of Appeal set out the defining characteristics of an easement, which they adopted from *Cheshire's The Modern Law of Real Property* (7th edn):

1. There must be a dominant and a servient tenement.
2. An easement must accommodate the dominant tenement.
3. Dominant and servient owners must be different persons.
4. A right over land cannot amount to an easement unless it is capable of forming the subject matter of a grant.

We will now look at each of these requirements in more detail.

11.2.1 **There must be a dominant and a servient tenement**

We have defined dominant and servient tenement at 11.2, and we also explained that an easement cannot exist in gross, because an easement is a right annexed or attached to land. Once an easement has been validly created, then it will run with the dominant tenement and be of benefit to successive owners of the land. So when the land is sold, for example, the benefit of the easement will pass to the new owner. The burden of the easement will also run with the servient tenement, so that it will be binding on future owners of that land. In other words, the easement continues through different ownerships of both the dominant and servient tenements.

11.2.2 **An easement must accommodate the dominant tenement**

To be an easement, the right claimed must benefit the land itself and not merely the owner of the dominant tenement personally. Firstly, the two tenements must be sufficiently close to each other. In *Bailey v. Stephens* (1862) 12 CB (NS) 91, it was famously stated that the owner of an estate in Northumberland could not validly grant a right of way over it to someone who owned an estate in Kent. While it might be very pleasant for the Kentish owner to walk over the estate in Northumberland, it could not possibly benefit his land in Kent!

In *Re Ellenborough Park* itself, the right to use the park was claimed not only by houses in the crescent facing the park, but also by the owners of some houses about 150 metres away. It was held that these houses were sufficiently close to benefit from the easement to use the garden. The dominant and servient tenements need not be next door to each other, but they must be close.

The right must also be of a kind that can benefit the dominant tenement. This will include a right that benefits a business or trade carried out on the dominant tenement.

 CASE CLOSE-UP

Moody v. Steggles (1879) 12 Ch D 261

The right to hang an inn sign on adjoining property was held to be an easement.

This case is supported by the approach taken by the Court of Appeal in a more recent case.

 CASE CLOSE-UP

Platt v. Crouch [2003] EWCA Civ 1110

The owners of a hotel on the Norfolk Broads claimed a right for guests to moor boats to adjacent land. This was accepted as an easement. Other rights, such as the right to place signs on nearby land and rights of way for hotel guests, were also accepted easements.

It seems, however, that the actual carrying out of the business itself cannot be an easement that accommodates the dominant tenement.

 CASE CLOSE-UP

Hill v. Tupper (1863) 159 ER 51

The claimant had been granted a lease of land next to a canal by the freeholder, together with an exclusive right to hire out pleasure boats on the canal. The defendant infringed that right by putting pleasure boats on the canal as well.

The claimant alleged that the right to hire out pleasure boats on the canal was an easement, so he could stop the defendant from infringing it.

The court refused his claim, because the right did not accommodate the dominant tenement and thus was not an easement. It was merely a personal right granted to the claimant under his lease.

11.2.3 The dominant and servient owners must be different persons

The two pieces of land benefiting from, and bearing the burden of, the easement must be owned by different persons: it is not possible to have an easement over your own land.

Where land is leased, however, the tenant may have easements over the landlord's property. This is, in fact, commonplace: for example, a tenant of a flat will often need a right of way over the landlord's property to reach his or her front door. Such an easement lasts as long as the leasehold estate.

11.2.4 The right must be capable of forming the subject matter of a grant

This means that the right claimed to be an easement must be capable of being granted by deed, which raises a number of points:

- the easement must have been granted by someone who had the power to do so and to a definite person;
- the easement must be sufficiently certain;
- the easement must be the sort of right normally recognized by the courts as such.

11.2.4.1 There must be a capable grantor and capable grantee

In order for there to be a grant of an easement, there must be someone who is capable of granting it. A statutory corporation with no power to grant easements would not be a capable grantor, for example.

There must also be a person (or persons) to whom an easement is capable of being granted: it is not possible to grant an easement to a fluctuating body of persons, such as 'all the inhabitants of a certain village' or 'all of the fishermen of [a particular] port'.

Such bodies of people may, however, have local customary rights that are similar to easements—see, for example, *Mercer v. Denne* [1905] 2 Ch 538, in which some fishermen established a customary right to dry fishing nets on the beach.

11.2.5 There must be certainty of description

The right must be definite enough to be described in a deed, or it could not have been granted. Examples that have fallen foul of this rule are claims to a right of indefinite privacy: *Browne v. Flower* [1911] 1 Ch 219, and the right to a view: *William Aldred's case* (1610) 9 Co Rep 57b. Other more recently rejected claims for easements include the right to drain water by percolation through the land: *Palmer v. Bowman* [2000] 1 All ER 22. However, in *Magrath v. Parkside Hotels Ltd* [2011] EWHC 143 (Ch) a right of fire escape over the servient land (not over a defined route but over the land in general) was held not to be too vague to be an easement. In *Coventry v. Lawrence* [2014]

UKSC 13, the Supreme Court considered whether it was possible to have an easement to create a noise over the servient tenement. The case concerned noise nuisance from a motocross stadium. The Supreme Court decided the case mainly on the law of nuisance, but also held that there could in principle be an easement to make a noise. However, the facts of the case itself did not establish such an easement.

11.2.6 The right must be of a type generally recognized by the law as an easement

There are a number of factors used in deciding whether a right is of the type that can be recognized as an easement:

- the right must be 'of the same kind' as existing easements;
- it should not oblige the servient owner to spend money;
- it should not amount to possession of the servient tenement—the servient owner must still be able to use the land.

11.2.6.1 Novel rights

To be an easement, a right must fall within the general category of rights that are recognized by the law as capable of existing as easements. This means that they must be analogous or similar to rights that have already been established as easements. Easements are proprietary rights running with the land, so the courts are wary of adding novel (new) rights to the list of those that will bind successive owners.

The categories of easements are not closed, however, and it is still possible for a new right to be recognized as an easement.

 CASE CLOSE-UP

Dyce v. Lady Hay (1852) 1 Macq 305

As long ago as 1852, the courts recognized that the law had to keep up with changing times.

It was held that: *'[t]he category of servitudes and easements must alter and expand with the changes that take place in the circumstances of mankind'*.

It is still possible to create new easements as times and circumstances change, but the courts are rather cautious in recognizing new easements.

One category that will not expand is that of negative easements. The two well-established negative easements are the right to light through a window—recognized in the Prescription Act 1832 (PA 1832)—and the right to support of a building—*Dalton v. Angus* (1881) App Cas 740. It seems unlikely that other negative rights will be added to this list.

 CASE CLOSE-UP

Phipps v. Pears [1965] 1 QB 76

The owner of a house demolished it, leaving the wall of the neighbouring house unprotected. The wall was damaged by the winter weather and the owner of the house claimed that he had been entitled to an easement of protection from the weather.

> Unfortunately for him, the Court of Appeal held that no such easement exists, so the claimant lost his case.
>
> This indicates that the courts will be unlikely to extend the category of negative easements.

This reasoning was also followed by Lord Hoffmann in a later case.

 CASE CLOSE-UP

Hunter v. Canary Wharf Ltd [1997] 2 All ER 426

The claimants brought an action in nuisance against the owners of Canary Wharf, on the grounds that the tall, metal-clad building had blocked television signals to their nearby houses.

Their action failed. In his speech, Lord Hoffmann considered whether an easement to receive uninterrupted television signals could exist.

He held that there could be no such easement, because the number of persons benefiting from it would be too vague and uncertain, and it would interfere too much with the use of the servient land.

The courts are unlikely to recognize any new negative easements, therefore, because of the restrictive effect they would have on neighbouring land. The balancing of competing rights to use land is nowadays best resolved under planning legislation, rather than by imposing new property law rights.

The reasoning applied in these two cases—that the use of the servient tenement should not be unduly restricted by an easement—can also be seen in other rules that help to determine whether a particular right can exist as an easement.

11.2.6.2 Expenditure of money

It is a general rule that the servient owner must not be obliged to spend money as a result of an easement. This is another reason why the claim to an easement of protection from the weather failed in *Phipps v. Pears*: the alleged servient owner would have had to pay to weatherproof the wall of the other house. In *Magrath v. Parkside Hotels Ltd*, one objection raised to the easement of fire escape was that it might oblige the servient owner to spend money maintaining the means of escape. It was held that the precise nature of the grant should be interpreted so as to avoid major expense by the servient owner.

There is only one exception to this general rule: the easement of fencing.

 CASE CLOSE-UP

Crow v. Wood [1971] 1 QB 77

This case concerned agricultural fencing to keep moorland sheep off a farm. An easement of fencing was recognized. This anomalous easement is of very ancient origin and is confined to agricultural land.

The servient owner is also under no duty to do any repairs or maintenance necessary to enable the dominant owner to enjoy the easement. The dominant owner, however, has a right of access to make repairs—*Jones v. Pritchard* [1908] 1 Ch 637.

 EXAMPLE

1. Anne has a right of way over her neighbour, Ben's, land. The right of way has become very overgrown. Ben is not obliged to cut down the plants; Anne must do this herself if she wishes to use the right of way.
2. Catherine has a right of drainage over Dan's land. The drains become blocked. Dan is not obliged to clear the drains, but Catherine may enter Dan's land to do so.

You may be surprised to learn that, where there is an easement of support, there is no obligation to keep the servient tenement in repair—the limit of liability is only that the servient owner must not pull down his or her own house!

The essentially negative aspect of easements also means that a servient owner cannot be obliged to grant a further easement to a third party, even if this means that their own easement might be rendered worthless.

 CASE CLOSE-UP

William Old International Ltd v. Arya [2009] EWHC 599 (Ch)

The claimant had an easement to run electricity cables over the defendant's land. However, the electricity supplier would not connect the supply unless the defendant servient owner also granted them a direct easement. It was held that the servient owner had no obligation to do so, as an easement cannot oblige the servient owner to enter into a contract or proprietary relationship with a third party.

11.2.6.3 Excessive use of the servient tenement

An easement is an incorporeal hereditament, which means that it does not entitle the dominant owner to possession of the servient land, as a freehold or leasehold estate does. It entitles the dominant owner to use the servient land for specific purposes, in common with the servient owner. It is in the nature of an easement that it cannot stop the servient owner from using his or her own land, which means that, if the right claimed has the effect of using up the whole of the servient land, it will be too extensive to be an easement.

> **CROSS REFERENCE**
>
> For more on incorporeal hereditaments, see Chapter 1.

 CASE CLOSE-UP

Copeland v. Greenhalf [1952] Ch 488

A wheelwright tried to claim an easement to store wheels, vehicles, and other articles on a strip of land close to his workshop.

It was held by Upjohn J that the right claimed really amounted to joint occupation of the strip of land with the owner. Therefore, the claim failed, because the right alleged by the claimant was too wide and extensive to be an easement.

This case indicates that problems are likely to arise in the areas of storage and of parking (which is essentially a special form of storage). However, despite the decision in *Copeland v. Greenhalf*, it is clear from other cases that such easements can exist.

 CASE CLOSE-UP

London and Blenheim Estates v. Ladbrooke Retail Parks Ltd [1992] 1 WLR 1278

The question of whether there can be a valid easement of parking was held to be one of degree. If the parking would amount to occupation of the land, it could not be a valid easement, but if there was room for both parking and other uses, an easement of parking could exist.

There have been a number of recent developments in the case law with respect to easements of parking, which are considered at 11.3.2.

Easements of storage have also been accepted in cases.

 CASE CLOSE-UP

Wright v. Macadam [1949] 2 KB 744

A tenant was allowed to use a shed on her landlord's property to store coal. It was found that this was a valid easement of storage.

There was no discussion in this case as to whether the easement was too excessive and the case was not cited in *Copeland v. Greenhalf*. It seems likely that it will be a matter of fact and degree, as it is with parking.

The point about excessive use was also considered in a different context in a more recent case concerning a shared garden.

 CASE CLOSE-UP

Mulvaney v. Gough [2002] EWCA Civ 1078

The claimant owned one of a group of cottages. Behind the cottages was an area of land owned by the defendants. The claimant, together with the other owners of the cottages, had been cultivating the area of land as a garden. The defendant created a path for vehicles through the garden, destroying some of it. This raised the question of whether the claimant had an easement to use the land as a garden.

The Court of Appeal held that there was an easement to use the area of land as a communal garden, but that this did not stop the servient owners from using the land as well. They were entitled to remove flowerbeds, etc. if it blocked access for their vehicles.

As you can see from these cases, there is no hard-and-fast rule as to when a use of land will be considered to be too extensive to be an easement. It is a matter of fact and degree in each case.

11.2.7 A comparison of easements with other rights

In working out what an easement *is*, it may be useful to have a look at what it *is not*. Thinking about the similarities and differences between easements and other rights leads to a better understanding of easements, and an appreciation of what other rights might be considered where an easement is inappropriate (see Table 11.1).

Table 11.1 A comparison of easements with other rights

Right	Similarities to an easement	Differences from an easement
Profit à prendre (the right to take part of the soil, minerals, or natural produce of the servient tenement-it is granted together with a licence to enter the land)	Both are proprietary rights that will bind future owners of the land	An easement does not allow anything to be taken from the land. An easement cannot exist in gross, but a profit can.
Licence (a permission to enter land or to use it for some purpose)	The same sorts of right can be granted by licence as by easement—for example, the right to walk or drive across land	A licence can grant exclusive occupation of land, unlike an easement. A licence can be created without formality. A licence can exist in gross. Most importantly, a licence is not a proprietary right in land and thus will not bind future landowners.
Restrictive covenant (a promise made by one landowner to another in a deed to refrain from doing something on land)	Both sorts of right can run with the land and concern two pieces of land. Both are used to regulate matters between neighbouring land.	Restrictive covenants run in equity only, whereas easements can exist in both common law and equity. Restrictive covenants must be granted expressly, whereas easements can be implied into conveyances and acquired by long use.
Public rights (rights exercisable by everyone, such as the right of passage along the highway, rights of navigation over tidal waters, rights of fishing in the sea, etc.)	The rights look similar to some that can be granted by easement—for example, a right of way looks similar to the right of passage along the highway	Easements are granted by one landowner to another, while public rights are not connected with land ownership, and are exercisable by everyone
Natural rights (rights that the common law has held as naturally part of the land. They are the right to support for land and the right to water in a defined channel, such as a river. The right to water also includes the right to drainage of water on to lower land.)	These two rights look very like easements of support and easements to take water	The natural right to support for land extends to land in its undeveloped state only. It does not include support for the buildings on the land. The right to support for a building may be granted as an easement. The natural right of drainage is by percolation through the soil, rather than through a defined ditch or drain.

(Continued)

Table 11.1 Continued

Right	Similarities to an easement	Differences from an easement
Customary rights (rights granted to inhabitants of a particular town or parish, or to a fluctuating group of people)	These rights are often rights to do something on land—for example, to dry fishing nets. They bind all owners of the affected land.	The rights are not dependent on land ownership. An easement cannot be granted to a fluctuating body of persons—*Mercer v. Denne*.

11.3 Common types of easement

It is useful to look at the most common types of easement, in order to see how easements work in practice and what problems can arise. Remember, however, that this list of easements is far from exhaustive and, as we have seen at 11.2.6.1, it is still possible for new easements to arise.

11.3.1 Rights of way

A right of way may be either general or limited: if it is general, it may be used in any way, whether with vehicles or on foot, and for any purpose connected with the land. A very important restriction on such easements, however, is that the right of way can be used to access only the dominant tenement, not other land belonging to the dominant owner. This is sometimes known as the rule in *Harris v. Flower* (1904) 74 LJ Ch 127 and it has been applied in recent cases.

Q | CASE CLOSE-UP

Das v. Linden Mews [2002] EWCA Civ 590, [2002] 2 EGLR 76

The claimants owned houses facing each other at the end of a mews (a private no-through road). At the very end of the mews were a courtyard and garden, owned by one of the claimants and used by both of them for parking.

The claimants managed to prove that they had rights of way over the mews to their houses. However, the rule in *Harris v. Flower* prevented them from using this right of way to drive to the courtyard and park there, because it was a separate tenement and the existing rights of way would not entitle them to drive to it.

The claimants tried to argue that their use of the right of way to get to the courtyard was merely 'ancillary' to their use to get to the dominant tenements (their houses), but this claim was rejected. The use of the easement in this way opened up a new and valuable use of the courtyard, namely parking. This was not ancillary to the use of the easement to reach the dominant tenement.

Note that the rule applies even if the extra land can be accessed through the dominant tenement. The right of way cannot be used to open up the other land. This is a rule that landowners are likely to find quite baffling, because it seems ridiculous that you cannot use a right of way to go onto one piece of land, then through that land to other land. It makes more sense if you remember that an easement is not like a public right of way: it is attached to one particular dominant tenement, so it cannot be used to benefit a different piece of land.

A limited right of way is one that has restrictions as to its use: perhaps in relation to the times at which it can be used—during daylight hours, for example—or the purposes for which it can be used. Some rights of way are restricted to use on foot; others are restricted to vehicular use or for driving cattle, etc.

The decision of the Court of Appeal in *Newman v. Greatorex* [2008] EWCA Civ 1318 illustrates a limited right of way.

 CASE CLOSE-UP

Newman v. Greatorex [2008] EWCA Civ 1318

The claimants were the owners of a residential property that included a covered passage which ran to the defendant's bar and beer garden. The claimants wished to stop the customers of the bar using the covered passageway. The defendants had a right of way over the passageway granted many years earlier in the following terms:

> ... to pass and repass from and to the said other premises belonging to [H] as now used by her tenant [C] ...

The Court of Appeal upheld the decision of the judge at first instance that the words 'as now used by her tenant [C]' were words of limitation. C had run a fishmonger's shop, not a bar. This meant that since C's customers would not have used the passageway, the bar's customers could not do so either.

Similarly, in *Dutta v. Hayes* [2012] EWHC 1727 (Ch), the owner of a stud farm could not use the right of way granted over neighbouring land for the purposes of his business, as it was restricted to agricultural use.

If a right of way is expressly granted, the court will construe (interpret) the terms of the right of way. If it is granted in general terms, some increase in use over the years is permitted, but there must not be an unreasonable increase in use.

 CASE CLOSE-UP

Jelbert v. Davis [1968] 1 All ER 1182

The dominant owner had a right of way *'at all times and for all purposes'* over a driveway leading to the highway, *'in common with all other persons having the like right'*.

The dominant land at the time of the grant was agricultural land. Later, the dominant owner opened a caravan park on the land, with space for up to 200 caravans. Lord Denning MR held that the dominant owner could not use the right of way for so many caravans. It was held to be a matter of fact and degree how many would, in practice, be excessive.

The circumstances at the time of the grant and the nature of the track over which the right of way runs will be very important.

CASE CLOSE-UP

White v. Richards (1993) 68 P & CR 105

A question arose as to the use of an expressly granted right of way over a track. The track was about 250 m long and about 2.7 m wide for most of that length. The right had been granted to the dominant owner to use the track 'with or without motor vehicles'.

The dominant owner began to use the track for the passage of up to sixteen large trucks a day, carrying rubble and building material. It was held that this sort of use of a narrow track was excessive and not within the terms of the grant.

Similarly, in the case of *St Edmundsbury and Ipswich Diocesan Board of Finance v. Clark* [1975] 1 WLR 468, the circumstances at the time of the grant of the easement showed it to be a right of way on foot only, rather than with vehicles. In the recent case of *Higson v. Guenault* [2014] EWCA Civ 703, the CA also held that the extent of a right of way reserved in a deed depends on the language of the deed, construed in the context of the circumstances surrounding its execution.

If the right of way is not expressly granted, but implied (see 11.4.3), the circumstances of the case will show what use is allowed. Therefore, in *Corporation of London v. Riggs* (1880) 13 Ch D 798, a right of way implied by necessity was limited to agricultural use only, because that was the use of the dominant land at the time that the easement was implied.

If the right of way is gained by prescription—that is, by long use (see 11.4.4)—its use during the prescription period will determine how it can be used in the future. The path or track cannot be improved to make it suitable for other uses.

 CASE CLOSE-UP

Mills v. Silver [1991] Ch 271

The defendants had a right of way gained by long use over a farm track. They employed builders to lay a stone road over the track so that it could be used in all weathers.

The Court of Appeal held that they had the right to repair the track, but not to improve it.

Nonetheless, similar, but more modern, use will be permitted: for example, a right of way originally used by horses and carts can be used in modern times by motor vehicles—*Lock v. Abercester Ltd* [1939] Ch 861.

A servient owner cannot insist on the deviation of a right of way from its original course, even if an alternative way is provided—*Heslop v. Bishton* [2009] EWHC 607 (Ch).

11.3.2 Rights of parking

As we saw earlier (11.2.6.3) easements of parking have been difficult to establish because there is a danger that the easement will be seen as too excessive a use of the servient tenement.

There have been a number of cases on this issue: In *Batchelor v. Marlow* (2001) 32 P & CR 36, the right to park six cars on a strip of land all day was determined to be too extensive to be an easement; the court held that the right to park the cars would render the servient owner's use of the land 'illusory'.

In *Hair v. Gillman* (2000) 80 P & CR 108, the right to park one car on land that was large enough for four cars was accepted as an easement.

The House of Lords' decision in *Moncrieff v. Jamieson* [2007] UKHL 42 contains some interesting points about the right to park, and whether or not it can be an easement. The case is persuasive only, as it was an appeal from a Scottish case. However, the law of servitudes in Scotland has similarities with the English law of easements, and English authorities were cited in the case.

🔍 CASE CLOSE-UP

Moncrieff v. Jamieson [2007] UKHL 42

The case concerned two pieces of land originally in common ownership. They were divided into two parts, one on the top of a cliff and the other below. The owner of the land at the bottom of the cliff was given a right of way to drive to his land over the other part. Clearly, he could not get the car down the steps on the cliff to park on his own land, and the right of way was useless without a right to park his car at the top of the cliffs. The House of Lords held that he did have the right to park.

This case clearly shows that a right to park may be implied into a right of way if that right would otherwise be of little value. Also, the right to park did not interfere with the servient owner's use of the land.

The decision in *Batchelor v. Marlow*, and the test it set out, was criticized. As Lord Scott of Foscote said at para. [59]:

> It is impossible to assert that there would be no use that could be made by an owner of land over which he had granted parking rights. He could, for example, build above or under the parking area. He could place advertising hoardings on the walls. Other possible uses can be conjured up. And by what yardstick is it to be decided whether the residual uses of the servient land available to its owner are 'reasonable' or sufficient to save his ownership from being 'illusory'? It is not the uncertainty of the test that, in my opinion, is the main problem. It is the test itself. I do not see why a landowner should not grant rights of a servitudal character over his land to any extent that he wishes.

The subsequent case of *Waterman v. Boyle* [2009] EWCA Civ 115 considered *Moncreiff v. Jameson*. The Court of Appeal held that a right to park will not readily be implied into an easement of way. It was the wholly exceptional circumstances in the *Moncrieff* case that led to that decision.

In the case of *Virdi v. Chana* [2008] EWHC 2901 (Ch), Judge Purle QC held that, despite the criticisms of *Batchelor v. Marlow* in *Moncrieff v. Jameson*, the case was not overruled, and remains a binding precedent. However, the right to park one car on a strip of land partly in the claimant's ownership was upheld, as the strip of land had no other viable use, so the defendant was not preventing the claimant from using it.

A similar right, that of mooring boats, was accepted as an easement in *Platt v. Crouch* [2003] EWCA Civ 1110.

11.3.3 **Rights of storage**

Rights of storage have been discussed at 11.2.6.3. It is clear that easements of storage can exist—*Wright v. Macadam* [1949] 2 KB 744—but remember that they must not be too extensive to prevent the servient owner from using his or her land.

11.3.4 **Rights of light**

A right of light is one of the few negative easements permitted by law. There is no natural right to light over land and no easement can be claimed in respect of light over a garden, for example, but it is possible to claim an easement of light through a *'defined aperture'*—that is, a window or glazed door. No particular quantity of light is guaranteed; the question is whether enough light is left for ordinary purposes: *Colls v. Home and Colonial Stores Ltd* [1904] AC 179.

> **ancient lights**
> rights to light that have been gained by long use

Most rights to light are gained by long use under PA 1832, s. 3. They are sometimes referred to as **ancient lights**. Rights to light can be very valuable and can substantially inhibit development on neighbouring land, as *HKRUK II (CHC) Ltd v. Heaney* [2010] EWHC 2245 (Ch) shows. The claimant had built two extra floors on its building which substantially diminished the light to the defendant's nearby building. The court ordered the offending extension to be demolished.

The Law Commission published a report on rights to light in December 2014. It did not recommend that prescription should be abolished as a means of acquiring a right to light, but did recommend changes in procedure.

11.3.5 **Right to air**

There can be no easement to receive air over the dominant land in general, because that would be too vague and would amount to a negative easement. It is, however, possible to have an easement of ventilation through defined vents or apertures—such as a ventilation shaft. Such a right was established in *Wong v. Beaumont Properties* [1965] 1 QB 173, in relation to a right to run a ventilation duct to a kitchen.

11.3.6 **Rights of support**

As well as the natural right to support for land in its unimproved state, easements of support for a building can be created. This occurs when one building relies on another for its structural stability—for example, houses in terraces share party walls, as do semi-detached houses. Flats obviously rely on those beneath them for support. Because an easement cannot impose a burden of expenditure on the servient land, the right of support prevents the owner of the adjoining house from knocking down his or her property, but there is no obligation to keep it in repair.

 CASE CLOSE-UP

Bradburn v. Lindsay [1983] 2 All ER 408

The claimant was the owner of a semi-detached house. The adjoining house fell into such disrepair that it had to be demolished, leaving the party wall unsupported.

Blackett-Ord VC held that the claimant had an easement of support. He accepted the earlier authorities that such an easement does not require the servient owner to maintain his or her property, but the claimant had also claimed in negligence and nuisance. The judge found the case made out on this point and awarded damages for the cost of repairs.

The owner of the servient land may, therefore, be liable in nuisance or negligence if the supporting house falls into disrepair and thus damages adjoining property. The fact that the dominant owner has the right to go onto the servient land and effect repairs does not negate that liability.

11.3.7 Rights of water

There are a number of easements connected with the use of water. They include the right to take water from the servient land—such as from a pond or well—and to let water out onto the servient land, through drains or ditches. Rights of drainage are particularly important, because it is comparatively rare for houses in towns to have entirely separate drainage systems; often drains run under other land before reaching public sewers.

Easements relating to water have to be distinguished from natural rights. For example, in *Palmer v. Bowman*, it was held that there was no easement of drainage by natural percolation of water through land (the natural flow of water through the soil, rather than through a ditch). An easement of drainage must be through a defined channel. Drainage through the soil is a natural right attaching to land, rather than an easement.

11.3.8 Right to fencing

This easement, unusual in that it requires the servient owner to spend money, has been discussed at 11.2.6.2.

11.3.9 Use of facilities

There have been many examples of different kinds of easement that permit the dominant owner to use facilities on the servient owner's land. They include *Miller v. Emcer Products* [1956] Ch 304, in which a right to use lavatories in a different part of the building was held to be an easement, and *Goldberg v. Edwards* [1950] Ch 247, in which the right to use a letterbox was accepted as an easement.

11.4 Acquisition of easements

11.4.1 Grant and reservation of easements

An easement may be acquired either by grant or reservation. The difference is best explained by an example.

From the example, you can see that an easement is granted over a landowner's own (retained) land, whereas an easement is reserved over land that the landowner is transferring to someone else. An easement is therefore granted by the servient owner, but reserved by the dominant owner.

It is important to note that some methods of acquiring easements apply only to a grant, not to a reservation.

 EXAMPLE

Figure 11.2 shows two adjoining houses. Originally they were both owned by the same person, Ken. The shaded area is a driveway serving both houses. Ken sold No. 2 to Lia and continued to live in No. 1.

In the transfer of No. 2 to Lia, Ken granted her a right of way over the half of the driveway on his land (the left-hand half of Figure 11.2). This is a *grant* of an easement by Ken.

> Ken also wanted to continue to use the whole driveway himself, so he reserved a right of way over the half of it on Lia's land (the right-hand half of Figure 11.2). This is a *reservation* of an easement by Ken.

Figure 11.2 Grant and reservation

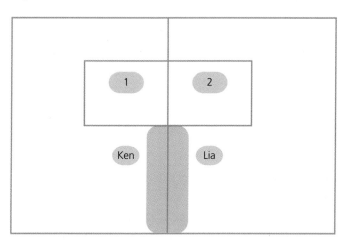

11.4.2 Express grant or reservation

11.4.2.1 Express grant

An easement is one of the rights listed in Law of Property Act 1925 (LPA 1925), s. 1(2)(a), as being capable of being a legal interest in land, provided that it is granted '*for an interest equivalent to an estate in fee simple absolute in possession or a term of years absolute*'. This means that the easement must be granted effectively in perpetuity (like a legal freehold) or for a determinate period (like a legal leasehold). An express grant of a legal easement must be made by deed (LPA 1925, s. 52(1)) and completed by registration.

> **CROSS REFERENCE**
>
> This rule is similar to that relating to legal and equitable leases—see Chapter 5.

If a deed is not used as required, the intended legal easement may operate as a contract to create a legal easement, provided that the agreement to create it is in writing complying with Law of Property (Miscellaneous Provisions) Act 1989 (LP(MP)A 1989), s. 2. A contract to create an easement would be specifically enforced by the courts, so an agreement in writing to create a legal easement will be treated as an equitable easement. If there is no writing, the right is most likely to take effect as a licence only.

 EXAMPLE

Gary is approached by three of his neighbours, who would all like to drive over the end of his garden to reach their land.

He executes a deed granting the first neighbour, Harriet, a right to drive over his land.

He writes a letter to the second neighbour, Ismat, promising her that he will grant her a right of way over his land.

He meets the third neighbour, Jack, in the local pub and tells him that he may drive over the land whenever he wishes.

Harriet will have a legal easement.

Ismat may have a valid contract to grant an easement (as long as the letter complies with LP(MP)A 1989, s. 2) and this will be treated as an equitable easement.

Jack has only a licence, which Gary may revoke at any time.

The express grant of a legal easement by a registered proprietor must be completed by registration to be a legal grant, because it is a registrable disposition within Land Registration Act 2002 (LRA 2002), s. 27(2)(d). This means that it does not operate at law until it is registered—LRA 2002, s. 27(1).

 EXAMPLE

If Gary's land is registered land, Harriet's easement will not take effect at law—that is, it will not be a legal easement—until it is registered. If Harriet does not apply for registration, it will continue to be an equitable easement, despite being granted by deed.

If there is some reason why Harriet cannot register the easement—perhaps because there is a restriction on the register preventing this—she must make sure that it is protected by notice as an equitable easement.

A legal easement can be granted only out of a legal estate. If the servient tenement is an equitable interest, then the easement can be equitable only.

An equitable easement (such as Ismat's right of way in the example above) must be noted on the charges register of the register of title, otherwise it will lose priority to a subsequent purchaser of the land—LRA 2002, s. 32. For an example of this see *Chaudhary v. Yavuz* [2011] EWCA Civ 1314.

Easements are often granted when land is divided, but they may be granted at any time.

11.4.2.2 Express reservation

An express reservation of an easement is often contained in the transfer of the land to the new (servient) owner. This situation is provided for in LPA 1925, s. 65.

 STATUTE

Law of Property Act 1925, s. 65(1)

A reservation of a legal estate shall operate at law without any execution of the conveyance by the grantee of the legal estate out of which the reservation is made, or any regrant by him, so as to create the legal estate reserved, and so as to vest the same in possession in the person (whether being the grantor or not) for whose benefit the reservation is made.

This section makes it clear that, if the transferor of an estate in land (Ken, in the example in Figure 11.2) reserves an easement over that land, the parties do not need to execute a transfer by deed in order for the easement to be validly granted. Without this provision, Lia (the transferee) would have to execute a deed to grant the easement, because only the owner of the servient (burdened) land can grant an easement over it.

For some time, it was not clear whether this was merely a 'word-saving' provision, or whether it had changed the way in which easements are reserved.

🔍 CASE CLOSE-UP

St Edmundsbury and Ipswich Diocesan Board of Finance v. Clark [1975] 1 WLR 468

This case concerned the question of whether a right of way was on foot only or included use by vehicles as well. One rule that was considered was whether any uncertainty in the grant should be construed in favour of the claimant church, which had sold the land and reserved the right of way, or the defendant purchaser, who was now the servient owner.

The usual rule is that uncertainty should be construed against the person making the grant (the *contra proferentum* rule)—but was that the dominant owner or the servient owner?

Usually, it is the servient owner who grants an easement, but where an easement has been reserved since 1925, LPA 1925, s. 65 provides that it operates without any regrant by the servient owner.

The Court of Appeal held that the presumption was not necessary to its decision, but *obiter dicta*, held that the reservation of an easement does operate by way of grant by the servient owner. LPA 1925, s. 65 is essentially a word-saving provision: it did not change the law on who actually makes the grant.

Easements may also be granted or reserved by statute. Easements created by statute are usually in favour of utility companies, such as suppliers of gas and electricity, and they will be legal easements.

11.4.3 Implied grant or reservation

An implied grant of an easement is one that is 'read into' a document transferring title to land from the 'servient' owner to the 'dominant' owner, just like an implied term in a contract. Of course, at the time of the transfer, there is no easement, because the 'servient' owner owns all of the land concerned and a landowner cannot have an easement against him- or herself. When land is divided, or leased, however, it is possible for an easement to be implied into the transfer—most commonly in favour of the transferee (an implied grant), but sometimes in favour of the transferor (an implied reservation).

EXAMPLE

Karen is planning to sell part of her land to Liam. It is possible that an easement over Karen's retained land may be implied into the transfer (implied grant of an easement) or that an easement over what is now Liam's land may be implied into the transfer (implied reservation).

If Karen decides to grant a lease of part of her land to Liam, it is also possible for easements to be implied into the lease, by way of either grant or reservation.

In order to discuss implied easements more easily, the terms quasi-easement, quasi-dominant, and quasi-servient are often used. 'Quasi-easement' indicates rights that are in the nature of easements, but which are not easements before the transfer, because the 'quasi-dominant' and 'quasi-servient' tenements are, at that time, in common ownership. In other words, in this context, *quasi* indicates 'not yet' or 'soon to be'.

11.4.3.1 Implied reservation of easements

There are two ways in which the reservation of an easement may be implied into a transfer:

- through necessity;
- by common intention.

It is important to remember that a transferor claiming an implied reservation of an easement has a higher burden of proof than a transferee claiming an implied grant of an easement. This is because a court will be more sympathetic to a person who cannot use the land transferred without an easement, under the principle of 'non-derogation from grant'. This principle means a person cannot grant something, but then hold back rights that would make the grant useful.

The opposite principle applies when a person grants something, such as a transfer of land, but then tries to claw back some benefit, such as an easement. If the transferor wished to reserve an easement over that land, it should have been done expressly—*Re Webb's Lease* (1951) Ch D 808—so the courts are rather more reluctant to imply a reserved easement.

Reservations of necessity

The reservation of an easement of necessity will be implied only if the land would be completely unusable without the easement. The most usual case of this would be where land is sold leaving no access to the highway, referred to in older cases as a 'landlocked close'. If the transferor of land has foolishly been left with no way of reaching the highway, a right of way will be implied by reservation of necessity.

'Necessity' is construed very strictly. Even if the remaining access to the land is very impractical, there will be no reservation of a way of necessity—see, for example, *Titchmarsh v. Royston Water Co.* (1900) 81 LT 673, in which the roadway was 20 ft below the level of the land, but no other way of necessity was implied by the court. In *Walby v. Walby* [2012] EWHC 3089 (Ch), it was held that there was no reservation of necessity of a right of drainage into the transfer of part of a farm. Since the absence of a right of drainage did not prevent the land being used, it would not be right to imply an easement of necessity. In *Yueng v. Potel* [2014] EWCA Civ 481, where there was a mismatch between the easements clause of a lease and the reservations clause, the more restrictive wording was held to be applicable, and the Court of Appeal held that there was no necessity to enter other parts of the premises to lay new gas pipes, even though it was sensible and convenient.

Reservation by common intention

These are easements reserved on the basis that it was the common intention of the parties that they should be created, based on their intended use of the land.

 CASE CLOSE-UP

Jones v. Pritchard [1908–10] All ER Rep 80

The defendant had sold one of a pair of semi-detached houses to the claimant. A dispute arose as to the use of the shared chimneys. Sensibly, it was held that there was a common intention that both parties should be able to use the chimneys.

In this case, both parties must have intended the chimneys to continue in use, so both the reservation of, and grant of, easements were implied to this effect. These could also be described as 'mutual easements'.

A more recent case on the reservation of a right of way by common intention concerned the sale of council houses to their tenants.

 CASE CLOSE-UP

Peckham v. Ellison [2000] 79 P & CR 276

The claimant was the owner of a former council house, one of a terrace of four houses sold off to the former tenants under the 'right to buy' provisions. Unfortunately, in selling the end house, the council forgot to reserve a right of way over the back garden and along the side of the house that had been used by the next-door neighbours to remove rubbish from the rear garden. The path was visible on the land and had been used by the owners of all four houses in the terrace.

The Court of Appeal held that there was a common intention to reserve a right of way. The court accepted that it was harder to show a reservation of an easement (on the authority of *Re Webb's Lease* (1951) Ch D 808), but held that the burden had been discharged in this case.

This case has been criticized as allowing the reservation too easily, but perhaps the court was influenced by the obvious layout of the properties and by the fact that it was not the council that suffered by the error, but the new owners of the houses.

In *Walby v. Walby* (discussed earlier) Morgan J refused to imply an easement of drainage by common intention, saying: '*Before the court can imply the reservation of an easement, it must be shown that the facts are not reasonably consistent with any explanation other than that such a reservation was intended*' (at para. [44]).

11.4.3.2 Implied grant of easements

There are four ways in which grants of easements can be implied into transfers of land:

- of necessity;
- by common intention;
- under the rule in *Wheeldon v. Burrows* (1879) 12 Ch D 31;
- under LPA 1925, s. 62.

Granted of necessity

Even in cases of implied grant, necessity has traditionally been construed very narrowly: the land must be completely unusable without the easement. In *Pearson v. Spencer* (1861) 1 B &S 571, it was held that, when implying an easement of necessity in these circumstances, any convenient way can be chosen, provided that it is reasonable. Once the way is decided upon, it cannot be changed—*Deacon v. South Eastern Railway Co.* (1889) 61 LT 377. The necessity must exist at the time of the transfer, rather than arise at some later date—*Corporation of London v. Riggs* (1880) 13 Ch D 798.

 CASE CLOSE-UP

Donovan v. Rana [2014] EWCA 99

A plot of land was sold at auction with the intention that a house would be built on it. A right to pass 'for all purposes connected with the use and enjoyment of the land but not for any other purpose' was expressly granted over the vendor's neighbouring land. The vendors claimed damages when their land was dug up to allow the running of utilities (water, gas, electricity, etc.) to the house.

An easement of way to allow the running of services and utilities was implied into the transfer.

An easement of necessity will be legal when it is implied into a legal transfer of land (because it is implied into the deed that transferred the land). It will be equitable if it is implied into an equitable transfer of the land.

Granted by common intention

Just as with implied reservation of an easement, a grant of an easement can be implied into transfers of land if the court finds that it was the common intention of the parties that there should be such an easement. In the old case of *Pwllbach Colliery Co. Ltd v. Woodman* [1915] AC 634 the House of Lords held that the court will readily imply the grant or reservation of an easement where it is necessary to give effect to the common intention of the parties with respect to the use of the land in the circumstances at the date of the transfer. This was applied in *Davies v. Bramwell* [2007] EWCA Civ 821 to imply a right of way wide enough to allow access to a ramp on the transfer of a garage. It was also cited in *Donovan v. Rana* and that case could be said to be decided on necessity or common intention, as the judge found that it must have been the common intention of the parties that a house with modern facilities be built. Common intention is perhaps best seen as an extension of necessity due to circumstances known to both parties at the time of the grant.

Sometimes, agreements such as leases are silent as to easements required by tenants. In that case, the courts will imply such easements as are needed to give effect to the agreement.

 CASE CLOSE-UP

Liverpool City Council v. Irwin [1977] AC 239

Tenancy agreements between the council and its tenants contained no mention of any rights for tenants at all.

The House of Lords held that, because the use of the stairs, lifts, and rubbish chutes was necessary for the tenants occupying dwellings in the block, the appropriate easements were to be implied into the tenancy agreements.

Another case shows that both parties must have known the intended use of the premises if an easement is to be implied.

 CASE CLOSE-UP

Wong v. Beaumont Properties [1964] 2 All ER 119

Basement premises were leased to the claimant for the purposes of carrying on a restaurant business. The lease contained covenants requiring the lessee not to create a nuisance through odours, etc. Despite this, the lessor refused permission to run a ventilation duct over his part of the premises.

Lord Denning MR held that, because the very purpose of the lease was that the basement should be used as a restaurant, which required ventilation, the grant of an easement of ventilation would be implied.

An easement implied by common intention will be legal when it is implied into a legal transfer of land (because it is implied into the deed that transferred the land). It will be equitable if it is implied into an equitable transfer of the land.

Under the rule in *Wheeldon v. Burrows*

This rule, as its name suggests, originates from the case of *Wheeldon v. Burrows* (1879) 12 Ch D 31, in which it was stated (at 49) that:

> in a grant of land, there may be implied in favour of the grantee those rights in the nature of easements which are continuous and apparent, and necessary to the reasonable enjoyment of the property granted, and which have been, and are at the time of the grant, used by the grantor for the benefit of the part granted.

The best way of explaining this rule is to look at an example.

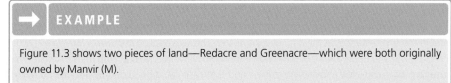

EXAMPLE

Figure 11.3 shows two pieces of land—Redacre and Greenacre—which were both originally owned by Manvir (M).

Manvir sells Greenacre to Nisha (N).

There is a path from Nisha's house to the public park at the side of Manvir's house. When Manvir owned Greenacre, he used the path to reach the park.

On the transfer of Greenacre to Nisha, the rule in *Wheeldon v. Burrows* will turn this quasi-easement into an easement in Nisha's favour and she will have a right of way over the path crossing Manvir's retained land.

Figure 11.3 Redacre and Greenacre

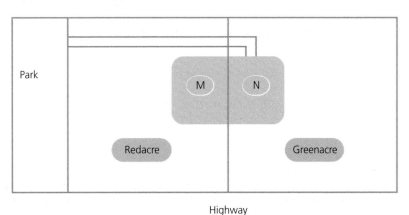

The rule also applies if both tenements are transferred at the same time. So, if in the last example, Manvir had sold Greenacre to Nisha and Redacre to Olu, Nisha would still have obtained an easement of right of way over the path under the rule in *Wheeldon v. Burrows*. In addition, both Nisha and Olu would have acquired mutual easements of support and of light.

Let us now look at the rule in a little more detail.

- Continuous and apparent

  An easement claimed under *Wheeldon v. Burrows* must be *'continuous and apparent'*. In other words, it must be fairly obvious that the easement exists and has done so for a long time. This requirement has not been construed very strictly: as long as an easement has been used over a substantial period of time and would be detected on a reasonably careful inspection of the land, it will meet these requirements. For example, it has been accepted that a worn track is sufficient indication of an easement of way: *Hansford v. Jago* [1921] 1 Ch 322.

- Necessary to reasonable enjoyment

  It is not clear whether the requirement that the easement is *'necessary to reasonable enjoyment'* is in addition to its continuous and apparent use, or is an alternative. Older cases seem to suggest that both must be satisfied, but more recent cases indicate that the two terms mean the same thing. In any case, it is clear that the 'necessity' in 'necessary to reasonable enjoyment' is not the same as that in easements of necessity. In the earlier example, for example, a right of way can still be implied even though Greenacre is not landlocked.

- Legal and equitable easements

  Both *legal and equitable easements* can be created under the rule in *Wheeldon v. Burrows*. If the grant of land into which the easement is implied is legal, then the easement is a legal one; if the grant of land is equitable only—for example, the grant of an equitable lease—then so is the easement.

 CASE CLOSE-UP

Borman v. Griffith [1930] 1 Ch 493

The claimant held a house, The Gardens, under an equitable lease for seven years. He used a driveway that ran across his landlord's property, although there was a separate access way to the back door of The Gardens. The landlord tried to stop the claimant using the driveway.

Maugham J held that the claimant was entitled to use the driveway, because it was plainly visible and was necessary for the reasonable enjoyment of the property. The right to use the driveway had not been excluded by the contract, so an easement of way over it was implied.

This case is a very good example of the application of *Wheeldon v. Burrows*. It was not necessary, in a strict sense, for the claimant to use the driveway, but the driveway was clearly intended for use by the occupier of The Gardens and had been used by the servient owner for that purpose when he occupied The Gardens. Note that the application of the rule could have been excluded by specific words in the contract granting the lease.

Under Law of Property Act 1925, s. 62

This statutory provision provides another way of implying easements into transfers of land. There is some overlap of this provision with the rule in *Wheeldon v. Burrows*, but there are also some differences.

 STATUTE

Law of Property Act 1925, s. 62 [General words implied in conveyances]

...

(2) A conveyance of land shall be deemed to include and shall by virtue of this Act operate to convey, with the land, all buildings, erections, fixtures, commons, hedges,

> ditches, fences, ways, waters, watercourses, liberties, privileges, easements, rights, and advantages whatsoever, appertaining or reputed to appertain to the land, or any part thereof, or, at the time of conveyance, demised, occupied, or enjoyed with or reputed or known as part or parcel of or appurtenant to the land or any part thereof.
>
> …

CROSS REFERENCE

For more on the items and rights that always form part of the land, see Chapter 1.

This section, and its predecessors, may originally have been intended only as a word-saving provision, confirming that a transfer of land carries with it all of the items (such as buildings and so on) and rights listed. This is open to the objection that such items and rights always form part of the land.

Whatever the merits of this argument, LPA 1925, s. 62 has come to be interpreted in a different way. It has been held that it operates to turn quasi-easements into easements on a transfer of the land and also to turn licences into easements.

The classic situations in which persons are affected by LPA 1925, s. 62 are those in which:

- a vendor has sold part of his or her legal estate in land, particularly if the part sold has been in separate occupation to the part retained;
- a lessor renews a lease, at a time when he or she owns a legal estate in land over which the lessee has been enjoying rights additional to those contained in the lease.

These situations are best explained by looking at the case law.

🔍 CASE CLOSE-UP

International Tea Stores v. Hobbs [1903] 2 Ch 165

A tenant was allowed to use an access path over his landlord's property. The landlord later conveyed the freehold to the tenant, making the former tenant the freehold owner of the land he had previously leased. After the transfer, the landlord tried to stop his former tenant from using the access path.

It was held that an easement to use the path had been implied into the conveyance by the predecessor to LPA 1925, s. 62. This meant that the tenant could continue to use the path.

This case clearly indicates the first of the situations outlined earlier. The landlord was a vendor selling off part of his land, which had formerly been in separate occupation (by his former tenant). Even though the right to use the path was by licence only, rather than a condition in either the lease or the transfer, it was turned or 'upgraded' into an easement by the equivalent of LPA 1925, s. 62.

Note that the party claiming the implied easement must provide evidence of the use of the quasi-easement before the division of the land: *Campbell v. Banks* [2011] EWCA Civ 61, in which the claimants failed to establish an implied easement because they could not prove any use of the bridleway in question for the benefit of their property prior to the division of the land.

🔍 CASE CLOSE-UP

Wright v. Macadam [1949] 2 KB 744

A tenant was allowed to use a coal shed situated on her landlord's premises. The lease was later renewed and no mention was made of the use of the coal shed. Afterwards, the landlord tried to claim extra rent for use of the shed.

The Court of Appeal held that the renewal of the lease had been a conveyance within LPA 1925, s. 62. Therefore, the licence to use the shed for storage of coal had become an easement. The landlord could neither stop the tenant from using the shed, nor charge her extra rent.

This case clearly illustrates the second situation described earlier. The lessor renewed the lease at a time when the tenant had been enjoying rights additional to those in her lease—namely, the right to store coal in a shed on the lessor's land. This right was turned into an easement by LPA 1925, s. 62.

Older cases indicate that the quasi-dominant and quasi-servient tenements must have been in separate occupation up to the date of the conveyance. In other words, there must have been different people living in each of the (quasi-) dominant and servient tenements.

 CASE CLOSE-UP

Long v. Gowlett [1923] 2 Ch 177

A miller tried to claim a right to go onto his neighbour's part of the river bank and clear weeds (to keep the river running freely).

It was held that no such right had been created by the conveyance of the land to the miller, because the same person had occupied the quasi-dominant and quasi-servient tenements before the conveyance—that is, there had been no prior diversity of occupation. It was held that the statute did not apply unless different persons had originally occupied the two pieces of land.

In *Long v. Gowlett*, Sargant J did give exceptions to the rule that there must have been prior diversity of occupation—namely, '*ways of necessity*', and '*continuous and apparent*' easements. It might be thought that this simply confirms the continued existence of the rule in *Wheeldon v. Burrows*, but it seems from later cases that continuous and apparent easements can be implied into conveyances by LPA 1925, s. 62, even where there is no prior diversity of occupation.

 CASE CLOSE-UP

Platt v. Crouch [2003] EWCA Civ 1110

In this case, it was held that the various rights claimed as easements when a hotel was sold did pass to the new owners under LPA 1925, s. 62. The rights, including rights of way and rights for hotel guests to moor boats, were claimed over neighbouring land that was also owned and occupied by the vendor of the hotel—so there was no prior diversity of occupation.

It was held that these were converted into easements by s. 62.

This has been followed by a very recent case.

 CASE CLOSE-UP

Wood v. Waddington [2015] EWCA Civ 538

The CA held that the claimants were entitled to two rights of way under LPA 1925, s. 62 where there had been no prior diversity of occupation. The rights were continuous and apparent and sufficient evidence of use was present. Use of a track once a month was held to be sufficient to show this. The fact that the claimants had started a livery business did prevent them using rights of way formerly used for domestic purposes.

It is possible to exclude the effect of s. 62 from a conveyance—see LPA 1925, s. 62(4). The vendors of the hotel in *Platt v. Crouch* had intended to do this but had left the clause out of the final contract, so were bound by s. 62.

Although LPA 1925, s. 62 is framed in very wide terms, it does not have the same effect on corporeal hereditaments (physical land) as it does on incorporeal hereditaments, such as easements. So, in *Commission for New Towns v. Gallagher* [2002] EWHC 2668 (Ch), s. 62 could not be used to establish ownership of a bridleway bordering the claimant's lands.

It is clear that there is some overlap between *Wheeldon v. Burrows* and LPA 1925, s. 62—but not all cases can be decided under both rules.

 THINKING POINT

Look back at the facts in the case of *Borman v. Griffith*. Could the claimant have used LPA 1925, s. 62, to establish an easement in that case?

The answer is no, because that case was about an equitable lease. LPA 1925, s. 62, applies only to '*a conveyance of land*', which means the transfer of a legal estate (whether freehold or leasehold), not the transfer of an equitable interest.

All easements implied under LPA 1925, s. 62 will be legal easements, because the section only applies to legal conveyances (transfers) of land.

11.4.3.3 Summary of implied easements

Table 11.2 shows the ways in which easements can be implied, and the differences and similarities between the methods.

Table 11.2 A summary of implied easements

Method	Grant	Reservation	Legal	Equitable	Main points
Necessity	Yes	Yes	Yes	Yes	If land is totally inaccessible or unusable without a right of way or other easement, one will be implied
Common intention	Yes	Yes	Yes	Yes	If the use of land contemplated by both parties makes such an easement necessary, one will be implied
Wheeldon v. Burrows	Yes	No	Yes	Yes	A grant of land carries with it any quasi-easements used by the transferor for the benefit of the part granted at the time of the transfer, as long as those rights are '*continuous and apparent*' and '*necessary for the reasonable enjoyment*' of the part granted

(Continued)

Table 11.2 Continued

Method	Grant	Reservation	Legal	Equitable	Main points
LPA 1925, s. 62	Yes	No	Yes	No	A conveyance of land carries with it all those rights in the nature of an easement that are 'enjoyed with or reputed or known as part or parcel of or appurtenant to the land'. This means that rights such as licences are turned into easements. This can apply to any kind of quasi-easement as long as there has been 'prior diversity of occupation', but only those that are 'continuous and apparent', if not.

11.4.4 Prescription

The creation of easements by **prescription** means that easements may be acquired by long use. This is a slightly quirky idea: if the dominant owner exercises the right (in the nature of an easement) for long enough, the law presumes that the servient owner must have granted the easement at some point in the past. This presumption is based upon the acquiescence of the servient owner to the continuous user by the dominant owner. We will discuss the meaning of 'continuous user' by the dominant owner and 'acquiescence' of the servient owner later in this chapter.

> **prescription**
> the acquisition of an easement by uninterrupted long use

The law is complicated by the fact that there are three types of prescription:

- common law;
- lost modern grant;
- the Prescription Act 1832.

The exact details of each of these types of prescription will also be discussed in the following sections, but it is important to note that all depend upon at least twenty years' use of the right by the claimant. They also have a number of other features in common.

11.4.4.1 'Continuous user' by the dominant owner

Firstly, prescription relies upon 'continuous user' (use) in fee simple by the dominant owner: the dominant owner must be either the owner of a freehold estate in land, or acting on behalf of a freehold owner.

An easement for life, or for a term of years, cannot be acquired by prescription. A tenant may, however, acquire an easement by prescription on behalf of his or her landlord, except against another tenant of the same landlord.

These rules mean that all easements gained by prescription are legal easements. This is a very important point, because students often think that they are equitable, perhaps because they seem to be created informally. Prescription means, however, that the easement has been deemed (assumed) to be granted by the servient owner and that it can only ever be a legal grant for the period of a fee simple—effectively forever.

The use of the right claimed as an easement must be continuous. If there have been long gaps in the use, prescription cannot be established. For example, a right of way used only three times at twelve-yearly intervals could not be claimed by prescription—*Hollins v. Verney* (1884) 13 QBD 304. Note that the use may be against successive owners of the servient land, as long as it is continuous. It does not matter that the servient land changes ownership.

EXAMPLE

Punita has been using an alleyway at the rear of her property to clear rubbish from her garden and to take it to the front of her property for collection for the last twenty-two years. During that time, the alleyway—which runs over the garden of a neighbouring house—has been owned by three different people.

Punita can still claim an easement of way by prescription, despite the changes in ownership of the servient land during the prescription period.

The use of the easement must be 'as of right'—the dominant owner must exercise it as if the right had been legally granted. From earliest times, the courts have expressed this as being use 'without force, without secrecy, without permission'—often expressed in Latin, *nec vi, nec clam, nec precario*.

> **nec vi, nec clam, nec precario**
>
> 'without force, without secrecy, without permission'

Without force *(nec vi)*

'Without force' means that the right claimed must have been exercised without physical force and not in the face of objections by the servient owner.

EXAMPLE

Punjab has been driving his car over Quentin's driveway in order to get access to his garage.

Quentin has objected to his use of the driveway from the beginning and has written letters to Punjab forbidding him to drive there.

Punjab would not be able to claim an easement of way by prescription, because he is not exercising the right '*without force*'.

In a case heard in the Upper-tier tribunal, *Winterburn v. Bennet* [2015] UKUT 59 (TCC), notices forbidding parking were enough to prevent a fish and chip shop owner from acquiring prescriptive rights of parking for himself and his customers.

Without secrecy *(nec clam)*

'Without secrecy' means that the use must have been open and not hidden.

EXAMPLE

Ross owns a factory that produces foul waste water. He constructs a pipe that discharges the water into a lake owned by Salman. The pipe enters the lake below the waterline, so Salman is unaware of it.

Ross cannot establish an easement of drainage by prescription, because his use is not '*without secrecy*'.

Without permission *(nec precario)*

'Without permission' means that the use must not have been in reliance upon a licence of some description. Good evidence of a licence would be shown by a written permission, or by the payment of a periodic fee, or because the servient owner chose to allow it. Note that it is possible for use to have started by permission, but later to have been exercised as of right. This will be a question of fact, dependent upon the circumstances of each case.

CASE CLOSE-UP

London Tara Hotel Ltd v. Kensington Close Hotel Ltd [2011] EWCA Civ 1356

A licence to use a service road ended when the servient land changed ownership. The new servient owner did not realize this and thought that the use of the road by the dominant owner was still by permission. It was nevertheless held that the servient owner had acquiesced to the use. The Court of Appeal held that 'as of right' was sufficiently defined by the 'nec vi, nec clam, nec precario' tests, and once these were established, no further criterion remained to be satisfied—the owner is taken to have acquiesced in the use.

If the right is exercised by the dominant owner in the mistaken belief that it had been validly granted, that will not prevent the long use giving rise to an easement by prescription—*Bridle v. Ruby* [1989] QB 169. However, there need not be subjective belief that there was such a right—the state of mind of the claimant is irrelevant, the claimant must simply use the alleged easement *as if* he or she had such a right: *R v. Oxfordshire County Council and Another, Ex parte Sunningwell Parish Council* [2000] 1 AC 335.

Illegal use

An easement by prescription cannot be based on use of the land that would be illegal even with the permission of the servient landowner. For example, it is usually illegal to discharge waste water into rivers without the consent of the Environment Agency. Therefore, an easement of drainage of such water into a river cannot be gained by prescription, because the servient owner could not legally have granted such an easement—see, for example, *George Legge and Son Ltd v. Wenlock Corporation* [1938] 1 All ER 37.

It is, however, possible to gain an easement by prescription if the right claimed would be illegal only if the servient landowner did not consent to the use. This is because the permission of the landowner is deemed to have been granted by the long use.

CASE CLOSE-UP

Bakewell Management Ltd v. Roland Brandwood and Ors [2004] UKHL 14

The claimant was the owner of common land that was bordered by houses belonging to the defendants. For many years, the defendants had been driving over the common land to reach their homes.

The claimant, following the decision of the Court of Appeal in *Hanning v. Top Deck Travel* (1993) 68 P & CR 14, claimed that the defendants could not establish easements of way by prescription, because driving on common land without the permission of the landowner is a criminal offence under LPA 1925, s. 193(4). The claimant had therefore tried to claim large sums of money from each householder in return for the express grant of an easement.

The House of Lords overruled *Hanning v. Top Deck Travel* and held that easements can be established by prescription if the right claimed (driving over common land, in this case) would be legal with the permission of the servient landowner.

This case shows the importance of easements in general, as well as the importance of the law of prescription. The houses bordering the common would have had a much lower value if there were no easement allowing the owners to drive onto their land.

11.4.4.2 Acquiescence by the servient owner

It must be shown that the servient owner acquiesced in the dominant owner's use of the right claimed. Clearly, this is closely related to 'use as of right', as shown in *London Tara Hotel Ltd v. Kensington Close Hotel Ltd* (discussed earlier), but there are some other factors to consider.

 CASE CLOSE-UP

Dalton v. Angus and Co. [1881–85] All ER Rep 1

It was held by Fry J that acquiescence was presumed if the servient owner had:

- a knowledge of the acts done;
- a power in him to stop the acts or sue in respect of them;
- an abstinence on his part from the exercise of such power.

It was held that an easement of support for a building had been acquired. The building had stood there, supported by the neighbouring building, for over twenty years, so the neighbouring owner had acquiesced in the use of the right of support.

It is therefore important that a landowner does not simply stand by and let someone exercise rights over his or her land. If the landowner does not object, the right will eventually become an easement.

As we have seen at 11.4.4.1, the presumed grant must be by the freehold owner. If the servient land is leased to a tenant at the time of the presumed grant, it may be argued that the tenant, rather than the freehold owner, had the power to stop the acts establishing the easement. However, this must be shown actually to be the case: the mere fact that the servient land was subject to a tenancy is not enough, by itself, to mean that there can be no acquiescence by the servient owner. In *Williams v. Sandy Lane (Chester) Ltd* [2006] EWCA Civ 1738, the Court of Appeal held that the freeholder did have the power to stop the claimants using the land, despite the tenancy. In *Llewellyn v. Lorey* [2011] EWCA Civ 37, however, it was held on the facts that the freeholder did not know about or have the power to stop the use of a track during the time the alleged servient land was tenanted, so had not acquiesced to the use.

11.4.4.3 Common law prescription

Common law prescription is based on use of the right in question since 'time immemorial'—that is since 1189. If the right has been used for at least twenty years, a presumption is raised that use has been since time immemorial.

This presumption can be rebutted by showing that the right could not have existed in 1189—for example, because the dominant and servient tenements have been in common ownership at some time since that date—or that the property in question could not have benefited from the right in 1189. A suburban house built in 1960 could hardly have benefited from a right of support in 1189, for example. For all intents and purposes, common law prescription is not useful in establishing modern rights.

11.4.4.4 Lost modern grant

To remedy the defects of common law prescription, the courts developed the fiction of the 'lost modern grant'. By this fiction, the court presumes that, if there has been twenty years' enjoyment of a right, a grant of that right must have been made and lost!

The presumption is a strong one—*Bryant v. Foot* (1867) LR 2 QB 161. The court will make the presumption even if there is no evidence at all of such a grant and even if there is evidence that no grant was ever made. If, however, there was no one who could have made such a grant (no capable grantor) the presumption will be rebutted.

CASE CLOSE-UP

Tehidy Minerals v. Norman [1971] 2 QB 528

In this case about rights of common acquired by prescription, it was held by the Court of Appeal that evidence that no such grant was ever made was irrelevant, as long as there was someone who could have made the grant.

It is important to note that the period of use need not be the last twenty years before the rights were disputed: it can be *any* period of twenty years. In *Tehidy Minerals v. Norman*, the Ministry of Defence had requisitioned the common from 1941 to 1960 and the owner of the common brought an action disputing their rights in 1966. This did not matter, because an earlier twenty years' continuous use (from 1921 to 1941) could be proved.

The doctrine of lost modern grant was recently used in the case of *Loose v. Lynn Shellfish Ltd* [2014] EWCA Civ 846 to claim the profit à prendre of a fishery. There was a dispute about the extent of the fishery, so the Court of Appeal had to interpret the supposed lost grant. They decided it would have been granted over the foreshore as it existed from time to time, best identified by the lowest astronomical tide.

11.4.4.5 The Prescription Act 1832

The Prescription Act 1832 (PA 1832) was supposed to rationalize the law on prescription, but instead complicated the law further by introducing a third type of prescription. It has not received many compliments over the years, and was recently criticized by Lord Neuberger MR in *London Tara Hotel Ltd v. Kensington Close Hotel Ltd.*

PA 1832, s. 1, deals with rights to profits à prendre and is discussed at 11.10. PA 1832, s. 2, deals with easements other than rights to light and s. 3 deals with easements of light.

Easements other than light

PA 1932, s. 2, provides for two different prescription periods in respect of easements other than light—that is, rights of way, etc.

STATUTE

Prescription Act 1832, s. 2

No claim which may be lawfully made at the common law, by custom, prescription, or grant, to any way or other easement, ... when such way or other matter as herein last before mentioned shall have been actually enjoyed by any person claiming right thereto without interruption for the full period of twenty years, shall be defeated or destroyed by showing only that such way or other matter was first enjoyed at any time prior to such period of twenty years, but nevertheless such claim may be defeated in any other way by which the same is now liable to be defeated; and where such way or other matter as herein last before mentioned shall have been so enjoyed as aforesaid for the full period of forty

> years, the right thereto shall be deemed absolute and indefeasible, unless it shall appear that the same was enjoyed by some consent or agreement expressly given or made for that purpose by deed or writing.

This section actually splits into two parts: the shorter period of twenty years and the longer period of forty years:

- If the easement has been actually enjoyed without interruption for twenty years, it shall not be defeated by proof that it began later than 1189, but it may be defeated in any other way possible at common law.

- If the easement has been enjoyed without interruption for forty years, it shall be deemed absolute and indefeasible, unless it appears that it was enjoyed by some consent or agreement expressly given in writing.

The Act specifies how the periods of twenty and forty years are to be measured; unlike lost modern grant, it is not possible to choose any period that the claimant wishes.

 STATUTE

Prescription Act 1832, s. 4

The 20 or 40 years must be:

> ... the Period next before some Suit or Action wherein the Claim or Matter to which such Period may relate shall have been or shall be brought into question; ...

PA 1932, s. 4, prescribes that it must be the period leading up to the action by which the legality of the right is questioned—in other words, the *last* twenty or forty years. The Act gives no rights to an easement unless, and until, an action is brought.

 THINKING POINT

Could the commoners in *Tehidy Minerals v. Norman* have used the PA 1832 to bring their claim?

No, because they could not rely on twenty years' use leading up to 1966, when the action was launched, as the common land had been requisitioned until 1960. They had to rely on an earlier period, so could use only the doctrine of lost modern grant.

The time also has to be '*without interruption*'. This is an action taken by the servient owner that prevents the use of the right claimed.

 STATUTE

Prescription Act 1932, s. 4

... no act or other matter shall be deemed to be an interruption, within the meaning of this statute, unless the same shall have been or shall be submitted to or acquiesced in for one year after the party interrupted shall have had or shall have notice thereof, and of the person making or authorizing the same to be made.

This means that, if the servient owner takes action to prevent the claimant from exercising the quasi-easement, time will not stop running unless the claimant does nothing about the interruption for a whole year. Once the interruption has lasted for one year, the time 'stops running'.

EXAMPLE

Tom has been exercising a right of way over Udish's land for the last nineteen and a half years, although he has no legal right to do so. Udish has now erected a barrier, making it impossible for Tom to continue using the right of way.

The barrier is a potential *'interruption'* within the meaning of s. 4. Tom cannot do anything about it immediately, because he has not been using the right for the whole of the prescription period—that is, twenty years.

As soon as the twenty-year period is up, however, Tom can bring an action under PA 1932, s. 2, using the shorter (twenty-year) period. This is because the interruption has not lasted for a whole year, so it does not stop the time running.

If, however, Tom were to do nothing until the barrier had been in place for a year, he would lose his right to claim an easement by prescription under the Act, because time would stop running at nineteen and a half years as soon as the interruption had been in place for a year.

Note that the starting of an action by the servient owner against the dominant owner will not count as an interruption; instead the twenty- or forty-year periods must be calculated backwards from the date the action starts—*Reilly v. Orange* [1955] 1 WLR 616.

Although both periods (twenty and forty years) are measured in the same way, their effects are different. Under the shorter period, the Act provides that the easement cannot be defeated by showing that it could not have existed in 1189, but it can be defeated in any other way known to the common law. So, it can be defeated by showing that it was not exercised 'as of right': for example, it was exercised secretly, or by force, or by permission. The twenty-year period is, therefore, a negative right under the Act: the Act prohibits the use of some of the common law defences to a finding of prescription, but not all of them.

The forty-year period operates in a more positive way. It provides that the right shall be *'absolute and indefeasible'* unless some written permission can be shown. This means that the right must still have been exercised as of right, without secrecy or force, but that initial oral permission from the servient owner will not defeat the claim. It also will not defeat the claim to show that use of the right began when the servient land was occupied by tenants under a lease, rather than a freehold owner.

Easements of light

Easements of light are dealt with separately from all other easements.

STATUTE

Prescription Act 1832, s. 3

When the access and use of light to and for any dwelling house, workshop, or other building shall have been actually enjoyed therewith for the full period of twenty years

> without interruption, the right thereto shall be deemed absolute and indefeasible, any local usage or custom to the contrary notwithstanding, unless it shall appear that the same was enjoyed by some consent or agreement expressly made or given for that purpose by deed or writing.

Under PA 1932, s. 3, all that the claimant need show is that the window in question has enjoyed access to, and use of, light for at least twenty years, and the absence of a written agreement. Notice that the words *'without interruption'* are also included in this section: if the access to light is interrupted for a period of at least one year, time stops running. The interruption may be physical—such as erecting a hoarding to block the light—or notional, under the Rights of Light Act 1959. Under that Act, the servient owner can register a notice of interruption as a local land charge. This notice acts as if it were blocking the light and therefore stops time running.

An easement of light does not depend upon a fictitious grant of an easement and it appears that a tenant can acquire an easement of light under this section. Only a freehold owner can acquire any other type of easement by prescription.

Note the Law Commission report LC356 published in December 2014, recommending changes to easements of light, particularly those obtained by prescription.

Deductions under the Act

PA 1932, ss. 7 and 8 provide for certain periods to be deducted in calculating time periods under the Act. Deductions are different to interruptions. If there is an interruption lasting at least a year, time stops running completely, and the claimant must use the right for another twenty years before any claim can be made. Where there is a deduction, however, time stops only for the period of the deduction; afterwards, time runs from where it left off.

 EXAMPLE

Vera had been exercising a right of way over a path on Wayne's land for ten years when Wayne erected a barrier preventing her from using it.

Two years later, the barrier blew down in a gale and Vera was able to use the path again for another ten years. Vera cannot bring an action against Wayne, because she has only ten years *'next before action'*.

If the two years had been a deduction rather than an interruption, Vera would now be able to bring a claim, as she could add together the ten years before the deduction and the ten years afterwards.

The deductions under PA 1932, s. 7, apply only to the shorter statutory period (twenty years). Any period for which the servient owner was aged under 18, a tenant for life under a settlement, or a patient under the Mental Health Act 1983, must be deducted.

The deductions under PA 1832, s. 8, apply only to the longer period (forty years). Any period for which the servient owner was a tenant for life under a settlement, or a tenant under a lease of more than three years, must be deducted.

EXAMPLE

Xena starts to use a path over Yvonne's land in 1980.

From 1990 to 1995, Yvonne is detained under the Mental Health Act 1983. Xena continues using the path until 2007, when Yvonne's successor in title brings an action in trespass against her.

The five years from 1990 to 1995 must be deducted in calculating whether Xena has twenty years' use, but the ten years' use until 1990 can be added to the twelve years' use since.

Therefore, Xena can show twenty-two years' use and can make a claim under the shorter period.

11.4.4.6 A summary of easements by prescription

Remember that all easements created by prescription are legal easements. The other characteristics of easements created by prescription can be summarized as in Table 11.3.

Table 11.3 A summary of easements by prescription

Type of prescription	Period	Requirements	Periods deducted
Common law	Use since 'time immemorial'—that is, 1189, although 20 years' use will raise a presumption of this	Can be defeated by showing that the easement could not have existed in 1189, or that it was not exercised as of right	Must be by a freehold owner against a freehold owner. Use must have begun when the freehold owner was in occupation—that is, the land must not have been leased.
Lost modern grant	Any period of 20 years	Can be defeated by showing that it was not exercised as of right	Must be by a freehold owner against a freehold owner. Use must have begun when the freehold owner was in occupation—that is, the land must not have been leased.
The PA 1832 (longer period)	The 40 years next before action—that is, the 40 years ending with the date on which a claim is made. If there has been an interruption lasting 1 year or more, time will stop running.	'Absolute and indefeasible' unless granted by some written permission, but must not have been used secretly or by force	Any period must be deducted for which the servient owner was a tenant for life under a settlement, or a tenant under a lease of more than 3 years
The PA 1832 (shorter period)	The 20 years next before action—that is, the 20 years ending with the date on which a claim is made. If there has been an interruption lasting 1 year or more, time will stop running.	Cannot be defeated by showing that it began after 1189, but can be defeated by showing it was not used as of right	Any period for which the servient owner was aged under 18, a tenant for life under a settlement, or a patient under the Mental Health Act 1983 must be deducted

11.5 Registration of easements

11.5.1 Registered land

11.5.1.1 Express grants

As noted at 11.4.2.1, the express grant of a legal easement by a registered proprietor must be completed by registration to be a legal grant, because it is a registrable disposition within LRA 2002, s. 27(2)(d). If the grant is not registered, the easement will remain equitable and must be registered as an equitable easement by notice on the charges register of the servient land, or it will not be binding on a purchaser of the servient land. The dominant owner will lose his or her right to use the easement.

Before the LRA 2002 came into force, it was possible for equitable easements—including those intended to be legal, but not registered—to be overriding interests, provided those easements were 'openly enjoyed and exercised'. This was due to the interpretation of Land Registration Act 1925, s. 70(1)(a) and certain Land Registry rules in the cases of *Celsteel v. Alton House Holdings Ltd* [1985] 1 WLR 204 and *Thatcher v. Douglas* [1996] 146 NLJ 282.

Since the LRA 2002 came into force on 13 October 2003, it is no longer possible for new equitable easements to be overriding interests. Under the transitional provisions in LRA 2002, Sch. 12, para. 9, however, any easement that was overriding before the LRA 2002 came into force continues to be an overriding interest until it is registered. In *Chaudhury v. Yavuz* [2011] EWCA Civ 1314 the Court refused to find that an unregistered equitable easement survived a sale of the servient tenement even where it was obvious on inspection of the land. It was not an overriding interest because there was no actual occupation of the servient tenement under LRA 2002, Sch. 3, para. 2. It was also held that the facts here did not lead to an equitable easement by estoppel by way of constructive trust.

11.5.1.2 Implied easements and those created by prescription

Legal easements that are not expressly granted—those that are implied or created by prescription—are overriding interests unless, and until, registered. Such easements are covered by LRA 2002, Sch. 3, para. 3.

The policy behind this is that it is unreasonable to expect such easements to be registered, because they are created by informal means. It is important to remember, however, that *easements implied into a legal transfer will be legal easements* (because they are implied into a deed) and that *easements created by prescription are always legal easements* (because they are deemed to be created by a deed, or because they are statutory). Students sometimes make the mistake of thinking that informally created easements must be equitable and, while this is an understandable error, it is very important to avoid making it.

Under LRA 2002, Sch. 3, para. 3 an easement that is an overriding interest will be binding on a purchaser of the servient land if it can be shown that:

- the purchaser actually knows of the easement;
- the easement is obvious on a reasonably careful inspection of the land over which it is exercisable;
- the easement has been exercised within the period of one year before the disposition.

 EXAMPLE

Zosia has just purchased a semi-detached house that is over twenty years old. After she has moved in, her neighbour, Abu, informs her that his drains go under her garden and that they are blocked. He wants to go onto her land to clear the drains. There is no mention of the drains in her register of title and she can see no sign of them on the surface of her land. Is Zosia bound by Abu's easement of drainage?

Zosia is bound as long as there is proof that the easement has been granted by implied grant (perhaps under *Wheeldon v. Burrows*, if the houses were originally sold by the same builder) or by long use, because the houses are over twenty years old. It does not matter that Zosia did not know of it and could not see the drains, as long as they have been used in the last year.

The aim of these provisions is to reduce the number of overriding easements. If the easement is not known to the purchaser, has not been exercised within the last year, and is not obvious on the face of the land, it will not bind the new owner of the servient land and will thus cease to exist. This policy goes along with a requirement on the parties to declare any overriding interests that are known, so that they can be registered. These policies should mean that there are fewer and fewer overriding easements. This accords with the 'mirror principle' of registration: the register should provide an accurate reflection of the rights and interests in the land.

> **CROSS REFERENCE**
> For more on the mirror principle, see Chapter 2.

11.5.2 Unregistered land

A legal easement granted over unregistered land is binding on all purchasers because it is a legal interest. An equitable easement over unregistered land must be registered as a Class D(iii) land charge under Land Charges Act 1972, s. 2(5).

> **CROSS REFERENCE**
> For more on the different classes of land charge, see Chapter 2.

11.6 Remedies for infringement of an easement

If an easement is infringed—for example, if the servient owner blocks a right of way—the dominant owner can take steps to remove the blockage, as long as no more force is used than is reasonably necessary, no injury is caused to others, and there is no danger of a breach of the peace. This remedy is called **abatement**.

The courts do not favour abatement as a remedy, however, and it is usually safer to bring an action against the servient owner. The court may grant an injunction, damages, or a declaration. For the rules on when the court will grant an injunction rather than damages, see the discussion on remedies for breach of covenant in Chapter 12, 12.7.1.

> **abatement**
> a remedy that, in relation to nuisances, allows for the removal, termination, or destruction of that nuisance under certain conditions

11.7 Extinguishment of easements

Extinguishment of easements means ways in which easements can cease to exist. Firstly, **unity of seisin** may occur. This means that the dominant and servient tenements come into joint ownership. As it is one of the main characteristics of an easement that the dominant and servient owners cannot be the same person, the easements will cease to exist. It is worth bearing in

> **unity of seisin**
> the ownership of two plots of land by the same (legal) person

mind, however, that, if the two tenements later come back into separate ownership, some of the former easements may revive under the rules in *Wheeldon v. Burrows* and LPA 1925, s. 62.

Secondly, the dominant owner may expressly release an easement, perhaps in return for a sum of money or other inducement. The release must be made by deed and followed by an application to cancel any relevant entries on the registers of title.

Thirdly, it is possible for an easement to be impliedly released if it can be shown to be permanently unexercisable, or to have been abandoned by the dominant owner. Abandonment is not presumed lightly; however, it must be shown that there was an intention to abandon the easement; mere non-use is not enough.

 Q | CASE CLOSE-UP

Benn v. Hardinge (1993) 66 P & CR 246

It was held by the Court of Appeal that a right of way that had not been used for 175 years had not been abandoned. The dominant owners had had another, more convenient way that had been available during that time. When that way became waterlogged, they were entitled to revert to the use of their easement.

If an easement has become impossible to use, it will be treated as impliedly extinguished, but if there is any chance that it might again become useable, extinguishment will not be presumed.

 Q | CASE CLOSE-UP

Jones v. Cleanthi [2006] EWCA Civ 1712

A tenant of a flat had a right to use an area on the ground floor for the disposal of rubbish, etc. The building of a brick wall blocked the tenant's access to that area. The landlord had been obliged to build the wall to comply with a statutory fire safety notice.

The Court of Appeal held that the easement was not extinguished and was only suspended. It was possible that, at some time in the future, fire safety regulations or the use of the property might change, so that the easement could be used again.

In *Williams v. Sandy Lane (Chester) Ltd*, fencing and earthworks that made a right of way less easy to use were not enough to show abandonment of it.

While easements are not easily extinguished, you should not forget the effects of LRA 2002, Sch. 3, para. 3. If the easement is not registered, but is an overriding interest, it will not bind a purchaser of the servient tenement unless:

- the purchaser actually knows of it;
- it is obvious on a reasonably careful inspection of the land over which the easement or profit is exercisable;
- it has been exercised within the period of one year before the disposition.

This will mean that unused easements that do not appear on the register and which are not apparent on the face of the land will effectively be extinguished on a sale of the servient tenement.

11.8 The Access to Neighbouring Land Act 1992

The Access to Neighbouring Land Act 1992 gives landowners useful rights to go onto neighbouring land to carry out necessary repair works to their own land and buildings, if they do not have a legal or equitable right of entry for those purposes.

Under this Act, an access order can be made by the county court. This order will not be a legal easement, but will be restricted, specifying the extent of access and any compensation to be paid. The access order must be registered if it is to bind future purchasers of the servient land.

Access orders are allowed for maintenance, but not for development of the land.

11.9 The Party Walls etc. Act 1996

The Party Walls etc. Act 1996 grants important rights to neighbouring landowners in respect of party walls. A party wall is one which:

- forms part of a building and projects beyond the boundary of the owner's land into neighbouring land; or
- is built on the land of one owner but separates buildings belonging to different owners.

Under the Act, a number of activities in relation to party walls can be carried out provided a notice is served on the adjoining owner:

- construction of a new party wall;
- repair of, or others works to, an existing party wall; and
- excavation work within a certain distance of the adjoining owner's buildings.

If the adjoining owner objects, a surveyor is appointed to arbitrate. The Act gives wide powers to enter the land of the adjoining owner to carry out works once agreed or arbitrated, right up to breaking down gates and doors to gain entry. The Act does not create legal easements, but is an alternative to an easement if a party wall is affected.

11.10 Profits à prendre

A profit à prendre is the right to take something from another person's land. This includes minerals, crops, and wild animals, but not water: a right to take water is an easement.

Profits may either be owned by one person to the exclusion of all others—that is, a **several profit** —or by one person in common with other persons—that is, a **profit in common, or a common**. Unlike easements, profits may exist in gross—that is, the owner of the profit does not need to be a landowner. A profit in gross can be registered at the Land Registry in its own right—LRA 2002, s. 2(a)(iv).

> **several profit**
> a profit à prendre that is enjoyed exclusively by one person

> **profit in common, or common**
> a profit à prendre that is enjoyed by one person in common with others

A legal profit à prendre must be granted either indefinitely—that is, for an interest equivalent to a fee simple absolute in possession—or for a fixed term (equivalent to a lease).

Profits may be granted expressly, either by statute or by deed, or they may be implied under LPA 1925, s. 62, in the same way as easements. They may be acquired by prescription under the common law, lost modern grant (for which the period is twenty years, as for easements), or under the PA 1832. Under PA 1832, s. 1, the periods for profits are thirty years (the shorter period) and sixty years (the longer period). An example of a profit à prendre obtained by prescription is *Loose v. Lyn Shellfish Ltd.* [2014] EWCA Civ 846.

11.11 Proposed reforms

The Law Commission report, *Making Land Work: Easements, Covenants and Profits à Prendre*, Law Com No. 327 (London: The Stationery Office, 2011) contains a number of suggested reforms to the law of easements and profits including:

- profits à prendre would no longer be able to be created by prescription;

- the law on acquisition of easements by prescription would be simplified;

- the law on implied easements and profits would be simplified, including the abolition of the way in which LPA 1925, s. 62 currently creates easements;

- the law on abandonment of easements would be changed to presume abandonment after non-use for twenty years;

- easements of parking would be clarified;

- in registered land only, it would be possible for easements to be created even if both pieces of land were owned by the same person, which would make developing housing estates much easier;

- in registered land, easements could not be released without removing them from the register;

- the jurisdiction of the Upper Tribunal would be extended to include discharging or modifying easements as well as restrictive covenants (see Chapter 12, 12.8 for the current jurisdiction of the Upper Tribunal).

Note also LC356 (December 2014) on reforming rights to light.

 ## Summary

1. Easements are important property rights owned by one landowner (the dominant owner) over land of another (the servient owner).

2. An easement must have the characteristics defined in *Re Ellenborough Park*:

- there must be a dominant and a servient tenement;

- an easement must accommodate the dominant tenement;

- dominant and servient owners must be different persons;

- a right over land cannot amount to an easement unless it is capable of forming the subject matter of a grant.

3. An easement can be either legal or equitable, but to be a legal right, an easement must be created by statute, deed, or prescription (long use).

4. Easements can be expressly granted or reserved.

5. Easements can be impliedly granted, or reserved by necessity or common intention. They can also be impliedly granted under the rule in *Wheeldon v. Burrows* and under LPA 1925, s. 62.

6. Easements can be acquired by long use at common law, under the doctrine of lost modern grant and under PA 1832.

7. Easements may be released or abandoned, but abandonment is not easily presumed.

8. Profits à prendre are rights to take some part of the soil or produce of other land. Unlike easements, they can exist in gross.

The bigger picture

- For more information on how to read and interpret easements found on registers of title, see Chapter 14, 14.2.3. For advice on answering exam questions on easements and profits, see Chapter 15, 15.10.

- If you need more information on the current law, criticisms of it, and proposals for reform, you cannot do better than to read the Law Commission report, *Making Land Work: Easements, Covenants and Profits à Prendre*, Law Com No. 327 (London: The Stationery Office, 2011).

? Questions

Self-test questions

1. Ali wishes to know if the right to park his car on the driveway of a neighbouring house is capable of being an easement. Advise Ali.

2. What is the difference between the public right of passage along the highway and an easement of way?

3. Betty has just moved into a house that has no access to the road for motor vehicles. Is she able to claim an easement of necessity over her neighbour's land?

Exam questions

1. (a) Carol has a lease of a small flat on the second floor. She is a keen cyclist and her landlord, David, has always allowed her to store her bicycle in his garden shed. Carol's lease was renewed last month. This week, she received a note from David saying that there is no longer room in his shed for her cycle, so she must remove it. What can Carol do?

   (b) Eddie has a garage at the back of his garden, in which he parks his car. He accesses the garage by driving along an alleyway between the gardens of the houses in his road and the neighbouring park. Yesterday, he received a letter from the local council, saying that it owns the alleyway and that he must now pay £300 per year to drive on it. Eddie has been using the alleyway for twenty-five years and his predecessor in title used it for fifteen years before that. Advise Eddie.

(c) Fred has an old well on his land that has not been used for many years. Last week, due to a drought order forbidding the watering of gardens with mains water, his neighbour Gina came onto Fred's land and took water from the well. Fred's register of title does show a right to take water in favour of Gina's land, but Fred had thought it was never going to be used. Advise Fred.

2. Is the law on acquisition of easements in need of reform?

 For suggested approaches to answering these questions visit the Online Resource Centre.

Further reading

Bogusz, B., 'The doctrine of lost modern grant: back to the future or time to move on?' [2013] Conv 198
This article considers the reforms in the Law Commission Report and the case of *London Tara Hotel Ltd v. Kensington Close Hotel Ltd* [2011] EWCA Civ 1356.

Douglas, S., 'How to reform section 62 of the Law of Property Act 1925' [2015] 1 Conv 13–25

Douglas, S., 'Reforming implied easements' [2015] 131(Apr) LQR 251–74
These articles comment on the proposals for reform of implied easements.

Fetherstonhaugh, G., 'Can reforming easements by prescription help find the light at the end of the right of way?' [2011] EG 74
This article considers the Law Commission report, *Making Land Work: Easements, Covenants and Profits à Prendre*, particularly as it applies to prescriptive easements.

Goymour, A., 'Easements, servitudes and the right to park' [2008] CLJ 20
This is an article on cases on parking as an easement.

Haley, M., 'Easements, exclusionary use and elusive principles—the right to park' [2008] Conv 244
This is an article on cases on parking as an easement.

Land Registry (2015) *Land Registry Practice Guide 52—Easements claimed by prescription,* **available online at https://www.gov.uk/government/publications/easements-claimed-by-prescription**
This guide gives clear guidance on how the Land Registry deals with claims for easements by prescription. It also gives a very clear outline of the law on prescription.

Land Registry (2015) *Land Registry Practice Guide 62—Easements,* **available online at https://www.gov.uk/government/publications/easements**
This guide sets out the rules on registration of easements. It is quite technical, but useful if you want to check whether a particular easement should have been registered.

Law Commission (2011) *Making Land Work: Easements, Covenants and Profits à Prendre*, Law Com No. 327 (London: The Stationery Office, 2011) available online at http://www.lawcom.gov.uk/wp-content/uploads/2015/03/lc327_easements_report.pdf

Law Commission (2014) *Rights to Light*, Law Com No. 356 (London: The Stationery Office, 2014) available online at http://www.lawcom.gov.uk/wp-content/uploads/2015/03/lc356_rights_to_light.pdf

McFarlane, B., 'Eastenders, Neighbours and Upstairs Downstairs: Chaudhary v Yavuz' [2013] Conv 74
This discusses the equitable easement in *Chaudhary v. Yavuz* [2011] EWCA Civ 1314, and the registration issues it threw up.

Murdoch, S., 'Not all rights can be taken for granted' [2009] EG 101
This is an article on cases on parking as an easement.

Paton, E. and Seabourne, G., 'Can't get there from here? Permissible use of easements after Das' [2003] Conv 127
This article looks at the case of *Das v. Linden Mews* and the rule in *Harris v. Flowers*. It also considers excessive use of an easement of way.

Online Resource Centre

www.oxfordtextbooks.co.uk/orc/clarke_directions5e/

For more advice relating to this chapter, including self-test questions and an interactive glossary, visit the Online Resource Centre.

12 Covenants in freehold land

□ **LEARNING OBJECTIVES**

By the end of this chapter, you will be able to:

- recognize a covenant in freehold land;
- identify the 'covenantor' and the 'covenantee';
- identify which land has the benefit of the covenant and which land has the burden;
- explain the problems with the enforceability of covenants, particularly when land changes hands;
- recognize the different approaches taken by common law and equity;
- explain the details of the passing of the benefit at law and understand the rule that the burden cannot pass at law;
- explain the passing of the benefit and burden of restrictive covenants in equity;
- discuss the various ways in which the burden of positive covenants may be enforced;
- identify the remedies for breach of covenant;
- recognize how covenants may be discharged;
- understand the most recent proposals for reform.

Introduction

In this chapter, we will be looking at covenants in freehold land. 'Covenant' is an old word for promise and this subject deals with promises made by freehold owners of land about their use of that land. This is a very complicated area, mainly because the common law has not accepted covenants as proprietary rights that every owner of the land with the benefit of a covenant could enforce, and which would bind every owner of land about which a promise has been made. As we shall see, equity has stepped in to solve this problem and some covenants are now capable of running with the land—but by no means all.

The law of freehold covenants is impossible to defend in its current form; it is over-complicated, confusing, and unhelpful. There have been numerous suggestions for reform over the years, most recently in the Law Commission report, *Making Land Work: Easements, Covenants and Profits à Prendre*, Law Com No. 327 (London: The Stationery Office, 2011), details of which you can find at 12.9. However, previous Law Commission reports were not implemented, and there is no reason yet to suppose that this one will have a happier fate. Consequently, we must grapple with the law in its unreformed state.

12.1 What is a covenant?

In this chapter, a **covenant** is a promise made by one landowner to another regarding the use of freehold land. The basic idea behind the use of covenants in freehold land is best illustrated by an example.

> **covenant**
> a promise contained in a deed

 EXAMPLE

Alexandra owns a house with a large garden. She decides to sell part of her garden to Bill, who is going to build a house on it. Obviously, this house will be very close to Alexandra's own house, so its appearance and the uses Bill will put it to will have an impact on Alexandra. She therefore wishes to impose conditions on Bill as to his use of the land.

In the transfer of part of her land to him, Alexandra requires Bill to promise the following:

1. To build only one house on the land.

2. To submit the plans of the proposed house to Alexandra for her approval before building.

3. To use the house as a private residence only and not to run any kind of business from the house.

4. To build a wall between his land and Alexandra's retained land, and to keep that wall in good repair.

In this example, Alexandra is using covenants to control what happens to nearby land, because it will have an impact on the enjoyment she gets from her own land and the value of that land. This is a very common use of covenants. Bill, as the person who makes the promises, is known as the **covenantor** and Alexandra, to whom the promises are made, is known as the **covenantee**.

> **covenantor**
> the person making a promise under covenant, who bears its burden— that is, who is bound to carry out the promise

> **covenantee** the person to whom a promise is made under covenant, who has its benefit—that is, who can enforce the promise against the covenantor

Another common use of covenants is where the developer of a housing estate imposes covenants on the purchasers of all of the houses, so that the housing estate maintains a particular character.

 EXAMPLE

Custombuild Ltd builds a small housing estate of private houses called Sunny Grange. The development is set in landscaped grounds and is built to a very high specification.

> Custombuild requires the purchaser of each house to promise the following:
>
> 1. to use the house only as a private dwelling (residential) house;
> 2. not to build any fences in the front garden of the house, so as to preserve the land-scaped design;
> 3. not to erect any satellite dishes or television aerials on the front facade or on parts of the roof that are visible from the road;
> 4. not to make any alterations to the house that affect its appearance from the road;
> 5. to pay a proportionate amount of the cost of upkeep of the private road leading to the houses.

Here, the covenants are intended to maintain the appearance of an estate of expensive houses. Anyone buying one of the houses would need to be aware of the restrictions and should only buy the house if willing to comply with them. In effect, a sort of private land law is being created for this estate, which places obligations on the owners that go beyond the general law. The owners are agreeing to restrict their use of the land and to pay for the private road.

12.2 Enforceability

> **CROSS REFERENCE**
>
> For the meaning of privity of contract, see Chapter 5.

When considering the original parties to a covenant, enforceability is not a problem. The parties have simply entered into a contract with each other. They have privity of contract and that contract can be enforced in the usual way, through a court action seeking either an **injunction** or damages as a remedy.

> **injunction** an order of the court that, in relation to a covenant, will demand that the covenantor comply with its terms

Let us have a think about how this would apply to Alexandra and Bill.

> **EXAMPLE**
>
> If Bill, in the first example, starts to build a house without submitting the plans to Alexandra for approval, she can go to court to get an injunction to stop the building until he carries out his promise.

However, once one or other of the original parties sells the land, things get more complicated.

> **THINKING POINT**
>
> Suppose that Alexandra has sold the land to Bill, who has entered into the agreed covenants. Bill decides not to live on the land and sells it instead to Dave. Would Dave be bound by the covenants entered into by Bill?

From a purely contractual viewpoint, they could not bind Dave, because he did not agree to them: there is no privity of contract between Alexandra and Dave. If Dave were not bound, however, such covenants would be of limited use in practice, because they would be easily destroyed by a sale of the burdened land. Bill and Dave might even hatch a plot to destroy the covenants, with Bill buying the land and agreeing to the covenants, knowing that Dave would buy it from him free of them and then do what he liked on the land.

 THINKING POINT

Alternatively, if Alexandra were to decide to sell her retained land to Edwina before Bill has built his house, could Edwina enforce the covenants against Bill? If not, Edwina may reduce the amount of money she would pay for the house, because she would not be able to stop uses of Bill's land that would annoy her.

What if both pieces of land were sold? Could Edwina enforce the covenants against Dave?

It is clear that contractual rules by themselves are not enough to deal with these questions.

If you think about the second example—that involving Custombuild Ltd, it also reveals problems that can arise after one or more of the original parties to the covenant have moved on.

 THINKING POINT

In our second example, the covenantors are all the purchasers of the houses and the covenantee is Custombuild Ltd.

If one of the purchasers breaches a covenant almost immediately, while houses are still being sold, Custombuild can enforce it through an action for breach of contract.

If, however, a breach happens many years later, Custombuild will have little or no interest in the matter. The company may even have ceased to trade or may be unwilling to act.

What would then happen to the owners of the houses on the estate?

If landowners are going to be able to make lasting agreements to keep a particular neighbourhood looking in a particular way, then it is essential for the law to provide some method of enforcing covenants outside the law of contract.

All of this points to one conclusion: the law of contract by itself is not enough to deal with covenants in land. We need to examine how far covenants can be said to be proprietary interests; interests that are part of the land and which run with it, in the same way that easements, for example, form part of the land.

Have a good look at Figure 12.1. It shows the various different scenarios that can arise and the questions that arise with them.

At the top are the two original parties to the covenant: the covenantee (A), who has the benefit of the covenant, and the covenantor (B), who has made the promise and has the burden of it. The

Figure 12.1 The passing of a covenant

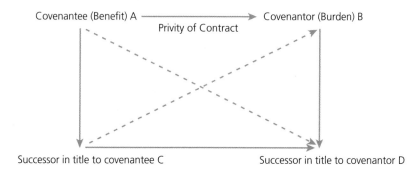

original covenantee can always enforce the covenant against the original covenantor, because there is privity of contract between them.

If the original covenantee's (A's) land changes hands and becomes the property of a successor in title (C), we need to know whether C can enforce the covenant against the original covenantor, B. In order to do this, we need to find out whether the *benefit* of the covenant has passed from A to C, so we need to look at the rules for the passing of the benefit.

Suppose instead that it is the covenantor (B) who disposes of his or her land. In this case, we would need to know whether the covenantee (A) could enforce the covenant against the successor in title of the covenantor (D). This means that the *burden* of the covenant needs to have passed to D, so we need to look at the rules for the passing of the burden.

Finally, imagine that both pieces of land have changed hands. The question now is whether the successor in title of the covenantee (C) can enforce the covenant against the successor in title of the covenantor (D). In other words, we need to know whether *both* the benefit *and* the burden have passed.

 THINKING POINT

When you are considering covenants it is very important to analyse the facts in this way. You need to work out who each party is and exactly what needs to be shown for the covenant to be enforceable. Is it just the passing of the benefit, or just the burden, or both? It is very important to discuss the passing of the benefit and the burden separately.

The rules for the passing of the benefit and burden of covenants unfortunately, are not straightforward. Unlike easements, covenants have not been accepted easily into the category of proprietary rights. One clue to this is the fact that they do not appear in the list of legal interests in land in Law of Property Act 1925 (LPA 1925), s. 1. The law on the passing of the benefit and the burden has developed over many years, and common law and equity have taken different paths. The resulting rules are unsatisfactory and have been the subject of criticism by academics, judges, and the Law Commission, including in its most recent report, *Making Land Work: Easements, Covenants and Profits à Prendre*, Law Com No. 327 (London: The Stationery Office, 2011), discussed at 12.9.

12.3 The original parties to the covenant

As discussed earlier, enforcement between the original covenantor and covenantee is a straight-forward matter of contract law. Complications are caused, however, by LPA 1925, s. 56(1), which extends the scope of persons who may be counted as original covenantees, and the Contracts (Rights of Third Parties) Act 1999 (C(RTP)A 1999), which enables the benefit of a contract to be given to those who are not parties to it.

12.3.1 Law of Property Act 1925, s. 56(1)

 STATUTE

Law of Property Act 1925, s. 56 [Persons taking who are not parties and as to indentures]

(1) A person may take an immediate or other interest in land or other property, or the benefit of any condition, right of entry, covenant or agreement over or respecting land or other property, although he may not be named as a party to the conveyance or other instrument.

...

This statutory provision was the subject of a confusing series of cases, in which it appeared, at one stage, that it had abolished the doctrine of privity of contract altogether. Lord Denning MR, in particular, was very keen to interpret the section as allowing anyone for whom the benefit of a covenant—or indeed, any contract—was made to enforce it.

However, it seems clear that this wide view of LPA 1925, s. 56(1) is incorrect.

CASE CLOSE-UP

***Beswick v. Beswick* [1968] AC 58**

An agreement was made between an uncle and a nephew. The uncle owned a coal business and, when he retired, he agreed to sell his business to his nephew. The nephew agreed to pay a pension to the uncle during his lifetime and, after his death, to his widow.

After the uncle died, the nephew did not pay the pension to the widow as agreed, so she wanted to sue him. Her problem was that she was not a party to the agreement.

In the Court of Appeal, Denning MR and Dankwerts LJ both used LPA 1925, s. 56, among other arguments, to hold that the widow could sue for her pension. The contract was made for her benefit, so, on a wide view of s. 56, the widow could enforce it.

In the House of Lords, however, it was held that she could sue only as the representative of her husband's estate—that is, if she stood in the shoes of her dead husband, who was, of course, a party to the contract. In that capacity, she could ask for a decree of specific performance: an order that the pension must be paid. The House of Lords did not adopt Lord Denning's wide view of s. 56 and two of the Law Lords (Lord Pearce and Lord Upjohn) expressly disapproved it.

It is now generally accepted that LPA 1925, s. 56(1) simply removes the old rule that a person must be expressly referred to by name in the deed of covenant to benefit from it. Those who are to benefit can instead be referred to by some generic, class description, such as 'the owners of Blackacre'—but they must be identifiable and in existence at the date of the covenant, and the covenant must clearly be intended to be made with them.

 EXAMPLE

Fozia owns two adjoining houses: The Laurels and The Beeches. In 1998, she sells The Beeches to Goumesh, who covenants *'with and for the benefit of Fozia, her successors in title, and the owners for the time being of the land adjoining The Beeches'* not to use the house for the purposes of running a business.

Harjot owns The Oaks, which adjoins The Beeches, at the date of the covenant. She will be able to take the benefit of the covenant under LPA 1925, s. 56(1), because, although she is not named in the covenant, she is an owner for the time being of land adjoining The Beeches, and she is identifiable and in existence at the date of the covenant.

But Fozia's successors in title—for example, Izzie in Figure 12.2—cannot use s. 56(1) to enable them to enforce the covenant, because they are not yet in existence and identifiable at the date of the covenant.

Figure 12.2 The covenant on The Beeches and The Laurels under the Law of Property Act 1925 only

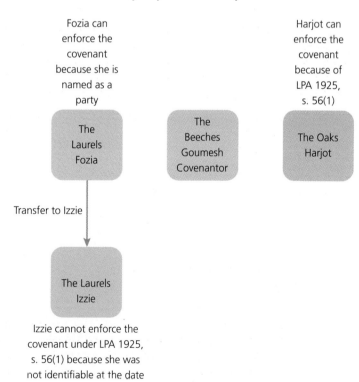

This view of LPA 1925, s. 56(1) is supported by the decisions in *White v. Bijou Mansions* [1937] Ch 610 and *Amsprop Trading v. Harris Distribution* [1997] 1 WLR 1025.

12.3.2 The Contracts (Rights of Third Parties) Act 1999

The Contracts (Rights of Third Parties) Act 1999 (C(RTP)A 1999) applies to all contracts made after 11 May 2000.

STATUTE

Contracts (Rights of Third Parties) Act 1999, s. 1 [Right of third party to enforce contractual term]

(1) Subject to the provisions of this Act, a person who is not a party to a contract (a 'third party') may in his own right enforce a term of the contract if—

   (a) the contract expressly provides that he may, or

   (b) subject to subsection (2), the term purports to confer a benefit on him.

(2) Subsection (1)(b) does not apply if on a proper construction of the contract it appears that the parties did not intend the term to be enforceable by the third party.

(3) The third party must be expressly identified in the contract by name, as a member of a class or as answering a particular description but need not be in existence when the contract is entered into.

…

C(RTP)A 1999, s. 1(1) gets rid of the problems caused by having to distinguish between a party *for whose benefit* a contract or covenant is made—such as the widow in *Beswick v. Beswick* (see 12.3.1)—and a person *with whom* a contract is made—such as Harjot in the previous example. Both will be able to enforce the contract in their own right, unless it appears that the parties did not intend the contract to be enforceable by them—C(RTP)A 1999, s. 1(2).

C(RTP)A 1999, s. 1(3) means that people in Izzie's position in the previous example will be able to enforce the covenant in their own right, because such a person does not need to be in existence at the time the contract is made.

This Act will therefore allow any person for whose benefit the covenant is made, including successors in title, to enforce it.

EXAMPLE

Imagine that the facts are the same as in the last example, but that the covenant was entered into on 12 May 2000.

Now, Fozia, Harjot, Izzie, and Jill can all enforce the covenant against Goumesh, because they are all people on whom the term (in this case, covenant) purports to confer a benefit under C(RTP)A 1999, s. 1(1). It does not matter that neither Izzie nor Jill was identifiable at the date of the covenant, because s. 1(3) states that they need not be in existence when the contract is entered into (see Figure 12.3).

Figure 12.3 The covenant on The Beeches and The Laurels under the Law of Property Act 1925 and the Contracts (Rights of Third Parties) Act 1999

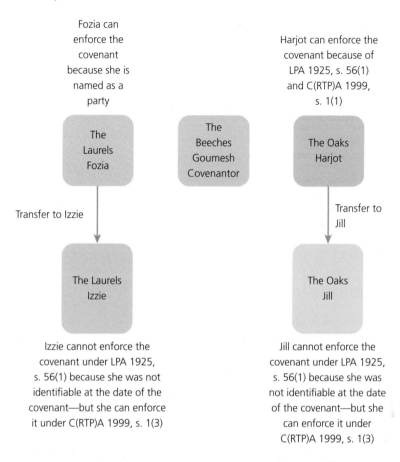

Fozia can enforce the covenant because she is named as a party

Harjot can enforce the covenant because of LPA 1925, s. 56(1) and C(RTP)A 1999, s. 1(1)

The Laurels
Fozia

The Beeches
Goumesh
Covenantor

The Oaks
Harjot

Transfer to Izzie

Transfer to Jill

The Laurels
Izzie

The Oaks
Jill

Izzie cannot enforce the covenant under LPA 1925, s. 56(1) because she was not identifiable at the date of the covenant—but she can enforce it under C(RTP)A 1999, s. 1(3)

Jill cannot enforce the covenant under LPA 1925, s. 56(1) because she was not identifiable at the date of the covenant—but she can enforce it under C(RTP)A 1999, s. 1(3)

You might think that the C(RTP)A 1999 means that there is no longer any need to worry about covenants surviving a change in the ownership of the land in question—but this is not true for two reasons. Firstly, the Act applies only to recent covenants. Lots of covenants were entered into before 11 May 2000 and the Act does not apply to them.

Secondly, the Act applies only to the benefit of the covenant, not the burden. Unfortunately, therefore, it is still important to understand the rules on the passing of the benefit and the burden of covenants.

12.4 The common law rules for passing of the benefit and burden of a covenant

The passing of the *benefit* will need to be considered whenever there is a change in ownership of the covenantee's land. The passing of the *burden* will need to be considered whenever there is a change in ownership of the covenantor's land.

THINKING POINT

Before you start reading, have another quick look at Figure 12.1.

We are now going to look at the first scenario, the transfer of the land to C and whether C can enforce the covenant against B.

There are two sets of rules to be considered, because common law and equity took different views on how far covenants should be enforceable by those other than the original parties. Once we have considered both sets of rules, we need to establish which set of rules to apply in any given situation.

12.4.1 The passing of the benefit at common law

The rules relating to when the benefit of a covenant will pass at common law are very old and can be summed up as follows.

The benefit of a covenant will pass to successors in title of the covenantee at common law if all four of the following conditions are met:

1. The covenant 'touches and concerns' land of the covenantee.

2. At the time when the covenant was made, it was intended that the benefit should run with the land to the covenantee's successors in title.

3. At the time the covenant was made, the covenantee held a legal estate in the land to be benefited.

4. The successor in title derives his or her title from, or under, the original covenantee.

An example of the application of these rules can be seen in the case of *Smith and Snipes Hall Farm Ltd v. River Douglas Catchment Board* [1949] 2 All ER 179.

CASE CLOSE-UP

Smith and Snipes Hall Farm Ltd v. River Douglas Catchment Board [1949] 2 All ER 179

The covenantor was the River Douglas Catchment Board, which had covenanted with a number of landowners (the covenantees) to maintain the banks of the Eller Brook, so as to prevent it from flooding their land.

The first claimant, Smith, was a successor in title to one of the original covenantees and he had granted a lease of the land to the second claimants, Snipes Hall Farm Ltd. The land in question was flooded on a number of occasions, until a major flood led the claimants to bring an action against the Board for breach of the covenant to keep the banks in repair. Because neither were the original covenantees, it had to be decided whether either, or both, of them had the benefit of the covenant.

In deciding this question, Tucker LJ said that it was necessary firstly to establish that the covenant touched and concerned the land. This meant that either it had to affect how the land could be occupied (mode of occupation) or it must directly affect the value of the land. Secondly, it had to be shown that the parties intended the covenant to run with the land and benefit future owners.

He decided that these tests were met, because the covenant was to prevent future flooding (so it affected the value of the land, by converting it from flooded meadow to agricultural land) and the works were to be maintained for all time, which indicated the intention of the parties that the benefit should pass to successors in title.

Tucker LJ then considered whether it was necessary for the covenantor to be a landowner. He quoted both from *The Prior's Case* (1368) and from *Rogers v. Hosegood* [1900] 2 Ch 395, and decided that the covenantor did not need to be a landowner. The defendant Board, in this case, did not own land burdened by the covenant, but this did not affect the running of the benefit at common law.

He also considered whether it was necessary that the benefited land should be identifiable and decided that it must be, although evidence beyond the deed itself could be brought to show what lands were intended to benefit.

Because both the claimants had legal estates in the land derived from the original covenantee (see the discussion of LPA 1925, s. 78(1), at 12.4.1.4), and the benefit had passed to them at common law under the other rules, they were able to sue in respect of the covenant and received damages for its breach.

This case provides a good overview of the common law on the passing of the benefit, but it is necessary to examine each of the rules in turn.

12.4.1.1 The covenant 'touches and concerns' land of the covenantee

The condition that the covenant must 'touch and concern' the land of the covenantee means that the covenant must not be a personal one, but must have something to do with the use of the land.

The tests of whether a covenant touches and concerns the land are said to be as follows:

1. The covenant is only of benefit to the person who owns the estate in the land; if it is separated from the land, it is of no more use to the covenantee.

2. The covenant affects the nature or quality of the land, how it can be used, or the value of the land of the estate owner.

3. The covenant is not expressed to be personal: it is not a promise made to a specific person.

These tests are taken from the decision of Lord Oliver of Aylmerton in the case of *P & A Swift Investments v. Combined English Store Groups* [1989] AC 632, 642.

The sorts of covenant that have been held to touch and concern land include:

- to use the property as a private dwelling house only;
- to do repairs on the land;
- not to build on the land.

> **CROSS REFERENCE**
>
> For more on the rules relating to easements, see Chapter 11.

It is impossible, however, to create a complete list of covenants touching and concerning land; instead, the facts must be looked at in each case. It is rather like the rule that an easement must accommodate the dominant tenement.

Note that it is only the land of the covenantee that need be affected by the covenant; it is not necessary for the covenantor to own any land at all in order for this requirement to be met. This was established in *The Prior's Case* (1368) and is illustrated by the decision in *Smith and Snipes Hall Farm Ltd v. River Douglas Catchment Board*, discussed at 12.4.1.

12.4.1.2 At the time when the covenant was made, it was intended that the benefit should run with the land to the covenantee's successors in title

As in *Smith and Snipes Hall Farm Ltd v. River Douglas Catchment Board*, it is necessary to show that the parties intended the benefit of the covenant to run with the land. In that case, the fact that the covenant was to prevent future flooding indicated that the parties intended the benefit to pass to successors in title to the original covenantees.

It is possible, however, for the intention to benefit future owners to be implied into covenants made after 1925, because of LPA 1925, s. 78(1).

 STATUTE

Law of Property Act 1925, s. 78 [Benefit of covenants relating to land]

A covenant relating to any land of the covenantee shall be deemed to be made with the covenantee and his successors in title and the persons deriving title under him or them, and shall have effect as if such successors and other persons were expressed.

For the purposes of this subsection in connexion with covenants restrictive of the user of land 'successors in title' shall be deemed to include the owners and occupiers for the time being of the land of the covenantee intended to be benefited.

...

This section means that covenants relating to land are deemed (assumed) to be made not only with the covenantee, but with his or her successors in title—thus indicating an intention that the covenant runs with the land. The effects of this section will be discussed in greater detail when considering the equitable rules for the passing of the benefit (see 12.5).

12.4.1.3 At the time the covenant was made, the covenantee held a legal estate in the land to be benefited

It is clear that the benefit of a covenant can run at common law only if the covenantee held a legal estate in the land: *Webb v. Russell* (1789) 3 TR 393. So, if the covenantee had only an equitable interest in the land, such as an equitable lease, only the equitable rules as to the passing of the benefit can be used.

12.4.1.4 The successor in title derives his or her title from, or under, the original covenantee

The successor in title to the original covenantee who wishes to show that the benefit of a covenant has passed at common law must show that he or she also has a legal estate in the land which can be traced back to the original covenantee.

It is thought that the common law originally required the successor to take the same legal estate in land as the covenantee—so that a tenant under a legal lease would not be able to take the benefit of a covenant made for the benefit of the freehold estate out of which the lease was granted. This rule has been changed by LPA 1925, s. 78, which allows a successor in title with any legal estate derived from the covenantee's estate to take the benefit. Therefore, in *Smith and Snipes Hall Farm Ltd v. River Douglas Catchment Board*, both the freehold successor in title (Smith) and the legal lessee (Snipes Hall Farm Ltd) were able to take the benefit of the covenant.

It is also clear that the benefit of the covenant attaches to each and every part of the covenantee's land, so that, if the land is later subdivided into more than one plot of land, any successor in title—that is, anyone owning any of those smaller plots—can enforce the covenant. This was held in the case of *Federated Homes v. Mill Lodge Properties* [1980] 1 All ER 371, which is discussed in more detail at 12.5.1.1.

 EXAMPLE

Look back at the first of our 'Fozia' examples (Figure 12.2).

In that example, Fozia is the original covenantee and Goumesh is the original covenantor.

Suppose that Fozia later divides The Laurels into two flats. She leases one flat to Kevin and the other to Laura. Both Kevin and Laura, who have legal leases in parts of the land owned by the original covenantee, will be able to enforce the covenant against Goumesh:

- the covenant touches and concerns Fozia's land;
- there is an intention to benefit successors in title, because they are mentioned in the covenant;
- Fozia had a legal estate in the land at the time of the covenant;
- Kevin and Laura have legal estates in that land derived from Fozia's estate.

It does not matter that their estates are not the same as Fozia's, nor that the land has been divided between them, because of LPA 1925, s. 78(1) (see Figure 12.4).

Figure 12.4 The benefit of the covenant on The Beeches and The Laurels under the common law

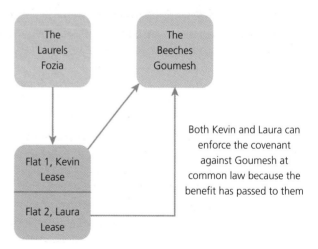

Both Kevin and Laura can enforce the covenant against Goumesh at common law because the benefit has passed to them

12.4.1.5 **Assignment of the benefit of a covenant at common law**

The benefit of a covenant may also be expressly assigned (transferred) at common law, as long as it is not a personal covenant. Assignment must be in writing and notice must be given to the covenantor—LPA 1925, s. 136.

EXAMPLE

Fozia might expressly assign the benefit of Goumesh's covenant to Izzie.

She would not, however, use assignment to pass the benefit to Kevin and Laura, because she would not then be able to sue on the covenant herself, despite retaining a freehold interest in the land. Once the benefit has been assigned at common law, the original covenantee can no longer sue on it.

12.4.2 The passing of the burden at common law

THINKING POINT

Look back at Figure 12.1.

We are now thinking about the transfer of the land from B to D, and whether A can enforce the covenant against D.

The common law rule about the passing of the burden of a covenant to a successor in title of the covenantor is perhaps the simplest rule of all—but it is also the most unhelpful: the burden of a covenant does not pass at common law, so successors in title cannot enforce it.

CASE CLOSE-UP

Austerberry v. Corporation of Oldham (1885) 29 Ch D 750

This is the leading case on the running of covenants at common law, and concerned a covenant to repair a road. The defendant Corporation had acquired the road from a previous owner, who had covenanted to keep it in good repair. The plaintiff, who claimed the benefit of that covenant, tried to enforce it against the Corporation. This meant that he had to show that the burden of the covenant had passed to the Corporation.

It was held that the burden of such a covenant could not run with the land. As Lindley LJ said (at 781):

> A mere covenant to repair, or to do something of that kind, does not seem to me, I confess, to run with the land in such a way as to bind those who may acquire it.

It is clear from this case that a covenant does not create an interest in land at common law—it is not like an easement. It therefore does not run with the land at common law.

Although a very old case, this remains good law today. It is not possible for the burden of a covenant to pass at common law. The rule in *Austerberry v. Corporation of Oldham* was confirmed in more recent times in the case of *Rhone v. Stephens* [1994] 2 AC 310. As Lord Templeman said in this case (at 317): '*the benefit of a covenant may run with the land at law but not the burden: see the Austerberry case*'.

So, if the covenantor's land has been transferred to a successor in title, the common law does not allow an action to be brought against that person, because he or she is not a party to the contract. Therefore, if the burden is to pass at all, it must pass in equity only.

12.5 The equitable rules for the passing of the benefit and the burden

CROSS REFERENCE

For a reminder of the differences between common law and equity in land law, see Chapter 2.

Because the common law did not permit the burden of a covenant to pass, equity came to supplement the law by allowing certain burdens to pass and by providing different rules for the passing of the benefit. For reasons that we will see later, however, equity generally did not concern itself with **positive covenants**, but only with **restrictive covenants**.

> **positive covenant** a covenant that requires the covenantor to do something—particularly something that requires the spending of money
>
> **restrictive covenant** a covenant that is negative in nature—that is, it restricts the use of the burdened land

A good way to think about the differences between positive and restrictive covenants is to look back at our very first example.

→ EXAMPLE

Consider the covenants entered into by Bill with Alexandra in the first example:

1. to build only one house on the land;
2. to submit the plans of the proposed house to Alexandra for her approval before building;
3. to use the house as a private residence only and not to run any kind of business from the house;
4. to build a wall between his land and Alexandra's retained land, and to keep that wall in good repair.

Which of these are restrictive covenants?

It might be thought that, because they are all expressed in positive terms—that is, 'to do' something, rather than 'not to do' something—that they are all positive. In fact, only covenant 4 is positive; the rest are restrictive. The test is whether it will cost money to carry out the covenant:

Covenant 1, despite its wording, restricts Bill from building more than one house on his land. It does not oblige him actually to build a house if he does not want to.

Similarly, covenant 2 restricts him from building without Alexandra's approval of the plans. If he does not build at all, he need not show her any plans.

Covenant 3 restricts his use of the house—he may not carry out any business there.

Covenant 4, on the other hand, is positive, because it obliges Bill to spend money on building and maintaining a wall. Covenant 4 would not be enforceable in equity.

It might be wondered why equity concerns itself only with restrictive covenants. This point was considered in *Rhone v. Stephens*, which confirmed the common law rule that the burden of covenants does not pass at common law.

 CASE CLOSE-UP

Rhone v. Stephens [1994] 2 AC 310

The covenant in question was to maintain a shared roof. This is clearly a positive covenant, because it requires the expenditure of money. The covenant could neither be enforced at common law against a successor in title to the original covenantor (see 12.4.2), nor could it be enforced in equity, because it was positive rather than restrictive.

Lord Templeman said that restrictive covenants, unlike positive covenants, do not impose an additional burden on the landowner. Restrictive covenants simply cut down the rights that the successor in title received when they acquired the land. In other words, the successor in title receives the land minus a particular right, such as the right to build on it.

Lord Templeman also explained that it was not possible for this rule to be changed except by legislation, because it would disturb property rights entered into on the basis of settled law.

Although there does not appear to be any actual rule that the benefit of positive covenants cannot pass in equity, there is certainly a rule that the burden of positive covenants can never pass. In practice, positive covenants are dealt with under the common law rules and restrictive ones under the equitable rules.

12.5.1 **The passing of the benefit in equity**

 THINKING POINT

Look back at Figure 12.1.

We are again thinking about the covenant passing from A to C.

According to *Renals v. Cowlishaw* (1878) 9 Ch D 125, 129, the benefit of a covenant will pass in equity if:

- the covenant touches and concerns land of the covenantee; and
- the benefit of the covenant was:
  - annexed to the land of the covenantee; or
  - expressly assigned to the successor in title; or
  - the land in question is part of a building scheme.

We have already looked at the requirement that the covenant must touch and concern the land of the covenantee when considering the common law rules (see 12.4.1.1), and it has the same meaning here. We do, however, need to look closely at the three possible ways in which the covenant could have been passed to a successor in title of the covenantee.

12.5.1.1 Annexation

> **annexation**
>
> the permanent attachment of the benefit of a covenant to the land of the covenantee, so that it passes with the land whenever it is transferred

Annexation means the permanent attachment of the covenant to the land of the covenantee—that is, the permanent 'fixing' or 'nailing' of the covenant to the land of the covenantee. Wherever the land goes, the covenant goes with it. If annexation can be successfully proven, then the benefit of the covenant will pass to any successor in title.

There are three types of annexation:

- express annexation;
- implied annexation;
- statutory annexation.

Express annexation

Express annexation occurs when the following conditions are met:

- the covenant indicates an intention that the benefit should become annexed to the land, so that it runs with the land; and
- the land for which the benefit of the covenant is made is identified or capable of identification; and
- either:
    - the covenant is for the benefit of the whole of the covenantee's land and the whole of that land has been assigned to the successors in title; or
    - the covenant is intended to be for the benefit of each and every part of the covenantee's land, and the covenant, in this case, is annexed to the part it actually benefits.

Firstly, the covenant must show by express wording an intention that the benefit should become annexed. Essentially, the wording of the covenant must show that the covenant is for the benefit of the land, not only for the owners in a personal capacity.

🔍 CASE CLOSE-UP

Rogers v. Hosegood [1900] 2 Ch 388

A covenant entered into by a purchaser of land that '*may enure to the benefit of* [the covenantees] *their heirs and assigns and others claiming under them to all or any of their lands adjoining or near to the* [burdened land]' was held to be annexed to the land of the covenantees.

The mention of the '*lands adjoining or near*' was important, as other cases show.

🔍 CASE CLOSE-UP

Renals v. Cowlishaw (1878) 9 Ch D 125, affirmed (1879) 11 Ch D 866

In this covenant, there was no mention of the lands of the covenantee and this was held to make annexation impossible.

This raises the second requirement for annexation, which is that the land must be identified or capable of identification. In this case, the land to be benefited was not identified and could not be identified. The court must be able to tell which lands benefit from the covenant.

If the benefited land is a small area, there is no problem with the covenant being annexed to the whole of the land, but if it is a large area of land—perhaps intended to be split into smaller lots in future—equity was initially reluctant to find that the benefit had been annexed to the whole of the benefited land—*Re Ballard's Conveyance* [1932] Ch 473.

These difficulties can be avoided if the covenant is expressed to be annexed to 'each and every part of' the benefited land. In that case, if the land is later split up, the benefit passes with any part of the land that it actually benefits—that is, any part of the land that will be affected by a breach of the covenant.

 CASE CLOSE-UP

Marquess of Zetland v. Driver [1939] Ch 1

The claimant's predecessor in title (the vendor) had sold a property to the defendant's predecessor in title (the purchaser). The purchaser entered into a covenant, which provided that:

> no act or thing shall be done or permitted thereon which in the opinion of the vendor may be a public or private nuisance or prejudicial or detrimental to the vendor and the owners or occupiers of any adjoining property or to the neighbourhood.

The covenant was expressed to be for:

> the benefit and protection of such part or parts of the [vendor's] land as should for the time being remain unsold or as should have been sold by the vendor or his successors in title with the express benefit of the covenants.

'*Vendor*' was defined so as to include successors in title to the original vendor.

The defendant, a successor in title to the covenantor, opened a fish-and-chip shop on the premises. The claimant—who owned much of the land originally owned by the vendor, including some in the immediate neighbourhood of the shop—objected to this, claiming that it was a nuisance and prejudicial to the neighbourhood.

The question arose as to whether the covenant was annexed to the retained land, especially because some of it was too far away to benefit from the covenant. The Court of Appeal was, however, able to distinguish the decision in *Re Ballard's Conveyance*, because, as Farwell J stated (at 10), when giving the judgment of the Court:

> in that case the covenant was expressed to run with the whole estate, whereas in the present case no such difficulty arises because the covenant is expressed to be for the benefit of the whole or any part or parts of the unsold settled property.

Because the claimant still owned land near to the shop, that land had the benefit of the covenant. The claimant was therefore able to enforce the covenant: the running of a fish-and-chip shop was found to be in breach of it and the shop had to close (see Figure 12.5).

Figure 12.5 A summary of the covenant in *Marquess of Zetland v. Driver*

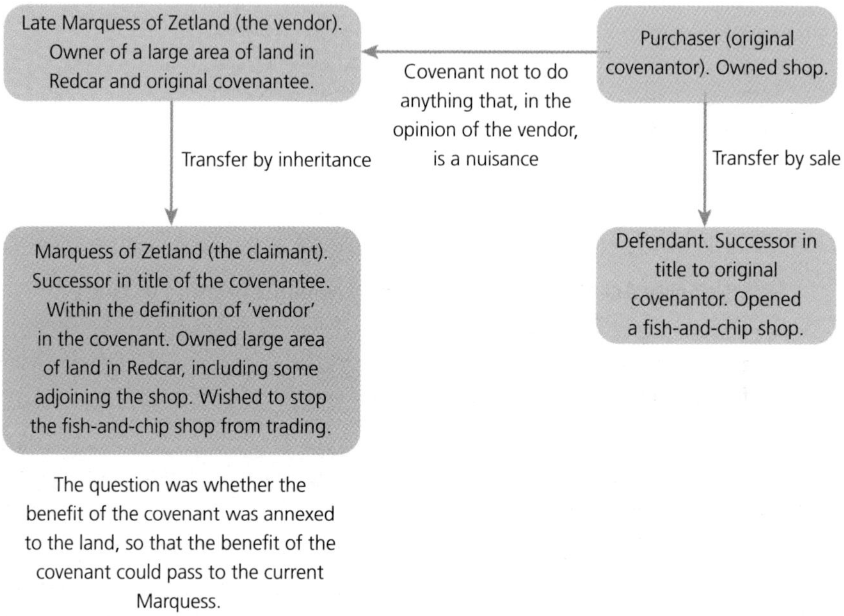

Late Marquess of Zetland (the vendor). Owner of a large area of land in Redcar and original covenantee.

Purchaser (original covenantor). Owned shop.

Covenant not to do anything that, in the opinion of the vendor, is a nuisance

Transfer by inheritance

Transfer by sale

Marquess of Zetland (the claimant). Successor in title of the covenantee. Within the definition of 'vendor' in the covenant. Owned large area of land in Redcar, including some adjoining the shop. Wished to stop the fish-and-chip shop from trading.

Defendant. Successor in title to original covenantor. Opened a fish-and-chip shop.

The question was whether the benefit of the covenant was annexed to the land, so that the benefit of the covenant could pass to the current Marquess.

After this case, most covenants contained references to 'each and every part' of the covenantee's land—but there was always the chance that someone might forget and that the benefit would not be annexed.

This is less likely after the decision in *Federated Homes v. Mill Lodge Properties*. In that case, it was suggested that LPA 1925, s. 78(1) (see later) meant that, once the benefit of a covenant was held to be annexed to the land, it was assumed to be annexed to each and every part unless the contrary were expressed.

Implied annexation

It has been established that annexation may be implied in circumstances under which it can be established that by reason of the circumstances surrounding it, the covenant must have been intended to benefit a defined piece of land.

CASE CLOSE-UP

Marten v. Flight Refuelling Ltd [1962] Ch 115

A covenant was entered into between the claimant's predecessor in title and the Air Ministry, which had compulsorily purchased the land, subject to a covenant against use as anything other than agricultural land.

After the war, the Air Ministry allowed a commercial company (Flight Refuelling) to occupy the land. The claimant sought a declaration that she had the benefit of the covenant and was entitled to enforce it.

It was held that the covenant had been intended to be for the benefit of the land. The claimant's estate was a single agricultural unit and she had inherited the whole of it. It was clear from the circumstances and the nature of the covenant that it was intended to be annexed, despite there being no clear words of annexation.

Cases of implied annexation are likely to be rare, because the court is unlikely to find an implied intention to benefit the land unless the circumstances are very clear.

Statutory annexation

The statute in question here is LPA 1925, s. 78(1), at which we looked at 12.4.1.2 in the context of the passing of the benefit at common law.

STATUTE

Law of Property Act 1925, s. 78 [Benefit of covenants relating to land]

A covenant relating to any land of the covenantee shall be deemed to be made with the covenantee and his successors in title and the persons deriving title under him or them, and shall have effect as if such successors and other persons were expressed.

For the purposes of this subsection in connexion with covenants restrictive of the user of land 'successors in title' shall be deemed to include the owners and occupiers for the time being of the land of the covenantee intended to be benefited.

We have already seen some of the effects of this section, but the case of *Federated Homes v. Mill Lodge Properties*, which we have also met before, interpreted s. 78 in such a wide way as to effect a statutory annexation of the benefit of any restrictive covenant made to the land after 1925.

CASE CLOSE-UP

Federated Homes v. Mill Lodge Properties [1980] 1 All ER 371

This case concerned three areas of land conveniently called the 'red', 'blue', and 'green' land.

All three areas were originally owned by M Ltd, which had obtained planning permission to develop them for housing at a certain density (number of houses per acre). M Ltd transferred the blue land to the defendants, who covenanted with them not to develop the land above 300 houses. The expressed purpose of the covenant was to protect the ability of M Ltd to build as many houses as it wished on the other land, because the density of housing was limited by the planning permission.

M Ltd sold the red and the green land to others. The transfers of the green land contained express assignments of the benefit of the covenant. The transfer of the red land to the claimant, however, did not assign the benefit of the covenant. The defendants planned to build more than 300 houses on the blue land, so the claimant brought an action under the covenant to stop them.

At first instance, it was held that the benefit of the covenant was neither expressly nor impliedly annexed to the land and that, because it had not been assigned, the benefit had not passed.

The Court of Appeal disagreed, however. It held that LPA 1925, s. 78 operated to annex the benefit of the covenant to the red land. A covenant that touches and concerns the land of the covenantee runs with the land for the benefit of successors in title, persons deriving title under the covenantee, and other owners and occupiers.

This is a very wide interpretation. It effectively means that the benefit of any restrictive covenant is annexed to the covenantee's benefited land, provided that the covenant is one that touches and concerns the land.

This interpretation of LPA 1925, s. 78 was highly controversial at the time and still raises some eyebrows. For one thing, it seems surprising that, if s. 78 had such a far-reaching effect, it took the courts over forty-five years to reach that conclusion about a provision enacted in 1925. It is also worth remembering that this is a decision of the Court of Appeal and so could yet be overruled by a Supreme Court decision. The Supreme Court has not yet been asked to consider the point.

Since 1980, a number of other cases have limited the very wide scope of LPA 1925, s. 78, as interpreted in *Federated Homes*. Firstly, in *Roake v. Chadha* [1984] 1 WLR 40, it was held that s. 78 would not annex the benefit of a covenant that is expressed to be personal. The covenant in that case was expressly stated not to pass to a subsequent purchaser unless expressly assigned.

More recently, the Court of Appeal considered LPA 1925, s. 78, again in *Crest Nicholson v. McAllister* [2004] EWCA Civ 410.

CASE CLOSE-UP

Crest Nicholson v. McAllister [2004] EWCA Civ 410

Land bordering Claygate Common in Surrey was sold off by a common vendor under a number of separate conveyances, called in court the '*Arthur conveyances*', the '*Humphreys conveyances*', the '*Roberts conveyances*', and the '*Wing conveyances*'. All of the relevant conveyances contained covenants restricting the use of the land to that of a private dwelling house and requiring the consent of the vendor to plans for building.

The Humphreys conveyances and one of the Roberts conveyances contained express words of annexation: '*[f]or the benefit of the property at Claygate aforesaid belonging to the Vendors or the part thereof for the time being remaining unsold*'. The Arthur conveyances and the other Roberts conveyance contained no express words of annexation, but did refer to the land being conveyed as being part of the '*Fee Farm Estate at Claygate*'.

In 2000, Crest Nicholson was seeking to buy the land conveyed by the Arthur, Humphreys, and Roberts conveyances in order to build a housing estate. The owner of the land originally conveyed by the Wing conveyances wanted to prevent the development. Whether she could do so depended on whether the benefit of the covenants in the Arthur, Humphreys, and Roberts conveyances was annexed to the land in the Wing conveyances.

The leading judgment was given by Chadwick LJ. He considered LPA 1925, s. 78, and its interpretation in *Federated Homes*.

Firstly, he identified one question left unanswered by the decision: whether it is still necessary, after *Federated Homes*, to show that the land to which the benefit is to be annexed is clearly identifiable.

Chadwick LJ referred to *Marquess of Zetland v. Driver* and held that this rule of annexation had not been removed by *Federated Homes*. Applying that rule to this case, the benefit of the covenants in the Arthur conveyances and one of the Humphreys conveyances was not annexed, because the land comprising the '*Fee Farm Estate*' was not sufficiently identified.

Secondly, Chadwick LJ approved the reasoning in *Roake v. Chadha*, finding that the covenants in the other Humphreys conveyance and the Roberts conveyances were intended to be personal in nature, and were therefore not annexed to the land (see Figure 12.6).

Figure 12.6 A summary of the covenant in *Crest Nicholson v. McAllister*

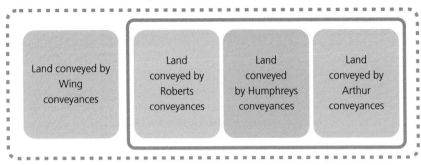

Land originally conveyed by common vendor

Land bought by Crest Nicholson for development

The question was whether the land in the Wing conveyances had the benefit of covenants given by the original purchaser of land in the Roberts, Humphreys, and Arthur conveyances to the common vendor— that is, was the benefit annexed to the Wing land?

It is clear from this case that covenants which, on their construction, are intended to be personal will not be annexed. It is also the case that the land intended to be benefited must be identified clearly in the covenant: if not, there can be no annexation. This is because the covenantor (and any successor in title of the burdened land) needs to be able to identify those who are likely to be able to enforce the covenant, especially after some time has elapsed from the date of the covenant.

The decision in *Crest Nicholson* has been applied in a number of High Court decisions. In *Sugarman v. Porter* [2006] EWHC 331 (Ch) the covenant was clearly intended to allow a covenantee selling land off in lots to retain control until the last lot was sold. It was held that this covenant was personal to the original covenantee and was not annexed by LPA 1925, s. 78(1).

A similar decision was reached in *Norwich City College v. McQuillan* [2009] EWHC 1496 (Ch), in relation to land which was gradually being sold off for development. However, everything depends upon the exact wording used.

> ## 🔍 CASE CLOSE-UP
>
> ### *Rees v. Peters* [2011] EWCA Civ 836
>
> The vendor owned an area of land which she divided into two parts which were known as Farne Court and Court Barn. She sold Farne Court, and entered into a covenant '*with the Purchasers and their successors in title … for the benefit of the property hereby conveyed, or the part thereof for the time being remaining unsold, and every part thereof …*', not to build on a particular part of the retained land without the consent of the purchasers.

In 1990 Court Barn was sold to the respondent (Peters), who was registered as proprietor. There was no mention of the covenants in the charges register, but Peters had actual notice of the covenants. Farne Court was sold a number of times, and each time the benefit of the covenants was assigned. In 2003 the appellants (Rees) were registered as the owners of Farne Court.

The court had to decide whether the benefit of the covenants was annexed to Farne Court, and whether the register should be rectified to add the covenants to the charges register of Court Barn. It was held that the wording indicated that the covenants were annexed to Farne Court. The reference to *'the part thereof for the time being remaining unsold'* was not intended to prevent annexation of the covenants to the land as a whole, only to prevent parts of Farne Court sold off later from claiming the benefit. It was also held that the covenants should be added to the charges register of Court Barn.

This case makes it very clear that whether a covenant is personal or not is a matter of construction of the exact words used in that particular document. If it is personal, LPA 1925, s. 78(1) is not relevant.

🔍 CASE CLOSE-UP

Holland Park (Management) Ltd v. Hicks [2013] EWHC 391 (Ch)

The claimants were a management company who owned the freehold of a block of flats, and the lessees were co-claimants. They argued that they had the benefit of a covenant requiring the consent of the covenantee to any plans submitted for planning permission. (The covenant had originally been entered into by a Brigadier Radford and a Miss De Froberville, and the two pieces of land involved are the same as in the case of *Radford v. De Froberville* [1977] 1 WLR 1262, which you may remember from studying contract law!) The covenants had been entered into by Miss De Froberville *'so as to bind the land hereby transferred and to benefit the vendor's property'*, and the parties were described with reference to their executors, administrators, and assigns.

It was held that there was nothing in the wording to exclude the operation of LPA 1925, s. 78(1). On the contrary, the wording clearly indicated that they were covenanting as land owners. The land to be benefited was also clearly identifiable from the documents. Therefore, the claimants, including the lessees, had the benefit of the covenants.

The construction of the exact words of the covenant is, therefore, still important after *Federated Homes*, and it may be that LPA 1925, s. 78(1) can be seen as shifting the burden of proof—it is for the covenantor to show that annexation was *not* intended.

Figure 12.7 summarizes how to determine whether or not a restrictive covenant has been annexed.

12.5.1.2 Assignment

assignment
the transfer of the benefit of a covenant to a particular person

assignor
the person assigning the covenant

assignee
the person receiving the benefit of the covenant by assignment

Assignment means the transfer of the benefit of a covenant by one person (the **assignor**) to another particular person (the **assignee**). This occurs at the time at which the land is transferred to that person. There are many differences between assignment and annexation:

- Annexation attaches the benefit to land, whereas assignment transfers it to a certain person.
- Annexation happens at the time at which the covenant is entered into, whereas assignment happens at the time the land is transferred, which may be many years after the covenant is entered into.
- Once a covenant is annexed to land, it passes with every transfer of the land; assignments must occur each time the land is transferred—and if the chain of covenants is broken, the benefit is lost.

Figure 12.7   A summary of the annexation of a covenant

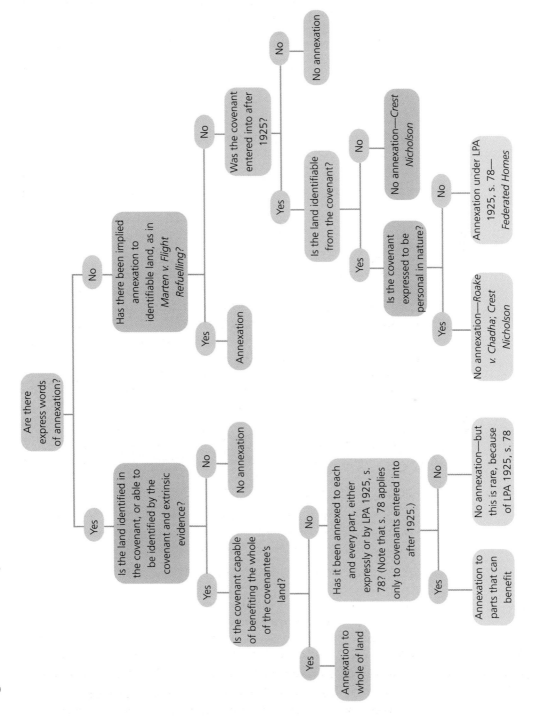

In equity, it is possible for the benefit to be assigned to owners of part of the benefited land only and there may consequently be several assignees. For example, in *Sugarman v. Porter* (see 12.5.1.1), the covenantee might have assigned the benefit of the covenant to the purchasers of each part of her land sold off had she wished to do so.

The three conditions that must be met for an assignee to take the benefit of a restrictive covenant in equity are found in the case of *Miles v. Easter* [1933] Ch 611 (also known as *Re Union of London and Smith's Bank Ltd's Conveyance*):

1. The covenant must have been taken for the benefit of land owned by the covenantee at the date of the covenant.

2. It must be possible to identify the benefited land.

3. The assignment must happen at the same time as the transfer of the land.

 EXAMPLE

Muman, who owns a house called The Briars, has the benefit of a restrictive covenant with Neta, who has promised that she will build only one dwelling house on her adjoining land, The Brambles.

The covenant is not annexed to Muman's land, because it states that the benefit is not to pass without express assignment. When Muman sells The Briars to Owen, he assigns the benefit of the covenant to him. This will mean that Owen can enforce the covenant against Neta, as long as all of the conditions in *Miles v. Easter* are met:

- the covenant must have been taken for the benefit of Muman's land (The Briars);
- the benefited land must be identified and the assignment take place at the same time as the transfer of the land to Owen.

It appears that these requirements are met, so Owen can enforce the covenant.

Suppose that Owen later transfers The Briars to Polly. He forgets to assign the covenant. Polly cannot enforce the covenant and Owen cannot later rectify his mistake, because, once he has parted with the land, he is no longer able to assign the benefit. The 'chain of assignments' has been broken.

If we suppose instead that Owen splits The Briars into two flats, he can then assign the benefit of the covenant to each of the two new owners, because it possible to assign the benefit to part of the benefited land.

12.5.1.3 Building schemes

The third way in which the benefit of a covenant can pass in equity is if the court finds the existence of a **building scheme** or a 'scheme of development'. The idea of a building scheme is most easily explained by thinking back to an example given earlier on in this chapter (reproduced here for your convenience).

building scheme a defined area of land sold by a single vendor in plots that are subject to restrictive covenants intended to benefit the whole

EXAMPLE

Custombuild Ltd builds a small housing estate of private houses called Sunny Grange. The development is set in landscaped grounds and is built to a very high specification.

Custombuild requires the purchaser of each house to promise the following:

1. to use the house only as a private dwelling (residential) house;

2. not to build any fences in the front garden of the house, so as to preserve the landscaped design;

3. not to erect any satellite dishes or television aerials on the front facade or on parts of the roof that are visible from the road;

4. not to make any alterations to the house that affect its appearance from the road;

5. to pay a proportionate amount of the cost of upkeep of the private road leading to the houses.

It is clear what the covenants in this example are intended to achieve: there is to be a sort of 'local land law' for this housing estate, which will preserve its appearance and character. Everyone who buys a house on the estate will agree to these terms and the houses will not be altered in any way that is visible from the street. If someone moves in who wants to put stone cladding on the front of his or her house, to erect a huge satellite dish, to fence off the front garden, to cover it in gravel, and to run a part-time car repair business, the neighbours will be able to enforce the covenants and stop these activities.

The problem, however, is in thinking about how the benefit of these covenants can be given to all the residents of the estate. Firstly, covenant 5 in the example is a positive covenant and, although the benefit can be made to pass, the burden will not run in equity, as we shall see at 12.6, so this covenant will have only limited enforceability. In practice, only the restrictive covenants will run with the land.

Who can enforce them would depend upon the order of sale, as shown in the example on the following page.

For this reason, equity developed a special set of rules for such building schemes or schemes of development. If such a scheme is held to exist, all of the owners of the houses (or flats) can enforce restrictive covenants against all of the other owners, as long as those covenants are registered. Both original covenantees and successors in title can enforce them, and it does not matter in which order the plots were sold.

The conditions that need to be met in order for a building scheme to exist were set out in classic form by Parker J in *Elliston v. Reacher* [1908] 2 Ch 374, 384:

1. Both the claimant and defendant derive title from a common vendor.

2. The vendor laid out his or her estate for sale in lots, and restrictive covenants were imposed on all the lots consistent with it being a single scheme of development.

3. These restrictions were intended by the vendor to be, and were, for the benefit of all of the lots sold.

4. The claimant and the defendants, or their predecessors in title, bought their land knowing about the restrictive covenants and knowing they were for the benefit of the scheme of development.

The first two requirements are not considered to be so important in the modern law. In *Re Dolphin's Conveyance* [1970] Ch 654, the land held to be part of the scheme was not all from one common vendor—but it was held that this did not matter, because the intention to create a building scheme was clear. In *Baxter v. Four Oaks Properties* [1965] Ch 816, the land was not laid out in lots before sales began, but this also was not fatal to the finding of a building scheme.

> ## ➡ EXAMPLE
>
> Suppose that Sunny Grange is laid out as shown in Figure 12.8.
>
> Custombuild first sells house A to Quentin. As a condition of the sale, Custombuild requires Quentin to enter into the covenants just detailed. The covenants are expressed to be for the benefit of Custombuild's retained land, Sunny Grange, which is clearly identified by a plan and the benefit is annexed to the land. This will mean that all of the houses, other than house A, are the benefited land.
>
> Next, Custombuild sells house B. This time, the benefited land is all of the houses, except the houses A and B.
>
> As the sales proceed round the close, eventually, when house F is sold, there is no more land to be benefited by the covenants and none of the owners of the other houses will have the benefit of the covenants entered into by the owner of house F. In other words, it is not possible to give the benefit of later covenants to earlier purchasers, either by annexation or by assignment.

Figure 12.8 A plan of Sunny Grange

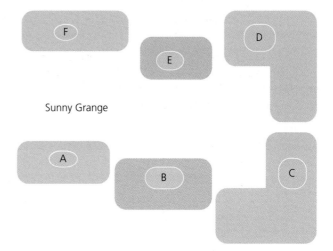

In the modern law, it is most important that the area of land that is the subject of the scheme is defined and that the obligations are reciprocal—that is, that all the parties have agreed to them and know that they are intended to bind everyone within the area—*Reid v. Bickerstaff* [1909] 2 Ch 305 and *Whitgift Homes Ltd v. Stocks* [2001] EWCA Civ 1732.

> ## 🔍 CASE CLOSE-UP
>
> ***Birdlip v. Hunter*** [2015] EWHC 808 (Ch)
> The claimant company bought a plot of land subject to a covenant not to build more than 'one or two detached residences' on it. These covenants applied to eighteen other plots of

land, one of which was owned by the defendants. The properties had originally been sold by the same vendor in 1909 and 1910, and referred to an 'Estate' which was not defined in the deeds, but which was marked on two plans which differed slightly.

The claimants wished to get the covenants removed under LPA s. 84(1) (see 12.8). The Upper Tribunal transferred the case to the High Court, to determine whether the covenants were enforceable under a building scheme for the benefit of the other properties on the estate.

Behrens J held that there was a building scheme. There was evidence that the boundaries of the scheme had been set out in the earliest (1908) plan; the covenants attached to each lot were substantially the same, and the variations immaterial. On the balance of probabilities, the covenants were intended to be for the common benefit of the purchasers as well as the vendor, so a building scheme had been made out.

THINKING POINT

So, is Sunny Grange likely to be a building scheme?

The two most important factors in the modern law are:

* that the land should be identifiable;
* that the purchasers know that there are intended to be reciprocal obligations—that is, a 'local law'.

Both of these are met here, as, in fact, are the earlier requirements that the land was sold by a common vendor and that it was laid out in lots. This means that all of the owners could sue all the other owners for breaches of the restrictive covenants, regardless of the order of sale and regardless of whether they were original covenantees or successors in title.

12.5.2 **The passing of the burden of restrictive covenants in equity**

THINKING POINT

Look back again at Figure 12.1.

We are now going to look at the second scenario, the passing of the covenant from B to D.

If the original covenantor has disposed of the land, it must be shown that the burden has passed to his or her successor in title if the covenant is to be enforced. Unlike the common law rules, which do not allow the burden of any covenants to pass to successors in title, equity does permit the burden of certain covenants to pass.

These are known as the rules in *Tulk v. Moxhay* (1842) 2 Ph 774, named after the case in which they were first set out. Next time you are in London, have a look at the little piece of land right in the middle of Leicester Square (see Photo 12.1)—it is, as we shall see, a piece of land law history with which you can impress your friends!

Photo 12.1 Leicester Square

© Pete Clarke

🔍 CASE CLOSE-UP

Tulk v. Moxhay (1842) 2 Ph 774

This case concerned the open area in the centre of Leicester Square in London. This was subject to a covenant:

> that [the covenantor], his heirs, and assigns should, and would from time to time, and at all times thereafter at his and their own costs and charges, keep and maintain the said piece of ground and square garden and the iron railing round the same in its then form, and in sufficient and proper repair as a square garden and pleasure ground, in an open state, uncovered with any buildings, in neat and ornamental order ...

The land passed into the hands of the defendant, who bought it with notice of the covenant, but who had not entered into such a covenant himself. He proposed to build on the land.

The Court upheld the covenant. Lord Cottenham LC enforced the covenant on the grounds that, in equity, a person cannot avoid a restriction placed on the land if they take with notice of it; otherwise, they would be in a better position than the person from whom they had bought the land. In particular, they may be unjustly enriched, because they would pay less for land subject to a covenant against building than for land that can be built upon.

The covenant was enforced, and the land remains open and unbuilt on to this day.

It is from this case that the rules in *Tulk v. Moxhay* developed, as follows:

1. The covenant must be restrictive.

2. At the date of the covenant, the covenantee owned land that was benefited by the covenant.

3. The original parties intended the burden to run with the land to bind successors.

4. The covenantor must take with notice of the covenant.

12.5.2.1 The covenant must be restrictive

It may be observed that some parts of the covenant in *Tulk v. Moxhay* itself appear to be positive in nature—maintaining the iron railings, and keeping it in neat and ornamental order, for example. The main point of the covenant, however, was that the land should not be built upon: that it should remain *'in an open state, uncovered with any buildings'*.

Later cases made it clear that it is only those covenants that are negative in substance that can be enforced in equity. In *Haywood v. Brunswick Permanent Benefit Building Society* (1881) 8 QBD 403, the Court of Appeal refused to enforce a covenant to repair on the authority of *Tulk v. Moxhay* and confirmed that the case was confined to restrictive covenants. As we have already seen in *Rhone v. Stephens* (at 12.5), it is clear that equity will intervene to pass the burden only of restrictive covenants.

12.5.2.2 At the date of the covenant, the covenantee owned land that was benefited by the covenant

It is clear that equity will not intervene to enforce a covenant in gross—that is, one unconnected with benefit to another piece of land.

CROSS REFERENCE

For the meaning of in gross, see Chapter 11.

So, to enforce a covenant against a successor in title to the covenantor, the claimant must show that:

*   the covenant was one that touched and concerned land;
*   at the date of the covenant, the covenantee retained land benefited by the covenant.

The meaning of touching and concerning land has already been discussed at 12.4.1.1, and has the same meaning here.

The second requirement means that:

*   the covenantee was the owner of land that could be benefited by the covenant; and
*   did not sell all that land at the time the covenant was entered into.

🔍 CASE CLOSE-UP

London County Council v. Allen [1914] 3 KB 642

The covenantee was the local council. The covenantor promised not to build on certain land without the council's permission.

When the covenantor's land was sold to someone else who started to build on the land, the council tried to enforce the covenant. The court held that it could not do so, because it did not own any land benefited by the covenant.

The whole point of the decision in *Tulk v. Moxhay* is that it enables a covenantee to protect his land by enforcing covenants against nearby landowners. If the covenant is not for the protection of land, it is not one that should be enforceable.

There are now some statutory exceptions to this rule in favour of local authorities, for example, but it remains good law for private individuals.

> **THINKING POINT**
>
> Rasul is thinking of selling his house and moving away. He is very fond of his neighbour, Sally. He wonders whether to oblige the purchaser of his house to enter into a covenant not to let the house to students, because he knows that Sally is scared of young people and dislikes their noise. Could Rasul enforce that covenant against the original purchaser? What about a successor in title to the original purchaser?

Rasul can enforce it against the original purchaser, because it is a matter of contract and, in the absence of illegality or public policy considerations, contracts are enforceable. Once the house is sold again, however, it would not be enforceable, because Rasul owns no land to be benefited by the covenant. It may also be held that the covenant does not touch and concern the land, unless it can be shown that a restriction against students enhances the value of the land.

12.5.2.3 The original parties intended the burden to run with the land to bind successors in title

Just as it is possible for the parties to intend the benefit of a covenant to be personal to the original covenantee only, it is equally possible for the parties to have intended that only the original covenantor should be bound by it. An intention that it should run with the land originally had to be shown by express words, but, since 1925, LPA 1925, s. 79, has implied an intention that the burden of a restrictive covenant should run with the land.

> **STATUTE**
>
> **Law of Property Act 1925, s. 79 [Burden of covenants relating to land]**
>
> (1) A covenant relating to any land of a covenantor or capable of being bound by him, shall, unless a contrary intention is expressed, be deemed to be made by the covenantor on behalf of himself his successors in title and the persons deriving title under him or them, and, subject as aforesaid, shall have effect as if such successors and other persons were expressed.
>
> This subsection extends to a covenant to do some act relating to the land, notwithstanding that the subject-matter may not be in existence when the covenant is made.
>
> (2) For the purposes of this section in connexion with covenants restrictive of the user of land 'successors in title' shall be deemed to include the owners and occupiers for the time being of such land.
>
> ...

Therefore, if a covenant has been made since 1925, it can be assumed that the burden is intended to run, unless the covenant makes it clear that it was not. If the covenant was entered into before 1925, it is necessary to look for words indicating that it was intended to bind successors in title—for example, the covenantor covenanting 'on behalf of [themselves] their successors in title and those deriving title under them'.

12.5.2.4 The covenantor must take with notice of the covenant

Looking back at the case of *Tulk v. Moxhay* itself, it can be seen that it was important to the reasoning of that decision that the successor in title had notice of the restriction. Restrictive covenants are interests in equity only, so they are dependent upon notice—or its modern equivalent, registration. It is necessary to look at unregistered land and registered land separately to establish the requirements.

Unregistered land

A covenant created since 1925 in unregistered land must be registered as a Class D(ii) land charge against the name of the estate owner whose land is intended to be burdened—that is, the original covenantor—Land Charges Act 1972 (LCA 1972), ss. 2 and 3. If it is properly registered, it will be binding on future purchasers of the burdened land—LPA 1925, s. 198. If it is not registered, it will not bind a purchaser for money or money's worth—LCA 1972, s. 4(2).

▶ **CROSS REFERENCE**

For more on classes of land charge, see Chapter 2.

Remember, however, that someone who acquires the land other than as a purchaser will take subject to a restrictive covenant even if it is not registered.

Covenants entered into before 1925 are still dependent upon the doctrine of notice and do not require to be registered.

Registered land

If the burdened land is registered land, the covenants must be entered as a notice in the charges register. They will also be noted in the property register of the benefited land if that is also registered land. A restrictive covenant can never be an overriding interest. If the restrictive covenant is properly noted in the charges register, it has priority over any registered disposition, such as a purchase of the estate—Land Registration Act 2002 (LRA 2002), s. 32.

It is important to note that the entry of a notice does not mean that the restrictive covenant is definitely enforceable. LRA 2002, s. 32(3) provides that 'the fact that an interest is the subject of a notice does not necessarily mean that the interest is valid'. In answering examination questions, therefore, it is vital to check that *all* of the rules in *Tulk v. Moxhay* have been met before deciding that the covenant runs with the land, even if it is registered.

12.5.3 When should the common law rules for the passing of the benefit be used and when should the equitable rules be used?

This is not a simple question. Firstly, positive covenants are usually dealt with by the common law. The covenant to repair and maintain a riverbank in *Smith and Snipes Hall Farm Ltd v. River Douglas Catchment Board* (see 12.4.1), for example, was dealt with under the common law rules for the passing of the benefit.

There seems to be no reason why the benefit of a restrictive covenant cannot also pass at common law—see, for example, *Rogers v. Hosegood* (at 12.5.1.1). Therefore, if a successor in title to the original covenantee wishes to sue the original covenantor, he or she can use the common law rules for the passing of the benefit.

If the burden of the restrictive covenant needs to pass in equity, because the original covenantor has parted with the land, however, the better view appears to be that the benefit needs to pass in equity as well—*Miles v. Easter (also known as Re Union of London and Smith's Bank Ltd's Conveyance)* (see 12.5.1.2).

12.6 Positive covenants

So far, we have established that the benefit of positive covenants can pass at common law and that there is no theoretical reason why they cannot pass in equity as well, although few, if any, cases use the equitable rules to pass the benefit of positive covenants. However, as we have already seen, the burden of positive covenants cannot pass at common law or in equity, because no burdens pass at common law—*Austerberry v. Corporation of Oldham* (see 12.4.2)—and only restrictive covenants pass in equity—*Haywood v. Brunswick Permanent Benefit Building Society* (see 12.5.2.1).

Therefore, it is not possible to create a straightforward positive covenant, such as a covenant to build and keep a wall in repair, or a covenant to keep a house in repair, that will run with the land so as to bind a successor in title to the covenantor. This explains why there are so few freehold flats in England and Wales: it is not easily possible to make the owner of the ground-floor flat keep his or her property in repair so that the flats above are supported. If the ground-floor owner neglects the property so that the flats above become unstable, there can be an action for breach of covenant only if he or she is the original covenantor. An easement of support is also not helpful in the case of neglect, because easements do not usually oblige the servient owner to spend money. It is, however, possible that there might be an action in nuisance—but this is a poor substitute for a straightforward obligation on the owner to maintain his or her property.

CROSS REFERENCE

For more on easements of support, see Chapter 11.

In this section, we will have a look at some of the ways of getting positive covenants to run with the land. Note that all of these methods are, to some extent, artificial—that is, they are all attempts to get round the inescapable fact that the burden of a positive covenant does not run with freehold land.

12.6.1 Granting a leasehold estate

CROSS REFERENCE

For more on the enforceability of covenants in leasehold land in comparison to that of those in freehold land, see Chapter 5.

The most straightforward way of ensuring that both the benefit and burden of positive covenants will run with the land is to grant a long leasehold—such as 125 years, or even longer—rather than transferring the freehold.

12.6.2 Leasehold enfranchisement

leasehold enfranchisement

the turning of a leasehold estate into a freehold estate by means of selling the reversion of the lease to the tenant

Leasehold enfranchisement means turning a leasehold estate into a freehold one by selling the reversion of the lease—that is, the freehold interest—to the tenant. The leasehold estate then merges into the freehold. Under the statutory provisions allowing leasehold enfranchisement—such as Leasehold Reform Act 1967 (LRA 1967), s. 8(1) and (3)—the freehold estate becomes subject to the same covenants as those to which the leasehold estate was subject.

12.6.3 Commonhold

CROSS REFERENCE

For more on commonhold, see Chapter 5.

Commonhold is a tenure introduced by the Commonhold and Leasehold Reform Act 2002. It enables those who own units in a registered commonhold scheme—for example, owners of individual flats in a block—to hold those units subject to a commonhold community statement, which can contain both positive and negative obligations. When a unit is sold, the new owner takes subject to all of the obligations in the commonhold community statement and the old owner is freed from them. Therefore, if land is held as part of a registered commonhold scheme, positive obligations will be enforceable.

12.6.4 Estate rentcharges

CROSS REFERENCE

For more on rentcharges, see Chapter 4.

An estate rentcharge is a payment of money due on a freehold estate that is created specifically to ensure the performance of positive obligations. If the money is not paid or the obligations are not met, a right of entry is reserved, which will allow the owner of the rentcharge to bring the freehold estate to an end.

Note that there is no right to enforce the covenants as such: the right is to bring the freehold to an end if the positive covenant is breached. The likely result, however, is that the successor in title to the covenantor will perform the covenants, because they risk their estate in land coming to an end if they do not do so.

12.6.5 Doctrine of mutual benefit and burden

Some positive covenants will be binding on successors in title under the doctrine that 'he who takes the benefit of a freehold grant must also take the burden'.

A good example of this doctrine at work can be seen in the case of *Halsall v. Brizell* [1957] Ch 169.

 CASE CLOSE-UP

Halsall v. Brizell [1957] Ch 169

In this case, the transfer of a house contained terms requiring the owners to pay a proportionate share of the maintenance of a private roadway and drainage—that is, a positive covenant to pay money for repairs and maintenance. The defendants, who were successors in title to the original covenantors, refused to pay.

Upjohn J agreed that there was no obligation to pay, because positive covenants do not run with the land. But on the basis *'that a man who takes the benefit of a deed is bound by a condition contained in it'*, the defendants could not continue to use the roadways or the sewers unless they also paid for the maintenance of them.

This meant that, in practice, the defendants were bound by the positive covenant to pay for repairs and maintenance.

This doctrine has not, however, been applied widely by the courts. There must be a very direct relationship between the benefits and the burdens; it is not enough that they are contained in the same document. So, for example, in *Rhone v. Stephens* (see 12.5), the defendant was not bound by a positive covenant to maintain a roof because she had the benefit of the support of her roof by the claimant's roof, or because there was drainage from her roof over the claimant's roof: those benefits were held to be too insubstantial.

The doctrine was considered again in the case of *Thamesmead Town v. Allotey* [1998] 3 EGLR 97.

 CASE CLOSE-UP

Thamesmead Town v. Allotey [1998] 3 EGLR 97

Peter Gibson LJ considered both *Halsall v. Brizell* and *Rhone v. Stephens*. He concluded that there were two conditions that had to be met for the doctrine of mutual benefit and burden to operate in respect of positive covenants:

1. The benefit and the burden must be directly related (as they were in *Halsall v. Brizell*).

> 2. It must be possible for the successor in title to the covenantor to be able to reject the burden as long as he or she does not take the benefit.

This was accepted and clarified by a further Court of Appeal decision in 2009.

 CASE CLOSE-UP

Davies v. Jones [2009] EWCA Civ 1164, [2010] 1 P & CR 22

Sir Andrew Morrit C held that for a positive covenant to be enforceable on the basis of mutual benefit and burden, three conditions must be satisfied:

1. The benefit and burden must be conferred in or by the same transaction.
2. The benefit and the burden must be directly related, and this is to be decided by construction of the deeds or other documents in the transaction.
3. The person on whom the burden is alleged to have been imposed must have or have had the opportunity of rejecting or disclaiming the benefit, not merely the right to receive the benefit.

These rules were applied again by the Court of Appeal in *Elwood v. Goodman* [2013] EWCA Civ 1103, a case—like *Halsall v. Brizell*—about contributions to the maintenance of a roadway. It was held that as a matter of substance, the right to use the roadway was clearly and obviously linked to the obligation to pay for repairs. Therefore a purchaser of part of the covenantor's land was liable to contribute to repairs to the roadway. It was also held that there is no need to register the burden of a positive covenant.

The doctrine is therefore limited to covenants that can be directly matched with a corresponding benefit in the same transfer, and the benefit has to be one that, at least in theory, the successor in title can reject if he or she does not wish to take on the burden. Therefore, only a limited number of positive covenants will be binding on successors in title under this rule.

12.6.6 Chains of indemnity covenants

It is possible to make positive covenants indirectly enforceable by a chain of **indemnity covenants**. The original covenantor remains liable on his or her original covenant, but takes an indemnity—that is, a promise to pay any damages awarded for a future breach of the covenant—from the successor in title. If the successor in title parts with the land, an indemnity covenant is taken from the next successor in title, and so on.

> **indemnity covenant** a promise on behalf of a successor in title to pay, to the original covenantor, any damages that might be awarded against him or her for a future breach of the covenant by the successor in title

If there is a breach of covenant, the original covenantor is sued. The only remedy that could be claimed is damages, because the original covenantor is no longer in a position to carry out the covenant—he or she would no longer have access to land to carry out maintenance to a wall, for example. Those damages would then be claimed under the indemnity covenant from the successor in title (see Figure 12.9).

Figure 12.9 Example of an indemnity covenant

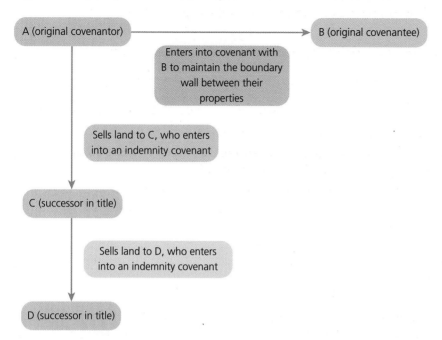

> **EXAMPLE**
>
> A, the original covenantor, has covenanted with B, the original covenantee, that he will maintain the boundary wall between their properties. Because this is a positive covenant, it will not run with A's land.
>
> When A sells the land to C, he obliges C to enter into an indemnity covenant with him, so that, if C breaches the covenant and B sues A, A can claim the damages from C.
>
> When C sells the land to D, he does the same.
>
> Suppose D breaches the covenant by letting the wall fall into disrepair. B cannot sue D, because he is not liable under the original covenant. B can sue A (provided he knows where he is) and can get damages. He cannot get a decree of specific performance (an order that A do the work), because A is no longer the owner of the land and cannot go onto it to carry out the work. A can sue C to get the damages back and C can sue D. Because D knows that he may be liable to C, he may decide to carry out the work instead.

As you can easily see, this is a very indirect method of enforcing the covenant. Financially, it is liable to break down if any of the successors in title disappears—and if the original covenantor cannot be found, the covenantee may be left without a remedy at all.

12.6.7 Covenants entered into by successors in title

The original covenantor might require a successor in title to enter directly into the same positive covenant with the covenantee. This would mean that the successor in title would, him- or herself, become an original covenantor (see Figure 12.10).

Figure 12.10 Example of a covenant entered into by successors in title

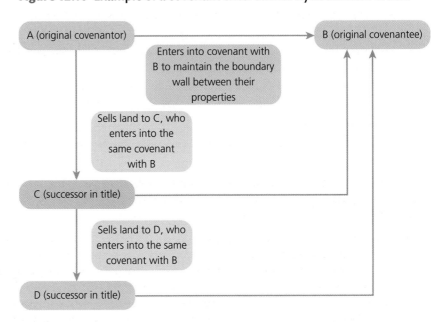

This can be made compulsory on the transfer of registered land if a restriction is entered into the proprietorship register of the covenantor's land under LRA 2002, s. 40 forbidding the covenantor from transferring the land unless the transferee enters into such a covenant with the covenantee. Unless such a restriction is registered, it is very likely that the requirement to oblige any successor in title to enter into a new covenant will not be met.

For example, such an obligation was imposed on the covenantors in *Thamesmead Town v. Allotey* (see 12.6.5), but Mr Allotey was not, in fact, obliged by the covenantors to enter into a fresh covenant with the covenantee.

12.6.8 The easement of fencing

▶ CROSS REFERENCE

For more on the easement of fencing, see Chapter 11.

There is an easement that requires the servient owner to maintain a fence. It is a very odd easement, because it requires the expenditure of money by the servient owner, which is usually not a feature of easements, but its existence was confirmed in the case of *Crowe v. Wood* [1971] 1 QB 77. It has therefore been suggested that a positive covenant to maintain a fence might be enforceable as an easement of fencing.

The easement seems, however, to be restricted to stockproof fencing on farms and not to extend, for example, to garden fencing. Also, in the recent case of *Sugarman v. Porter* [2006] EWHC 331 (Ch), Peter Smith J refused to construe a covenant to maintain fencing as an easement, because it was drafted as a covenant. It appears, therefore, that it is unlikely that a positive covenant to maintain a fence will be enforced as an easement.

12.7 Breach of covenant

Usually, when you are dealing with a question on covenants, it is because the covenantor (or a successor in title) either has already done something that may be in breach of the covenant, or is threatening to do so.

In this case, there will be four main points that you will need to consider:

1. Does that person have the burden of the covenant—that is, has the burden passed to him or her?

2. Who can enforce the covenant against that person—that is, has the benefit passed to the person who wants to enforce it?

3. Is the action or proposed action actually a breach of the covenant—that is, does it fall within the list of things that the covenant requires or, as is more likely, prohibits?

4. What remedies can be obtained?

The first two questions are dealt with by looking at the rules for the passing of the benefit and the burden.

The third question—is the action in breach of covenant?—involves interpreting the covenant just as you would any contractual term. Does the action fall within what is forbidden by the covenant? It is usually up to the claimant to prove that the action is in breach.

To give some examples, in *Mortimer v. Bailey* [2004] EWCA Civ 1514 (see 12.7.1), the Court had to decide whether the covenantee's consent to building an extension had been unreasonably withheld in order to know whether there had been a breach of covenant. This was clearly a fact that had to be decided on the evidence, before the question of remedies was discussed. In *Margerison v. Bates* [2008] EWHC 1211 (Ch), there was a covenant which provided that any alteration to a bungalow on the burdened land must be approved by the original covenantee, who was now deceased. It was held that, on the true construction of the covenant, no consent was now required for alterations—the covenant had died with the original covenantee. Finally, in *Dennis v. Davies* [2009] EWCA Civ 1081, it was held that building an extension which obstructed the covenantee's river view was in breach of a covenant against 'nuisance or annoyance'. These are just a few examples of questions of construction of the covenant; different facts will give rise to different answers.

The last question, about remedies, is very important, and is discussed separately next.

12.7.1 Remedies for breach of covenant

Once it has been established that there has been a breach of a covenant, and that the parties have the benefit and the burden respectively, it must be decided what remedies the court can award. At common law, the usual remedy for the breach of any contract is damages. Damages are therefore available between the original covenantor and covenantee, and if the benefit of a covenant has run at common law. Where the burden of a restrictive covenant has run, however, the remedies must of course be equitable, because the burden does not run at common law.

The most usual remedy that the parties want is an injunction—that is, an order of the court that something be done or not done. There are various stages at which an injunction may be sought.

 EXAMPLE

Raj has the benefit of a covenant under which his neighbour, Saul, has covenanted not to build more than one house on his land. Raj discovers that Saul has applied for planning permission to build four houses.

Raj can apply for an injunction preventing Saul from building more than one house.

Suppose that Raj does not find out that Saul has applied to build more than one house until he starts building. He arrives home one day to find footings for four houses being dug. He can apply to court for an injunction to stop the building work from continuing.

> Finally, suppose that Raj has been abroad for a year. He arrives home to find four houses already built on Saul's land. He can apply for a mandatory injunction to have the houses pulled down.

Injunctions, like all equitable remedies, are discretionary, so they may not be granted in certain circumstances. To see when the court is likely to grant an injunction, we have to look at the case law.

A major problem is that a claimant seeking an interim injunction to stop work going ahead must usually give an undertaking to pay damages to the defendant if the covenant turns out not to be enforceable, or if the proposed action is not in breach of covenant. This can put many covenantees off, because it will be very expensive if they are proved wrong. On the other hand, if they do not make it clear that they object, a mandatory injunction to pull down the building might be refused on the grounds that the covenantee delayed in acting. If no injunction is granted, damages may be awarded instead, a power originally conferred under Lord Cairns' Act (the Chancery Amendment Act 1858). However, the courts are keen not to allow the covenantor to 'buy himself out of the covenant' against the wishes of the covenantee by awarding damages, rather than an injunction.

The leading case on when an injunction or damages should be granted is *Shelfer v. City of London Electric Lighting Co. Ltd (No. 1)* [1895] 1 Ch 287. Smith LJ laid down four principles (at 322). Damages may be given instead of an injunction if:

1. the injury to the [claimant's] legal rights is small; and

2. is one which is capable of being estimated in money; and

3. is one which can be adequately compensated by a small money payment; and

4. the case is one in which it would be oppressive to the defendant to grant an injunction.

These rules were applied in *Jaggard v. Sawyer* [1995] 2 All ER 189, in which an injunction was refused. The covenantor had built in breach of covenant and the claimant was seeking an injunction that would render the new, unauthorized house landlocked. It was held that damages would be adequate compensation, because the injury to the claimant's legal rights was small, and it would be oppressive to grant the injunction.

 CASE CLOSE-UP

Coventry v. Lawrence [2014 UKSC] 13

In this case concerning noise nuisance from a motocross track, the 'Shelfer criteria' were criticized by the Supreme Court.

Lord Neuberger held:

the prima facie position is that an injunction should be granted;

the legal burden is on the defendant to show why an injunction should not be granted.

However, the application of the *Shelfer* criteria must not 'be a fetter on the exercise of the court's discretion';

- It would normally be right to refuse an injunction if the four tests were satisfied.

- The fact that those tests are not all satisfied does not mean that an injunction should be granted.

Lord Sumption held that the decision in *Shelfer* is out-of-date, and that it is unfortunate that it has been followed 'so recently and so slavishly'.

Lords Clarke, Mance and Carnworth broadly agreed with the opinions of Lords Neuberger and Clarke on these points.

It is therefore clear that the strict application of the *Shelfer* criteria is no longer thought to be good law. This leaves the authority of previous cases on these points in some doubt.

In *Gafford v. Graham* (1998) 77 P & CR 73, it was held by the Court of Appeal that to get an injunction, the covenantee must act promptly upon discovering a breach of covenant. A riding school was built on land burdened by a covenant, but as the covenantee had stood by and watched it being built without seeking an interim injunction, only damages were available as a remedy. In addition, breaches of covenant which had occurred three years previously had been acquiesced to by the covenantee, and no remedy at all was available.

Subsequent decisions of the Court of Appeal made it clear, however, that it is not always necessary to get an interim injunction, and that delay in issuing proceedings may not always be fatal to a claim for an injunction.

 CASE CLOSE-UP

Mortimer v. Bailey [2004] EWCA Civ 1514

The claimants had the benefit of a covenant under which the defendants' predecessor in title had covenanted not to build on the land without the approval of the plans by the claimants, such consent not to be unreasonably withheld. The defendants went ahead with building an extension, thinking that the claimants' refusal to approve the plans would be held to be unreasonable.

The claimants applied for an interim injunction, but did not get one. They made it very clear in writing that they objected to the building and pursued a claim for a mandatory injunction to have it knocked down. By the date of the hearing, however, the building was almost complete. Despite this, the judge granted a mandatory injunction that the extension should be demolished.

The Court of Appeal upheld the mandatory injunction, so the extension built in breach of covenant had to be knocked down.

In *Hicks v. Holland Park Management* [2014] EWHC 2962 (Ch), an interim injunction restraining a landowner from applying for planning permission was refused. An upcoming change in planning policy would have made the detriment to D substantial and unquantifiable, so on the balance of convenience the injunction was refused.

In *Jacklin v. Chief Constable of West Yorkshire* [2007] EWCA Civ 181, an injunction was granted in respect of an easement of way despite considerable delay on the part of the claimant because the court was not satisfied that it would be oppressive to grant the injunction, even though the first three *Shelfer* principles were agreed to have been met. Similarly, in *HKRUK II (CHC) Ltd v. Heaney* [2010] EWHC 2245 (Ch), a two-storey extension was ordered to be demolished because it blocked the claimant's right to light.

In *Harris v. Williams-Wynne* [2006] EWCA Civ 104, the claimant did not seek a mandatory injunction to knock down the building, because he realized that he had delayed in asserting his rights. It was held that he could get damages instead, based on the amount that could have been charged for releasing the covenant. If he had waited even longer and his right to sue had been lost by acquiescence, then there would have been no damages either.

We can summarize the outcomes of these cases as follows:

- A claimant who wants to get an injunction to stop a breach of covenant should act decisively and make it clear that the breach will be pursued, and that damages are not an acceptable alternative. An interim injunction need not be sought, although sometimes it may be better to do so—*Gafford v. Graham; Mortimer v. Bailey; Jacklin v. Chief Constable of West Yorkshire.*

- Until recently cases proceeded on the basis that all four principles in *Shelfer v. City of London Electric Lighting Co. Ltd* had to be met for damages to be awarded instead of an injunction. Damages will usually be based on the amount that the covenantor would have had to pay to get a release of the covenant, which is generally fixed after hearing expert evidence—*Jaggard v. Sawyer; Harris v. Williams-Wynne.*

- If there is too long a delay, the covenantee may be held to have acquiesced to the breach and neither an injunction nor damages will be available—*Gafford v. Graham.*

- The courts take a dim view of covenantors who proceed with a breach of covenant (or any other property right) despite clear objections, and will award even a mandatory injunction to knock down buildings if the case requires it: *Mortimer v. Bailey.* It seemed until very recently that the courts were perhaps more willing than formerly to grant injunctions—*Jacklin v. Chief Constable of West Yorkshire; HKRUK II (CHC) Ltd v. Heaney.* However, in *Coventry v. Lawrence* [2014] UKSC 13, the Supreme Court indicated that a more flexible approach should be taken, and this is likely to influence decisions in the future.

12.8 Modification and discharge of covenants

You will have seen by now that it is perfectly possible for restrictive covenants to run with the land forever, binding each new successor in title. This means that many old and obsolete covenants may still be enforceable, at least in theory. This could inhibit perfectly reasonable development of land and make it unusable.

 EXAMPLE

Tim has just bought a huge, dilapidated house. He would like to renovate it and turn it into flats, but there is a covenant restricting the use of the house to that of a single residence only, which was created in 1930 and which appears to be for the benefit of neighbouring land.

Tim could simply go ahead and renovate anyway, hoping that no one has the benefit of the covenant any more, or that they will not bother to enforce it. If he does so, however, he runs a risk that the successor in title of the covenantee may object and obtain either an injunction or damages against him.

Fortunately for Tim, in the example above, he may be able to resolve these problems with the aid of LPA 1925, s. 84.

> ## 📖 STATUTE
>
> ### Law of Property Act 1925, s. 84 [Power to discharge or modify restrictive covenants affecting land]
>
> (1) The [Upper Tribunal] shall (without prejudice to any concurrent jurisdiction of the court) have power from time to time, on the application of any person interested in any freehold land affected by any restriction arising under covenant or otherwise as to the user thereof or the building thereon, by order wholly or partially to discharge or modify any such restriction on being satisfied—
>
> (a) that by reason of changes in the character of the property or the neighbourhood or other circumstances of the case which the [Upper Tribunal] may deem material, the restriction ought to be deemed obsolete; or
>
> (aa) that (in a case falling within subsection (1A) below) the continued existence thereof would impede some reasonable user of the land for public or private purposes or, as the case may be, would unless modified so impede such user; or
>
> (b) that the persons of full age and capacity for the time being or from time to time entitled to the benefit of the restriction, whether in respect of estates in fee simple or any lesser estates or interests in the property to which the benefit of the restriction is annexed, have agreed, either expressly or by implication, by their acts or omissions, to the same being discharged or modified; or
>
> (c) that the proposed discharge or modification will not injure the persons entitled to the benefit of the restriction;
>
> and an order discharging or modifying a restriction under this subsection may direct the applicant to pay to any person entitled to the benefit of the restriction such sum by way of consideration as the Tribunal may think it just to award under one, but not both, of the following heads, that is to say, either—
>
> (i) a sum to make up for any loss or disadvantage suffered by that person in consequence of the discharge or modification; or
>
> (ii) a sum to make up for any effect which the restriction had, at the time when it was imposed, in reducing the consideration then received for the land affected by it.
>
> (1A) Subsection (1)(aa) above authorises the discharge or modification of a restriction by reference to its impeding some reasonable user of land in any case in which the [Upper Tribunal] is satisfied that the restriction, in impeding that user, either—
>
> (a) does not secure to persons entitled to the benefit of it any practical benefits of substantial value or advantage to them; or
>
> (b) is contrary to the public interest;
>
> and that money will be an adequate compensation for the loss or disadvantage (if any) which any such person will suffer from the discharge or modification.
>
> (1B) In determining whether a case is one falling within subsection (1A) above, and in determining whether (in any such case or otherwise) a restriction ought to be discharged or modified, the [Upper Tribunal] shall take into account the development plan and any declared or ascertainable pattern for the grant or refusal of planning permissions in the relevant areas, as well as the period at which and context in which the restriction was created or imposed and any other material circumstances.

(1C) It is hereby declared that the power conferred by this section to modify a restriction includes power to add such further provisions restricting the user of or the building on the land affected as appear to the [Upper Tribunal] to be reasonable in view of the relaxation of the existing provisions, and as may be accepted by the applicant; and the [Upper Tribunal] may accordingly refuse to modify a restriction without some such addition.

(2) The court shall have power on the application of any person interested—

(a) to declare whether or not in any particular case any freehold land is, or would in any given event be, affected by a restriction imposed by any instrument; or

(b) to declare what, upon the true construction of any instrument purporting to impose a restriction, is the nature and extent of the restriction thereby imposed and whether the same is, or would in any given event be, enforceable and if so by whom.

...

Taking subsection (2) first, Tim might apply to the court to find out whether his land is still affected by the covenant and who, if anyone, can enforce it (for examples of such cases, see *Norwich City College v. McQuillan* [2009] EWHC 1496 (Ch) and *Birdlip v. Hunter* [2015] EWHC 808 (Ch)).

If it is discovered that the land is still affected, Tim can apply to the Upper Tribunal (formerly known as the Lands Tribunal) for the covenant to be discharged or modified under any of the grounds in LPA 1925, s. 1, namely that:

- the covenant is obsolete—LPA 1925, s. 1(a);
- the covenant impedes some reasonable public or private use of the land—LPA 1925, s. 1(aa);
- those entitled to the benefit consent to the discharge or modification—LPA 1925, s. 1(b);
- the discharge will not injure those who benefit from the covenant—LPA 1925, s. 1(c).

> **➡ EXAMPLE**
>
> Tim might argue that the restriction is obsolete, perhaps because other houses in the area are now divided into flats (s. 1(a)), or that the covenant impedes some reasonable private use of the land (s. 1(aa)) and that its discharge will not injure the persons entitled to the benefit.

In *Re University of Westminster* [1998] 3 All ER 1014, it was held that the Tribunal must exercise its jurisdiction judicially, even if the application to discharge a covenant is not opposed by anyone. This means that it must think about the evidence both for and against discharging the covenant, whether or not anyone turns up to argue the case for keeping it. The applicant (the university) was not entitled to have the covenants discharged simply because nobody responded to its application to the Tribunal.

Just because a covenant is old does not mean that it will be discharged. For example, in the case *In The Matter Of Hamden Homes Ltd* (2002) Lands Tribunal (N J Rose) LTL 30/1/2002, the Tribunal would not discharge a covenant restricting the owners to building only one house on each plot of land, even though it was created in 1930. The developers argued that modern houses have much smaller gardens, but the Tribunal found that the covenant protected the character of the residential area.

Note that the Tribunal must consider the local authority's development plan for the area and the pattern of any planning decisions before exercising its discretion.

It is interesting to compare restrictive covenants and easements in this respect: there is no equivalent section allowing an easement to be modified or discharged, no matter how old it is and how much it impedes development of the land.

The Housing Act 1985, s. 610, allows the county court to vary a restrictive covenant restricting the division of a house into two or more tenements—for example, flats—if it impedes the letting of a house for residential use. This provision may also assist Tim in the earlier examples.

12.9 Proposals for reform

The Law Commission report, *Making Land Work: Easements, Covenants and Profits à Prendre*, Law Com No. 327 (London: The Stationery Office, 2011) recommends replacing covenants with a new interest in land, the 'land obligation'. This would work essentially like an easement, and be registered in the same way. Land obligations could be either positive or restrictive; however, the Law Commission thought that flats would continue to work better in either leasehold or commonhold than as freeholds.

The jurisdiction of the Upper Tribunal would be extended to cover both positive and negative land obligations.

Visit the Online Resource Centre.

 Summary

1. A covenant is a promise contained in a deed.

2. There is privity of contract between covenantee and covenantor.

3. The meaning of covenantee has been extended by LPA 1925, s. 56(1) and the C(RTP)A 1999.

4. The benefit of positive covenants runs at common law, provided that the requirements are satisfied.

5. The burden of positive covenants does not run with the land, either at law or in equity.

6. Both the benefit and burden of restrictive covenants run in equity, provided that the requirements are satisfied:

    • The benefit runs if the covenant touches and concerns land, and the benefit is annexed or assigned, or the land forms part of a building scheme.

    • The burden passes if the rules in *Tulk v. Moxhay* are satisfied.

7. There are various devices for attempting to enforce positive covenants against successors in title to the original covenantor, but none of them is straightforward.

8. Remedies for breach of covenant include injunctions and damages.

9. The right to an injunction may be lost by delay and damages in equity may be lost by acquiescence.

10. Restrictive covenants that are obsolete or impede a reasonable use of land, or which confer no benefit, may be discharged by the Upper Tribunal, under LPA 1925, s. 84.

The bigger picture

- For an example of how to work out if a covenant is likely to be enforceable from information in the charges register, see Chapter 14, 14.4.2. For ideas on how to answer exam questions on covenants, see Chapter 15, 15.11.

- For criticism of the law on freehold covenants and proposals for reform, you cannot do better than to read the relevant parts of the recent Law Commission report, *Making Land Work: Easements, Covenants and Profits à Prendre*, Law Com No. 327 (London: The Stationery Office, 2011).

? Questions

Self-test questions

1. Does a covenantee have the benefit or the burden of a covenant?

2. Abi has the benefit of a covenant entered into by Belinda that Belinda will maintain the fence between their gardens. Belinda has sold her land to Carl. Can Abi oblige Carl to carry out repairs to the fence?

3. Doug has the benefit of a covenant entered into by Ed that Ed will not build on his land without Doug's consent. Will the benefit of this covenant pass to Fiona if she buys Doug's land? Will the burden pass to Greg if he buys Ed's land?

4. What remedies would be open to Fiona if she were to sue Greg for breach of covenant?

Exam questions.

1. Abe was the owner of a detached house with a large garden. In 2009, he sold part of his garden to Ben. In the transfer, Ben covenanted as follows:

   - to build only one bungalow on the purchased land, the plans for which were to be approved by Abe;

   - to build a wall between the purchased land and Abe's retained land;

   - to contribute to the cost of maintaining the driveway which serves both houses, and over which both properties have a right of way.

   Ben did nothing with the land for some years, mainly because he fell ill shortly after buying it. In 2015, he sold the purchased land to Cerys. A number of problems have arisen in respect of her use of the land. Firstly, she has refused to build the wall between the two plots, saying that that obligation was personal to Ben. Secondly, she has started to build a large house on the land, without consulting Abe, and despite his objections. Thirdly, she has refused to contribute to resurfacing the driveway even though it is the lorries from her building work that have damaged the surface. Advise Abe.

2. In *Rhone v. Stephens* [1994] 2 AC 310, Lord Templeman said (at 317): '*the benefit of a covenant may run with the land at law but not the burden: see the Austerberry case*'.

Explain the effect this rule has had on English land law, and indicate how the law might be reformed.

 For suggested approaches to answering these questions visit the Online Resource Centre.

 Further reading

Bullock, A., 'Federated Homes revisited' (2005) 155 NLJ 238
This article discusses *Federated Homes* in the light of the later decision in *Crest Nicholson*. It is a very helpful article on statutory annexation.

Clark, P., 'The benefit of freehold covenants' [2012] 2 Conv 145
This article discusses the application of LPA 1925, s. 78(1) and *Rees v. Peters* [2011] EWCA Civ 836.

Francis, A. 'Construing Covenant Chaos' [2007] NLJ 206
This article discusses the interpretation of restrictive covenants, particularly with regard to consent clauses.

Goulding, S., 'Privity of estate and the enforcement of real covenants' (2007) 36(3) CLWR 193
This article discusses the theoretical reasons why English law does not permit the enforcement of positive covenants, and how the US courts arrived at a different conclusion. It is quite difficult and theoretical, but contains an interesting insight into the origins of the law.

House of Commons Committee on Positive Covenants Affecting Land (1965) *Report of the Committee on Positive Covenants Affecting Land*, Cmnd 2719, London: HMSO
This is the report of the Wilberforce Committee, which recommended reform of the law on positive covenants. The reforms have not been implemented.

http://www.lawcom.gov.uk/wp-content/uploads/2015/03/lc327_easements_report.pdf
This website contains the Law Commission report, *Making Land Work: Easements, Covenants and Profits à Prendre*, Law Com No. 327 (London: The Stationery Office, 2011), which contains the latest proposals for reform.

https://www.gov.uk/appeal-upper-tribunal-lands/legislation-and-previous-decisions
The website of the Upper Tribunal (Lands Chamber) contains decisions made by the Tribunal, along with other useful information.

Law Commission (1984) *Transfer of Land: The Law of Positive and Restrictive Covenants*, Law Com No. 127 (HC 201)
This Law Commission report has a draft Bill attached. Its proposals were not implemented.

Law Commission (1991) *Obsolete Restrictive Covenants*, Law Com No. 201 (HC 546)
This Law Commission report contains proposals for reform of the law that were not implemented.

O'Connor, P., 'Careful what you wish for: positive freehold covenants' [2011] Conv 191
This article discusses positive covenants and whether there are drawbacks to enforcing them.

Snape, J., 'The burden of positive covenants' [1994] Conv 477
This article also discusses positive covenants in the light of the decision in *Rhone v. Stephens*.

Walsh, E. and Morris, C., 'Enforcing positive covenants' [2015] 4 Conv 316–23
This article discusses positive covenants and suggested reforms.

Online Resource Centre

www.oxfordtextbooks.co.uk/orc/clarke_directions5e/

For more advice relating to this chapter, including self-test questions and an interactive glossary, visit the Online Resource Centre.

13 Mortgages

◻ LEARNING OBJECTIVES

By the end of this chapter, you will be able to:

- understand what a 'mortgage' is and how it works;
- identify the statutory measures in place to protect the mortgagor;
- identify the rights and remedies of the mortgagee.

Introduction

The UK is a nation of homeowners. Unlike their friends in many other European countries, the British seem to dislike renting and prefer to buy their own home (hence perhaps the old maxim 'An Englishman's home is his castle'). The problem, however, is that property in the UK is expensive. Most people are only able to buy their own home with the help of a mortgage from a bank or building society.

The theory behind a mortgage is simple. The bank lends an individual the money to buy his or her home and, in return, the homeowner pays the bank interest on the loan and (usually) some of the outstanding debt (also called 'capital') every month.

A mortgage is different from other kinds of loan, however, because it is 'secured' on the property itself. You will have seen the caveat: 'Your home is at risk if you do not keep up the repayments on the loan.' This means that, if, for some reason, the homeowner does not pay the bank its money, the bank has the right to take certain steps to recover the amount that it is owed. This can include repossessing the property and selling it—even if the homeowner does not want this to happen.

What most people do not realize as they sign on the dotted line of the mortgage application form, is that not only have they purchased a lovely new home, they also have become involved in a sophisticated legal agreement, with its own statutory framework and centuries of case law.

13.1 Terminology

This area of land law seems to have more than its fair share of confusing terminology, so it is important to understand a few of the key terms right at the start.

One of the most confusing descriptions is that given to the borrower—the mortgagor—and the lender—the mortgagee. When most people think about buying a home, they talk about the bank granting them a mortgage: in fact, legally, it is the other way around! The homeowner grants a mortgage (or charge) to the bank over his or her home and is thus known as the **mortgagor**. In return for the charge, the bank lends the homeowner the money to buy the property. Because the bank is effectively receiving the mortgage, it is described as the **mortgagee**.

> **mortgagor** the borrower, who grants the mortgage to the bank
>
> **mortgagee** the lender, who, in return for receiving the mortgage, lends the money

You may also see references to different types of mortgage—in particular, to a repayment mortgage and an interest-only mortgage. Detailed consideration of these is outside the scope of this book, but to help you to understand a little more how mortgages work in practice—and to help you to impress the bank when you go and ask it for a mortgage—we will look very briefly at the meaning of these terms.

repayment mortgage

a type of mortgage arrangement under which the mortgagor repays both interest and capital each month

Under a **repayment mortgage**, the borrower (mortgagor) repays both some interest and some capital each month to the bank. Most mortgages are taken out over a long time—typically twenty-five years. If the mortgagor has a repayment mortgage, then, by the end of that twenty-five years, he or she will have repaid the whole of the loan for the property and any interest on that loan due to the bank: the mortgagor will then own his or her home completely.

interest-only mortgage

a type of mortgage arrangement under which the mortgagor repays only interest each month, with capital to be repaid in full at the end of the mortgage term

Under an **interest-only mortgage**, the mortgagor pays only interest to the bank each month; he or she does not repay any of the capital. At the end of the mortgage term, the mortgagor will still owe the mortgagee the whole of the amount borrowed. The mortgagor must then either sell the property to repay the bank or pay the bank back from other assets that he or she might have—usually from the proceeds of an investment vehicle that the mortgagor has arranged specifically for this purpose.

Looking at the two possibilities, you might wonder why anyone would choose an interest-only mortgage. There are various reasons for doing so, but one of the most common is that the monthly repayments are lower. The number of interest-only mortgages has started to fall in recent years, as lenders perceive them as more risky: currently, a number of lenders face the prospect of borrowers being unable to repay the mortgage debt at the end of the term, because their chosen investment vehicle has not produced sufficient capital growth to enable them pay off the debt completely.

CROSS REFERENCE

For a reminder of the meanings of fee simple and term of years absolute, see Chapters 3 and 5.

13.2 Creating a mortgage

A long time ago, the most common means of granting a mortgage was for the borrower (mortgagor) to transfer his or her fee simple (or freehold) interest in the land entirely to the lender (mortgagee), under an agreement that, when the money was repaid in full, on the due date, the mortgagee would transfer the fee simple back to the mortgagor.

Originally, this was very strictly applied. If the mortgagor was even one day late with his or her payment, or had almost repaid the debt in its entirety but just failed to do so by the date of repayment, it meant that the mortgagee could keep the land for itself. The mortgagor then lost both his or her land and all of the repayments made on the loan.

Equity recognized that this situation caused great hardship to the mortgagor. As a result, the concept of the **equitable right of redemption** was introduced. What this meant essentially was that there were now two crucial dates in the life of the mortgage. The first date, usually fixed at six months after the creation of the mortgage, is the legal date of redemption. At this point, the mortgagor has a legal, contractual right to redeem—that is, to repay—the mortgage. Of course, neither the mortgagor nor the mortgagee really expects this so quickly after the mortgage has been set up—but nevertheless, at this point, the mortgagor is legally entitled to do so should he or she so choose.

> **equitable right of redemption** the right of a mortgagor to repay all of the capital, interest, and costs involved in their mortgage arrangement at any time and thereby wholly own his or her property

If the mortgagor does not redeem the mortgage at this stage, he or she acquires what is known as the equitable right of redemption. This continues for the remainder of the mortgage term. Equity says that, if the mortgagor chooses to, he or she can redeem the mortgage at any point, as Figure 13.1 helps to demonstrate.

Figure 13.1 The legal and equitable rights of redemption

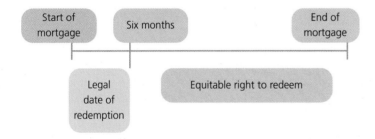

After the 1925 legislation, it was no longer possible to create a mortgage by the mortgagor transferring the fee simple to the mortgagee. As we shall see in the next section, the Law of Property Act 1925 (LPA 1925) provided that there are now only two possible ways of creating a legal mortgage—but the equitable right of redemption continues to play an important part in the modern law of mortgages.

Mortgages can be created in both registered and unregistered land, but note that a first legal mortgage of unregistered freehold land will be a trigger for registration of the land—Land Registration Act 2002 (LRA 2002), ss. 4(1)(g) and 6(2)(a).

▶ CROSS REFERENCE
For more on first registration, see Chapter 4.

Mortgages can be both legal and equitable, and there may also be a number of mortgages on one piece of land. For the majority of this chapter, we will be considering the law in relation to legal mortgages. Equitable mortgages and multiple mortgages will be considered separately at the very end of the chapter.

13.3 Legal mortgages

13.3.1 Creating a legal mortgage

 STATUTE

Law of Property Act 1925, s. 85(1)

A mortgage of an estate in fee simple shall only be capable of being effected at law either by a demise for a term of years absolute, subject to a provision for cesser on redemption, or by a charge by deed, expressed to be by way of legal mortgage.

---

legal mortgage
a mortgage that is created by legal charge (in registered land) and completed by means of certain formalities

---

demise
a lease

Although LPA 1925, s. 85(1) looks rather complicated, it basically says that there are two ways of creating a **legal mortgage**—that is, a mortgage 'effected at law':

- grant by demise;
- grant by legal charge.

13.3.1.1 Grant by demise ('term of years absolute')

If the mortgagor owns the fee simple of the property, then he or she can grant a legal mortgage over it by **demise** to the bank. 'Demise' means simply a lease. Once the mortgagor has paid back to the bank all of the money borrowed and all of the interest due under the mortgage arrangement, the lease will automatically come to an end and the bank's interest in the property will cease. This is what is meant by a 'cesser on redemption'.

In this situation, both the mortgagor and the mortgagee have a legal estate in the land.

Sometimes the mortgagor owns only a leasehold interest in the property—this is very common when somebody buys a flat, rather than a house. In this case, he or she can still raise a mortgage by granting a lease to the bank, provided that the lease granted is for a lesser period than the lease that the mortgagor holds—LPA 1925, s. 86.

In agreements such as this, the parties usually provide that the mortgage monies may be repaid within a year of the mortgage date. This is to prevent the lender making it difficult in any way for the mortgagor to repay the mortgage (see 13.3.2.1).

This method of creating legal mortgages was rather difficult and became less popular over the years. With registered land, it is no longer possible to create a mortgage by granting a lease. LRA 2002, s. 23(1)(a) provides that the only way that a legal mortgage of registered land can be created is by means of a legal charge. In practice, although it is still possible to create a legal mortgage over unregistered land by means of granting a lease, it is extremely rare. We will therefore concentrate our efforts on the most important means of creating a legal mortgage over land.

13.3.1.2 Legal charge ('charge by deed')

---

legal charge
a legal interest in land that acts to secure the payment of money

---

A **legal charge** essentially grants the mortgagee a legal interest in the mortgagor's land until the mortgage is repaid. It has to be made by deed—LPA 1925, s. 85—and, in the case of registered land, it must be registered in the charges register of the land register. As with any legal interest, this protects the owner of the interest by notifying all potential dealers in the land of its existence.

13.3.2 Rights of the mortgagor

The essence of a mortgage is that it is a debt secured on a property or land. The intention of the mortgagor is that he or she will repay the debt and be allowed to enjoy his or her land without interference. The land is simply security for the debt: it provides the mortgagee with a tangible asset that it can sell to recover its money if the mortgagor fails to repay the debt. The mortgagor's intention is not to allow the mortgagee to obtain the land for itself: when the loan has been repaid, the lender's interest in the land disappears.

⟩ CROSS REFERENCE

For more on the registering of charges, see Chapter 4.

The mortgage takes effect as a contract, agreed between the mortgagor and mortgagee. Most residential mortgage contracts these days are fairly standard in their wording—but as with any contract, the parties can agree to include whatever terms they choose into the contractual document.

The law is very careful to protect the interests of the mortgagor, who is often in a more vulnerable position than the mortgagee. Remember that, although the mortgage industry is now well regulated, this was not always the case. The very nature of the mortgage transaction may give rise to unfairness. Particularly where residential properties are involved, the two contracting parties may well be in very different bargaining positions: the mortgagor may well be very anxious to raise money through the mortgage and may be prepared to agree to something that is not in his or her interests. The mortgagee, on the other hand, is often a commercial organization that has the upper hand in the negotiations.

The bundle of rights given by the law to the mortgagor is known as the mortgagor's **equity of redemption** and will be discussed further later. Before we go on, however, you should check that you understand each of the following terms:

- Equitable right of redemption
  This is the right that the mortgagor acquires to repay all of the capital, interest, and costs involved under the mortgage arrangement, once the legal date of redemption has passed, and thereby wholly own his or her property (see 13.2).

- Equity of redemption
  This is the bundle of rights that the law gives to the mortgagor, only one of which is the equitable right of redemption.

- Equity
  You may have heard the term 'equity' in the media. The **equity** in a property refers to the value that is the difference between the value of the property and the amount of outstanding mortgage debt. This might be more fully described as the value of the mortgagor's equity of redemption.

equity of redemption
the bundle of rights given by law to the mortgagor, which includes the equitable right of redemption

equity
the value that is the difference between the monetary worth of a property and the amount of outstanding mortgage debt

---

→ EXAMPLE

Sian's house is worth £100,000. She bought it with the help of a £75,000 interest-only mortgage. The difference between these two figures is Sian's equity in the property—that is, £25,000. If she were to sell the house and repay the mortgage, this is what she would be left with.

In the 1990s, the term **negative equity** was frequently heard. During the 1980s, when property prices were high, many people had taken out large mortgages to buy their homes; after a property crash, house prices dropped sharply, leaving many people owing more money than their homes were worth.

> **negative equity** a negative value that arises when the monetary worth of a property is less than the amount of outstanding mortgage debt

EXAMPLE

The value of Sian's house may have fallen to £50,000. Rather than having equity in the property, Sian would now have negative equity. If she were to sell the property for £50,000, she would be unable to repay the whole £75,000 to the mortgagee and would have to find another £25,000 from somewhere to repay the debt.

13.3.2.1 Clogs and fetters

> **clogs and fetters**
> any provision in a mortgage deed that restricts the mortgagor's equity of redemption

One of the ways in which equity protects the mortgagor—and we are now talking about equity as a part of law rather than the equity held in a property—is to prevent the mortgagee from attaching any unfair restrictions or applying any unfair conditions to the mortgage contract. This protection is often referred to as the prohibition of **clogs and fetters** on the mortgage. For those interested in the original meaning of these words—a 'clog' was a weight attached to the hind leg of an animal to stop it wandering off and a 'fetter' was a kind of chain, or shackle, attached to someone's ankle, to restrict that person's movement. This poetic description simply means that the mortgage must be free from unnecessary restrictions and undue burdens.

Cases in this area fall into two main categories:

- attempts by the mortgagee to restrict the mortgagor's equity of redemption;
- attempts by the mortgagee to gain a collateral advantage from the mortgagor—for example, by making it a condition of the mortgage that the mortgagor must buy products only from the mortgagee.

> **unconscionability**
> gross unfairness or morally wrong behaviour that should go against the conscience of an honest person, stemming from the idea that a person's conscience must be affected for equity to intervene

These will now be considered in more detail. As we will see, greater regulation of the mortgage industry has led to a more flexible interpretation of the prohibition on clogs and fetters, and if the court does not detect any **unconscionability** in the transaction, it may well allow it to stand.

13.3.2.2 The right to redeem

The mortgagor's right to redeem the mortgage by repaying the debt with interest is fundamental to the law of mortgages. The right has been protected for many centuries. In *Santley v. Wilde* [1899] 2 Ch 474 Lindley MR said (at 475) that there must be no 'clogs or fetters' on the equity of redemption:

> A clog or a fetter is something which is inconsistent with the idea of security; a clog or fetter is in the nature of a repugnant condition … If I gave a mortgage on a condition that I shall not redeem, that is a repugnant condition.

The court will generally not be impressed if the mortgagee tries to restrict the mortgagor's right to redeem in any way. If the mortgagee tries to impose such a condition on the mortgagor, the court will look very closely at the agreement, the bargaining power of the respective parties, and the circumstances surrounding the mortgage. If two equal parties freely entered into an agreement, then the court will not necessarily interfere.

THINKING POINT

How might the mortgagee try to restrict the mortgagor's right to redeem?

The mortgagee might try to prevent redemption altogether, or specify that only a certain person is allowed to redeem the mortgage, or impose a condition that the mortgage is not allowed to be redeemed for a very long time.

Two contrasting cases neatly illustrate the circumstances in which a court will and will not allow a term that postpones the right of redemption.

CASE CLOSE-UP

Fairclough v. Swan Brewery Co. Ltd [1912] AC 565

The mortgaged property was leasehold and the lease ran for 172 years. In the mortgage contract, the mortgagee imposed a term that prevented the mortgagor from redeeming the mortgage until six weeks before the end of the lease. The Privy Council decided that this term was void: it effectively denied the mortgagor the right to redeem the mortgage at all!

If, however, the clause postponing the redemption of the mortgage is not oppressive and does not completely negate the right to redeem, the court may well allow it to stand.

It will not simply help the mortgagor to escape from a contract that is not favourable to him or her.

CASE CLOSE-UP

Knightsbridge Estates Trust Ltd v. Byrne [1939] Ch 441

Two commercial organizations entered into a mortgage agreement on a freehold property that prohibited the mortgagor from redeeming the mortgage for forty years. When interest rates dropped, the mortgagor wanted to redeem the mortgage early.

The court held that the term was not unreasonable. The contracting parties were both businesses negotiating at arm's length and the term was neither unconscionable nor oppressive.

The key element that the court will look for is unconscionability. A clause will be deemed unfair and unconscionable only if it can be shown that 'one of the parties to it has imposed the objectionable terms in a morally reprehensible manner, that is to say, in a way which affects his conscience'—*Multiservice Bookbinding Ltd v. Marden* [1979] Ch 84, 110, per Browne-Wilkinson J. This case is interesting because it brings together some of the issues about which we have been thinking.

CASE CLOSE-UP

Multiservice Bookbinding Ltd v. Marden [1979] Ch 84

The mortgage agreement in this case contained a number of clauses that the mortgagor claimed were unconscionable. These included:

- postponing the redemption of the mortgage for ten years;
- capitalizing any interest after twenty-one days (which meant, effectively, that the mortgagor, if it fell behind with its payments, could end up paying interest on the interest);
- index-linking the value of the amount loaned and interest payable to the Swiss Franc.

At the end of the ten-year period, currency fluctuations had significantly increased the capital amount due under the mortgage. The mortgagee (lender) was an individual and the mortgagor (borrower) was a small, but successful, company. The mortgagor had acted with independent legal advice. In addition, the value of the mortgaged premises had significantly increased since it was purchased.

 THINKING POINT

Do you think that the mortgage was deemed to be unconscionable in this case?

The terms of the mortgage were upheld. Although the agreement was somewhat harsh, it was not unconscionable. The mortgagor had entered into it freely and was under no pressure to accept the terms. In addition, there was no evidence of 'sharp practice' by the mortgagee and the mortgagor had also had the advantage of legal advice.

13.3.2.3 Collateral advantages

The mortgagor is also given protection against the mortgagee obtaining an additional advantage by including secondary conditions in the mortgage agreement.

For example, in *Noakes v. Rice* [1902] AC 24, the mortgagee, a brewery, imposed a condition on the mortgagor, a pub landlord, that he must buy all of his beer from the mortgagee, not only during the whole mortgage term, but also after the mortgage had been redeemed. This kind of agreement is known as a **solus tie**, in that it ties the mortgagor into buying products only from the mortgagee. This was found to be a clog on the mortgagor's equity of redemption, largely because the mortgagor was bound by the clause even after the mortgage had been redeemed, which the court said was harsh and oppressive.

solus tie
a type of agreement that binds the mortgagor into buying products only from the mortgagee

Again, the key to the court setting aside such a clause will be unconscionability. The courts have shown an increasing willingness to accept that, while the collateral term should not clog the equity of redemption, there is no reason why the parties should not make a perfectly reasonable business arrangement outside—but alongside—the mortgage agreement.

 CASE CLOSE-UP

Kreglinger v. New Patagonia Meat and Cold Storage Co. Ltd [1914] AC 25

The two parties were in the same industry: the mortgagor was a small meat-preserving company; the mortgagee was a firm of woolbrokers. The agreement contained a term that, for five years after the mortgage started, the mortgagor would only sell its sheepskins (a by-product of the meat-preserving business) to the mortgagee. The mortgagee would pay market value for them and also would not demand repayment of the loan for the five-year period.

The mortgage was paid off after two and a half years and the mortgagor argued that the term was unfair, because the agreement to sell the sheepskins only to the mortgagee continued for a further two and a half years after the redemption of the mortgage.

The House of Lords said that the agreement was neither unfair nor unconscionable. Viscount Haldane LC said that the Court should look at the substance of the agreement rather than its form. Although the clause was contained in the mortgage agreement, it was essentially a separate agreement: a 'collateral bargain'. It did not fetter the equity of redemption and was simply a trade agreement between two commercial parties.

Although the Court would carefully protect the mortgagor from clogs and fetters on the equity of redemption, it would not interfere in a legitimate business agreement. Lord Mersey (at 46) described the doctrine of clogs and fetters as *an unruly dog, which, if not securely chained to its own kennel, is prone to wander into places where it should not be'*.

The House of Lords put the dog firmly back in its kennel.

13.3.2.4 Options to purchase

Another means by which the mortgagee can fetter the equity of redemption is by including in the agreement a clause allowing it to acquire the mortgaged land for itself. This is often in the form of an option to purchase the mortgaged land. This undermines the whole purpose of the mortgage agreement and, generally, the court does not like such a clause.

As we will see, however, the guiding principle is again unconscionability.

 CASE CLOSE-UP

Samuel v. Jarrah Timber and Wood Paving Corporation Ltd [1904] AC 323

The mortgagor granted a mortgage on some debenture stock (a type of financial asset) in order to obtain £5,000 in cash. The mortgage agreement contained a clause giving the mortgagee the right to purchase the stock at any time within the next year at an agreed rate.

The House of Lords held that this was a clog on the equity of redemption. It expressed its reluctance to do this, however, because the parties were in equal bargaining positions and at arm's length.

One of the key factors in the House of Lords' decision in this case seems to be the timing of the agreement to grant an option to purchase the property. In *Jarrah*, the option was included within the mortgage agreement itself. In *Reeve v. Lisle* [1902] AC 461, the House of Lords upheld an option to purchase the mortgaged property, because it was agreed ten or eleven days *after* the mortgage agreement. It was, therefore, a separate transaction from the mortgage itself.

Although, in the vast majority of modern residential mortgages, the issue of the mortgagee acquiring the property for itself simply will not arise, it does still appear in some cases involving mortgage agreements between private individuals.

CASE CLOSE-UP

Jones v. Morgan **[2001] EWCA Civ 995, [2002] 1 EGLR 125**

The mortgagor and mortgagee were acquaintances. The mortgagee agreed to lend the mortgagor money to convert an old farmhouse into (originally) a residential home and (eventually) flats. The mortgage agreement was varied in order to allow the mortgagor to sell some of the mortgaged land to release funds and repay some of the debt. The varied agreement also said that the mortgagor would transfer half of the remaining property to the mortgagee. The court at first instance decided that this was a clog on the equity of redemption.

The Court of Appeal somewhat reluctantly agreed that the term was a clog on the equity of redemption. Although the agreement to transfer the land was made at a date later than the original mortgage, it was essentially part of the mortgage transaction itself. Lord Phillips MR described the doctrine of clogs on the equity of redemption as '*an appendix to our law which no longer serves a useful purpose and would be better excised*' (at [86]).

13.3.3 Rights and remedies of the mortgagee

So far, we have looked at the ways in which the law protects the mortgagor. Traditionally, the mortgagor was always seen as the vulnerable party, at risk of exploitation by the big, bad mortgagee—but times have changed. Buying a property with the help of a mortgage has become an everyday reality for millions of people and the increased regulation of the mortgage industry reflects this. The law recognizes that the mortgagee requires protection as well—many people every year fail to make their mortgage repayments and, although banks are often sympathetic and helpful, they have a legitimate need to protect their own commercial interests. Just as the law protects the right of the mortgagor to redeem the mortgage, it also protects the right of the mortgagee to recover the money that it has lent to the mortgagor.

The mortgagee has five potential remedies to recover its money:

- an action on the mortgagor's personal covenant to repay the mortgage;
- the right to repossess the mortgaged premises;
- the right to appoint a receiver;
- the power to sell the mortgaged premises;
- the right of foreclosure.

The mortgagee does not have to choose which of these remedies it wants to pursue: it can pursue any, or all, of them concurrently. Indeed, with the exception of foreclosure—which is perhaps the most extreme remedy—the mortgagee will often combine the remedies to maximize the prospects of recovering the money that it is owed.

An example may help you to understand this.

➡ **EXAMPLE**

Graham has fallen months behind with his mortgage repayments and has no realistic prospect of ever repaying the arrears. The mortgagee, Binkleys Bank, has decided that it must take steps to recover the outstanding amount.

It seeks possession of the property. The property will be much easier to sell if potential buyers do not have to see the (understandably grumpy) mortgagor when they come to look round the property.

This links in to the second remedy: it will sell the property to recover as much of its money as it can.

If the sale of the property does not raise enough money to pay off the mortgage debt, it will sue Graham on his personal covenant to repay in order to recover the outstanding balance.

13.3.3.1 Suing on the personal covenant

We have already seen that a mortgage is essentially a contract, under which the mortgagor agrees to repay the sum borrowed, together with any interest due under the agreement. If this term is breached and the mortgagor does not repay the debt, then the mortgagee can sue the mortgagor in common law. This right continues after the mortgagee has repossessed and sold the property, and subsists even if the mortgagor transfers his or her interest in the mortgaged property to someone else (although, in practice, the transferee would indemnify the mortgagor against this).

THINKING POINT

Why might this not appear to be very useful to the mortgagee, initially?

Generally, if somebody has fallen behind with his or her mortgage repayments, it is an indication that his or her financial position is very poor. Even if the mortgagee obtains a court order to make the mortgagor pay back what he or she owes, it is of little use if the mortgagor has no money or assets whatsoever! That is why this remedy is almost always combined with repossession and sale.

The right of the mortgagee to sue on the mortgagor's covenant continues for twelve years from the date that the right to receive the money accrued—Limitation Act 1980 (LA 1980), s. 20(1). This date will usually be specified in the mortgage agreement. The House of Lords rejected any suggestion that the sale of the mortgaged property starts a further twelve-year period—*West Bromwich Building Society v. Wilkinson* [2005] UKHL 44, [2005] 1 WLR 2303. The twelve-year period relates only to the capital money owed under the mortgage—this is the initial amount borrowed by the mortgagor. The mortgagor may also owe interest arrears, but the mortgagee has only six years to recover this outstanding amount—LA 1980, s. 20(5), and *Bristol and West plc v. Bartlett* [2002] EWCA Civ 1181, [2002] 4 All ER 544.

So although initially this may not seem to be a terribly useful remedy, in practice, it can be helpful to the mortgagee. The mortgagor's financial fortunes can change considerably in twelve years and someone who could not manage his or her mortgage repayments many years ago may well now have acquired the capital to repay the shortfall in full. It should also be noted that, under LA 1980, s. 29(5), any fresh payment or acknowledgement of the mortgage debt will cause the limitation period to start again, from the date of the payment or letter. In *Bradford and Bingley plc v. Rashid* [2006] UKHL 37, the House of Lords held that two letters from a legal advice centre, written on the mortgagor's behalf, were not protected by legal privilege and were admissible in court. Because the letters had effectively acknowledged the debt, they caused the time period to run afresh, thus giving the mortgagee another (unexpected!) opportunity to recover its money.

13.3.3.2 **The right to possession**

It may come as a surprise to you to learn that the mortgagee has a right to enter into possession of the mortgaged premises 'as soon as the ink is dry' on the mortgage agreement, unless that agreement provides to the contrary—*Four-Maids Ltd v. Dudley Marshall (Properties) Ltd* [1957] Ch 317, 320. There is no need for the mortgagor to have fallen behind in his or her mortgage repayments. In *Ropaigealach v. Barclays Bank plc* [1999] 4 All ER 235, Clarke LJ commented (at 253) that 'many mortgagors would be surprised to discover that a bank which had lent them money to buy a property for them to live in could take possession of it the next day'.

Of course, in normal circumstances most banks and building societies have no interest in entering into possession of the property: the property is intended to be occupied usually by the mortgagor and, as long as the mortgagee is receiving its money, both parties are happy. The mortgagee will want to recover the premises, however, if the mortgagor defaults on his or her mortgage payments and the mortgagee decides to sell the property. Houses sell better with vacant possession: disgruntled mortgagors continuing to live in the premises understandably put off buyers!

Although the mortgagee has the right to take possession of the premises, it will very rarely do so—particularly if the premises are occupied—without a court order. This is largely because the mortgagee runs the risk of breaking the criminal law under Criminal Law Act 1977, s. 6(1) if the mortgagor in possession is in any way treated violently or threatened with violence in the course of obtaining possession—and it is unlikely that many mortgagors will obey meekly when asked to leave the premises. If the premises are unoccupied, however, the mortgagee can step in and repossess the property. This may have serious consequences for the mortgagor, as we shall soon see.

Hope for the mortgagor

If the mortgage is secured on a dwelling house—meaning that it is held over residential, rather than commercial, property—the court throws the mortgagor a potential lifeline.

In making a decision as to whether to grant the order for possession, the court has an inherent discretion to allow a stay of the order for a short time to allow the mortgagor some time to organize his or her affairs—*Birmingham Citizens Permanent Building Society v. Caunt* [1962] Ch 883.

More important, however, is the statutory protection afforded to the mortgagor by the Administration of Justice Act 1970 (AJA 1970).

 STATUTE

Administration of Justice Act 1970, s. 36

(1) Where a mortgagee under a mortgage of land which consists of or includes a dwelling-house brings an action in which he claims possession of the mortgaged property, not being an action for foreclosure in which a claim for possession of the mortgaged property is also made, the court may exercise any of the powers conferred on it by subsection (2) below if it appears to the court that in the event of its exercising the power the mortgagor is likely to be able within a reasonable period to pay any sums due under the mortgage or to remedy a default consisting of a breach of any other obligation arising under or by virtue of the mortgage.

(2) The court—

   (a) may adjourn the proceedings; or

   (b) on giving judgment, or making an order, for delivery of possession of the mortgaged property, or at any time before the execution of such judgment or order, may—

> (i) stay or suspend execution of the judgment or order, or
>
> (ii) postpone the date for delivery of possession, for any such period or periods as the court thinks reasonable.
>
> …

AJA 1970, s. 36 provides the mortgagor with a real opportunity to stop the process of repossession if he or she can demonstrate to the court that he or she has the means to pay back 'any sums due under the mortgage' within a 'reasonable' time.

Both of these terms have caused some confusion. 'Any sums due' could, of course, imply not only the mortgage arrears, but the whole of the mortgage debt, particularly if the mortgage agreement contained a penalty clause requiring repayment of the whole amount if the mortgagor defaulted—*Halifax Building Society v. Clark* [1973] Ch 307. AJA 1973, s. 8(1), clarified the position by providing that the court could treat only the amount in arrears as 'sums due', provided that it also took into account the mortgagor's ability to pay any further instalments that had subsequently become due—AJA 1973, s. 8(2). Essentially, then, the court will look at the mortgagor's ability to pay all of the sums due to the time at which the case is heard. In practice, it will also surely have in mind the mortgagor's likely ability to make payments in the immediate future.

The second term that has caused some difficulty is whether the mortgagor can repay the arrears over 'a reasonable time'. In previous years, this was considered to be a two-year period—but *Cheltenham and Gloucester Building Society v. Norgan* [1996] 1 WLR 343 changed this and the strong presumption now is that the starting point for the court, in working out what is a 'reasonable time', is considered to be the remainder of the life of the mortgage. Note that this is indeed only a starting point and not an automatic right for the mortgagor. The court will exercise its discretion and decide according to the circumstances of the individual case.

Q CASE CLOSE-UP

Cheltenham and Gloucester Building Society v. Norgan [1996] 1 WLR 343

Evans LJ helpfully summarized the considerations that were likely to be relevant in the court's exercise of its discretion:

1. How much can the borrower reasonably afford to pay, both now and in the future?
2. If the borrower has a temporary difficulty in meeting his obligations, how long is the difficulty likely to last?
3. What was the reason for the arrears that have accumulated?
4. How much remains of the original mortgage term?
5. What kind of a mortgage is it? What are the terms of the contract? When is the principal due to be repaid?
6. Should the court exercise its power to disregard the accelerated payment provisions (AJA 1973, s. 8)?
7. Is it reasonable to expect the lender, in the circumstances of the particular case, to recoup the arrears of interest: (i) over the whole of the original term; or (ii) within a shorter period; or even (iii) within a longer period?

The mortgagor must be able to demonstrate a realistic prospect of paying the arrears, not simply a hope or possibility. He or she must also make a full and frank disclosure of income and expenditure, to enable the court to properly make its decision about whether or not to exercise its discretion—*Jameer v. Paratus AMC* [2012] EWCA Civ 1924.

 EXAMPLE

1. Fiona has fallen behind with her mortgage repayments and the bank has applied for an order to repossess her home. She tells the court that she was only in arrears because she had lost her well-paid job in the City, but that she has just started another one and is earning more than she earned before. Is the court likely to grant a postponement of the possession order?

Probably. Fiona has some tangible evidence that her financial position has significantly improved. The court may well think that, in these circumstances, it should exercise its discretion.

2. Imagine instead that Fiona goes to court and tells them that she will be able to make the payments, because she is convinced that she will win the lottery on Saturday. What is the court likely to say now?

Fiona is likely to have to start packing. The court is unlikely to exercise its discretion on the basis of a hope or wish. The rights of the mortgagee must also be considered and it has the right to recover its money.

The protection afforded by AJA 1970, s. 36 is obviously very valuable to the mortgagor. Remember, however, that it only applies when the mortgagee has sought an order for possession: if the mortgagee manages to acquire possession of the property without a court order, the court is unable to exercise its discretion.

This can be seen in the somewhat unfortunate case—at least for the mortgagors—of *Ropaigealach v. Barclays Bank plc.*

 CASE CLOSE-UP

Ropaigealach v. Barclays Bank plc [1999] 4 All ER 235

A husband and wife fell behind with their mortgage repayments, and the bank wrote to them several times individually, finally notifying them of its intention to repossess the property and to sell it at auction. On the date notified, the bank took possession and the house was sold. The couple were not at the property, because it was undergoing refurbishment and both claimed that they had received no letter from the bank.

The couple claimed that the statutory protection afforded to mortgagors under AJA 1970, s. 36 would be undermined unless the court construed that section to mean that it would be unlawful for a mortgagee to enter into possession unless by a court order.

The Court of Appeal held that the court could only exercise its powers under s. 36 if the mortgagee had begun an action for possession. If the mortgagee was legally entitled to take possession of the property, then it need not seek a court order to do so. This means effectively that if a mortgagee is able to take possession of the premises without a court order, then the mortgagor will not be afforded the protection of s. 36.

Ropaigelach left many property lawyers uncomfortable about the loophole in the protection for mortgagors. However, a recent case in this area of law has led to widespread calls for an urgent review of AJA 1970, s. 36. In *Horsham Properties Group v. Clark* [2008] EWHC 2327 (Ch), the statutory mechanism of s. 36 was once again bypassed perfectly legally by a different means.

Q CASE CLOSE-UP

Horsham Properties Group v. Clark [2008] EWHC 2327 (Ch)

The mortgagors took out a mortgage with GMAC. The property was described as a buy-to-let property, although the mortgagors appeared to be living in it. As with any legal mortgage, the lender had a statutory power of sale, implied into the mortgage agreement, under LPA 1925, s. 101. The mortgage agreement also contained provisions which specified that if the borrowers were more than one month in arrears with their mortgage payments, the lender could sell the property or appoint a receiver of the property.

The mortgagors fell behind with their repayments, and GMAC appointed receivers of the property, which sold it to Coastal Enterprises Ltd, which in turn transferred it to Horsham Properties. During this time, the mortgagors remained in possession of the property. Once Horsham owned the property, it began possession proceedings to remove the mortgagors, on the grounds that, by purchasing the property, it had overridden the rights of the mortgagors and, consequently, that the mortgagors were now trespassers.

We have just seen in *Ropaigelach* that a mortgagee does not have to seek a court order before it takes possession of a mortgaged property, and that if it does not seek a court order for possession, then AJA 1970, s. 36 is not triggered. *Horsham* adds a different dimension to the issue of triggering the court's discretion under s. 36.

The problem for the mortgagors in *Horsham* was that the application for possession was not made by the mortgagee, but by the purchaser of the property and, under these circumstances, s. 36 is not engaged. The court has no discretion to postpone possession. The mortgagors claimed that this was incompatible with the Human Rights Act 1998 (HRA 1998), and could only be compatible if s. 36 was construed to extend to applications for possession made by a purchaser, as well as a mortgagee.

Briggs J rejected both arguments. The exercise of a statutory power of sale under LPA 1925, s. 101 was not incompatible with the HRA 1998, and s. 36 could not be triggered in the context of a claim for possession by a purchaser.

Immediately after *Horsham*, the Ministry of Justice called for an urgent review of the implications of the decision. Reaction to this was divided: the residential mortgage industry, represented by the Council of Mortgage Lenders (CML), argued that existing safeguards were sufficient. Those involved in helping mortgagors in defending against repossession, such as the Citizens' Advice Bureau, welcomed the review and recommended urgent action.

Proposed reforms

Following *Horsham*, the Home Repossession (Protection) Bill 2008–09 (a Private Members' Bill) was introduced into the House of Commons. It proposed that before exercising the power of sale in respect of residential properties (see 13.3.3.4), the mortgagee must apply for a court order before taking possession of the property. This would then trigger the court's discretion under s. 36 to adjourn the possession proceedings, or to postpone the possession. This Bill was withdrawn before its second reading in the House. Following this, a second Private Members' Bill, the Secured Lending Reform Bill 2010–11, was introduced, which was similarly unsuccessful. The CML has so far successfully argued that its members should be allowed to regulate themselves, without changes to their legal rights. Its members have agreed voluntarily not to seek to sell an owner-occupied (i.e. residential, rather than buy-to-let) property, without first obtaining a court order for possession. Immediately after the proposed reforms, a variety of schemes designed to assist struggling homeowners emerged. However, as economic circumstances have improved, these have been discontinued and there is currently only one scheme running across the whole of the UK, the Support for Mortgage Interest scheme ('SMI'). Additional help is provided in Scotland and Wales. Even with this scheme, the government has announced plans to make major changes in 2018.

Pre-action protocol

pre-action protocol
a statement of best practice about pre-action conduct which has been approved by the Head of Civil Justice

In November 2008, a new **pre-action protocol** for possessions based on mortgage arrears came into effect. Pre-action protocols are intended to reduce the likelihood that the parties in a dispute will go to court, by encouraging them to fully discuss and try to settle the dispute between themselves.

The protocol applies to all first charge residential mortgages in the UK. Its aim is to improve communication between lenders and borrowers, and to encourage the solution of problems with arrears at an early stage, in order to avoid, where possible, the need for repossession proceedings.

The protocol does not alter the legal rights of the mortgagee, but it does encourage lenders to postpone possession proceedings wherever possible, particularly if the mortgagor is already trying to sell the mortgaged property him- or herself. Beginning possession proceedings should be seen as a last resort by mortgagees, and when determining applications for possession of mortgaged premises, the court will look at whether (and to what extent) lenders have complied with the protocol.

Time limits

Lenders generally prefer to let defaulting mortgagors stay in their homes for as long as possible. However, *Ashe v. National Westminster Bank* [2008] EWCA Civ 55, [2008] 1 WLR 710 has raised some concern that this might not always happen.

🔍 CASE CLOSE-UP

Ashe v. National Westminster Bank [2008] EWCA Civ 55, [2008] 1 WLR 710

Mr and Mrs Babai owned a long leasehold property in Stockport. There was a mortgage over the property, with Halifax plc. In 1989, they granted a second legal charge (mortgage) over the property to National Westminster Bank plc ('the Bank'), to secure Mr Babai's debts with the bank. In 1992, following a period of non-payment, the bank made a formal request for payment, but took no steps to recover possession of the property. The parties negotiated payment by instalments, and some payments were made. The last was a payment of £40 in January 1993. In March 1993, Mr Babai was made bankrupt. Correspondence continued intermittently but no further payments were made. In 2006, a new trustee in bankruptcy, Mr Ashe, began proceedings. He argued that the bank's right to take action accrued when the legal charge was granted (1989), and accrued afresh at the date of the last payment (1993). As more than twelve years had passed since that date, the bank's right to possession of the property was statute-barred under LA 1980, ss. 15 and 17 and, as a result, it had lost its legal interest in the property.

The bank argued that although its contractual right to sue Mr Babai was time-barred (see 13.3.1), its right to possession of the property had not been extinguished as Mr Babai was not 'adversely possessing' the property, but was with the bank's consent. The bank's right of action had not yet accrued.

The bank argued this because LA 1980, s. 15 sets a twelve-year limit to recover land. The twelve-year period begins when the right of action (which includes the right to enter into possession) accrues. LA 1980, s. 17 provides that at the end of that period the rights of the person entitled to recover the land will be extinguished. LA 1980, Sch. 1, para. 8 provides that the right of action only accrues when there is a person in adverse possession of the land. The Court held that this paragraph also applies to claims by legal mortgagees against mortgagors in possession. Time only began running against the bank, then, when the Babais began to be in adverse possession of the property.

The Court decided that the Babais were indeed in adverse possession of the property, according to the meaning of that term in *J. A. Pye (Oxford) Ltd v. Graham* [2003] 1 AC 419. In *Ashe v. National Westminster Bank*, Mummery LJ commented (at [92]):

> [t]he focus is not on the nature of the possession but on the capacity of the person in possession. Ordinary possession of land is adverse possession so far as the person out of possession and the 1980 Act is concerned. Mr & Mrs Babai were in possession of the property. The bank was not in possession of the property nor was anyone else.

The bank's right of action accrued when the charge was made and then again at the date of the last payment. As more than twelve years had passed since that date, the interest of the bank had been extinguished.

Lenders were anxious that a decision such as this would have serious consequences for them, and might lead to them seeking possession of mortgaged premises much earlier than they otherwise would have done, to ensure that an *Ashe* type situation would not occur. Mummery LJ dismissed these concerns, stating that mortgagees would only need to take 'modest steps' to protect themselves, such as obtaining small payments and acknowledgment of debt from mortgagors. This would cause time to run afresh.

Duties of the mortgagee in possession

Once the mortgagee has obtained possession of the property, it has some serious responsibilities in respect of the mortgaged property. In most cases, it will make sense for the mortgagee to make a quick sale and recover its money.

Before sale, or if the mortgagee decides to rent the property out, it is responsible for the physical state of the property. The mortgagee must also obtain the best rent possible and must not benefit personally from the arrangement—*White v. City of London Brewery Company* (1889) 42 Ch D 237. If it leaves the property empty, the mortgagee will be liable to pay the rent itself. Given these somewhat onerous requirements, if the mortgagee wishes to keep, rather than to sell, the mortgaged property, it may well make sense to appoint a receiver to look after it.

13.3.3.3 Appointing a receiver

The mortgagee has a statutory right under LPA 1925, ss. 101(1)(iii) and 109, to appoint a **receiver**. This right can only be exercised, however, when the mortgagee becomes entitled to exercise the power of sale: LPA 1925, s. 109(1) (see 13.3.3.4).

A receiver is someone who essentially takes over the management of the mortgaged property. He or she receives rents and other income from the property, and pays the property's expenses,

receiver

a person appointed by the court to protect and preserve property during the course of litigation applying whatever money is left over to paying back the money owed under the mortgage—that is, interest arrears and, if directed by the mortgagee, capital. If anything is left over after these payments, it is paid to the mortgagor.

Receivers are most often appointed when the mortgaged premises are commercial. Indeed, the receiver may well take over the running of the mortgagor's business at the premises, although he or she is under no obligation to do so.

The advantage to the mortgagee of appointing a receiver is that he or she is deemed to be the agent of the mortgagor—LPA 1925, s. 109(2)—and so the mortgagee has no responsibility for his or her actions. The receiver has a duty to act in good faith, of course, and must manage the property with due diligence.

13.3.3.4   Power of sale

Most mortgage agreements contain a provision that expressly gives the mortgagee the **power of sale**. Even if the agreement does not contain such a clause, the mortgagee has a statutory power of sale under LPA 1925, s. 101(1)(i).

> **power of sale** the right of a mortgagee to sell a mortgaged property under certain circumstances

 STATUTE

Law of Property Act 1925, s. 101

A mortgagee, where the mortgage has been made by deed, shall ... have the following powers ...

    (i)   A power, when the mortgage money has become due, to sell, or to concur with any other person in selling, the mortgaged property ...

    ...

As soon as the legal date for redemption of the mortgage has passed—which, as we have seen at 13.2, is usually six months after the creation of the mortgage—the power of sale for the mortgagee arises. That power is not, however, exercisable until one of the conditions in LPA 1925, s. 103 has been met.

 STATUTE

Law of Property Act 1925, s. 103

A mortgagee shall not exercise the power of sale conferred by the Act unless and until—

    (i)   Notice requiring payment of the mortgage money has been served on the mortgagor or one or two of the mortgagors, and default has been made in payment of the mortgage money, or part thereof, for three months after such service; or

    (ii)   Some interest under the mortgage is in arrear and unpaid for two months after becoming due; or

    (iii)   There has been a breach of some provision in the mortgage deed or in this Act ...

The notice detailed in LPA 1925, s. 103(i) must be made in writing—LPA 1925, s. 196(1). Note also that only one of these conditions must be met—each is separated by the word *'or'*.

An example may help at this point.

> **EXAMPLE**
>
> Nadia grants a mortgage by deed to Burns Bank plc. It is an ordinary legal mortgage. Six months after the creation of the mortgage, the power of sale arises in Burns Bank's favour. Nadia continues to make payments for a few years, but then runs into financial difficulties. She defaults on two payments.
>
> One day, she receives a letter from Burns Bank, demanding that she repay the arrears on her mortgage. Unfortunately, Nadia still makes no payment. Three months after the date of the letter, Burns Bank's power of sale becomes exercisable. At this point, it can legally sell Nadia's home.

If the mortgagee sells the property before the power of sale becomes exercisable, the mortgagor can sue the mortgagee—LPA 1925, s. 104(2)(d).

Purchaser from a mortgagee

It is worth noting at this point that the purchaser of a property from a mortgagee will acquire good title from the mortgagee. The sale of the property will convey to the purchaser the mortgagor's original estate in the land—so, for example, if the mortgagor owned a freehold property, so too will the purchaser. He or she does not even need to investigate whether the power of sale has become exercisable—LPA 1925, s. 104(2)(d). If the purchaser actually knows that the power of sale had not become exercisable, however, he or she will not get good title—*Lord Waring v. London and Manchester Assurance Co. Ltd* [1935] Ch 310.

Once the property has been sold, the mortgagor's equity of redemption is destroyed—*National and Provincial Bank v. Ahmed* [1995] EGLR 127.

CROSS REFERENCE

For more on establishing good title, see Chapter 4.

Proceeds of sale

Once the sale has taken place, the mortgagee becomes a trustee of the proceeds of sale for the mortgagor. The proceeds must be applied according to the order laid down in LPA 1925, s. 105.

After paying off prior mortgages, if any, the mortgagee must apply the funds as follows:

1. all costs, charges, and expenses incurred by the mortgagee in selling the property—for example, estate agents' fees;

2. interest, costs, and any other money due under the mortgage (including the capital);

3. the residue to the mortgagor—or, indeed, any subsequent mortgagees, if there is more than one mortgage on the land.

The mortgagee's duties on sale

When a mortgagee attempts to sell a repossessed property, to some extent there will be a conflict of interest between mortgagee and mortgagor. Although it might appear that both would want to obtain the best price possible for the property, the reality is that the mortgagee simply wants to recover its money: it will not be interested in engaging in protracted negotiations with potential buyers to obtain the best price for the mortgagor. The law recognizes this tension and tries to balance the interests of both parties.

The mortgagee is not in the position of trustee for the mortgagor—*Cuckmere Brick Co. Ltd v. Mutual Finance Ltd* [1971] Ch 949. It does, however, owe the mortgagor a duty of care. This duty is rooted in equity, because of the relationship between mortgagor and mortgagee, rather than in the tort of negligence—*Parker-Tweedale v. Dunbar Bank plc* [1991] Ch 12. The mortgagee must act in good faith in the transaction. The mortgagee's motive in selling the property is not relevant, unless the sale is prompted by a motive that is completely unrelated to its wish to recover its debt, in which case, it may be an improper exercise of the mortgagee's power—*Meretz Investments NV v. ACP Ltd* [2006] EWHC 74 (Ch). In this case, it was held that, as long as one of the motives prompting the sale was to recover the mortgagee's debt, the mortgagee's exercise of the power of sale would be valid.

Time and mode of sale

Once the power of sale becomes exercisable, the mortgagee can choose when it sells the property. It is under no obligation to wait for better market conditions, although it must try to obtain the true market value of the property when it does decide to sell—*Cuckmere Brick Co. Ltd v. Mutual Finance Ltd* [1971] Ch 949. The mortgagee cannot sell it at a knock-down price, simply to recover its money—*Palk v. Mortgage Services Funding plc* [1993] Ch 330.

Although no specific mode of sale is prescribed by law, the mortgagee must ensure that all information relevant to the potential market value of the property is made known, in order to obtain the 'true market value'. In *Cuckmere Brick*, for example, no mention was made in the sales publicity of the fact that the land had a valuable planning permission already granted, which would have considerably increased its market value. In this case, the mortgagee was liable for a breach of its duty towards the mortgagor and had to compensate him accordingly.

Assessing 'true market value'

To obtain a realistic market value, the property should usually be offered on the open market, or at public auction, or, at the very least, be valued by a professional before it is sold. In *Meah v. GE Money Home Finance Ltd* [2013] EWHC 20 (Ch) the true 'market value' of a property was described as what *'a willing purchaser is prepared to pay for the property to a willing vendor after the property has been exposed to the market for a reasonable period of time'* (at 23). It is not necessarily the value ascribed to a property by experts. Sometimes it is difficult for the court to assess whether the property has been sold at a true market value. In *Michael v. Miller* [2004] EWCA Civ 282, the Court of Appeal suggested (at [135]) that:

> a mortgagee will not breach his duty to the mortgagor if in the exercise of his power to sell the mortgaged property he exercises his judgment reasonably; and to the extent that that judgment involves assessing the market value of the mortgaged property the mortgagee will have acted reasonably if his assessment falls within an acceptable margin of error.

The mortgagee has a duty to take reasonable care to sell the property for the best price reasonably obtainable. It will only have breached that duty, if it is *'plainly on the wrong side of the line'* in terms of the valuation (*Aodhcon LLP v. Bridgeco Ltd.* [2014] EWHC 535 (Ch) at 154.

The best way for the court to assess this is to look at the steps taken by the mortgagee to sell the property and then to consider whether the mortgagee's decision to sell at a particular price was reasonable, given all of the circumstances of the case. If the court finds that the property has been sold for less than it should have been, the mortgagee will be liable to pay the difference between the price obtained and the true market value to the mortgagor.

The way that the property was marketed during the sale may be a highly relevant factor.

Q | CASE CLOSE-UP

***Bishop v. Blake* [2006] EWHC 831 (Ch)**

In this case, the mortgaged property was a pub. The mortgagor granted a lease, without the consent of the mortgagee, for twenty-five years. This amounted to a breach of a term of the mortgage, which required that consent must be obtained from the mortgagee. At this point, the mortgagee's power of sale became exercisable and she subsequently sold the pub for £225,000 to a company connected to the tenants.

The mortgagor claimed that the sale was improper, because the property had been sold at a serious undervalue.

The court found that the mortgagee had sold the property at an undervalue. It reached this conclusion by examining the steps that the mortgagee had taken to sell the property and assessing the reasonableness of those steps in all of the circumstances of the case.

The judge found that the only marketing done by the mortgagee (in fact, by her agent) had been one small advertisement in the trade press (described by the judge as 'pathetic'), with inadequate contact details. The property had only been offered directly to the tenant and the tenant's first offer had been immediately accepted. This was despite the fact that the offer was £25,000 less than the (conservative) valuation of the property already given by a local surveyor.

After looking at an expert witness valuation from each of the parties, the judge awarded the mortgagor the difference between the sum received (£225,000) and the true market value of the property at the date of sale (£340,000): a warning to mortgagees that they must take all reasonable steps to obtain true market value, rather than concentrating exclusively on recovering their money!

Note, though, that even if there were shortcomings in the way that the mortgagee marketed the property, provided that the property was eventually sold at '*the best price reasonably achievable*', the court will accept that outcome—*Meah v. GE Money Home Finance Limited* [2013] EWHC 20 (Ch). In addition, the mortgagee is under no obligation to make the property any more marketable or to increase its potential market value, for example by repairing or refurbishing it—*Lloyds Bank v. Bryant* (1996) NPC 31.

Business premises

The mortgagee has no duty to undertake to continue the mortgagor's business after repossessing business premises, at least as long as the business ceased before the mortgagee entered into possession—*AIB Finance Ltd v. Debtors* [1998] 2 All ER 929. If the business property is repossessed as a going concern, however, then the mortgagee may well have a duty to sell it as a going concern, as part of its general duty to obtain a true market value for the property.

Limitation on the time of sale

As we have just seen, once the power of sale has become exercisable, the mortgagee can sell the property whenever it pleases. It has no duty to wait for the property market to improve, in order to obtain more money for the mortgagor.

Equally, however, the court does not allow it to delay a sale, in the hope of obtaining a better price, if that would mean the mortgagor sinking further into debt. This might happen, for example, in a depressed housing market, when, because of low property prices, the mortgagee would be unlikely to recover all of the debt. Under these circumstances, the mortgagee might decide to rent out the property until the market improved and then sell. The problem for the mortgagor, however, is that all of the time that the house is not sold, his or her debt will continue to increase. In these circumstances, the court offers the mortgagor a remedy under LPA 1925, s. 91(2).

 STATUTE

Law of Property Act 1925, s. 91(2)

Any person entitled to redeem mortgaged property may have a judgment or order for sale instead of for redemption in an action bought by him either for redemption alone, or for sale alone, or for sale or redemption in the alternative.

This means that, if the mortgagee does not want to sell the property but the mortgagor does, the court may grant an order forcing the mortgagee to sell.

 CASE CLOSE-UP

Palk v. Mortgage Services Funding plc [1993] Ch 330

This case was heard at a time when many homeowners were struggling with high interest rates and a depressed property market, leading to negative equity (see 13.3.2).

Mr and Mrs Palk had a £300,000 mortgage secured on their family home. Following the economic recession and failure of Mr Palk's business, the Palks decided to try to sell the property. They found a buyer prepared to pay £283,000. By this time, they owed the mortgagee £358,587, including arrears, and the mortgagee refused to allow the sale.

The mortgagee sought possession of the property, but did not intend to sell it. Instead, it wanted to wait until property prices recovered, to try to get back more of its debt. It wanted to rent the property in the meantime.

The court heard that, even offsetting the rental income against the mortgage debt, the Palks' debt to the mortgagee would increase by £30,000 for each year during which the house was not sold. Already, by the time of the court hearing, the debt had increased to £409,000. By this stage, Mr Palk was bankrupt, so Mrs Palk applied to the court for an order to sell the property, against the mortgagee's wishes, under LPA 1925, s. 91(2).

The court made an order for sale. This was making legal history, because there were no known cases in which a court had ordered a sale against the mortgagee's wishes, if it meant that the mortgagee would not recover all of its money. The circumstances of the case were such that fairness demanded a sale, to avoid plunging the mortgagors into even more debt and the mortgagee was given the opportunity of buying the property itself, if it believed that prices would rise.

This seems to be a very sensible decision by the court. It may appear to be slightly hard on the mortgagee, but do not forget that, even after sale, the mortgagee could sue Mrs Palk on her personal covenant to recover the balance (see 13.3.3).

The interesting case of *Polonski v. Lloyd's Bank Mortgages Ltd* [1998] 1 FLR 896 established that, in exercising its discretion under LPA 1925, s. 91(2), the court was not limited to consideration of purely financial matters.

🔍 CASE CLOSE-UP

Polonski v. Lloyd's Bank Mortgages Ltd [1998] 1 FLR 896

In this case, once again, the homeowner applied to the court for an order for sale of the mortgaged property under LPA 1925, s. 91(2). The owner was a woman who had bought the property with her partner. He had left, leaving her with two small children and difficult financial circumstances. Her mortgage was paid through housing benefits. The homeowner wanted to sell the property, in order to move to a better area, with better schools for the children and more job opportunities for her. Unfortunately, the offer that she received on the house would not fully repay the mortgage debt—it would leave around £12,000 of debt outstanding. The lender bank wanted to postpone the sale until house prices rose, in the hope that it would then recover the whole of its debt. Rather unusually, because the mortgage repayments were being paid by the state, there was no issue of the debt steadily increasing, as in *Palk*.

Jacobs J decided to make an order for sale, against the lender's wishes. He said that, in exercising his discretion under s. 91(2), he was entitled to look at all of the circumstances of the case. The court was not restricted to considering 'purely financial matters', but also could look at social matters, such as those raised by the homeowner. The homeowner had perfectly good reasons for wanting to move and had in no way been financially irresponsible.

Note too that the pre-action protocol on mortgage arrears (see 13.3.3.2) encourages the mortgagee to consider postponing starting possession proceedings if the mortgagor has taken or will take 'reasonable steps' to sell the house him- or herself. Reasonable steps include making sure that the property has been offered for sale at an appropriate price, and with professional advice. If the mortgagee agrees not to start proceedings in order to allow the mortgagor to try to sell the property, the protocol requires that the mortgagor must undertake to allow the mortgagee to communicate with professionals involved in the sale—for example, the estate agent. This is a useful provision for most mortgagors, as they are more likely to obtain a better price for the property than the mortgagee. This will benefit both parties: more of the mortgage debt will be repaid and the mortgagor may even have some money left over to fund his or her accommodation needs.

13.3.3.5 Foreclosure

The very drastic remedy of **foreclosure** is very seldom seen these days. It is only available to the mortgagee on application to the Chancery Division, and by a procedure that is somewhat ancient and appealing (although, of course, not to the mortgagor).

The reason that foreclosure is no longer used is that it has the effect of extinguishing the mortgagor's equity of redemption of the property in its entirety. The foreclosure order vests the whole of the mortgagor's estate in the mortgagee: effectively, the mortgagee steps into the shoes of the mortgagor and the mortgagee becomes registered as the proprietor of the land. The mortgagee does not have to pay the mortgagor any increase in the value of the property over and above the debt. For this reason, the court is unlikely to make an order if the value of the property exceeds the mortgage debt.

Equally, foreclosure will not be attractive to the mortgagee if there is negative equity in the property, because the order also extinguishes the personal covenant of the mortgagor, meaning that the mortgagee cannot pursue him or her for any shortfall.

In exceptional cases, the court can reopen an order for foreclosure and afford some relief to the mortgagor. This is so unusual, however, that it will not be further considered here.

> **foreclosure**
> a remedy under which the court orders a date by which the mortgagor must pay off his or her debt, or on which his or her property will be lost to the mortgagee

13.3.4 **Undue influence**

We have seen that equity is quick to protect mortgagors from any unconscionable behaviour on the part of the mortgagee. It also acts to ensure that the mortgagor is not subjected to any **undue influence** to enter into the mortgage, either at the hands of the mortgagee or from a third party. Undue influence includes any inappropriate pressure to sign a mortgage agreement that the mortgagor may not understand. It can also include misrepresentation of the implications of the agreement that the mortgagor is being encouraged to sign. If the mortgagor can establish that his or her agreement was obtained in this way, then the court will set aside the mortgage (in respect of the deceived mortgagor).

We will look, firstly, at a case law example to explain what 'undue influence' actually means and then we will consider the effect on the mortgagee. Finally, we will think about how the mortgagee might avoid such claims in the future.

> **undue influence**
>
> influence exerted by another that prevents a person from exercising independent judgement in relation to any decision

---

 CASE CLOSE-UP

Barclays Bank v. O'Brien [1993] 3 WLR 786

The facts

In this case, Mr and Mrs O'Brien took out a second mortgage secured against their property to support Mr O'Brien's failing business. Mrs O'Brien was somewhat unwilling to take out a further loan against her home, but Mr O'Brien was extremely persistent. He assured her that the loan was only for £60,000 and that it would be cleared in three weeks. On the strength of this, Mrs O'Brien signed the necessary paperwork. Unfortunately, the loan was actually for £135,000 and, of course, Mr O'Brien ran into financial difficulties.

The mortgagee bank was aware that the additional loan was to prop up Mr O'Brien's failing business. It had produced a letter advising Mrs O'Brien to obtain independent legal advice, but she did not read this. It neither explained the implications of the second loan to her, nor checked that she had obtained independent legal advice.

Undue influence can take many forms, not just threats or physical force, but other 'unacceptable forms of persuasion' (Lord Nicholls in *Royal Bank of Scotland v. Etridge (No. 2)* [2001] UKHL 44, [7]) such as one party taking unfair advantage of another, in a situation where there is a relationship of trust and confidence between the parties. It can arise where a 'vulnerable' person has been exploited, for example, where someone has taken advantage of their '*mental infirmity … youth or old age or … economic dependency*' (at 9)—*Liddle v. Cree* [2011] EWHC 3294 (Ch). It can also involve the influencing party deliberately not disclosing relevant information. In *Hewitt v. First Plus Financial Group plc* [2010] EWCA Civ 312, the Court of Appeal held that a husband's failure to disclose that he was having an affair before obtaining his wife's (reluctant) agreement to refinance the property amounted to undue influence. However, in *The Royal Bank of Scotland plc v. Chandra* [2010] EWHC 105 (Ch), Richards J made a clear distinction between inadvertent non-disclosure and '*deliberate concealment or suppression of material facts*' (at [140]). Only the latter, in his view, constituted undue influence.

The case of *Barclays Bank v. O'Brien* neatly demonstrates the difficulties with the doctrine of undue influence. If the undue influence or misrepresentation had come from the mortgagee, then it would seem reasonable that the mortgagee should be prevented from recovering its money. In most of these cases, however, the undue influence does not come from the mortgagee: it comes from a third party—often, but not always, a husband, who exercises undue influence over his wife to obtain her consent to a mortgage agreement that will usually confer little benefit on her. The mortgagee itself is essentially innocent and yet it is unable to recover the money that it legitimately lent to the influenced mortgagor. On the other hand, the influenced mortgagor is also innocent, because her agreement to the loan has been falsely obtained.

The courts have attempted to strike a balance, then, between the commercial interests of the mortgagee and the need to protect the influenced mortgagor.

Q CASE CLOSE-UP

Barclays Bank v. O'Brien [1993] 3 WLR 786

In the House of Lords, Lord Browne-Wilkinson, after reviewing the authorities, outlined the traditional distinction between different categories of undue influence (adopted from *BCCI SA v. Aboody* [1990] 1 QB 923):

Actual undue influence The claimant must positively prove that she was subjected to undue influence to enter into the transaction.

Presumed undue influence In certain cases, the claimant only needs to show that there was a relationship of trust and confidence between her and the alleged influencer. Once she has done this, the burden shifts to the influencer to prove that the claimant entered the transaction of her own free will. This category was divided into Class 2A—for which the law presumed such a relationship (as, for example, doctor and patient)—and Class 2B—for which there was no automatic presumption of such a relationship, but the claimant could prove that such a relationship existed. Generally, the husband and wife relationship would fall into this category. Lord Browne-Wilkinson accepted that '*the risk of undue influence affecting a voluntary disposition by a wife in favour of a husband is greater than in the ordinary run of cases where no sexual or emotional ties affect the free exercise of the individual's will*'.

Note that the House of Lords in *Royal Bank of Scotland v. Etridge (No. 2)* doubted the usefulness of these categories and developed a rather more straightforward test for notice. Lewison J in *Thompson v. Foy* [2009] EWHC 1076 (Ch) describes the categories of undue influence as '*no more than different ways of proving the same thing*' (at [100]). Both types of undue influence must be proved, but the advantage of presumed undue influence is that it may be proved with the aid of an evidential presumption. Presumed undue influence arises where there is a relevant relationship, in which one party placed trust and confidence in the other in respect of management of their financial affairs, together with a transaction which on the face of it requires further explanation. Once this is established, the presumption is that undue influence has occurred, and the burden of proof shifts to the alleged influencer, who must then rebut this presumption.

Q CASE CLOSE-UP

Barclays Bank v. O'Brien [1993] 3 WLR 786

If the bank is put on notice of the risk of undue influence, it should take steps to ensure that the wife's agreement has been properly obtained. If not, it will run the risk of having the transaction set aside. It is put on notice if:

1. the transaction is not, on the face of it, to the financial advantage to the wife;

2. there is a substantial risk in transactions of that kind that, in procuring the wife to act as surety, the husband has committed a legal or equitable wrong that entitles the wife to set aside the transaction.

In *Royal Bank of Scotland v. Etridge (No. 2)*, the House of Lords interpreted (at [44]) that Lord Browne-Wilkinson's words *'be taken to mean, quite simply, that a bank is put on inquiry whenever a wife offers to stand surety for her husband's debts'*. This does not mean that the bank is put on notice every time a couple applies for a joint mortgage; it will only be put on notice when, for example, a joint application is made that involves the wife agreeing to a second mortgage to fund debts of her husband. Note too that, although we have been talking in terms of wives and husbands, the bank is equally put on notice when a similar application is made by an unmarried couple, *'whether heterosexual or homosexual, where the bank is aware of the relationship'*—*Royal Bank of Scotland v. Etridge (No. 2)*, at [47]—or by applicants in other close family relationships. In *Abbey National Bank plc v. Stringer* [2006] EWCA Civ 38, for example, the son was found to have exercised undue influence over his elderly, illiterate mother.

Although these examples all relate to various relationships between the applicants, it is important to remember that, in broad terms, it is not the relationship between the parties that will put the lender on notice, but the nature of the transaction itself. If the application is made by people in any non-commercial relationship and one of the applicants is mortgaging his or her share of the property in order to guarantee a loan that would benefit the other applicant, then the lender will be put on notice and must comply with the steps suggested below.

In a commercial relationship, the court will carefully consider the facts of the case. If it is a 'sensible commercial relationship' and the claimant had received independent legal advice that she chose not to follow, in the absence of evidence of undue influence, the court would not interfere in a transaction even though it may be disadvantageous to the claimant (*Brown v. Stephenson* [2013] EWHC 2531 (Ch)).

Inevitably, each of these cases turns on its facts, and the appellate courts will be very reluctant to overturn a finding of the lower courts where the judge will have had the opportunity to hear the witness evidence. In *Crossfield v. Jackson* [2014] EWCA Civ 1548, Gloster LJ says: 'A decision as to whether there is a relationship of trust and confidence as between two people, and whether a transaction has been procured by undue influence, is necessarily highly fact sensitive and justifiably dependent upon the view formed by the judge of the principal protagonists' (at para. 21).

Barclays Bank v. O'Brien was one of a list of cases that started to suggest to the mortgagee the steps that it would need to take in order to protect itself from claims of undue influence. The most important of these steps was to advise the wife to take independent legal advice. In *Royal Bank of Scotland v. Etridge (No. 2)*, the House of Lords, firstly, clarified when the mortgagee would be put on notice that undue influence was a possibility and, then, suggested a whole sequence of steps that the mortgagee was required to take in order to escape a claim being levied against it.

🔍 CASE CLOSE-UP

Royal Bank of Scotland v. Etridge (No. 2) [2001] UKHL 44

The House of Lords made it clear that, for past cases, the bank would be protected if it had obtained confirmation from the solicitor acting for the wife in the transaction that he had explained the risks of the transaction to the wife.

For future cases, it outlined the necessary steps that a bank should take.

The bank should write to the wife and ask her for the name of the solicitor that she would like to act for her in the transaction. If the wife does not respond, the bank should not proceed.

The bank must then obtain the husband's consent to disclose his financial information to the solicitor and, if consent is obtained, should disclose this information. If the husband does not consent, the bank should not proceed.

The solicitor must have a private, face-to-face meeting with the wife alone. The solicitor should explain the transaction to the wife in everyday, non-technical language.

The House of Lords set out 'core minimum' content for the advice that the solicitor should give:

(i) The solicitor should explain the nature of the documents that the wife will be asked to sign and explain the practical consequences for the wife of signing the documents.

(ii) The solicitor should then outline the seriousness of the risks involved in entering the transaction.

(iii) He or she should inform the wife that she has a choice: she does not have to sign the papers if she does not want to do so.

(iv) Finally, the solicitor should then ask the wife if she wants to proceed with the transaction and also ask whether she is happy for the solicitor to confirm to the bank that he or she has explained it to her.

The bank should obtain from the solicitor a confirmation that step (iii) has been satisfactorily carried out.

If the bank completes the 'modest obligations' outlined above, it will protect itself against future claims of undue influence in this (domestic) context.

The steps outlined above appear to be clear and largely workable for the lender.

THINKING POINT

Who do you think this decision actually helps?

It may be seen as helping the victim of undue influence, by preventing it occurring. If the bank ensures that the solicitor has carefully and clearly explained the risks that the wife is taking, then she may decide not to enter into the transaction at all. Unfortunately, the very nature of 'undue influence' may well mean that she goes ahead with it anyway—and then loses any legal protection completely.

The decision is much more likely to be helpful to the bank. The House of Lords has effectively given the lending institution a checklist of actions to complete and, if it does this systematically, then it will be protected. A cynic might also say that the decision also effectively shifts the burden of risk from the mortgagee bank to the advising solicitor.

The recent case of *HSBC Bank plc v. Brown* [2015] EWHC 359 (Ch) is interesting because it adds some detail to the application of *Etridge* for both lenders and solicitors. The case involved an elderly parent (Mrs Brown) acting as a surety for her son, in circumstances which were clearly not to her financial advantage. The son defaulted in his payments to HSBC and HSBC sought to enforce the charge against his mother's property. HSBC argued that it was entitled to rely on a certificate of execution from a solicitor which stated that Mrs Brown had received independent legal advice: this meant essentially that it had complied with the *Etridge* guidelines.

However, the court found that HSBC had not properly taken some very important preliminary steps: it appeared to the court that there was no evidence that HSBC had written to Mrs Brown to require her to obtain independent legal advice, nor had it required her to provide HSBC with the name of her solicitor. There was also no evidence that HSBC had provided Mrs Brown's solicitor with sufficient detail of her son's financial affairs in order that he might properly advise her. The court also found that the solicitor had failed to give the core minimum advice specified in *Etridge* and so neither the lender nor the solicitor had taken appropriate steps to ensure that Mrs Brown had taken independent legal advice. As a result, the charge on the property was unenforceable and cancelled.

13.3.4.1 'Back door' tactics

CROSS REFERENCE

For more on bankruptcy, see Chapter 10.

Even if the wife establishes undue influence and has the transaction set aside as against her, the mortgagee may have a means of securing a sale of the property. We have seen that the mortgagee has a range of remedies against the defaulting mortgagor, all or any of which it may pursue concurrently. If the mortgagee is defeated on one remedy, it is entitled to pursue another.

🔍 CASE CLOSE-UP

Alliance and Leicester plc v. Slayford [2001] All ER 1

Mr Slayford acquired a mortgage to buy out his first wife's interest in the family home, in which he was living with his then girlfriend (subsequently Mrs Slayford II). It was a condition of this mortgage that the property was in Mr Slayford's sole name. Mrs Slayford II agreed to sign away her rights, if any, in the family home. Over the years, Mr Slayford took out further advances secured on the property. The inevitable happened and he was unable to make the repayments. The bank applied to the court for an order for possession.

At this point, Mrs Slayford II raised a defence of undue influence, saying that she had not understood what she was signing. The defence succeeded and the judge refused the bank's application for possession against Mrs Slayford II, adjourning the application in respect of Mr Slayford.

The bank decided to pursue another tactic. It decided to sue Mr Slayford on his personal covenant, with a view to making him bankrupt—but you may, at this point, be wondering how such an action would help the bank to recover its money.

A trustee in bankruptcy is an interested person under Trusts of Land and Appointment of Trustees Act 1996, s. 14. It can apply to the court for an order for sale of the property. The court will consider the application under Insolvency Act 1980, s. 335A, which provides that, if the application is made more than one year after the declaration of bankruptcy, the court will make the order unless there are exceptional circumstances. In this way, it would be likely to receive at least some of its money.

The court said that the mortgagee bank was perfectly entitled to do this. There was nothing to stop a mortgagee using a different remedy when an earlier attempt had not been successful.

13.3.4.2 European Mortgage Credit Directive

The European Mortgage Credit Directive, which comes into effect in March 2016, aims to set minimum regulatory requirements in the way in which Member States regulate mortgages and protect borrowers. The UK government's stated objective is to minimize the impact of the Directive on the UK market, not least because the market is already very well regulated. The detail of the Directive is outside the scope of this book, but the Directive has particular implications for second charge and buy-to-let mortgages. It also means that equitable mortgages will be brought within the

Financial Conduct Authority's remit, just as legal mortgages already are. We will consider equitable mortgages in more detail below.

13.4 Equitable mortgages

An **equitable mortgage** may come into being in a number of ways. Firstly, if a mortgagor has only an equitable interest in the property, he or she is only able to grant an equitable mortgage over it. Even if he or she attempts to create a legal charge, it will only take effect in equity. An example of this might be if somebody has a life interest in the land, under a trust.

Secondly, an equitable mortgage will be created when the formal requirements for the grant of a legal mortgage have not been carried out. For example, if the legal mortgage is not registered on the charges register in registered land, the mortgage will take effect only as an equitable mortgage. Similarly, if an attempt is made to grant a legal mortgage, but it is not executed by deed, then— provided that it conforms to the other requirements of Law of Property (Miscellaneous Provisions) Act 1989 (LP(MP)A 1989), s. 2—it will take effect as an equitable mortgage.

Before the LP(MP)A 1989, it used to be possible to create an equitable mortgage simply by depositing the title deeds of the property with the mortgagee. The formal requirements of that Act now mean that this will not be enough to create an interest in land: both parties now need to sign a written contract containing all of the express terms of the agreement.

> **equitable mortgage**
> a mortgage under which the mortgagee does not acquire a legal interest in the land

> ▶ **CROSS REFERENCE**
> For more on a life interest held under trust, see Chapter 10.

13.4.1 **Remedies of the equitable mortgagee**

The remedies of the equitable mortgagee are largely similar to the remedies of the legal mortgagee, with a few exceptions.

The most important difference is that the equitable mortgagee does not have the right to enter into possession, or automatic power of sale, unless the mortgage agreement specifically allows it. The equitable mortgagee must apply to the court for an order in each case. If the equitable mortgage has been made by deed, however, it now appears that a court order is not necessary (*Swift 1st Ltd v. Colin* [2011] All ER 271).

Additionally, an equitable mortgagee can only appoint a receiver if the mortgage has been created by deed, or by an order of the court.

13.5 Priority of mortgages

As we said at the start of this chapter, it is possible to grant more than one mortgage over one piece of land. These mortgages can be either legal, equitable, or a mixture of both. When a homeowner needs to raise money, granting a further mortgage may seem to be a sensible idea: it means that his or her principal asset—his or her home—is working for him or her. Unfortunately, the more mortgages on a property, the more mortgage repayments the mortgagor needs to make each month and, in many cases, the more likely he or she is to be unable to meet those financial commitments.

When a mortgaged property is sold, there is a prescribed order in which the selling mortgagee must pay off any mortgages on the property. We have seen that LPA 1925, s. 105, says that any prior mortgages must be paid off first, even before paying the selling mortgagee's costs of sale. If

> ▶ **CROSS REFERENCE**
> For more on the charges register, see Chapter 4.

the selling mortgagee is also the first mortgagee, then he or she may recover his or her own debt before applying the funds to subsequent mortgages (see 13.3.3.4).

The real problem, however, is that there is often not enough money to satisfy all of the mortgagees and this is when the order of payment between them becomes very important.

13.5.1 **Registered land**

⟩ CROSS REFERENCE

For more on electronic conveyancing, see Chapter 3.

Land registration has made sorting out the priorities of mortgagees much simpler than it was before 1925. All of the charges on a property must be entered in the charges register of the land register. A legal mortgage only becomes 'legal'—that is, it only takes effect in law—when it has been completed by registration—LRA 2002, s. 27(2)(f). An equitable mortgage must be entered as a 'notice' in the charges register—LRA 2002, ss. 34–36. Note that each entry is dated and also gives the name of each mortgagee.

The general rule with registered land is that the earliest registered legal charge takes priority over every other charge. Note that the relevant date here is the date of registration rather than of creation—LRA 2002, s. 48(1). This is an incentive for the mortgagee to register as promptly as possible. When electronic conveyancing comes into existence, the charge will automatically be registered as soon as it is created, avoiding any potential problems.

A registered legal charge will also take priority over any earlier equitable charges that have not been protected by notice in the land register. Equitable interests protected as a notice also take priority over all later charges (see Figure 13.2).

Figure 13.2 The priorities of mortgages held over registered land

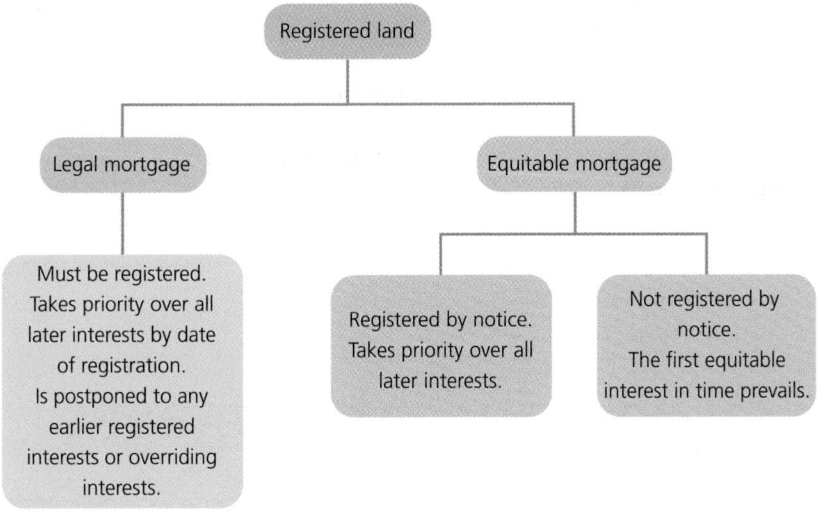

13.5.2 **Unregistered land**

⟩ CROSS REFERENCE

For more on legal interests binding the world, see Chapter 2.

The rules relating to the priority of mortgages in unregistered land are complicated and only the basic principles are outlined here.

The first legal mortgagee of unregistered land is entitled to hold the title deeds to the land. This is valuable protection for the mortgagee, because if the mortgagor tries to create any further mortgages over the land, the potential mortgagee will want to examine the title deeds before entering into any agreement. This way, the first mortgagee is warned of any further dealings in the property. The first legal mortgagee will therefore have priority over all subsequent mortgagees. Remember that 'legal interests bind the world'.

If the mortgagee does not have the title deeds, the charge must be registered as a Class C land charge in the land charges register (see Figure 13.3). The priority of charges will then be decided by date order (see Figure 13.4).

> CROSS REFERENCE
> For more on classes of land charge, see Chapter 4.

Figure 13.3 The priority of mortgages of legal estates in unregistered land

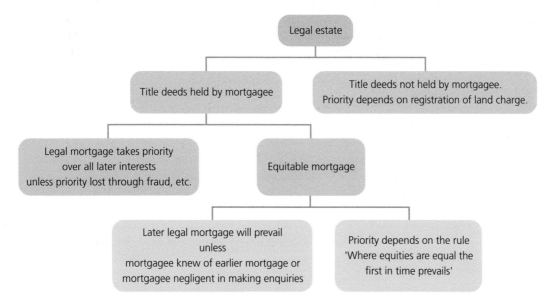

Figure 13.4 The priority of mortgages of equitable interests in unregistered land

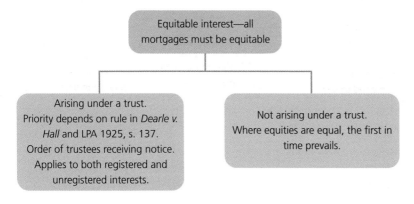

13.5.3 Tacking

Sometimes, rather than taking out a number of different loans with different mortgagees, a mortgagor will ask for a further advance of money from an existing mortgagee. This procedure is known as **tacking**—that is, the new loan is added, or 'tacked' to, the mortgagor's other loans.

tacking
the adding of a further advance of money under an existing mortgage agreement, subject to certain conditions

Tacking is usually done with the agreement of any other mortgagees of the property, although for registered land, LRA 2002, s. 49 provides some specific circumstances under which tacking will enable a mortgagee making an additional advance to gain priority over a mortgagee that lent between the list loan and the 'tacked' one. Remember that, by agreeing to this, the subsequent mortgagee could increase the likelihood that it will not recover its money.

 EXAMPLE

Ceri has two legal mortgages over his property, which is registered land. The first is with Grimleys Bank, for £100,000; the second is with Bradleys Building Society, for £50,000. Grimleys Bank has priority over Bradleys BS, because it is entered first on the land register in date order.

Ceri needs to raise more cash, so he asks Grimleys for an additional loan of £50,000. It agrees.

Ceri runs into financial difficulties, and Grimleys repossesses and sells his home. It only recovers £150,000.

If Bradleys had agreed to the tacking, then all £150,000 would have gone to Grimleys; if it had not, then £100,000 would have gone to Grimleys in relation to the first advance and £50,000 to Bradleys—and there would be nothing left to pay back Grimleys' second advance of £50,000.

 # Summary

1. A mortgage is a debt secured on land—*Santley v. Wilde*.

2. A legal mortgage in registered land can now be created only by means of a legal charge— LRA 2002, s. 23(1)(a).

3. The two key dates in the life of the mortgage are the legal date of redemption (usually six months after the creation of the mortgage) and the equitable date of redemption (for the remainder of the mortgage term).

4. The mortgagor has a bundle of rights that are known as the 'equity of redemption'.

5. There must be no restriction on the mortgagor's equity of redemption; neither must there be any clogs and fetters on it.

6. If the mortgagee attempts to gain any unconscionable advantage by means of the mortgage, the courts will strike it down. In deciding whether something is unconscionable, the court will look at all of the circumstances of the case, including the equality of the bargaining positions of the parties.

7. The mortgagee has five potential remedies to recover the debt: an action on the personal covenant of the mortgagor; repossession; sale; appointment of a receiver; foreclosure.

8. The doctrine of undue influence is important in the law of mortgages.

9. A mortgagee will be put on notice if the mortgage transaction is such that a wife is acting as surety for her husband's debts. This also applies to cohabitees and other close family relationships.

10. Provided that the mortgagee bank follows the steps outlined by the House of Lords in *Royal Bank of Scotland v. Etridge (No. 2)*, it will be protected against a claim for undue influence.

The bigger picture

- If you want to see how this area of land law fits into the rest of your studies, you can look at Chapter 14, especially 14.4.

- For some guidance on what sort of exam questions come up in this area, see Chapter 15, 15.12.

- There have been some interesting developments in situations where the mortgagee seeks possession of the property and discovers that the mortgagor has let the property to a tenant without its permission. See the Mortgage Repossessions (Protection of Tenants etc.) Act 2010.

- For a really careful and thorough explanation of the doctrine of undue influence, you might like to read *Evans v. Lloyd* [2013] EWHC 1725 (Ch). Although it discusses the doctrine in relation to gifts rather than mortgages, it reviews the history of the doctrine, and discusses in detail what the court needs to establish in order to show undue influence. The facts of this case are also interesting.

? Questions

Self-test questions

1. Bob and Andy both own large plots of land very near to each other. Bob decides that he wants to build on part of his land, but he does not have the money to complete the project by himself. Andy agrees to lend him £150,000, secured on Bob's land. He insists that the mortgage agreement contains the following clauses:

   - The mortgagor may not redeem the mortgage for ten years.

   - The mortgagor shall use only the mortgagee's field during the building project to store all of the building materials and the mortgagor shall pay the mortgagee a reasonable sum for the use of his field.

   - The mortgagee has the right to purchase one-half of the mortgaged land at market value within five years of the date of this agreement.

Advise Bob whether a court is likely to decide whether all, or any, of these terms will be binding on him.

2. Terry is now six months behind with his mortgage repayments and the bank has written to him twice: firstly, asking for immediate payment, and then informing Terry that it is starting proceedings for possession. Terry is a self-employed roofer. He has not paid his mortgage, because he had a bad fall from a ladder and broke his leg. When he is unable to work, he does not get paid. His leg has now healed and he is due to begin work again next week. His wife, Abigail, has also just returned to full-time work after a year's maternity leave. Terry does not want to lose his home. What can the bank do? Is there anything that might help Terry to keep his home?

Exam questions

1. Suki purchased her property four years ago with a mortgage of £300,000. She has been unable to keep up her mortgage repayments for the past six months and now wants to sell her home. Unfortunately, the area in which she lives has become rather run down and she can only find a buyer willing to pay £280,000 for her house. She has asked the mortgagee to consent to a sale, but it has refused. Instead, it has applied for a possession order. It does not want to sell her home, but wants her instead to rent it out for two years. This is because it believes that the government is soon to announce a major regeneration programme in the area, which will significantly increase the value of the property. Advise Suki.

2. Sharon's husband, Irvine, has asked her to sign some papers that he says are necessary to help his business. He explains that they need a second mortgage over their family home, to raise some cash. He is very vague about the amount that they will be borrowing and has told her not to worry: that it is a short-term measure. The bank has sent her a letter asking her to nominate a solicitor, but Irvine has told her not to bother with 'all that legal stuff'. Advise Sharon.

 For suggested approaches to answering these questions visit the Online Resource Centre.

Further reading

Clements, L. M., 'Residential mortgages and the Administration of Justice Acts 1970 and 1973: a case for reform' [1999] 3 Web JCLI
This article offers a useful critical review of the AJAs.

Dixon, M., 'Mortgage duties and commercial property transactions' [2006] Conv 278
This is an interesting article on the mortgagee's duty to act in good faith when selling the property.

Evans, S., 'A scrutiny of powers of sale arising under an equitable mortgage: a case for reining these in' [2015] Conv 123
A critical analysis of the implications of the decision in *Swift 1st Ltd v. Colin* in respect of equitable mortgages. It also contains a very clear explanation of the powers of sale in legal mortgages.

Greer, S., 'Watching the clock' (2008) 158 NLJ 7317

This looks in more detail at the issue of time limits and the mortgagee seeking possession.

Hanbury, W., 'Limiting the shortfall' (2006) 156 NLJ 7215

This article looks at how mortgagees can pursue a shortfall in debts recovered after sale of the mortgaged property.

Mujih, E., 'The role of the solicitor in guarantee cases 10 years after *Royal Bank of Scotland v Etridge* (No. 2)' JIBLR [2012] 520

This interesting article reviews post-*Etridge* cases and concludes that competent solicitors have little to be anxious about, provided that the guidelines are followed, and that the scope of solicitors' responsibilities in such cases has not been widened.

Pawlowski, M. and Greer, S. J., 'Constructive notice and independent legal advice: a study in lending institution practice' [2001] Conv 229

This article offers empirical research into the practices of lending institutions when advising applicants potentially acting under undue influence.

Pawlowski, M. and Greer, S. J., 'Undue influence: back door tactics?' [2001] Fam Law 275

This article discusses the tactics employed by the mortgagee in *Alliance & Leicester plc v. Slayford*.

Pre-action protocol

For more on the pre-action protocol on mortgage arrears, see https://www.justice.gov.uk/courts/procedure-rules/civil/protocol/prot_mha and also the CML website at http://www.cml.org.uk

Royal Bank of Scotland v. Etridge (No. 2)

It really is worth reading this case in its entirety.

Online Resource Centre

www.oxfordtextbooks.co.uk/orc/clarke_directions5e/

For more advice relating to this chapter, including self-test questions and an interactive glossary, visit the Online Resource Centre.

PART 5

THE BIGGER PICTURE

14

Completing the puzzle

☐ **LEARNING OBJECTIVES**

By the end of this chapter, you will be able to:

- understand more about how land law works in practice;
- identify the various parts of the land register and explain their purpose;
- explain the individual entries on the land register, and identify the rights and interests in land to which they relate;
- recognize a filed plan and appreciate its purpose.

Introduction

We have now reached the end of the road on our journey through land law. If you have read the book from cover to cover (and, of course, we hope that you have), you will now be armed with lots of useful information about various aspects of land law—from mortgages to easements, and covenants to co-ownership.

While all of these chapters will obviously be helpful to you as you prepare for your land law exam or coursework, we believe that this chapter may well be the most useful chapter of all. In this chapter, we will try to draw together all of the different strands of knowledge that you have worked hard to acquire and show you how they fit together in practice. By looking at a register of title for an imaginary piece of land in 'Maryford, Greenfordshire', we will take you step-by-step through each of the entries on the register, to build up a complete picture of all of the rights and interests in the land. This is the final piece of the land law jigsaw, which will put all of the various parts of the puzzle into their rightful places and give you a practical context in which to put everything you have already read about in this book.

14.1 The register of title

Form 14.1 **Register of title for Anne's Cottage**

Edition Date: 1 December 2009

Entry No.	*A. PROPERTY REGISTER*
	containing the description of the registered land and the estate comprised in the title
	Greenfordshire: Maryford
1.	(28 October 1990) The Freehold land shown edged with red on the plan of the above title filed at the Registry and known as Anne's Cottage, Maryford.
2.	(28 October 1990) The mines and minerals are excepted.
3.	(28 October 1990) The boundary of the land where it abuts the River Mary is the High Water Mark of Medium Tides from time to time.
4.	(28 October 1990) The land has the benefit of the following rights granted by a Conveyance of the land in this title and other land dated 10 July 1952 made between (1) JOSEPH SMITH and (2) EVAN JONES and LINDA JONES: "TOGETHER WITH the right to pass with or without vehicles over the land tinted green on the said plan" NOTE: The green land referred to is reproduced on the filed plan.

Entry No.	*B. PROPRIETORSHIP REGISTER*
	Stating the nature of the Title, name address and description of the proprietor of the land and any entries affecting the right of disposal thereof
	TITLE ABSOLUTE
1.	(28 June 1999) MANVIR SINGH and HARTPREET SINGH of Anne's Cottage, Maryford.
2.	(28 June 1999) RESTRICTION Except under an order of the Registrar no disposition by the proprietors of the land shall be registered without the consent of the Greenford Building Society.

Entry No.	*C. CHARGES REGISTER*
	Containing charges, encumbrances etc. adversely affecting the land and registered dealings therewith
1.	(30 April 2000) The land edged green on the filed plan is subject to a lease dated 25 March 2000 made between (1) MANVIR SINGH and HARPREET SINGH and (2) JENNIFER BOWLES for a term of 25 years from 25 March 2000 at an annual rent of £300.
2.	A Conveyance of the land in this title and other land dated 14 July 1933 made between (1) Benjamin Lapin (vendor) and (2) Joseph Smith (purchaser) contains covenants details of which are set out in the schedule of restrictive covenants hereto.
3.	REGISTERED CHARGE dated 1 June 1999 to secure the monies including the further advances therein mentioned. PROPRIETOR of Charge dated 1 June 1999 Greenford Building Society of Greenford House, High Street, Greenfordshire GN2 8GA.

Entry No.	Schedule of restrictive covenants
	The purchaser for the benefit of the retained land of the vendor hereby covenants on behalf of himself and his successors in title and those deriving title under him:
1.	Not to allow any shed caravan house on wheels or other temporary buildings adapted or intended for use as a dwelling or sleeping apartment to be erected or placed or used or allowed to remain on the land hereby conveyed (hereinafter referred to as the said land) except temporary structures in connection with any building work actually in progress.
2.	Not to erect any building on any part of the said land except private dwellinghouses professional offices consulting rooms nursing or maternity homes or flats or maisonettesfor use as private dwellings with private garages thereto. END OF REGISTER

14.2 The property register: the description of the land

The first part of a register of title—the property register—contains a description of the registered land. It tells us whether the land is freehold or leasehold and describes certain features of the land (see Form 14.1).

Figure 14.1 Filed plan for Anne's Cottage

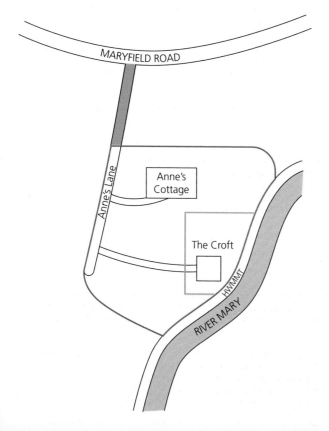

14.2.1 **Freehold land**

> (28 October 1990) The Freehold land shown edged with red on the plan of the above title filed at the Registry and known as Anne's Cottage, Maryford.

The date shown in the register '(28 October 1990)' (see Form 14.1) is the date on which the entry was made in the register. This is the date on which this title was first registered. Before that date, it is likely that Anne's Cottage, Maryford, was unregistered land, which was then registered following a transfer of the land at that date.

THINKING POINT

What else does the property register tell us about the land?

It tells us that the land is freehold land.

❯ CROSS REFERENCE

For more on freehold land, see Chapter 3.

We know that the legal freehold estate is technically called the 'fee simple absolute in possession'. It is the largest estate that anyone other than the Crown can hold in land in England and Wales. Although you will remember that—thanks to the system of tenure—all land is technically held of the Crown, for all practical purposes the freehold estate is equivalent to outright ownership of the land.

THINKING POINT

Have a look at Figure 14.1—the filed plan. Try to identify the land about which we are thinking.

The plan is attached to the register of title. It gives a potential purchaser a picture of the boundaries of the land described in the register. In this example, it shows the extent of the land outlined in red. Often it is quite tricky to get an accurate picture of the land from the description in the register, so it is important to look carefully at the plan to interpret what is described.

The plan can also give us clues as to what is included within the definition of the land. In this example, there are two buildings on the land: Anne's Cottage itself and another building called 'The Croft'. Both of these buildings will form part of the land.

THINKING POINT

What else will form part of the land, even though you cannot see it from the plan?

Remember that the definition of land is very wide.

❯ CROSS REFERENCE

For a definition of land, and more on fixtures, see Chapter 1.

When the owner bought this piece of land, he or she would not only have purchased the land and buildings, but also any plants or trees on the land. A visit to the land may be necessary to identify other fixtures—for example, there may be sheds, summerhouses, and garden ornaments. Whether they form part of the land will depend upon the tests in *Holland v. Hodgson* (1872) LR 7 CP 328, and upon the degree of annexation and the purpose of annexation.

14.2.2 Corporeal hereditaments: the extent of land

(28 October 1990) The mines and minerals are excepted.

This entry is part of the definition of the extent of this piece of land, in that it specifically excludes mines and minerals from the title. Remember that land is three-dimensional—that is, it includes not only the surface of the land, but also the airspace above it and the underground space below it.

▶ CROSS REFERENCE

For more on the three-dimensional extent of land, see Chapter 1.

Usually, mines and minerals would be included within the title unless they belonged to the Crown by prerogative right or by statute. In this example, they are clearly excluded, and belong to someone else.

(28 October 1990) The boundary of the land where it abuts the River Mary is the High Water Mark of Medium Tides from time to time.

This is an interesting entry. It defines one of the boundaries to the land. Usually, boundaries are not defined, but simply marked on the filed plan. This boundary, however, has been fixed more precisely, because it is a boundary with a tidal river. The foreshore (the area between the high and low tides) is generally owned by the Crown, unless it has been granted to someone else. Anne's Cottage does not include the foreshore, because the boundary is to be the high-water mark. The river itself is not included within the title. If the river had been non-tidal, there would have been a presumption that it was owned up to the mid-point by the owners of the land on either side.

▶ CROSS REFERENCE

For more on foreshore and ownership to the mid-point, see Chapter 1.

The owners of Anne's Cottage also need to be aware that the public have rights of fishing and navigation over tidal waters, which may affect the owners' privacy.

▶ CROSS REFERENCE

For more on rights of fishing and navigation over tidal waters, see Chapter 1.

14.2.3 Incorporeal hereditaments: the right of way

(28 October 1990) The land has the benefit of the following rights granted by a Conveyance of the land in this title and other land dated 10 July 1952 made between (1) JOSEPH SMITH and (2) EVAN JONES and LINDA JONES:

"TOGETHER WITH the right to pass with or without vehicles over the land tinted green on the said plan"

NOTE: The green land referred to is reproduced on the filed plan.

This last entry in the property register contains an example of an incorporeal hereditament—that is, an intangible right that forms part of the land. Look, firstly, at the nature of the right granted here: it is a right to 'pass with or without vehicles'.

> ### 💬 THINKING POINT
>
> What kind of a right is this?

This is a right of way, which is one of the most common types of easement.

Look again at the filed plan in Figure 14.1. You will soon see how important this right will be to the owners of Anne's Cottage. The property is not, apparently, situated on a public highway. There is Maryfield Road to the north, but that can be reached only by crossing neighbouring land, probably by going along Anne's Lane. Part of Anne's Lane is within the boundary of this title, but the part tinted green on the plan is not.

▶ CROSS REFERENCE

For more on easements, see Chapter 11.

It appears from this entry that Anne's Cottage was transferred (conveyed) to Evan and Linda Jones by Joseph Smith, who was then the owner of the land over which the lilac-tinted part of Anne's Lane runs. As part of that transfer, he granted them an easement of way with or without vehicles over the part of the lane that was on his land. This is an express grant of an easement, because Joseph Smith expressly granted it to the Joneses.

 THINKING POINT

Have a look again at the plan in Figure 14.1. Which would be the dominant tenement and which would be the servient tenement?

The dominant tenement is Anne's Cottage and the servient tenement is the land tinted green on the plan—originally Joseph Smith's land. It does not matter whether Joseph Smith still owns the land or not, because an easement is a proprietary right that passes with the dominant land and binds all owners of the servient land, provided it is properly registered.

 THINKING POINT

What if Joseph Smith had not expressly granted an easement here? Might an easement have come into being in any other way?

It looks as though, originally, both the dominant and servient tenements were in common ownership—that is, they were once both owned by Joseph Smith. This means that you need to think carefully about implied easements here. Remember that there are four methods of implying the grant of an easement:

- of necessity;
- by common intention;
- the rule in *Wheeldon v. Burrows* (1879) 12 Ch D 31;
- Law of Property Act 1925 (LPA 1925), s. 62.

 THINKING POINT

Do you think that any, or all, of these could be used to imply an easement here?

See the Online Resource Centre for possible answers to this question.

Alternatively, could long use of this track have given rise to an easement by prescription?

▶ CROSS REFERENCE

For more on easements as overriding interests, see Chapter 11.

If there is no express grant of an easement, but one has been implied or acquired by prescription, it may not appear in the property register. An expressly granted easement must be registered—Land Registration Act 2002 (LRA 2002), s. 27(2)(d). An easement that is implied or which arises by prescription may, however, be an overriding interest under LRA 2002, Sch. 3, para. 3.

14.3 The proprietorship register

As its name suggests, this part of the register tells us who is the proprietor—or owner—of the property. There may be one owner, or more than one owner, but you will never see more than four names in the proprietorship register, because the number of legal owners of the land is limited to four.

This part of the register gives the name of the owner, the address of the property, and advises any potential purchasers of the property of any restrictions that may exist on the owner's ability to sell the property. It also gives the class of the owner's title to the property. In this example, the owner's title is 'title absolute', which is the best class of title obtainable.

We will now think about each of the entries in more detail.

(28 June 1999) MANVIR SINGH and HARPREET SINGH of Anne's Cottage, Maryford.

Here, we can see that the two legal owners of Anne's Cottage are Manvir and Harpreet Singh—but this entry gives us much more information than just their names!

THINKING POINT

We know that the land is co-owned, because there are two registered proprietors. Can you think of anything else that this fact tells us—or does not tell us?

All we know at present is that the legal title to the land is owned by two people. We also know that they must hold the legal title as joint tenants, because the law does not permit them to hold it any other way.

We know that a trust has arisen, because whenever there is more than one legal owner, a trust arises automatically. Manvir and Harpreet are therefore both the legal owners of the land, and they are trustees of the land.

However, we know nothing about the equitable ownership of the land—the beneficiaries of the trust. Remember that the land register only gives details of the legal title, because one of the fundamental principles governing land registration is the 'curtain principle'—that is, that trusts are kept off the face of the register. The register, then, does not give us the identity of the beneficiaries of this trust of land.

THINKING POINT

Who are the likely beneficiaries of the trust?

It is likely that Manvir and Harpreet hold the land on trust for themselves. This still does not tell us how they actually hold the equitable interest. They may hold the land as joint tenants, or as tenants in common. The key difference between the two is that, if they hold it as joint tenants, they both own the whole. If one dies, the principle of survivorship means that the remaining joint tenant takes on the former joint tenant's share. If they hold it as tenants in common, they each own their own quantifiable share.

CROSS REFERENCE
For more on the proprietorship register, see Chapter 2.

CROSS REFERENCE
For more on class of title, see Chapter 2.

CROSS REFERENCE
For more on joint tenants, see Chapter 8.

CROSS REFERENCE
For more on automatic trusts in co-ownership, see Chapter 9.

CROSS REFERENCE
For more on the curtain principle, see Chapter 2.

CROSS REFERENCE
For more on types of co-ownership and the principle of survivorship, see Chapter 8.

To make it easier for potential purchasers, if the land is to be co-owned, the registrar must enter a restriction in the register to ensure that potential purchasers comply with the overreaching provisions. The registrar obtains this information from Form TR1 that purchasers of land complete. Remember, however, that purchasers are not obliged by law to provide information about how they wish to hold the land in equity: it is entirely up to them whether or not they choose to provide it. The registrar does not have to enter a restriction when the owners hold the land as joint tenants in both law and equity. The absence of such a restriction will, therefore, suggest to the purchaser that the owners hold the land wholly as joint tenants.

THINKING POINT

Would the purchaser of Anne's Cottage need to worry about the equitable ownership of the land?

> **CROSS REFERENCE**
> For more on overreaching, see Chapter 2.

The answer to this question is probably not. Provided that the purchaser pays his or her purchase money to two trustees—in this case, Manvir and Harpreet—he or she would be protected from any subsequent claims made by equitable owners of the land. Once the money is paid to two trustees, the overreaching mechanism is triggered, and the interest of the equitable owners is swept off the land and into the proceeds of sale.

> **CROSS REFERENCE**
> For more on resulting and constructive trusts, see Chapter 9.Evirtanuntes,

If the purchase money is not paid to two trustees—which is sometimes the case if the land is owned by only one legal owner—the potential purchaser runs the risk that the interest of any unidentified equitable owner may become binding on him or her. If the equitable owner's interest is combined with actual occupation of the land, then he or she may have an overriding interest that is binding on the purchaser. This situation is difficult for the purchaser, because many equitable interests arise informally, by means of resulting or constructive trusts. Thankfully for any purchaser of Anne's Cottage, this will not affect him—provided, of course, that he pays the purchase money to both Manvir and Harpreet.

(28 June 1999) RESTRICTION Except under an order of the Registrar no disposition by the proprietors of the land shall be registered without the consent of the Greenford Building Society.

> **CROSS REFERENCE**
> For more on restrictions, see Chapter 2.

As the name of this entry implies, this signifies a restriction on the Singhs' powers to dispose of their land. Unless the Land Registrar permits it, no disposition or sale of the land can be registered without obtaining the consent of the Greenford Building Society.

THINKING POINT

Why do you think the Greenford Building Society would want to have the power to consent to registering a 'disposition' of the land?

As we will see when we look at the charges register, the Singhs have granted Greenford Building Society a mortgage over the property. Greenford's investment is tied up in Anne's Cottage and it will want to be kept informed of any 'dispositions' that the Singhs may wish to make. Do not forget that although 'disposition' can mean a sale or the granting of a lease, it can also mean the grant of a mortgage. If the Singhs grant another mortgage over the land to a different lender, this restriction warns the lender that, in order to register the second mortgage, Greenford's consent must be obtained. Note that the restriction does not mean that the Singhs cannot deal with their land as they wish. Rather, it means that the registrar will not register the disposition without Greenford's consent. If it is not registered, the purchaser will only acquire an equitable interest in the land

> **CROSS REFERENCE**
> For more on mortgages, see Chapter 13.

Similarly, this restriction alerts potential purchasers to the fact that there is a mortgage on the land. The purchaser will obviously want the previous owner's mortgage debt to be paid off before his or her own title is registered.

14.4 The charges register

The charges register shows all of the burdens on the land.

14.4.1 The lease

> (30 April 2000) The land edged green on the filed plan is subject to a lease dated 25 March 2000 made between (1) MANVIR SINGH and HARPREET SINGH and (2) JENNIFER BOWLES for a term of 25 years from 25 March 2000 at an annual rent of £300.

Have a look at the plan in Figure 14.1. You will see that a parcel of the land has been bordered in green. The extract from the land register tells us that this piece of land has been leased to Jennifer Bowles. The Singhs own the freehold of the land and have decided to grant a lease over part of it. In order to be a valid lease, the Singhs must confer on Jennifer exclusive possession of the property for a term, but not necessarily at a rent. The term of the lease here is for twenty-five years and, in return for occupying the land, Jennifer Bowles pays the Singhs £300 per year. She is also likely to have paid the Singhs a premium—that is, an upfront amount of money—for the lease. Jennifer acquires an estate in the land for the duration of the lease, but, at the end of twenty-five years, the land reverts back to the Singhs. They hold the reversionary interest in the land. The Singhs are the landlords of the property and Jennifer is the tenant.

▶ CROSS REFERENCE
For more on leases, see Chapter 5.

Remember that, in order for this to be a legal lease, certain formalities must have been complied with when the parties entered into the agreement. It must have been made by deed and registered, because the lease is for more than seven years. As a consequence, the leasehold estate will have its own entry in the land register, with its own title number.

The lease agreement itself is essentially a contract between the parties. It will contain various clauses—known as covenants—by which both the landlords and the tenant will have agreed to do, and not do, certain things. Some of these covenants are express—for example, Jennifer will have agreed to pay the Singhs an annual rent—but some will be implied into the lease by common law—for example, the right to quiet enjoyment.

▶ CROSS REFERENCE
For more on express and implied terms in a lease, see Chapter 5.

14.4.2 The covenants

The second entry in the charges register contains a reference to covenants:

> A Conveyance of the land in this title and other land dated 14 July 1933 made between (1) Benjamin Lapin (vendor) and (2) Joseph Smith (purchaser) contains covenants details of which are set out in the schedule of restrictive covenants hereto.

 THINKING POINT

What are covenants in freehold land? Can you remember what they do?

Covenants are promises made by one landowner to another in a deed.

In this case, the deed was the conveyance of the land from Benjamin Lapin to Joseph Smith in 1933. The existence of the covenants attached to this title is noted in the register itself, but the details of the covenants themselves are set out in a schedule at the end of the register.

▶ CROSS REFERENCE
For more on covenants, see Chapter 12.

Schedule of restrictive covenants

The purchaser for the benefit of the retained land of the vendor hereby covenants on behalf of himself and his successors in title and those deriving title under him:

1. Not to allow any shed caravan house on wheels or other temporary buildings adapted or intended for use as a dwelling or sleeping apartment to be erected or placed or used or allowed to remain on the land hereby conveyed (hereinafter referred to as the said land) except temporary structures in connection with any building work actually in progress.

2. Not to erect any building on any part of the said land except private dwellinghouses professional offices consulting rooms nursing or maternity homes or flats or maisonettes for use as private dwellings with private garages thereto.

THINKING POINT

Can you work out who the covenantor and covenantee were? Is the land in this title the benefited land or the burdened land?

These covenants are contained in the charges register, so we know that Anne's Cottage is the burdened land. Those interests that third parties have over the land and which therefore burden the land are always contained in the charges register. If the covenants had been for the benefit of Anne's Cottage, the covenants would have been mentioned instead in the property register.

We can see, from looking at the details of the covenants in the schedule, that the original covenantee was somebody called Benjamin Lapin, who was selling the land in 1933, and that the covenants were taken for the benefit of his retained land. The original covenantor was the purchaser of the land at the time at which the covenants were made—that is, Joseph Smith. We know from the property register that, some years later, in 1952, Joseph Smith must have divided his land, selling Anne's Cottage (the land in this title) to the Joneses, who are predecessors in title to the Singhs, who own the land now (see Figure 14.2).

Figure 14.2 Summary of covenants held against Anne's Cottage

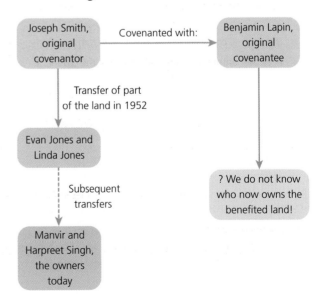

The fact that these covenants appear in the register does not automatically mean that they are enforceable. In this respect, they are different to the registered charge—that is, the mortgage—for example. Because covenants are entered onto the register by notice, rather than being registrable dispositions, they are not guaranteed to be valid interests—LRA 2002, s. 32(3). It is therefore necessary to examine whether these covenants are still enforceable.

This will depend upon two conditions being satisfied. Firstly, we would need to determine whether they are binding on the Singhs as successors in title to the original covenantor. Secondly, we would need to establish whether anyone now has the benefit of the covenants and can enforce them.

14.4.2.1 Has the burden of the covenants passed to the Singhs?

THINKING POINT

Have another look at the schedule of covenants given earlier. What kinds of covenant are they?

The covenants at which we are looking here are restrictive, or negative, covenants, because they restrict what the landowner may do with their land.

THINKING POINT

Can you remember which type of covenant can 'run with the land'? Remember, at common law, the burden never passes. Only certain covenants can pass in equity.

Restrictive covenants, unlike positive ones, may be binding on successors in title of the original covenantor in equity. They may run with the land, but only if the rules in *Tulk v. Moxhay* (1842) 2 Ph 774 are met:

* The covenant must be restrictive.
* At the date of the covenant, the covenantee owned land that was benefited by the covenant.
* The original parties intended the burden to run with the land to bind successors.
* The covenantor must take with notice of the covenant.

> **CROSS REFERENCE**
> For more on restrictive covenants and *Tulk v. Moxhay*, see Chapter 12.

THINKING POINT

Do you think that the conditions in *Tulk v. Moxhay* have been met here?

It would appear likely that the conditions in the rules in *Tulk v. Moxhay* are met here. We will work through them in turn.

1. Are the covenants restrictive?

   Yes, clearly, the covenants are restrictive in nature—they prohibit certain acts on the land.

2. At the date of the covenant, did the covenantee own land that was benefited by the covenant?

   Yes again—the original covenantee did own land to be benefited by the covenants, as the covenant makes express reference to the 'retained land of the vendor', and these are covenants which 'touch and concern' the land.

3. Did the original parties intend the burden to run with the land to bind successors?

   Yes—there are express words indicating that the burden of the covenant was intended to run with the land. The purchaser (covenantor) covenanted 'on behalf of himself and his successors in title and those deriving title under him'.

4. Did the covenantor take with notice of the covenant?

   Yes. Because the covenants are registered, the Singhs have taken with notice of the covenants.

The Singhs, therefore, would be bound by these restrictive covenants—but that is only half the story. It is also likely to be necessary to show that the benefit of the covenants has passed to someone who can enforce them against the Singhs, because it is rather unlikely that Benjamin Lapin himself (the original covenantee in 1933) is still alive and still owns any of the land originally benefited.

14.4.2.2 Does anyone now have the benefit of the covenants?

» CROSS REFERENCE

For more on the passing of the benefit of the covenant, see Chapter 12.

Because the burden passed in equity, the benefit needs to pass in equity as well. The benefit of a restrictive covenant will pass in equity if:

- the covenant touches and concerns land of the covenantee;
- the benefit of the covenant was either:
  - annexed to the land of the covenantee;
  - expressly assigned to the successor in title; or
  - the land in question is part of a building scheme.

> **THINKING POINT**
>
> Do you think the equitable rules have been met here? Has the benefit been annexed or assigned? Is there any evidence of a building scheme?

You cannot tell for sure, but you can apply the cases and make a reasoned guess.

The first requirement is met. These covenants do 'touch and concern' the land of the covenantee, because they affect how the burdened land can be used. This therefore brings us to the second requirement. There is no evidence here of a building scheme, so we should look for either annexation or assignment. The wording of the covenant here does refer to the covenantee's retained land, which may be sufficient for express annexation, or there may be statutory annexation under LPA 1925, s. 78, and the decision in *Federated Homes v. Mill Lodge Properties* [1980] 1 All ER 371.

» CROSS REFERENCE

For more detail on *Federated Homes v. Mill Lodge Properties*, see Chapter 12.

In either case, it must be shown that the land benefited by the covenant is identifiable, either by express words or necessary implication in the conveyance that created the covenants. If the benefited land has since been divided up among more than one owner it will also need to be shown that the covenant was annexed to each and every part of the benefited land—but this happens automatically under *Federated Homes v. Mill Lodge Properties*.

14.4.2.3 So are these covenants enforceable?

Without further investigation, it is not possible to assume that there is no one who can enforce these covenants, because the benefit could well have been annexed to the benefited land. Alternatively, there could have been an express assignment of the benefit to a successor in title. Therefore, the Singhs would have to be careful to establish whether anyone is, in fact, interested in enforcing the covenants if they were to wish to do anything on the land that is prohibited by them—for example, if they were to wish to build a workshop. They would need to read the covenants quite carefully, in order to see what they prohibit. For example, the second covenant permits use of the land as professional offices and consulting rooms, as well as private dwelling houses.

THINKING POINT

If the Singhs were to want to use the property as a beauty parlour, would this be within the terms of the covenant? Is that a 'professional office' or 'consulting room'? What about if they were to wish to practise as mediums or fortune-tellers?

It is often necessary to interpret covenants to see if the proposed use would be a breach. This can be quite difficult at times. Interpretations of similar words in earlier cases may be useful as precedents, but often the court is asked to decide on the meaning of a word used many years ago and to decide how it applies in a modern context.

14.4.2.4 Can the Singhs do anything about the covenants?

If they wish to use the land for a purpose that may be prohibited by the covenant, they could apply under LPA 1925, s. 84, for a declaration as to whether the covenants are still enforceable and by whom, and then apply for the covenants to be discharged or modified.

As a general rule, it is wise to take note of restrictive covenants and not to assume that they are unenforceable, because the court could order prohibited uses of the land to stop or award expensive damages.

14.4.3 The registered charge

> REGISTERED CHARGE dated 1 June 1999 to secure the monies including the further advances therein mentioned.
>
> PROPRIETOR of Charge dated 1 June 1999 Greenford Building Society of Greenford House, High Street, Greenfordshire GN2 8GA.

This entry tells us that there is a mortgage— a 'REGISTERED CHARGE'—on the land. Most people buy their property with the assistance of a mortgage and the Singhs are no exception. The Singhs granted Greenford Building Society—the 'PROPRIETOR of Charge'—a mortgage and, in return, Greenford lent the Singhs the money to purchase the property. This loan was secured on the property, Anne's Cottage. The Singhs are the mortgagors and Greenford Building Society is the mortgagee. If the Singhs fail to keep up their mortgage repayments, then Greenford has the right to repossess the property and to sell it in order to recover its money.

The mortgage will have been created by deed and has obviously been completed by registration, because it appears on the land register. It will therefore be a legal mortgage. It also appears from the reference to 'further advances' that the Singhs obtained additional funds from Greenford after the property was purchased. Again, it is very common for homeowners to raise additional funds by securing the money on their home, perhaps in order to improve the property. Once the Singhs have

CROSS REFERENCE

For more on mortgages, see Chapter 13.

repaid the mortgage money (and any interest due under the mortgage) to Greenford, Greenford's interest in the land will come to an end and this entry, together with the restriction discussed at 14.3, will be removed from the land register.

14.5 Interests that are not shown on the register

In this chapter, we have looked at the actual entries on the register and at the filed plan that accompanies it. We have sometimes speculated about interests that do not appear on the register at all—for example, easements that are implied or created by prescription (see 14.2.3) and interests of equitable co-owners (see 14.3).

THINKING POINT

These rights are examples of overriding interests. What are overriding interests and how do we know if they exist?

Overriding interests are interests that are binding on a purchaser of the land even though they are not registered. This might seem to be rather a large gap in the effectiveness of the land registration system. Nevertheless, it generally seems to work.

> **CROSS REFERENCE**
>
> For more on unregistered overriding interests, see Chapter 4.

LRA 2002, Schs 1 and 3 set out a comprehensive list of overriding interests. Schedule 3 will apply to our example, because that Schedule deals with interests that override a registered disposition of the land. This means that it applies when land that is already registered is transferred, which is what happened when Anne's Cottage was transferred to the Singhs.

> **CROSS REFERENCE**
>
> For more on actual occupation, see Chapter 4.

LRA 2002, Sch. 3 contains a list of interests that includes:

- short leases (of up to seven years);
- interests of persons in actual occupation (note that the interests must have been actually known to the purchaser, or he or she must have been able to discover them on a reasonably careful inspection of the land at the time of the disposition);
- a legal easement or profit à prendre, which was not expressly created (or it would have to be registered) and which is actually known to the purchaser, or which could have been discovered on a reasonably careful inspection of the land at the time of the disposition, or which has been used by the dominant owner within the last year;
- customary rights;
- local land charges;
- certain mineral rights;
- certain other miscellaneous rights, including manorial rights, and rights in respect of tithes and church buildings (chancel repairs). These rights are being phased out as overriding rights, and will be rendered unenforceable by any transfer for value after 12 October 2013 unless registered before the transfer.

It is not always possible to be sure that you have spotted all of the overriding interests in land. Some are easier to identify than others—for example, it should usually be possible to tell that someone is occupying all, or part, of the land, which might indicate the presence of a tenant under a short lease or a person in actual occupation of the land. This underlines the importance of visiting the land, as well as looking at the register. Any person in actual occupation should be questioned, because if he or she does not disclose his or her rights, they will not bind a purchaser. Nonetheless, the rights of such a person can be very important: it is possible that a person in actual occupation may have adversely possessed the land before 13 October 2003 and may have good title to the land. It would clearly be a disaster to buy land that had already been adversely possessed!

Not all easements are as easily spotted—for example, if drains run under the land, they may be invisible, but if used in the last year before a disposition of the land, they will be overriding. The moral of the story, therefore, is that the register cannot tell us everything. Although, in registered land, it is always our starting point, we must make our own investigations to ensure that we have a full picture of the rights and interests in the land. It is perhaps fitting that our finishing point should be to go back to the land itself and think about what we find there.

▶ CROSS REFERENCE
For more on adverse possession, see Chapter 6.

14.6 Drawing it all together

Our conclusion consists of two figures. The first of these—Figure 14.3—draws together all of the various aspects of land law that we have discussed in this book. The second—Figure 14.4—draws together the particular aspects of land law that we have identified from the land register extract relating to Anne's Cottage.

Figure 14.3 Drawing together land law

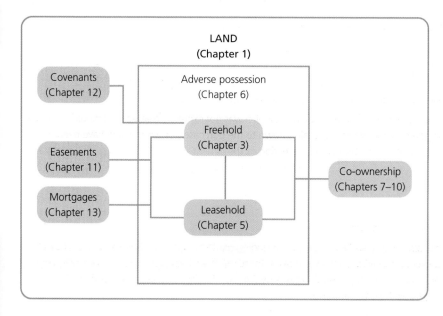

Figure 14.4 Drawing together Anne's Cottage

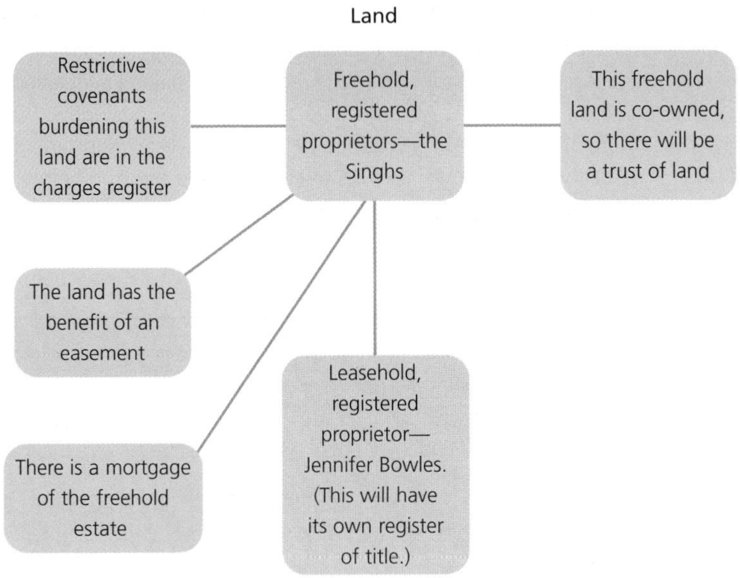

Land

Restrictive covenants burdening this land are in the charges register

Freehold, registered proprietors—the Singhs

This freehold land is co-owned, so there will be a trust of land

The land has the benefit of an easement

Leasehold, registered proprietor—Jennifer Bowles. (This will have its own register of title.)

There is a mortgage of the freehold estate

The outer box in Figure 14.3 indicates that all of the estates and interests within it are capable of forming part of the land. In the middle of the box, there are the two legal estates: the freehold and the leasehold. There must always be a freehold estate in any parcel of land—unless it is owned by the Crown—but there may or may not be a leasehold estate. Either of the estates may be held in co-ownership or in succession, in which case a trust of land will be imposed. Both freehold and leasehold land (and some equitable interests) can be mortgaged, and can be subject to easements and profits à prendre.

Covenants can affect both freehold and leasehold land, but do not forget that the rules for each are quite different.

Both freehold and leasehold estates may be adversely possessed, as indicated by the inner box.

Figure 14.4 shows the interests that we have found in this particular register of title. The land is freehold, but a leasehold estate is binding on part of it. The freehold is co-owned by Manvir and Harpreet Singh, who, as well as being the legal owners and trustees, will have equitable interests under a trust of land. There may also be other beneficiaries, but there is no sign of this on the register.

The land has the benefit of an easement of way over neighbouring land.

It is also subject to a mortgage (registered charge) and to restrictive covenants affecting the use of the land.

Summary

1. Land law should be looked at in a practical context: although you need to know the legal rules governing the individual aspects, it is important to remember that these form part of a wider system that affects our everyday lives.

2. The framework for land law in the twenty-first century is the system of land registration.

3. Whatever you are looking at in your study of land law, you should try to understand how each right or interest will be reflected on the land register.

4. There is some information about the land that the register does not provide: for example, it does not give details of the beneficiaries under a trust of land.

5. There may be some interests that are not reflected on the land register which will still be binding on a purchaser, such as overriding interests.

 ## Further reading

Of course, the further reading for this chapter is essentially the earlier chapters in this book—but we have a few additional suggestions that you might find useful.

https://www.gov.uk/government/organisations/land-registry
The Land Registry website contains lots of useful, practical information about land registration.

https://www.gov.uk/search-property-information-land-registry
The land register is a public document. For a small fee, you can find online the land registry entry for any registered title in England and Wales.

LRA 2002
While we do not suggest that you sit down and read this document in its entirety, the best place to start when considering land registration is this surprisingly user-friendly statute.

Exam technique and the perils of question spotting

By the end of this chapter, you will be able to:

● plan and manage a revision programme for exams in land law;

● understand the different approaches required for problem and essay questions;

● identify the most frequently examined areas of each of the topics covered in this book.

Introduction

Exams strike terror into the heart of even the most hard-working student. In this chapter, we will offer you some general advice about how to prepare for your land law exam and we will then look at some of the kinds of questions that are likely to appear on your exam paper.

However, we must start with a disclaimer: although we can generalize, in terms of likely topics and suggested approaches, different institutions set different kinds of exam, with different kinds of questions. Some set questions on specific areas of land law, such as easements or leases; others set questions that mix up a number of land law topics in a single question. Make sure that you attend lectures and seminars throughout the year, as well as any revision lectures, in order to understand your institution's approach. Listen to what your tutors tell you—they often slip in hints! Above all, look at previous years' exam papers and practise some past questions. If you really understand a topic, you will be able to apply that understanding and knowledge to every question that is thrown at you.

15.1 Revision

Before we begin, let us pose a question: what does 'revision' mean?

Revision is supposed to be all about going over information that you have already acquired. This means that, in order to revise a topic, you must have acquired the information in the first place! Boring though it may sound, there is no substitute for attending classes throughout the year, and building up a body of knowledge and notes. As we see every year, students who try to cram a year's worth of land law into the final month of the academic year usually fail. If you avoid such an approach, you will be in a really good position to do well in your land law exam. The following advice will hopefully be useful to you, both in your preparation and during the exam itself.

15.1.1 How to begin the revision process

It might sound obvious, but your first step is to ensure that you have some idea of which bits of the land law syllabus will be tested in the exam. Some institutions will test you on the whole syllabus, but others may have already assessed you on some of it, perhaps in coursework, and so will not examine you on the same material. Your tutor will almost certainly give you guidance on this, and do not forget to look at your institution's website.

Once you have identified the areas that you need to revise, you can begin the process. You need to allow yourself time for this, so it is worth beginning well in advance of the exam period.

15.1.2 Look at what you already have

During the year, you will have acquired thousands of pieces of paper and/or digital files. Set aside a few hours and, for each topic, gather together the following:

* all of your lecture notes;
* notes from seminars;
* notes that you may have made from textbooks;
* notes on journal articles;
* case notes.

Your reaction to the pile in front of you will depend on how much work you have done through the year: if the pile is large, you may feel daunted by it—but by the end of the revision process, you will have distilled a huge amount of information into a manageable form. If, on the other hand, you are faced with a rather small, sorry-looking pile, you may begin to panic. Again, there is no need for this, if you have started revising in time to fill in any gaps in your studying.

15.1.3 Look at what you need

You will probably already have some idea of the topics that you are going to attempt in the exam. Now is the time to fill in any gaps, both in your knowledge and your understanding.

In terms of knowledge, make sure that you have complete sets of lecture and seminar notes. Look at the topic as a whole and think about whether you need to make additional notes on areas that you have missed. Consider whether there are any 'must-read' cases that you never quite got round to reading. Now is the time to start doing this.

Filling in gaps of understanding is equally—if not more—crucial. Most students can regurgitate their lecture notes in an exam and scrape through it. Really good students, however, display their understanding of the topic in their application of the law (knowledge) to the facts in the question set. As you read through your notes, really make sure that you are not just learning the topic by heart, useful though such learning is. Instead, every so often, stop and think for a while about what you have read: Do you understand it? Can you think of real-life examples? Why would what you are learning matter, in real life? Can you draw a diagram of the facts of a question? (Not everyone finds diagrams useful, but they can be a good way of seeing if you have grasped the facts.)

The best way to assess your understanding of a topic is to try to answer a past exam question on it. At the beginning of the revision process, you may find it useful to do this as an 'open-book' exercise—that is, by reading the question, and trying to answer it with the assistance of textbooks and notes, taking as long as necessary to do so. Towards the end of your revision, it may be more useful to do a question under 'exam' conditions. Sit somewhere quiet and try to answer the question on your own, with no notes. Restrict yourself to the time that you would have for the question in the real exam and, at the end of that time, stop.

Both of these exercises are only useful if, after you have done them, you reflect on what you have learned. It will immediately become obvious to you if you have a gap in your knowledge and you can then remedy that gap straight away. If you are writing to time and you do not manage to complete the answer, you know that you need to work on your time management or structure. Many tutors will be only too glad to look through your work and offer some advice. Later in this chapter, we will be looking at suggested approaches to questions on various topics.

15.1.4 Distilling your notes

Some students find it useful to work towards summarizing their notes into one or two sheets of A4, covering the main points and cases. Nearer the exam, they focus on these summaries, rather than trawl through the whole of their notes. This is a good idea, but only if you have gone through the processes suggested earlier and filled in any gaps.

15.2 The exam

So, you have thoroughly revised your chosen topic and the day of the exam has arrived. The key to exam success is to remain calm.

Practical measures help. Allow yourself plenty of time to find, and get to, the exam room. If the exam is being held in a building that you have never visited before, or on a different campus from usual, go there a day or so before the exam to make sure that you know exactly where you are going.

In addition, trust your revision process—do not try to cram everything into your head at the last minute, or it could muddle you up! Make sure that you have a pen and a spare, and anything else that your institution requires you to bring, such as an ID card.

15.2.1 Top exam tips

- Read the instructions at the beginning of the paper. If it requires you to answer two questions from a first section and two questions from a second, then do as it asks.
- Some institutions allow reading time, so make sure that you use it wisely.
- Read the paper through. Every year, somebody forgets to turn a page and misses part of a question!
- Select your questions and reread them, highlighting the relevant information. Focus on what the examiner is actually asking you to do.

- Take a few minutes to plan your answer. This is especially important when answering essay questions. Take a few minutes to read through your answer, to make sure that you have not forgotten anything important.

- Stick to your time allocation for each question—do not be tempted to spend longer on one question at the expense of the others. This has a snowball effect and often leaves you with very little time to answer the last question on the paper.

- Do not panic! If you mind goes completely blank (and it happens to us all at some point), take a few deep breaths and calm yourself down.

15.2.2 Question spotting

There are obvious perils in question spotting, if by that you mean learning only half the course and hoping that questions on the topics that you have learnt will appear on the exam paper! There is, however, nothing wrong with looking back through old exam papers to see which questions are old favourites and so likely to come up this year—as long as you remember that 'likely' does not mean 'certain'. Your lecturers may have got tired of a particular question or even question format.

You should also pay careful attention to important new cases and legislation—after all, examiners are likely to be interested in new developments in the law. Attend any revision lectures offered and listen out for such tips. Please do not badger your lecturers with questions about what will come up, however, because they are not likely to tell you and may well get fed up with being asked. It is vitally important to allow yourself some choice of topics, so that you have a degree of choice about which questions to answer on the day of the exam. After all, you may read the paper and find a really difficult question on a topic that you thought was straightforward. If you have revised a variety of topics, you will then be able to do a different question.

With this proviso, there is nothing wrong with looking at what questions are likely to be asked on the topics that you have studied. Therefore, in the rest of this chapter, we take each topic in turn and indicate what is most likely to be asked. Unfortunately, we cannot offer any guarantees.

15.3 The nature of land

By 'the nature of land', we mean the topics covered in Chapter 1, 'What is land?' This is often an introductory topic, so may not be on your exam papers—or it may come up as a small part of a wider question. As always, do some research to see what your exam is likely to contain.

If this area is on your paper, the following topics are the most likely to come up:

- the extent of land—for example, airspace and subterranean space;
- whether certain objects form part of the land—for example, garden sheds, statues, light fittings, etc.;
- who owns objects found on the land—treasure, objects buried in the land, items dropped on the surface of land.

These areas may come up separately, or together.

▶ CROSS REFERENCE
See Chapter 1.

15.3.1 **The extent of land**

Remember that land is three-dimensional. Check that you know the definition of land in Law of Property Act 1925 (LPA 1925), s. 205(1)(ix), and that you have some cases to use as authority to back up what you say. Do not forget that incorporeal rights (such as easements) form part of the land and that there are special rules relating to water.

You may be asked whether overhanging objects are a trespass onto the land. In these questions, the answer depends upon whether the part of the airspace that they are occupying forms part of the land. Look at the cases in Chapter 1 and use them to construct an argument. Similar questions may also arise in respect of subterranean space in the light of the decision in *Bocardo v. Star Energy* [2010] UKSC 35 and the Infrastructure Act 2015, s. 43.

15.3.2 **Whether objects form part of land**

A question of this type is about what is generally known as 'fixtures and fittings'. If it is a problem question, rather than an essay, you will need to decide whether certain objects form part of the land. It is essential to be able to cite the main test in *Holland v. Hodgson* (1872) LR 7 CP 328 and the further refinement in *Elitestone v. Morris* [1997] 1 WLR 687 and to be able to apply them, using other cases as examples. You may not be able to come to a certain answer, however, if the object is one that is not discussed in any case. In that event, you should do your best to come up with a sensible answer that is based on the reasoning in the cases.

Remember the rules on tenants' fixtures and apply them after you have decided whether or not the object is a fixture at all under the general rules.

Some exams may have questions on real and personal property. Remember the anomalous position of leasehold land, which is 'land', but not 'real property' (or 'realty').

15.3.3 **Objects lost and found on land**

The best way to deal with this area is to know how the law concerning objects found in and on land differ, and what effect the law of treasure has. We would suggest that a useful guide is Figure 1.2 in Chapter 1. If you follow that figure and know some cases to use as authority, you should not go too far wrong!

15.4 The structure of land law

The material covered in Chapter 2 is quite theoretical in nature and probably better suited to essay questions than to problem solving.

▶ CROSS REFERENCE

See Chapter 2.

The main questions that can be asked include:

- the contributions of common law and equity to modern land law;
- the policy of the 1925 property legislation;
- why land registration was introduced.

Some courses will also ask detailed questions about unregistered land—but, because the vast majority of titles are now registered, this is becoming less common. You should nonetheless have at least a basic understanding of the registration of land charges and the reasons why the system is defective.

You should be able to compare registered and unregistered land.

15.4.1 **Common law and equity**

If you are asked about the differences between common law and equity, you need to be prepared to delve a little bit into the history of land law and to explain how equity came about. You should, however, also relate what you know to modern land law.

 THINKING POINT

Which areas of land law might you draw upon to show the effects of equity in modern land law?

Hint: do not confine yourself to the areas mentioned in Chapter 2—think broadly across all areas of land law!

There are quite a number of differences between common law and equity from which you might choose: co-ownership, in which the trust plays such an important part; mortgages, with the equity of redemption; covenants in freehold land, in which equity allows the burden of restrictive covenants to run with the land—something that the common law does not allow. You might also talk about equity's role in 'rescuing' leases and other formal transfers not made by deed—think about *Walsh v. Lonsdale* (1882) LR 21 Ch D 9.

15.4.2 **The policy of the 1925 property legislation**

Again, it is important here to know a little of the history of land law so that you can explain why the reforms in the 1925 property legislation were so necessary and important.

The main aims can be expressed as follows:

- the reduction of legal estates in land to two and limits on the types of interest in land that could be legal—LPA 1925, s. 1;
- the introduction of land registration, to overcome the problems of the doctrine of notice;
- the introduction of 'overreaching'.

As you can probably tell, these three points would lead to a fairly lengthy essay if explained properly! You need to understand the structure of land law and the reasons for these reforms if you are to do well on such a question—but do not attempt it if you like to state 'what the law is' rather than 'why the law is like it is'!

15.4.3 **Land registration**

You might be asked general questions about why land registration was introduced, or more detailed ones about how land registration works (the mechanics of it).

The first question requires you to know what the law was before land registration was introduced (history again!) and what defects in the law it was intended to remedy. Clearly, there are overlaps here with the questions listed earlier—you will need to discuss common law and equity, the doctrine of notice, registration of land charges and its defects, and the policy of the 1925 property legislation. You should take care to focus on how land registration addresses each of these issues, rather than writing a general essay: in other words, keep coming back to the question!

The second type of question is dealt with later.

15.5   The freehold estate

❱ CROSS REFERENCE

See Chapter 3.

This is an area that is very important to understanding land law. Questions on the freehold estate may include:

- the distinction between a fee simple absolute and a conditional or determinable fee;
- the process of transferring land, although this is unlikely to be at a detailed level, because conveyancing is more usually studied during professional training after your degree.

There may also be more general questions about the differences between transferring registered and unregistered land.

15.5.1   The fee simple absolute

Questions here may be problem-type questions along the lines of: 'Which of these interests create a legal estate in the land?' You would then get a series of hypothetical situations in which land is transferred 'to Jack for life' or 'to Joe provided he never passes an exam in land law', etc.—a condition that you may well feel is fairly easy for Joe to meet as you sit there pondering upon the effect of the transfer!

The trick is to remember that the legal freehold is the fee simple absolute in possession. All of the parts of the definition must be met for the estate to be legal. Learn what each part of the definition means and when it will be satisfied. In our first example, Jack has only an equitable interest, because a life interest is not a 'fee'. In the second example, Joe has what looks like a conditional fee, which is not a fee simple, but which is nevertheless treated as one by LPA 1925, s. 7. He may therefore have a legal estate in the land.

All of this is quite technical, but if you learn it carefully and practise doing examples, it is possible to do very well on this type of question. It is a bit like a puzzle: as long as you follow the rules carefully, you can always work it out!

15.5.2   Transfers of land

Questions relating to transfers in land are likely to overlap with those above, and include questions on registration, and comparisons between unregistered and registered land. They may also include questions on formality, such as the need for a deed, or the requirement of writing in a contract for the sale of land and the possible exceptions to this rule. You should be aware of the decision in *Cobbe v. Yeoman's Row* [2008] UKHL 55 and *Whittaker v. Kinnear* [2011] EWHC 1479 (QB).

15.6   Land registration

❱ CROSS REFERENCE

See Chapter 4.

It is possible that you may be set specific questions on points of registration, including how certain interests may be registered. In most courses, however, you are also supposed to deal with registration alongside the substantive interests. So, for example, in a question on easements, you would be expected to mention (if it was relevant to the question) that an unregistered express easement will remain equitable and could easily be lost on a transfer of the land (see *Chaudhary v. Yavuz* [2011] EWCA Civ 1314) or (again if it is relevant) that an easement acquired by prescription is an overriding interest.

Specific questions on registration include:

- descriptive or critical essays on how registration works—for example, what overriding interests are and their effect;
- problem questions on problems caused by registration—for example, on land wrongly included in a registered title;
- questions of alteration of the register, rectification, and indemnity.

15.6.1 Essays on registration

The important thing to remember about registration is that you cannot really discuss it in a vacuum. You need to know how it works with interests in land. So, for example, if you are asked to discuss how overriding interests work, you should be prepared to draw on material from trusts of land, such as the case of *Williams & Glyn's Bank v. Boland* [1981] AC 487, and material on easements. You will probably need to know why the Land Registration Act 2002 (LRA 2002) was enacted to reform the original law in the LRA 1925 and you should have looked at relevant parts of the Law Commission reports that preceded the LRA 2002. This is another area that you should avoid if you really do not like discussing policy!

15.6.2 Problem questions

The sorts of things you may be asked in terms of problem questions will include such matters as land that is found to have unregistered easements affecting it, land that has been wrongly included in the title by mistake, etc. You will often be asked to advise which interests have priority over the new registered proprietor. You will need to be aware of the differences between first registration and registrable dispositions. These are often quite technical questions, but if you understand registration and can tell the difference between a registered disposition, an overriding interest, and a notice in the charges register, you could do very well.

Remember to learn about when the register can be altered and when compensation (indemnity) will be paid for mistakes. One important point to remember is that indemnity is never payable for an overriding interest, even if it turns out to render the title worthless.

In any case, you will need a good understanding of registration to really do well in land law. Registration can form a part of any question on any topic, so you would be very foolish not to look at it all in your revision!

15.7 Leases

The topic of leases is potentially huge and you should be careful not to narrow down your revision in the hope of a question on one particular aspect of leases, unless your tutor tells you that it is safe to do so. Questions in this area can be both essay and problem questions. Remember too that the LRA 2002 changed the registration requirements for leases. Table 5.1 in Chapter 5 summarizes these changes and may well be worth committing to memory.

» CROSS REFERENCE
See Chapter 5.

The following broad topics are frequently set as exam questions:

- essential requirements of a lease;
- leases and licences;
- leasehold covenants.

15.7.1 Essential requirements of a lease

Generally, a question on this aspect of the topic is likely to be an essay question. You will equally need to be able to identify in a problem question whether a lease is indeed a lease, however, and so the essential requirements of a lease are the starting point in any question on leases.

Firstly, think about how the lease was created: have all the requirements been met to make it a legal lease? Or does it only take effect in equity? Make sure that you understand not only the requirements for each type of lease, but also the differences between legal and equitable leases.

The usual starting point for defining a lease is LPA 1925, s. 205(xxvii)—but this must be read with Lord Templeman's definition of a lease in *Street v. Mountford* [1985] AC 809, which said that a lease involved the grant of exclusive possession, for a term at a rent. Do not forget, however, that the courts rejected the 'at a rent' requirement in *Ashburn Anstalt v. Arnold* [1989] Ch 1.

In your answer, you will probably need to address each of these requirements in turn, and explain to the examiner what 'exclusive possession', 'term certain', and 'rent' actually mean. This applies both to questions on the essential requirements of a lease and to questions on the lease/licence distinction (below).

15.7.2 Distinguishing between leases and licences

This aspect of the topic may be set as either an essay or as a problem question. Essay questions may well focus on particular cases, such as *Bruton v. London and Quadrant Housing Trust* [2000] 1 AC 406, which have raised interesting questions about previously settled law. Examiners often give a problem scenario that is very similar to some of the cases, involving a group of students occupying a flat, or a young couple renting a room. *Street v. Mountford* itself provides the structure for your answer: Do they have exclusive possession for a term certain? Explain what this means and apply it to the facts of the question. Is there a rent? This may be indicative of a tenancy, but not necessarily. Are the four unities present? Look at the agreement itself and identify any sham clauses. Even if there is exclusive possession, does the situation fall under one of the exceptions in *Street v. Mountford*?

15.7.3 Leasehold covenants

We think that an entire question on leasehold covenants may well be outside the scope of an LLB land law exam, although some universities offer a separate landlord and tenant law option that covers them in more detail. You may, however, be presented with a copy of a lease and asked to comment on its contents. You should be aware of all of the main landlord's and tenant's covenants, whether express or implied.

The really tricky part of this area of law is the assignment and running of leasehold covenants. Remember that this has become much simpler since the Landlord and Tenant (Covenants) Act 1995, so identify whether the lease you are dealing with was made before or after 1995. Finally, remind yourself of the various ways of ending a lease.

 THINKING POINT

The most useful exercise if you are planning to answer a question on leases is to read the case of *Street v. Mountford* in its entirety. It is not a long case, and will really help you to understand both the essential requirements of a lease and the lease/licence distinction.

15.8 Adverse possession

Some courses give little attention to adverse possession, but the number of recent cases and changes in legislation mean that it may still be examinable. You will have to judge how interested your own lecturers are in adverse possession and how likely it is to come up as a topic.

CROSS REFERENCE
See Chapter 6.

Questions on adverse possession are likely to include:

*   essay questions on the changes in the LRA 2002, the reasons for this, etc., and the decisions in *J. A. Pye v. United Kingdom*. These may appear as general essays on the theme of: 'Is adverse possession still justified in registered land?' Questions may also involve references to LASPOA 2012, s. 144, criminalizing squatting in residential buildings;
*   problem questions about land being adversely possessed for certain periods and the application of either the old or the new law, or—most likely—both. Again, such questions may include the application of LASPOA 2012, s. 144.

15.8.1 Essay questions: critical analysis of the law

If you intend to complete an essay question on adverse possession, you really need to have read some of the arguments for and against the changes in the law introduced by the LRA 2002, and the criticisms made of the old law by ECtHR in *J. A. Pye v. United Kingdom*, although the Grand Chamber eventually rejected these criticisms. You should get some help from the further reading section in Chapter 6. It will not be enough to simply describe the old law and the new law, and the decisions in *J. A. Pye v. United Kingdom*—you need to have thought about the issue of adverse possession, and to have read the views of the Law Commission and leading academics. There is plenty to write about in an essay like this, so be careful of time management.

15.8.2 Problem questions on adverse possession

A problem question on adverse possession will probably contain a description of a series of actions taken by a squatter on someone else's land over a number of years. The first thing you should do is to note whether the land being adversely possessed is registered or unregistered land. It is fairly likely that registered land will feature in the question somewhere, because all the changes to the law have affected registered land—but you might well be asked to compare the law for both registered and unregistered land. This may take the form of an additional question, such as: 'How would your advice differ if the land were unregistered?'

Next, create a timeline, setting out the dates you are given in the question, and also including the relevant date for the LRA 2002. This might look something like Figure 15.1.

In this timeline, we can see that the squatter first moved onto the land in November 1988, but did not fence it until November 2001. This means that we will have to decide if adverse possession began at either of those two dates and which is most likely. We can see that the date on which adverse possession began will be very important if the land is registered. If we take the earlier date, the Limitation Act 1980 (LA 1980) applies. If we take the later date, an application must be made under the LRA 2002, rather than the LA 1980.

If you get the facts of the problem clear and you can remember the important statutory dates, you should be able to answer any problem question.

Figure 15.1 Timeline relating to adverse possession

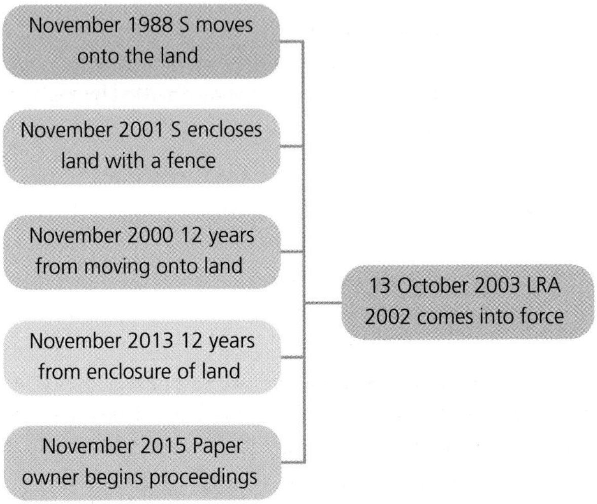

November 1988 S moves onto the land

November 2001 S encloses land with a fence

November 2000 12 years from moving onto land

November 2013 12 years from enclosure of land

November 2015 Paper owner begins proceedings

13 October 2003 LRA 2002 comes into force

15.9 Co-ownership and the Trusts of Land and Appointment of Trustees Act 1996

▶ CROSS REFERENCE
See Chapters 7–10.

Co-ownership of land is a huge subject and you may be asked either a narrow question on one particular area of it—for example, constructive trusts—or a wider question that encompasses several different aspects of co-ownership. To some extent, this will dictate your approach. A narrow question will require demonstration of a greater depth of knowledge than a more general question, which will require a breadth of discussion. Either way, the best starting point is to make sure that you have a really good understanding of the way in which each of the various aspects of the subject fit together in practice.

We will look at the topic step by step in order to build up a picture of it as a whole.

15.9.1 The legal title

At the very start, we need to ascertain who owns the legal title to the property and who owns the equitable title to the property.

THINKING POINT

What is the easiest way to find out who is the legal owner of the property in registered land?

Look at the land register. In the proprietorship register, it will have the name of the legal owner of the land. If there is more than one name, then the land will be co-owned.

CROSS REFERENCE
See Chapter 8.

Remember that the legal title does not tell you about the equitable ownership of the property. However, there is a presumption that equity follows the law, so that the equitable title reflects the legal title. This is a presumption that can be rebutted by evidence to the contrary.

The next step will be to work out the equitable interests in the property. When quantifying shares in the property, the court will now follow the guidance in *Jones v. Kernott* [2011] UKSC 53.

CROSS REFERENCE
See Chapter 9.

15.9.2 **The equitable title**

15.9.2.1 **Two legal owners**

Remember that, whenever there is more than one legal owner of land, a trust arises. The legal owners are the trustees and are usually also the beneficiaries, although there may be other beneficiaries who are not legal owners. The legal owners can hold the legal title only as joint tenants. If there are two or more legal owners, then, following *Stack v. Dowden* [2007] UKHL 17, and confirmed in *Jones v. Kernott*, the starting presumption will be that the legal owners also own the equitable title as joint tenants.

This may or may not, in fact, be the case. The onus is on the person claiming to have a tenancy in common to prove that this is, indeed, so. Remember that the key difference between joint tenancy and tenancy in common is that if one of the joint tenants dies, the other joint tenant automatically acquires his or her share of the property by means of the doctrine of survivorship. In an exam question involving two legal owners, you will need to think about this.

Try to see if there is any evidence of the joint tenancy being severed. There are fundamentally five different ways in which severance can occur:

- statutory;
- by written notice;
- by an owner acting on his or her own share;
- by mutual agreement or mutual conduct;
- by forfeiture.

You should know all of these methods in some detail.

CROSS REFERENCE
See Chapter 8.

Finally, remember the extremely important concept of overreaching. Provided that the purchaser of a property pays the purchase money to two trustees, then all, or any, equitable interests in the land are overreached and the purchaser takes free of them. The equitable owners will then only have an interest in the proceeds of sale.

15.9.2.2 **One legal owner**

Often, in co-ownership questions, there will be only one legal owner of the land. Again, following *Stack v. Dowden*, the starting presumption will be that the sole legal owner is also the sole equitable owner. The person claiming to have an equitable share in the land must prove otherwise.

If you are not told about any formal express declarations of trust in the land, you need to start thinking about whether anyone has acquired an equitable interest informally.

CROSS REFERENCE
See Chapter 7.

THINKING POINT

Can you remember how equitable interests can arise informally in land?

They may arise informally through the operation of a resulting or constructive trust.

▶ **CROSS REFERENCE**

See Chapter 9.

Resulting trusts arise by a direct contribution to the purchase price of the property. If someone has paid a contribution towards purchasing the house, by means of a deposit or other payment, he or she will acquire an equitable interest in the property.

Constructive trusts, on the other hand, arise from the common intention of the parties. Although the case law in this area can be complicated, broadly adhering to the following should help you to decide whether a constructive trust has arisen.

Express common intention constructive trusts arise if:

* there is evidence that the parties have discussed co-ownership of the property—even if there has been no discussion of shares; and
* the person claiming to have an equitable interest in the property under a constructive trust has acted to his or her detriment on the strength of these discussions.

Inferred common intention constructive trusts arise if:

* the party claiming an equitable interest has made a direct financial contribution to the purchase price of the property; and
* the person claiming to have an equitable interest in the property under a constructive trust has acted to his or her detriment, believing him- or herself to have an equitable interest in the property.

Be aware of the current debate around the continued relevance of the *Rosset* guidelines outlined above, but remember that they are still good law. This may well be an interesting topic for examiners to explore. *Jones v. Kernott* has established guidelines for the court to follow in quantifying shares in the family home for both joint legal owner and sole legal owner cases. A relatively new Supreme Court decision on such an important area of law is likely to be popular with examiners, so you should make sure that you read this case, and the interpretations of it in the lower courts.

15.9.2.3 Beware the hidden equitable owner!

If you have identified a hidden equitable owner, by following the guidelines noted earlier, then you need to proceed with caution.

Remember that:

equitable interest + actual occupation = overriding interest that will be binding on the purchaser.

You then need to think about whether the person who has an equitable interest is in actual occupation of the property. If he or she is in actual occupation and the purchaser has not overreached the equitable interest by paying the purchase money to two trustees, then the purchaser will be bound by that interest, even though there was no indication of it on the land register.

15.9.3 The statutory framework

Much of the law which we have looked at so far is rooted in case law. In answering a question on co-ownership you will, however, need to be very familiar with the provisions of the Trusts of Land and Appointment of Trustees Act 1996 (TOLATA 1996).

> CROSS REFERENCE

See Chapter 10.

This is largely a matter of working your way through the main provisions of the statute, perhaps with the help of Chapter 10. It is a very straightforwardly written statute, which essentially does what it says on the tin! You need to be particularly aware of TOLATA 1996, ss. 14 and 15. Section 14 provides co-owners of land with a mechanism to resolve disputes by making an application to court for it to decide the matter and s. 15 indicates the factors that the court must take into account in reaching its decision.

15.10 Easements and profits

Questions on easements and profits can take the form of either an essay or a problem question. For both of them, you will need a good knowledge of easements. In our experience, profits are taught in less depth, but it is useful to know in what ways they are similar to easements and in what ways they differ.

Questions that can arise include:

> CROSS REFERENCE

See Chapter 11.

- essay questions on the nature of easements and profits, and on acquisition of easements and profits by implied grant or prescription;
- problem questions, in which an easement or profit is being claimed.

15.10.1 Essay questions

These areas are frequently the subject of critical questions, perhaps asking why informal methods of creation remain in existence and whether they are justified. The questions on the nature of easements and profits may centre on the idea of the categories of easements not being closed, and the rule that easements must not be too extensive. You will need to have thought about these areas in some depth to get good marks for such a question.

You should always use cases as authority for your opinions and you should if possible have read articles discussing these points. A simple description of the law is not enough to get good marks—you must be able to criticize it.

You could well be asked about the proposed reforms in the Law Commission report, *Making Land Work: Easements, Covenants and Profits à Prendre*, Law Com No. 327 (London: The Stationery Office, 2011), so if you plan to answer a question on easements, make sure that you have read this report.

15.10.2 Problem questions

Problem questions in this area of law usually involve a scenario in which individuals are attempting to prove, or disprove, the existence of an easement or profit. For example: 'Bill has been driving his car over the end of Ben's garden for many years. When Ben sells his land, the new owner stops Bill from driving over it any longer. Does Bill have any right of way over the garden?' Hopefully, you will be able to recognize that a right of way is an easement and that this is the area of law you must address!

Just as with essay questions, there are two main areas to consider:

- Is this right capable of being an easement?
- If so, how was the easement acquired?

15.10.2.1 Is it capable of being an easement?

In order to answer the first question, you should learn the characteristics of an easement in *Re Ellenborough Park* [1956] Ch 131 and be able to apply them to your facts. One really important characteristic to establish is that of the dominant and servient tenement—make sure that, for each easement claimed, you identify which land is the dominant tenement and which is the servient. Draw a diagram if it helps!

For example, the Bill and Ben example above might be drawn as in Figure 15.2.

Figure 15.2 Establishing the dominant and servient tenements under an easement

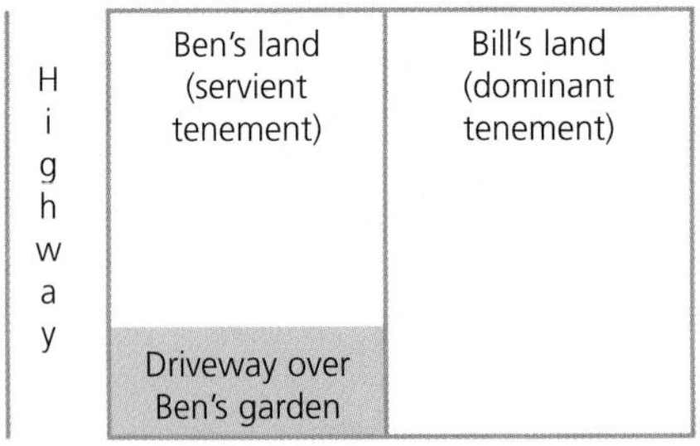

	Ben's land (servient tenement)	Bill's land (dominant tenement)
H i g h w a y		
	Driveway over Ben's garden	

If it is fairly obvious that the right is capable of being an easement, do not spend hours on this point. If the right is a right of way, for example, between neighbouring landowners, you need not spend much time on establishing that it is within the category of rights that can be easements. If, however, it is an unusual or new easement, or one that causes problems, such as parking, spend longer, because this may well be one of the main points of the question.

15.10.2.2 How was the easement acquired?

You should have a checklist in your head of the various ways of acquiring an easement and work through them. You should not write it out as a list, however: instead, select only the bits you need and apply them to the question (see Figure 15.3).

If you have that structure in your head, you should be able to answer most problem questions.

15.11 Covenants in freehold land

In our experience, questions on covenants in freehold land nearly always come as problem questions, in which you are asked to decide whether either the benefit of a freehold covenant, or the burden, or both, have passed to successors in title of the original covenantee and/or covenantor. However, in the light of the Law Commission Report, *Easements, Covenants and Profits à Prendre*, you could be asked an essay question about the proposed reforms to the law of covenants in freehold land. If so, you need to have thought about the defects of the present law and to have read the report thoroughly!

Figure 15.3 A summary of ways of acquiring easements

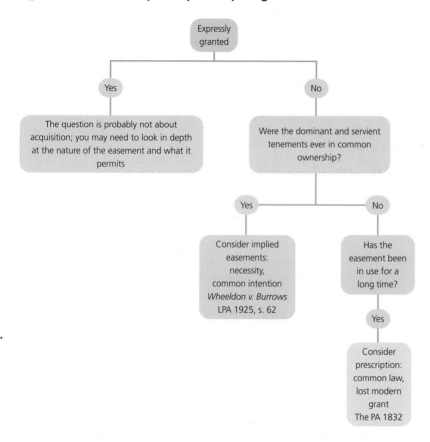

The first step with a problem question is to read it very carefully indeed and work out who the parties are. You might find that drawing a diagram helps here. See, for example, Figure 14.2 in Chapter 14.

▶ CROSS REFERENCE
See Chapter 12.

You need to identify which land has the benefit and which land has the burden, who was the original covenantee and who was the original covenantor. It is vital that you do this—and tell the examiner that you have done it. If you get it wrong, at least the examiner will know what you decided and can give you credit for law applied correctly to what you thought the facts were! Once you have identified the parties, work out if you need to discuss the passing of the benefit, or the burden, or both.

Most questions will include restrictive covenants. Remember to state that the burden cannot run at common law, so that you need to consider the equitable rules. It generally seems to make sense to start with the burden under *Tulk v. Moxhay* (1848) 2 Ph 774, and you need to learn these rules and apply them one at a time to the question. Always deal completely with the burden before going on to look at the benefit; never jump about between the two.

If the covenants are positive, you may need to consider the common law rules for the passing of the benefit. The burden cannot pass, but you should consider the various possible ways around this and decide if any of them are likely to apply. Favourites with examiners seem to be the fencing easement in *Crow v. Wood* [1971] 1 QB 77 and the benefit/burden doctrine in *Halsall v. Brizell* [1957] Ch 169.

Remember to consider whether there is any actual, or proposed, breach of the covenant and also what remedies are available—there have been a number of new cases on this area including *Coventry v. Lawrence* [2014] UKSC 13. You may also need to consider whether the covenant can be discharged or modified under LPA 1925, s. 84.

15.12 Mortgages

If you are lucky enough to find an exam question entirely on mortgages, it is likely to be on one of the following four areas:

- the mortgage itself—how it was created; whether there are any 'clogs and fetters';
- the rights of the mortgagee;
- the rights and remedies of the mortgagor;
- undue influence.

⟫ CROSS REFERENCE
See Chapter 13.

Less examined topics include tacking and the priority of mortgages—but, remember: if you have been taught it on your course, then it is fair game for the examiner, unless you are told otherwise!

Although the law and some of the concepts involved in mortgages can be complicated, this is a more straightforward exam topic, because it has a built-in structure. The fundamental rules are largely based on statute, which gives us an immediate framework on which to peg our answer.

This topic might be set either as a problem question or as an essay. Either way, as long as you really understand the topic, you will be able to adapt to whatever the examiner throws at you.

15.12.1 Read the question: Who are you advising?

When you have read the question, work out who are the mortgagor (borrower) and mortgagee (lender). Under exam pressure, you may get a little flustered, so write this on your exam paper to remind yourself. Then try to work out who you are advising: Are you advising a mortgagor, who has had clogs and fetters attached to his or her agreement? Or a mortgagor who has fallen behind with his or her repayments? Or a mortgagee who wants to know how it may recover its money? Is there a suggestion of undue influence? Be aware of the recent case law in this area.

As with any question in any exam, you will get more marks for attempting to answer the question set. Tempting though it might be to write everything you have learnt about the remedies of the mortgagee, it will gain you no favour with an examiner who has asked you a question about the rights of a mortgagor. Work out from the start which information the examiner requires and be brave enough to leave out irrelevant material.

15.12.2 What kind of mortgage is it?

Think about how the mortgage has been created. Work out whether it complies with the requirements needed to create a legal mortgage or whether it only takes effect in equity. It is unlikely that detailed questions will be set on the creation of the mortgage, but it is useful to think about this, as a starting point.

15.12.3 Look at the mortgage agreement itself and its implications for the mortgagor

If you are given details of the mortgage agreement, think about whether there are any restrictions on the mortgagor's right to redeem, or other clogs and fetters. If there are, can they be justified? Are they unconscionable (in which case, the courts will not allow them)?

15.12.4 Has the mortgagor fallen behind with his or her repayments?

If so, there may well be implications for both mortgagor and mortgagee. The mortgagor is in danger of losing his or her home, and the mortgagee may well want to recover its investment. You may well be asked to advise one or other of the parties.

If you are advising the mortgagee, then think about the remedies available and consider whether it should exercise one or some of them. Most questions will focus on the mortgagee's right to repossess and sell the property. If this is the case, does the mortgagor have any potential protection under Administration of Justice Act 1970, s. 36? Read the facts of the question carefully. Does he or she have a realistic chance of paying back the arrears?

This protection should also, of course, be pointed out to the mortgagor, if you are advising him. This is an interesting topic and one that is frequently examined.

If the mortgagee does decide to repossess and sell the house, then it has certain duties in respect of the sale and the application of the sale proceeds. Again, look out for new cases, because examiners like them! Although they may not change the law dramatically, new cases do allow examiners to revisit a familiar old problem.

 Summary

1. Good preparation is the key to doing well in your land law exam.

2. This means attending classes throughout the year, ensuring that you understand topics as you go through them, and asking your tutor to clarify any points as necessary.

3. Gather together your revision notes, and fill in gaps in your knowledge and understanding.

4. Practise past exam questions and reflect on your answers: in what areas might you improve? It may be in your knowledge or your structure.

5. Prepare for the exam itself and allow for exam nerves.

6. Read the exam paper and the questions thoroughly.

7. Make sure that you are answering the question set, rather than the one for which you have prepared.

8. Reread your answer and amend any careless mistakes or omissions.

Further reading

Finch, E. and Fafinski, S. (2013) *Legal Skills*, 4th edn, Oxford: Oxford University Press
This is a useful book on legal skills, including writing answers to questions, etc.

McVea, H. and Cumper, P. (2006) *Exam Skills for Law Students*, 2nd edn, Oxford: Oxford University Press
This is a book focusing specifically on exam skills.

Sayles, V. (2014) *Land Law Concentrate*, 4th edn, Oxford: Oxford University Press

Strong, S. (2014) *How to Write Law Essays and Exams*, 4th edn, Oxford: Oxford University Press
This book focuses on problem questions and how to answer them.

Wilkie, M. et al. (2015) *Questions and Answers: Land Law*, 10th edn, Oxford: Oxford University Press
These are revision and exam guides to land law. Many tutors dislike such books, as they can oversimplify the law. However, if you use them to supplement your own notes and reading rather than as an alternative, you may find them useful.

Glossary

1925 property legislation a series of Acts of Parliament that came into effect on 1 January 1926. These Acts consolidated earlier piecemeal changes in the law—particularly from 1922–24—and brought them all together as a body of law, which made substantial changes to the common law of property.

abatement a remedy that, in relation to nuisances, allows for the removal, termination, or destruction of that nuisance under certain conditions

absolute complete; unconditional; not qualified

ad medium filum 'to the mid line'

administrators personal representatives in cases of intestacy—that is, in which there is no will (cf executors)

adverse possession the possession of land by someone other than the registered proprietor or unregistered owner, without that proprietor or owner's consent

agreed notice a notice on registered land that is either requested or agreed to by the proprietor, or the validity of which satisfies the registrar (cf unilateral notice)

allodial land land that is owned outright, rather than as an estate held of a lord

alteration any change to the register

ancient lights rights to light that have been gained by long use

animus possidendi an intention to possess the land to the exclusion of all others

annexation the permanent attachment of the benefit of a covenant to the land of the covenantee, so that it passes with the land whenever it is transferred

assignee the person receiving the benefit of covenant or lease by assignment (cf assignor)

assignment 1. (of leases) the transfer of the whole of the remainder of the term of a lease; 2. (of covenants in freehold land) the transfer of the benefit of a covenant to a particular person

assignor the person assigning the covenant or lease (cf assignee)

bankruptcy a state under which a person has been judged by a court to be insolvent, involving the appointment of an administrator to distribute the bankrupt's assets among his or her creditors

bare trust a trust under which the trustee has no obligation other than to hold property on trust for an adult beneficiary who is absolutely entitled to the property

bona fide 'in good faith'

bona fide purchaser of the legal estate for value without notice broken down, this phrase refers to someone who has bought the legal estate in the land—the 'purchaser of the legal estate'—who has acted honestly in the purchase—that is, in good faith or 'bona fide'—and has bought the land without knowing about the equitable interest in the land—that is, 'without notice'

break clause a clause that allows the parties to bring a lease to an end at various specified points in advance of the lease's end

building scheme a defined area of land sold by a single vendor in plots that are subject to restrictive covenants intended to benefit the whole

caution against first registration a notice lodged with the Land Registry by any person claiming to have ownership of, or an interest in, unregistered land that obliges the Registry to notify that person of any application for first registration of title to that land

certain term a period that has a specified beginning and end

charge a legal or equitable interest in land, securing the payment of money

charges register third part of the register of title, containing charges or encumbrances over land such as mortgages, easements, and restrictive covenants burdening the land

chattels all property that is not real property, including leasehold land, and is also often used as the opposite to fixture. Leasehold land came to have such importance, however, that it was called a 'chattel real', because it has many of the characteristics of real property.

clogs and fetters any provision in a mortgage deed that restricts the mortgagor's equity of redemption

commonhold a way of owning property that features shared areas, for which ownership needs to remain in central ownership and maintenance

commonhold association the formal body that commonhold leaseholders must establish to manage the common parts of the property so held

common law the law developed by the Royal Courts—that is, the law applicable to the whole country, not purely local law (cf equity)

concurrent interest the owners all hold an interest in the land at the same time (cf successive interest)

condition precedent a condition that must be met before the estate comes into being (cf condition subsequent)

condition subsequent a condition that may be fulfilled after the estate has been created (cf condition precedent)

conditional fee simple an estate that might last forever, but which may be brought to an end on the satisfaction of a condition subsequent (cf determinable fee simple)

contingent remainder a future interest that can only come into being on meeting a condition precedent (cf vested remainder)

conveyance the transfer of a legal estate in land from one person to another

conveyancer a person who specializes in the transfer of estates in land—usually a solicitor or licensed conveyancer

conveyancing the process of transferring a legal estate in land from one person to another

corporeal hereditaments any real property, having a physical form (cf incorporeal hereditaments)

covenant a promise contained in a deed

covenantee the person to whom a promise is made under covenant, who has its benefit—that is, who can enforce the promise against the covenantor

covenantor the person making a promise under covenant, who bears its burden—that is, who is bound to carry out the promise (cf covenantee)

cuius est solum eius est usque ad coelum et ad inferos 'he who owns the land owns everything reaching up to the very heavens and down to the depths of the earth'

curtain principle the principle in registration of title that the details of any trusts affecting the land should be kept off the title

deed a formal document that makes it clear, on its face, that it is intended to be a deed and which is executed as a deed

demesne land 'land belonging to [the monarch] in right of the Crown'

de minimis of the rule *de minimis non curat lex*, or 'the law does not take account of trifles'

demise a lease

determinable fee simple an estate that may last forever, but which may be cut short by a specified but unpredictable event (cf conditional fee simple)

determined ended; terminated

discontinuance the act of giving up possession, often an act of simply abandoning the land (cf dispossession)

disponee the person to whom a registrable disposition is made

dispossession the act of being dispossessed—that is, of another person assuming ordinary possession of the land (cf discontinuance)

distress the seizure of goods as security for the performance of an obligation

dominant owner the owner of the land that benefits from the easement (cf servient owner)

dominant tenement a piece of land that benefits from an easement (cf servient tenement)

easement a right enjoyed by the owner of land to a benefit from other land

electronic conveyancing, or e-conveyancing the transfer of land by electronic, rather than paper-based, means

equitable charge an equitable interest in land that acts to secure the payment of money

equitable interest an interest in land that is recognized by equity (cf legal estate)

equitable lease a lease that grants an interest in land on terms that correspond to those of a legal lease, but without completion of the legal formalities

equitable mortgage a mortgage under which the mortgagee does not acquire a legal interest in the land (cf legal mortgage)

equitable right of redemption the right of a mortgagor to repay all of the capital, interest, and costs involved in their mortgage arrangement at any time and thereby wholly own his or her property

equity 1. the law developed by the Lord Chancellor and the Court of Chancery to remedy defects in the common law; 2. an equitable right or claim; 3. the value that is the difference between the monetary worth of a property and the amount of outstanding mortgage debt

equity of redemption the bundle of rights given by law to the mortgagor, which includes the equitable right of redemption

escheat the right of the lord to the tenant's land if he were to die without leaving an heir. This survives into modern times as the right of the Crown to land left without an owner (*bona vacantia*), although it is now regulated by the Administration of Estates Act 1925. Common law escheat survives under which land is disclaimed by a debtor on insolvency (bankruptcy).

estate the length of time for which land has been granted to a tenant under the system of tenure. It means the duration of the grant. Note that this is a use of the word 'estate' that differs from the general use of the word; estate is used in this technical sense in land law.

estate in remainder an interest that gives its owner the present right to future enjoyment (cf in possession)

estate in reversion an interest that is retained by the grantor, because the fee simple estate in the land has not been transferred to anyone

exclusive occupation sole occupation of all, or part, of a property

exclusive possession possession of a property to the exclusion of all others, including the landlord

executors personal representatives named in the will (cf administrators)

express covenants terms that are expressly stated in a lease (cf implied covenants)

express trust a trust created by the express intention of the settlor (cf resulting and constructive trusts)

fee the estate is inheritable, meaning that it can be left in a will after someone dies

fee simple an estate that is inheritable for as long as there are general heirs of the owner (cf fee tail)

fee simple absolute in possession this refers to the legal freehold estate

fee tail an estate that is inheritable for as long as there are lineal descendants of the owner (cf fee simple)

feudal system a political, economic, and social system under which only the monarch was able to own land outright

first registration of title the first time that title to an estate in land is registered at the Land Registry and at which point it therefore changes from unregistered land to registered land

fixed-term lease a lease that is entered into for a fixed period of time

fixture an object that is attached to the land in such a way and for such a reason that it becomes part of the land

foreclosure a remedy under which the court orders a date by which the mortgagor must pay off his or her debt, or on which his or her property will be lost to the mortgagee

foreshore the land between the high-water mark and low-water mark

forfeiture the bringing to an end of an estate as the consequence of an offence or a breach of an undertaking

four unities of joint tenancy the four conditions that must be satisfied in order for a joint tenancy in equity to exist—that is, possession, interest, time, and title

franchise a right, conferred by the Crown on a subject, to do something specific on certain land, eg hold a market

frustration the termination of a contract as a result of an event that renders its performance impossible or illegal, or otherwise prevents its fulfilment

gazanging the vendor pulling out of the sale altogether at the last moment

gazumping the process of a third party offering, or the vendor accepting, a higher offer on a property on which a sale price has already been agreed, but for which agreement no binding contract is yet in place (cf gazundering)

gazundering the process of the purchaser demanding a lower price on a property after a sale price has already been agreed, but for which agreement no binding contract is yet in place (cf gazumping)

heir someone who inherits property under a will

implied covenants terms that are implied into a lease by law (cf express covenants)

inchoate incomplete or unformed

incorporeal hereditaments intangible rights in land (cf corporeal hereditaments)

indemnity covenant a promise on behalf of a successor in title to pay, to the original covenantor, any damages that might be awarded against him or her for a future breach of the covenant by the successor in title

indemnity principle an indemnity (compensation) is payable by the state if loss is caused by errors in the register

in gross not attached to land

injunction an order of the court that obliges somebody to do something or refrain from doing something

in loco parentis 'in place of a parent'

in personam a right enforceable against certain persons or classes of persons (cf *in rem*)

in possession the estate must confer upon its owner the immediate right to enjoy the land, or the rents and profits of the land, from the date of the grant (cf estate in remainder)

in rem a right enforceable against everyone— that is, a right in the property itself (cf *in personam*)

in reversion at some point in the future (cf in possession)

interest-only mortgage a type of mortgage arrangement under which the mortgagor repays only interest each month, with capital to be repaid in full at the end of the mortgage term (cf repayment mortgage)

joint tenancy the legal or equitable co-ownership of land by persons who together own the whole of the land (cf tenancy in common)

landlord or lessor the person granting the lease, which is sometimes described as 'letting' the property

landlord's covenants clauses in a lease specifying the obligations of the landlord under the lease (cf tenant's covenants)

land registration the system of registering certain legal estates and interests in land

lease or tenancy any such term refers to a lease: shorter leases tend to be called tenancies, longer leases tend to be referred to as leases—but often, for all practical purposes, the terms are used interchangeably

leasehold covenant a clause in a lease, specifying certain obligations on the part of either party

leasehold enfranchisement the turning of a leasehold estate into a freehold estate by means of selling the reversion of the lease to the tenant

legal charge a legal interest in land that acts to secure the payment of money

legal estate an estate in land that is recognized by the common law (cf equitable interest)

legal interests interests in land that can exist at common law, rather than in equity

legal lease a lease that creates an estate in land for a term of years absolute and with certain formalities (cf equitable lease)

legal mortgage a mortgage that is created by legal charge (in registered land) and completed by means of certain formalities (cf equitable mortgage)

licence a personal arrangement between licensor and licensee under which the licensee may occupy the licensor's property for a specified purpose

limitation period statutory time limit after which no action to reclaim land under adverse possession can be started

market value a full rent at current economic rates

mirror principle the principle in registration of title that the register should be a mirror of the estates and interests affecting the land

mortgage a way of using land as security for a loan. Properly, the name for the charge over land that is the security for the loan granted by a bank to the purchaser of the land, rather than the name for the loan itself.

mortgagee the lender, who, in return for receiving the mortgage, lends the money (cf mortgagor)

mortgagor the borrower, who grants the mortgage to the bank (cf mortgagee)

nec vi, nec clam, nec precario 'without force, without secrecy, without permission'

negative equity a negative value that arises when the monetary worth of a property is less than the amount of outstanding mortgage debt

notice 1. an entry against a registered title lodged by a person with a specified interest in the land; 2. in unregistered land, knowledge of an equitable interest

overreaching the process by which interests in land are converted into corresponding interests in money arising from the sale of the land

overriding interests certain rights and interests in land that need not be protected by land registration, but which will bind the proprietor and any subsequent purchaser unless overreached

paper owner the person who holds the documentary title—the 'papers'—to the land

periodic tenancy a lease or tenancy in which rent is payable at fixed intervals and which continues indefinitely from one rent period to the next, until being terminated by notice

permissive waste waste that is caused by the tenant's neglect (cf voluntary waste)

personal property, or personalty all property that does not comprise freehold land or incorporeal hereditaments (cf real property, or realty)

personal representatives those responsible for looking after the property of someone who has died, who might, for example, make sure that any bequests made in the deceased person's will are carried out

physical possession actual occupation or control of land

positive covenant a covenant that requires the covenantor to do something—particularly something that requires the spending of money

postponement when an interest in land is not binding on its new registered proprietor (cf priority)

power of attorney a formal instrument by which one person empowers another to act on his or her behalf

power of sale the right of a mortgagee to sell a mortgaged property under certain circumstances

pre-action protocol a statement of best practice about pre-action conduct which has been approved by the Head of Civil Justice

premium (or fine) a sum that is sometimes charged by a landlord as the 'price' of granting a lease, which is usually seen in commercial or long leases

prescription the acquisition of an easement by uninterrupted long use

presumption of advancement the presumption that, in certain types of relationship, a person who makes a transfer of or contribution to the purchase of a property held in the name of another is doing so for the benefit of that other

prior adverse interests interests that come before an estate in time and that are not for the present landowner's benefit

priority when an interest in land is binding on its new registered proprietor (cf postponement)

privity of contract the relationship that exists between parties to a contract that allows each to sue, or be sued, under the contract

privity of estate the relationship that exists between landlord and tenant under the same lease that allows each to enforce his or her obligations against the other

profit à prendre the right to take natural produce from another person's land

profit in common, or common a profit à prendre that is enjoyed by one person in common with others (cf several profit)

property register first part of the register of title, containing a description of the land by address and postcode, and including incorporeal hereditaments, such as easements over other land and restrictive covenants benefitting the land

proprietary estoppel a doctrine under which the courts can grant a remedy if a landowner has implicitly or explicitly led a claimant to act detrimentally under the belief that he or she would be granted rights in the land

proprietary rights rights that are not personal to the original parties, but which are binding on future owners

proprietorship register second part of the register of title giving the names of the registered proprietor, the type of title, and any restrictions to which the registered proprietor is subject when dealing with their title

quicquid plantatur solo, solo cedit 'whatever is fixed to the land becomes part of it'

real property, or realty this term refers to freehold land (cf personal property, or personalty)

receiver a person appointed by the court to protect and preserve property during the course of litigation

rectification a change to the register that is made to correct a mistake and which prejudicially affects the title of the registered proprietor

registered land land to which the title is registered with the Land Registry. Title to such land is guaranteed by the Land Registry and is proven by a search of the register (cf unregistered land).

registrable disposition a transfer of an estate or interest in registered land that is to be registered in the name of the new proprietor

registration gap the period of time between the date of the transfer of property and the date of land registration

relativity of title the doctrine that all rights to land are relative and that the person with the best title will be entitled to the land

rentcharge a charge for the payment of money that is held over freehold land

repayment mortgage a type of mortgage arrangement under which the mortgagor repays both interest and capital each month (cf interest-only mortgage)

repudiation an indication that a breach of contract will occur in the future, leading to the end of that contract

restriction a limitation on the right of a registered proprietor to deal with the land or charge in a registered title

restrictive covenant a covenant that is negative in nature—that is, it restricts the use of the burdened land

resulting and constructive trusts forms of implied trust that arise by operation of law (cf express trust)

reversion the interest that the landlord retains in the land after the lease has finished

right of re-entry a legal or equitable right to resume possession of land

satisfying the equity the fulfilment of the equitable right or claim

secured creditor someone who has lent money to the owner of the property, and has 'secured' the loan on the property itself, meaning that, if the owner fails to meet the payments on the loan, the creditor can recover the money that it has lent by (usually) repossessing and selling the property

servient owner the owner of the land that bears the burden of the easement (cf dominant owner)

servient tenement a piece of land that bears the burden of an easement (cf dominant tenement)

settlement a disposition of land under which a trust is created designating beneficiaries and the terms on which they are to take the land

settlor a person who creates a trust

several profit a profit à prendre that is enjoyed exclusively by one person (cf profit in common, or common)

severance the conversion of a joint tenancy in equity into a tenancy in common

sole owner a person registered as the sole legal proprietor of land, who may or may not be the sole equitable owner

solus tie a type of agreement that binds the mortgagor into buying products only from the mortgagee

specific performance a remedy for breach of contract that demands the fulfilment of obligations under the contract

squatter a person in adverse possession of land

subinfeudation the process of making new grants of land under the feudal system

subletting the granting of a sublease by someone who is himself or herself a tenant, for a period shorter than that of his or her own (head) lease

substitution the process of transferring estates in land under which one owner takes the place of another

successive interest one owner's interest in the land is followed by another owner's interest in the land (cf concurrent interest)

surrender the giving up of a tenant's interest in a property to his or her landlord, which might be in the form of a deed (express) or as a consequence of the actions of both parties (implied)

tacking the adding of a further advance of money under an existing mortgage agreement, subject to certain conditions

tenancy at sufferance a lease or tenancy that arises when a tenant stays on in a property after a lease is ended, but to which occupation the landlord has not indicated agreement or otherwise

tenancy at will a lease or tenancy, which usually arises by implication, that can be terminated by the landlord or tenant at any time

tenancy by estoppel a lease or tenancy that exists despite the fact that the person who granted it had no right to do so

tenancy in common the equitable co-ownership of land by persons in equal or unequal shares (cf joint tenancy)

tenant or lessee the person to whom the lease is granted

tenant's covenants clauses in a lease specifying the obligations of the tenant under the lease (cf landlord's covenants)

tenant's fixtures fixtures attached to rented property by a tenant that the tenant is entitled to remove

tenure 1. *freehold tenure*—in the feudal system, the grant of an estate in land by a lord to a tenant. The tenant 'holds the land of the lord' for the period defined by the estate. 2. *leasehold tenure*—the relationship between a landlord and a tenant in leasehold land

term of years absolute this refers to the leasehold estate

title deeds the documentary evidence that shows how land came to its present owner

treasure trove under common law before 1997, items of gold and silver found in a concealed place, apparently having been hidden by their owner and not reclaimed, to which the Crown had the right of possession, now replaced by the Treasure Act 1996

trust an arrangement by which someone (called a 'settlor') transfers property to others (called 'trustees') on terms that the trustees will hold that property for the benefit of certain persons (called the 'beneficiaries')

trustee in bankruptcy a person in whom the property of a bankrupt is vested for the benefit of the bankrupt's creditors

trust for sale a trust under which the trustees were obliged to sell the property and hold the proceeds in trust for the beneficiaries

trust of land any trust of property that comprises or includes land

unconscionability gross unfairness or morally wrong behaviour that should go against the conscience of an honest person, stemming from the idea that a person's conscience must be affected for equity to intervene

undue influence influence exerted by another that prevents a person from exercising independent judgement in relation to any decision

unilateral notice a notice on registered land to which the proprietor will not agree, which consequently represents a disputed interest (cf agreed notice)

unity of seisin the ownership of two plots of land by the same (legal) person

unregistered land land to which the title has not yet been registered at the Land Registry. Title to such land has to be proven by documentary evidence, known as 'title deeds' (cf registered land).

vested remainder the present right to a future interest (cf contingent remainder)

voluntary waste waste that is caused by a voluntary action of the tenant (cf permissive waste)

waste any permanent alteration of tenanted property that is caused by the tenant's action or neglect

Index

E